Locatelli and the Violin Bravura Tradition

STUDIES ON ITALIAN MUSIC HISTORY

EDENDUM CURAVIT
FULVIA MORABITO

VOLUME IX

PUBLICATIONS OF THE CENTRO STUDI OPERA OMNIA LUIGI BOCCHERINI
PUBBLICAZIONI DEL CENTRO STUDI OPERA OMNIA LUIGI BOCCHERINI
PUBLICATIONS DU CENTRO STUDI OPERA OMNIA LUIGI BOCCHERINI
VERÖFFENTLICHUNGEN DER CENTRO STUDI OPERA OMNIA LUIGI BOCCHERINI
PUBLICACIONES DEL CENTRO STUDI OPERA OMNIA LUIGI BOCCHERINI
LUCCA

Locatelli and the Violin Bravura Tradition

EDITED BY

FULVIA MORABITO

BREPOLS

TURNHOUT

MMXV

The present volume has been made possible with assistance from

D/2015/0095/64

ISBN 978-2-503-55535-5

Printed in Italy

CONTENTS

Preface

2014 marked the 250ᵗʰ anniversary of the death of two great virtuoso violinists: Pietro Antonio Locatelli and Jean-Marie Leclair *l'aîné*. This important celebration stimulated the compilation of the present volume, which focuses on the origin and development of the violin bravura tradition, from the end of the seventeenth century to the early years of the twentieth. Rather than providing a systematic survey of the subject, this book collects a few of case studies that highlight a phenomenon originating in Italy and gradually spreading to the rest of Europe.

Locatelli spent his formative years in the chapel of Santa Maria Maggiore in Bergamo, his native town. In 1711 he left for Rome, intending perhaps to refine his skills under the guidance of one of the highest musical authorities of the time: Arcangelo Corelli. We do not know if this aim was realised: Corelli, severely ill, died soon after Locatelli's arrival. What is certain is that the young virtuoso absorbed the then prevailing Corellian style, at least until 1723, when he left Rome to begin his career as a traveling virtuoso, performing both in Italy (in Vivaldi's Venice and Mantua) and abroad (Munich, Berlin, Frankfurt, Kassel), before settling permanently in Amsterdam in 1729. Jean-Marie Leclair, born in Lyon but a student of the Piedmontese violin virtuoso Giovanni Battista Somis, a pupil of Corelli, was based in Paris, at least until 1737, when a dispute with the Turin violinist Giovanni Pietro Ghignone (*alias* Jean-Pierre Guignon) about the leadership of the orchestra of the then French King Louis XV[1], took him regularly to the Netherlands, as a guest of the Princess Anne of Orange. Leclair was to return permanently to Paris in 1743.

It was in Kassel that the destinies of Locatelli and Leclair were to converge. A chronicle by Jacob Wilhelm Lustig, organist of Groningen, describes a musical duel held in December 1728 at the court of Carl I, Landgrave of Hesse-Kassel. On that occasion Locatelli played «like a devil», Leclair «like an angel», each reflecting the two respective dominant violin styles: the Italian (virtuosic, acrobatic, representing the edge of the executive possibility, even at the expense of tone) and the French (more sober, but much more expressive, lyrical, and concerned with tone quality). If the veracity of the story remains disputable (no documentation certifies that the meeting took place) it is possible that the two violinists met subsequently — regularly, even — in the Netherlands: but this remains another hypothesis lacking confirmatory evidence. In addition, the received assumption is that Locatelli instructed Leclair, influencing the composition of his Op. 5. It is erroneous to speak about Locatelli's influence on Leclair's Op. 5; it was composed

---

[1]. Which resolved in favour of the Italian-French violinist.

before the supposed tuition of Leclair by Locatelli; a genuine influence on Leclair's Op. 9 is however detectable[2].

Determining the influence of the Italian master on Leclair is not just a matter of stylistic comparison, since that discipleship, even if only 'spiritual', was to establish Locatelli as one of the most influential inspirations of the glorious '*école française de violon*', of which Leclair was among the founders[3].

The objective of this volume is to separate factual evidence from those unfounded beliefs perpetuated by decades of literature. In fact, no documents attest to regular interaction between Locatelli and Leclair. The fact nonetheless remains that Locatelli, at that time as at the present, was a key figure in the history of violin music. He was the author of *L'Arte del violino*, 12 Concertos for solo violin with 24 Capriccios *ad libitum*, Op. 3, a *Kunstbuch* which, although eschewing the systematic structure of a treatise, explores and reveals the idiomatic potentialities of an instrument then relatively 'young', implementing the technique of both the left hand and the bow. Thus, Locatelli's legacy, was certainly acquired more-or-less directly by Leclair and by the 'French violin school', from its start a formidable sounding-board of the Italian violin tradition.

Since the seventeenth century Italy, and in particular Northern Italy, has acted as a seedbed of violin virtuosity: Biagio Marini, Carlo Farina, Salomone Rossi, Giovanni Battista Buonamente and Marco Uccellini being among its first and most important representatives. Their musical output, bold and sometimes bizarre as it was, found a counterpart in the more lyrical school of Bologna, with Giuseppe Torelli as one of its leaders, responsible for the education of the *divino* Arcangelo (Corelli), who was the bearer of a sober, elegant, but not dry style — especially in terms of ornamentation — and initiator of a school destined to exercise a lasting, supranational influence. Among the students of Corelli, are early-eighteenth-century figures of high calibre such as Francesco Geminiani, Francesco Maria Veracini and Somis, the aforementioned master of Leclair. Renewed impetus towards extreme virtuosity came from Antonio Vivaldi and Locatelli himself; the more restrained and expressive Giuseppe Tartini instituted at Padua the 'School of the Nations', an advanced study programme (as we say today), attended by around seventy students, including the beloved Pietro Nardini. With these foundations, the echoes of the Italian violin school reverberated throughout Europe, taking root in France with particular tenacity.

With its lively concert life, thanks not least to the establishment of the public Concert spirituel (1725 onwards), the Concert des amateurs (1769-1780) and the Concert de la Loge Olympique (1786-1789), France became the cradle of the violin bravura tradition. If at first the scene was dominated by two disciples of Somis, the said Leclair and Ghignone/

---

[2].   See Rudolf Rasch's article in the present volume.

[3].   If not the proper founder, in the words of FÉTIS, François-Joseph. *Notice biographique sur Nicolo Paganini, suivie de l'analyse de ses ouvrages et précédée d'une esquisse de l'histoire du violon*, Paris, Schonenberger, 1851, p. 27. *Cfr.* also Étienne Jardin's article in the present volume.

Guignon[4] it was then the turn of Tartini's pupil Pierre Pagin, protagonist of the Concert spirituel during the 1740s, who passed into the annals of history for being resoundingly decried as the champion of the Italian style. Then emerged Pierre Gaviniès, presumably a student of Leclair, and Giovanni Mane Giornovichi, *alias* Ivan Mane Jarnović, possibly a student of the 'pyrothechnical' Antonio Lolli, a disciple of Pasquale Bini, emanating in turn from the Tartini school. The turning-point of the French violin school came with the ascent and success of another Piedmontese: Giovanni Battista Viotti, a pupil of Gaetano Pugnani (Somis school). Facilitated by his inseparable Stradivari and the newly introduced, versatile Tourte bow, Viotti achieved a powerful, eloquent sound, at times dramatic, supporting an intense, expressive interpretation, distanced from the display of sterile, self-referential virtuosity. So began the romantic sensibility.

After Viotti had initiated what may be called the 'second generation' of the French violin school, his legacy inspired the didactic fundamentals of the Conservatoire of Paris, founded in 1795, as a hotbed of artists: for the first time in history students were called upon to undertake a comprehensive and systematic course of studies, including knowledge of the repertoire of the greatest masters of the past. Directly responsible for the dissemination of Viotti's teachings was his putative pupil Pierre Baillot, professor of violin of the newly established Institution. His *Méthode de violon* provided the training manual of the Conservatoire; it was published in 1803 and written in collaboration with the Institute colleagues Pierre Rode (one of the principal disciples of Viotti), and Rodolphe Kreutzer, pupil of Anton Stamitz — a leading member of the Mannheim School. Also belonging to the Viotti school was the Belgian Charles-Auguste de Bériot, traditionally considered the founder of the so-called 'Franco-Belgian violin school': this label, coined by German critics in the context of a juxtaposition between national and French violin tradition, does not denote any particularly distinctive features, apart from the disqualification of spectacular or sensationalized virtuosity. The teachings of de Bériot provided the basis for the formation of many virtuosos, including Henry Vieuxtemps, eventual teacher of Eugène Ysaÿe.

Paganini achieved a major synthesis of the Italian and French violin traditions. He can be considered the most worthy follower of Locatelli: in his Capriccios Op. 1 he admirably brought together the technical achievements of the many virtuosos who preceded him. These represented the swan-song of the Italian violin bravura tradition, which for decades had been downgraded to the status of 'spectator' rather than 'protagonist'.

Beyond the conceptual Italian-French 'axis', including its more mature Belgian offshoots, there were two territories in which violin repertoire was also cultivated: the Anglo-Saxon and the Germanic.

At the beginning of the eighteenth century, Great Britain, and especially London, was subjugated by the Italian violin tradition, part of a culture whose resonance was

---

[4]. The latter was appointed *Roi des violons* by Louis xv in person.

being maximised by aristocrats returning from the *grand tour*. The violinists of the *bel Paese* became protagonists of the intense concert life of the UK as well as the burgeoning publishing market (witness the plethora of editions by John Walsh). The attitude of the English towards extreme virtuosity was hostile, however; such virtuosity was perceived as an expression of barbarism, completely devoid of good taste, above all when it involved the imitation of the sounds of nature (birds singing, animal sounds, and so forth). Similar reactions were provoked by 'redundant' ornamentation. Virtuosic ostentation and exaggerated ornamentation even became a metaphor for excess and degeneration, with moral connotations of the lustful and salacious.

In light of the above — and not without ambivalent reactions from critics and the public — the English stage was trod by Geminiani, Veracini, Pietro Castrucci (Corellian school), Vivaldi, Felice Giardini (another student of Somis), Carlo Chiabrano (grandson of Somis), Pugnani, Lolli, Giornovichi, and finally Viotti, who won almost unanimous praise. This Italian hegemony was gradually eroded by the presence of some prominent members of the German violin school. Except for a few minor figures such as Matthew Dubourg (pupil of Geminiani), Thomas Linley (student of Nardini), and a few others (such as the brothers Alfred and Henry Holmes), Great Britain never established a strong national violin tradition.

Even the German school, comprising musicians born in Austria, Bohemia and Hungary, was largely indebted to the Italian violins virtuosos at the beginning of the eighteenth century. Starting from Johann Georg Pisendel, a pupil of Torelli and Vivaldi, and an exponent of Locatelli's compositions (his private library contained several works by the elder Italian), was a progression to Leopold Mozart author of the *Versuch einer gründliche Violinschule* (1756), one of the most seminal contemporary treatises, and thence to the court of Mannheim as stimuli for the international resonance of contemporary violin repertoire. As the centre for one of the most important orchestras in Europe, Mannheim also produced Johann, Carl and Anton Stamitz, Christian Cannabich, the Czech Franz Xaver Richter and Wilhelm Cramer, disseminator of Austro-German symphonic repertoire in London. From 1772 Cramer led the orchestra of the Bach-Abel Concerts and, in 1785, founded the Professional Concerts. Johann Peter Salomon, responsible for Haydn's visit to London in 1791, was said to be a student of the Czech Franz Benda (student of Carl Heinrich Graun, in turn a student of Tartini). German musical taste was substantially influenced by Louis Spohr, a pupil of the Mannheimer Franz Eck. Congruent with English 'good taste', Spohr's musical sensibility was oriented towards a serious style, free from entertaining frills, restrained even in the use of vibrato, construing it as a kind of ornament emphasizing the pathos of short passages. In this Spohr differed from Fritz Kreisler, Austrian by birth but educated in Paris, and famous for his 'continuous vibrato'. Spohr was teacher of August Wilhelmj and Ferdinand David, the latter becoming conductor of the Gewandhaus Orchestra and professor at the Leipzig Conservatory, institutions then newly founded by Mendelssohn. Under the guidance of David emerged the Hungarian Joseph Joachim.

All of these figures were entrusted by history with the task of disseminating the German Classical- and Romantic-era repertoire[5].

This, moreover, is the historical background to the contributions of this volume, which, as mentioned previously, do not cover every facet of the phenomenon of violin virtuosity: absent, for instance, is the bravura tradition in Spain, Poland, Scandinavia etc. The outlined scenery represents what might be described as the coarse texture of a fabric whose dyes have gradually merged in many nuances. The various national violin traditions, since their dawning, interacted with steadily increasing intensity, generating the hybridization of dominant styles, performing techniques, repertoire, both highbrow and popular. Even the term 'school' should be applied cautiously, because of the international dimension of composers' careers, the development of the international publishing market and, not least, the emergence of the travelling-virtuosos, one of the most incisive and «corroding»[6] institutions of music history[7].

---

[5]. The present preface have been inspired by all the contributions of the present volume. Other considered texts have been: McVEIGH, Simon. 'The Violinists of the Baroque and Classical Periods', in: *Cambridge Companion to the Violin*, edited by Robin Stowell, Cambridge-New York, Cambridge University Press, 1992 (Cambridge companions to music), pp. 46-60; STOWELL, Robin. 'The Nineteenth Century Bravura Tradition', in: *ibidem*, pp. 61-78; WEN, Eric. 'The Twentieth Century', in: *ibidem*, pp. 79-91; McVEIGH, Simon. 'Italian Violinists in Eighteenth-Century London', in: *The Eighteenth-Century Diaspora of Italian Music and Musicians*, edited by Reinhard Strohm, Turnhout, Brepols, 2001 (Speculum musicae, 8), pp. 139-176; SUCHOWIEJKO, Renata. 'Virtuoso: an Incarnation of God or Evil? Some Thoughts about Violin Virtuosity in the 19th Century', in: *Instrumental Music and the Industrial Revolution*, edited by Roberto Illiano and Luca Lévi Sala, Bologna, Ut Orpheus Edizioni, 2010 (Ad Parnassum Studies, 5), pp. 99-106; BORER, Philippe. 'Paganini's Virtuosity and Improvisatory Style', in: *Beyond Notes: Improvisation in Western Music of the Eighteenth and Nineteenth Centuries*, edited by Rudolf Rasch, Turnhout, Brepols, 2011 (Speculum musicae, 16), pp. 191-215; RICCO, Renato. 'Charles-Auguste de Bériot e l'improvvisazione virtuosistica per violino', in: *ibidem*, pp. 218-236; MILSOM, David. 'The Franco-Belgian School of Violin Playing: Towards an Understanding of Chronology and Characteristic, 1850-1925', in: *Ad Parnassum: A Journal of Eighteenth- and Nineteenth-Century Instrumental Music*, II/21 (April 2013); JARDIN, Étienne. 'Les violonistes en concert à Paris (1822-1848)', in: *ibidem*, pp. 21-41. On more specific topics see also METZNER, Paul. *Crescendo of the Virtuoso: Spectacle, Skill, and Self-Promotion in Paris during the Age of the Revolution*, Berkeley-Los Angeles, University of California Press, 1998 (Studies on the history of society and culture, 30); *Giovanni Battista Viotti: A Composer between the Two Revolutions*, edited by Massimiliano Sala, Bologna, Ut Orpheus Edizioni, 2006 (Ad Parnassum studies, 2); ROWE, Mark W. *Heinrich Wilhelm Ernst: Virtuoso Violinist*, Aldershot, Ashgate, 2008; BROWN, Clive. *Classical and Romantic Performance Practice 1750-1900*, Oxford, Oxford University Press, 1999; *Nicolò Paganini: Diabolus in Musica*, edited by Andrea Barizza and Fulvia Morabito, Turnhout, Brepols, 2010 (Studies on Italian music history, 5); *Henryk Wieniawski and the Bravura Tradition*, edited by Maciej Jabłoński and Danuta Jasińska, Poznań, Henryk Wieniawski Musical Society, 2011 (Henryk Wieniawski, Complete works, B series); KAWABATA, Maiko. *Paganini: The 'Demonic' Virtuoso*, Woodbridge, Boydell & Press, 2013.

[6]. With the words of VEINUS, Abraham. *The Concert*, London, Cassel, 1948.

[7]. See the following volumes recently published: *«En pèlerinage avec Liszt»: Virtuosos, Repertoire and Performing Venues in 19th-Century Europe*, edited by Fulvia Morabito, Turnhout, Brepols, 2014 (Speculum musicae, 24), and *Piano Culture in 19th-Century Paris*, edited by Massimiliano Sala, Turnhout, Brepols, 2015 (Speculum musicae, 26).

PREFACE

The majority of the contributions to this volume comprise a selection of the papers presented at the international conference *P. A. Locatelli and J.-M. Leclair: Legacy in the 19th Century*, held in Bergamo on 17-19 October 2014. The event was organized by the Centro Studi Opera Omnia Luigi Boccherini (Lucca), the Fondazione MIA (Bergamo) and the Palazzetto Bru Zane – Centre de musique romantique française (Venice), in collaboration with the Italian National Edition of the Complete Works of Pietro Antonio Locatelli. The scientific committee consisted of Annalisa Barzanò (Bergamo), Sergio Durante (Padua), Roberto Illiano (Lucca), Étienne Jardin (Paris-Venice), Fulvia Morabito (Lucca), Paola Palermo (Bergamo), Rudolf Rasch (Utrecht) and Massimiliano Sala (Bergamo). The keynote speakers were Sergio Durante (University of Padua, President of the cited Locatelli Complete Edition), Rudolf Rasch (Utrecht University) and Neal Zaslaw (Cornell University, Ithaca, NY).

I would like to thank all the Institutions involved in the conference. Special thanks go to Fondazione MIA (in particular to Fabio Bombardieri and Claudio Pelis, the Fondazione's respective President and Councilor), and to Fondazione della Comunità Bergamasca Onlus. A particular aknowledgement goes also to my colleague Roberto Illiano, for his work on the volume, to Michael Talbot for his advice, and to Rohan H. Stewart-MacDonald and Naomi Matsumoto for their careful assistance with the revision of the English texts.

Fulvia Morabito
Lucca, March 2015

PIETRO ANTONIO LOCATELLI AND JEAN-MARIE LECLAIR

Leclair, Locatelli and the Musical Geography of Europe

Rudolf Rasch
(Utrecht)

The careers of the composers Jean-Marie Leclair (1697-1764) and Pietro Antonio Locatelli (1695-1764) have many things in common. Both of them were important performers on the violin and both composed an important body of music for the violin. And both travelled to other countries to show off their capabilities on their instrument. Born only two years apart, in 1697 and 1695 respectively, both of them died in 1764.

Their careers crossed one another a few times. The first time must have been in Kassel, in Germany, where, at the court of Landgrave Carl of Hesse-Kassel apparently there was a concert where both Locatelli and Leclair performed. The date of this encounter is usually set at December 1728, when Locatelli was indeed paid by the Court of Kassel. The only account on the event is from more than half a century later, given by the Dutch organist of German extraction, Jacob Wilhelm Lustig, organist in Groningen, in a footnote added to his translation into Dutch of the German translation of Charles Burney's *The Present State of Music in France and Italy* (London, T. Becket and Co., 1771)[1], published in Groningen in 1786 as *Rijk Gestoffeerd Verhaal van de Eigenlijke Gesteldheid der Hedendaagsche Toonkunst* [Richly Decorated Account of the Real State of Music Today][2]:

---

[1]. *Carl Burney's* [...] *Tagebuch einer musikalischen Reise* [...] *aus dem Englishen übersetzt von C. D. Ebeling*, 3 vols., Hamburg, Bode, 1772-1773.

[2]. Burney, Charles. *Rijk gestoffeerd verhaal van de eigenlijke gesteldheid der hedendaagsche Toonkunst* [...] *Vertaald en Opgeluisterd door Jacob Wilhelm Lustig*, Groningen, J. Oomkens, 1786, pp. 389-390, note 168: «When he [Locatelli] and Leclair once let themselves hear at the same time at the court of Kassel, the court-jester had said already at the beginning: that lad walks over the violin as a hare, and at the end: he [Leclair] plays like an angel, the other [Locatelli] as a devil. The former succeeded, with a little-exercised left hand, in conquering the hearts by his unusually pure and lovely tone; whereas the latter [Locatelli], by producing, grindingly, extremely difficult things, mainly tried to bring the listeners in a state of astonishment. However, regarding the saddle-steadiness of the metre, which, alas!, the French musician usually do not

> Toen Hy [Locatelli] en *Le Clair* zich eens ter zelver Tijd hooren
> lieten op 't Hof te Kassel, had de Hofnar reeds in 't begin gezegd: die Karel
> loopt op de Viool, als een Haas; en, by het Slot: die [Leclair] speelt als
> een Engel; en de eerste [Locatelli], als een Duivel. Gene [Leclair] wist,
> by een weinig geoeffende linker Hand, door zynen ongemeen zuiveren
> en lieflijken Toon, de Harten te vermeesteren; terwijl deeze [Locatelli],
> door groote Zwaarigheden, al knarssende, 'er uit te halen, voornaamlijk
> trachtde, de Toehoorders tot Verwondering te brengen. Doch, aangaande
> het Zadelvaste in de Maat, den franschen Musiekeren in 't gemeen, helaas!
> niet volkomen eigen (not. 28 pag. 32), konde men ligt merken, dat de
> eerstgemelde, by zyn Solospeelen, buiten het Spoor raakte, zo dra hy niet
> zeer omzigtig op zyne Hoede bleef.

How exact this account is, one cannot say. It must be noted here that the characterisations of the violin playing of the two masters follow exactly the traditional prejudices about Italian and French music and musicians in the eighteenth century and this does not add much weight to the credibility of Lustig's report.

The second time their careers crossed one another will be dealt with later.

There are also important differences between the careers of Locatelli and Leclair.

Leclair was born in Lyon, in 1697, and spent his youth there[3]. Certainly he was in Turin at several occasions in the 1720s, also to study violin with Giovanni Battista Somis. From 1723 to his death he was based in Paris, a stay only occasionally interrupted by foreign travels.

John Walsh reprinted Leclair's *Second livre de sonates pour le violon et pour la flûte traversière avec la basse continue* (Paris, Author-Boivin-Le Clerc, 1728), an edition announced as «Solo's for a Violin or German Flute, with a Thorough Bass for the Harpsichord or Bass Violin, Compos'd by Mr. Le Clair, lately come from Italy. Opera Secunda», in the *Country Journal* of 20 July 1728[4]. The phrase «lately come from Italy» of course suggests Leclair's presence in the English capital, but this must be doubted. Apparently no copy of Walsh's edition of Leclair's second book is extant. Later on Walsh reprinted other works by Leclair; there is no reason to think of any involvement of the composer himself.

The first is the visit to Kassel in 1728 already mentioned, which is, by the way, not documented in any contemporary document as far as Leclair is involved. Lustig has to be believed on his word, more the half a century later.

---

master completely, one could easily notice that the first mentioned [Leclair], when playing solo, got off the track, as soon as he did not pay attention to it very carefully».

  3. There seem to be no general studies about Leclair after PINCHERLE, Marc. *Jean-Marie Leclair l'aîné*, Paris, La Colombe, 1952 (Euterpe), and, ZASLAW, Neal. *Materials for the Life and Works of Jean-Marie Leclair l'aîné*, Ph.D. Diss., New York (NY), Columbia University, 1970.

  4. SMITH, William C. – HUMPHRIES, Charles. *A Bibliography of the Musical Works Published by the Firm of John Walsh during the Years 1721-1766*, London, The Bibliographical Society, 1968, pp. 926-927.

Sometimes it is supposed or considered possible that Leclair went to Amsterdam with Locatelli after the event in Kassel: «Leclair apparently worked with Locatelli at this time, perhaps returning to Amsterdam with him», writes the *New Grove* article about Leclair[5]. As far as my knowledge goes, there is no shred of evidence that Leclair was with Locatelli in Amsterdam at that time.

More certainty there is about a trip to Holland in the years 1740-1743, when he was director of the musical establishment of the rich Jewish merchant Francisco López de Liz in The Hague[6]. This appointment ended with López de Liz's bankruptcy early in 1743. The contract allowed Leclair to take a leave for three month every years, and at least one of these leaves was spent in Leeuwarden, the capital of the province of Frisia. There was, at that time, the court of Anne of Hanover, Princess of Orange, wife of William, Prince of Orange, Stadholder of Frisia. Leclair's sojourn in Leeuwarden is mentioned, again, by Lustig who wrote a one-paragraph biographical note on Leclair for his collection of biographical notes about Dutch musicians that was published in Friedrich Wilhelm Marpurg's *Kritische Briefe über die Tonkunst, Zweyter Band, Vierter Theil*[7]. There it reads:

> Er [Leclair] pflegte ehedem jährlich ein Vierteljahr unsere Princessin [Anna] zum Concert zu besuchen.

Leclair's visit to Leeuwarden is confirmed by the letter of dedication added to his *Quatrième livre de sonates à violon seul avec la basse continue* [...] *Œuvre* IX (Paris, Author-Le Clerc-Le Clerc-Boivin, [1743]). Here it is read[8]:

> Je l'ai éprouvé, Madame, pendant tout le tems que j'ai passé dans vôtre Cour, où vous m'aviés fait l'honneur de m'appeller.

Unfortunately, there is no archival evidence to provide more detail about Leclair's visit to Leeuwarden. The receipts of the payments that Leclair received from López de Liz, suggest that Leclair was in Leeuwarden in the summer of 1741.

---

5. Zaslaw, Neal. 'Leclair, Jean-Marie', in: *The New Grove Dictionary of Music and Musicians*, Second edition, 29 vols., London, Macmillan Publishers, 2001, vol. XIV, pp. 445-448.

6. See Id. *Materials for the Life and Works* [...], *op. cit.* (see note 3).

7. Marpurg, Friedrich Wilhelm. *Kritische Briefe über die Tonkunst*, 3 vols., Berlin, Friedrich Wilhelm Birnstiel, 1759-1763, vol. II/4, '123. Brief', pp. 463-476: «He [Leclair] formerly used to visit every year for three months our princess [Anne of Hannover] for her concerts»; see Enschedé, Jan Willem. 'Biografische aanteekeningen over musici door J. W. Lustig, Organist van de Martinikerk te Groningen', in: *Tijdschrift van de Vereeniging voor Nederlandse Muziekgeschiedenis*, VIII/2 (1906), pp. 146-165.

8. «I have experienced that, Madame, during the time I have passed at your Court, where you have done me the honour of calling me to».

A Son Altesse Royale Madame
La Princesse D'Orange.

Madame

Le gout de V.A.R. pour les vraïs beautés de la Musique, et la Connoissance
profonde que vous avés des principes de cet Art, ne sont pas les seuls motifs qui m'ont
inspiré la confiance de vous offrir cet ouvrage - je sçai que non - contente d'aimer tous les
talens, vous faites gloire de les proteger. je l'ai éprouvé, Madame, pendant tout le tems
que j'ai passé dans vôtre Cour, où vous m'aviés fait l'honneur de m'apeller. Les aplaudissemens
sont la récompense la plus flateuse dés Arts. le souvenir de ceux que j'ai reçus de V.A.R.
est plus precieux pour moi, que celui de vos bienfaits. je ferai toute ma vie de nouveaux
efforts pour les justifier.

Je Suis

Madame

Avec le plus respectueux attachement

de Votre Altesse Royale

Le tres humble et tres
obeissant Serviteur.
LE CLAIR l'aîné

ILL. 1: Dedication of Jean-Marie Leclair, *Quatrième livre de sonates à violon seul avec la Basse continue*
(Paris, 1743).

One of the payments for his service to López de Liz was cashed in Amsterdam, on 3 March 1741[9], and this is, as far as known, the only piece of hard evidence that Leclair ever was in that city. If he went to see Locatelli at that occasion, is impossible to tell, but it may well have been so.

Such a visit, at least, is reported in a passage in the 'Necrologe de M. Le Clair' by François-Joachim de Pierre de Bernis (1715-1794), published in *Le Necrologe des hommes célèbres de France, Année 1766*[10]:

> C'est dans ce dessein qu'il fit un voyage en Hollande, où il s'occupa moins de ses succès, & de l'accueil qui lui fit la Princesse d'Orange, que du plaisir d'entendre le célèbre Locatelli; il profita avidement des lumières qu'il daigna lui communiquer sur les profondeurs de l'harmonie.

De Bernis goes on by signalling an influence of Locatelli in Leclair's *Troisième livre de sonates à violon seul avec la basse continue*, but in this respect he must be mistaken. The *Troisième livre* (Op. 5) was published in 1734. If he actually meant the *Quatrième livre* of 1743, one could agree with him: here clearly reminiscences of Locatelli's virtuoso style can be heard, while such reminiscences are certainly missing in the *Troisième livre*.

There may be even a quotation from Locatelli's *Sonate* [...] *Opera sesta* in Leclair's *Quatrième livre*. The opening passage of the first movement of Sonata III, in D major, strongly reminds one of the opening passage of the first movement of Locatelli's Sonata Op. 6 No. 3.

Locatelli's geographical career is quite different from that of Leclair. Born in Bergamo, he spent his youth and had his first music instruction there[11]. Around 1710 he went to Rome for further lessons and earned a living as violinist. If he really was a pupil of Corelli, as the tradition wants, is doubtful if not improbable. At some point in the 1720s he went to Germany, but many details of this journey are still unclear. In any case he was in Kassel in 1728, as shown above. Soon afterwards he must have gone to Amsterdam, where he would stay for the rest of his life. No further travels are documented.

---

[9]. See ZASLAW, Neal. *Materials for the Life and Works* [...], *op. cit.* (see note 3), p. 76.

[10]. BERNIS, François-Joachim de Pierre, de. 'Necrologe de M. Le Clair', in: *Le Necrologe des hommes célèbres de France, Année 1766*, Paris, Moreau, 1767. «With this aim he made a trip to Holland, where he occupied himself less with his successes and the way he was received by the Princess of Orange, than by the pleasure of hearing Locatelli. He profited avidly from the insights he was willing to communicate about the depths of harmony». Quoted from the 1775 Maastricht edition, where the article is on pp. 119-131. De Bernis became cardinal in 1769.

[11]. There are three biographies of Locatelli: KOOLE, Arend. *Leven en Werken van Pietro Antonio Locatelli da Bergamo, 1695-1764* [*sic*]: «*Italiaans Musycqmeester tot Amsterdam*», Amsterdam, Jasonpers, 1949; DUNNING, Albert. *Pietro Antonio Locatelli: Der Virtuose und seine Welt*, 2 vols., Buren, Frits Knuf, 1981; and MORABITO, Fulvia. *Pietro Antonio Locatelli*, Palermo, L'Epos, 2009 (Constellatio musica, 17).

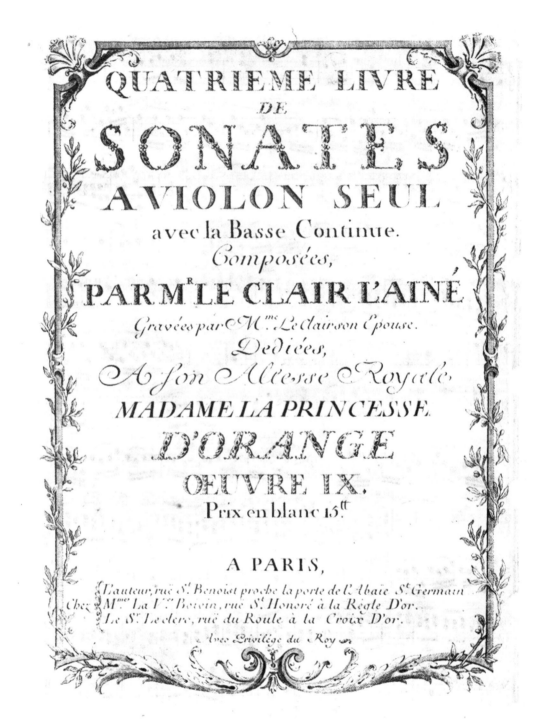

ILL. 2: Title page of Jean-Marie Leclair, *Quatrième livre de sonates à violon seul avec la Basse continue* (Paris, 1743).

Comparing the careers of Locatelli and Leclair they represent two different types: Leclair staying in his own country, Locatelli settling in another country, many miles away. This difference makes it necessary to say some general words about the role in music history of travel and moving from one country to another.

In fact the movements of musicians through the geography of Europe are part and parcel of the musical history of Europe not only in the eighteenth century, but at all times. From Medieval times onwards musicians and composers have travelled, and these travels have shaped the history of music in many significant aspects. Musicians from the north, mainly the southern parts of the Netherlands and the northern parts of France travelled to Italy to develop the 'central style' of fifteenth- and sixteenth-century music. Italian musicians swarmed off all over Europe during the eighteenth century and brought Italian musical genres to every corner of the Continent. Czech musicians and composers fulfilled their own roles outside the Czech Lands in the eighteenth century.

Movements of musicians can be studied from two points of view, that of the musician himself and that of the location. Let us first look at the musician.

A distinction can to be made between three kinds of movement, which will be called travel, stay and settlement.

A *visit* means going somewhere without the intention of settlement, not even for a short period.

A stay can be a *short stay* in the same place somewhere for a couple of months to a couple of years. A *longer stay* may last from a few years to, let us say, ten to fifteen years. A characteristic of a 'stay' is that, in principle, there is the intention to move on later.

Settlement means going to be based somewhere in a permanent or at least semi-permanent way. Of course, when a musician settles somewhere his plans how long to stay or whether to move on or not may not yet have been articulated.

If the careers of musicians are viewed from the point of view of settlement, three basic career types for musicians can be defined:

1. The *national career*: birth, education and professional career occur on the same place or at least in the same region or national entity. Of course, there may be travels or short foreign stays, but there is always the return to the home base. Easy examples that come to one's mind are Bach and Mozart.

2. The *foreign career*: birth (and probably education too) in one place or at least in the same region or national entity, but the professional career in another part of Europe (or of the world), in a single place or region. Also in this type of career there may be travels and short stays elsewhere. The careers of Lully and Handel may serve as examples.

3. The *international career*: birth and (probably education too) in one place or at least in the same region or national entity, the professional career in several different places or regions of Europe (or of the world), including the place or region of origin.

The distinctions are very simple and very crude and are bound to cause problems in many individual cases. Some comments only about the problems of place and time are useful.

First of all there is the 'problem of place'. It is not so difficult to call England, France, Spain and Italy cultural entities, despite the substantial regional varieties within this entities. But what about the German-speaking part of Europe? The borders of the various German and Austrian 'states' have moved considerably over time, especially if the considerations are stretched to the Middle Ages on the one end and to the present day on the other. Large regions were at some periods of time connected with a central authority in a German land, established in Vienna, Berlin or elsewhere, which were not so in other periods. These regions include the Netherlands, the East of France, Northern Italy and large parts of Eastern Europe. Not only the borders moved, within these borders the regional variety is so large that it is often difficult to speak of a single cultural entity or identity.

The second problem is the 'problem of time'. How long should a musician be in a place to have an effect on his classification into one of the four categories? Jean-Marie Leclair's two-year stay in The Hague certainly is certainly not enough to classify his career as international, but what about the German career years of George Frideric Handel or the French years of Igor Stravinsky? It seems that usually a minimum stay of five years is required to speak of real settlement, but this is just a working hypothesis and there may be exceptions to this rule. The concept of 'longer stay' is in fact a compromise category between those of 'short stay' and 'settlement'.

The place or places where a composer developed his career determines the 'cultural entity' to which a composer generally belonged, at least in our eyes. For the composer itself it probably was not always a very important question, but ever since the nineteenth century nationality has been an important category in musical historiography. The country or area to which a composer is considered to belong has, for example, considerable influence on which musicological communities study the life and works of the composer, which countries or cities have societies for the promotion of the composer's works and which publishers produce his Complete Works edition. Although many composers are being studied all over the world, the largest concentration of scholars dealing with a certain composer is usually found (not counting the United States) in the country to which the composer has been assigned by the musicological community. This works in a simple way for composers who were born and raised in one country and worked there all or most of their lives, but is more complicated for composers with foreign and international careers. Often, there is a win-win situation for composer with an international career: the life and work of Handel is studied in both Germany and England, that of Locatelli both in Italy and the Netherlands. Interest in Leclair should be looked for especially in France (and, of course, the United States).

About the way in which composers dealt with their national identities themselves will be said some words later on in this article.

It is now time to look at the musical geography of Europe from the other side, that of the location. This point of view starts with the question which career types did the musicians and composers have that were active at a certain place at a certain time. Where did they come from and for how long were they at that place? In order to answer this question it is necessary to make an overview of all musicians of whom data are available and then check systematically both their extraction and their residency in the location at issue. I have done this exercise for the Dutch Republic and it became soon clear that the musicians and composers active there in the seventeenth and eighteenth centuries could fall in any of the categories described so far[12].

First there are composers who were both born and had their main career in the Dutch Republic. Examples of composers who spent their entire lives (apart from occasional travels) in the Dutch Republic are Jan Pieterszoon Sweelinck, organist in Amsterdam, Jacob van Eyck, carillon player in Utrecht and composer for the recorder, Constantijn Huygens, musical amateur in The Hague, and Unico Wilhelm van Wassenaer, also musical amateur in The Hague.

Then there are composers who were born outside the Dutch Republic but spent nearly their complete professional careers in the Dutch Republic. Henricus Albicastro (probably born in Biswang in Bavaria, officer in the Dutch army, musical amateur) and Christian Ernst Graf (born in Rudolstadt in Thuringia, music director of the Prince of Orange in The Hague) are the best known examples. For them their career in the Dutch Republic was a foreign career.

And then there are musicians/composers with international careers, careers that developed partly outside the Dutch Republic, partly inside. A distinction into two subgroups must be made, when one is studying this category in the musical history of a certain country or region. The first subgroup includes the composers with careers that started in the country under study but ended elsewhere, the second subgroup includes the careers that started somewhere else but ended in the country or region studied. If this is applied to the Dutch Republic the first subgroup includes names such as those of Johann Schenck, Pieter Hellendaal and Willem de Fesch. They were born and first worked in the Dutch Republic, but moved later to Germany (Schenck) or England (Hellendaal, De Fesch), where they continued their career.

To the second subgroup belongs Pietro Antonio Locatelli, who was born in Bergamo in Italy, first worked in Italy and internationally (in particular in Germany) and then settled in Amsterdam for what was to be the second half of his life.

---

12. RASCH, Rudolf. *Geschiedenis van de Muziek in de Republiek der Zeven Verenigde Nederlanden 1572-1795* (= Mijn Werk op Internet, Deel Een), Hoofdstuk Vier: Componisten, <http://www.let.uu.nl/~Rudolf. Rasch/personal/Republiek/Republiek04-Componisten.pdf> (accessed 30 January 2015).

In addition there are musicians who stayed in the Dutch Republic for just a couple of months to a couple of years. Examples from the second half of the eighteenth century are Franz Xaver Richter, Carl Stamitz and Jan Ladislav Dussek. Mozart was in the Dutch Republic for half a year, in 1765-1766, but this should perhaps better be classified as travel, and the same applies probably to Giuseppe Torelli's visit to the Republic in 1698. Jean-Marie Leclair also belongs to this group, because of his stay in The Hague as music director of Francisco López de Liz. Among the musicians and composers who resided between five and fifteen years in the Dutch Republic may be mentioned the Italians Santo Lapis and Giovanni Battista Zingoni.

Musical travellers visiting the Dutch Republic can be documented in large numbers, especially in the eighteenth century. Not only Mozart, but also Beethoven has given concerts at the Stadholder's Court in The Hague (in 1783). Other musical travellers of name who have toured through the Dutch Republic include Mattheson, Francesco Maria Veracini, Carlo Tessarini, George Frideric Handel, Carl Philipp Emanuel and Wilhelm Friedemann Bach, Abt. Vogler and many more.

A not unimportant question related to the presence of musicians and composers from elsewhere in a certain place at a certain time is to what extent they brought the musical culture from their country of origin with them and to which extent this was a factor in musical life (and musical history). One can rather safely say that the presence of foreign musicians has contributed enormously to the spread of musical culture from one place, region or country to other places, regions or countries. This is especially so where concentrations of foreigners of the same kind could be found, such as the Italian musicians and composers in London in the eighteenth century.

In other cases transnational influences were strong because of the presence of foreign musical institutions, such as Italian *opera seria* in Middle and Western Europe in the seventeenth and eighteenth centuries, Italian *opera buffa* in mid-eighteenth-century Paris and French *opéra-comique* in Holland in the second half of the eighteenth century.

A significant impact on musical life was also exerted by the presence of printed editions (or manuscripts) of foreign music, an impact that could be felt without the physical presence of musicians of corresponding origin. Examples of this phenomenon are the numerous editions of Lully's works produced in Holland during the decades around 1700[13], and the massive amount of editions of Corelli's works produced in Amsterdam,

---

[13]. See SCHNEIDER, Herbert. 'The Amsterdam Editions of Lully's Orchestral Suites', in: *Jean-Baptiste Lully and the Music of the French Baroque: Essays in Honor of James R. Anthony*, edited by John Hajdu Heyer, in collaboration with Catherine Massip, Carl B. Schmidt and Herbert Schneider, Cambridge-New York, Cambridge University Press, 1989, pp. 113-130, and SCHMIDT, Carl B. 'The Amsterdam Editions of Lully's Music: A Bibliographical Scrutiny with Commentary', in: *Lully Studies*, edited by John Hajdu Heyer, Cambridge, Cambridge University Press, 2000, pp. 100-165.

London and Paris in almost the entire eighteenth century[14]. This foreign presence could, of course, be strengthened when the foreigners in a certain musical centre themselves also published their work there. Locatelli, who published all of his works in Holland, most often in Amsterdam[15], is a case in point.

The impact of Leclair's stay in Holland is much more restricted. He will have played his own music there, but to which extent he may have introduced works of other French composers is completely unknown. The music library of López de Liz, for whom Leclair worked, which was inventoried after López de Liz's bankruptcy, shows the normal domination of Italian music in Dutch music collections of the time[16]. Leclair's short-time presence in Leeuwarden did not leave any permanent traces there. The only Dutch publication of his works is a reprint of his sonatas for two violins *senza basso* Opus 3 produced by Gerhard Fredrik Witvogel as *Six sonates à deux violons sans basse* […] *Troisième œuvre* probably in 1739.

Foreign musicians with long periods of settlements, if not the rest of their lives, in their adopted homelands could follow different policies in positioning themselves in the musical life of that new homeland. One was that of emphasizing their foreign background and using this foreign background as a recommendation for their work. Pietro Antonio Locatelli is certainly an example of this approach. After his settlement in Amsterdam around 1730, he called himself «Maestro di musica italiano» and continued to published al his works with Italian titles and with Italian dedications, even if the dedicatees were Dutchmen. Using Italian as the language for musical publications was not so difficult in Amsterdam in the first half of the eighteenth century. The publishing house of Estienne Roger had, from 1696 onwards, published an enormous amount of Italian music, always with the original Italian titles and so on (but, however, with French imprints)[17]. Most Italianate instrumental music composed by transalpine composers (such as Henricus Albicastro, Johann Christian Schickhardt and Willem de Fesch) was published in Amsterdam with Italian titles also. Roger's business successor, Michel-Charles le Cène, followed this policy but usually made his imprints Italian also.

Sometimes an Italian identity was adopted by musicians who were not born in Italy nor had ever worked there, certainly for no other reason to gain prestige as a musician

---

14. See MARX, Hans-Joachim. *Die Überlieferung der Werke Arcangelo Corellis: catalogue raisonné*, Cologne, Arno Volk Verlag, 1980 (Arcangelo Corelli, Historisch-kritische Gesamtausgabe der musikalischen Werke, Supplementband, [5bis]).

15. Only the *Concerti* […] *Opera ottava* were published in Leiden.

16. SCHEURLEER, Daniel François. 'Een Haagsche Muziekliefhebber uit de 18ᵉ eeuw', in: *Tijdschrift van de Vereniging voor Nederlandse Muziekgeschiedenis*, IX/1 (1909), pp. 41-64.

17. See RASCH, Rudolf. '«Il cielo batavo»: I compositori italiani e le edizioni olandesi delle loro opere strumentali nel primo Settecento', in: *Italienische Instrumentalmusik des 18. Jahrhunderts: Alte und neue Protagonisten*, edited by Enrico Careri and Markus Engelhardt, Laaber, Laaber-Verlag, 2002 (Analecta musicologica, 32), pp. 237-266.

or composer[18]. Bavarian-born Johann Heinrich von Weissenburg styled himself Henricus Albicastro, a simple translation of his surname. Dutch-born Quirinus van Blankenburg pulled the same trick, using the Italian name Castelbianco. By doing so he earned two articles in Johann Gottfried Walther's *Musikalisches Lexicon*, one under Blankenburg, one under Castelbianco. By a strange coincidence the names Weissenburg and Blankenburg share the same meaning. The Dutch *secondo Settecento* provides two more Italianate pseudonyms. The musician and composer Johann Andreas Kauchlitz, of Bohemian descent, consistently added the Italianization Colizzi to his name. (Colizzi is a fairly normal Italian surname.) And Christian Gottlieb Tübel, a German musician living in Amsterdam in the 1760s, playfully reversed his last name and gave it an Italian ending: Lebutini. To this day his works are listed in the RISM volumes under both Tübel and Lebutini[19].

A second policy open to immigrant musicians was to integrate into their new environment and to become a musician just like any local musician. This policy was followed especially by German musicians and by musicians coming from the Southern Netherlands who settled in the Dutch Republic. Socially this can be seen by their marriages to Dutch women, from the composition of music on Dutch text or of music in genres that have a close connection with Dutch musical life such as compositions for the accompaniment of the psalms in the Dutch Reformed Church.

To conclude the following remarks. It is useful to study music history, whether it is seen as the history of musical life or as the sum of the biographies of individual musicians and the oeuvres of individual composers, from the point of view of geographical concepts (cities and towns, regions, countries) and their corresponding geographical identities. In order to understand the music of individual composers it is necessary to realise in what kind of context they worked. To understand the music history of a certain place at a certain time, it is necessary to be aware of the origins and backgrounds of the musicians and composers that made this music history.

---

[18]. See ID. 'The Italian Presence in the Musical Life of the Dutch Republic', in: *The Eighteenth-Century Diaspora of Italian Music and Musicians*, edited by Reinhard Strohm, Turnhout, Brepols, 2001 (Speculum musicae, 8), pp. 177-210.

[19]. RISM L 1273 and T 1307-1310.

Locatelli a Bergamo: documenti d'archivio

Paola Palermo
(Bergamo)

I DOCUMENTI D'ARCHIVIO BERGAMASCHI relativi a Pietro Antonio Locatelli sono stati reperiti da chi scrive nell'arco degli ultimi vent'anni e via via censiti in numerose pubblicazioni[1]. Gran parte della documentazione archivistica è stata raccolta, cronologicamente ordinata e riproposta nel volume x dell'Opera Omnia locatelliana, alle sezioni 'Documenti sulla vita e le opere' (pp. 135-195) e 'Lettere' (pp. 247-249)[2].

Le fonti documentarie locatelliane si conservano attualmente nei maggiori istituti culturali della città di Bergamo:

1. Civica Biblioteca 'Angelo Mai' e sezione staccata biblioteca musicale 'G. Donizetti';
2. Archivio di Stato;
3. Archivio Storico Diocesano.

Fonti conservate alla Civica Biblioteca 'Angelo Mai'

Archivio Fumagalli

L'archivio Fumagalli è intitolato a Giuseppe Fumagalli (1920-1998), commercialista bergamasco e musicofilo, discendente di Locatelli per tramite di Caterina, una delle cinque

---

[1]. PALERMO, Paola. *La musica nella basilica di Santa Maria Maggiore a Bergamo dal 1657 al 1711: studio archivistico*, tesi di laurea, 3 voll., Cremona, Università degli studi di Pavia, 1995; EAD. 'La musica nella basilica di Santa Maria Maggiore a Bergamo all'epoca dell'infanzia di Locatelli', in: *Intorno a Locatelli: studi in occasione del tricentenario della nascita di Pietro Antonio Locatelli, (1695-1764)*, 2 voll., Lucca, LIM, 1995 (Speculum musicae, 1/1-2), vol. i, pp. 653-748; EAD. 'La famiglia d'origine di Pietro Antonio Locatelli', in: *Bergomum*, LXLI/2 (1996), pp. 189-208; EAD. – PECIS CAVAGNA, Giulia. *La cappella musicale di Santa Maria Maggiore a Bergamo dal 1657 al 1810*, Turnhout, Brepols, 2011 (Studies on Italian music history, 6), pp. 129-134; PALERMO, Paola. 'Pietro Antonio Locatelli da 'Bergamo': luoghi e fonti archivistiche bergamasche che raccontano il compositore', in: *Atti dell'Ateneo di Scienze, Lettere ed Arti di Bergamo*, LXXV (2011-2012), pp. 115-122.

[2]. LOCATELLI, Pietro Antonio. *Catalogo tematico, lettere, documenti & iconografia*, a cura di Albert Dunning, Magonza, Schott, 2001 (Locatelli complete edition, 10), pp. 259-265.

sorelle del musicista, che il 5 maggio 1705 andò in sposa a Giovanni Battista Fumagalli. Il padre di Giuseppe Fumagalli, anch'egli di nome Giuseppe, già nel 1948 si era adoperato per dimostrare l'illustre discendenza, tanto da stilare un albero genealogico della famiglia Fumagalli (ILL. 1)[3]. Il figlio proseguì l'opera di valorizzazione del compositore costituendo, nel 1969, l'*Associazione Collegium Musicum Pietro Antonio Locatelli*, promuovendo inoltre studi, monografie, edizioni musicali e concerti; ebbe quindi contatti con i principali studiosi locatelliani (Arend Koole[4] e Albert Dunning[5]) e con direttori d'orchestra (da Gianandrea Gavazzeni a Claudio Scimone), raccogliendo una grande quantità di materiale. L'archivio Fumagalli, donato nel febbraio 2001 alla Civica Biblioteca 'Angelo Mai', raccoglie documenti databili dal 1919 al 2000; si tratta di lettere che il Fumagalli mandò ai suoi corrispondenti, fotografie, discorsi dattiloscritti, ricevute, l'atto di fondazione dell'*Associazione Collegium Musicum Pietro Antonio Locatelli*, monografie, articoli di periodici, partiture, dischi, audio e videocassette, locandine, programmi di sala.

L'Archivio Doti Andrea Locatelli[6]

L'archivio storico fondo Doti Locatelli, di proprietà della Congregazione dei padri Somaschi di Genova fino al 1981, fu acquistato e donato alla Biblioteca Mai dallo studioso Carlo Locatelli, discendente della gens Locatellia originaria della Valle Imagna. Vi si conservano 576 fascicoli disposti in ordine cronologico (con estremi dal 1559 al 1794) disposti in 11 cartelle, dei quali il numero 10 contiene le camicie originali e il numero 11 le copie fotostatiche degli atti conservati presso l'Archivio Storico dei Padri Somaschi di Genova.

L'analisi dell'intero archivio[7] ha permesso di individuare, oltre ad un corposo nucleo di documenti inerente alcuni componenti della famiglia Locatelli[8], tra cui anche i bisnonni Filippo e Caterina originari di Mapello e i nonni Pietro e Domenica provenienti da Filago, anche:

[3]. Biblioteca Civica 'A. Mai' di Bergamo (d'ora in avanti BCB), Archivio Giuseppe Fumagalli 35 (tubo), albero genealogico della famiglia Fumagalli in due copie.

[4]. Sua la monografia *Leven en werken van Pietro Antonio Locatelli da Bergamo, 1695-1794 [sic]: «Italiaans musycqmeester tot Amsterdam»*, Amsterdam, Jasonpers, 1949.

[5]. Sua la monografia DUNNING, Albert. *Pietro Antonio Locatelli. Der Virtuose und seine Welt*, 2 voll., Buren, Frits Knuf, 1981, disponibile anche in traduzione italiana a cura di Oddo Piero Bertini, *Pietro Antonio Locatelli. Il virtuoso, il compositore e il suo tempo*, Torino, Fogola, 1983.

[6]. Andrea Locatelli da Mapello (Mapello, Bergamo, ? - Roma 1596), con istrumento rogato dal notaio Panizza, legò 6000 scudi ai padri Somaschi di san Biagio in Monte Citorio, con l'obbligo di dotare ogni anno di 50 scudi due zitelle indigenti e di comprovata moralità, appartenenti alla sua famiglia o della sua terra d'origine oppure di un altro luogo, ma con le qualità richieste. Il legato fu versato dall'erede testamentario Gerolamo Locatelli sotto forma di beni stabili, censi e denari.

[7]. PALERMO, Paola. 'La famiglia d'origine […]', *op. cit.* (si veda nota 1).

[8]. BCB, Archivio Doti Andrea Locatelli, MMB 954–957 e MMB 959–960. *Ibidem*, p. 190.

Albero genealogico della Famiglia Fumagalli

composto nel 1948 dal Dott. Rag. Giuseppe Fumagalli fu Luigi di Bergamo
e da Giovanni (Gino) fu Gaetano perchè più cara sia la memoria degli Antenati e meno facile la dimenticanza

Capostipite

Giovanni Battista Fumagalli olim Francesco
nato il 23-V-1707 in Bergamo Via Corsarola e morto il 29-V-1773 - Sposato con Locatelli Caterina fu Filippo nata il 9-V-1707 e morta il 9-XI-1782
(sorella di Pietro Antonio Locatelli, celebre professore di violino, nato il 3-IX-1695 e morto ad Amsterdam il 1-IV-1764)

Prima generazione dal Capostipite

Maria n. 1736 † 6-V-1819 sposa nel 1761 Giovanni Paolo Ronzoni corriere veneto — **Lucia** n. ? † 1798 sposa nel 1760 il Conte Bondurri — **Caterina** n. 1748 † 1822 sposa Gerolamo Forini morto nel 1786 — **Gaetano** n. 5-VII-1750 † 19-IX-1803 sposa il 21-I-1779 Maddalena Maironi da Ponte n. 5-8-1757 † 28-I-1829

Seconda generazione dal Capostipite

Dei sedici figli di Gaetano Fumagalli e di Maddalena Maironi da Ponte: Giovan Battista, Caterina, Giovanna, Giovan Battista, Caterina, Giuseppe, Giuseppe, Giuseppe, Caterina, Giovanna, Giuseppe, Luigi, Maria, Maria Anna, Francesco e Luigi Maria non sopravvissero che cinque.

Terza generazione dal Capostipite

Quarta generazione dal Capostipite

Quinta generazione dal Capostipite

Sesta generazione dal Capostipite

Settima generazione dal Capostipite

Ramo dei figli di Pietro fu Zaverio (Buenos Ayres) — Ramo dei figli di Cesare fu Cesare — Ramo dei figli di Cirillo (Kiria) di Camillo (Shanghai) — Ramo dei figli di Luigi di Camillo

ILL. 1: Biblioteca Civica 'A. Mai' di Bergamo, Archivio Giuseppe Fumagalli 35 (tubo), albero genealogico della famiglia Fumagalli.

- l'albero genealogico della famiglia Locatelli[9];
- l'attestazione di battesimo di Pietro Antonio, di suo fratello e delle sue sorelle, redatta il 3 settembre 1721[10]; la carta dotale della madre Lucia Crocchi (attestata anche Trotto, Trotta o Trotti), che nel 1694 sposerà Filippo Andrea;
- due lettere, datate 27 settembre e 8 novembre 1730, in cui Filippo Andrea si rivolge al cardinale Camillo Cybo chiedendo di intercedere presso i Padri Somaschi di San Nicolò affinché venga assegnata la dote alle sue due figlie nubende: Caterina, che si sposerà con Giovanni Battista Fumagalli, e Antonia, che andrà in sposa a Giuseppe Albani. Dalla lettera del 27 settembre si apprende che, trascorso l'inverno da venire, Pietro Antonio si recherà da Amsterdam a Bergamo e poi a Roma.

RICOSTRUZIONE DELL'ALBERO GENEALOGICO DEI BISNONNI PATERNI DI PIETRO ANTONIO

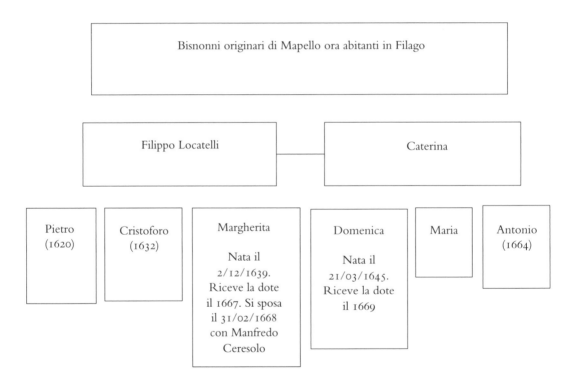

9. BCB, Archivio Doti Andrea Locatelli, MMB 960, 5868. L'albero genealogico è riprodotto in: PALERMO, Paola. 'La famiglia d'origine […]', op. cit. (si veda nota 1), pp. 198-199 e riproposto, solo per il ramo della famiglia di Pietro Antonio, a partire dai bisnonni, a p. 197.

10. BCB, Archivio Doti Andrea Locatelli, MMB 959, 5849-B. Riproduzione in: PALERMO, Paola. 'La famiglia d'origine […]', op. cit. (si veda nota 1), pp. 202-203. Si veda anche: LOCATELLI, Pietro Antonio. Op. cit. (si veda nota 2), p. 135.

Locatelli a Bergamo: documenti d'archivio

Ricostruzione dell'albero genealogico dei nonni paterni di Pietro Antonio

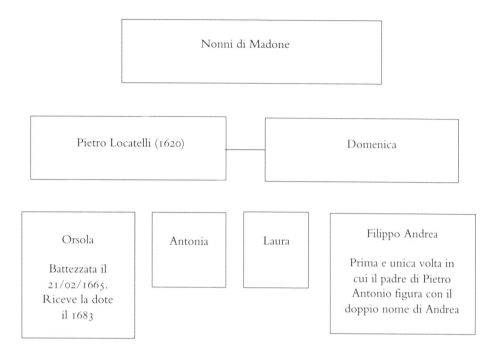

Ricostruzione dell'albero genealogico dei genitori di Pietro Antonio

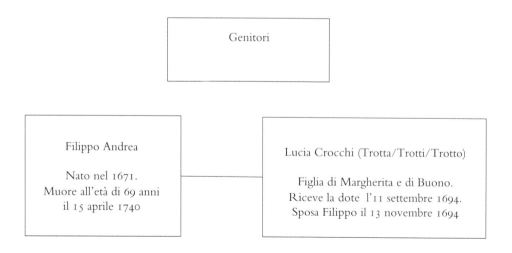

Ricostruzione dell'albero genealogico dei fratelli di Pietro Antonio

Figli di Filippo Andrea e Lucia

Pietro Antonio	Elena Margherita	Domenica Anna Maria
Nasce il 03/09/1695 Muore il 30/03/1764	Nasce il 08/08/1697	Nasce il 10/05/1699 Muore il 21/04/1759

Antonia	Caterina	Giovanni Gaetano Omobono	Anna Lucia
Nasce il 02/03/1703 Sposa Giuseppe Albani il 10/11/1729. Ha un figlio di nome Mariano Gaetano	Nasce il 05/05/1705 Sposa Giovanni Battista Fumagalli il 25/11/1738 Muore il 09/11/1782	Nasce il 18/04/1709	Nasce il 09/08/1710

Ricostruzione dell'albero genealogico della sorella Caterina

Giovanni Battista Fumagalli	Caterina Locatelli
Nasce il 21/05/1707 da Angela e Francesco. Muore il 30/04/1773	

Anna Maria Vittoria	Elisabeth Maria	Anna Lucia
Nasce il 24/09/1739)	Nasce il 08/04/1744	Nasce il 17/12/1741. Si sposa il 25/07/1760 con il Conte Ogni Santo Bonduri. Hanno due gemelli Giovanni Battista Pietro e Guerino che muoiono il 12/03/1762. Muore nel 1798

Giuseppa Caterina Maria	Gaetano Vincenzo Francesco
Nasce il 20/03/1746 Sposa Gerolamo Forini il 09/05/1770	Nasce il 04/07/1750. Muore il 19/09/1803. Sposa Maddalena Maironi da Ponte il 21/01/1779

Archivio del Consorzio della Misericordia Maggiore (MIA)

Nel periodo in cui Francesco Ballarotti opera come maestro di cappella presso la basilica di Santa Maria Maggiore, Pietro Antonio Locatelli presta ivi servizio in qualità di violinista. Il musicista si tratterrà a Bergamo fino al 1711, anno in cui partirà per Roma.

Nell'Archivio della Misericordia Maggiore sono stati reperiti pochi documenti riguardanti Locatelli, attraverso i quali è però possibile ricostruire almeno in parte il periodo giovanile e i suoi rapporti col mondo musicale bergamasco, con particolare riferimento alla basilica di Santa Maria Maggiore. Dalle fonti documentarie pervenuteci sappiamo che Locatelli è presente, come «violino di ripieno», durante due delle solennità liturgiche più importanti dell'anno 1710 — all'età di 14 anni —, anticipando così il suo esordio in Santa Maria di 9 mesi rispetto alla condotta avvenuta il 5 gennaio 1711, che lo vede tra i musicisti dell'organico stabile. Nella prima 'Notta delle Parti, è stromenti' è attestato che nel mese d'aprile dell'anno 1710, durante la Settimana Santa e il giorno di Pasqua, partecipa a cinque funzioni ed è retribuito con 15 lire[11]. Ancora, nella seconda lista di pagamento si attesta che Locatelli serve la basilica, in qualità di unico suonatore di violino, il 15 agosto per la festa dell'Assunta, ricevendo come compenso 9 lire[12].

Il 5 gennaio 1711, all'età di 15 anni, Locatelli supplica i reggenti del Consorzio della Misericordia Maggiore affinché venga ingaggiato come musicista condotto, in qualità di terzo violino[13]. La richiesta viene letta e accettata il giorno stesso dai Reggenti del *Pio Luogo*, deliberando così, col verbale che segue, la sua assunzione[14].

Dopo aver prestato servizio nella basilica della sua città natale per un anno e mezzo come musicista non condotto e per nove mesi come terzo violino dell'organico stabile, Locatelli decide di recarsi a Roma, città che rispetto alla provinciale Bergamo gli avrebbe dato maggiori opportunità per sviluppare le sue potenzialità; la richiesta da parte di Locatelli non ci è pervenuta, ma nel volume di *Scritture (contratti)*, comprendente documenti tra il 1711 ed il 1723, è riportata una delibera con cui il Consorzio accetta la domanda di Locatelli[15].

---

[11]. BCB, *Spese* 1398, c. 568ʳ. *Cfr.* anche Palermo, Paola – Pecis Cavagna, Giulia. *Op. cit.* (si veda nota 1), pp. 129-130 e p. 132; Locatelli, Pietro Antonio. *Op. cit.* (si veda nota 2), p. 136.

[12]. BCB, *Spese* 1398, c. 597ʳ. *Cfr.* Palermo, Paola – Pecis Cavagna, Giulia. *Op. cit.* (si veda nota 1), p. 132; Locatelli, Pietro Antonio. *Op. cit.* (si veda nota 2), p. 136.

[13]. BCB, *Scritture (suppliche)* 1458, c. 426ʳ. *Cfr.* anche Palermo, Paola – Pecis Cavagna, Giulia. *Op. cit.* (si veda nota 1), pp. 132-133; Locatelli, Pietro Antonio. *Op. cit.* (si veda nota 2), p. 247.

[14]. BCB, *Terminazioni* 1290, f. 8ᵛ. *Cfr.* anche Palermo, Paola – Pecis Cavagna, Giulia. *Op. cit.* (si veda nota 1), p. 133; Locatelli, Pietro Antonio. *Op. cit.* (si veda nota 2), p. 137.

[15]. BCB, *Scritture (contratti)* 1312, f. 58ʳ. *Cfr.* anche Palermo, Paola – Pecis Cavagna, Giulia. *Op. cit.* (si veda nota 1), p. 133; Locatelli, Pietro Antonio. *Op. cit.* (si veda nota 2), p. 137.

Per il servizio prestato presso la cappella bergamasca, Locatelli riceve due pagamenti, contenuti nel Giornale del Consorzio, relativo agli anni 1709-1712[16].

Fondo Mayr

Nel fondo, che raccoglie circa 3500 pezzi provenienti in gran parte dalla biblioteca musicale appartenuta all'illustre compositore bavarese Johann Simon Mayr, si conserva un corposo volume autografo, intitolato *Biografie di scrittori*[17] in cui, oltre alla biografia di Locatelli[18], è presente una lettera scritta dal giovane musicista al padre Filippo Andrea da Roma il 17 marzo 1714[19].

Altro

Un altro documento conservato alla Biblioteca Mai e degno di particolare attenzione, perché sul soggiorno mantovano del compositore non ci è giunta alcuna altra documentazione, è la nomina di Pietro Antonio Locatelli a 'Virtuoso' della corte di Mantova da parte del principe Filippo Langravio di Hesse-Darmstadt in data 15 marzo 1725[20].

Archivio storico del Comune di Bergamo, sezione Antico regime

Appresa la morte del fratello, il 30 aprile 1764 Caterina Locatelli si reca dalle autorità competenti di Bergamo perché le venga riconosciuto il diritto di successione sull'eredità di Pietro Antonio[21]. Questo risulta essere, dal punto di vista cronologico, il primo di un'importante serie di documenti collegati fra loro, che riguarda una causa intrapresa dal nipote di Pietro Antonio, il reverendo Gaetano, orfano di Giuseppe Albani e di Antonia Locatelli, sorella del compositore, contro la zia Caterina. L'intera documentazione è stata individuata nell'Archivio Notarile presso l'Archivio di Stato di Bergamo.

---

[16]. BCB, *Giornali* 1227, f. 465. *Cfr.* anche PALERMO, Paola – PECIS CAVAGNA, Giulia. *Op. cit.* (si veda nota 1), p. 134; LOCATELLI, Pietro Antonio. *Op. cit.* (si veda nota 2), p. 137.

[17]. BCB, Fondo Mayr, Salone N 9.7.

[18]. BCB, Fondo Mayr, Salone N 9.7, ff. 216-228.

[19]. BCB, Fondo Mayr, Salone N 9.7, ff. 213-215.

[20]. BCB, Specola Doc. 972.

[21]. BCB, Archivio storico del Comune di Bergamo, Sezione antico regime, Ufficio Pretorio, filza non numerata (in corso di inventariazione), 30 aprile 1764, f. 59. Parziale trascrizione in PALERMO, Paola. 'La famiglia d'origine [...]', *op. cit.* (si veda nota 1), p. 206. *Cfr.* anche LOCATELLI, Pietro Antonio. *Op. cit.* (si veda nota 2), p. 186.

Biblioteca Musicale Donizetti

La biblioteca, alcuni anni fa, ha ricevuto in dono dalla famiglia Fumagalli, nella persona del figlio di Giuseppe dottor Giovanni, una copia dell'edizione critica dell'Opera Omnia di Locatelli, pubblicata in dieci volumi da Schott dal 1994 al 2002. Si conservano inoltre pregevoli edizioni a stampa e copie manoscritte nel fondo Missiroli e nel fondo Piatti-Lochis.

FONTI CONSERVATE ALL'ARCHIVIO DI STATO DI BERGAMO, ARCHIVIO NOTARILE

Lo spoglio degli 'Indici delle Parti', onde risalire a eventuali atti in cui una delle parti si riferisse a persone legate da vincolo di parentela alla famiglia Locatelli, ha permesso di individuare poco più di una decina di documenti.

Il primo atto, in ordine cronologico, risale al 14 settembre 1694: si tratta della dote che attesta l'avvenuto matrimonio tra la giovane Lucia, figlia di Buono Trotto, entrambi oriundi di Brescia ma abitanti a Bergamo, e Filippo Andrea, figlio del fu Pietro Locatelli, abitante anch'egli a Bergamo[22].

Il secondo documento è l'atto di acquisto del 15 maggio 1754, con cui Giovanni Battista Fumagalli, marito di Caterina Locatelli, sorella del compositore, compra una casa al prezzo di 316 scudi, situata in Borgo Canale[23].

Il resto della documentazione riguarda, invece, la causa intercorsa tra Gaetano Albani, nipote di Pietro Antonio, e la zia Caterina. Con atto del 2 maggio 1764, Gaetano rivendica dinanzi al notaio i propri diritti di erede legittimo di Pietro Antonio al pari della zia Caterina e, al contempo, nomina proprio rappresentante legale David van Mollem Sijndervalt. Lo stesso giorno anche Caterina Locatelli si reca dal notaio Panigoni ed elegge a proprio procuratore il già citato David van Mollem Sijndervalt, ribadendo che l'eredità del fratello le spetta di diritto[24]. L'intervento di un amico scongiura la lite tra zia e nipote, e l'accordo, ratificato da una transazione del notaio Gaetano Longaretti, prevede la suddivisione dell'eredità del compositore in tre parti uguali: i due terzi sarebbero spettati a Caterina e la rimanente terza parte a Gaetano Albani[25].

---

[22]. Archivio di Stato di Bergamo, (d'ora in avanti ASB), Archivio Notarile, Locatelli Alessandro Antonio n. 4760, 14 settembre 1694.

[23]. ASB, Archivio Notarile, Locatelli Alessandro Antonio n. 11818, f. 385.

[24]. ASB, Archivio Notarile, Panigoni Giovanni n. 9008, 2 maggio 1764. *Cfr.* anche PALERMO, Paola. 'La famiglia d'origine […]', *op. cit.* (si veda nota 1), pp. 207-208; LOCATELLI, Pietro Antonio. *Op. cit.* (si veda nota 2), pp. 186-194.

[25]. ASB, Archivio Notarile, Longaretti Gaetano, n. 12596, f. 59. *Cfr.* anche PALERMO, Paola. 'La famiglia d'origine […]', *op. cit.* (si veda nota 1), p. 207; LOCATELLI, Pietro Antonio. *Op. cit.* (si veda nota 2), pp. 189-190.

Il 7 ottobre 1764, sotto congiunta richiesta di Caterina Locatelli e Gaetano Albani, il notaio Longaretti emette una procura con cui designa *Li SS.ri David Van Mollem Sijndervalt, e compagni d'Amsterdam* rappresentanti dei suddetti eredi di Pietro Antonio Locatelli. Il compito dei procuratori fu quello di provvedere alla vendita dei beni mobili e immobili dell'eredità Locatelli «et convertir il tutto in contanti, e dinaro»[26].

Il primo aprile 1765 il notaio Gaetano Longaretti emette una seconda procura, con cui i legittimi eredi di Locatelli incaricano il conte Ogni Santo Bonduri di «conseguire, esigere e ricevere l'eredità tutta del fù sig.r Pietro Antonio Locatelli»[27].

Il conte Santo o Ogni Santo Bonduri, figlio del nobile Giovanni Battista e di Maria Caterina Bonduri — entrambi originari di Gandino[28] —, è il marito di Lucia, una delle tre figlie di Giovanni Battista Fumagalli e Caterina Fumagalli, sorella di Pietro Antonio[29].

Fonti conservate presso l'Archivio Storico Diocesano

Presso l'archivio Storico Diocesano di Bergamo si conserva, e da qualche anno è consultabile, l'archivio della chiesa di Sant'Agata al Carmine in Bergamo, parrocchia dove viveva la famiglia Locatelli e dove nacque Pietro Antonio. Qualche mese fa, grazie alla disponibilità e alla cortesia di don Luigi Marchetti, Veronica Vitali e Andrea Zonca, ho potuto analizzare per la prima volta detto archivio[30] e trovare altre informazioni che permettono di completare o perfezionare le notizie sulla famiglia d'origine e sulle famiglie che andarono imparentandosi con i Locatelli, e cioè i Fumagalli, i Bonduri e gli Albani.

Per quanto riguarda la famiglia Locatelli, partendo dall'albero genealogico della famiglia (trisnonni, bisnonni, nonni, genitori, figli)[31], sono riuscita a dettagliare ulteriormente il ramo della famiglia di Pietro Antonio rispetto a quanto avevo scoperto anni fa. In particolare, in detto archivio si conservano i *Libri Baptizatorum* originali di Pietro Antonio (Ill. 2), dei

26. ASB, Archivio Notarile, Longaretti Gaetano, n. 12596, f. 12. *Cfr.* anche Palermo, Paola. 'La famiglia d'origine […]', *op. cit.* (si veda nota 1), pp. 207; Locatelli, Pietro Antonio. *Op. cit.* (si veda nota 2), pp. 190-192.

27. ASB, Archivio Notarile, Longaretti Gaetano, n. 12596, f. 44. *Cfr.* anche Palermo, Paola. 'La famiglia d'origine […]', *op. cit.* (si veda nota 1), p. 207; Locatelli, Pietro Antonio. *Op. cit.* (si veda nota 2), pp. 192-194.

28. ASB, Archivio Notarile, Gregori Bernardo, n. 10543, 30 ottobre 1759. *Cfr.* anche Palermo, Paola. 'La famiglia d'origine […]', *op. cit.* (si veda nota 1), pp. 207-208.

29. Palermo, Paola. 'La famiglia d'origine […]', *op. cit.* (si veda nota 1), p. 207.

30. L'archivio è attualmente consultabile grazie a un elenco di consistenza, prezioso strumento di corredo realizzato da Veronica Vitali.

31. BCB, Archivio Doti Andrea Locatelli, MMB 960, 5868. L'albero genealogico è riprodotto in Palermo, Paola. 'La famiglia d'origine […]', *op. cit.* (si veda nota 1), pp. 198-199 e riproposto, solo per il ramo della famiglia di Pietro Antonio, a partire dai bisnonni, a p. 197.

suoi fratelli e delle sorelle[32], che confermano i dati riportati nelle fedi di battesimo stilate il 3 settembre 1721 presenti nell'archivio delle doti Locatelli conservate in Biblioteca Mai[33]. Inoltre, se nel mio primo lavoro sulla famiglia Locatelli, apparso sulla rivista *Bergomum* del 1996[34], avevo trovato presso l'Archivio di Stato di Bergamo l'atto di dote di Lucia, mamma di Pietro Antonio, e papà Filippo Andrea, datato 14 settembre 1694[35], ora ho identificato l'atto di matrimonio dei genitori, che si sposarono il 13 novembre 1694 (ILL. 3)[36]. Ancora, ho rinvenuto l'atto di morte della sorella Domenica Anna Maria, rimasta nubile, che risale al 21 aprile 1759[37]; la sorella Antonia si sposerà con Giuseppe Albani il 10 novembre 1729[38]. Infine, ho rinvenuto l'atto di morte del padre Filippo Andrea Locatelli, morto all'età di 69 anni il 15 aprile 1740[39], quindi nato nel 1671.

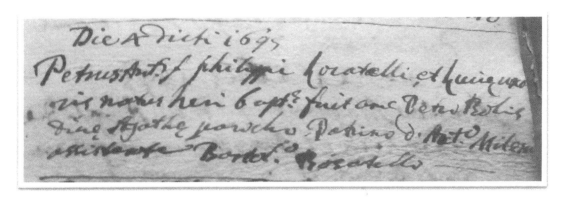

ILL. 2: Atto di Battestimo di Pietro Antonio Locatelli (Archivio Storico Diocesano di Bergamo, Archivio ex Chiesa di S. Agata, Atti di nascita e battesimo dal 1684 al 1801, n. 16, p. 57).

Per quanto riguarda la famiglia Fumagalli, imparentata con i Locatelli, perché Caterina, la sorella di Pietro Antonio, sposerà Giovanni Battista Fumagalli, partendo dall'albero genealogico stilato nel 1948 da Giuseppe, padre del dott. Giuseppe Fumagalli, «perché più cara sia la memoria degli Antenati e meno facile la dimenticanza»[40], ho stabilito, tramite i documenti dell'Archivio di Stato incrociati con quelli dell'ex chiesa di Sant'Agata, che

[32]. Archivio Storico Diocesano di Bergamo, (d'ora in avanti ASDB), Archivio ex Chiesa di S. Agata, Atti di nascita e battesimo dal 1684 al 1801, n. 16, p. 57 (Pietro Antonio), p. 65 (Elena Margherita), p. 72 (Domenica Anna Maria), p. 91 (Antonia), p. 106 (Caterina), p. 132 (Giovanni Gaetano), p. 139 (Anna Lucia).

[33]. BCB, Archivio Doti Andrea Locatelli, MMB 959, 5849-B.

[34]. PALERMO, Paola. 'La famiglia d'origine […]', *op. cit.* (si veda nota 1), pp. 189-208.

[35]. ASB, Archivio Notarile, Locatelli Alessandro Antonio n. 4760, 14 settembre 1694.

[36]. ASDB, Archivio ex Chiesa di S. Agata, Atti di matrimonio dal 1643 al 1781, n. 32, c. 102[v].

[37]. ASDB, Archivio ex Chiesa di S. Agata, Atti di morte e sepolture dal 1643 al 1792, n. 62, p. 233.

[38]. ASDB, Archivio ex Chiesa di S. Agata, Atti di matrimonio dal 1643 al 1781, n. 32, c. 139[r].

[39]. ASDB, Archivio ex Chiesa di S. Agata, Atti di morte e sepolture dal 1643 al 1792, n. 62, p. 211.

[40]. BCB, Archivio Giuseppe Fumagalli 35 (tubo), albero genealogico della famiglia Fumagalli in due copie.

Atto di matrimonio dei genitori di Pietro Antonio Locatelli (ASDB, Archivio ex Chiesa di S. Agata, Atti di matrimonio dal 1643 al 1781, n. 32, c. 102ᵛ).

– Caterina e Giovanni Battista si sposano il 25 novembre 1738 (ILL. 4)[41];

– Giovanni Battista nasce da Angela e Francesco Fumagalli il 21 e non il 23 maggio 1707[42] e muore il 30 aprile[43] e non il 29 maggio 1773.

Per finire, dall'albero genealogico risulta che Caterina e Giovanni Battista hanno tre figlie e un figlio, ma dalle carte d'archivio risultano quattro figlie e un figlio:

– la primogenita Anna Maria Vittoria (e non Maria), nasce il 24 settembre 1739 (e non nel 1736)[44];

– Anna Lucia, nata il 17 dicembre 1741[45], morirà nel 1798 e sposerà il conte Ogni Santo Bonduri il 25 luglio 1760[46]. Ogni Santo è figlio di Giovanni Battista di Gandino. È stato rintracciato anche l'atto di morte dei gemelli di Lucia e Santo, di nome Giovanni Battista Pietro e Guerino, avvenuta il 12 marzo 1762[47];

---

[41]. ASDB, Archivio ex Chiesa di S. Agata, Atti di matrimonio dal 1643 al 1781, n. 32, c. 150ᵛ.

[42]. ASDB, Archivio ex Chiesa di S. Agata, Atti di nascita e battesimo dal 1684 al 1801, n. 16, p. 120.

[43]. ASDB, Archivio ex Chiesa di S. Agata, Atti di morte e sepolture dal 1643 al 1792, n. 62, p. 265.

[44]. ASDB, Archivio ex Chiesa di S. Agata, Atti di nascita e battesimo dal 1684 al 1801, n. 16, p. 263.

[45]. ASDB, Archivio ex Chiesa di S. Agata, Atti di nascita e battesimo dal 1684 al 1801, n. 16, p. 272. Nel documento il cognome riportato di Anna Lucia non è Fumagalli, ma Locatelli, cioè quello della madre.

[46]. ASDB, Archivio ex Chiesa di S. Agata, Atti di matrimonio dal 1643 al 1781, n. 32, c. 163ᵛ.

[47]. ASDB, Archivio ex Chiesa di S. Agata, Atti di morte e sepolture dal 1643 al 1792, n. 62, p. 239.

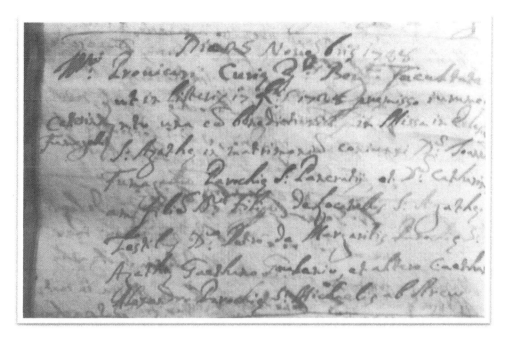

Ill. 4: Atto di matrimonio di Caterina e Giovanni Battista Fumagalli (ASDB, Archivio ex Chiesa di S. Agata, Atti di matrimonio dal 1643 al 1781, n. 32, c. 150ᵛ).

- Elisabeth Maria, che non compare nell'albero genealogico stilato da Fumagalli, nasce l'8 aprile 1744[48];
- Gioseppa Caterina Maria, nata il 20 marzo 1746[49] e non nel 1748, sposerà Gerolamo Forini il 9 maggio 1770[50];
- Gaetano Vincenzo Francesco, che nasce il 4 (e non il 5) luglio 1750[51] e che sposa Maddalena Maironi da Ponte il 21 gennaio 1779[52].

[48]. ASDB, Archivio ex Chiesa di S. Agata, Atti di nascita e battesimo dal 1684 al 1801, n. 16, p. 280.
[49]. ASDB, Archivio ex Chiesa di S. Agata, Atti di nascita e battesimo dal 1684 al 1801, n. 16, p. 287.
[50]. ASDB, Archivio ex Chiesa di S. Agata, Atti di matrimonio dal 1643 al 1781, n. 32, c. 173ᵛ.
[51]. ASDB, Archivio ex Chiesa di S. Agata, Atti di nascita e battesimo dal 1684 al 1801, n. 16, p. 296.
[52]. ASDB, Archivio ex Chiesa di S. Agata, Atti di matrimonio dal 1643 al 1781, n. 32, c. 181ʳ.

Locatelli's Influence on Leclair: Myth or Reality?

Neal Zaslaw
(Ithaca, NY)

T HE INVESTIGATION BEGINS with two full-length obituaries of Leclair, which appeared in 1764 and 1767 respectively. The writer of the first of these, Farmian de Rozoi (or Rozoy), was a minor literary figure of mid-18th-century Paris, who knew Leclair personally. Despite a few errors, Rozoi's tribute to Leclair, published in the establishment journal the *Mercure de France*, was remarkably well informed. But all he had to say about Leclair's time in Holland was, «The desire to travel caused [Leclair] to go to Holland, where Her Royal Highness the Princess of Orange heaped kindnesses upon him». In the decades following Rozoi's obituary, it was widely quoted, paraphrased and plagiarized.

The author of the second extended obituary, «Le comte du B***»[1], was among the ranks of those plagiarists. The Comte du B*** did, however, offer a fuller account of Leclair's decision to visit Holland, describing him as a genuinely modest man, and then continuing in a vein apparently intended to refute Rozoi's comment:

> Awareness of his true worth caused him to acknowledge that he was satisfied with his works but, always ready to revise his opinion in favor of those whose opinions he judged superior, he would submissively correct them [his works]. Born with rather modest talent, which he was able alter only by dint of hard work, Leclair found that knowledge earned in the art of composition served only to put him on his mettle to acquire more such knowledge. To this end he traveled to Holland, where he busied himself less with his success and the honorable welcome given him by the Princess of Orange, than with the pleasure of hearing the celebrated Locatelli. *Leclair*

---

[1]. LE COMTE DU B*** [François-Joachim de Pierre de Bernis, comte de Lyon]. 'Éloge de M. Leclair', in: *Nécrologe des hommes célèbres de France: par une société de gens de lettres* (1767); also attributed (falsely) to 'le Comte de Brassac', presumably Louis Hercule Timoléon de Cossé-Brissac (1734-1792), 8e duc de Brissac. De Bernis presumably knew Leclair from their common Lyons connection. This passage, uncredited, was copied *verbatim* in Louis Abel de Bonafons, l'abbé de Fontenay in his *Dictionnaire des artistes* (1776).

> *profited eagerly from the enlightenment about harmonic profundities that Locatelli deigned to impart to him.* This was evident soon after his return to France, and it was with admiration that *people recognized the grand manner of the master in the masterpieces of the pupil. It is above all his third book of sonatas* [Op. 5] *in which this progress was palpable.* The first [book] had the sole merit of simple, fluent melody; he had already in his second [book] deployed the riches resulting from the use of double stops[2].

Whatever truth may reside in this narrative, it has fundamental flaws. Although Leclair's time at the Court of Orange fell during the period *c*1740-1743, his Op. 5 was published in 1734. And while it is certainly true that Leclair's Op. 5 contains harmonic profundities, and while I might have a difficult time proving it, I venture to say that, beyond the common harmonic progressions of the period, Locatelli's harmonic complexities and Leclair's arise from differing motivations and they function according to somewhat different principles. To my ear at least, those principles can be summarized this way: Locatelli's use of chromaticism arises in the first instance from considerations of melody and voice-leading, whereas Leclair's use testifies to his keen interest in sonorities and timbres.

Leclair's first scholarly biographer, the formidable Laurence de la Laurencie[3], accepted Count de Bernis' remarks at face value and strove diligently to find Locatelli-inspired ideas in Leclair's violin sonatas. A first comparison, not with Leclair but with his slightly older contemporary, Jean Baptiste Senaillé, could just as well have been illustrated by examples drawn from Leclair's sonatas. Here La Laurencie contrasted a French aspect of Senaillé's style with an Italianate one said to be like those favored by Locatelli (Ex. 1).

---

[2].   Emphasis added. «La conscience de son proper mérite lui faisait avouer ingénuement qu'il était satisfait de ses ouvrages; mais, toujours prêt à sacrifier son avis à celui qu'il jugeait le meilleur, il les corrigeait avec docilité. Né avec des dispositions assez ingrates, qu'il ne put changer qu'à force de travail, ses connoissances acquises dans l'art de la composition, n'excitaient en lui que l'émulation d'en acquérir de nouvelles. C'est dans ce dessein qu'il fit un voyage en Hollande, où il s'occupa moins de ses succès, & de l'accueil honorable qui lui fit la Princesse d'Orange, que du plaisir d'entendre le célèbre Locatelli; il profita avidement des lumières qu'il daigna lui communiquer sur les profondeurs de l'harmone; on s'en apperçut bientôt à son retour en France; & ce fut avec admiration que l'on reconut la grande manière du maître dans les chefs-d'œuvre de l'écolier. C'est sur-tout dans la troisième livre de ses sonnates, où ce progrès parait sensible: le premier n'a que le mérite d'une mélodie simple & facile; il avait déja déployé dans le second toutes les richesses dont il était redevable à la pratique de la double corde». Note that «harmony» (or «harmonic») was sometimes used in a generic sense to mean music in general.

[3].   LA LAURENCIE, Lionel de. *L'école française de violon de Lully à Viotti: études d'histoire et d'esthétique*, 3 vols. Paris, Delagrave, 1922-1924, vol. 1, pp. 269-340. La Laurencie noticed de Bernis's error in chronology and suggested that he must have meant Leclair's Fourth Book, Op. 9, which was mostly complete before he left for Holland, but which could have been revised in light of his experiences there prior to being engraved by his wife and published in Paris in 1743.

Ex. 1: Characteristic French air and Locatelli-like movement from Jean Baptiste Senaillé's Violin Sonata, Bk. 5, No. 6 (La Laurencie, vol. 1, p. 176).

Dans d'autres, s'épanche la langueur distinguée et la tendresse mélancolique de l'air français :

avec la chute assombrie sur la sensible; [ou bien, comme dans le *Largo* de la Sonate VI du cinquième Livre, le musicien adoptera un thème morcelé, une mélodie coupée d'arrêts, cheminant par petites incises, telles que celles qui sont si fréquentes dans les mouvements lents de Locatelli[1].

While asserting that Leclair's characteristic strengths were very much his own, La Laurencie involked Locatelli's name with regard to Leclair's use of trochaic rhythms and of leaps from the G string to notes on the E string (Exx. 2, 3 and 4).

Ex. 2: An Italianate figure in Leclair's Violin Sonata, Bk. 2, No. 4, prior to his putative contact with Locatelli (LA LAURENCIE, Lionel de. *Op. cit.* [see note 3], vol. 1, p. 320).

A Locatelli, et bien avant son voyage en Hollande, il prend certains tours et certains dispositifs thématiques. Ainsi, l'*Allegro* C de la Sonate IV (II* Livre) présente une série de formules rythmiques :

dont Locatelli fait fréquemment état et, en étudiant les concertos de Leclair, nous retrouverons encore trace de l'influence que l'auteur des *Caprices* a exercée sur le violoniste français.

Ex. 3: Comparison between large leaps in Leclair's Violin Sonata, Op. 9, No. 10 (with another example of the rhythmic figure of Ex. 2) and in Locatelli's Bk. 4, No. 4 (LA LAURENCIE, Lionel de. *Op. cit.* [see note 3], vol. 1, p. 325).

Le *Vivace* 3/4 de la Sonate X présente un formidable écart de trois octaves :

après lequel on relève les figurations A, si fréquentes dans l'œuvre de Locatelli :
De même, il lance (Sonate IV du quatrième Livre) ce trait escarpé à la chute

vertigineuse :

Ex. 4: Other large leaps from Leclair's Violin Sonata, Bk. 4, No. 8 (LA LAURENCIE, Lionel de. *Op. cit.* [see note 3], vol. I, p. 328).

1. *Aria* de la Sonate VII (1er *Livre*).
2. *Allegro moderato* C de la Sonate IX (IVe *Livre*).
3. *Allegro assai* C de la Sonate I (IVe *Livre*).
4. *Allegro moderato* C de la Sonate IX (IVe *Livre*).
5. *Ciaconna* finale de la Sonate VIII (IVe *Livre*).

And finally Locatelli is credited with inspiring Leclair's use of a syncopated figure in 3/4 meter (Ex. 5).

Ex. 5: Related melody types from Leclair's Violin Concerto, Op. 7, No. 1, and Locatelli's Violin Sonata, Op. 6, No. 12 (LA LAURENCIE, Lionel de. *Op. cit.* [see note 3], vol. I, p. 334).

En étudiant les sonates de Leclair, nous avons indiqué que Locatelli avait exercé une indéniable influence sur leur thématique. Les concertos apportent une confirmation de cette assertion. Que l'on compare, par exemple, ce passage du Concerto I du premier Livre :

avec celui que nous trouvons dans la Sonate XII de l'op. VI de Locatelli :

Behind La Laurencie's attempts to exemplify de Bernis' assertion that Leclair's style was altered by his encounter with Locatelli, lies a flawed methodology — a methodology by which one begins with a *conclusion* rather than an *hypothesis*, and then seeks evidence to confirm (but not to contradict) that pre-established goal. La Laurencie's examples of the putative influence of Locatelli upon Leclair are by-and-large common-coin figurations, idioms, topoi, even clichés: internationally circulating ideas found in much European music of the period. Instances of this are found in La Laurencie's examples of Leclair's use of trochaic rhythms (Exx. 2-3). The trochaic rhythm, found all over Europe at that period, in two-note and three-note versions, has been called the Lombard rhythm and the Scottish snap; it is also a mainstay of Hungarian folk and folk-derived music, and it was also a favorite of Henry Purcell[4].

---

4. The three-note version of this ornament is also related to the *coulée* of the French *clavecinistes* and the English 'slide'.

And the leaps from the G string to the E string (Exx. 3-4)? At first glance they look rather like some of the leaps in Locatelli's *Capricci* for unaccompanied violin (Op. 3; 1733), but they aren't. Locatelli required the violinist to leap in a split second from one double-stopped contortion to another left-hand contortion. Leclair, who was well known for his command of double, triple and quadruple stops, requires only one note at a time, and he allows the player an open G string and a rest to cross strings and shift.

Thus, when three decades later the Marc Pincherle distilled La Laurencie's research on Leclair into a small monograph, he was duly skeptical of the latter's examples of 'influence':

> From the Italians Leclair assimilated above all [the styles of] Corelli, G.-B. Somis, Tartini, Locatelli, Vivaldi. To judge solely by thematic resemblances, the influence of the last of these [Vivaldi] seems to have been preponderant. Even certain turns of phrase that people [La Laurencie!] had believed came directly from Locatelli have as their source the Red Priest's *L'estro aromonico* or *La stravaganza*. We also note in passing that among the themes and virtuosic formulas that Leclair and Locatelli have in common, the borrowing doesn't always have the same significance[5].

Pincherle then proceeded to suggest that, as far as national styles were concerned, influence flowed in both directions, quoting the Marquis d'Argens, who wrote that he had witnessed «[Antonio] Montanari, first violinist of Rome, enchanted with Leclair's sonatas»[6]. This is intriguing but does little to alter the fact that, whereas the French were obsessed with Italian music (whether for or against it), the Italians typically could take or leave French music — mostly the latter.

Later in his monograph (p. 74) Pincherle returned to the Locatelli-Leclair conundrum, supplementing his earlier remarks:

> The points of contact between Leclair and Locatelli are primarily in the realms of instrumental writing, of ornamentation, of virtuosic devices. As for melodic invention, it seems that [Leclair's] dependency isn't very great, in as much as the figurations, the rhythms employed by Locatelli, which people [La Laurencie!] confidently attribute to him, had their origins with Vivaldi.

Pincherle's point about the weakness of La Laurencie's demonstrations of Locatelli's influence on Leclair is well taken, but here he falls into a different untenable position, trying to substitute a single source of inspiration (Vivaldi) for another (Locatelli), rather than recalling his own earlier point about the multifarious influences that impinge upon any alert creative artist[7].

---

5. Pincherle, Marc. *J.-M. Leclair: la vie, l'œuvre, discographie*, Paris, La Colombe, 1952 (Euterpe), p. 57.

6. Argens, Jean-Baptiste de Boyer d'. 'Lettre ii: Sur la musique, l'opéra et la comédie', in: Id. *Mémoires et lettres de M. le marquis d'Argens*, London, aux dépens de la compagnie, 1755.

7. As Pincherle writes, contradicting himself: «[…] les influences italiennes sont multiples […]»; Pincherle, Marc. *Op. cit.* (see note 6), p. 92.

Before moving on to other possible approaches to understanding the relationship between Leclair and Locatelli, here is a document new to Leclair research, which bears on matters discussed here, even if only tangentially.

[Lord Beauchamp to Lord Hertford:]

Lyons, April 4 N.S., 1743

[…] I suppose you go to town [London] once a week to the opera as you intended. I hope it goes to your satisfaction, and that it is well filled to keep the house warm. Our operas [in Lyons] are finished all [*recte*: until] after *Pâques*, and instead we have a thing they call a *concert spirituel*, which is all sung in Latin in a great *salle* of the *Maison de Ville*, so we have all the noise and scream without the amusement of the scenery and dancing. We have a famous violin who plays there; he is the brother of the man who plays first fiddle at the opera [Jean-Marie *le cadet*]; his name is Le Clair [*l'aîné*]. He comes from the Princess of Orange's Court, where he has been for two years, and has now got leave to come hither for three months, because he is of this town and all his relations live here. I like him better than any French fiddle I have heard, because he plays in an Italian taste, which is vastly condemned here, and which is a great objection to his playing, among the judges of this country […][8].

This document establishes a date by which Leclair had returned to France, previously determined only by the somewhat later public announcement of Op. 9: «On grave actuellement la neuvième *Œuvre, IV. Livre* de M. le Clair, desiré depuis long-tems mais qu'on ne pouvoit espérer qu'au retour de l'Autuer à Paris, où il est nouvellement arrivé»[9]. The beginning of his residence in Holland is harder to pin down. Daniel François Scheurleer long ago published archival documents revealing that Leclair held a position as director of music for the wealthy, scandal-ridden «Portugese» Jew, Francisco López de Liz, at his mansion in The Hague[10]. These documents reveal that from no later than 1740 until López de Liz's bankruptcy in 1743, Leclair was in The Hague with Duliz for nine months of each year; for the other three months he served the Princess of Orange in Leeuwarden[11]. In each place he led an 'orchestra' of fewer than a dozen musicians.

★★★

---

8. HUGHES, Helen Sard. *The Gentle Hertford: Her Life and Letters*, New York, Macmillan, 1940, p. 248. When Charles Burney visited the Concert spiritual in 1770, his negative reaction to French singing was similar to that expressed by Lord Beauchamp in this letter. Contra Lord Beauchamp, an essay in the *Mercure de France* claimed that Leclair played equally well in the French and Italian styles (August 1738, pp. 1721-1737).

9. *Mercure de France*, June 1743, p. 1193.

10. SCHEURLEER, Daniel François. 'Jean-Marie Leclair l'aîné in Holland', in: *Sammelband der Internationale Musikgesellschaft*, X (1908-1909), pp. 259-262.

11. Princess Anne was British; she was musically talented and had been taught by Handel. For a fine run-down of her very considerable connections with music, see KING, Richard G. 'Anne of Hanover and Orange (1707-59) as Patron and Practitioner of the Arts', in: *Queenship in Britain 1660-1837: Royal Patronage, Court Culture and Dynastic Politics*, edited by Clarissa Campbell Orr, Manchester, Manchester University Press, 2002, pp. 162-192.

There is something else peculiar about de Bernis's suggestion of Locatelli's influence on Leclair: insofar as Locatelli was discussed in French writings of the period, he may have been the most severely criticized of the numerous Italian violinist-composers. His music and his manner of performance were experienced as lacking taste, moderation, beauty. And not only by the French. Here, for instance, is an account by two English amateurs who visited Locatelli in Amsterdam in April 1741:

> Locatelli must surely be allowed by all to be a *terre moto*. […] *Quels coups d'archet! Quel feu! Quelle vitesse!* […] He plays with so much fury upon his fiddle, that in my humble opinion, he must wear out some dozens of them in a year. […] He has the most affected look just before he begins to play, that I ever saw in my life […][12].

By far the most vivid, if satirical, portrayal of Locatelli performing is found in Diderot's *Le neveu de Rameau*. Here is that scene:

> HIM [Rameau's nephew]: […] Take a good look at this wrist. It used to be stiff as the devil. These ten fingers were like so many sticks stuck into a wooden metacarpal. And these tendons were old cords of catgut — drier, stiffer, and more inflexible that those used to turn a lathe operator's wheel. But I've tormented, broken, and abused them so much. You don't want to move, but, by God, I say that you will and that's that!
> And as he said this, with his right hand he grabbed the fingers and wrist of his left hand and bent them back and forth. The tips of his fingers were touching his arm. His joints were cracking. I was afraid he'd end up dislocating the bones.
> ME [Diderot]: Be careful, I say to him. You're going to injure yourself.
> HIM: Don't worry. They can stand it. For ten years I've given them a hard time. Whatever they felt like, the little buggers had to get used to it and learn to stop the notes and fly over the strings. So right now they're working. Yes, they're working fine. At that moment he takes on the pose of a violin player. He hums an allegro by Locatelli, and his right arm imitates the movement of the bow, while the fingers of his left hand seem to move along the length of the fingerboard. If it goes out of tune, he stops, tightens or loosens the string and plucks it with his finger nail, to make sure that it's in tune. He resumes playing the piece where he left off. He keeps time with his foot, and thrashes about with his head, feet, hands, arms, and body. You've perhaps had occasion to see [Domenico] Ferrari or [Carlo] Chiabran or some other virtuoso at the Concert spirituel in the same sort of convulsions, presenting me with a picture of the same sort of agony and causing me to suffer almost as much; for isn't it a painful thing to behold the torment of someone who busies himself

---

12. DUNNING, Albert. *Pietro Antonio Locatelli. Der Virtuose und seine Welt*, 2 vols., Buren, Frits Knuf, 1981, vol. I, pp. 148-149.

portraying pleasure to me. If he simply must show me a condemned man, erect a curtain between him and me to hide him from me.

In the midst of his agitation and cries, if a long-held note presented itself — one of those harmonious spots when the bow is drawn slowly across several strings at once — his face took on an ecstatic expression, his voice softened, and he listened in rapture. He was sure the chords were resonating in his ears and mine. Then, placing his instrument under his left arm using the same hand with which he had held it, and letting his right hand and the bow fall, he said, «Well, what do you think of that?»

Me: Wonderful.

Him: That was all right, I thought. That sounded almost like the others[13].

This scene, set by Diderot in the well-frequented precincts of the Parisian Café de la Régence, has been imagined by many artists, one example of which is reproduced in Ill.1.

---

[13]. Diderot, Denis. *Le neveu de Rameau* (1761 but unpublished), translation by Ian C. Johnston, modified by N. Z. «Lui. – Et puis vous voyez bien ce poignet; il était raide comme un diable. Ces dix doigts, c'étaient autant de bâtons fichés dans un métacarpe de bois; et ces tendons, c'étaient de vieilles cordes à boyau plus sèches, plus raides, plus inflexibles que celles qui ont servi à la roue d'un tourneur. Mais je vous les ai tant tourmentées, tant brisées, tant rompues. Tu ne veux pas aller; et moi, mordieu, je dis que tu iras; et cela sera. | Et tout en disant cela, de la main droite, il s'était saisi les doigts et le poignet de la main gauche; et il les renversait en dessus; en dessous; l'extrémité des doigts touchait au bras; les jointures en craquaient; je craignais que les os n'en demeurassent disloqués. | Moi. – Prenez garde, lui dis-je; vous allez vous estropier. | Lui. – Ne craignez rien. Ils y sont faits; depuis dix ans, je leur en ai bien donné d'une autre façon. Malgré qu'ils en eussent, il a bien fallu que les bougres s'y accoutumassent, et qu'ils apprissent à se placer sur les touches et à voltiger sur les cordes. Aussi à présent cela va. Oui, cela va. | En même temps, il se met dans l'attitude d'un joueur de violon; il fredonne de la voix un allegro de Locatelli, son bras droit imite le mouvement de l'archet; sa main gauche et ses doigts semblent se promener sur la longueur du manche; s'il fait un ton faux; il s'arrête; il remonte ou baisse la corde; il la pince de l'ongle, pour s'assurer qu'elle est juste; il reprend le morceau où il l'a laissé; il bat la mesure du pied; il se démène de la tête, des pieds, des mains, des bras, du corps. Comme vous avez vu quelquefois au Concert spirituel, Ferrari ou Chiabran, ou quelque autre virtuose, dans les mêmes convulsions, m'offrant l'image du même supplice, et me causant à peu près la même peine; car n'est-ce pas une chose pénible à voir que le tourment, dans celui qui s'occupe à me peindre le plaisir; tirez entre cet homme et moi, un rideau qui me le cache, s'il faut qu'il me montre un patient appliqué à la question. Au milieu de ses agitations et de ses cris, s'il se présentait une tenue, un de ces endroits harmonieux où l'archet se meut lentement sur plusieurs cordes à la fois, son visage prenait l'air de l'extase sa voix s'adoucissait, il s'écoutait avec ravissement. Il est sûr que les accords résonnaient dans ses oreilles et dans les miennes. Puis, remettant son instrument sous son bras gauche, de la même main dont il le tenait, et laissant tomber sa main droite, avec son archet. Eh bien, me disait-il, qu'en pensez-vous? | Moi. – A merveille. | Lui. – Cela va, ce me semble; cela résonne à peu près, comme les autres»; <http://www.gutenberg.org/ebooks/13862> (consulted 31 August 2014). For further discussion of this famous scene, see Heartz, Daniel. 'Locatelli and the Pantomime of the Violinist in *Le neveu de Rameau*', in: *Diderot Studies XXVII*, edited by Diana Guiragossian Carr, Geneva, Droz, 1998, pp. 115-127.

ILL. 1: An anonymous rendering (1875) of Diderot's fictional description (1761-1762, revised 1773-1774) of Jean-François Rameau 'performing' a sonata by Locatelli in the Café de la Régence, Paris.

★★★

So far the discussion of evidence for a relationship between Locatelli and Leclair has, following de Bernis' obituary, been limited to the period 1740-1743. But there is an account unknown to La Laurencie, which suggests that the two violinists met earlier in Kassel. Before considering that document, however, an excursis on the topos 'Angels and Devils' — a metaphor employed by the writer of the Kassel anecdote. The battles between good and evil spirits in the Bible are found in passages in the Old and New Testaments, sometimes as abstract forces and other times embodied as good and bad angels contending against each other. As early as Hildegard of Bingen the iconography of the conflict over which side would capture humans' souls was well established, and it remained fundamentally unchanged for centuries (ILL. 2).

ILL. 2: Hildegard von Bingen, *The Soul Leaving the Body at Death*. Detail of a miniature in the *Liber Scivias* (SAURMA-JELTSCH, Lieselotte E. *Die Miniaturen im «Liber Scivias» der Hildegard von Bingen*, Wiesbaden, Reichert, 1998), vision I, 4; miniature 7.

At some later date the devil became associated with violin playing. That this strand of the iconography — the association of the violin with the devil and death — was already well established by no later than the seventeenth century is shown by art works of the period as well as an amusing anecdote. When the Lubeck-born violin virtuoso Thomas Baltzar came to England in 1655, nothing like his playing in high positions, double stops, and scordatura had been heard there before. The sensation aroused by his playing was recorded by the diarists John Evelyn and Anthony Wood. Evelyn heard Baltzar in London at the house of Nicholas L'Estrange and wrote that he «plaid on that single Instrument a full Consort, so as the rest, flung-downe their Instruments, as acknowledging a victory». For his part, Wood described a musical gathering of Oxford dons at which Baltzar

> [...] played to the wonder of all the auditory; and exercising his finger upon
> the instrument several wayes to the utmost of his power. Wilson, thereupon,
> the public professor, the greatest judge of Musick that ever was, did, after his
> humoursome way, stoop down to Baltzar's feet, to see whether or not he had
> a huff on, that is to say, to see whether he was a devil or not, because he acted
> beyond the parts of a man[14].

---

[14]. BOYDEN, David D. *The History of Violin Playing from its Origins to 1761*, London, Oxford University Press, 1965, p. 236.

The violinist as devil also strayed into the iconographies of the Temptation of St. Anthony and the Ecstasy of St. Francis (ILL. 3), as a bad angel tempting the saints to fleshly pleasures.

ILL. 3: *St. Francis in Ecstasy* by Guercino (after 1623). Muzeum Narodowe, Warsaw (M.OB.644).

And another topos was involved, one directly relevant to Locatelli and Leclair's supposed encounter in Kassel: 'Musical Competitions'. This topos that can be traced to the Greek myth of the satyr Maryas challenging Apollo to a musical duel. Losing, the satyr was flayed alive by Apollo for his hubris. Note the violin in the upper right-hand corner of ILL. 4.

ILL. 4: *Apollo Flaying Maryas* by Guercino (1618). Galleria Palatina, Palazzo Pitti, Florence.

In the generations after Leclair and Locatelli the diabolical fiddler remained a familiar theme: Tartini dreaming his devil's trill sonata, for instance, or Paganini portrayed as if in the 'Witch's Sabbath' of the finale of Berlioz's *Symphonie fantastique*, down to Stravinsky's *Histoire du soldat* and beyond. Keeping such connections in mind, we can now turn to the account of Locatelli and Leclair performing for the Court of Kassel. The anecdote was recorded in convoluted Dutch in 1786 by the German-born organist and composer Jakob Wilhelm Lustig, who appended it as a footnote to his Dutch translation of Charles Burney's *The Present State of Music in France and Italy*[15].

---

15. London, T. Becket, 1771.

[...] Whoever heard *Loccatelli* improvise 55 years ago knows what grimaces he exhibited before emerging from his trance, crying out repeatedly, «*Ah! que dites-vous de cela?*» Once, when he and *Le Clair* performed at the Court of Kassel, the court jester soon remarked, «That fellow [Locatelli] hops around the violin like a rabbit», and when they finished, «[Leclair] plays like an angel and [Locatelli] like a devil». [Leclair] with his little-practiced left hand, knew how to conquer hearts with his uncommonly sweet and lovely tone, while [Locatelli] sought, principally by means of great technical difficulties, while gnashing his teeth [*al knarssende*], to transport his listeners to a state of astonishment. When, however, it was a matter of riding the beat securely in the saddle — in which French musicians are (alas!) often lacking — one couldn't help noticing that in [Leclair's] solos as soon as he failed to pay very careful attention, he rode [his metaphorical metrical horse] off the road! [...][16].

It is unclear from Lustig's wording whether he was claiming to have witnessed the event himself or was simply relaying someone else's account. It is also unclear why a court jester was put forward as a music critic. Whoever was reporting certainly knew nothing about French unmeasured preludes. And what can we make of Leclair's 'little-practiced left hand' when we see the virtuosity called for by his music and read repeated observations by writers who heard him that his playing was always impeccable? Assuming that Lustig's report was not a complete fiction, what could its basis have been?

In 1957 Christiane Englbrecht published a previously unknown archival document recording a payment to Locatelli for an appearance at the Court of Kassel in 1728. The relevant text reads: «Dem italienischen Musico Locatelli wegen gethaner Auffwartung 7. xbr. 80 rthlr.»[17]. No mention of Leclair; however eighty Reichsthaler was a handsome sum, perhaps intended also to cover the services of others who performed with Locatelli — but that is speculation. A chronology of Leclair's known whereabouts during 1728 shows

---

[16]. BURNEY, Charles. *Rijk gestoffeerd verhaal van de eigenlijke gesteldheid der hedendaagsche Toonkunst* [...] *Vertaald en Opgeluisterd door Jacob Wilhelm Lustig*, Groningen, J. Oomkens, 1786, p. 390, note 168: «[...] wie, 55 Jaar geleden, *Loccatelli* heeft hooren fantaseeren, die weet, wat Grimacen daar by voorvielen: aller Hy, weer tot zich zelven komende, zomwijlen uitriep: «Ah! que dites-vous de cela?» Toen Hy [Locatelli] en *Le Clair* zich eens ter zelver Tijd hooren lieten op 't Hof te Kassel, had de Hofnar reeds in't begin gezegd: die Karel loopt op de Viool, als een Haas; en, by het Slot: die [Leclair] speelt als een Engel; en de eerste [Locatelli], als een Duivel. Gene [Leclair] wist, by een weinig geoeffende linker Hand, door zynen ongemeen zuiveren en lieflijken Toon, de Harten te vermeesteren; terwijl deeze [Locatelli], door groote Zwaarigheden, al knarssende, 'er uit te halen, voornaamlijk trachtde, de Toehoorders tot Verwondering te brengen. Doch, aangaande het Zadelvaste in de Maat, den franschen Musiekeren in't gemeen, helaas! niet volkomen eigen (not. 28 pag. 32), konde men ligt merken, dat de eerstgemelde, by zyn Solospeelen, buiten het Spoor raakte, zo dra hy niet zeer omzigtig op zyne Hoede bleef». I am grateful to Rudolf Rasch for his comments on this document. Lustig's «Ah! que dites-vous de cela?» would seem to echo Diderot's «Eh bien, me disait-il, qu'en pensez-vous?»; but Diderot's fantasy remained unpublished until the nineteenth-century.

[17]. ENGELBRECHT, Christiane. 'Die Hofkapelle des Landgrafen Carl von Hessen-Kassel', in: *Zeitschrift des Vereins für Hessische Geschichte und Landeskunde*, LXVIII (1957), pp. 166-167.

him publishing his Op. 2 and giving seven performances at the Concert spirituel between 17 April and 6 May. He may have been in London around 20 July. His Concert spirituel appearances then resumed, five more between 15 August and 22 November, after which no further performances by him until 16 June 1729. So Leclair's presence in Kassel on or about 7 December may have been just barely possible, even if no hard evidence confirms that he was actually there at that time.

★★★

In the end possible conclusions are elusive. After Leclair's death, two men who knew him wrote that he had worked with Locatelli in Holland, and that Locatelli's influence could be detected in some of Leclair's music. Whether or not Leclair actually played with Locatelli in 1728, Locatelli's works were readily available in Amsterdam and Parisian publications, so this remains in the realm of possibility.

The notion that Locatelli's influence upon Leclair's derived from the latter's time in Holland in 1740-1742, however, is unconvincing. By that time Leclair's style was firmly in place and the majority of his violin compositions had already been composed. After all, before he left for Holland he had already published his Opp. 1-8, and the Leclairs had announced in the press that Opp. 9 and 12 would be published during the winter of 1738[18]. In the event they were not published then and, as we have already noted, when Leclair returned to Paris in 1743, the Leclairs then advertised that the Op. 9 was belatedly in the press[19].

And finally, I do not believe that anyone has yet convincingly demonstrated, by comparisons between the violin compositions of these two masters of their craft, what that influence consisted of and how it was manifested. The careful passing-down of skills, ideas and explanations from master to pupil is itself a topos that has been persistent in the writing of music history. Numerous examples of it are unimpeachably documented, no matter how they may be explained or understood and whether or not there was anxiety on the part of the pupil. In this investigation the jury is still out, but so far it remains questionable that that kind of relationship existed between Locatelli and Leclair.

POSTSCRIPT

While this article was already in press, Zoe Weiss pointed out to me the following angel/devil comparison between the gambists Marais and Forqueray in Hubert le Blanc's *Defense de la basse de viole contre les entrèprises du violon et les prétentions du violoncel* (Amsterdam, Pierre Mortier, 1740), p. 59: «La Viole s'étoit vue favorisée par le Roi *Louis* XIV dans ses Nourissons, le Père *Marais* pour ses Pièces, & *Forcroi* le Père pour ses Préludes tirans sur la Sonate. L'un avoit été déclaré jouer comme un Ange, & l'autre jouer comme un Diable».

---

18. *Le Mercure de France*, January 1737, p. 109.
19. See note 9 above.

RETROUVER LECLAIR
(1794-1874)

Étienne Jardin
(PARIS)

LES RECHERCHES CONCERNANT la redécouverte des musiciens du passé au cours du XIXe siècle français se focalisent généralement sur des institutions de concert[1] ou d'enseignement musical[2] et adoptent l'échelle d'une ville[3], d'un pays ou même d'un continent[4] pour s'interroger sur l'évolution du canon musical et la place que les siècles précédents y tiennent. Quand cette perspective s'inverse et que — à l'image de l'étude de Joël-Marie Fauquet et Antoine Hennion sur Bach[5] ou de Jean-Claire Vançon sur Rameau[6] — l'on suit la trajectoire posthume d'un compositeur baroque ou classique dans le siècle romantique, c'est généralement en s'appuyant sur une figure incontournable de l'histoire de la musique européenne. Jean-Marie Leclair (1697-1764) n'a clairement pas la même place que Bach et Rameau dans les pratiques et l'imaginaire du monde musical français du XIXe siècle et, très rapidement, il a paru nécessaire de construire l'étude de sa notoriété posthume autour des questions relatives à la disparition de ses œuvres avant d'aborder la redécouverte à la fois du musicien et de ses productions. Retrouver Leclair,

---

[1]. Voir CAMPOS, Rémy. *La Renaissance introuvable? Entre curiosité et militantisme: la Société des concerts de musique vocale religieuse et classique du prince de la Moskowa, 1843-1846*, Paris, Klincksieck, 2000 (Epitome musical, 6).

[2]. Voir SIMMS, Brian Randolph. *Alexandre Choron (1771-1834) as a Historian and Theorist of Music*, Ph.D. Diss., New Haven (CT), Yale University, 1971.

[3]. Voir GRIBENSKI, Fanny. 'Présenter la musique ancienne: les avatars du concert-conférence à Paris dans les années 1880-1890', in: *La musique ancienne entre historiens et musiciens*, dirigé par Xavier Bisaro et Rémy Campos, Genève, Droz-Haute École de Musique de Genève, 2014 (Musique & recherche, 3), pp. 63-103.

[4]. Voir ELLIS, Katharine. *Interpreting the Musical Past. Early Music in Nineteenth-Century France*, Oxford-New York, Oxford University Press, 2005. Voir aussi WEBER, William. *The Great Transformation of Musical Taste: Concert Programming from Haydn to Brahms*, Cambridge-New York, Cambridge University Press, 2008.

[5]. FAUQUET, Joël-Marie – HENNION, Antoine. *La Grandeur de Bach: l'amour de la musique en France au XIXe siècle*, Paris, Fayard, 2000 (Les chemins de la musique).

[6]. VANÇON, Jean-Claire. *Le Temple de la Gloire. Visages et usages de Jean-Philippe Rameau en France entre 1764 et 1895*, thèse de doctorat, Paris, Paris-Sorbonne, 2009.

c'est ce que les musicologues français du tournant des XIXᵉ et XXᵉ siècles s'attacheront à faire pleinement en lui consacrant des articles biographiques[7] ou des critiques des rééditions de ses œuvres[8]. Le violoniste et ses sonates sortent alors d'un purgatoire du goût musical français dans lequel ils semblent être restés depuis, au moins, la chute de Robespierre. C'est cette période transitoire qui nous intéressera ici.

Dans un premier temps, on tentera d'expliquer la disparition des œuvres de Leclair dans les concerts parisiens en observant les pièces pour violon qui sont effectivement programmées à Paris entre 1794 et 1815. On s'attardera ensuite sur le rapport que le Conservatoire et plus particulièrement le professeur Pierre Baillot entretiennent avec Leclair; et nous décrirons enfin quelques étapes qui jalonnent la popularisation du compositeur depuis la monarchie de Juillet jusqu'aux débuts de la Troisième République. Plutôt que d'avancer des raisons esthétiques ou politiques de son retour en grâce, en suivant le chemin permettant de retrouver Leclair, on tentera de montrer comment la musique du passé — ici essentiellement instrumentale — reprend une place dans le canon musical français.

DISPARITION

Afin de constater l'absence des œuvres de Leclair à Paris au début du XIXᵉ siècle, nous avons d'abord utilisé le répertoire des concerts tenus dans cette ville entre 1794 et 1815, répertoire élaboré sous la direction de Cécile Duflo, Patrick Taïeb et nous-mêmes dans le cadre du projet de cherche sur les programmes de concert en France (RPCF)[9]. Ce répertoire regroupe 841 événements qui ont eu lieu dans la capitale française entre la chute de Robespierre et celle de Napoléon. Il en propose une reconstitution normalisée des programmes en se basant sur des éléments trouvés dans la presse[10] ou dans des fonds

---

[7].   Voir LA LAURENCIE, Lionel de. 'Jean-Marie Leclair l'aîné. Premier Symphoniste du Roi. D'après des documents inédits', in: *Sammelbände der Internationalen Musikgesellschaft*, VI/2 (1905), pp. 250-273. Voir aussi ID. 'Une assertion de Fétis: Jean-Marie Leclair l'aîné à l'orchestre de l'Opéra', in: *La Revue musicale*, IV/20 (1904), pp. 496-503.

[8].   Voir DUVAL, Gaston. 'Un cas nouveau de vandalisme musical: J.-M. Leclair, violoniste-compositeur parisien (1687-1764)', in: *La Revue musicale*, III/9 (1903), pp. 358-362.

[9].   Au sujet de ce groupe de recherche et de ses méthodes, voir le dossier 'Société internationale de musicologie. Le Répertoire des programmes de concert en France' paru dans *Bulletin de l'Association internationale des bibliothèques, archives et centres de documentation musicaux (AIBM) – Groupe français*, n° 17 (2009), pp. 41-92. Le répertoire des concerts parisiens entre 1794 et 1815 est en cours de publication sur la base Dezède (en ligne: <dezede.org>).

[10].   La liste alphabétique des journaux consultés pour établir ce répertoire est la suivante: *Affiches, Annonces et Avis divers*; *Correspondance des amateurs musiciens* puis *Correspondance des professeurs et amateurs de musique*; *Courrier de l'Europe et des spectacles*; *Courrier des spectacles*; *Décade philosophique*; *Gazette de France*; *Journal de l'Empire*; *Journal de Paris*; *Journal des arts, de littérature et de commerce*; *Journal des arts, des sciences et de littérature*; *Journal des débats et des décrets*; *Journal des spectacles, de musique et des arts*; *Journal des théâtres et des fêtes nationales*;

d'archive. Dans ce répertoire, on ne trouve à aucun endroit le nom de Leclair: non seulement on n'y rencontre aucune trace de l'exécution de ses œuvres entre 1794 et 1815, mais la presse ne mentionne pas non plus le compositeur, ne serait-ce que pour indiquer une filiation personnelle ou esthétique avec un violoniste contemporain. Si, alors, on ne joue pas des œuvres de Leclair, que joue-t-on? Bien que cette question nous mène légèrement hors de notre sujet, elle doit néanmoins être posée afin de nous orienter sur les raisons de la désaffection pour Leclair: doit-elle être directement liée à ses œuvres, ou répond-elle à une attitude plus générale?

Avant d'analyser l'ensemble des pièces interprétées par des violonistes dans les concerts parisiens entre 1794 et 1815, il faut néanmoins signaler qu'il reste de grandes zones d'imprécisions relatives à ce répertoire. Les sources dont nous disposons aujourd'hui pour l'aborder donnent peu de détail sur le contenu exact des partitions interprétées et les appellations génériques 'air varié pour violon', 'concerto pour violon' ou 'symphonie concertante pour violon', sans précision du nom du compositeur, sont très souvent les seules disponibles[11]. On pourrait émettre l'hypothèse que derrière ces dénominations vagues se cache, parfois, une œuvre de Leclair. Cependant, l'analyse du répertoire identifiable rend cette idée peu crédible.

La liste des compositeurs d'œuvres pour violon, classée dans l'ordre chronologique de leur naissance, est la suivante:

Gaviniès (1728-1800);	Aubert (1763-1830);	Boucher (1778-1861);
Rey (1734-1810);	Demar (1763-1832);	Guénée (1779-1850);
Désormery (1740-1810);	Himmel (1765-1814);	Gasse (1780-1825);
Fridzeri (1741-1825);	Kreutzer (1766-1831);	Habeneck (1781-1849);
Giornovichi (1745-1804);	Ladurner (1766-1839);	Lafont (1781-1839);
Cambini (1746-1825);	Eck (1767-1838);	Pradher (1782-1843);
Barrière (1748-1818);	Romberg (1767-1841);	Mazas (1782-1849);
Mestrino (1748-1789);	Grasset (1769-1839);	Dupierge (1784-?);
Stamitz (1750-?);	Duranowski (c1770-1834);	Spohr (1784-1859);
Taskin (1750-1829);	Baillot (1771-1842);	Vidal (1789-1867);
Viotti (1755-1824);	Labarre (1771-?);	Fémy (1790-1842);
Pleyel (1757-1831);	Lamare (1772-1823);	Attaccy;
Blasius (1758-1829);	Lemoyne (1772-1815);	Grattel;
Lefèvre (1759-1820);	Rode (1774-1830);	Henry;
Dussek (1761-1812);	Libon (1775-1838);	Mlle Roussel.
Janiewick (1762-1848);	Giorgis (1777-?);	

Journal du commerce, de politique et de littérature; *L'Ami des citoyens*; *Le Mercure français*; *Le Moniteur universel*; *Le Narrateur universel*; *L'Observateur des spectacles, de la littérature et des arts*; *Le Publiciste*; *Revue philosophique, littéraire et politique* et *Tablette de Polymnie*.

11. Voir JARDIN, Étienne. 'Le concert dans la presse parisienne. 1794-1815', in: *Bulletin de l'Association internationale des bibliothèques, archives et centres de documentation musicaux (AIBM) – Groupe français*, n° 17 (2009), pp. 65-69.

Hormis un «concerto pour violon» de Mestrino interprété par August Duranowski le 13 juin 1800 au concert de la rue St-Nicaise[12], toutes les occurrences d'œuvres pour violon — seul ou en formation de musique de chambre — sont dues à des compositeurs vivants au moment de leur exécution. On peut par ailleurs détailler cette première information en répartissant ce groupe de compositeurs en fonction de leur date de naissance:

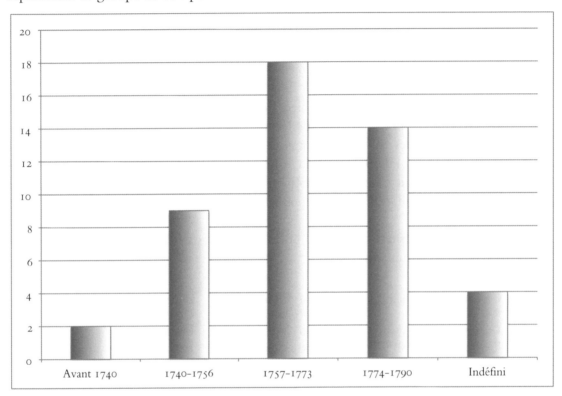

La majeure partie des compositeurs joués dans les concerts parisiens entre 1794 et 1815 est née après la mort de Leclair; et les plus anciens d'entre eux sont nés plus de trente ans après le violoniste qui nous intéresse ici. Une dernière information paraît importante à signaler: sur les 48 compositeurs recensés, une majorité (54%) est constituée d'instrumentistes pouvant défendre eux-mêmes leurs œuvres à Paris.

Au début du XIXe siècle, la place que pourraient occuper les œuvres de Leclair est presque entièrement occupée par des productions contemporaines, majoritairement composées par des violonistes en activité. Le «nouveau commerce de la virtuosité» décrit par Alexandre Dratwicki[13] se trouve en plein essor et l'intérêt porté à la musique du

---

[12].   Voir *Journal de Paris*, 12 juin 1800 [23 prairial an VIII].

[13].   DRATWICKI, Alexandre. *Un nouveau commerce de la virtuosité: émancipation et métamorphoses de la musique concertante au sein des institutions musicales parisiennes (1780-1830)*, Lyon, Symétrie, 2006 (Musicologie).

passé — notamment celles de l'époque de Louis XV et Louis XVI — est faible, sinon nul. Parmi les commentateurs des concerts, rares sont aussi ceux s'indignant de cette course à la nouveauté qui se joue au sein du monde des violonistes. On notera néanmoins la remarque du rédacteur de *Journal de l'Europe* qui, en mai 1810, s'inquiète que «les jeunes compositeurs […] se hâtent trop, non pas de composer, mais de faire part au public de leurs thèmes»:

> […] je crois qu'ils doivent exécuter longtemps les compositions des grands maîtres avant de hasarder leurs propres ouvrages. Je recommande aux jeunes violons les sonates de Tartini, les concertos de Viotti: il y a là de quoi les exercer utilement: quand ils seront parvenus à exécuter parfaitement ces chefs-d'œuvre, ils pourront s'applaudir de leur talent pour l'exécution[14].

L'idée que la formation d'un musicien passe par l'apprentissage des répertoires des époques qui le précède sera largement admise au début du siècle suivant: dans le Paris de l'Empire, elle reste encore très minoritaire. Pour que la musique du passé vienne seconder les productions contemporaines, il faudrait en premier lieu que les institutions d'enseignement musical, et notamment le Conservatoire de Paris (créé en 1795), s'en fassent les promoteurs.

BAILLOT ET LECLAIR

Professeur titulaire au Conservatoire de Paris depuis 1799 jusqu'à sa mort en 1842, Pierre Baillot (1771-1842) est une figure centrale pour saisir l'évolution du violon dans cette école de musique au cours des premières décennies du XIXᵉ siècle[15]. Il nous permet d'abord d'accéder au point de vue initial des professeurs de violon de l'établissement grâce à la *Méthode de violon*, signée Baillot, Rode et Kreutzer, mais «rédigée» par Baillot seul et éditée en 1803. Cette publication didactique est l'une des premières méthodes instrumentales du Conservatoire (après le cor et la clarinette) et a pour mission de diffuser le plus largement possible les principes fondamentaux de la nouvelle école française[16].

La seule allusion directe aux générations précédentes de violonistes dans cette méthode se trouve à la fin de la 2ᵉ page d'introduction: un petit paragraphe intitulé 'Des différents caractères' dans lequel on cite les noms de Corelli (1653-1713), Tartini (1692-

---

[14]. *Journal de l'Europe*, 3 mai 1810.

[15]. Voir FRANÇOIS-SAPPEY, Brigitte. 'Pierre Marie François de Sales Baillot (1771-1842) par lui-même: étude de sociologie musicale', in: *Recherches sur la musique française classique*, XVIII (1978), pp. 126-211. Voir aussi FAUQUET, Joël-Marie. *Les sociétés de musique de chambre à Paris, de la Restauration à 1870*, Paris, Aux Amateurs de livres, 1986 (Domaine musicologique, 1).

[16]. Voir HONDRÉ, Emmanuel. 'Les méthodes officielles du Conservatoire', in: *Le Conservatoire de musique de Paris: regards sur une institution et son histoire*, dirigé par Emmanuel Hondré, Paris, Association du bureau des étudiants du Conservatoire national supérieur de musique, 1995, pp. 73-107.

1770), Gaviniès, Pugnani (1731-1798) et bien sûr Viotti — extrêmement influent sur la première génération des professeurs de violon au Conservatoire:

> Cet instrument, fait par sa nature pour regner dans les concerts et pour obéïr à tous les élans du génie, a pris les différens caractères que les grands maîtres ont voulu lui donner: simple et mélodieux sous les doigts de CORELLI, harmonieux, touchant et plein de graces sous l'archet de TARTINI, aimable et suave sous celui de GAVINIÉS, noble et grandioso sous celui de PUGNANI, plein de feu, plein d'audace, pathétique, sublime entre les mains de VIOTTI, il s'est élevé jusqu'à peindre les passions avec énergie et avec cette noblesse qui convient autant au rang qu'il occupe qu'à l'empire qu'il exerce sur l'âme[17].

Alors que Baillot fait l'effort de citer des compositeurs qui ne sont pas joués en concert à Paris (comme Corelli, Tartini et Pugnani) et qui appartiennent, pour certains, à un passé dépassant la mémoire d'homme, il ne cite pas Leclair.

Trente ans plus tard (1834), dans *L'Art du violon*, Baillot reprend ce même passage au sein de l'introduction. Cette fois, cependant, le texte désormais intitulé 'Virtuoses les plus célèbres' se termine par un appel de note de bas de page renvoyant à ce court paragraphe:

> Ce passage est extrait de la 1re Méthode que nous avons rédigée pour le Conservatoire. Tant d'années écoulées depuis sa publication nous ont mis plus à portée de connaître et d'apprécier les beautés de la musique de Leclair, et ce nom célèbre ne peut en être rappelé par nous qu'avec l'admiration qui lui est due. Un auteur que nous citons à l'article des *Sons soutenus*, Hubert Leblanc, parle de ses ouvrages en ces termes: «Les trois douzaines sonates des livres de M. Leclair étalèrent en pompe la majesté du jeu du violon»[18].

Citant l'auteur de *Défense de la basse de viole contre les entreprises du violon et les prétentions du violoncelle* (1740), Baillot place enfin Leclair dans la lumière, mais ne le fait qu'en note de bas de page.

Nous savons — par Baillot lui-même — que le violoniste a été en contact direct avec des œuvres de Leclair au cours de l'intervalle séparant la rédaction des deux méthodes. Dans un document intitulé *Voyage dans le midi de la France* — compilation par Baillot des lettres qu'il adresse à sa femme au cours d'une tournée qui le mène, entre janvier et mai 1812, de Bordeaux à Lyon —, il relate ainsi sa rencontre avec Barthélémy de Marin, comte de Carranrais:

---

17. BAILLOT, Pierre(-Marie-François de Sales) – RODE, Pierre – KREUTZER, Rodolphe. *Méthode de violon*, Paris, Au Magasin de musique du Conservatoire, [1803], p. 2.

18. BAILLOT, Pierre(-Marie-François de Sales). *L'Art du violon: nouvelle méthode*, Paris, Au Dépôt central de la musique, [1835], p. 5.

> Je suis parti de Toulouse le 14 [mars 1812] pour aller à Rieux. M. Auguste de Marin m'a mené chez ses parents. Nous y arrivâmes à 4 h du soir après nous être arrêtés 1 h à Muret, patrie de Dalayrac. J'avais vu M. de Marin père à Rome, il y a 26 ans. C'est un beau vieillard, passionné pour le violon et qui m'a fait entendre des sonates de Leclair et de Tartini qu'il joue avec feu et avec un certain petit doigt dont il a presque le droit de s'enorgueillir à 75 ans[19].

Cette audition particulière des sonates de Leclair est-elle la première pour Baillot? Le fait qu'elle soit donnée par un musicien amateur âgé de plus de trente ans que lui[20] renforce le constat dressé plus haut: celui d'une désaffection des musiciens de la génération de Baillot pour les artistes du début du XVIIIᵉ siècle.

En plus de le signaler dans l'introduction de *L'Art du violon* au rang des virtuoses du passé, Baillot place Leclair à la fin de cet ouvrage dans le «Catalogue des auteurs dont les compositions servent à l'enseignement dans les classes de violon du Conservatoire»[21]. Cette indication est d'autant plus précieuse que — si les œuvres de Leclair sont effectivement étudiées dans cette école — elles ne sont en revanche jamais interprétées au cours des concerts ou exercices publics organisés par le Conservatoire tout au long du XIXᵉ siècle[22]. Cette introduction de Leclair dans le répertoire de formation des élèves date probablement de la période de rédaction de *L'Art du violon*: le début des années 1830, période au cours de laquelle nous savons que Baillot a joué (ou a envisagé de jouer) une pièce de Leclair au cours d'une «séance historique» de musique de chambre.

Cette séance s'inscrit dans la lignée des séances de musique de chambre que le violoniste organise à Paris depuis 1814 — activité qui fait de Baillot le premier musicien français à proposer ce type d'audition dans un cadre public[23]. Le répertoire de ces séances ordinaires est néanmoins essentiellement centré sur les productions de Boccherini, Haydn, Mozart, Beethoven et Baillot lui-même. Trois séances de musique ancienne viennent varier cette programmation: la première en 1818, la deuxième en 1833 et une dernière en 1837. Au concert de musique ancienne de 1818, il fait entendre des œuvres de Corelli, Händel, Geminiani, Tartini et Barbella[24]. À celui de 1833, on retrouve sensiblement les

---

[19]. ID. *Voyage dans le midi de la France*, manuscrit, Bibliothèque nationale de France, fonds Baillot.

[20]. Le comte de Marin est né en 1738.

[21]. BAILLOT, Pierre(-Marie-François de Sales). *L'Art du violon: nouvelle méthode*, op. cit. (voir la note 18), p. 271. Leclair apparaît dans le tableau consacré aux «Compositeurs morts».

[22]. Aucune œuvre de Leclair n'apparaît dans les programmes des exercices des élèves reconstitués par Constant Pierre dans son ouvrage sur le Conservatoire (PIERRE, Constant. *Le Conservatoire national de musique et de déclamation: documents historiques et administratifs*, Paris, Imprimerie nationale, 1900, pp. 476-510).

[23]. Voir FAUQUET, Joël-Marie. *Op. cit.* (voir la note 15).

[24]. Le programme manuscrit conservé par les descendants de Pierre Baillot porte les indications suivantes: «Musique ancienne. / 14 février 1818. / 1. Concerto de Corelli (le 1ᵉʳ) / 2. Trio de Handel (le 1ᵉʳ) / 3. Concerto de Geminiani (le 1ᵉʳ) / 4. Concerto de Tartini (en *ut*) / - / 5. Concerto de Corelli (le 8ᵉ,

mêmes compositeurs, accompagnés de Bach. Le programme se termine par des œuvres de Mozart et Beethoven, interprétées par les enfants de Baillot, et permettant de faire un lien entre les œuvres anciennes et le répertoire devenu usuel à Paris à cette époque[25]. On peut y sentir l'influence des auditions organisées par Alexandre Choron[26] à l'Institution de musique religieuse, rue de Vaugirard (depuis 1827), ou encore celle des concerts historiques de Fétis[27] (1832).

Le dernier concert de ce type organisé par Baillot chez lui, rue Pigalle, intègre de manière encore plus explicite le modèle des concerts historiques de Fétis. Il présente, sur la droite du programme, «l'âge du morceau de musique» calculé approximativement, et les morceaux de musique sont organisés du plus ancien (une «Chanson flamande du 13ᵉ siècle») au plus récent (une «Sonate de Boccherini» de 1768). Il existe deux versions manuscrites de ce programme conservées dans le fonds des descendants de Pierre Baillot: on dénombre, sur le premier, neuf numéros; et 10 numéros sur le second. L'œuvre supplémentaire est le 8ᵉ numéro du second programme: «Le Tombeau de Leclair, sonate» que Baillot date de 1760. Sommes-nous alors devant la première preuve d'une audition de Leclair à Paris depuis la chute de Robespierre? Ou la disparition de Leclair dans le premier programme montre-t-elle qu'après avoir envisagé de jouer cette sonate, Baillot s'est ravisé[28]?

Sans qu'ils permettent d'assurer que *Le Tombeau* a bien été joué au cours de ce concert, on trouve au cours des années qui le suivent quelques indices dans la *Revue et Gazette musicale de Paris* laissant à penser que Baillot s'est bien fait entendre dans une sonate de Leclair à cette époque:

---

pour la Nuit de Noël) / 6. Sonate de Tartini (la Didon abandonnée) / 7. Concerto de Geminiani (le 2ᵉ) / 8. Concerto de Tartini (en *si* mineur) / 9. Andante de Barbella (la Ninna Nonna)».

[25]. Le programme manuscrit conservé par les descendants de Pierre Baillot porte les indications suivantes: «Séance historique du Concerto donnée particulièrement chez moi fb. Poissonnière 101, le samedi 13 avril 1833. / 1. 8ᵉ Concerto de Corelli, fait pour la Nuit de Noël. / 2. 2ᵉ et 1ʳᵉ partie du 3ᵉ Concerto de Geminiani. / 3. Concerto de Pergolese (en *si*♭) / 4. 3ᵉ Concerto de Haendel / 5. Concerto de Sébastien Bach (en *la* min.) / 6. Concerto de Tartini (en *si* min) / 7. *La Nina Nonna* chant de nourrice de Barbella / 8. Fantaise de Mozart pour le piano exécuté par René [Baillot] / 9. Concerto en *ut* mineur de Beethoven exécuté par Augustine [Baillot]».

[26]. Voir SIMMS, Brian Randolph. *Op. cit.* (voir la note 2) notamment le chapitre 'The Historical Concerts', p. 123 et suivantes. Voir aussi BOETTCHER, Tilmann. *Les exercices publics d'Alexandre Choron: à travers la presse de l'époque*, mémoire de maîtrise, Paris, Université de Paris IV-Sorbonne, 1995.

[27]. Voir CAMPOS, Rémy. *François-Joseph Fétis musicographe*, Genève, Droz-Haute École de Musique de Genève, 2013 (Musique & recherche, 2), pp. 600-604. Pierre Baillot a participé au concert historique du 16 décembre 1832 organisé par Fétis en y interprétant un *Concerto passeggiato* de Cavalieri. Voir FRANÇOIS-SAPPEY, Brigitte. *Op. cit.* (voir la note 15), p. 192.

[28]. C'est l'interprétation retenue par FRANÇOIS-SAPPEY, Brigitte. *Op. cit.* (voir note 15), p. 192.

Ill. 1a: première version du programme du Concert historique du violon donné par Baillot le mardi 29 novembre 1837, rue Pigalle. © Fonds particulier, numérisation effectuée par le Palazzetto Bru Zane.

ILL. 1b: deuxième version du programme du Concert historique du violon donné par Baillot le mardi 29 novembre 1837, rue Pigalle. © Fonds particulier, numérisation effectuée par le Palazzetto Bru Zane.

CONCOURS DU CONSERVATOIRE.

(Troisième article.) [...]

Nous aurions préféré entendre une de ces vieilles sonates de Bach ou de Mozart, comme on savait les faire autrefois. Car nous en demandons bien pardon à Fontenelle, mais son mot célèbre: Sonate, que me veux-tu? n'est tout simplement qu'une sottise. Pour vous en convaincre, priez M. Baillot de vouloir bien vous jouer quelques morceaux de Corelli ou de Leclair; et quand vous aurez entendu cette musique à la fois expressive et pathétique, vous serez de notre sentiment[29].

[...] Baillot prit une non moins remarquable position; il fit revivre les anciennes écoles de France et d'Italie. La double corde, la cadence, le trille brillant et rapide sur le trait, le staccato mordu avec verve, une inconcevable liberté d'archet, telles sont les qualités que ses rivaux eux-mêmes se plurent dès l'abord à lui reconnaître, et qui donnèrent une physionomie rétrospective, classique et toute pittoresque à sa manière d'enseigner l'art du violon; il fit revivre Tartini, Leclair et Locatelli; on peut dire même que c'est à l'école de Baillot que s'est formée celle de Belgique, qui jette maintenant un si vif éclat[30].

Publiés dans deux numéros successifs de la *Revue et Gazette musicale de Paris* et sans doute écrits par le même rédacteur (Henri Blanchard), ces deux passages permettent d'imaginer que Baillot, à la fin de sa vie, interprétait volontiers des œuvres de Leclair dans un cadre privé. En vieillissant, l'auteur de *L'Art du violon* aurait-il amplifié ses préoccupations historiques? Souhaitait-il alors consciemment apparaître comme le présente Blanchard: le point d'aboutissement d'un lignée ancienne de violonistes et le fondateur d'une école franco-belge? Un autre indice de la place que prend Leclair dans la classe de Baillot se trouve enfin dans une lettre qu'il adresse à Cherubini en décembre 1838 dans le but de fonder une classe de musique d'ensemble au Conservatoire:

21 décembre 1838.

Monsieur,

Le désir de régulariser et compléter les études des élèves de ma classe m'a fait sentir depuis très longtemps la nécessité de leur faire prendre connaissance de tous les ouvrages classiques écrits pour le violon depuis les plus anciens compositeurs connus jusques aux plus modernes. C'est pourquoi mes élèves ont tous étudié les sonates de Corelli, Leclair, Tartini, Locatelli, Geminiani, Bach, Pugnani et successivement les solos de Viotti, Kreutzer, Rode, etc., mais les auteurs que je viens de citer et d'autres encore tels que Haendel, Haydn, Mozart et Beethoven, ces auteurs, dis-je, ont fait expressément pour le violon des morceaux d'ensemble qu'il serait d'autant plus important de faire connaître et pratiquer aux élèves que chaque jour on perd davantage la trace de leurs beautés et qu'ils renferment en eux-mêmes l'histoire de l'art si utile et si intéressante[31].

---

29. *Revue et Gazette musicale de Paris*, 15 août 1839.
30. BLANCHARD, Henri. 'Physiologie du violon', in: *Revue et Gazette musicale de Paris*, 23 août 1839.
31. Cité dans FRANÇOIS-SAPPEY, Brigitte. *Op. cit.* (voir la note 15), p. 199.

L'entrée du compositeur dans le répertoire d'apprentissage des violonistes ne fera que s'accentuer dans la deuxième partie du XIXe siècle — comme le prouvent, par exemple, la méthode d'Eugène Sauzay (*Le Violon harmonique*, 1889[32]) ou les recommandations de répertoire que Vincent d'Indy formule au conservatoire de Saint-Étienne en 1909[33]. Néanmoins, les étapes qui jalonnent la reconnaissance de Leclair ne se situent pas toutes dans le milieu académique. Pour que ses œuvres retrouvent le chemin des concerts et des éditeurs, il faut en effet qu'elles répondent à une attente du public. Or, pour que cette attente existe, il faut que le public connaisse son nom.

Popularisation de Leclair

L'incroyable développement de la presse musicale sous la monarchie de Juillet témoigne d'un besoin d'information sur l'actualité lyrique et instrumentale du moment, mais également d'un besoin de connaissances sur l'histoire de la musique et sur la vie des compositeurs[34]. Si certains articles peuvent prendre un caractère très sérieux, d'autres emploient un ton bien plus romanesque pour dépeindre le destin des musiciens du passé. Ils s'alignent en cela sur les abondants détails que l'on rapporte alors au sujet des grands solistes du temps, notamment Paganini, en n'ayant que rarement le souci de donner des informations véridiques. L'assassinat de Leclair et l'incertitude qui règne sur les circonstances de celui-ci sont, en cela, une aubaine pour sa notoriété à l'époque romantique.

En 1845, le violoniste trouve ainsi une place non négligeable dans un feuilleton publié par la *Revue et Gazette musicale de Paris* intitulé *Souvenirs d'un octogénaire*. Le premier épisode de ce feuilleton paraît dans le numéro du 22 juin en étant précédé d'un 'Avertissement de l'Éditeur' au cours duquel Maurice Bourges présente les circonstances au cours desquelles il a été amené à sauver les mémoires de Joseph-Hyacinthe Ferrand (1709-1791) que l'un de ses hériter, négociant de vin à Bordeaux, s'apprêtait à brûler. Ce personnage, fils d'un fermier général et ami des musiciens de son temps, aurait ainsi — d'après Maurice Bourges — passé les dernières années de sa vie à rédiger des souvenirs que l'éditeur de 1845 décide de produire «dans leur abandon primitif»[35], donc *a priori* sans en altérer le

---

[32]. Sauzay, Eugène. *Le Violon harmonique: ses ressources, son emploi dans les écoles anciennes et modernes. Étude complétée par un cours d'harmonie à l'usage des violonistes*, Paris, Firmin-Didot, 1889. Certains exemples utilisés dans cette méthode sont tirés des œuvres de Leclair.

[33]. Voir Jardin, Étienne. 'Entre art et loisir: définir la politique éducative d'un conservatoire. L'exemple de Saint-Étienne à la Belle Époque', in: *Revue de Musicologie*, XCVI/1 (2010), p. 113. Dans son «Aperçu d'un plan d'études, sous forme de répertoire», pour les cours de violon élémentaires, d'Indy préconise notamment l'apprentissage des «Sonates françaises du XVIIIe siècle, de Leclair, Senaillé, Aubert, etc.».

[34]. Voir notamment Reibel, Emmanuel. *L'écriture de la critique musicale au temps de Berlioz*, Paris, Honoré Champion, 2005 (Musique-musicologie, 39).

[35]. *Revue et Gazette musicale de Paris*, 22 juin 1845.

contenu ni en corriger les nombreuses erreurs de date. La publication de ce feuilleton en seize chapitres occupe le bas des quatre ou cinq premières pages de la *Revue et Gazette musicale de Paris* jusqu'au début du mois d'octobre 1845. Trois chapitres nous intéressent particulièrement ici: le chapitre VI, 'Locatelli, et l'amputation par amour' (27 juillet 1845), le chapitre IX, 'Fanchonnette' (17 août 1845) et le chapitre X, 'La petite maison'.

Le premier chapitre est la transcription d'une lettre que Leclair aurait écrite à Ferrand en lui faisant part à la fois de son admiration pour Locatelli et d'une anecdote le concernant: pour gagner le cœur d'une femme, Locatelli aurait tenté de se faire amputer une jambe, opération arrêtée à la dernière minute par la jeune femme en question qui, devant ce geste extrême, aurait consenti à l'épouser. Les chapitres IX et X sont le récit des circonstances entourant la mort de Leclair. L'héroïne de cette deuxième histoire est la nièce du compositeur, «Fanchonnette», danseuse à l'Opéra de Paris. Leclair aurait tenté de protéger cette jeune fille des périls de la vie d'artiste qu'une mère vénale l'aurait encouragé à suivre. Enlevée un soir, après une représentation de *Castor et Pollux* de Rameau[36], par un aristocrate anglais, Fanchonnette est secourue par son oncle qui se sacrifie pour lui permettre de s'enfuir. De nombreux détails du récit permettent de fortement douter de sa véracité et même de remettre en question la provenance du texte. Sa construction répond si bien aux codes du feuilleton de l'époque qu'on ne peut que supposer que Maurice Bourges en est — sinon l'auteur unique — du moins le coauteur. La popularisation du nom de Leclair prenant appui sur les circonstances de sa mort connaît un autre exemple dans cette même revue un peu moins de dix ans plus tard quand, dans les 'Ephémérides musicales' du 22 octobre 1854, on fait figurer en haut de liste: «22 octobre 1764. Jean-Marie Leclair est assassiné à Paris».

Des publications plus sérieuses s'intéressent par la suite à ce violoniste. François-Joseph Fétis s'y attèle dès la première édition de sa *Biographie universelle des musiciens* (1840) puis dans l'introduction de sa *Notice biographique sur Nicolo Paganini* (1851) intitulée 'Esquisse de l'histoire du violon'[37]. Leclair y est désigné comme le fondateur de l'école française de violon: «La gloire de poser les bases d'une école de violon en France était réservée à Jean-Marie Lecler [*sic*], élève de Soumis, et violoniste de grand talent, qui naquit à Lyon, en 1697»[38]. Chez Fétis, cet intérêt relatif pour Leclair, se poursuit dans la deuxième édition de *Biographie universelle des musiciens* (tome V, 1863) dans laquelle il donne bien plus d'ampleur

---

36. Une première incohérence est ici flagrante: Jean-Marie Leclair a été assassiné le 22 octobre 1764 alors que les représentations de *Castor et Pollux* de Rameau ont lieu, au cours de l'année 1764, entre le 24 janvier et le 6 avril. Voir la base de données chronopera (<http://chronopera.free.fr>).

37. Dans ce texte, Fétis orthographie mal le nom de Leclair (noté «Lecler»), ce qui est étonnant quand Choron, dans son *Dictionnaire historique des musiciens* (1810), utilise la bonne orthographe et que Fétis lui-même écrit «Leclair» dans la première édition de la *Biographie universelle*.

38. FÉTIS, François-Joseph. *Notice biographique sur Nicolo Paganini, suivie de l'analyse de ses ouvrages et précédée d'une esquisse de l'histoire du violon*, Paris, Schonenberger, 1851, p. 27.

à ses recherches tout en faisant un certain nombre d'erreurs qui seront relevées par Lionel de La Laurencie dans un article paru dans *La Revue musicale* en 1904[39].

Paradoxalement, alors que les musicographes désignent de plus en plus fréquemment Leclair comme le père de l'école française de violon, c'est sous l'impulsion d'un violoniste allemand, Jean Becker (1833-1881), que le Français réapparaît dans les concerts parisiens au cours des années 1860. Le 3ᵉ «concert historique» qu'il propose à Paris en 1863 est annoncé ainsi: «Cette fois, c'est un spécimen des écoles française et belge que déroulera l'éminent violoniste dans une série de morceaux empruntés aux maîtres les plus célèbres, depuis Leclair jusqu'à Alard»[40].

Si l'on se base sur les informations contenues uniquement dans la *Revue et Gazette musicale de Paris* (informations évidemment très partielles) ce concert est la seule occurrence d'audition publique d'une œuvre de Leclair sous le Second Empire. Pour que ce nom apparaisse de nouveau dans des programmes parisiens, il faut encore attendre une dizaine d'années et l'audition d'une *Sonate de violon* aux Concerts Pasdeloup.

Dimanche 1ᵉʳ novembre 1874
3ᵉ concert de la 1ʳᵉ série; de 0,75 F à 5 F

1. Meyerbeer (G.), *Festmarsch (Schiller-Marsch)*
2. Beethoven (L. van), *Symphonie nᵒ 2 Op. 36 en ré maj.*
3. Dubois (Th.), *Air de ballet (Scherzo)*
4. Mendelssohn (F.), *Concerto pour piano nᵒ 1 Op. 25 en sol min.* – Jaëll (M.)
5. Leclair (J.-M.), *Sonate pour violon, par tous les premiers violons*
6. Wagner (R.), *Tannhäuser*, Ouverture[41]

Intercalée entre un concerto pour piano de Mendelssohn et une ouverture de Wagner, l'apparition de cette sonate de Leclair est d'autant plus exceptionnelle quand on considère l'intégralité de la programmation des concerts populaires. Sur les 190 compositeurs que Pasdeloup fait entendre au Cirque d'hiver de 1861 à 1887, seulement 18 (soit 9,5%) n'ont pas vécu au XIXᵉ siècle[42]. La présence ici de la sonate de Leclair paraît, par ailleurs, d'autant plus incongrue qu'elle n'est pas jouée par un soliste, mais interprétée par l'ensemble des premiers violons. Il s'agit cependant d'une pratique relativement commune au XIXᵉ siècle et que l'on rencontre dans les auditions de la Société des concerts du Conservatoire dès

39. LA LAURENCIE, Lionel de. 'Une assertion de Fétis [...]', *op. cit.* (voir la note 7).
40. *Revue et Gazette musicale de Paris*, 5 avril 1863.
41. Reconstitution du programme par Yannick Simon. Le répertoire des programmes des Concerts Pasdeloup sera bientôt disponibles sur la base Dezède (<dezede.org>).
42. SIMON, Yannick. *Jules Pasdeloup et les origines du concert populaire*, Lyon, Symétrie, 2011 (Collection Symétrie recherche. Série Histoire du concert), p. 139.

1832[43]. Elle permet notamment de faire entendre des œuvres de musique de chambre dans le cadre de concerts symphoniques. À en croire la *Revue et Gazette musicale de Paris*, le morceau de Leclair a été «très goûté malgré l'archaïsme de ses formes et la brusquerie de ses cadences»[44].

D'autres éléments permettent de constater le fort impact que cette audition va avoir sur la renommée de Leclair à Paris. Au cours du mois suivant ce concert populaire, le violoniste Pablo de Sarasate (1844-1908) joue une œuvre de Leclair intitulée *Le Tambourin* au cours d'un concert de musique de chambre[45]; en janvier 1876, Pasdeloup programme de nouveau cette sonate et, le 29 octobre suivant, il est imité par Édouard Colonne qui programme un «Andante d'une sonate de Leclair» au cours de l'un de ses concerts du Châtelet. L'œuvre est également interprétée par tous les 1ers violons et l'on apprend dans *Le Ménestrel*[46] qu'elle a été bissée.

Cette entrée de Leclair au concert amplifie, par ailleurs, sa présence dans les catalogues d'éditeurs musicaux[47]. Les publications que l'on observe au début de la Troisième République peuvent toutes être considérées comme des produits dérivés du concert populaire de 1872 et nous permettent d'ailleurs de connaître plus précisément l'identité de celle-ci. En 1874, les éditions Mackar, dans la collection qu'elles consacrent aux œuvres exécutées aux concerts Pasdeloup[48] présentées sous la forme de transcription pour piano («Répertoire des Concerts populaires»), publient la transcription de la «Gavotte de la 2e sonate, 1er livre, composée en 1720 par J. M. Leclair l'aîné», par Frédéric Demarquette. Cette transcription pour piano seul connaît une déclinaison pour piano à quatre mains, piano et violon (par Amédée Berthemet), piano et flûte (par Paul Taffanel), ou encore piano et violoncelle (par

---

[43]. Au cours du concert du 1er avril 1832, la Société des concerts du Conservatoire fait entendre des «Fragments de quatuor de Beethoven» exécutés par tous les violons, altos et basses de l'orchestre. Voir les programmes de cette société reconstitués par D. Kern Holoman (<http://hector.ucdavis.edu/SdC/>).

[44]. *Revue et Gazette musicale de Paris*, 1er novembre 1874.

[45]. *Revue et Gazette musicale de Paris*, 8 novembre 1874.

[46]. *Le Ménestrel*, 5 novembre 1876.

[47]. Les premiers efforts pour rééditer Leclair semblent avoir été fournis par Victor Moret au milieu des années 1860. Celui-ci publie en effet, entre 1865 et 1870, trois numéros d'opus arrangés, transcrits ou inspirés par le violoniste du XVIIIe siècle: *Une fleur du passé. Andante d'une sonate de Leclair (1720) arrangé pour violon avec accompagnement de piano* en 1865; *Duo concertant pour piano et violon sur des réminiscences de Le Clair (1720)* en 1868; et *24 Morceaux extraits des Sonates de Jean Marie Leclair […] arrangées pour piano* en 1870. Cette production sera complétée en 1892 par une *Suite Louis XV, en 4 parties extraites des œuvres de J-M. Leclair pour deux violons avec accompagnement de piano Op. 97*. La grande liberté que prend Moret avec les œuvres de Leclair est lisible dès la page de titre de ces ouvrages où le nom du transcripteur apparaît en caractère cinq à six fois plus grands que ceux de l'auteur original.

[48]. Cet éditeur n'est pas le seul à proposer ce type de transcription. Voir notamment le cas, étudié par Yannick Simon, des éditions proposées par Ernest-Wilhem Ritter et Joseph-Gustave Biloir; SIMON, Yannick. 'Transcription et popularisation des classiques. Le cas du répertoire des Concerts populaires (1863-1879)', in: *Quatre siècles d'édition musicale: mélanges offerts à Jean Gribenski*, sous la direction de Joann Élart, Étienne Jardin et Patrick Taïeb, Bern, Peter Lang, 2014 (Étude de musicologie, 5), pp. 251-256.

Ernest Nathan). Un an plus tard, l'éditeur Armand Dignat publie exactement la même gavotte, cette fois dans une transcription pour violon et piano par Adolphe Herman. Ce à quoi répondent les éditions Mackar en 1877 en rééditant la transcription de Berthemet (dans la collection 'Transcriptions classiques').

Une analyse sommaire montrerait que les transcriptions de Berthmet et Herman prennent des partis très différents pour transcrire l'œuvre originale en version pour violon et piano. Ils apparaissent très nettement dès les deux premiers systèmes de ces éditions: Herman fait entrer le violon dès le début, ouvrant l'œuvre en anacrouse alors que Berthemet lui fait précéder six temps de piano seul; le piano marque presque uniquement les temps chez Berthemet alors qu'Herman propose une main droite tout en croches avec de multiples nuances. Ces éditions pourraient être destinées à deux publics différents — Herman exigeant de la part des deux interprètes plus de dextérité —; elles pourraient également correspondent à deux visions opposées du répertoire ancien et du respect de l'œuvre originale[49]. On ne doit cependant par perdre de vue que la transcription d'Herman, parue un an après celle de Berthemet, avait tout intérêt à s'éloigner le plus possible de la première version afin d'éviter tout procès.

On l'aura constaté: c'est par très petites touches que la figure de Leclair se dessine dans le panthéon musical des Français du XIXᵉ siècle. L'évolution de sa notoriété est sensible au cours de la période, mais n'est ni constante ni extraordinaire. Il est parvenu à entrer dans le programme des cours de violon du Conservatoire sous la monarchie de Juillet, très probablement sous l'impulsion de Pierre Baillot, et est parvenu à s'y maintenir au moins jusqu'à la fin du siècle par l'intermédiaire de ses héritiers dans l'établissement (notamment Charles Dancla et Eugène Sauzay). Cette place, progressivement, permet sans doute à Leclair de toucher l'ensemble des écoles de musique du territoire national grâce aux méthodes pédagogiques publiées par l'établissement, mais également aux relais du Conservatoire dans les principales villes de France. Personnage au destin atypique, intéressant les littérateurs, il est suffisamment présent dans les esprits au début de la Troisième République pour que deux sociétés de concert le programment à quelques mois d'écart et que deux éditeurs se livrent une bataille pour l'éditer. Il ne s'agit néanmoins que de transcriptions d'un seul passage de l'une de ses œuvres. C'est à la génération suivante que reviendra la charge de pleinement retrouver Leclair. Le compositeur bénéficie alors de la vogue que l'ensemble des compositeurs de son temps connaît à la Belle Époque, à l'heure où la modernité française, dans le cadre des efforts qu'elle fournit pour oblitérer la période romantique, entre en discussion avec le XVIIIᵉ siècle.

---

49. Sur la question de l'édition de musique ancienne en France sous la Troisième République, voir notamment VANÇON, Jean-Claire. 'Éditer Rameau à Paris entre 1840 et 1895', in: *ibidem*, pp. 271-292.

Leclair's *goûts réunis* in His *Quatre livres de sonates pour violin et basso continuo*, Opp. 1, 2, 5 & 9
Diatonicism, Chromaticism, Voice Exchange, Bimodality, and Enharmonic Modulation

Walter Kurt Kreyszig
(Saskatoon - Vienna)

In memory of Allen Forte (1926-2014)[1]

THE DECADES AROUND 1700, marked by an important shift in behavioural ethics, that is, from an ethics centered largely around the aristocracy to one with a more solid bourgeois orientation[2], left an undeniable impact on culture, including music, as revealed in the music theoretical discourse of Johann Mattheson[3]. In music, the period of the early- to mid-eighteenth century with rich and multifaceted approaches to compositional practice[4]

---

[1]. During the 1980-1981 academic year, the author had the privilege of enrolling in a doctoral class on music pedagogy of tonal music with Allen Forte, Battell Professor of the Theory of Music at Yale University (New Haven, Connecticut, U.S.A). As part of this seminar, Allen Forte guided the author in an extended study on figured bass practices in Johann Sebastian Bach's *Trio Sonata for flute, violin, and basso continuo* from his *Musikalische Opfer*, BWV 1079. The author wishes to thank Roberto Illiano, Fulvia Morabito, and Neal Zaslaw for their comments on the paper. Furthermore, the author wishes to thank Daniel Béland (Canada Research Chair) for his suggestions on the French translations.

[2]. On the longevity of this issue, see, for example, KOCKSA, Jürgen. 'Bürgertum und Bürgerlichkeit als Problem der deutschen Geschichte vom späten 18. zum frühen 20. Jahrhundert', in: *Bürger und Bürgerlichkeit im 19. Jahrhundert*, edited by Jürgen Kocksa, Göttingen, Vandenhoeck & Ruprecht, 1987 (Sammlung Vandenhoeck), pp. 21-63; VIERHAUS, Rudolf. 'Der Aufstieg des Bürgertums vom späten 18. Jahrhundert bis 1848/49', in: *ibidem*, pp. 64-78; BUDDE, Gunilla. *Blütezeit des Bürgertums: Bürgerlichkeit im 19. Jahrhundert*, Darmstadt, Wissenschaftliche Buchgesellschaft, 2010; SCHULTZ, Andreas. *Lebenswelt und Kultur des Bürgertums im 19. und 20. Jahrhundert*, Berlin-Boston, De Gruyter, ²2014 (Enzyklopädie deutscher Geschichte, 75).

[3]. KUTSCHKE, Beate. 'Johann Mattheson's Writings on Music and the Ethical Shift Around 1700', in: *International Review of the Aesthetics and Sociology of Music*, XXXVIII/1 (June 2007), pp. 23-38; see also HARRISS, Ernest. 'Johann Mattheson's Influence on the Next Generation of Music Scholars', in: *Studien zu den deutsch-französischen Musikbeziehungen im 18. und 19. Jahrhundert: Bericht über die erste gemeinsame Jahrestagung der Gesellschaft für Musikforschung und der Société Française de Musicologie Saarbrücken 1999*, edited by Herbert Schneider, Hildesheim-New York, Georg Olms, 2002 (Musikwissenschaftliche Publikationen, 20), pp. 167-178; see also *Johann Mattheson als Vermittler und Initiator: Wissenstransfer und die Etablierung neuer Diskurse in der ersten Hälfte des 18. Jahrhunderts*, edited by Wolfgang Hirschmann and Bernhard Jahn, Hildesheim-New York, Georg Olms, 2010.

[4]. For an overview of compositional practices, see, for example, LESTER, Joel. *Compositional Theory in the Eighteenth Century*, Cambridge (MA), Harvard University Press, 1992.

and the corresponding intense writings of Joseph Riepel[5] and Heinrich Christoph Koch[6], with a continuation in the nineteenth century[7], was characterized by a gradual supplanting of the *gelehrte Stil* in favour of the *stile galante*[8]. The latter aesthetic category first received attention by members of the Berlin School of Composition[9], including Johann Joachim Quantz[10], Carl Philipp Emanuel Bach[11], Friedrich Wilhelm Marpurg[12], and Johann Philipp

5. RIEPEL, Joseph. *Anfangsgründe zur musicalischen Setzkunst* […], 5 vols., Frankfurt, Johann Jakob Lotter, 1752-1768; *Joseph Riepel: Sämtliche Schriften zur Musiktheorie*, edited by Thomas Emmerig, Vienna, Böhlau, 1996 (Wiener Musikwissenschaftliche Beiträge, 20); see also TWITTENHOFF, Wilhelm. *Die musiktheoretischen Schriften Joseph Riepels*, Halle/Saale, Buchhandlung des Waisenhauses, 1935 (Beiträge zur Musikforschung, 2); SCHWARZMAIER, Ernst. *Die Takt- und Tonordnung Joseph Riepels: Ein Beitrag zur Geschichte der Formenlehre im 18. Jahrhundert*, Regensburg, Gustav Bosse, 1938 (Regensburger Beiträge zur Musikwissenschaft, 4); KNOUSE, Nola Reed. 'Joseph Riepel and the Emerging Theory of Form in the Eighteenth Century', in: *Current Musicology*, no. 41 (Spring 1986), pp. 47-62; ECKERT, Stefan. *Ars Combinatoria, Dialogue Structure, and Musical Practice in Josef Riepel's Anfangsgründe zur musikalischen Setzkunst*, Ph.D. Diss., Stoney Brook (NY), State University of Stony Brook, 2000.

6. KOCH, Heinrich Christoph. *Versuch einer Anleitung zur Composition*, 3 vols., Rudolstadt-Leipzig, Bey A. F. Böhme, 1782-1793; also as Studienausgabe, Hannover, Siebert, 2007; see also FEIL, Arnold. *Satztechnische Fragen in den Kompositionslehren von F. E. Niedt, J. Riepel und H. C. Koch*, Heidelberg, Gehrer & Grosch, 1955; KOVALEFF BAKER, Nancy. *From Teil to Tonstück: The Significance of the «Versuch einer Anleitung zur Composition» by Heinrich Christoph Koch*, Ph.D. Diss., New Haven (CT), Yale University, 1976; WAGNER, Günther. 'Anmerkungen zur Formtheorie H. C. Kochs', in: *Archiv für Musikwissenschaft*, XCI/2 (1984), pp. 86-112.

7. KOCH, Heinrich Christoph. *Op. cit.* (see note 6); see also DAHLHAUS, Carl. *Die Musiktheorie im 18. und 19. Jahrhundert. 2: Deutschland*, Darmstadt, Wissenschaftliche Buchgesellschaft, 1989 (Geschichte der Musiktheorie, 11).

8. HOFFMANN-ERBRECHT, Lothar. 'Der «galante Stil» in der Musik des 18. Jahrhunderts: Zur Problematik des Begriffs', in: *Studien zur Musikwissenschaft*, XXV (1962), pp. 252-260; FINSCHER, Ludwig. 'Galanter und gelehrter Stil: Der kompositionsgeschichtliche Wandel im 18. Jahrhundert', in: *Europäische Musikgeschichte*, 2 vols., edited by Giselher Schubert, Sabine Ehrmann-Herfort and Ludwig Finscher, Kassel, Bärenreiter, 2002, vol. I, pp. 587-665.

9. For an overview of the *stile galante*, see HORN, Wolfgang. 'Galant, Galanterie, Galanter Stil', in: *Handwörterbuch der musikalischen Terminologie: im Auftrag der Akademie der Wissenschaften und der Literatur zu Mainz von Hans Heinrich Eggebrecht*, edited by Albrecht Riethmüller and Markus Bandur, Stuttgart, Franz Steiner, 2005; see also OTTENBERG, Hans-Günter. *Die Entwicklung des theoretisch-ästhetischen Denkens innerhalb der Berliner Musikkultur von den Anfängen der Aufklärung bis Reichardt*, Leipzig, Deutscher Verlag für Musik, 1978 (Beiträge zur Musikwissenschaftlichen Forschung in der DDR, 10).

10. QUANTZ, Johann Joachim. *Versuch einer Anweisung die Flöte traversiere zu spielen* […], Berlin, Johann Friedrich Voss, 1752; also as facsimile, with an introduction by Barthold Kuijken, Wiesbaden, Breitkopf & Härtel, 1988.

11. BACH, Carl Philipp Emanuel. *Versuch über die wahre Art, das Clavier zu spielen*, 2 vols., Berlin, Königliche Hof-Buchdrucker Christian Friedrich Henning, 1753-1762; *Carl Philipp Emanuel Bach: Versuch über die wahre Art das Clavier zu spielen*, edited by Tobias Plebuch, 3 vols., Los Altos (CA), Packard Humanities Institute, 2011 (Carl Philipp Emanuel Bach, Complete works, series 7: Theoretical writings); see also COHEN, Peter. *Theorie und Praxis der Clavierästhetik Carl Philipp Emanuel Bachs*, Hamburg, Verlag der Musikalienhandlung Wagner, 1974 (Hamburger Beiträge zur Musikwissenschaft, 13).

12. MARPURG, Friedrich Wilhelm. *Handbuch bey dem Generalbasse und der Composition mit zwey-, drey-, vier-, fünf-, sechs- sieben-, acht- und mehreren Stimmen*, 3 vols. and *Anhang in einem Band* […] *worinn Probexempel vorgelegt werden*, Berlin, Wittwe Schütz Lange, 1755-1760, Rpt. Hildesheim-New York, Georg Olms, 2002.

Kirnberger[13], all of whom commented on a development that had begun as early as 1700[14], but was more rigorously pursued by Johann Sebastian Bach[15], foremost in his *Musikalische Opfer*, BWV 1079 (composed 1747)[16] and subsequently adopted by Bach's sons[17], especially by Wilhelm Friedemann Bach[18] and to a lesser degree also by C. P. E. Bach[19]. In fact, this

---

[13].   KIRNBERGER, Johann Philipp. *Die Kunst des reinen Satzes in der Musik, aus sicheren Grundsätzen hergeleitet und mit deutlichen Beyspielen erläutert*, 2 vols., Berlin-Königsberg, Bey G. J. Decker und G. L. Hartung, 1774-1779. Further on the *stile galante* in Kirnberger's music theoretical discourse, see MEKEEL, Joyce. 'The Harmonic Theories of Kirnberger and Marpurg', in: *Journal of Music Theory*, IV/2 (1960), pp. 169-193; ALDRICH, Pauline. 'Rhythmic Harmony as Taught by Johann Philipp Kirnberger', in: *Studies in Eighteenth-Century Music: A Tribute to Karl Geiringer on His 70th Birthday*, edited by Howard C. Robbins Landon and Roger E. Chapman, London-New York, Allen & Unwin, 1970, pp. 37-52; BEACH, David W. *The Harmonic Theories of Johann Philipp Kirnberger: Their Origins and Influences*, Ph.D. Diss., New Haven (CT), Yale University, 1975; see also BORRIS, Siegfried. *Kirnbergers Leben und Werk und seine Bedeutung im Berliner Musikkreis um 1750*, Kassel, Bärenreiter, 1933.

[14].   See, for example LOESER, Martin. 'Musik als Teil galanten Handelns: Überlegungen am Beispiel der Hamburger Musikkultur um 1700', in: *Gattungsgeschichte als Kulturgeschichte: Festschrift für Arnfried Edler*, edited by Christine Siegert, Katharina Hottmann, Sabine Meine, Martin Loeser and Axel Fischer, Hildesheim-New York, Georg Olms, 2008 (Ligaturen, 3), pp. 79-91.

[15].   See, for example, EPPSTEIN, Hans. 'Johann Sebastian Bach und der galante Stil', in: *Aufklärungen. Band 2. Studien zur deutsch-französischen Musikgeschichte im 18. Jahrhundert: Einflüsse und Wirkungen*, edited by Wolfgang Birtel and Christoph-Hellmut Mahling, Heidelberg, Carl Winter Universitätsverlag, 1986 (Annales Universitatis Saraviensis, Reihe: Philosophische Fakultät, 20), pp. 29-218.

[16].   Further on this topic, see, for example, BUTLER, Gregory. 'The «Galant» Style in J. S. Bach's «Musical Offering» Widening the Dimensions', in: *Bach: Journal of the Riemenschneider Bach-Institute Baldwin-Wallace College*, XXXIII/1 (2002), pp. 57-68; see also MARSHALL, Robert. 'Bach the Progressive: Observations on His Later Works', in: *The Musical Quarterly*, LXII/3 (July 1976), pp. 328-354. On the interpretation of Bach's late oeuvre from a humanist perspective, with reference to Johannes Kepler (1571-1630) and Andreas Werkmeister (1645-1706), see GECK, Martin. 'Concordia discors: Bachs Kontrapunkt gegen die Pythagoreer unter seinen Liebhabern verteidigt' in: *Philosophie des Kontrapunkts*, edited by Ulrich Tadday, Munich, Text & Kritik, 2010 (Musik-Konzepte: Die Reihe über Komponisten, Sonderband, Neue Folge), pp. 5-20.

[17].   BESSELER, Heinrich. 'Bach als Wegbereiter', in: *Archiv für Musikwissenschaft*, XII/1 (1955), pp. 1-39; GECK, Martin. «*Denn alles findet bei Bach statt*»: *Erforschtes und Erfahrenes*, Stuttgart-Weimar, Metzler, 2000, pp. 109-117; see also EGGEBRECHT, Hans Heinrich. 'Über Bachs geschichtlichen Ort', in: *Deutsche Vierteljahrsschrift für Literaturwissenschaft und Geistesgeschichte*, XXXI (1957), pp. 527-556; BÜSCH, Georg – NAGEL, Ingo. 'An der Schwelle zur Klassik: Die Kammermusik Johann Sebastian Bachs, der galante Stil seiner Söhne und der Einfluß auf Joseph Haydns Streichquartette', in: *Ensemble: Magazin für Kamermusik*, VI/3 (2008), pp. 34-38.

[18].   See, for example, WOLLNY, Peter. *Studies in the Music of Wilhelm Friedemann Bach: Sources and Style*, Ph.D. Diss., Cambridge (MA), Harvard University, 1993; see also MÜLLER-BLATTAU, Joseph. 'Bindung und Freiheit: Zu Wilhelm Friedemann Bachs Fugen und Polonaisen', in: *Festschrift Wilhelm Fischer zum 70. Geburtstag überreicht im Mozartjahr 1956*, edited by Hans Zingerle, Innsbruck, Selbstverlag des Sprachwissenschaftlichen Seminars der Universität Innsbruck, 1956 (Innsbrucker Beiträge zur Kulturwissenschaft, Sonderdruck, 3), pp. 82-98; HENZEL, Christoph. 'Zu Wilhelm Friedemann Bachs Berliner Jahren', in: *Bach-Jahrbuch*, LXXVIII (1992), pp. 107-112; ID. 'Nachtrag zu Wilhelm Friedemann Bachs Berliner Jahren', in: *Bach-Jahrbuch*, XC (2004), pp. 229-231.

[19].   See for example, SCHULENBERG, David L. *The Instrumental Music of Carl Philipp Emanuel Bach*, Ann Arbor (MI), UMI Research Press, 1984 (Studies in musicology, 77).

development of the musical language had already been predicted by Adolf Bernhard Marx, who in his *Die Musik des 19. Jahrhunderts und ihre Pflege* (Leipzig, 1855)[20], a publication which had attracted the attention of Franz Liszt[21], prophesized the end of counterpoint with the pinnacle of the *gelehrte Stil* reached in the oeuvre of J. S. Bach[22], and that already with a view into the future of compositional practice commented on by members of the Berlin circle during the second half of the eighteenth century, among them Marpurg[23]. In fact, it was Marpurg who had also attested to the longevity of Bach's legacy[24], as Bach in his oeuvre exceeded beyond the *gelehrte Stil* and the *stile galante*, embracing elements of a number of compositional trends, including the *Empfindsamkeit*[25], the *stylus phantasticus*[26], and the *Sturm und Drang*[27], with such vastness of approaches displayed serving as a fount for emulation

[20]. MARX, Adolf Bernhard. *Die Musik des 19. Jahrhunderts und ihre Pflege: Methode der Musik*, Leipzig, Breitkopf & Härtel, 1855, ²1873; see also EDLER, Arnfried. 'Die Musikanschauung von Adolf Bernhard Marx', in: *Beiträge zur Geschichte der Musikanschuung in 19. Jahrhundert*, edited by Walter Salmen, Regensburg, Gustav Bosse, 1965 (Studien zur Musikgeschichte des 19. Jahrhunderts, 1), pp. 103-112.

[21]. LISZT, Franz. 'Marx und sein Buch *Die Musik des neunzehnten Jahrhunderts und ihre Pflege*', (1855), in: *Gesammelte Schriften von Franz Liszt*, translated from French into German by La Mara (vol. 1) and Lina Ramann (vols. 2-6), Leipzig, Breitkopf & Härtel, 1880-1883.

[22]. Further on the prophecy of Marx, see SÜHRING, Peter. 'Kontrapunktische Kindheit der Musikgeschichte: Adolf Bernhard Marx' geschichtsphilosophische These vom notwendigem Ende des Kontrapunkts nach Bach', in: *Philosophie des Kontrapunkts […]*, *op. cit.* (see note 16), pp. 48-59; see also FINSCHER, Ludwig. 'Bach in the Eighteenth Century', in: *Bach Studies*, edited by Don O. Franklin, Cambridge-New York, Cambridge University Press, 1989, pp. 281-296.

[23]. See, for example, SERWER, Howard. *Friedrich Wilhelm Marpurg (1718-1795): Music Critic in a Galant Age*, Ph.D. Diss., New Haven (CT), Yale University, 1969.

[24]. On the longevity of Bach's legacy, see, for example, LEISINGER, Ulrich. '«Das Erste und Bleibenste was die deutsche Nation als Musikkunstwerk aufzuzeigen hat»: Johann Sebastian Bachs Werke im Berliner Musikleben des 18. Jahrhunderts', in: *Jahrbuch des Staatlichen Instituts für Musikforschung Preußischer Kulturbesitz*, (1995), pp. 66-79. On the reception of Bach's legacy during the early nineteenth century, see, for example, BEISSWENGER, Kirsten. 'Zwischen 1750 und 1850 erschienene «Berliner» Drucke Bachscher Werke', in: *Jahrbuch des Staatlichen Instituts für Musikforschung Preußischer Kulturbesitz*, (1993), pp. 106-130; see also DAHLHAUS, Carl. 'Zur Entstehung der romantischen Bach-Deutung', in: *Bach-Jahrbuch*, LXIV (1978), pp. 192-210.

[25]. See, for example, RECKOW, Fritz. 'Die «Schwülstigkeit» Johann Sebastian Bachs, oder «Melodie versus Harmonie»: Ein musiktheoretischer Prinzipienstreit der europäischen Aufklärung und seine kompositions- und sozialgeschichtlichen Implikationen', in: *Aufbruch aus dem Ancien régime: Beiträge zur Geschichte des 18. Jahrhunderts*, edited by Helmut Neuhaus, Vienna-Cologne, Böhlau, 1993, pp. 211-243.

[26]. See for example, SCHLEUNING, Peter. 'Johann Sebastian Bach and the *stylus phantasticus*', in: *Bach und die Stile: Bericht über das 2. Dortmunder Bach-Symposion 1998*, edited by Martin Geck, in collaboration with Klaus Hofmann, Dortmund, Klangfarben Musikverlag, 1999 (Dortmunder Bach-Forschungen, 2), pp. 197-204; see also COLLINS, Paul. *The Stylus phantasticus and Free Keyboard Music of the North German Baroque*, Aldershot, Ashgate, 2005.

[27]. See, for example, SCHLEUNING, Peter. 'The Chromatic Fantasia of Johann Sebastian Bach and the Genesis of Musical «Sturm und Drang»', in: *The Harpsichord and Its Repertoire: Proceedings of the International Harpsichord Symposium, Utrecht 1990*, edited by Pieter Dirksen, Utrecht, STIMU-Foundation for Historical

by contemporaries and composers of the following generations[28]. Once the *stile galante* had been fully developed by continental composers[29], with Georg Philipp Telemann leading the way, and that given his proclivity towards this particular idiom combined with his tremendous output of repertory[30], the features of this new overriding principle of shaping a symmetrical construct, with a focus on thematic structure and cadential organization[31], all embedded within periodicity[32] and diatonicism[33] and placed within the strict adherence to

---

Performance Practice, 1992, pp. 217-229; see also HARRISS, Ernest. 'Johann Adolf Hasse and the «Sturm und Drang» in Vienna', in: *Hasse-Studien*, III (1996), pp. 24-53.

[28]. Further on this topic, see, for example, WOLFF, Christoph. 'Bach und die Idee musikalischer Vollkommenheit', in: *Jahrbuch des Staatlichen Instituts für Musikforschung Preußischer Kulturbesitz*, (1996), pp. 9-23; see also HINDEMITH, Paul. *Johann Sebastian Bach: Heritage and Obligation*, London, Oxford University Press, 1952.

[29]. For an overview of the *stile galante*, see, for example, BÜCKEN, Ernst. 'Der galante Stil: Eine Skizze seiner Entwicklung', in: *Zeitschrift für Musikwissenschaft*, VI (1923), pp. 418-430; HOFFMANN-ERBRECHT, Lothar. '«Der galante Stil» in der Musik des 18. Jahrhunderts: Zur Problematik des Begriffs', in: *Festschrift für Erich Schenk: zum 60. Geburtstage gewidmet von Kollegen, Freunden und Schülern*, Graz-Vienna-Cologne, Böhlau, 1962 (Studien zur Musikwissenschaft, 25), pp. 252-260; SHELDON, David A. 'The Galant Style Revisited and Re-Evaluated', in: *Acta Musicologica*, XLVII/2 (1975), pp. 240-269; ID. 'Exchange, Anticipation, and Ellipsis: Analytical Definitions of the Galant Style', in: *Music East and West: Essays in Honor of Walter Kaufman*, edited by Thomas Noblitt, New York, Pendragon Press, 1981 (Festschrift series, 3), pp. 225-241; DAHLHAUS, Carl. 'Galante Stil und freier Satz', in: *Die Musik des 18. Jahrhunderts*, edited by Carl Dahlhaus, Laaber, Laaber-Verlag, 1985 (Neues Handbuch der Musikwissenschaft, 5), pp. 24-32; HEARTZ, Daniel. *Music in European Capitals: The Galant Style, 1720-1780*, New York, W. W. Norton, 2013; GJERDINGEN, Robert O. *Music in the Galant Style*, Oxford-New York, Oxford University Press, 2007.

[30]. Further on Telemann's contribution to the *stile galante*, see, for example, FLEISCHHAUER, Günter. 'Die «galante» und die kontrapunktische Schreibart Telemanns im Urteil Friedrich Wilhelm Marpurgs', in: *Telemann und seine Freunde: Kontakte, Einflüsse, Auswirkungen: Bericht über die Internationale Wissenschaftliche Konferenz anläßlich der 8. Telemann-Festtage der DDR, Magdeburg, 15. und 16. März 1984*, 2 vols., edited by Bernd Baselt, Magdeburg, Zentrum für Telemann-Pflege und -Forschung, 1986, vol. II, pp. 71-81.

[31]. WALDURA, Markus. 'Zukunftsweisende Momente in Johann Matthesons musikalischem Periodenbegriff', in: *Musik, Wissenschaft und ihre Vermittlung: Bericht über die Internationale Musikwissenschaftliche Tagung der Hochschule für Musik und Theater Hannover, 26.-29. September 2001*, edited by Arnfried Edler and Sabine Meine, Augsburg, Wissner, 2002 (Publikationen der Hochschule für Musik und Theater Hannover, 12), pp. 289-292.

[32]. RATNER, Leonard G. 'Eighteenth-Century Theories of Musical Period Structure', in: *The Musical Quarterly*, XLII/4 (October 1956), pp. 439-454; ID. *Classic Music: Expression, Form, and Style*, New York-London, Schirmer Books-Collier Macmillan, 1980; VIAL, Stephanie D. *The Art of Musical Phrasing in the Eighteenth Century: Punctuating the Classical 'Period'*, Rochester, University of Rochester Press, 2008 (Eastman studies in music).

[33]. RATNER, Leonard G. 'Harmonic Aspects of Classic Form', in: *Journal of the American Musicological Society*, II/3 (Autumn 1949), pp. 159-168.

the *tactus*[34] directly associated with the theory of the pulse[35] found wide acceptance in the music theoretical discourse. In fact, Mattheson wholeheartedly embraced the *stile galante* as a point of departure of his formulating of the *Affektenlehre*[36] as well as the invention of an *Incisionslehre*[37], with the latter serving as a didactic model for the comprehensive discussion of the *Melodielehre*[38], a concept which was adopted by a number of theorists, including

[34]. For an overview, see FROBENIUS, Wolf. 'Tactus', in: *Handwörterbuch der musikalischen Terminologie* [...], *op. cit.* (see note 9), 1971. For the early development of this concept, see DAHLHAUS, Carl. 'Zur Theorie des Tactus im 16. Jahrhundert', in: *Archiv für Musikwissenschaft*, XVII/1 (1960), pp. 22-39; HECKMANN, Harald. 'Der Takt in der Musiklehre des siebzehnten Jahrhunderts', in: *Archiv für Musikwissenschaft*, X/2 (1953), pp. 116-139; DAHLHAUS, Carl. 'Zur Entstehung des modernen Taktsystems im 17. Jahrhundert', in: *Archiv für Musikwissenschaft*, XVIII/3-4 (1961), pp. 223-240. The strict adherence to the *tactus* is also characteristic of the classic era; see HENNEBERG, Gudrun. *Theorien zur Rhythmik und Metrik: Möglichkeiten und Grenzen rhythmischer und metrischer Analyse, dargestellt am Beispiel der Wiener Klassik*, Tutzing, Hans Schneider, 1974 (Mainzer Studien zur Musikwissenschaft, 6); BUDDAY, Wolfgang. *Grundlagen musikalischer Formen der Wiener Klassik: An Hand der zeitgenössischen Theorie von Joseph Riepel und Heinrich Christoph Koch, dargestellt an Menuetten und Sonatensätzen (1750-1790)*, Kassel, Bärenreiter, 1983; MAIER, Siegfried. *Studien zur Theorie des Taktes in der 1. Hälfte des 18. Jahrhunderts*, Tutzing, Hans Schneider, 1984 (Frankfurter Beiträge zur Musikwissenschaft, 16); SCHWINDT-GROSS, Nicole. 'Einfache, zusammengesetzte und doppelt notierte Takte: Ein Aspekt der Takttheorie im 18. Jahrhundert', in: *Musiktheorie*, IV/3 (1989), pp. 203-222; BRUMBELOE, Joseph Leonard. *Formal Grouping in the Theory and Musical Practice of the Eighteenth Century*, Ph.D. Diss., Bloomington (IN), Indiana University, 1991; WALDURA, Markus. 'Marpurg, Koch und die Neubegründung des Taktbegriffs', in: *Die Musikforschung*, LIII/3 (2000), pp. 237-253; BOCKMAIER, Claus. *Die instrumentale Gestalt des Taktes: Studien zum Verhältnis von Spielvorgang, Zeitmaß und Betonung in der Musik*, Tutzing, Hans Schneider, 2001 (Münchner Veröffentlichungen zur Musikgeschichte, 57); MAURER ZENCK, Claudia. *Vom Takt: Überlegungen zur Theorie und kompositorischen Praxis im ausgehenden 18. und beginnenden 19. Jahrhundert*, Vienna, Böhlau, 2001.

[35]. ERIG, Richard. 'Zum «Pulsschlag» bei Johann Joachim Quantz', in: *Tibia: Magazin für Freunde alter und neuer Bläsermusik*, VII/3 (1982), pp. 168-175; PETERSEN, Peter. 'Die «Rhythmuspartitur»: Über eine neue Methode zur rhythmisch-metrischen Analyse pulsgebundener Musik', in: *50 Jahre Musikwissenschaftliches Institut in Hamburg: Bestandsaufnahme – Aktuelle Forschung – Ausblick*, Frankfurt, Peter Lang, 1999 (Hamburger Jahrbuch für Musikwissenschaft, 16), pp. 83-110.

[36]. BUELOW, George J. 'Johann Mattheson and the Invention of the *Affektenlehre*', in: *New Mattheson Studies*, edited by George J. Buelow and Hans-Joachim Marx, Cambridge, Cambridge University Press, 1983, pp. 393-407; see also THIEME, Ulrich. 'Die Affektenlehre im philosophischen und musikalischen Denken des Barock – II. Die Affekte und ihre Darstellungsmittel', in: *Tibia: Magazin für Freunde alter und neuer Bläsermusik*, VIII/1 (1983), pp. 241-245.

[37]. FEES, Konrad. *Die Incisionslehre bis zu Johann Mattheson: Zur Tradition eines didaktischen Modells*, Pfaffenweiler, Centaurus-Verlagsgesellschaft, 1991 (Musikwissenschaft, 2).

[38]. MATTHESON, Johann. *Der vollkommene Capellmeister* [...], Hamburg, Christian Herold, 1739; also as facsimile, edited by Margarete Reimann, Kassel, Bärenreiter, 1954 (Documenta musicologica, Reihe I: Druckschriften-Faksimiles, 5); also edited by Fredericke Ramm, Kassel, Bärenreiter, 1999 (Bärenreiter Studienausgabe); see also FELLERER, Karl Gustav. 'Zur Melodielehre im 18. Jahrhundert', in: *Studia Musicologica Academiae Scientiarum Hungaricae*, III/1-4 (1962), pp. 109-115; BUELOW, George J. 'The Concept of *Melodielehre*: A Key to Classic Style', in: *Mozart-Jahrbuch*, (1978/1979), pp. 182-195; PETERSEN-MIKKELSEN, Birger. *Die Melodielehre des «Vollkommenen Capellmeister» von Johann Mattheson: Eine Studie zum Paradigmenwechsel in der Melodielehre des 18. Jahrhunderts*, Eutin, B. Petersen-Mikkelsen, 2002 (Eutiner Beiträge zur Musikforschung,

Johann Friedrich Daube[39], Kirnberger[40], Koch[41], Christoph Nichelmann[42], and Riepel[43], with emphasis on beauty and naturalness of the *Klangrede*[44] with its subdivisions into periods and phrases[45] — notions set forth in his *Kern melodischer Wissenschaft* (Hamburg, 1737)[46], functioning within the confines of the *stile galante*[47] and in a decisively broader realm of the *Empfindsamkeit*[48].

Already during the first half of the eighteenth century, composers proceeded with a gradual widening of the harmonic language, by cautiously introducing chromaticisim side-

---

12); Pozzi, Egidio. 'Il primo Settecento e la *Melodielehre* di Mattheson, Riepel e Kirnberger', in: *Melodia, stile, suono*, edited by Gianmario Borio, Rome, Carocci, 2009 (Storia dei concetti musicali, 3), pp. 53-70.

[39]. Daube, Johann Friedrich. *Anleitung zum Selbstunterricht in der musikalischen Komposition, sowohl für die Instrumental- als Vocalmusik*, Vienna, Daube, 1798, see also Karbaum, Michael. *Das theoretische Werk Johann Friedrich Daubes – Der Theoretiker Johann Friedrich Daube: Ein Beitrag zur Kompositionslehre des 18. Jahrhunderts*, Ph.D. Diss., Vienna, Universität Wien, 1969; Wallace, Barbara K. *A. J. F. Daube's General-Bass in drey Accorden (1756): Translation and Commentary*, Ph.D. Diss., Denton (TX), North Texas State University, 1983.

[40]. Kirnberger, Johann Philipp. *Op. cit.* (see note 13).

[41]. Koch, Heinrich Christoph. *Op. cit.* (see note 6).

[42]. Nichelmann, Christoph. *Die Melodie nach ihrem Wesen, sowohl als nach ihren Eigenschaften*, Danzig, J. C. Schuster, 1755; also Hamburg, C. Herold, 1755; see also Christensen, Thomas. 'Nichelmann contra C. P. E. Bach: Harmonic Theory and Musical Politics at the Court of Frederik the Great', in: *Carl Philipp Emanuel Bach und die europäische Musikkultur des mittleren 18. Jahrhunderts: Bericht über das Internationale Symposium der Joachim Jungius-Gesellschaft der Wissenschaften Hamburg, 29. September – 2. Oktober 1988*, edited by Hans-Joachim Marx, Göttingen, Vandenhoeck & Ruprecht, 1990 (Veröffentlichungen der Joachim Jungius-Gesellschaft der Wissenschaften Hamburg, 62), pp. 189-220.

[43]. Riepel, Joseph. *Op. cit.* (see note 5).

[44]. Klassen, Janina. 'Klang-Rede und musikalische Syntax', in: *Musik & Ästhetik*, xi/41 (January 2007), pp. 43-61.

[45]. Mattheson, Johann. *Der vollkommene Capellmeister* […], *op. cit.* (see note 38), Kapitel 'Ab- und Einschnitte der Klangrede'; see also Waldura, Markus. 'Zu Johann Matthesons Lehre von den Ab- und Einschnitten der Klang-Rede', in: *Musiktheorie*, xv/3 (2001), pp. 195-219.

[46]. Mattheson, Johann. *Kern melodischer Wissenschaft, bestehend in den auserlesensten Haupt- und Grundlehren der musicalischen Setzkunst oder Composition, als ein Vorläufer des Vollkommenen Capellmeisters*, Hamburg, Christian Herold, 1737; see also Ackermann, Peter. 'Johann Mattheson und die Anfänge der Melodielehre', in: «*Vanitatis fuga, aeternitatis amor*»: *Wolfgang Witzenmann zum 65. Geburtstag / Wolfgang Witzenmann in occasione del suo 65° compleanno*, edited by Sabine Ehrmann-Herfort and Markus Engelhardt, Laaber, Laaber-Verlag, 2005 (Analecta musicologica, 36), pp. 355-369.

[47]. On the applicability of the *Incisionslehre* in the instrumental repertories, see Gutknecht, Dieter. '«Sing-Gedicht» und «Klang-Rede»: Matthesons Theorie vom Sinngehalt der Instrumentalmusik', in: *Die Sprache der Musik: Festschrift Klaus Wolfgang Niemöller zum 60. Geburtstag*, edited by Jobst Peter Fricke, Regensburg, Gustav Bosse, 1989 (Kölner Beiträge zur Musikwissenschaft, 165), pp. 239-249.

[48]. Ehrmann-Herfort, Sabine. '«Das vornehmste […] in der Music ist eine gute, fliessende, bewegliche Melodie»: Johann Mattheson und die Empfindsamkeit', in: *Aspekte der Musik des Barock: Aufführungspraxis und Stil – Bericht über die Symposien der Internationalen Händel-Akademie Karlsruhe, 2001-2004*, edited by Siegfried Schmalzriedt, Laaber, Laaber-Verlag, 2006 (Veröffentlichungen der Internationalen Händel-Akademie Karlsruhe, 8), pp. 227-250.

by-side with diatonicism, and that in an effort to enlarge the harmonic palette. Indeed, this practice emerged gradually, with its initial stages still very much tied to the compositional rigour associated with the aesthetic category of the *stile galante*, though in an effort to impart a heightened expressivity, foreshadowing the genuine *Empfindsamkeit* (also known as the sensitive, emotional, expressive style)[49], an aim consciously pursued by Telemann, especially in his chamber music works published in Hamburg[50], which earned him tremendous praise from his contemporaries, foremost from the pen of Quantz[51], whose reflections on issues of style, with special focus on the *stile galante*[52], paved the way for its codification as well as its careful delineation from the *empfindsame Stil*. Subsequently, this move was often directly associated with the expansion of compositional practices, specifically the reliance on genres and idioms associated with the *Empfindsamkeit*[53], characterized by the sudden unexpected modulations[54] and changes in mood as well as the fully notated extended ornamentation, communicated not only in the *Versuch* of C. P. E. Bach[55], but also readily recognized in many of his works[56], including his keyboard compositions, among them the character

---

[49]. See, for example, LICHTENHAHN, Ernst. 'Der musikalische Stilwandel im Selbstverständnis der Zeit um 1750', in: *Carl Philipp Emanuel Bach und die europäische Musikkultur des mittleren 18. Jahrhunderts* […], *op. cit.* (see note 42), pp. 65-77.

[50]. Further on this topic, see, for example, ZOHN, Steven. *Music for a Mixed Taste: Style, Genre, and Meaning in Telemann's Instrumental Works*, Oxford, Oxford University Press, 2008, especially pp. 459-461.

[51]. QUANTZ, Johann Joachim. *Op. cit.* (see note 10), 10. Hauptstück, Paragraphs 14-15; see also ZOHN, Steven. 'New Light on Quantz's Advocacy of Telemann's Music', in: *Early Music*, XXV/3 (August 1997), pp. 441-461.

[52]. Further on this topic, see SCHÄFKE, Rudolf. 'Quantz als Ästhetiker: Eine Einführung in die Musikästhetik des galanten Stils', in: *Archiv für Musikwissenschaft*, VI/2 (July 1924), pp. 213-242.

[53]. On the *Empfindsamkeit* see, for example, BONSONNET, Felix R. 'Die Bedeutung des Begriffs «Empfindsamkeit» für die deutsche Musik des 18. Jahrhunderts', in: *Gesellschaft für Musikforschung: Bericht über den Internationalen Musikwissenschaftlichen Kongress, Bonn 1970*, edited by Carl Dahlhaus, Hans-Joachim Marx, Magda Marx-Weber and Günther Massenkeil, Kassel, Bärenreiter, 1971, pp. 352-355; COWART, Georgia J. 'Sense and Sensibility in Eighteenth-Century Musical Thought', in: *Acta Musicologica*, LVI/2 (July-December 1984), pp. 251-266; KUBOTA, Keiichi. 'Über die musikalische «Empfindsamkeit»', in: *Die Musikforschung*, XXXIX/2 (April-June 1986), pp. 139-148; BAASNER, Frank. *Der Begriff der 'sensibilité' im 18. Jahrhunderts: Aufstieg und Niedergang eines Ideals*, Heidelberg, Carl Winter, 1988 (Studia romanica, 69); see also KRUEGER, Renate. *Das Zeitalter der Empfindsamkeit: Kunst und Kultur des späten 18. Jahrhunderts in Deutschland*, Vienna-Munich, Schroll, 1972; WEGMANN, Nikolaus. *Diskurse der Empfindsamkeit: Zur Geschichte eines Gefühls in der Literatur des 18. Jahrhunderts*, Stuttgart, Metzler, 1988; MÜLLER, Ruth E. *Erzählte Töne: Studien zur Musikästhetik im späten 18. Jahrhundert*, Stuttgart-Wiesbaden, Franz Steiner, 1989 (Beihefte zum Archiv für Musikwissenschaft, 30).

[54]. Further on this topic, see, for example, ROSE, Juanelva M. *The Harmonic Idiom of the Keyboard Works of Carl Philipp Emanuel Bach*, Ph.D. Diss., Santa Barbara (CA), University of California, 1970.

[55]. BACH, Carl Philipp Emanuel. *Op. cit.* (see note 11).

[56]. BERG, Darrell M. 'C. P. E. Bach und die empfindsame Weise', in: *Carl Philipp Emanuel Bach und die europäische Musikkultur* […], *op. cit.* (see note 42), pp. 93-105.

pieces, fantasias, rondos, and approximately one third of his solo sonatas[57], and observed also in his chamber music, concertos, and symphonies[58]. In fact, in the context of the *Empfindsamkeit*, those genres proved to be a fertile ground for the exploration of melody and form[59], not by a rigid scheme controlled by the eighteenth-century periodicity, later favoured by the masters of Viennese classicism[60], but rather by a compositional practice based on the concept of feeling, first captured in the *Versuch einer Anleitung zur Composition*

[57]. ALLIHN, Ingeborg. 'Die *Pièces caractèristiques* des C. P. E. Bach: Ein Modell für die Gesprächskultur in der zweiten Hälfte des 18. Jahrhunderts', in: *Carl Philipp Emanuel Bach: Musik in Europa — Bericht über das Internationale Symposium vom 8. März bis 12. März 1994 im Rahmen der 29. Frankfurter Festtage der Musik in der Konzerthalle 'Carl Philipp Emanuel Bach' in Frankfurt (Oder)*, edited by Hans-Günter Ottenberg, Frankfurt an der Oder, Konzerthalle 'Carl Philipp Emanuel Bach', 1998 (Carl-Philipp-Emanuel-Bach-Konzepte: Sonderband, 2), pp. 94-107; OTTENBERG, Hans-Günter. 'Zur Fantasieproblematik im Schaffen C. P. E. Bachs', in: *Die Einflüsse einzelner Interpreten und Komponisten des 18. Jahrhunderts auf die Musik ihrer Zeit: Konferenzbericht der VIII. Wissenschaftlichen Arbeitstagung, Blankenburg/Harz, 27. Juni bis 29. Juni 1980*, edited by Eitelfriedrich Thom, Blankenburg/Harz, Kultur- und Forschungsstätte Michaelstein, 1980 (Studien zur Aufführungspraxis und Interpretation von Instrumentalmusik des 18. Jahrhunderts, 13), pp. 74-80; RICHARDS, Annette. *The Free Fantasia and the Musical Picturesque*, Cambridge-New York, Cambridge University Press, 2001 (New perspectives in music history and criticism); CLERCX, Suzanne. 'La forme du Rondo chez Carl Philipp Emanuel Bach', in: *Revue de Musicologie*, XVI (1935), pp. 148-167; PFINGSTEN, Ingeborg. '«Er übersetzte, indem er phantasierte, die Sprache des Verstandes in die Sprache der Empfindungen: denn dazu diente ihm die Musik»: Zum Themabegriff Carl Philipp Emanuel Bachs in seinen späten Klaviersonaten', in: *Carl Philipp Emanuel Bach: Beiträge zu Leben und Werk*, edited by Heinrich Poos, Mainz, Schott, 1993 (Schott Musikwissenschaft), pp. 97-117; WAGNER, Günther. 'Die Entwicklung der Klaviersonate bei C. Ph. E. Bach', in: *Carl Philipp Emanuel Bach und die europäische Musikkultur [...]*, op. cit. (see note 42), pp. 231-243; BERG, Darrell M. 'Die Orgelsonaten Carl Philipp Emanuel Bachs', in: *Carl Philipp Emanuel Bach: Musik in Europa [...]*, op. cit. (see above), pp. 245-260.

[58]. SCHMID, Ernst Fritz. *Carl Philipp Emanuel Bach und seine Kammermusik*, Kassel, Bärenreiter, 1931; WADE, Rachel W. *The Keyboard Concertos of Carl Philipp Emanuel Bach*, Ann Arbor (MI), UMI Research Press, 1981 (Studies in musicology, 48); EDLER, Arnfried. 'Die Klavierkonzerte Carl Philipp Emanuel Bachs im Kontext der zeitgenössischen Gattungsgeschichte in Norddeutschland', in: *Carl Philipp Emanuel Bach: Musik in Europa [...]*, op. cit. (see note 57), pp. 261-278; SUCHALLA, Ernst. 'Carl Philipp Emanuel Bach, Wegbereiter der Musik seiner Zeit: Eine stilkritische Untersuchung seiner Snfonien', in: *Carl Philipp Emanuel Bach und die europäische Musikkultur [...]*, op. cit. (see note 42), pp. 269-282; WAGNER, Günther. *Die Sinfonien Carl Philipp Emanuel Bachs: Werdende Gattung und Originalidee*, Stuttgart-Weimar, Metzler, 1994; see also ID. 'Die Sinfonien Carl Philipp Emanuel Bachs in der Bewertung von Zeitgenossen und Nachgeborenen', in: *Carl Philipp Emanuel Bach: Musik in Europa [...]*, op. cit. (see note 57), pp. 481-495.

[59]. See, for example, TISHKOFF, Doris P. *Sensibility in the Eighteenth Century as Seen in the Fantasias from the 'Für Kenner und Liebhaber' of Carl Philipp Emanuel Bach*, 3 vols., Ph.D. Diss., Ann Arbor (MI), University of Michigan, 1983.

[60]. On the pervasiveness of periodicity, especially in the era of Viennese classicism, see, for example, KREYSZIG, Walter Kurt. 'Traditionalität, Originalität und Experimentierfreudigkeit in Wolfgang Amadeus Mozarts *Lodi-Quartett*, KV 80 (=73f) im Vorfeld seiner Annäherung zum klassischen Streichquartett als Gattung der Wiener Klassik: Zu den beiden Fassungen des *Trios* als Zeugnis der Zusammenarbeit von Vater und Sohn', in: *Die Wiener Klassiker und das Italien ihrer Zeit: Festschrift für Christian Speck zum 60. Geburtstag*, edited by Petra Weber, Paderborn, Wilhelm Fink, 2015 (Studien zur Musik, 19), pp. 113-160; see also

(Rudolstadt-Leipzig, 1782-1793) of Koch[61], who based his thoughts on the philosophy of Johann Georg Sulzer[62]. In fact, this newly emerging aesthetics of composition, linked to the natural declamation of music first observed in language with its inflections — a principle which partly guided Telemann in his compositional process[63] and which his godson, C. P. E. Bach, readily resorted to in music[64], the so-called *redende Prinzip* coined by C. P. E. Bach[65], with the analogy between the language of music and the verbal language explored by Franz Joseph Haydn in his instrumental oeuvre[66] — gave rise to a broadened harmonic language, one in which a gradual balance between diatonicism and chromaticism was achieved. However, already prior to the full efflorescence of the *Empfindsamkeit* after the mid-eighteenth century, composers did display an interest in a broadening of the harmonic palette, specifically by infusing the diatonic harmonic progressions with some attention to chromaticism.

One of the earliest composers to devote special attention to chromaticism and display considerable reliance on this increasingly more important facet in the defining

---

Wiener Klassik: Ein musikgeschichtlicher Begriff in Diskussion, edited by Gernot Gruber, Vienna, Böhlau, 2002 (Wiener Musikwissenschaftliche Beiträge, 21).

61. KOCH, Heinrich Christoph. *Op. cit.* (see note 6); see also WALDURA, Markus. 'Zum Begriff des «Gefühls» in Heinrich Christoph Kochs *Versuch einer Anleitung zur Composition*', in: *Aufbrüche – Fluchtwege: Musik in Weimar um 1800*, edited by Helen Geyer and Thomas Radecke, Cologne, Böhlau, 2003 (Schriftenreihe der Hochschule für Musik Franz Liszt, 3), pp. 61-69.

62. SULZER, Johann Georg. 'Recherche sur l'origine des sentiments agréables & desagréables', in: *Histoire (Mémoires) de l'Académie Royale des Sciences et de Belles lettres [de Berlin] pour l'année* MDCCLI, Berlin, Haude et Spener, 1753; see also *Johann Georg Sulzers vermischte philosophische Schriften, aus den Jahrbüchern der Akademie zu Berlin gesammelt*, compiled by Christian Friedrich von Blankenburg, Part 1, Leipzig, Bey Weidmanns Erben und Reich, 1773; Part 2 […] *nebst einigen Nachrichten von dem Leben und den Schriften des Herrn J. G. Sulzer, von Christian Friedrich von Blankenburg*, Leipzig, Bey Weidmanns Erben und Reich, 1781. Further on Sulzer's aesthetics, see, for example, HEYM, Ludwig Maximilian. *Darstellung und Kritik der ästhetischen Ansichten Johann Georg Sulzers*, Leipzig, Druck von O. Schmidt, 1894; TUMARKIN, Anna. *Der Ästhetiker Johann Georg Sulzer*, Frauenfeld-Leipzig, Huber, 1933 (Die Schweiz im deutschen Geistesleben, 79-80); see also GERHARD, Anselm. '«Man hat noch kein System von der Theorie der Musik»: Die Bedeutung von Johann Georg Sulzers *Allgemeine Theorie der Schönen Künste* für die Musikästhetik des ausgehenden 18. Jahrhunderts', in: *Schweizer im Berlin des 18. Jahrhunderts*, edited by Martin Fontius and Helmut Holzhey, Berlin, Akademie-Verlag, 1996 (Aufklärung und Europa), pp. 341-353.

63. FLEISCHHAUER, Günter. 'Zum «redenden Prinzip» in der Instrumentalmusik Georg Philipp Telemanns', in: *Konferenzbericht des Kolloquiums Carl Philipp Emanuel Bach in unserer Zeit. 4.-6. März 1984*, edited by Hans-Günter Ottenberg, Frankfurt an der Oder, Konzerthalle C. P. E. Bach, 1985 (Bachkonzepte, 2), pp. 41-48.

64. See, for example, BUSCH, Gudrun. *«Redendes Prinzip», instrumentale «Klangrede» und Klavierlied im Schaffen Carl Philipp Emanuel Bachs*, edited by Eitelfriedrich Thom, Blankenburg/Harz, Kultur- und Forschungsstätte Michaelstein, 1989 (Kultur- und Forschungsstätte Michaelstein: Sonderbeitrag, 7).

65. SCHERING, Arnold. 'Carl Philipp Emanuel Bach und das «redendes Prinzip» in der Musik', in: *Jahrbuch der Musikbibliothek Peters*, XLV (1938), pp. 13-29.

66. KRONES, Hartmut. '«Meine Sparche verstehet man durch die ganze Welt»: Das «redende Prinzip» in Joseph Haydns Instrumentalmusik', in: *Wort und Ton im europäischen Raum: Gedenkschrift für Robert Schollum*, edited by Hartmut Krones, Vienna, Böhlau, 1989, pp. 79-108.

of the overall compositional practices, especially beginning in the early nineteenth century, was Jean-Marie Leclair *l'aîné*, noted composer[67] and violin virtuoso[68], and a main contributor to the solo sonata with *basso continuo* in France[69] as well as founder of the French Violin School[70]. Remarkably in an era when there was indeed little reliance upon chromaticism as a principal facet in the defining of contemporary compositional practice, Leclair advanced the then sparing use of chromaticism to new heights, and that in openly embracing chromaticism within his overall compositional techniques[71], as readily displayed in his *Quatre livres de sonates pour violin et basso continuo*[72], comprising a

---

[67]. For an overview of his instrumental oeuvre, comprising fourteen *opera*, see Beckmann, Gisela. *Die französische Violinsonate mit Basso continuo von Jean-Marie Leclair bis Pierre Gaviniès*, Hamburg, Verlag der Musikalienhandlung Karl Dieter Wagner, 1975 (Hamburger Beiträge zur Musikwissenschaft, 15), p. 39.

[68]. *Jean-Marie Leclair: virtuose et compositeur, 1697-1764*, edited by Benoît Dratwicki and Thomas Leconte, Versailles, Édition du Centre de Musique Baroque de Versailles, 2005; see also Lemoine, Micheline. 'La technique violinistique de Jean-Marie Leclair', in: *Aspects inédits de l'art instrumental en France des origines à nos jours*, special number of *La Revue musicale*, no. 226 (1955), pp. 117-143.

[69]. La Laurencie, Lionel de. 'L'origine de Jean-Marie Leclair l'aîné, violoniste-compositeur', in: *Le Courier musical*, VII (1904), pp. 321-324; Id. 'Sur les oeuvres de Jean-Marie Leclair l'aîné', in: *Le Courier musical*, VII (1904), pp. 597-605; Id. 'Le rôle de Leclair dans la musique instrumentale', in: *La Revue musicale*, IV/4 (1 February 1923), pp. 12-20; Appia, Edmond. 'Les sonates à violon seul et basse continue de Jean-Marie Leclair, l'aîne: 1697-1764', in: *Schweizerische Musikzeitung*, XC/6 (June 1950), pp. 293-299; Id. 'The Violin Sonatas of Leclair', in: *The Score*, III (June 1950), pp. 3-19; Preston, Robert E. *The Sonatas for Violin and Figured Bass by Jean-Marie Leclair l'aîné*, Ph.D. Diss., Ann Arbor (MI), University of Michigan, 1959; Coates, John E. *The Instrumental Music of Jean-Marie Leclair l'aîné*, M.M. Thesis, Birmingham (UK), University of Birmingham, 1960; Hulse, Mary Jane. *The Music of Jean-Marie Leclair and Its Historical Significance*, M.M. Thesis, Northhampton (MA), Smith College, 1962.

[70]. La Laurencie, Lionel de. *L'école française de violon de Lully à Viotti: études d'histoire et d'ésthetique*, 3 vols., Paris, Delagrave, 1922-1924.

[71]. Preston, Robert E. 'The Treatment of Harmony in the Solo Violin Sonatas of Jean-Marie Leclair', in: *Recherches sur la musique française classique*, VII (1967), pp. 154-163.

[72]. For a modern edition of these works edited by Robert E. Preston for A-R-Editions (Madison, WI), see Leclair, Jean-Marie. *Sonatas for Violin and Basso continuo, Opus 1*, 1995 (Recent researches in the music of the Baroque era, 76); Id. *Sonatas for Violin and Basso continuo, Opus 2*, 1988 (Recent researches in the music of the Baroque era, 58); Id. *Sonatas for Violin and Basso continuo, Op. 5, Op. 9, and Op. 15, Part I: Opus 5, Sonatas I-V*, 1968 (Recent researches in the music of the Baroque era, 4); Id. *Sonatas for Violin and Basso continuo, Op. 5, Op. 9, and Op. 15, Part II: Opus 5, Sonatas VI-XII*, 1969 (Recent researches in the music of the Baroque era, 5); Id. *Sonatas for Violin and Basso continuo, Op. 5, Op. 9, and Op. 15, Part III: Opus 9, Sonatas I-VI*, 1970 (Recent researches in the music of the Baroque era, 10); Id. *Sonatas for Violin and Basso continuo, Op. 5, Op. 9, and Op. 15, Part IV: Opus 9, Sonatas VII-XII*, 1971 (Recent researches in the music of the Baroque era, 11); see also Id. *Zwölf Sonaten für Violine und Generalbass nebst einem Trio für Violine, Violoncell und Generalbass*, edited by Robert Eitner, Leipzig, Breitkopf & Härtel, 1903 (Publikationen älterer praktischer und theoetischer Musikwerke, 27); Id. *Premie livre de sonates, Œuvres III*, edited by Alexandre Guilmaunt, and Joseph Debroux, Paris, Max Eschig, c1905 (Les maîtres violonistes de l'école française du XVIIIᵉ siècle); *Alte Meistersonaten für Geige und Klavier*, edited by Karl Geiringer, Vienna, Universal Edition, 1937 (Universal Edition, 10914). For an inventory of this repertory, see, for example, Bachmann, Alberto. *Jean-Marie Leclair: A Biographical*

total of forty-eight sonatas[73] in addition to one posthumous sonata, Op. 15[74], all of which are rich in the fusion of Italian and French styles of composition, resulting in a rather novel approach to composition — what François Couperin in his *Les goûts réunis* (Paris, 1724) had prophesized in the *goût réunis*[75] and what Quantz in the closing chapters his widely disseminated *Versuch* (Berlin, 1752)[76] described as the *stilus mixtus* or *vermischter Stil*[77] — a compositional idiom that had already been explored by J. S. Bach[78].

Leclair's initial dual career path as a dancer and musician[79] is reflected in his compositional oeuvre. To that end, already the four volumes of sonatas for violin and *basso continuo* bear witness to his interest and penchant for the dance, such as the *gavotte*, in its melodic squareness and harmonic rigour, especially the stylized dance and its presence

---

Sketch and a Thematic Catalogue of His Works, with a Portrait Extracted from an Unidentified Periodical, [s.l.], [s.n.], 1913; WOLLHEIM, Heinrich. *Thematisches Verzeichnis sämtlicher im Druck erschienenen Werke von Jean Marie Leclair l'aîné*, Berlin, [s.n.], 1929; ZASLAW, Neal. *Jean-Marie Leclair l'aîné: Biography and Chronological Thematic Catalogue*, M.A. Thesis, New York (NY), Columbia University, 1965; RHYHN, Anne-Marie. 'La thématique des sonates pour violon et basse continue de Jean-Marie Leclair «Aine»', in: *Mémoire de licence dactyl: lettres Genève*, Geneva, [s.n.], 1973, pp. 68-69.

[73]. For an overview of these publications, see BECKMANN, Gisela. *Op. cit.* (see note 67), pp. 41-45.

[74]. PRESTON, Robert E. 'Leclair's Posthumous Solo Sonata: An Enigma', in: *Recherches sur la musique française*, VII (1967), pp. 154-163.

[75]. COUPERIN, François. *Les goûts réunis, ou nouveaux concerts à l'usage de toutes les sortes d'instruments de musique augmentés d'une grande sonade en trio intitulée Le Parnasse, ou l'apothéose de Corelli* [...], Paris, l'auteur, 1724; see also MELLERS, Wilfrid. *François Couperin and the French Classical Tradition*, London, Dennis Dobson, 1950; TUNLEY, David. *François Couperin and 'The Perfection of Music'*, Farnham, Ashgate, 2014. The fusion of styles noted by Couperin is also found in Leclair's concertos; see KING, Richard G. *Les goûts-réunis and Leclair's concertos*, M.M. Thesis, Edmonton (AB), University of Alberta, 1984; see also FADER, Don. 'The goûts-réunis in French Vocal Music (1695-1710): Through the Lens of the «Recueil d'airs sérieux et à boire»', in: *Revue de Musicologie*, XCVI/2 (2010), pp. 321-363.

[76]. On the dissemination of this treatise, see REILLY, Edward R. 'The Dissemination of the Versuch', in: ID. *Quantz and His Versuch: Three Studies*, [New York], American Musicological Society, 1971 (Studies and documents, 5), pp. 40-92.

[77]. QUANTZ, Johann Joachim. *Op. cit.* (see note 10), 18. Hauptstück, Paragraphs 87-89. For a further exploration of the *stilus mixtus*, see, for example, KREYSZIG, Walter Kurt. 'Quantz's *Adagio in C-Major for Flute and basso continuo* (QV 1:7) in His *Versuch* (1752): Baroque Ornamentation in the Context of the Mid-18th Century Music Theoretical Discourse and Compositions in the *stilus mixtus*', in: *Ad Parnassum: A Journal of Eighteenth- and Nineteenth-Century Instrumental Music*, X/20 (October 2012), pp. 139-171.

[78]. Further on this topic, see, for example SIEGELE, Ulrich. 'Bachs vermischter Geschmack', in: *Bach und die Stile* [...], *op. cit.* (see note 26), pp. 9-17.

[79]. Further on Leclair's career, see, for example, ZASLAW, Neal. 'Leclair, Jean-Marie', in: *The New Grove Dictionary of Music and Musicians*, Second edition, 29 vols., edited by Stanley Sadie, London, Macmillan, 2001, vol. XIV, pp. 444-448: 445-446; BRAUN, Lucinde. 'Leclair, Jean-Marie, gen. l'aîné', in: *Die Musik in Geschichte und Gegenwart: Allgemeine Enzyklopädie der Musik, begründet von Friedrich Blume. Zweite, neu bearbeitete Ausgabe*, 26 vols., edited by Ludwig Finscher, Kassel [...], Bärenreiter; Stuttgart-Weimar, Metzler, 1994-2008, *Personenteil*, vol. X (2003), cols. 1416-1419: 1416-1417.

in the *sonata da camera*[80], in its contrast to the *sonata da chiesa*[81] with an emphasis on the learned counterpoint[82]. In 1723 Leclair launched his *Premier livre de sonates* in Paris under the 'Privilège general du roi'[83], following in the footsteps of the violinist and composer François Duval[84], the first composer to publish sonatas under the protection of King Louis XV[85], the latter to whom Leclair dedicated his *Troisième livre de sonates*, and that in gratitude of Leclair's appointment as *ordinaire de la musique du roi* by the King in 1733. Leclair's remaining three volumes of sonatas for violin and *basso continuo* appeared in more or less regular intervals, with the hiatus between the first and second volumes accounted for by Leclair's sojourn in Turin in 1726[86], where, according to Quantz[87], he took violin lessons with the acclaimed violinist and composer Giovanni Battista Somis, the director of the Royal Orchestra in Turin[88].

---

[80]. Further on the *sonata da camera*, see, for example, Daverio, John. 'In Search of the «sonata da camera» before Corelli', in: *Acta Musicologica*, LVII/2 (July-December 1985), pp. 195-214; Mangsen, Sandra S. 'The Sonata da camera Before Corelli: A Renewed Search', in: *Music & Letters*, LXXVI/1 (February 1995), pp. 19-31.

[81]. Further on the *sonata da chiesa*, see, for example, Bonta, Stephen. 'The Uses of the «sonata da chiesa»', in: *Journal of the American Musicological Society*, XXII/1 (Spring 1969), pp. 54-84. Further on the distinction between the *sonata da camera* and the *sonata da chiesa*, see, for example, Sehnal, Jiří. 'Zur Differenzierung der «sonata da chiesa» und «sonata da camera» in der zweiten Hälfte des 17. Jahrhunderts', in: *Colloquium Musica cameralis, Brno 1971*, edited by Rudolf Pečman, Brno, Mezinárodní hudební Festival, 1977 (Colloquium on the history and theory of music at the International musical festival in Brno, 6), pp. 303-310; Daverio, John. *Fornal Design and Terminology in the Pre-Corellian 'Sonata' and Related Instrumental Forms in the Printed Sources*, Ph.D. Diss., Boston (MA), Boston University, 1983.

[82]. On the learned counterpoint, see, for example, Boyd, Malcolm. *Bach's Instrumental Counterpoint*, London, Barrie and Jenkins, 1967; Dreyfus, Laurence. *Bach and the Patterns of Invention*, Cambridge (MA), Harvard University Press, 1996; Yearsley, David Gaynor. *Bach and the Meanings of Counterpoint*, Cambridge-New York, Cambridge University Press, 2002 (New perspectives in music history and criticism).

[83]. For a reproduction of this document, see Bachmann, Alberto. *Les grands violinistes du passé*, Paris, Librairie Fischbacher, 1913, p. 138; see also La Laurencie, Lionel de. 'Jean-Marie Leclair l'aîné: Premier symphoniste du Roi, d'après des documents inédits', in: *Sammelbände der Internationalen Musikgesellschaft*, VI/2 (January 1905), pp. 250-273; Id. 'À propos des protecteurs de J.-M. Leclair l'aîné', in: *Zeitschrift der Internationalen Musikgesellschaft*, IX (November 1907), pp. 61-65.

[84]. Dufourcq, Norbert – Bénoît, Marcelle. 'Les musiciens de Versailles à travers les minutes notariales de lamy versées aux Archives Départementales de Seine-et-Oise', in: *Recherches sur la musique française classique*, III (1963), pp. 189-206.

[85]. Brenet, Michel. 'La librairie musicale en France de 1653 à 1790 d'après les Registres de privilèges', in: *Sammelbände der Internationalen Musikgesellschaft*, VIII/3 (1907), pp. 401-466.

[86]. Bénoît, Marcelle. *Musiques de cour, chapelle, chambre, écurie: Versailles et les musiciens du roi, 1661-1733*, Paris, Picard, 1971.

[87]. *Herrn Johann Joachim Quantzens Lebenslauf, von ihm selbst entworfen* (dated Potsdam, August, 1754), included in Marpurg, Friedrich Wilhelm. *Historisch-kritische Beyträge zur Aufnahme der Musik*, 5 vols., Berlin, G. A. Lange, 1754-1760; also as facsimile of autobiography in Kahl, Friedrich. *Selbstbiographien deutscher Musiker des XVIII. Jahrhunderts (mit Einleitungen und Anmerkungen)*, Cologne, Stauffen-Verlag, 1948, pp. 104-157: 143.

[88]. Fino, Giocondo. 'Un grande violinista torinese ed una famiglia di violinisti: Giovanni Battista Somis, 1686-1763', in: *Il momento* (Turin, 25-26 October 1927); Becherini, Bianca. 'Un musicista italiano del XVIII

Past examinations of Leclair's sonatas have focussed largely on the performance practice[89]. This observation is all the more peculiar, as Leclair himself offered very little written commentary on the performance of the solo violin sonatas[90]. In this way, Leclair stands clearly apart from his Italian predecessors, in particular Arcangelo Corelli, whose sonatas for violin and *basso continuo* have received considerable attention[91] as a result of reworkings focussed on the addition of substantial written ornamentations[92], not only by the composer himself but also by his contemporaries, among them the violin virtuoso and pedagogue Francesco Geminiani[93], the violinist, composer, and student of Geminiani, Matthew Dubourg[94], known

secolo: Giovan Battista Somis', in: *Musicisti piemontesi e liguri: per la XVI settimana musicale, 13-21 settembre 1959*, edited by Adelmo Damerini and Gino Roncaglia, Siena, Accademia Musicale Chigiana, 1959 (Chigiana, 16), pp. 7-15; BURDETTE, Glenn. *The Violin Sonatas of G. B. Somis*, Ph.D. Diss., Cincinnati (OH), University of Cincinnati, 1993.

[89]. See, for example, MARTINEAU, Lorraine. *Violin Technique in the Sonata in E♭ Major by Jean-Marie Leclair*, M.M. Thesis, Rochester (NY), University of Rochester, 1941; CHEVALIER, Roberta Denise. *Ornamentation and Fingering in the Sonatas of Jean-Marie Leclair l'aîné*, M.A. Term Project, Stanford (CA), Stanford University, 1976; ROBERTS, Hollis E. *A Performance Style Analysis of Jean-Marie Leclair's Sonata No. 3 in D major, Op. 9*, Senior Paper in Music Performance, Spartanburg (SC), Converse College, 2006; see also SEAGRAVE, Barbara. *The French Style of Violin Bowing and Phrasing from Lully to Jacques Aubert (1650-1730), as Illustrated from Ballets and Dance Movements from Violin Sonatas of Representative Composers*, Ph.D. Diss., Stanford (CA), Stanford University, 1958; RAMIREZ, Marc A. *Program Notes for the Unaccompanied Violin Duos of Jacques Auber (1689-1753) Opus 15 and Jean-Marie Leclair l'aîné (1697-1764) Opus 3: French Bowing Traditions Applied to the Dance Movements*, D.M.A. Thesis, College Park (MD), University of Maryland, 1998. The emphasis on the examination of the musical text also pertains to Leclair's concertos; see, for example, WIENS, Victor D. *A Comparative Study of Four Editions of J. M. Leclair's Violin Concerto, Opus 10, No. 6*, M.M. Thesis, London (ON), University of Western Ontario, 1978.

[90]. See, for example, LECLAIR, Jean-Marie. *Sonatas for Violin and Basso continuo, Opus 1 […]*, *op. cit.* (see note 72), pp. x-xi; ID. *Sonatas for Violin and Basso continuo, Opus 2 […]*, *op. cit.* (see note 72), pp. ix-xi.

[91]. On the reception of Corelli's oeuvre, see, for example, ALLSOP, Peter. *Arcangelo Corelli: New Orpheus of Our Times*, Oxford, Oxford University Press, 1999.

[92]. Further on this topic, see, for example, BOYDEN, David D. 'The Corelli «Solo» Sonatas and Their Ornamental Additions by Corelli, Geminiani, Dubourg, Tartini, and the «Walsh Anonymous»', in: *Musica Antiqua: III. Acta scientifica*, edited by Lissa Zofia, Bydgoszcz, Filharmonia Pomorska im. I. Paderewskiego, 1972 (Musica antiqua Europae orientalis, 3), pp. 591-607; see also BOYDEN, David D. 'Corelli's Solo Violin Sonatas «Grac'd» by Dubourq', in: *Festschrift Jens Peter Larsen, 1902-1972*, edited by Nils Schiørring and Carsten E. Hatting, Copenhagen, Hansen, 1972, pp. 113-125; REICH, Sandra. *Corelli-Verzierungen des 'Manchester Anonymus'*, Master Thesis, Basel, Schola Cantorum Basiliensis, 1990.

[93]. McARTOR, Marion Emmett. *Francesco Geminiani, Composer and Theorist*, Ph.D. Diss., Ann Arbor (MI), University of Michgan, 1951; BOYDEN, David D. 'Geminiani and the First Violin Tutor', in: *Acta Musicologica*, XXXI/3-4 (July-December 1959), pp. 161-170; ID. 'A Postscript to: «Geminiani and the First Violin Tutor»', in: *Acta Musicologica*, XXXII/1 (January-March 1960), pp. 40-47. For an overview of Geminiani's treatises, see CARERI, Enrico. 'I sei trattati di Francesco Geminiani', in: *Musica senza aggettivi: studi per Fedele D'Amico*, 2 vols., edited by Agostino Ziino, Florence, Leo S. Olschki, 1991 (Quaderni della RIdM, 25), pp. 85-122.

[94]. BOYDELL, Brian. 'Dubourg, Matthew', in: *Die Musik […]*, *op. cit.* (see note 79), *Personenteil*, vol. V (2001), col. 1480.

for his exceptional performance of a solo by Corelli[95], and the composer, violin virtuoso and pedagogue Giuseppe Tartini, author of treatises on performance practice[96] and music theory[97]. Less attention has been devoted to the vastness of Leclair's approaches to the compositional practices, related to the adoption of the Italian style and the juxtaposition of this idiom with the musical traditions of his native France[98], with the dichotomy between Italian and French idioms within a single sonata[99], sometimes even within a single movement[100], informing much of Leclair's formulating of his own compositional style and technique. With Leclair's compositional legacy accessible in both published facsimiles and reliable modern editions in addition to nearly his entire contribution in recordings, we are in a most fortunate position to refocus our attention on the examination of Leclair's oeuvre[101], with its immense richness of style and proclivity towards a fusion of French and Italian compositional practices that hitherto had often existed side by side, but had

---

[95]. ID. 'Dubourg, Matthew', in: *The New Grove Dictionary* […], *op. cit.* (see note 79), vol. VII, p. 633.

[96]. TARTINI, Giuseppe. *Traité des agréments de la musique*, Paris, Pietro Denis, 1771; also in modern edition, edited by Erwin R. Jacobi with English translation by Cuthbert Girdlestone, Celle-New York, H. Moeck, 1961. For a discussion of this treatise, see, for example, GOLDIN, M. *The Violinistic Innovations of Giuseppe Tartini*, Ph.D. Diss., New York (NY), New York University, 1955; ELMER, Minnie Agnes. *Tartini's Improvised Ornamentation, as Illustrated by Manuscripts in the Berkeley Collection of Eighteenth-Century Italian Instrumental Music*, M.A. Thesis, Berkeley (CA), University of California, 1962; VITALI, Danilo. *Il 'Trattato degli abbellimenti' di G. Tartini*, Ph.D. Diss., Rome, Università degli Studi di Roma, 1995; see also PETROBELLI, Pierluigi. *Tartini, le sue idee e il suo tempo*, Lucca, LIM, 1992 (Musicalia, 5).

[97]. TARTINI, Giuseppe. *Trattato di musica secondo la vera scienza dell'armonia*, Padua, Stamperia del Seminario, 1754; also as facsimile, New York, Broude Brothers, 1966 (Monuments of music and music literature in facsimile, series II: Music literature, 8); also in English translation by JOHNSTON, Fredric B. *Tartini's «Trattato di musica secondo le vera scienza dell'armonia»: An Annotated Translation with Commentary*, Ph.D. Diss., Bloomington (IN), Indiana University, 1985; see also RUBELI, Alfred Ulrich. *Das musiktheoretische System Giuseppe Tartinis*, Winterthur, Keller, 1958; PLANCHART, Alejandro Enrique. 'A Study of the Theories of Giuseppe Tartini', in: *Journal of Music Theory*, IV/1 (April 1960), pp. 32-61; RUBELI, Alfred. *Traktat über die Musik: Gemäß der wahren Wissenschaft von der Harmonie*, Düsseldorf, Verlag der Gesellschaft zur Förderung der Systematischen Musikwissenschaft, 1966 (Orpheus Schriftenreihe zu Grundfragen der Musik, 6); POLZONETTI, Pierpaolo. *Tartini e la musica secondo natura*, Lucca, LIM, 2001; *Giuseppe Tartini: le opere teorico-didattiche*, edited by Margherita Canale Degrassi, SEdM, <http://www.sedm.it/sedm/it/metodi-trattati/45-le-opere-teorico-didattiche.html>.

[98]. The presence of Italian musicians during this era accounts for the ready adoption of the Italian style by a Frenchman; see *The Eighteenth-Century Diaspora of Italian Music and Musicians*, edited by Reinhard Strohm, Turnhout, Brepols, 2001 (Speculum musicae, 8).

[99]. See, for example, Jean-Marie Leclair, Sonata No. 8 in G major, Op. 1; in: LECLAIR, Jean-Marie. *Sonatas for Violin and Basso continuo, Opus 1* […], *op. cit.* (see note 72), pp. 103-119.

[100]. See, for example, Jean-Marie Leclair, Sonata No. 6 in D major, Op. 2, *Allegretto ma poco* (opening movement); in: ID. *Sonatas for Violin and Basso Continuo, Opus 2* […], *op. cit.* (see note 72), pp. 59-69: 59-63.

[101]. This message has been most elegantly conveyed by Neal Zaslaw in his critical remarks on Leclair's legacy communicated in the form of a tribute; see ZASLAW, Neal. 'Editorial: Jean-Marie Leclair l'aîné (1697-1764)', in: *Ad Parnassum: A Journal of Eighteenth- and Nineteenth-Century Instrumental Music*, XII/24 (October 2014), pp. v-vi.

perhaps not received the attention they so rightly deserve. It is precisely here where Leclair undoubtedly found his niche as a composer, with the fusion of the two national styles offering unprecedented possibilities worthy of exploration.

Already in the *Premier livre de sonates*, Op. 1 (Paris, 1723)[102], Leclair displays his fondness for a harmonic palette enriched with dissonant progressions. The fourth movement, marked *Tempo Gavotta*, from the Sonata in D major, Op. 1 No. 4, a work which opens with an *Adagio*, Italian in style with attention to the inflection of French ornamentation, in which Leclair displays his penchant for *les goûts reunis*, serves as a case in point[103]. Laid out in a tripartite structure (measures 1-68; measures 68-113 marked *Altro*; measures 113-121), with the first two large-scale segments articulated by a partial repeat of material, and the interpolation of a lengthy segment (measures 68-113), marked by a sudden change in the key, that is from, D major to D minor, the parallel minor of the home key, Leclair embraces the many facets of the Italian compositional style, with the brief concise melodies couched within an overriding symmetry, largely comprising two-measure units, their incessant repetition, including both exact restatements (for example, measures 32-34) and varied restatements (for example, measures 64-66) of the melodic materials within a diatonic frame, the infusion of melodic/rhythmic diminutions over a lengthy pedal point (for example, measures 50-55), or the spinning out of the theme in melodic sequences (for example, measures 83-87), in the so-called *Fortspinnungstechnik*[104], as a means of replacing the consequent of the antecedent-consequent phrase structure[105]. On occasion, throughout this movement, the unfolding of the thematic/motivic material with emphasis on the predominant homophony or simple counterpoint, controlled by diminutions, without distorting the regular harmonic rhythm, a hallmark of the *stile galante*, is interrupted by a sudden change in the harmonic rhythm (measures 36-42). Leclair inserts a lengthy pedal point on f♯, the dominant of B minor (the relative of the homekey of this movement and of this sonata as a whole) with a prominent display of a series of seventh chords and the eventual resolution by step in a 7-6 suspension (measure 40) and a close of this eight-measure period on the tonic chord (of B minor) in measure 44. In the following period, Leclair resorts to a varied statement of the *Gavotta* theme now altogether stripped of its diminutions but retaining its overall harmonic profile, stressed by the quarter-note double stops in the violin (measures 45-48) and the separately notated viol part, emphasizing the *basso continuo* line, with this scoring reminiscent of the performance

102. Leclair, Jean-Marie. *Premier livre de sonates à violin seul avec la basse continue*, Paris, Leclair, Boivin, le Clerc, 1723, engraved by Louis-Hector Hue (Hüe); dedicated to Monsieur Bonnet.

103. Id. *Sonatas for Violin and Basso continuo, Opus 1* […], *op. cit.* (see note 72), pp. 55-61.

104. Further on this technique, see, for example, Fischer, Wilhelm. 'Zur Entwicklungsgeschichte des Wiener Klassischen Stils', in: *Studien zur Musikwissenschaft*, III (1915), pp. 24-84.

105. Further on this topic, see, for example, Hill, John Walter. *Baroque Music: Music in Western Europe, 1580-1750*, New York, W. W. Norton, 2005 (The Norton introduction to music history), pp. 346ff.

practice in vogue at the Court of Louis XIV[106]. For the consequent of this period (measures 49-52), Leclair resorts to the eight-note diminutions in both violin and viol over another pedal point in the *basso continuo* (measures 50-56), this time placing emphasis on the note e (as the dominant of A major), yet with a conscious attention to the preserving of the *Affektenlehre*, especially in Leclair's careful adherence to the overall layout of the dance itself[107]. Here, Leclair displays the close relationship between the two string parts, by resorting to a series of voice exchanges (measures 50-52) a compositional technique, first observed in polyphonic repertories of the Middle Ages, with special attention to the organum[108]. For, with the examination of the concept of the voice exchange, defined as an exchange of phrases, normally of short duration, between two voices, we have entered the world of medieval music, specifically with reference to two-part counterpoint, often in contrary motion, in vogue throughout the twelfth century[109], what the music theorist Johannes de Garlandia describes as the «repetitio diversae vocis»[110], with specific examples found in Notre Dame polyphony[111]. However, this compositional device is not restricted to two-voice polyphony, but eventually also occurs in three- and four-voice organa of

[106]. RYCROFT, Marjorie E. 'Aspects of National Styles in Gamba Music of the Eighteenth Century', in: *Nationalstile und europäisches Denken in der Musik von Fasch und seinen Zeitgenossen: Bericht über die Internationale Wissenschaftliche Konferenz am 21. und 22. April 1995 im Rahmen der IV. Internationalen Fasch-Festtage in Zerbst*, edited by Konstanze Musketa, Dessau, Anhaltische Verlagsanstalt, 1997 (Fasch-Studien, 5), pp. 99-108; see also SADIE, Julie Anne. *The Bass Viol in French Baroque Chamber Music*, Ann Arbor (MI), UMI Research Press, 1980 (Studies in musicology, 26).

[107]. SPARSHOTT, Francis. 'Reflections on *Affektenlehre* and Dance Theory in the Eighteenth Century', in: *The Journal of Aesthetics and Art Criticism*, XXXVI/1 (Winter 1998), pp. 21-28.

[108]. WAELTNER, Ernst Ludwig. *Die Lehre vom Organum bis zur Mitte des 11. Jahrhunderts*, 2 vols., edited by Gabriele E. Mayer and Hans Schmid, Tutzing, Hans Schneider, 1975-2002 (Münchner Veröffentlichungen zur Musikgeschichte, 13, 44); see also *Ad organum faciendum: Lehrschriften der Mehrstimmigkeit in nachguidonischer Zeit*, edited by Hans Heinrich Eggebrecht and Frieder Zaminer, Mainz, Schott, 1970 (Neue Studien zur Musikwissenschaft, 3); APFEL, Ernst. *Die Lehre vom Organum, Diskant, Kontrapunkt und von der Komposition bis um 1480*, Saarbücken, Musikwissenschaftliches Institut der Universität des Saarlandes, 1987.

[109]. RECKOW, Fritz. 'Organum', in: *Gattungen der Musik in Einzeldarstellungen: Gedenkschrift Leo Schrade, in Verbindung mit Freunden, Schülern und weiteren Fachgelehrten*, edited by Wulf Arlt, Ernst Lichtenhahn and Hans Oesch in collaboration with Max Haas, Bern-Munich, Francke, 1973, pp. 434-496.

[110]. REIMER, Erich. *Johannes de Garlandia: De mensurabili musicae – Kritische Edition mit Kommentar und Interpretation der Notationslehre*, 2 vols., Wiesbaden, Franz Steiner, 1972 (Beihefte zum Archiv für Musikwissenschaft, 10-11), vol. 1, p. 95; see also WAITE, William R. *The Rhythm of Twelfth-Century Polyphony: Its Theory and Practice*, New Haven (CT)-London, Yale University Press-Oxford University Press, 1954 (Yale Studies in the History of Music, 3).

[111]. Further on Notre Dame polyphony, see, for example, CROCKER, Richard L. – HILEY, David. *The Early Middle Ages to 1300*, Oxford-New York, Oxford University Press, 1990 (The New Oxford History of Music, 2), pp. 557-635: 564-625; see also FLINDELL, Edwin Frederick. *An Explanation of the Origins and Nature of Notre Dame Modal Polyphony in the Twelfth Century: A Musical Genre Integral to the Development of Gothic Art and Medieval Culture*, Lewiston (NY), The Edwin Mellen Press, 2014.

Magister Perotinus of Paris[112], as for example in his four-voice *Sederunt*[113] with the *voces organales* laid out in *discantus* (note-against-note) style[114] — on the whole what appears to signal a major shift in musical paradigms taking place in the early decade of the thirteenth century[115] and continuing through the latter half of the thirteenth century, as gleaned from the late-thirteenth century anonymous rondellus motet *Fulget coelestis curia/O Petre flos/ Roma gaudet* from the *Worcester Fragments*, comprising two three-voice segments laid out as a *rondellus* with its intricate voice exchange comprising all three voices[116]. Though rare, voice exchanges on special occasion are found in the *gelehrte Stil* of composition, as for example, in J. S. Bach's two-voice canon *Quaerendo invenietis* from the *Musikalisches Opfer*, BWV 1079[117], as an exemplification of his exceptional skills pertaining to the

---

[112]. SCHMIDT, Helmut. *Die drei- und vierstimmigen Organa*, Kassel, Bärenreiter, 1933; FLOTZINGER, Rudolf. *Perotinus musicus: Wegbereiter abendländischen Komponierens*, Mainz, Schott, 2000; see also POUCKE, Peter van. *Magister Perotinus magnus: Organa quadruple generaliter, inleidende reconstructieve studie*, Ph.D. Diss., Ghent, Rijksuniversiteit Ghent, 1983.

[113]. There are numerous editions of this particular composition; see, for example, *Die drei- und vierstimmigen Notre-Dame Organa: Kritische Gesamtausgabe*, edited by Heinrich Husmann, Leipzig, Breitkopf & Härtel, 1940; *Les Quadruples et Triples de Paris*, edited by Edward H. Roesner and Michel Huglo, Monaco, Éditions de l'Oiseau-Lyre, 1993 (Le Magnus Liber Organi de Notre-Dame de Paris, 1). Further on this work, see, for example, FLOTZINGER, Rudolf. 'Zu Perotin und seinem «Sederunt»', in: *Analysen: Beiträge zu einer Problemgeschichte des Komponierens — Festschrift Hans Heinrich Eggebrecht zum 65. Geburtstag*, edited by Werner Breig, Reinhold Brinkmann and Elmar Budde, Wiesbaden, Franz Steiner, 1984 (Beihefte zum Archiv für Musikwissenschaft, 23), pp. 14-28; see also MACHABEY, Armand. 'A propos des quadruples pérotiniens', in: *Musica Disciplina: A Yearbook of the History of Music*, XII (1958), pp. 3-25. Interestingly enough, Perotinus's setting of *Sederunt* has also preoccupied later composers; see, for example, TRAUB, Andreas. 'Eine Perotin-Bearbeitung Hindemiths', in: *Hindemith-Jahrbuch*, XXIII (1994), pp. 30-60.

[114]. Further on the *discantus* as a compositional technique, see, for example, FLOTZINGER, Rudolf. *Der Discantussatz im Magnus Liber und seine Nachfolger, mit Beiträgen zur Frage der sogenannten Notre-Dame Handschriften*, Vienna, Böhlau, 1969 (Wiener Musikwissenschaftliche Beiträge, 8).

[115]. Further on this topic, see, for example, ID. *Von Leonin zu Perotin: Der musikalische Paradigmenwechsel in Paris um 1210*, Bern, Peter Lang, 2007 (Varia musicologica, 8).

[116]. For a modern edition of this rondellus motet, see *Norton Anthology of History of Western Music in Two Volumes*, edited by Claude V. Palisca, New York, W. W. Norton, 1980, vol. 1, pp. 89-91; see also HARRISON, Frank L. *Music in Medieval Britain*, London, Routledge and Paul, 1958 (Studies in the history of music), pp. 141-149.

[117]. BACH, Johann Sebastian. *Das musikalische Opfer*, edited by Christoph Wolff, Kassel, Bärenreiter, 1974 (Johann Sebastian Bach, Neue Ausgabe sämtlicher Werke, Reihe 8: Kanons, Musikalische Opfer, Kunst der Fuge, 1); see also Böss, Reinhard. 'Stimmentausch und Spiegelungstechniken im Canon à 2 «Quaerendo invenietis» als beispielhafte Kennzeichen für Bachs «ars canonica», Das musikalische Opfer', in: *Alte Musik als ästhetische Gegenwart: Bach, Händel, Schütz — Bericht über den Internationalen Musikwissenschaftlichen Kongress, Stuttgart, 1985*, 2 vols., edited by Dietrich Berke and Dorothea Hanemann, Kassel, Bärenreiter, vol. 1, pp. 329-341; see also WUIDAR, Laurence. 'De l'emblème au canon: Étude iconographique et essai herméneutique de Kircher à Bach', in: *Imago musicae: International Yearbook of Musical Iconography*, XXI-XXII (2004-2005), pp. 263-287.

ars canonica[118]. Even in repertories of the *stile galante*, this compositional device surfaces in instrumental music, as, for example, in the *Musique de table* (Hamburg, 1733) of Telemann. In the *Allegresse* (Movement 3) of Production 3 of this publication, Telemann elegantly conceals two examples of voice exchange, placed in close proximity within a segment that abounds in a series of imitative exchanges between the two oboes proceeding in parallel thirds with the two violins also progressing in parallel thirds. In measures 42-44, we notice two identical statements within the imitative structure, with a third statement (measure 44) deviating by the final sixteenth note, necessitated to allow the individual parts to proceed with the continuation of the melodic line[119].

Resorting to this most venerable compositional device, Leclair underscores the significance of the viol part, not merely as a reinforcement of the *basso continuo* line but rather at times as the genuine melody-bearing line, here closely modelled upon the diminutions displayed in the violin part, with this particular part writing suggesting a close emulation of the trio-sonata, a genre characterized by an already lengthy history on Italian soil[120], with Corelli most likely serving as the model[121]. Throughout the middle segment of the *Tempo Gavotta*, the *Altro* in D minor, Leclair upholds the trio texture of the earlier segment. An initial passage (measures 79-81) features the violin in double and triple stops and the viol in eighth-note diminutions over the *basso continuo* part, with an emphasis on double suspensions, that is, 7-6 progressions in conjunction with 4-3 progression[122],

---

[118]. BLANKENBURG, Walther. 'Die Bedeutung des Kanons in Bachs Werk', in: *Bericht über die Wissenschaftliche Bachtagung der Gesellschaft für Musikforschung, Leipzig, 23. bis 26. Juli 1950*, edited by Walther Vetter and Ernst Hermann Meyer, Leipzig, C. F. Peters, 1951, pp. 250-258; Böss, Reinhard. *Die Kunst des Rätselkanons im Musikalischen Opfer*, 2 vols., Wilhelmshaven, F. Noetzel, 1991; see also WOLFF, Christoph. *Der stile antico in der Musik Johann Sebastian Bachs: Studien zu Bachs Spätwerk*, Wiesbaden, Franz Steiner, 1968 (Beihefte zum Archiv für Musikwissenschaft, 6); BEICHE, Michael. 'Imitatio / Nachahmung', in: *Handwörterbuch der musikalischen Terminologie* […], *op. cit.* (see note 9), 1988; ID. 'Fugue / Fuga', in: *Handwörterbuch der musikalischen Terminologie* […], *op. cit.* (see note 9), 1990; WALKER, Paul. *Theories of Fugue from the Age of Josquin to the Age of Bach*, Rochester-Woodbridge, University of Rochester Press, 2000 (Eastman studies in music, 13).

[119]. TELEMANN, Georg Philipp. *Tafelmusik*, 3 vols., edited by Johann Philipp Hinnenthal, Kassel, Bärenreiter, 1959-1963 (Georg Philipp Telemann: Musikalische Werke, 12-14), vol. XIV, pp. 26-28: 27; see also KREYSZIG, Walter Kurt. '«I hope that this work will one day bring me fame»: On Georg Philipp Telemann's *Musique de table* (Hamburg, 1733) as a Testimony of Exceptional Spiritual Nourishment in the Context of the *stilus mixtus*', paper presented at the 16th *Biennial International Conference on Baroque Music*, University of Music and Dramatic Arts Mozarteum Salzburg, 9-13 July 2014.

[120]. ALLSOP, Peter. *The Italian 'Trio' Sonata from the Origins until Corelli*, Oxford-New York, Clarendon Press-Oxford University Press, 1992 (Oxford monographs on music).

[121]. FINSCHER, Ludwig. 'Corelli als Klassiker der Triosonate', in: *Nuovi studi corelliani: atti del Secondo congresso internazionale Fusignano (5-8 settembre 1974)*, edited by Giulia Giachin, Florence, Leo S. Olschki, 1978 (Quaderni della RIdM, 4), pp. 23-29; see also MANGSEN, Sandra. *Instrumental Duos and Trios in Printed Italian Sources, 1600-1675*, 2 vols., Ph.D. Diss., Ithaca (NY), Cornell University, 1989.

[122]. On the suspension in earlier polyphonic repertories of the seventeenth century, see, for example, KREYSZIG, Walter Kurt. 'William Mahrt's Notion of Gregorian Chant as a Polyphonic Fundamentum:

slightly displaced, so as to increase the tension that Leclair has built up systematically from the beginning of this movement. To this end, the appearance of accentuated ninth chords at the beginning of measures 84, 85, 86, and 87 serve as yet another confirmation of Leclair's interest in his gradual yet persistent increase of the overall intensification of the drama, with these dissonances serving as a most appropriate rhetorical gesture in the context of conceptional changes to eighteenth-century periodicity[123] — what a number of German theorists, including Christoph Bernhard[124], Johann David Heinichen[125] (according to Charles Burney the 'Rameau of Germany'[126]), Mattheson[127] (who, like Heinichen had

Gregorio Allegri's *Miserere* (1638) and Historiography', in: *Chant and Culture: Proceedings of the Conference of the Gregorian Institute of Canada, University of British Columbia, August 6-9, 2013*, edited by Armin Karim and Barbara Swanson, Lions Bay (BC), The Institute of Medieval Music, 2014 (Musikwissenschaftliche Abhandlungen/Musicological studies, 105), pp. 161-189: 168-170.

[123]. Further on this topic, see, for example, WALDURA, Markus. 'Musical Rhetoric and the Modern Concept of Musical Period: A New Perspective on 18th-Century German Theories of Musical Periodicity', translated by Frank Heidlberger, in: *Theoria: Historical Aspects of Music Theory*, XIII (2006), pp. 5-41.

[124]. BERNHARD, Christoph. *Tractatus compositionis augmentatus* (c1657), ms., published in *Die Kompositionslehre Heinrich Schützens in der Fassung seines Schülers Christoph Bernhard*, edited by Joseph Müller-Blattau, Leipzig, Breitkopf & Härtel, 1926. Further on the dissonances, see FEDERHOFER, Hellmut. 'Christoph Bernhards Figurenlehre und die Dissonanz', in: *Die Musikforschung*, XLII/2 (April 1989), pp. 110-127; see also 'The Treatises of Christoph Bernhard', edited and translated by Walter Hilse, in: *The Music Forum*, III (1973), pp. 1-196; DEGGELLER, Kurt. 'Materialien zu den Musiktraktaten Christoph Bernhards', in: *Basler Studien zur Interpretation alter Musik*, edited by Veronika Gutmann, Winterthur, Amadeus, 1980 (Forum Musicologicum, 2), pp. 141-168; FIEBIG, Folkert. *Christoph Bernhard und der stile moderno: Untersuchungen zu Leben und Werk*, Hamburg, Verlag der Musikalienhandlung Wagner, 1980 (Hamburger Beiträge zur Musikwissenschaft, 22); BARTEL, Dietrich. *Musica poetica: Musical Rhetorical Figures in Geman Baroque Music*, Lincoln (NB), University of Nebraska Press, 1997.

[125]. HEINICHEN, Johann David. *Neu-erfundene und gründliche Anweisung wie ein Music-Liebender auff gewisse vortheilhafftige Arth könne zu vollkommener Erlernung des General-Basses [...]*, Hamburg, Benjamin Schiller, 1711; also as facsimile edition, edited by Wolfgang Horn, Kassel, Bärenreiter, 2000 (Documenta musicologica, Reihe I: Druckschriften-Faksimiles, 15); also as revised version ID. *Der General-Bass in der Composition, Oder: Neue und gründliche Anweisung, wie ein Music-Liebender mit besonderem Vortheil durch die Prinzipien der Composition, nicht allein den General-Bass [...]*, Dresden, Johann David Heinichen, 1728; also as facsimile, Hildesheim-New York, Georg Olms, 1969; see also BUELOW, George J. 'Heinichen's Treatment of Dissonance', in: *Journal of Music Theory*, VI/2 (Winter 1962), pp. 216-273; HORN, Wolfgang. 'Johann David Heinichen und die musikalische Zeit: Die *quantitas intrinseca* und der Begrif des Akzenttaktes', in: *Musiktheorie*, VII/3 (1992), pp. 195-218.

[126]. BURNEY, Charles. *A General History of Music, from the Earliest Ages to the Present Period*, London, by the Author, 1789, 2 vols., edited with critical and historical notes by Frank Mercer, New York, Harcourt, Brace and Company, 1935, vol. II, p. 459; see also GRANT, Kerry S. *Dr. Charles Burney as Critic and Historian of Music*, Ann Arbor (MI), UMI Research Press, 1983 (Studies in musicology, 62); McLEOD, Alexander Kenneth. *Charles Burney's Philosophy of Musical Criticism*, M.A. Thesis, Hamilton (ON), McMaster University, 1991.

[127]. GÖTTERT, Karl-Heinz. 'Rhetorik und Musiktheorie im frühen 18. Jahrhundert: Ein Beitrag zu Johann Mattheson', in: *Poetica: Zeitschrift für Sprach- und Literaturwissenschaft*, XVIII (1986), pp. 274-287; see also LENNEBERG, Hans. 'Johann Mattheson on Affect and Rhetoric in Music', in: *Journal of Music Theory*, II/1-2 (November-April 1958), pp. 47-84, 193-236; HARRISS, Ernest. 'Johann Mattheson and the Affekten-, Figuren-

a close connection with the French Enlightenment[128]), and Johann Gottfried Walther[129] had classified as a *Verzögerung*, and that as a justification of the most unusual disposition of this dissonance[130]. Throughout the *Premier livre de sonates*, Leclair displays a penchant for infusing diatonic structures with carefully placed chromaticism, occasionally even with an increase of dramatic gestures over an extended period, and that without resolving the dissonant build-up immediately but rather at the end of a lengthy passage. In the *Allegro* of Sonata in D major, Op. 1 No. 10[131], Leclair displays such prominent use of chromaticism, here with the intent of delaying the large scale progression from the dominant chord in measure 10 to the tonic chord in measure 19, with the intercalation of an extended passage unfolding over a dominant pedal, progressing from a root position chord (measures 10-11) to a seventh chord (measure 12), to a ninth chord in fourth inversion (measure 13), to a second inversion chord on A (measure 14) to a second inversion chord on A with a flattened sixth (measure 15) resulting in a strident cross relation ($c\sharp$ in measure 14 against the $c\natural$ in measure 15), which in turn leads to another seventh chord on D$\sharp$ (measure 16), a third-inversion ninth chord on A, which resolves via a dominant chord and a subsequent dominant-seventh chord (measure 18) to the already mentioned tonic chord in measure 19. Leclair's most colourful display of chromaticism is reminiscent of Antonio Vivaldi's extended use of dissonances within the harmonic frame, largely based on a bass progression with a stepwise motion leading to a length pedal point in the *Largo*, subtitled 'Il sonno' from his Concerto No. 2 in G minor for Flute and Orchestra, Op. 10, RV 104 (published in Amsterdam in 1728)[132], whose autograph along with five other

und Rhetorik-Lehren', in: *La musique et la rite sacré e profane: actes du XIIIe Congrès de la Société Internationale de Musicologie, Strasbourg, 29 août - 3 septembre 1982*, edited by Marc Honegger and Paul Prevost, 2 vols., Strassbourg, Association des Publications près les Universités de Strasbourg, 1986, vol. II, pp. 517-531.

[128]. See, for example, FORCHERT, Arno. 'Fanzösische Autoren in den Schriften Johann Matthesons', in: *Festschrift Heinz Becker zum 60. Geburtstag am 26. Juni 1982*, edited by Jürgen Schläder and Reinhold Quandt, Laaber, Laaber-Verlag, 1982, pp. 382-391.

[129]. WALTHER, Johann Gottfried. *Praecepta der musicalischen Composition* (1708); preserved as autograph in Manuscript Weimar, Thüringische Landesbibliothek, Musiksammlung Q 341C, part of Stiftung Weimarer Klassik, Hezogin Anna Amalia Bibliothek. Further on this treatise, see, for example, RATHERT, Wolfgang. 'Zur Überlieferung der «Praecepta der musicalischen Composition» von Johann Gottfried Walther', in: *Ständige Konferenz für Mitteldeutsche Barockmusik in Sachsen, Sachsen-Anhalt und Thüringen: Jahrbuch*, (2000), pp. 83-92; see also SCHMITZ, Arnold. 'Die Figurenlehre in den theoretischen Werken Johann Gottfried Walthers', in: *Archiv für Musikwissenschaft*, IX/2 (January 1952), pp. 79-100; BENARY, Peter. *Die deutsche Kompositionslehre des 18. Jahrhunderts (im Anhang: Johann Adolph Scheibe: Compendium musices)*, Leipzig, Breitkopf & Härtel, 1961 (Jenaer Beiträge zur Musikforschung, 3).

[130]. Further on this topic, see SHELDON, David A. '«The Ninth Chord» in German Theory', in: *Journal of Music Theory*, XXVI/1 (Spring 1982), pp. 61-100.

[131]. LECLAIR, Jean-Marie. *Sonatas for Violin and Basso continuo, Opus 1* [...], *op. cit.* (see note 72), pp. 138-142.

[132]. VIVALDI, Antonio. *Concerto in Sol minore per flauto, fagotto, archi e cembalo 'La notte', F. XII, n. 5*, edited by Angelo Ephrikian, Milan, Ricordi, 1949 (Opere Antonio Vivaldi, 33); see also TALBOT, Michael. *Vivaldi*, New York, Schirmer Books-Maxwell Macmillan International, 1993 (The master musicians), p. 121.

concertos is preserved in the Biblioteca Nazionale in Turin[133]. In the *Largo*, the large-scale chromatic gestures are of programmatic significance[134], namely, serving as a portrayal of the sombre quality of the sleep as conveyed in the long ascents and descents of limited range in the flute, as an effective imagery associated with the depiction of the night ('la notte'), the subtitle of this concerto, with the expansion of the melodic idea of 'Il sonno' occurring in the movement for sleeping inebriates ('Ubriachi dormienti') in the Concerto No. 3 in F major ('L'autunno'), RV 293 of Vivaldi's *Le quattro stagioni*, Op. 8[135]. As a typical Italianate gesture, a similar build-up of tension within the overriding harmonic plan is found at the beginning of the slow movement of Geminiani's Concerto grosso No. 3 in C major after Corelli's Op. 5[136],

[133]. RYOM, Peter. *Répertoire des œuvres d'Antonio Vivaldi: les compositions instrumentales*, Copenhagen, Engstrøm & Sødring AS Musikforlag, 1986, p. 171.

[134]. On the significance of programmatic gestures in Vivaldi's instrumental oeuvre, see PINCHERLE, Marc. *Antonio Vivaldi et la musique instrumentale*, Paris, Librairie Floury, 1949, pp. 205ff.

[135]. VIVALDI, Antonio. *Concerto in Fa maggiore per violino, archi e organo (o cembalo) 'L'autunno', F. I, n. 24*, edited by Gian Francesco Malipiero, Milan, Ricordi, 1950 (Opere Antonio Vivaldi, 78); see also ROBBINS LANDON, Howard Chandler. *Vivaldi: Voice of the Baroque*, London, Thames and Hudson, 1993, pp. 63-65; EVERETT, Paul. *Vivaldi: The Four Seasons and Other Concertos, Op. 8*, Cambridge, Cambridge University Press, 1996 (Cambridge music handbooks), pp. 76, 85-87; BROVER-LUBOVSKY, Bella. *Tonal Space in the Music of Antonio Vivaldi*, Bloomington (IN), Indiana University Press, 2008 (Music and the early modern imagination), pp. 144-145, 191.

[136]. GEMINIANI, Francesco. *[6] Concerti grossi [...] composti delli sei soli della prima parte dell'opera quinta d'Arcangelo Corelli*, London, William Smith and John Barrett, 1726, for two violins, viola, and violoncello, or two violins and *basso continuo*; see also ID. *6 Concertos after Corelli, Opp. 1 & 3 (H. 126-131 − 3 Concertos from 'Select Harmony' (H 121-123) − 2 Unison Concertos (H 124-125)*, edited by Christopher Hogwood, Bologna, Ut Orpheus Edizioni, 2010 (Francesco Geminiani, Opera Omnia, 8). For an inventory of Geminiani's *Concerti grossi*, see CARERI, Enrico. *Francesco Geminiani (1687-1762)*, Oxford, Clarendon Press, 1993, pp. 268-270; see also HENRIED, Robert. 'Francesco Geminiani's Concerti grossi, Op. 3', in: *Acta Musicologica*, IX/1-2 (January-June 1937), pp. 22-30; CARERI, Enrico. 'Francesco Geminiani e il culto inglese per Corelli', in: *Studi Corelliani V: atti del Quinto congresso, Fusignano*, edited by Stefano La Via, Florence, Leo S. Olschki, 1996 (Quaderni della RIdM, 33), pp. 347-373. On the preeminent status of Corelli's Opus 5, see, for example, MOSER, Andreas. 'Zur Frage der Ornamentik in ihrer Anwendung auf Corellis Op. 5', in: *Zeitschrift für Musikwissenschaft*, 1 (1918/1919), pp. 287-293; RINALDI, Mario. *Il problema degli abbellimenti nell'Op. V di Corelli*, Siena, Ticci, 1947 (Quaderni dell'Accademia Chigiana, 10); BETZ, Marianne. 'Verzierungspraxis im italienischen Stil am Beispiel der Sonate Op. 5/9 von A. Corelli', in: *Tibia: Magazin für Freunde alter und neuer Bläsermusik*, VIII/2 (1983), pp. 343-350; DIACK JOHNSTONE, Harry. 'Yet More Ornaments for Corelli's Violin Sonatas, Op. 5' in: *Early Music*, XXIV/4 (November 1996), pp. 623-633; SELETSKY, Robert E. '18th-Century Variations for Corelli's Sonatas Op. 5', in: *Early Music*, XXIV/1 (February 1996), pp. 119-130; ZASLAW, Neal. 'Ornaments for Corelli's Violin Sonatas, Op. 5', in: *Early Music*, XXIV/1 (February 1996), pp. 95-115; FIKENTSCHER, Saskia. *Die Verzierungen zu Arcangelo Corellis Violinsonaten, Op. 5: Ein analytischer Vergleich unter besonderer Berücksichtigung der Beziehung von Notation und Realisation*, Lucca, LIM, 1997 (Quaderni di Musica/Realtà, 35); see also PINCHERLE, Marc. 'De l'ornamentation des sonates de Corelli', in: *Feuillets d'Histoire du Violon*, Paris, Legouix, 1927, pp. 133-142; MARX, Hans-Joachim. 'Some Unknown Embellishments of Corelli's Violin Sonatas', in: *The Musical Quarterly*, LXI/1 (January 1975), pp. 65-76; WALLS, Peter. 'Performing Corelli's Violin Sonatas', in: *Early Music*, XXIV/1 (February 1996), pp.

obviously regarded as Geminiani's tribute to Corelli[137], though without attributing any programmatic significance.

In the Sonata in B minor, Op. 1 No. 12[138], Leclair displays his compositional skills and showcases the virtuosity of Italian violin playing in a heightened manner. A symmetrically conceived work, with the two *Largo* movements, abounding in writing rich in double stops for violin 1. Each of these movements is followed, respectively, by two *Allegro* movements, both of which display a *fugato* style, the only movements in all of Opus 1 to show an obvious emulation of learned counterpoint, Leclair supplements the already rich and diverse counterpoint, with an emphasis on linear progressions, especially in the solo violin, as expressed in the carefully notated double stops, occurring in all four movements of this sonata, with numerous chromatic inflections, especially at the close of the *Allegro ma non troppo* (measures 66-73), as readily gathered form the heavily figured *basso continuo* part — a facet which we also observe in the oeuvre of J. S. Bach, for example in the *Larghetto* (second movement) of his Concerto No. 4 in A major for Harpsichord and Strings, BWV 1055 (composed *c*1738), where the inclusion of the *continuo* figures is restricted to the approach of the final cadence[139]. Of special interest is the passage with the dominant pedal on f♯ signalling the close of the intital *Allegro* with its slow conclusion in the notated *Adagio*. Here, the gradual decrease of the harmonic rhythm, already emphasized by the presence of the pedal point, is further underscored by the increase in complexity of the linear motions, readily gathered from the solo violin writing and the increase in figured bass symbols towards the end of this movement, with this full-voiced style accompaniment, of Italian origin, advocated in *Der General-Bass in der Composition* (Dresden, 1728) of Heinichen[140], who acknowledged the *basso continuo* as the foremost tool for learning the method of counterpoint. Here, the seventh chords are arranged in an increasing occurrence, namely from a single appearance in measure 69 to two appearances

---

133-142; Sackmann, Dominik. *Bach und Corelli: Studien zu Bachs Rezeption von Corellis Violinsonaten Op. 5 unter besonderer Berücksichtigung der 'Passaggio-Orgelchoräle' und der langsamen Konzertsätze*, Munich, Emil Katzbichler, 1999 (Musikwissenschaftliche Schriften, 36); Mangsen, Sandra. 'Geminiani the Arranger: A Re-Evalution', in: *Geminiani Studies*, edited by Christopher Hogwood, Bologna, Ut Orpheus Edizioni, 2013 (Ad Parnassum studies, 6), pp. 331-367.

[137].   Geminiani's admiration for Corelli is expressed in yet another generally ignored homage for the latter composer; see Barblan, Guglielmo. 'Un ignoto omaggio di Francesco Geminiani ad Arcangelo Corelli', in: *Musiche italiane rare e vive da Giovanni Gabrieli a Giuseppe Verdi: per la 19. Settimana musicale 22-30 luglio 1962*, edited by Adelmo Damerini and Gino Roncaglia, Siena, Accademia musicale Chigiana, 1962, pp. 51-55.

[138].   Leclair, Jean-Marie. *Sonatas for Violin and Basso continuo, Opus 1* […], *op. cit.* (see note 72), pp. 162-177.

[139].   Bach, Johann Sebastian. *Concerto IV für Cembalo und Streicher A-Dur, BWV 1055*, in: Id. *Konzerte für Cembalo*, edited by Werner Breig, Kassel, Bärenreiter, 1999 (Johann Sebastian Bach, Neue Ausgabe sämtlicher Werke, Reihe 7: Orchesterwerke, 4), pp. 161-189: 177.

[140].   Heinichen, Johann David. *Der General-Bass* […], *op. cit.* (see note 125); see also Buelow, George J. 'The Italian Influence in Heinichen's *Der General-Bass in der Composition* (1728)', in: *Basler Jahrbuch für Historische Musikpraxis*, XVIII (1994), pp. 47-65.

in measure 71, to three appearances in measure 72, and the final seventh chord in the closing measure in conjunction with the v-i cadence, so as to suggest an harmonic accelerando into the notated *Adagio*. In the *Largo* with its brief opening point of imitation between the solo violin and the *basso continuo*, Leclair intensifies the chromaticism in the harmonic progressions, by adding ninth chords on the downbeats of measures 4, 7, 9, 10, and so forth, with these formations in part arising out of the double stops in the violin.

In the *Deuxième livre de sonates*, Op. 2 (Paris, c1728)[141], Leclair continues to adopt the Baroque style of composition with greater attention devoted to the fugal movements, now, unlike the single occurrence in the final sonata of Op. 1, surfacing in three sonatas, that is, in Sonata No. 3 in B♭ major, Sonata No. 8 in G major, and Sonata No. 12 in B minor. Beyond that, Leclair displays a greater flexibility with regard to the overall organization of the individual sonatas, with nine sonatas comprising four movements, two sonatas embracing three movements and one sonata with four or five movements, depending on the interpretation of the *Altro* as a separate movement or as an integral part of the closing movement of Sonata No. 1 in E minor. In the *Deuxième livre de sonates*, Leclair resorts to a considerable widening of the melodic range in his conceiving of themes, a facet which also leaves an imprint on his widening of the expressive means, as reflected in the rich array of melodic intervals at his disposal, including intervals of the augmented second, diminished thirds, augmented fourth, and diminished seventh. This considerable change in the compositional process is readily gathered in the *Sonata in C major*, Op. 2 No. 3[142] — a work for which Leclair, in the obvious absence of the technique of double stops, identifies both violin and flute[143], the latter as the galant instrument *par excellence* as the solo instrument, with the choice left to the performer[144]. In the *Allegro*, we witness the aforementioned facets of his style. Within the overall spectrum of expressivity enlarged, even in the absence of double stops, Leclair expands the harmonic profile of the movement with a more diversified *basso continuo* line, one which is characterized not only by the greater preponderance of seventh chords, but also by the greater diversity within this category of chords, including the expansion of a seventh chord to a ninth chord in measure 17. In the ensuing *Largo* with its lilting 12/8 meter suggesting an Italianate *siciliano*, generally unfolding in a diatonic frame, Leclair places

---

[141]. LECLAIR, Jean-Marie. *Second livre de sonates pour le violon et pour la flute traversière avec la basse continue*, Paris, Leclair-Boivin-Le Clerc, c1728; dedicated to Monsieur Bonnet.

[142]. ID. *Sonatas for Violin and Basso continuo, Opus 2* [...], *op. cit.* (see note 72), pp. 26-34.

[143]. Within his *Quatre livres de sonates*, Leclair draws attention to the alternate scoring, with the violin replaced by the 'flûte allemande' (in the case of the Sonata in C major, Op. 1 No. 2; Sonata in E minor, Op. 2 No. 1; Sonata in C major, Op. 2 No. 3; Sonata in G major, Op. 2 No. 5; Sonata in B minor, Op. 2 No. 11; Sonata in G major, Op. 9 No. 7), or the 'flûte traversière' (in the case of the Sonata in E minor, Op. 1 No. 6). For the Sonata in D major, Op. 2 No. 8, Leclair identifies the following instrumentation «à trois: violin ou flûte / viole / violoncelle» [i.e. clavecin ou violoncelle].

[144]. BLAKELY, Brandy L. *Jean-Marie Leclair's Flute and Violin Sonatas*, Senior Thesis, Santa Cruz (CA), University of California, 2002.

an even more pronounced emphasis on the chromaticism enriched with dissonant intervals, as is readily gathered from Leclair's figured bass symbols.

In the *Troisième livre de sonates*, Op. 5 (Paris, *c*1734)[145], Leclair focusses more intensely on the linearity between melody and bass, thus steering clear of the bass line as a subsidiary to the solo line, with the latter dichotomy more readily observed in the *Premier livre de sonates* and in the *Deuxième livre de sonates* of Leclair's *opus*. Unlike Leclair's earlier compilations of sonatas, the sonatas included in the *Troisième livre de sonates* display a wider range of tonalities both within a given sonata[146] and with an individual movement. Here, the opening movement of the Sonata in A minor, Op. 5 No. 7[147] attests to a richer harmonic palette with regard to the modulations to D minor (the subdominant of A minor in measure 6), C major (the mediant of A minor in measure 8) before reverting back to A minor (the homekey) in the first ending, though briefly. Although chromaticism, on the whole, plays a significantly lesser role in the sonatas of the *Troisième livre de sonates*, with the opening movement of the Sonata No. 7 in A minor constituting no exception, as readily gathered from the somewhat sparser notation of the figured bass, at least in the first half of this movement, the opening gesture in the violin, especially the interval f-$g\sharp$, part of the harmonic minor mode, stated in monophony, and the adoption of this figure in the *basso continuo*, though not in strict imitation of the interval content, but rather in the natural minor mode, is rather unusual, even for a composer as innovative as Leclair. Apart from the rather the rapidly changing key areas within each half of the binary form, Leclair highlights a melodically rather peculiar passage, with the initial $f\sharp$ subject to reinterpretation as an $f\natural$ (at the opening of measure 12), and in the corresponding passage with the $d\sharp$ subject to reinterpretation as $d\natural$ (at the opening of measure 40), with the *basso continuo* briefly reverting to a segment for *tasto solo* in measures 11-13 and measures 39-41, respectively, so as to highlight this peculiar interval disposition of the melody, in each case featuring the identical interval content of the passage in the violin over a brief dominant pedal, with this passage on the whole capturing an element of the *Empfindsamer Stil*, with a focus on the expression of true and natural feeling rather than the adherence to a more uniform *Affekt* of the *stile galante*[148], as articulated in *Der vollkommene Capellmeister* (Hamburg, 1739) of Mattheson[149], with a careful delineation between compositional style

[145]. LECLAIR, Jean-Marie. *Troisième livre de sonates à violon seul avec la basse continue*, Paris, Leclair-Boivin-Le Clerc, *c*1734; dedicated to Her Royal Highness, Madame the Prince of Orange.

[146]. See BECKMANN, Gisela. *Op. cit.* (see note 67), pp. 43-44.

[147]. LECLAIR, Jean-Marie. *Sonatas for Violin and Basso continuo, Opus 5* […], *op. cit.* (see note 72), pp. 14-15.

[148]. BEINROTH, Fritz. 'Zu Fragen des Wandels in der Affekten- und Nachahmungslehre in der Musikästhetik des 18. Jahrhunderts unter besonderer Berücksichtigung der Berliner Schule', in: *Carl Philipp Emanuel Bach in unserer Zeit* […], *op. cit.* (see note 63), pp. 17-25.

[149]. MATTHESON, Johann. *Der vollkommene Capellmeister*, *op. cit.* (see note 38).

and genre[150], as well as in the *Versuch* (Berlin, 1752) of Quantz[151] and, at least in part, in the *Versuch* (1753-1762) of C. P. E. Bach[152].

In the *Quatrième livre de sonates*, Op. 9 (Paris, 1743)[153], Leclair explores a number of new territories in terms of infusing unexpected meanings into the tonal language of this period, with the resulting compositional practises revealing an obvious gradual abandoning of the *stile galante* in favour of the *Empfindsamer Stil*, in vogue during the second half of the eighteenth century. Leclair illustrates the novelty of his melodic and harmonic language in the closing movement of his Sonata in D major, Op. 9 No. 3[154], identified in the original print by the term *Tambourin / Presto*, with Leclair here capturing the old Provenance dance in 2/4 meter from the era of the Middle Ages, accompanied by a pipe and tambour, the latter instrument also known as a *tambour de Basque*[155], an instrumental combination in vogue in the Netherlands[156], where Leclair had spent considerable time. Leclair transfers this idiom to his Sonata in D major, with the violin performing rapid passages in a semi-rhapsodic style, including passages in diminutions (for example, measures 92-102) alternating with passages in double stops (for example, measures 103-105) to the relentless quarter-note rhythm of the unfigured basso part. On a number of occasions throughout this movement, Leclair replaces the steady pulsation of the basso line with a more colourful harmony, fusing

[150]. KRUMMACHER, Friedhelm. 'Stylus versus genus: Zum systematischen Denken Johann Matthesons', in: *Festschrift Arno Forchert zum 60. Geburtstag am 29. Dezember 1985*, edited by Gerhard Allroggen and Detlef Altenburg, Kassel, Bärenreiter, 1986, pp. 86-95.

[151]. QUANTZ, Johann Joachim. *Op. cit.* (see note 10).

[152]. BACH, Carl Philipp Emanuel. *Op. cit.* (see note 11); see also SOINNE, Paavo. 'Tempus, Affectus und Artikulation in Carl Philipp Emanuel Bachs «Versuch über die wahre Art das Clavier zu spielen»', in: *Fragen der Aufführungspraxis und Interpretation von Werken Carl Philipp Emanuel Bachs – ein Beitrag zum 200. Todestag: Konferenzbericht der 16. Wissenschaftlichen Arbeitstagung Michaelstein 1988*, edited by Thom Eitelfriedrich, 2 vols., Blankenburg/Harz, Die Kultur- und Forschungsstätte Michaelstein, 1989 (Studien zur Aufführungspraxis und Interpretation der Musik des 18. Jahrhunderts, 37/38), vol. I, pp. 41-53; PEČMAN, Rudolf. 'C. Ph. E. Bach und die Affektenlehre: Bemerkungen zur Aufführungspraxis', in: *Rudolfu Pečmanovi k sedmdesátinám / Rudolf Pečman zu seinem 70. Geburtstag*, Brno, Masarykova Univerzita, 2001 (Studia minora Facultatis philosophicae Universitatis brunensis, 36-37), pp. 17-22.

[153]. LECLAIR, Jean-Marie. *Quatrième livre de sonates à violon seul avec la basse continue*, Paris, Leclair-Boivin-Le Clerc, 1743; engraved by Madame Leclair; dedicated to Her Royal Highness, Madame the Princess of Orange.

[154]. ID. *Sonatas for Violin and Basso continuo, Opus 5, Opus 9, and Opus 15, Part III: Opus 9, Sonatas I-VI* […], *op. cit.* (see note 72), pp. 42-47.

[155]. MOECK, Hermann. 'Einhandflöte mit Trommel: Historisches und Folkloristisches kurzgefaßt', in: *Tibia: Magazin für Holzbläser*, XXI/3 (1996), pp. 168-175; MONTAGU, Jeremy. 'Was the Tabor Pipe always as We Know It?', in: *The Galpin Society Journal*, L (March 1997), pp. 16-30; ID. 'Significación del conjunto flauta-tamboril', in: *Txistulari: Boletin de la Asociación de Txistularis del Pais Vasco-Navarro*, no. 172 (October 1997), pp. 69-74; see also LIBIN, Laurence. *A Checklist of Western European Flageolets, Recorder and Tabor Pipes*, New York, Metropolitan Museum of Art, 1976.

[156]. BOSMANS, Wim. *Eenhandsfluit en trom in de Lage Landen / The Pipe and Tabor in the Low Countries*, Peer, Alamire, 1991.

chromaticism with diatonicism (for example, measures 82-111), as a means of integrating this particular dance, lifted out of its originally modal environment of the Middle Ages, into the tonal environment of the eighteenth-century. An even more innovative widening of the harmonic palette occurs in the *Adagio* of the Sonata in A minor, Op. 9 No. 5[157], where Leclair, in a rather systematic fashion, explores the juxtaposition of the major and minor parallel keys, what Robert Preston has captured in the term 'bimodality'[158]. Beginning in the key of F♯ major, the submediant of the homekey of the sonata, Leclair, in the course of this movement, reaches eleven keys, each of which is identified by a modulation serving as a means of establishing the particular key[159]. Beyond that, Leclair includes a small cross above the violin part, generally interpreted as an ornament, with the particular execution left to the discretion of the performer deciding within the frame of *le bon goût*[160], so as to further identify the principal points of incision within this rather unusual movement — a movement in which Leclair offers an extreme response to the *redende Prinzip* of C. P. E. Bach.

Beginning with the early eighteenth century, composers and theorists alike on occasion proceeded outside the traditional harmonic frame, restricted to relatively few keys, especially those with few flats or sharps in the respective key signatures, so as to also allow the participation of natural (valveless) instruments. In his *Exemplarische Organisten-Probe* (Hamburg, 1719)[161], Mattheson encouraged composers to expand their harmonic horizons in suggesting to embrace the entire chromatic gamut in their compositional practice, that is, resorting to all twenty-four keys. This enlarged harmonic space is systematically explored by J. S. Bach in his *Das Wohltemperierte Clavier* (Leipzig, 1722)[162], by Heinichen in his *Der*

---

[157]. LECLAIR, Jean-Marie. *Sonatas for Violin and Basso continuo, Opus 5, Opus 9, and Opus 15, Part III: Opus 9, Sonatas I-VI* […], *op. cit.* (see note 72), pp. 79-81.

[158]. ID. *Sonatas for Violin and Basso continuo, Opus 5, Opus 9, and Opus 15, Part I: Opus 5, Sonatas I-V* […], *op. cit.* (see note 72), p. xii.

[159]. The succession of keys reached is as follows: C major (measure 4), C minor (measure 6), C minor (measure 8), B♭ minor (measure 13), E♭ major (measure 15), F minor (measure 19), B♭ major (measure 21), G minor (measure 25), C major (measure 27), E major (measure 29), E major (measure 32).

[160]. GEMINIANI, Francesco. *Rules for Playing in a True Taste on the Violin, German Flute, Violoncello and Harpsichord, particulary the Thorough Bass Exemply'd in a Variety of Compositions on the Subjects of English, Scotch and Irish Tunes*, London, [s.n.], 1739; also 1745; ID. *A Treatise of Good Taste in the Art of Musick*; London, [s.n.], 1749; QUANTZ, Johann Joachim. *Op. cit.* (see note 10); see also GEMINIANI, Francesco. *Rules for Playing in a True Taste, Op. 8 (H. 400) – A Treatise of Good Taste in the Art of Musick (H. 401)*, edited by Peter Walls, Bologna, Ut Orpheus Edizioni, 2012 (Francesco Geminiani, Opera Omnia, 12); DART, Thurston. 'Francesco Geminiani and the Rule of Taste', in: *The Consort*, XIX (1962), pp. 122-128.

[161]. MATTHESON, Johann. *Exemplarische Organisten-Probe im Artikel vom General-Bass* […], Hamburg, Im Schiller- und Kissnerischen Buch-Laden, 1719; also as new edition Mainz, Schott, 1956; also REDDICK, Harvey P. *Johann Mattheson's Forty-Eight Thorough-Bass Test-Pieces: Translation and Commentary*, 2 vols., Ph.D. Diss., Ann Arbor (MI), University of Michigan, 1989.

[162]. BACH, Johann Sebastian. *Das Wohltemperierte Klavier I*, BWV 846-869; *II*, BWV 870-893 edited by Alfred Dürr, Kassel, Bärenreiter, 1989 and 1995 (Johann Sebastian Bach, Neue Ausgabe sämtlicher Werke, Reihe V: Klavier- und Lautenwerke, 6.1; 6.2); see also BRUYCK, Carl Debrois van. *Technische und ästhetische*

General-Bass in der Composition (Dresden, 1728)[163], and by Georg Andreas Sorge in his *Clavier-Übung* (Nuremberg, 1739 and 1742)[164], with the latter theorist guided by the circle of fifths in his arrangement of the succession of keys. The circle of fifths as the basis for a rigorous traversing of the tonal space plays an important role in the *Adagio* of Leclair's Sonata in E♭ major, Op. 9 No. 9[165], — a movement in which the composer experiments with harmonic profiles, and that beyond what has been proposed by his predecessors. In this movement, the juxtaposition of major and minor keys is superceded by an enharmonic modulation, as indicated in the change of the key signature from the initial A♭ major (in measure 1) to C♯ minor (in measure 10) and a return to A♭ major (in measure 24), with the movement ending in B♭ major. Within the tripartite division of the movement, a division suggested by the aforementioned harmonic layout, Leclair resorts to the circle of fifth (in descending motion) from A♭ major to D♭ major (in measure 5) and G♭ major (measure 6), and a conclusion on E♭ major (in measure 10) as the major incision point to Section B (measures 10-24), marked by the sudden shift of periphery, namely from the flat key (A♭ major) to the sharp key (C♯ minor, the relative minor of E major), with which Leclair signals the climax, regarding the harmonic profile, prior to the return to Section A (measures 24-32) marked by a return to the same tonal organization as in the initial Section A. While the reliance on the circle of fifth plays a prominent role in the music-theoretical discourse from the second half of the eighteenth century, especially in the disclosing of the rules of harmony, as for example in Vincenzo Manfredin's *Regole armoniche* (Venice, 1775)[166], a volume with a broad agenda devoted to basic exercises in the twenty-four keys, the fingerings of scales, the basic chord progressions, the disclosure of the rule of the octave, and the formation of cadences, Leclair, in his setting

Analysen des Wohltemperierten Klaviers: Nebst einer allgemeinen, Sebastian Bach und die sogenannte kontrapunktische Kunst betreffenden Einleitung, Leipzig, Breitkopf & Härtel, 1867; Keller, Hermann. *Das Wohltemperierte Klavier von Johann Sebastian Bach: Werk und Wiedergabe*, Kassel, Bärenreiter, 1965; Dirst, Matthew Charles. *Bach's Well-Tempered Clavier in Musical Thought and Practice, 1750-1850*, Ph.D. Diss., Stanford (CA), Stanford University, 1996; Ledbetter, David. *Bach's Well-Tempered Clavier: The 48 Preludes and Fugues*, New Haven (CT)-London, Yale University Press, 2002; Wornell Engels, Marjorie. *Bach's Well-Tempered Clavier: An Exploration of the 48 Preludes and Fugues*, Jefferson (NC), McFarland, 2006.

163. Heinichen, Johann David. *Der General-Bass in der Composition* [...], *op. cit.* (see note 125).

164. Sorge, Georg Andreas. *Clavier-Übung, in sich haltend das I. und II. halbe Dutzend*, Nürnberg, Balthasar Schmidt, [1739]; Id. *Clavier-Übung, in sich haltend das III. und IV. Halbe Dutzend*, Nürnberg, Balthasar Schmidt, [1742]; also as facsimile edition, Utrecht, Musica Repartita, 1995 and 1996; see also Miller, Franklin S. *The Keyboard Music of Georg Andreas Sorge*, Ph.D. Diss., Ypsilanti (MI), Michigan State University, 1974.

165. Leclair, Jean-Marie. *Sonatas for Violin and Basso continuo, Opus 5, Opus 9, and Opus 15, Part IV: Opus 9, Sonatas VII-XII* [...], *op. cit.* (see note 72), pp. 47-48.

166. Manfredini, Vincenzo. *Regole armoniche o sieno Precetti ragionati per apprendere li prinicipj della musica* [...], Venice, Guglielmo Zerletti, 1775. For a facsimile edition, see Id. *Regole armoniche*, Facsimile of the 1775 Venice edition with an annotated English translation by Robert Zappulla, edited by Massimiliano Sala, Turnhout, Brepols, 2013 (Musical treatises, 1). Further on Manfredini's contribution to this topic in the broader context of the eighteenth-century music-theoretical discourse, see Rasch, Rudolf. 'Vincenzo Manfredini and the Circle of Fifths', in: *ibidem*, pp. 61-72.

forth of the enharmonic modulation in the *Adagio* of the Sonata in E♭ major, Op. 9 No. 9, is undoubtedly without a precedent in either contemporary repertory or critical reception thereof. In fact, with the most unusual harmonic organization displayed in this movement, Leclair achieves a new a compositional aesthetic, heightened with an unprecedented level of emotion that contravenes the emphasis on an overriding order and rational thinking, all charateristics of Enlightenment philosophy, but replacing it with an approach to composition rooted in a more intuitive experience, with a focus on the emotions, already present in the clavichord works of C. P. E. Bach[167], and as such forecasting the anti-rational approach associated with the *Sturm and Drang* aesthetics of the late 1760s and early 1770s[168], as most prominently displayed in the instrumental writing of Haydn, with a climax of reached in his Symphony No. 45 in F♯ minor ('Abschiedssinfonie'), Hob. I/45 (composed in 1772) with its most perplexing harmonic plan unfolding within a throughcomposed form[169], in anticiaption of the Romantic era[170].

[167]. RUMMENHÖLLER, Peter. 'Carl Philipp Emanuel Bach und der Sturm-und-Drang in der Musik', in: *Sturm und Drang in Literatur und Musik: XXIX. Internationale Wissenschaftliche Arbeitstagung, Michaelstein, 11. bis 13. Mai 2001*, edited by Siegmund Bert, Blankenburg/Harz, Stiftung Kloster Michaelstein, 2004 (Michaelsteiner Konferenzberichte, 65), pp. 51-56.

[168]. EGGEBRECHT, Hans Heinrich. 'Das Ausdrucks-Prinzip im musikalischen Sturm und Drang', in: *Deutsche Vierteljahrsschrift für Literaturwissenschaft und Geistesgeschichte*, XXIX (1955), pp. 323-349; also in ID. *Das musikalische Denken: Aufsätze zur Theorie und Ästhetik der Musik*, Wilhelmshaven, Noetzel, 1977 (Taschenbücher zur Musikwissenschaft, 46); PETROBELLI, Pierluigi. 'Haydn e lo Sturm und Drang', in: *Haydn e il suo tempo: atti del convengo di studi, Siena, 28-30 agosto 1979*, Florence, Leo S. Olschki, 1984 (Chigiana, 36; n.s. 16), pp. 65-72; FINSCHER, Ludwig. 'Sturm und Drang in der Musikgeschichte', in: *Ludwig Finscher auf seiner Japan-Reise: Vorträge und Symposium*, edited by Usaburo Mabuchi, Tokyo, Academia Music & Company, 1986, pp. 111-140. Further on the relationship between *Empfindsamkeit* and *Sturm und Drang*, see, for example, RUMMENHÖLLER, Peter. 'Sprachähnlichkeit von Musik im Zeitalter der Empfindsamkeit und des Sturm und Drang', in: *Musiktheorie*, edited by Helga de la Motte-Haber and Oliver Schwab-Felisch, Laaber, Laaber-Verlag, 2005 (Handbuch der systematischen Musikwissenschaft, 2), pp. 127-138.

[169]. For a detailed analysis of the harmonic plan and the overriding formal construct, see WEBSTER, James. *Haydn's 'Farewell' Symphony and the Idea of Classical Style: Through-Composition and Cyclic Integration in His Instrumental Music*, Cambridge-New York, Cambridge University Press, 1991 (Cambridge studies in music theory and analysis); see also TODD, R. Larry. 'Joseph Haydn and the Sturm und Drang: A Reevaluation', in: *The Music Review*, XLI/3 (August 1980), pp. 172-186; BONDS, Mark Evan. 'Haydn's «cours complet de la composition» and the Sturm und Drang', in: *Haydn Studies*, edited by W. Dean Sutcliffe, Cambridge-New York, Cambridge University Press, 1998, pp. 152-176; WEBSTER, James. 'Haydns Symphonik zwischen «Sturm und Drang» und «Wiener Klassik»: Zur Ästhetik der gehobenen Unterhaltungsmusik', in: *Das symphonische Werk Joseph Haydns: Referate des Internationalen Musikwissenschaftlichen Symposions Eisenstadt, 13.-15. September 1995*, edited by Gerhard J. Winkler, Eisenstadt, Burgenländisches Landesmuseum, 2000 (Wissenschaftliche Arbeiten aus dem Burgenland, 103), pp. 79-101; GRIM, William Edward. *Haydn's Sturm und Drang Symphonies: Form and Meaning*, Lewiston (NY), Edwin Mellen Press, 1990 (Studies in the history and interpretation of music, 23); KRONES, Hartmut. 'Annotationen zum Sturm und Drang bei Joseph Haydn', in: *Sturm und Drang in Literatur und Musik* […], *op. cit.* (see note 167), pp. 109-122.

[170]. BROOK, Barry S. 'Sturm und Drang and the Romantic Period in Music', in: *Studies in Romanticism*, IX/4 (January 1970), pp. 269-284.

Notwithstanding the vastness of approaches displayed in the aforementioned *Quatre livres de sonates*, the examination of this extensive body of chamber music is not suggestive of a grouping of the repertory according to the all too often cited classification concerning an early period, a middle period, and a late period of composition[171], so readily relied upon. In his comprehensive entry on Jean-Marie Leclair prepared for the *New Grove Dictionary*, Neal Zaslaw cautions that

> […] one cannot speak of an 'early' or 'late' style in Leclair's music. His remarkably consistent style was as advanced in 1723 as it was outmoded in 1753. Although none of his works can be dated other than by the *terminus ad quem* provided by their first publication, there is some evidence that Leclair, like Corelli[172], composed the bulk of his music early in his career and published it little by little; the increase in harmonic complexity found by Preston[173] in the four books of violin sonatas is perhaps due to Leclair's preferring to publish the less problematic works first[174].

The uniformity of Leclair to which Zaslaw alludes here pertains to the composer's overall consistency with regard to the conciseness of his melodies captured within the *tactus*, a hallmark of the *stile galante*, with the brevity of phrases providing an ideal platform for the *Fortspinnungstechnik*, often with careful attention to melodic sequences, which in turn are placed within the corresponding unfolding of the consistent overall diatonic frame, which Leclair enlivens frequently with carefully controlled chromaticism. As far as the publications of this repertory are concerned, Leclair, in his particular assembling of the individual sonatas for publication may indeed point to an interest in music pedagogy, with such interest perhaps kindled by the famous violin virtuoso, Pietro Antonio Locatelli[175]. Locatelli's music, which enjoyed wide dissemination in prints across Europe[176], may indeed have provided some inspiration for Leclair. Here, Locatelli's Opus 3, the *Arte del violino* of 1734[177], a collection

---

[171]. The first composer to suggest such a classification scheme of his musical compositions is Ludwig van Beethoven, and that in a letter to Bernhard Schotts Söhne in Mainz, dated Vienna, 22 January 1825; see BEETHOVEN, Ludwig van. *Briefwechsel – Gesamtausgabe*, 8 vols., edited by Sieghard Brandenburg, Munich, G. Henle, 1996, vol. VI, *1825-1827*, pp. 10 and 127 (no. 1925). The autograph of this letter is preserved at the Stadtbibliothek in Mainz.

[172]. See, for example, RINALDI, Mario. *Arcangelo Corelli*, Milan, Edizioni Curci, 1903; PINCHERLE, Marc. *Corelli et son temps*, Paris, Le Bon Plaisir, 1954 (Amour de la musique).

[173]. LECLAIR, Jean-Marie. *Sonatas for Violin and Basso continuo* […], *op. cit.* (see note 72).

[174]. ZASLAW, Neal. 'Leclair', in: *The New Grove Dictionary* […], *op. cit.* (see note 79), vol. XIV, p. 446.

[175]. DUNNING, Albert. *Pietro Antonio Locatelli: Der Virtuose und seine Welt*, 2 vols., Buren, Frits Knuf, 1981.

[176]. LOCATELLI, Pietro Antonio. *Catalogo tematico, lettere, documenti & iconografia*, edited by Albert Dunning, Mainz, Schott, 2001 (Locatelli complete edition, 10); see also MORABITO, Fulvia. 'Locatelli, Pietro Antonio', in: *Die Musik in Geschichte und Gegenwart* […], *op. cit.* (see note 79), *Personenteil*, vol. XI (2004), cols. 357-362: 359-360.

[177]. LOCATELLI, Pietro Antonio. *L'arte del violino: 12 Concerti cioè, violino solo, con 24 Capricci ad libitum* […], Amsterdam, Michel-Charles le Cène, *con privilegio*, plate no. 572/573. For an inventory of this *opus*, see

of twelve violin concertos[178] modelled after Vivaldi's concertos, and twenty-four caprices, *ad libitum*[179], in its exceptionally broad conception, what Fulvia Morabito has considered as a *Kunstbuch*[180], focussed on the vast gamut of technical and expressive dimensions bridging the spheres of composition and performance[181]. These observations indeed further substantiate Zaslaw's aforementioned comments and in turn explain Leclair's written annotations, though often decisively brief in nature. Readily available in reprints[182], Locatelli's Opus 3, owing to its fusion of creative facets and pedagogical vision, was attractive not only to Leclair but also to a broader audience, as this publication paved the future for nineteenth-century repertories, with their focus on virtuosity. This claim in turn is substantiated from the numerous editions of Locatelli's Capriccios from Opus 3, which appeared during the early nineteenth century[183] and beyond[184].

DUNNING, Albert. *Pietro Antonio Locatelli: Der Virtuose* [...], *op. cit.* (see note 175), vol. II, pp. 47-59.

[178]. The *Violino principale* of the Concerto No. 4 in E major is also preserved in manuscript Stockholm, Kunglige Musikaliska Akademien; the remaining manuscript parts of this concerto are no longer extant; see DUNNING, Albert. *Pietro Antonio Locatelli: Der Virtuose* [...], *op. cit.* (see note 175), vol. II, p. 55.

[179]. Beyond that, the *24 Capricci* are also transmitted in manuscript Paris, Bibliothèque nationale Vm⁷ 1686, Capriccios 1-24, comprising only the violon solo part without the resolution of the abbreviations; see *ibidem*, p. 55.

[180]. MORABITO, Fulvia. 'Editorial', in: *Ad Parnassum: A Journal of Eighteenth- and Nineteenth-Century Instrumental Music*, XI/23 (April 2014), pp. v-ix: vi.

[181]. PORTA, Enzo. 'La tecnica violinistica dell'*Arte del violino* di Pietro Antonio Locatelli', in: *Intorno a Locatelli: studi in occasione del tricentenario della nascita di Pietro Antonio Locatelli (1695-1764)*, edited by Albert Dunning, 2 vols., Lucca, LIM, 1995 (Speculum musicae 1), vol. II, pp. 879-952.

[182]. (a) *L'Arte del violino: XII Concerti cioè, violino solo, con XXIV Capricci ad libitum* [...] *Opera terza*, Paris, Le Clerc le cadet-Le Clerc-Mme. Boivin, gravé par le Sr. Huë, [1742]; with the violoncello solo part preserved in Den Hague, Gemeente Museum; (b) *L'Arte del violino: XII Concerti cioè, violino solo, con XXIV Capricci ad libitum* [...] *Opera terza*, Paris, Au Bureau du Journal de musique, gravé par le Sr. Huë, [c1773], with only the violoncello solo part extant, with copy preserved in Bergamo, Istituto musicale Gaetano Donizetti; (c) *L'arte de violino: XII Concerti con XXIV capricci ad libitum* [...] *Opera terza*, Paris, Des Lauriers, [c1781], with only the violoncello solo part extant, with copy preserved in London, British Library (*olim* British Museum); see DUNNING, Albert. *Pietro Antonio Locatelli: Der Virtuose* [...], *op. cit.* (see note 175), vol. II, p. 54.

[183]. (a) *Le Labyrinthe. Caprice énematique du célèbre Locatelli, portant cette devise: facilis aditus, difficilis exitus*, preserved in Paris, Bibliothèque nationale, in printed collection of violin pieces by Michel Woldemar (includes Locatelli, Capriccio No. 23), presumably part of WOLDEMAR, Michel. *Études élémentaires du violon dédié à J. B. Cartier*, Paris, Cousineau père & fils, *c*1800. These *Études* contain an edition of the Capriccio No. 23 «arrange pour deux violins, par Woldemar»; the second violin part contains the heading «Rève de l'auteur»; (b) *Caprices intitulé L'art du Violon composés par P. Locatelli. Nouvelle édition dediée aux mânes de J. B. Viotti*, Paris, J. Frey, [1824]; with rare copy preserved in Zürich, Zaentralbibliothek, Collection Erwin Jacobi; (c) CHORON, Alexandre(-Étienne) – SALA, Nicola. *Principes de composition des écoles d'Italie* [...], Paris, Alphonse Leduc, 1808, vol. III, p. 330ff (includes Locatelli, Capriccios Nos. 3 and 4); (d) CARTIER, Jean-Baptiste. *L'Art du violon* [...] *seconde edition, revue et corrigée*, Paris, [s.n.], ²1798, p. 280 (includes Locatelli, Capriccio No. 4). According to Dunning, the indications, such as «Arpeggio del diavolo» in Michel Woldemar's *Études* point to a decisively romanticized version; see DUNNING, Albert. *Pietro Antonio Locatelli: Der Virtuose* [...], *op. cit.* (see note 175), p. 56.

[184]. (a) LOCATELLI, Pietro Antonio. *Vingt-six Caprices. Enseignement complet du violon*, edited by Georges Catherine, Paris, Alphonse Leduc, [1919]; contains Capriccios Nos. 1-24 of Op. 3 and the solo violin part

Within the *Quatre livres de sonates pour violon* of Leclair, we notice a gradual increase in attention to details pertaining to a steady broadening of the harmonic language, especially with regard to a decisive application of chromaticism, thereby redefining the relationship between diatonicism and chromaticism, initiated by Leclair himself, with this equilibrium coming to full fruition only during the mid-nineteenth century. In an era characterized by the pre-eminence and resultant codification of the French style of composition[185], a development which many non-French musicians saw as an impediment to their overall approach and enjoyment of the repertoire of the *ancien régime*[186], Leclair indeed appears to

---

of last movement of Locatelli, Concerto No. 12 in D major, Op. 3 as well as the 'Capriccio Prova del intonatione' from the Sonata No. 12 in D minor, Op. 6 (*12 Sonate a violino solo e basso da camera*); (b) ID. *L'arte del violino, 25 Capricci*, edited by Romeo Franzoni, Milan, Ricordi, [1920]; contains Capriccios Nos. 1-24 of Op. 3 and the 'Capriccio Prova del intonatione' from the Sonata No. 12 in D minor, Op. 6; (c) ID. *L'Art du violon, 25 Caprices pour violon seul*, revised edition by Edouard Nadaud, Paris, Costallat, [c1920]; same content as under (b); (d) ID. *25 Caprices pour violon* [...], transcription for Alto by Léon Raby, Op. 77, Leipzig, Hofmeister, 1937; same content as under (c); see DUNNING, Albert. *Pietro Antonio Locatelli: Der Virtuose* [...], *op. cit.* (see note 175), vol. II, p. 56. Beyond that, Dunning has identified a number of publications which contain only selected pieces of Locatelli: (a) DAVID, Ferdinand. *Die hohe Schule des Violinspiels: Werke berühmter Meister des 17. und 18. Jahrhunderts, zum Gebrauch am Conservatorium der Musik in Leipzig und zum öffentlichen Vortrag 1, No. 1-10*, Leipzig, Breitkopf & Härtel, 1860; includes Capriccio No. 23; (b) ID. *Capriccio No. 7 per violino con accompagnamento di pianoforte*, edited by Luigi Cornago, Milan, Camista, 1941; (c) ID. *3 Stücke für Violine und Klavier frei bearbeitet*, edited by Paul Klengel, Berlin, Nikolaus Simrock, 1919; contains the *Andante* (third movement) from Sonata No. 12 in A minor, Op. 6 and the *Allegro* (second movement) from the Sonata No. 2 in F major, Op. 6; also the Capriccio No. 23 from Op. 3 (with an added piano part); (d) ID. *Suite für Violine allein*, edited by Florizel von Reuter, [s.l.], Eulenburg, [s.d.], contains arrangement of six Capriccios; (e) ID. *Le Labyrinthe de l'harmonie, pour violon seul*, edited by Delphin Alard, Mainz, Schott, [s.d.] (Maitres classiques du violon, 25); (f) LONGO, Alessandro. *Biblioteca d'oro*, Milan, Ricordi, [s.d.], vol. III, No. 4; contains Capriccio No. 23 from Op. 3 in an arrangement for piano; (g) WITTING, Carl. *Die Kunst des Violinspiels: Eine Sammlung der besten Werke für dieses Instrument von Corelli (1653) bis auf unsere Zeit*, 2 vols., Wolfenbüttel, L. Holle, [s.d.]; contains Capriccios Nos. 2, 4, 12, 15, 16, 18, 21, 22 of Op. 3; (h) *Studien für die Violine aus der ältesten und älteren Zeit*, edited by Karl Böhmer, Berlin-Posen, Bote & Bock, [s.d.], Verlagsnummer 9500, Heft 1, Nos. 1-6; contains Capriccio Nos. 14, 7, 12, 19, 18 from Op. 3; see DUNNING, Albert. *Pietro Antonio Locatelli: Der Virtuose* [...], *op. cit.* (see note 175), vol. II, pp. 56-57.

[185]. Further on this topic, see, for example, PRICE, Charles Gower. *The Codification and Perseverance of a French National Style of Instrumental Composition Between 1687 and 1737: Montéclair's Serenade au concert (1697)*, Ph.D. Diss., Stanford (CA), Stanford University, 1973; see also BATES, Carol Henry. 'The Early French Sonatas for Solo Instruments: A Study in Diversity', in: *Recherches sur la musique française classique*, XXVII (1991/1992), pp. 71-98.

[186]. Further on this topic, see MCCLARY, Susan. 'Temporality and Ideology: Qualities of Motion in Seventeenth-Century French Music', in: *Structures of Feeling in Seventeenth-Century Cultural Expression*, edited by Susan McClary, Toronto-Buffalo, University of Toronto Press in association with the UCLA Center, 2013 (UCLA Center Clark Library series, 14), pp. 315-337; also in: *Echo. A Music-Centered Journal*, II/2 (Fall 2000) [online]; see also BRENET, Michel. *Les concerts en France sous l'Ancien Régime*, Paris, Librairie Fischbacher, 1970; SAINT-ARROMAN, Jean. *L'interprétation de la musique française, 1661-1789*, Paris, H. Champion, 1983; ÉLART,

have provided a response to the one-sidedness of seventeenth-century French repertoire, indeed suggesting a compositional alternative to this longstanding practice. With his *Quatre livres de sonates* Leclair has left an important legacy on French soil, both as a composer in his fusion of the Italian and French national styles and as a noted violin virtuoso — thus exhibiting qualities which were captured in the writings of contemporaries, among them the theorist, composer and violoncellist Charles-Henri Blainville. In his *L'ésprit de l'art musical* (Paris, 1754)[187], a volume devoted to the reflection upon the dichotomy between melody and harmony, Blainville, familiar with the *basso continuo* practice of Corelli[188], refers to Leclair as «the Corelli of France»[189], obviously in paying tribute to Leclair's emulation of Corelli's style on French soil[190]. Indeed, in this respect, Leclair is not the sole composer with a prominent orientation towards Corelli, but follows the footsteps of Locatelli, who continued the tradition established by Corelli[191], with Corelli, an enthusiastic champion of the French style[192], on occasion adopting the *stile mixtus* in the juxtaposition of French and Italian compositional practices[193]. Here, Leclair embraces the tradition of two ardent

Joann. *Musiciens et repertoires de concert en France à la fin de l'Ancien régime*, Ph.D. Diss., Rouen, Université de Rouen, 2005.

[187]. BLAINVILLE, Charles-Henri. *L'ésprit de l'art musical, ou réflexions sur la musique, et ses differentes parties*, Geneva, Charles-Henri Blainville, 1754.

[188]. BOUVIER, Xavier. 'Response à la critique de Rameau des basses de Corelli: Un manuscript inédit de Charles-Henri Blainville (1711-c1777)', in: *Schweizer Jahrbuch für Musikwissenschaft*, Neue Folge 18 (1998), pp. 181-208 [issue: *Jean-Jacques Rousseau und sein Umfeld*]; see also PEYROT, J. 'Un tentative pour créer un nouveau mode au XVIIIe siècle: Charles-Henri Blainville et le mode mixte', in: *La Tribune de Saint Gervais*, XVII/12 (1911), pp. 281-286.

[189]. «Le Corelli de la France»; BLAINVILLE, Charles-Henri. *Op. cit.* (see note 187).

[190]. Further on the dissemination of Corelli's compositional practice in France, see, for example, PINCHERLE, Marc. 'Corelli et la France', in: *Studi Corelliani: atti del Primo congresso internazionale, Fusignano, 5-8 settembre 1968*, edited by Adriano Cavicchi, Florence, Leo S. Olschki, 1972 (Quaderni della RIdM, 3), pp. 13-18; VAN HEYGHEN, Peter. 'De Corelli van Frankrijk: Les Muffatti wept licht op', in: *Tijdschrift oude Muziek*, XXV/3 (August 2010), pp. 10-14; see also SPAMPINATO, Graziella. *A. Corelli e il suo influsso sulla scuola del Settecento*, thesis, Catania, Università degli studi di Catania, 1970.

[191]. Further on the continuation of the compositional traditions of Corelli in the oeuvre of Locatelli, see, for example, LEPORE, Angela. 'La sonata a tre in ambito Corelliano', in: *Intorno a Locatelli […], op. cit.* (see note 181), vol. II, pp. 527-599. Curiously enough, Lepore does not mention Leclair and his close association with the oeuvre of Corelli.

[192]. FERREIRA, Manuel Pedro. 'The «French Style» and Corelli', in: *Studi Corelliani V […], op. cit.* (see note 136), pp. 379-391.

[193]. Further on the *stilus mixtus* in Corelli's oeuvre, see, for example, ALLSOP, Peter. '«Da camera e da ballo — alla francese et all'italiana»: Functional and National Distinctions in Corelli's sonate da camera', in: *Early Music*, XXVI/1 (February 1998), pp. 87-96. Further on the coexistence of French and Italian styles, see MORCHE, Gunther. 'Corelli und Lully: Über den Nationalstil', in: *Nuovi studi Corelliani […], op. cit.* (see note 121), pp. 65-78.

admirers of Corelli, namely, George Frideric Handel[194] and Telemann[195], both of whom adopted Corelli's style of composition in some of their own music[196]. Undoubtedly, the influence of Corelli was felt beyond these composers, as J. S. Bach in the slow movements of his concertos must have drawn some inspiration from the older master[197].

In his *Historisch-Kritische Beyträge* (Berlin, 1754-1760), Marpurg, versed in both the *basso continuo* practice[198] and the *stile galante*[199], includes a reference to Leclair «who is acknowledged in France as one of the first violinists»[200], presumably reflecting on a number of Leclair's activities in Paris, including the publication of his *Premier livre de sonates*, dedicated to his patron Joseph Bonnier in 1723[201], and Leclair's debut with his own works in the Concert spirituel in 1728[202], and that following his concertizing in London and Kassel[203], where the Landgrave Carl von Hesse-Kassel had maintained a Hofkapelle[204], and finally his sojourn in Holland where he could have encountered Locatelli in 1741[205].

[194]. ZASLAW, Neal. 'Handel and Leclair', in: *Current Musicology*, no. 9 (Fall 1969), pp. 183-189; see also McGRADY, Richard E. 'Corelli's Violin Sonatas and the Ornamentation of Handel's Recorder Sonatas', in: *Recorder and Music*, III (1971), pp. 357-359; EDWARDS, Owan. 'The Response to Corelli's Music in Eighteenth-Century England', in: *Studia musicologica norvegica*, II (1976), pp. 51-96.

[195]. FINSCHER, Ludwig. 'Corelli und die «Corellisierenden Sonaten» Telemanns', in: *Studi Corelliani* […], *op. cit.* (see note 190), pp. 75-95; see also SCHENK, Erich. 'Corelli und Telemann', in: *Accademia musicale Chigiana*, XXIV (1967), pp. 79-95; CHANG, Young-Shim. *Italian Influences in the 'Corellisierenden Sonaten' of Telemann*, M.M. Thesis, Denton (TX), University of North Texas, 1995.

[196]. In his Concerti grossi Op. 6, Handel adopted the older Concerti Op. 6 of Corelli as a model; see also KEYM, Stefan. 'Händel und die Sonatentradition Corellis', in: *Händel-Jahrbuch*, LVI (2010), pp. 289-313.

[197]. On the alleged influence of Corelli upon Johann Sebastian Bach, see, for example, SACKMANN, Dominik. 'Bachs langsame Konzertsätze unter dem Einfluß von Arcangelo Corelli: Vom Ostinatoprinzip zum Primat der expressiven Solostimme', in: *Bach und die Stile* […], *op. cit.* (see note 26), pp. 303-326.

[198]. See, for example, SHELDON, David A. *Marpurg's Thoroughbass and Composition Handbook: A Narrative Translation and Critical Study*, Stuyvesant (NY), Pendragon Press, 1989 (Harmonologia series, 2).

[199]. *Ibidem.*

[200]. «[…] welcher nunmehr in Frankreich für einen der ersten Violinisten paßiret»; as cited in: MARPURG, Friedrich Wilhelm. *Historisch-Kritische Beyträge* […], *op. cit.* (see note 87), vol. 1, p. 236; English translation by Walter Kurt Kreyszig.

[201]. LECLAIR, Jean-Marie. *Sonatas for Violin and Basso continuo, Opus 1* […], *op. cit.* (see note 72), p. xiii.

[202]. PIERRE, Constant. *Histoire du Concert spirituel, 1725-1790*, Paris, Société Française de Musicologie, 1975, ²2000 (Publications de la Société Françaises de Musicologie, III/3).

[203]. Further on Leclair's stay in Kassel, see LUSTIG, Jacob Wilhelm. *Rijk gestoffeerd verhaal van de eigenlijke gesteldheid der hedendaagsche Toonkunst, of Karel Burneys (Doctor in de Muziekkunde)* […], Groningen, J. Oomeskens, 1786, p. 389, article 168; also cited in LOCATELLI, Pietro Antonio. *Catalogo tematico* […], *op. cit.* (see note 176), p. 145; also in DUNNING, Albert. *Pietro Antonio Locatelli: Der Virtuose* […], *op. cit.* (see note 175), vol. 1, p. 119.

[204]. ENGELBRECHT, Christiane. 'Die Hofkapelle des Landgrafen Carl von Hessen-Kassel', in: *Zeitschrift des Vereins für Hessische Geschichte und Landeskunde*, LXVIII (1957), pp. 141-173.

[205]. There is no evidence concerning this encounter (see the articles by Rudolf Rasch and Neal Zaslaw in this volume).

Beyond that, in an era of emphasis placed upon the institutionalization of the curriculum in music in France[206], Leclair's founding of the French violin school, as the ideal platform for the teaching of repertory and technique, including the exploration of performance practice issues related to his own oeuvre, drew further notoriety to his contribution as a composer and performing artist, to which several reviewers alluded in their respective comments. François-Joseph Fétis remarked that

> Leclair was a genuine artist at heart. Proof of this claim comes from the trip which he made to Holland in order to meet Locatelli, although he [Leclair] was no longer younger. The innovations with which the Italian violinist shared with him [Leclair] were not without influence on his [Leclair's] taste, as one detects traces in his posthumous oeuvre of his sonatas published by his wife [...][207].

Evidence concerning the longevity of Leclair's fame through at least the mid-nineteenth century is provided in a lengthy homage by Maurice Bourges, who assures his readers of his *Souvenirs* an important niche for Leclair, based on a letter from Leclair's hand, when he writes that

> In my papers I found again a letter of the poor and famous Leclair, and I want to secure him a niche in my Souvenirs. This [document] is an homage to the sincere friendship that has united us for a long time. Some day I shall relate the mysterious and tragic end of this musician, so distinguished by [his] heart and talent. Leclair was a genuine artist passionate about the violin like hardly anyone else, with a soul also pure, also as candid as that of Corelli, incapable of jealousy, an enthusiast with regard to the merit of his rivals. The letter which I have inserted in these Memoires was addressed to my by Leclair during his stay in Amsterdam. This [letter] gives the impression of the good faith of this great home in his relationships with his followers; this [letter] captures a moment of the simplicity of his heart. Here, I transcribe this letter in such a manner as his [i.e. Leclair's] hand has drawn it[208].

---

206. See, for example, GESSELE, Cynthia. *The Institutionalization of Music Theory in France, 1764-1802*, Ph.D. Diss., Princeton (NJ), Princeton University, 1989.

207. «Leclair était un véritable artiste de cœur; on en a la preuve par le voyage qu'il fit en Hollande pour entendre Locatelli, quoiqu'il ne fût déjà plus jeune. Les nouveautés que lui fit connaître le violoniste italien ne furent pas sans influence sur son goût: on en remarque des traces dans l'oeuvre posthume de ses sonates publié par sa femme [...]»; as cited in FÉTIS, François-Joseph. *Biographie universelle des musiciens et bibliographie générale de la musique*, 8 vols., Brussels, Leroux, 1835-1844, vol. v, p. 245; English translation by Walter Kurt Kreyszig.

208. «Je retrouve dans mes papiers une lettre du malheureux et célèbre Leclair, et je veux lui donner d'une place dans mes Souvenirs. C'est un hommage rendu à la sincere amitié qui nous a si longtemps unis; je raconterai quelque jour la fin mystérieuse et tragique de ce musicien si distingué par le cœur et le talent. Leclair a été un artiste véritable, passionné pour le violon comme on ne l'est guère, d'une âme aussi pure, aussi candide que celle de Corelli, incapable de jalousie, enthousiaste du mérite de ses rivaux. La lettre

On the whole, reviewers concentrate their remarks foremost on the notoriety of Leclair as a performing musician. Nevertheless, as Fétis noted, Leclair's fame undoubtedly exceeded beyond his virtuosity, linked directly to his important contributions as a composer. Indeed, the latter role of Leclair has received little attention in nineteenth-century literature. Sir John Hawkins, as one of the principal promoters of a new era of music historical discourse beginning in the second half of the eighteenth cenutury[209], acknowledges the close affinity between Leclair's two spheres of activities, when he remarks that «Le Clair [sic] is celebrated for the spirit and energy of his manual performance, and these compositions are in some sort a proof of it»[210]. Although in his comments, Hawkins refers to Leclair's Six Sonatas for two violins and bass, Op. IV[211], engraved by Madame Leclair, as one example selected from Leclair's substantial instrumental oeuvre[212], this reciprocal interaction between performance and compositional practice most definitely also pertains to Leclair's *Quatre livres de sonates pour violin*, the fourth volume of which was engraved by Leclair's wife, with this body of chamber music chartering the course for early nineteenth-century harmonic practices.

que j'ai insère dans ces Mémoires me fut adressée par Leclair pendant son séjour à Amsterdam; elle donne l'idée de la bonne foi de cet excellent homme dans ses relations avec ses émules; c'est un monument de la simplicité de son cœur. Je transcris ici cette lettre telle que sa main l'a tracée»; as cited in BOURGES, Maurice. 'Souvenir d'un octagenaire — Chapitre VI', in: *Revue et Gazette musicale*, XII/30 (13 July 1845), pp. 240-245; also in: LOCATELLI, Pietro Antonio. *Catalogo tematico* […], *op. cit.* (see note 176), pp. 233-237: 233; DUNNING, Albert. *Pietro Antonio Locatelli: Der Virtuose* […], *op. cit.* (see note 175), vol. I, p. 328; see also NOSKE, Frits. 'En chirughisch avontuur toegeschrieven aan Pietro Locatelli', in: *Mens en Melodie*, IX (1954), pp. 255-257.

[209]. For an overview of this discourse focussed on the continuous unfolding of historiography, as promoted in the writings of the aforementioned Burney; see, for example, HEGAR, Elisabeth. *Die Anfänge der neueren Musikgeschichtsschreibung um 1770 bei Gerbert, Burney und Hawkins*, Strasbourg, Heitz & Co., 1932 (Sammlung musikwissenschaftlicher Abhandlungen/Collection d'études musicologiques, 7).

[210]. HAWKINS, John, sir. *A General History of the Science and Practice of Music*, 2 vols., London, J. Alfred Novello, 1853, vol. II, p. 900.

[211]. LECLAIR, Jean-Marie. *Sonates en trio pour deux violons et la basse continue*, Op. 4 (c1730).

[212]. See footnote 67.

Dialogues, Duels, Diets: Leclair, the French Violin School, and the 2-Violin Repertoire

Guillaume Tardif
(Edmonton, AB)

Introduction

Two hundred and fifty years have passed since the deaths of violinists-composers Pietro Antonio Locatelli (1695-1764) and Jean-Marie Leclair *l'aîné* (1697-1764)[1]. The following chart shows how their published productions share many similarities in time, volume, and genre:

	Locatelli	Leclair
1720-1730	Op. 1 *concerti grossi*	Opp. 1-2 *sonatas*
1730-1740	Opp. 2-6 *sonatas, concerti ('L'arte del violino'), ouvertures, trios*	Opp. 3-8 *duets, sonatas, trios, concerti, récréations de musique (trios)*
1740-1750	Opp. 7-8 *concerti, trios*	Opp. 9-10 *concerti, sonatas, opera (Scylla and Glaucus)*, Op. 12 *duets*
1750-1760		Op. 13 *overtures and trios*
1760-1770	Op. 9 *concerti*	Opp. 14-15 (posth.) *trio sonata and solo sonata*

In contrast to Locatelli, Leclair wrote many duets — or, to be exact, *Sonates à deux violons sans basse* (two sets of 6 sonatas, Opp. 3 and 12). These duets are many a modern violinist's introduction to the 'founder of the French violin school'[2]. Leclair's duets, historically among the first in the genre, are a cornerstone of today's duet concert programs — for example when colleagues visit each other and perform together to signify *dialogue*, or otherwise stage friendly *duels*[3].

---

[1]. Leclair was mysteriously stabbed and killed at his home on 22 October 1764.

[2]. An expression generally used. See Zaslaw, Neal. 'Leclair, Jean-Marie', in: *Grove Music Online*, at <http://www.oxfordmusiconline.com>, accessed 13 December 2014.

[3]. To this day, such *dueling* events still occur, such as the recent 'Dueling Strads' concert featuring music by Leclair, Frolov, Moszkowski and others, played by 'duelists' Vladimir Gluzman and Philippe Quint; this

A comprehensive study of the violin duet genre has apparently not yet been written, nor has a comprehensive catalogue of duets been compiled. What do we know about the genre and Leclair's duets in particular? How did the genre evolve over time? Taking Leclair and the beginnings of the French violin school in the first half of the 1700s as starting point, this study will examine the duet repertoire from Leclair to Ysaÿe. It offers an opportunity to consider important aspects of the genre with regard to history, composition, style, creativity, and pedagogy. To conclude this discussion, a working catalogue of duets, organized according to a genealogical principle (i.e. 'schools', or clusters of artists related to a teacher), may serve as a basis for further research.

THE DUET REPERTOIRE: NEGLECTED BUT SIGNIFICANT

Duets have generally stood in the shadow of other genres like the trio sonata, the concerto, or the 'solo accompanied' repertoire. A survey of the repertoire however shows that duets are very present throughout the history of the violin. In fact, nearly *every* violinist-composer since the early 18th century[4] has written for two unaccompanied violins[5]. Therefore, to study the 2-violin duet repertoire from a genealogical perspective[6], with Leclair at its root, represents an opportunity to take a fresh look at the history of the instrument.

Duet writing and duet playing are creative practices that have been cultivated across Europe, from one generation of violinists to the next. However, considering that the genre appears to emerge with French violinists in the second quarter of the 18th century, with uninterrupted threads from Leclair to Eugène Ysaÿe, it is not unreasonable to cast Leclair as a pioneer and leader in the genre, and the duet as being prominently associated with the French violin school. In other words, the violin duet stands as a legacy of the French violin school.

The duet is essentially the smallest chamber music ensemble and obviously implies the notion of collaboration and cooperation, or 'dialogue'. Considering the collegial relationship and the teacher-student relationship, this collaboration may take place between players of the same generation or across generations[7]. However, when two violinists play side-by-side, the audience is also presented with the question of differential appreciation or

---

event was sponsored by the Strad Society and the Chicago dealer Bein & Fushi (2013 Catalogue). We note here that duet playing is not part of national or international violin competitions.

    4.   That is, since the times of Stradivari (1644-1737) and Guarneri (1698-1744).

    5.   Corelli, Locatelli, Tartini, Vivaldi, and later, Vieuxtemps and Sarasate are notable exceptions of composers who apparently left us no duets.

    6.   Allegorically, the teacher and student can be described as an interdependent 'duet' relationship.

    7.   Some older, established players will at times feature a much younger student in a duet performance, communicating over a generational gap.

comparison; therefore, duets also naturally evoke competition, or 'duel', and emulation[8]. These notions extend into the pedagogical context, or pedagogical 'diet', and to the question of creativity[9].

Just as basso continuo may consist of any number and type of bass instruments, baroque duets often imply versatility: violin duets could quite easily be played on other treble instruments ('double treble'), as long as proper attention is given to the limits of each instrument's range. Flutes, oboes, or treble viols ('dessus') are often listed as possible alternatives to violins — though wind instruments cannot play double-stops. Witness to a time of transition from older to newer instruments, Leclair indicated that his duets could be played on viols or on violins. Composers writing duets in this manner could hope to reach a significantly larger amateur market interested in enjoyable musical conversations. Furthermore, as a tool to support method instruction, duet writing was generally regarded as very useful.

In his time, Leclair perfected a genre that can be regarded as an ideal mixture of Italian and French influences, in the spirit of Couperin's 'Les Goûts-Réunis' (1724). After his early training as dancer and violinist in Lyons and Turin, Leclair established himself in Paris, where he took compositional lessons with André Chéron (student of Bernier, a colleague of Charpentier)[10]. Chéron apparently helped Leclair design bass lines for his first two sets of 12 Sonatas Op. 1 (1723) and Op. 2 (1728)[11]. This training must have been particularly important when Leclair tackled the challenge of his 'senza basso' duets Op. 3 (1730)[12], which we assume he started writing during his study leave with violinist Giovanni Battista Somis (student of Corelli)[13] in Turin. Somis apparently held the duet genre in high

---

[8]. A vocal musical tradition in Brazil is based on 'poetic duel'. See TRAVASSOS, Elizabeth. 'Ethics in the Sung Duels of North-Eastern Brazil: Collective Memory and Contemporary Practice', in: *British Journal of Ethnomusicology*, IX/1 (2000), pp. 61-94: 69. Extended to the violin, it calls for aggressive playing, in close imitation (e.g. CERVO, Dimitri. *Três Momentos Brasileiros* for 2 violins, 2007).

[9]. Duet as '*do-it*'.

[10]. See MONTAGNIER, Jean-Paul. 'Bernier, Nicolas', in: *Grove Music Online, op. cit.* (see note 2).

[11]. Op. 1 was first published in 1723; Op. 2 was first published in 1728. According to Laurencie, La Borde mentions that the bass might have been provided by Chéron himself, a statement that Robert Preston contests, saying that Leclair instead learned mostly through observation. See LECLAIR, Jean-Marie. *Sonatas for Violin and Basso Continuo, Op. 5, Op. 9, Op. 15*, edited by Robert E. Preston, 4 vols., New Haven, A-R Editions, 1968-1971 (Recent researches in the music of the baroque era, 4-5, 10-11).

[12]. Op. 4 (also published in 1730) focuses on trio sonatas; Opp. 5-8 were published during the period 1734-1737.

[13]. Leclair's own performance style was generally contrasted with his more showy Italian counterparts (Leclair *vs* Locatelli, or Leclair *vs* Guignon). Lustig suggested that Leclair's playing was that «of an angel», in contrast to the 'devilish' Locatelli, see ZASLAW, Neal. 'Leclair, Jean-Marie', *op. cit.* (see note 2). This however did not mean that Leclair's playing style was less than vigorous. His playing was reported to be «surprisingly vigorous for his age»; see LA LAURENCIE, Lionel de. *L'école française de violon de Lully à Viotti: études d'histoire et d'esthétique*, 3 vols., Paris, Delagrave, 1922-1924, Rpt. 3 vols., Geneva, Minkoff, 1971, vol. I, p. 314. While it is possible that Leclair's manner was by and large more attuned to the softer manner of viols still in favor in France

regard and might have inspired Leclair to develop his own duets during that time. Somis' own later set of duets, *Ideali trattimenti da camera* (1747, pub. Paris, 1750)[14] suggests — without further explanation by the author –that the duet genre features an ideal balance (or 'treatment') for both players. These duets are ideally conversational, accessible, versatile, rewarding, and simply ideal for all occasions.

CHARACTERISTICS OF LECLAIR'S DUETS

Leclair writes tuneful 'sonates' (which he also calls 'duos')[15] that clearly embrace the Corellian tradition[16] and often remind of Couperin and Rameau[17]. As a subgenre of the solo or trio sonata[18], the *sonate à deux violons* is a multi-movement work (usually fast/slow/fast, with the occasional slow introduction) in one main key[19]. They occasionally feature French dances (e.g. gavotte, gigue) or air; however, all movements are listed in Italian (e.g. «gavotta», «gigua» [*sic*], «aria»).

The subtle, virtuosic challenge of duet performance consists of a dynamic and intimate negotiation in time, without a balancing third party. The duet 'conversations' alternate movements of canonic or polyphonic writing (exchanging voices, imitative counterpoint) with harmonized melody (monody). As is typical with trio sonatas, the upper voices of duets often engage in lock-step (or parallel) thirds and sixths, anchored with resonant basses on the main beats. Harmonic tension is balanced and varied with the effective use of suspensions and simple, well-managed tonal plans[20]. Considering that Leclair was not

---

(*Le Mercure de France* compares M. Cupis to Leclair and Guignon: «très capable de réunir en lui le sentiment, le tendre et le doux de M. Leclerc, avec le feu, le brillant, le surprenant de Guignon» [in *ibidem*, vol II. p. 83]), Leclair was also described as a temperamental individual, and a masculine player (see note 35 below).

[14]. The *Ideali trattimenti da camera* Op. 7 includes 12 short duets for violins, flutes, or viols; perhaps a coincidence, its first appearance came in the same year that Leclair published his second book of duets, Op. 12 (1747). Somis' work was published in 1750 in Paris, by Leclair's usual publishers (Boivin, Le Clerc).

[15]. See preface to Op. 12. All other notation in the parts are in Italian, including movement titles and instrumentation 'violino primo'.

[16]. Similarly, the 'senza basso' solo violin works of J. S. Bach (solo sonatas and partitas, 1720) or G. P. Telemann (12 fantasias, 1735) represent a subgenre of the solo sonata with continuo — which itself can be regarded as a sub-genre of the trio sonata.

[17]. For example, in bb. 8-9 from the end of Gavotta (in Op. 3 No. 4) Leclair proposes a modally mixed lead-in that Rameau also used in 'Les Sauvages', in *Les Indes Galante* (first performed in 1735).

[18]. The trio sonata texture is ideally balanced for triad-based music: a clear bass line leads to strong cadences, on top of which a melody is devised. A third voice follows or contrasts the top or bottom voice. Corelli's (1653-1713) sonatas (e.g. Op. 5) established the two types of movements that were much imitated: an opening slow movement (punctuated by cadenza-like passages) followed by a fugal movement.

[19]. With the occasional relative minor middle movement, or a temporary change of mode mid-way through a rondeau.

[20]. See LA LAURENCIE, Lionel de. *Op. cit.* (see note 13), vol. I, p. 314: «On remarquera, une fois de plus, le rapprochement que de Rozoi cherche à établir entrer le style de Rameau et celui de Leclair».

unfamiliar with re-scoring his own material[21], it is not impossible that he first sketched these duo sonatas as trios before integrating/transposing the bass line[22].

In order to enrich the overall sonority and to create kaleidoscopic effects, Leclair uses a variety of double-stops, open-string drones, fast register shifts, string crossings, and Vivaldi-like figurations. Time and again, Leclair astutely crafts melodies that inherently suggest two voices; he also sets melodic segments that can take the role of a functional bass ('walking bass' melodies). These 'solo duetting'[23] solutions exploit the violin's capacity to a greater degree, moving from simple melody to multi-dimensional structures (polyphonic, harmonic, and, up to a point, orchestral)[24]. These techniques also appear in the increasingly sophisticated solo violin works — essentially recreating the 'ideal' trio sonata texture[25], only with less players[26]. In this respect, Leclair's duet writing directly contributes to the development of violin virtuosity, perhaps more than we usually assume.

LECLAIR'S DIALOGUES AND DUELS

Leclair's duets suggest the possibility that Leclair and Locatelli actually met, exchanged ideas as colleagues, and perhaps even performed together[27]. If indeed a joint concert was arranged in Kassel in late 1728[28], following Leclair's appearances in between April and October of the same year[29], it is not impossible that the two artists played some of his Op. 3, as these duets might have been completed, but not yet published. Another possibility

---

[21]. For example, the instrumental arrangements (Overtures and Trios Op. 13) that he extracted from his opera.

[22]. The final product was published as parts, not as a score; this is more practical for performance.

[23]. 'Solo duetting' (our term) takes place when a single player presents musical structures that apparently involve two melodic streams, either in double-stops or close melodic patterns.

[24]. Conceptually, 'solo duetting' in violin playing may be the equivalent of 'perspective' in the visual arts; 'solo duetting' in the duet genre creates the illusion of a fuller texture, at times 'quartet-like' or 'symphonic'.

[25]. Ideal for its clear division of labor in the context of triadic harmony.

[26]. Tartini's fugue in A (Op. 1 No. 3) for solo violin and bass shares thematic similarity with Bach's solo violin fugues; Locatelli's Capriccios, and in particular 'Labyrinth' (from Op. 3 No. 12, publ. 1733) demonstrate the increasing fascination for 'solo duetting'. This process of virtuosic 'reduction of means' reaches a limit with Paganini, who, in unaccompanied solos, further limits possibilities to three, two, and finally only one string (!).

[27]. ZASLAW, Neal. 'Leclair, Jean-Marie', op. cit. (see note 2).

[28]. Said to have taken place 7 November 1728. See ENGELBRECHT, Christiane. 'Die Hofkapelle des Landgrafen Carl von Hessen-Kassel', in: *Zeitschrift des Vereins für Hessische Geschichted und Landeskunde*, LXVIIII (1957), pp. 141-173. According to Ludwig Finscher, Locatelli was performing his Op. 2 No. 3 in Frankfurt am Main, a few weeks earlier (on October 20). See HILL, John Walter. 'Review. Albert Dunning, *Pietro Antonio Locatelli: Der Virtuose und seine Welt'*, in: *The Journal of Musicology*, 1/4 (October 1982), pp. 471-474. Op. 2 is listed as transverse flute sonatas, published in 1732 (interestingly, Guignon's Op. 1 is also listed for flute).

[29]. POUGIN, Arthur. *Le violon, les violonistes et la musique de violon du XVIᵉ au XVIIIᵉ siècle*, Paris, Fischbacher, 1924, p. 195.

is that Leclair was inspired to write duets after meeting Locatelli. Finally, the duets might have simply been written for amateurs of reliable technique, students, and professionals with whom he collaborated.

A rivalry in Paris between Leclair and his younger Italian colleague Jean-Pierre Guignon (student of Somis) apparently came to a head during a night of concerto performances showcasing the two violinists on 24 December 1734[30]. With the King as judge, the outwardly ambitious Guignon, himself a student of Somis and a successful composer of duets, secured half of the orchestra leader's appointment[31], a situation that did not sit well with the proud Leclair and eventually led to his resignation in 1736[32]. Prior to facing Leclair, Guignon had enjoyed a similar dueling success[33] in 1725 at his Concert spirituel début vis-à-vis another well-established member of the King's violins, Jean-Jacques-Baptiste Anet (student of Corelli)[34]. For Guignon, whose playing was quintessentially Italian — fiery, and spectacular[35], but also delicate and graceful — 'dueling' had been rewarding. First, it thrust him in the Parisian music elite. Following Leclair's departure[36], his jockeying for position led to his 1741 appointment as 'Roy des Ménétriers', a post he held for 32 years, and as

---

[30]. Guignon was known to the Parisian public since his debut with the initial Concert spirituel in 1725. He entered the Chapelle Royale in 1733, adding to his service in the Duke of Carignan's orchestra.

[31]. Following that performance, the King appointed them to serve alternately, a month at a time, as solo violinists of the Royal Chapel.

[32]. La Laurencie, Lionel de. *Op. cit.* (see note 13), vol. I, p. 282, relays a different story, from Marpurg. The political overtones surrounding this story are not clear: the violinists might have been only pawns in a game played by more powerful masters (the Duke of Savoy, Prince of Carignan-Savoy, etc.).

[33]. «In 1725, Guignon appeared with Anet at the Concert spirituel, the occasion was particularly contrived to pit the exponents of the French and Italian violin playing against one another»; see Sadie, Julie Anne. 'France', in: *Companion to Baroque Music*, compiled and edited by Julie Anne Sadie, foreword by Christopher Hogwood, London, J. M. Dent, 1990, p. 122.

[34]. «Another Piedmontese violinist, Giovanni Pietro Ghignone, settled in Paris permanently. At first he was set up to represent the alien Italian style, taking part in a national 'duel' with Jean[-Jacques]-Baptiste Anet at the Concert spirituel in 1725. Five years later he became musician of the Prince of Carignan [the Duke of Savoy's relative who moved to Paris in 1718 and had employed Somis since 1709 in Turin], but he was rapidly accepted into Parisian musical life, entering the service of the King in 1733 and becoming a French citizen in 1741 under the name Jean-Pierre Guignon»; see McVeigh, Simon – Hirshberg, Jehoash. *The Italian Solo Concerto (1700-1760): Rhetorical Strategies and Style History*, Woodbridge, Boydell, 2004, p. 39.

[35]. Pougin, Arthur. *Op. cit.* (see note 29), p. 223: « […] très habile virtuose, brillant surtout par la grâce, l'élégance et la légèreté, Guignon méritait, par un jeu dont la distinction n'excluait pas la hardiesse, les succès qui ne l'abandonnèrent jamais au cours de sa longue carrière. Il fut, disait-on, le rival souvent heureux de Leclair, dont l'exécution plus mâle contrastait avec sa souplesse et sa grâce italiennes. Mais là s'arrêtait forcément la comparaison, les compositions de Guignon ne pouvant supporter l'examen auprès de celles de Leclair».

[36]. The reasons for this rivalry are not well-known; they might have started in Turin around Somis, perhaps extended in the performing space in the manner of playing, or even extended to the teaching realm. La Laurencie, Lionel de. *Op. cit.* (see note 13), vol. II, p. 63. «Les anciens biographes du musicien ajoutent que sa [Guignon's] maison fut pendant toute sa vie une école gratuite et publique pour les jeunes

violin teacher for the Dauphin. In the latter case, Guignon's 'duetting' partner Cassanéa de Mondonville had first been approached; Guignon's appropriation of this position cost him his relationship with Mondonville[37].

Leclair's resignation was followed by more publications (engraved by his new wife, Louise Roussel) and an extended stay in the Netherlands. From 1738, Leclair was invited to the Dutch court of one of Locatelli's music-lover patrons, Anne of Hannover (Princess Royal and Princess of Orange, and student of Handel)[38], where Locatelli and Leclair might have (again?) met, exchanged[39], and played together. Thankful to his host, Leclair dedicated his fourth book of sonatas Op. 9, which in preface offered a 'warning' ('Avertissement')[40] «to those who wish to play according to the Author's taste»; in effect, Leclair was signaling annoyance with some questionable (Italianizing?) performance practices[41].

Public debates on the question of the primacy of the Italian or the French taste were not to disappear any time soon[42]. With changing fashions during the long reign of Louis XV (1715-1774), Leclair's style remained mostly true to the ideals of 'Les Goûts-Réunis', though trending toward the universalizing, lighter features of the pre-Revolutionary style galant[43]. Leclair's duets are first and foremost gentle dialogues, with a concern for elegance and characterization. They are a by-product of a musical world still intimately linked to dance and aristocratic or bourgeois entertainment. Stylistically, his music admirably fits the theater of Marivaux and the paintings of Watteau. The idea of a dialogue between the arts was visibly of interest to Leclair, who, upon his permanent return to Paris, set for himself to create an opera. The brief success of his *Scylla and Glaucus* in 1746 was followed by the

---

gens désireux de s'adonner au violon et qui paraissaient avoir des dispositions, assertion toute à l'honneur du désintéressement de l'artiste. Il forma ainsi plusieurs bons élèves».

[37]. Mondonville and Guignon had toured France together, notably stopping in Lyons. See SUPIČIĆ, Ivo. *Music in Society: A Guide to the Sociology of Music*, Stuyvesant (NY), Pendragon Press, 1987 (Sociology of music, 4), p. 111.

[38]. Leclair, otherwise stationed in The Hague, was the guest of that court for three months each year from 1738 to 1743. See ZASLAW, Neal. 'Leclair. Jean-Marie', *op. cit.* (see note 2).

[39]. Locatelli's recent Op. 3 *L'arte del violino* (1733) would have undoubtedly interested Leclair.

[40]. See PRESTON, Robert E. 'Introduction' in: LECLAIR, Jean-Marie. *Op. cit.* (see note 11), p. xvi.

[41]. *Ibidem*. Leclair points at unnecessary changes of tempi between minor and major modes, and 'disfigured melodies' because of ornamentation. He might have been critical of amateurs, students, or… of Italian players in general (who were famous for indulging elaborate ornamentation — and perhaps of Guignon in particular?). In less-than-expert hands, improvised flights of fancy can easily fall into areas of dubious taste and lead to musical problems (i.e. cacophony, loss of time, etc.). Leclair also hints that his published music circulates well (to the point that he will need to replace the original plates), and that he expects the same care from the players that he himself puts in the writing. A splendid lesson, indeed, in very few words.

[42]. See for example, la *querelle des bouffons*, in 1752.

[43]. In 1763-1764, W. A. Mozart, at 8 years old, visited and performed at the court as part of his European tour. Mozart left Paris in April 1764 for London, a few months before Leclair was killed. See SADIE, Stanley. *Mozart: The Early Years, 1756-1781*, New York, W. W. Norton & Co., 2006, pp. 47-50.

publication of a second and last book of 6 Sonatas for two violins Op. 12. Combined with the first set, his 12 duo sonatas in effect — if not by design — cover all the usual keys from D to D. The particular motivation for writing more duets at the time might have had something to do with teaching[44].

PEDAGOGICAL 'DIET'

Leclair's duets not only punctuate and remind of his life's professional dialogues and duels; they are also a window through which we can get a glimpse of his pedagogy[45]. Leclair introduced many of his best students to the Parisian audiences via their duet performances at the Concert spirituel. Of note, L'abbé *le fils* (Joseph-Barnabé Saint-Sévin, *dit*)[46] and Pierre Gaviniès were acclaimed as teenage virtuosi in 1741 «in the performance of a duo sonata by their teacher»[47]; and later: «Leclair aimait alors beaucoup à produire ses élèves; c'est ainsi que, le 19 mai 1746, un autre de ses disciples, Dupont, joue avec L'abbé *le fils*, 'au goût des auditeurs', une sonate à deux violons qui était probablement de la composition de Leclair»[48].

From these accounts, it is possible to infer that duet playing was an important part of Leclair's pedagogy and — *teacher teaches what teacher learned* — probably an important part of his own training and regular practice. However, this needs to be understood with the knowledge that only a few works for two violins 'senza basso' were circulating before 1730[49], and that Leclair's training was somewhat off the regular course (thanks to Somis, his focus shifted from being a dancer and dance master to becoming a violinist and composer)[50]. In Leclair's time, violin teaching undoubtedly involved frequent duet playing, whether in preparing trio sonatas with a student or adapting the figured bass line of a solo violin sonata or concerto on the violin. The emergence of methods of instruction that included duets as 'second-line accompaniments' carried on these practices, with the expectation that

44. Leclair's own domestic duet however was turning into a *duel*, and he took separate residence from 1758.

45. A pedagogy appreciated through his students. See LA LAURENCIE, Lionel de. *Op. cit.* (see note 13), vol. I, p. 314: «Il laissa d'excellents élèves, dont L'abbé *le fils*, Dauvergne et Berton, qui, "par leurs succès, déclare de Bernis, ajoutent à sa gloire et que la nature a formés — sans doute pour perpétuer nos plaisirs". Enfin, un 'Supplément à la lettre' insérée par de Rozoi dans le *Mercure* de novembre 1734 signalait un autre disciple de Leclair, nommé Geoffroy, et qui marchait à grands pas sur les traces de son maître. Geoffroy était au service du duc de Gramont».

46. L'abbé *le fils*, for example, published his violin treatise in 1761.

47. LA LAURENCIE, Lionel de. *Op. cit.* (see note 13), vol. II, p. 216: «Le sieur Gaviniès, âgé de treize ans, et le sieur L'abbé, à peu près du même âge, jouèrent une *symphonie* à deux violons de M. Le Clair [*sic*] avec toute la précision et la vivacité convenables; ils furent applaudis par une très nombreuse assemblée».

48. *Ibidem*, p. 217. «Likely» («probablement»), as it was perhaps not yet published.

49. The Catalogue mentions only Robert Valentine, Jacques Aubert, Jean-Jacques-Baptiste Anet, Willem de Fesch — and likely only Aubert and Anet are relevant in this case.

50. POUGIN, Arthur. *Op. cit.* (see note 29), pp. 191-194.

teachers would appreciate the benefits of playing duets with their students. With Leclair's reputation growing rapidly from 1728 onwards[51], there is little doubt that he must have attracted talented students and that his duets must have received serious attention, therefore setting a solid model to influence many after him. New books of duets became available by violinists such as Guignon (c1736), Mangean (1744), Vibert (1750), Miroglio *le cadet* (1753), and others. Perhaps encouraged by their illustrious older brother, Jean-Marie Leclair 'the Younger' and Pierre Leclair both later published their own sets of duets (1750 and 1764)[52].

To the practitioner, duets may be instrumental in developing a superior sense of intonation, tone, timing, ensemble, and style (or to borrow Baillot's word, «accent»[53]). Furthermore, duets offer hands-on materials to help develop effective sight-reading, and responsibility and responsiveness in performance[54]. Switching roles in a duet is a simple and effective way for the teacher to demonstrate the interpretive possibilities of each line, and an opportunity for the student to appreciate the same[55]. The student is therefore introduced to the subtle and important arts of interpretation and accompanying, which depend on the mastery of more advanced musical concepts, such as harmonic rhythm, phrase structure, and form. Duet playing may also stimulate a healthy dose of emulation between students and therefore influence the speed of their overall development.

While it is common today to see spontaneous, improvised 'duetting' taking place in fiddling, gypsy, or jazz circles, it is certainly rare to witness the same in the string classes of conservatories and universities. If sight-reading duets is still practiced as part of Conservatory wind instruction, it is not usually the case for violin instruction, and this, despite a wealth of materials. The large focus that is placed on the solo and orchestral repertoire clearly relegates the teachings of duet playing to the periphery. We ask at this point: is there a correlation between duet playing and the types of musicians that are trained

---

[51]. *Ibidem*, p. 195.

[52]. Jean-Marie Leclair *le cadet*, b. 1703, published two-violin sonatas *sans basse* Op. 2 (1750); Pierre Leclair, b. 1709, *6 sonates de récréation à 2 violons* Op. 1 (1764); Jean-Benoît Leclair (duet works unknown).

[53]. BAILLOT, Pierre(-Marie-François de Sales) – RODE, Pierre – KREUTZER, Rodolphe. *Méthode de Violon*, Paris, Au Magasin de musique, [1803].

[54]. The videos of Jascha Heifetz's masterclasses show him participating in quartet sight-reading with his students and reading a violin duet (Halvorsen-Handel) with his student Pierre Amoyal. A clear sense of emulation, interaction, and fun are portrayed in these videos. See *Heifetz Master Classes*, DVD, West Long Branch (NJ), Kultur, 2011.

[55]. See LE ROUX, Didier. 'Le mythe de la basse continue', in: *Le Plectre*, no. 21 (December 2001), <http://leplectre.plectra-music.net/2002/viewArticle.asp?idTopic=27&idMT=3&idArticle=13>, accessed 11 December 2014. «Troisième cas: les sonates pour violon où la partie d'accompagnement, en clé de sol, est destinée visiblement à un second violon (doubles cordes, arpèges). Ces recueils peuvent avoir pour titre «sonates pour violon» sans préciser l'accompagnement (Bertheaume Op. 2, Op. 4; Bruni 1er livre; Fiorillo en manuscrit), "sonates pour le violon avec accompagnement d'un second violon" (Bruni Op. 4) ou même: "sonates pour violon et basse" (Bruni 2e livre, Baumbach: variations), ce qui montre bien que le mot "basse", qui était souvent synonyme de violoncelle à cette époque, pouvait aussi à l'occasion désigner un violon».

today? Is there also a correlation between duet playing and the thread of creativity that we witness among violinists up to Ysaÿe (who is often described as 'the last violinist-composer')?

Some violin teachers will still at times spontaneously engage in improvising a second line, or provide chords ('harmonizing'[56]) to create a more stimulating musical environment (for example, to a repetitive etude, a well-known concert solo, or even a scale[57]). The practices of creating 'second lines' to an air or a caprice, or 'reducing a concerto's orchestral score'[58] to accompany a student soloist, can be a stimulating and creative exercises. On one hand, the duet arrangement of a caprice may propose a 'background-foreground' transformation, in which the virtuoso etude becomes the perceived accompaniment of a new counter-melody (e.g. Wieniawski, Paganini-Bachmann[59]). On the other hand, orchestral reductions featuring sequences of double- and triple-stops played by a single violin accompanying another, create virtuosic and vibrant duet textures that also challenge the usual meaning of accompaniment[60]. These types of duets are rarely intended for the amateur[61].

So far, this paper has brought attention to the neglected genre of the violin duet. In particular, it situated Leclair's fundamental contributions in the context of his career as performer, composer, and teacher. With Leclair's example in mind, we argued that the practice of duet playing and duet composing passed from one generation to the next can yield new insights into aspects of the development of violin virtuosity, as well as partly explain the remarkable creative thread from Leclair to Ysaÿe. To conclude this discussion,

---

[56]. See SAUZAY, Eugène. *Le Violon harmonique: ses ressources, son emploi dans les écoles anciennes et modernes: étude complétée par un cours d'harmonie a l'usage des violonistes*, Paris, Librairie Firmin-Didot, 1889. Thanks to Philippe Borer for pointing out this remarkable and neglected resource.

[57]. Rode, Baillot, Campagnoli and Rolla are among those demonstrating the power of such harmonized exercises.

[58]. Again, thanks to Philippe Borer for identifying scores of concertos with second-line accompaniments (Sibelius, Tchaikovsky, Mozart, Wieniawski, etc. as arranged by Marteau, Bachmann, Ysaÿe, Ševčik, Hubay, and Philippe Borer).

[59]. Paganini is also reported to have played duets with Antonio Rolla, in presence of Alessandro, who might or might not have taught Paganini. It is worth noting that Paganini's graduating assignment with Paër (recommended by Rolla) was to write a violin-cello duet. See BORER, Philippe. *The Twenty-four Caprices of Niccolò Paganini: Their Significance for the History of Violin Playing and the Music of the Romantic Era*, Ph.D. Diss., Hobart, University of Tasmania, 1995, p. 88. The style of Paganini was apparently rooted in creative practices, see ID. 'Paganini's Virtuosity and Improvisatory Style', in: *Beyond Notes: Improvisation in Western Music of the Eighteenth and Nineteenth Centuries*, edited by Rudolf Rasch, Turnhout, Brepols, 2011 (Speculum musicae, 16), pp. 191-215: 200-203.

[60]. When did the concept of 'accompaniment' take hold in the musical language? 'A melody being accompanied by chords' gives precedence to the melody. However, if one considers the centrality of the bass line ruling the harmonic possibilities and the musical form, the argument is quickly turned upside down: the upper, ornamental and ornamented voice(s) is (are) in fact 'accompanying' the bass.

[61]. In its earlier manifestations, French duet music is often of a lighter character or 'diversional' in nature, with titles such as *amusements* and *musettes*. Many composers would specify that the music was composed with the amateur in mind; Paganini, in his Op. 1, took a difference stand and called upon 'the Artists'.

we propose a new working catalogue of duets, organized according to a genealogical principle (i.e. 'schools', or clusters of artists related to a teacher). This catalogue's resources may serve as a basis for further research and help the reader appreciate the richness of the duet repertoire.

CATEGORIZING THE DUET REPERTOIRE

The following catalogue, which aims to categorize the duet repertoire, draws from digitized scores in the Petrucci Music Library (mostly first prints), encyclopedias (*Grove Music Online*), violin methods (which contain many pedagogical duets), existing listings of duets (in particular, Bachmann and Farish[62]), and historical studies of the French violin school (La Laurencie, Pougin). Brief biographical notes complement the listing of works in order to help the reader situate the composers. The composers' names are <u>underlined</u>, the works are *italicized*, and names of particular significance in the development of the genre have been set in **bold**. The notation (> Corelli) means 'student of Corelli'[63], and (> X> Y) means 'student of Y, who was student of X'.

In duets, roles are attributed in a more or less equal way. The most absolute equality of voices belongs to the *canon* or *canonic sonatas*, where only the very end is slightly adjusted for a bass-like final cadence. In the conversational sonata, dialoguer, or *air varié* (often sourcing from opera), some specialization might take place. Further, in the *duo brillant* (as in *quatuor brillant*), *sérénade*, *duo concertant*, and the étude or *caprice*, the first and second violin become increasingly differentiated, reflecting either a pedagogical purpose or a one-sided virtuosity. In these cases, the second violin provides a supporting role in the lower register (for example, playing rhythmic double-stops) while the first line assumes the more virtuosic role.

Violin Duets – Early French
<u>Jean-Jacques-Baptiste Anet</u>[64] (1676-1755) (>Corelli in 1695-1696), appeared at the first Concert spirituel in 1725[65]: Books of *Musettes* (1726, 1730, 1734); <u>Julien-Amable Mathieu</u> (1734-1811): *6 sonates* Op. 3 (1764)[66]; <u>Jacques Aubert</u> (1689-1753) (>Sénaillé), first violin at the Opéra from 1728, appeared at the Concert spirituel from 1729 to 1739[67], known to have composed the first French violin concerto[68]: *Pièces (3 Suites)* Op. 15 (c1734)[69], *Pièces*, première suite (1723), *Sonates* Op. 24 (1738), *Les jolis airs* Opp. 27-29 (c1740-1745), Op.

---

[62]. See BACHMANN, Alberto. *An Encyclopedia of the Violin*, translated by Frederick H. Martens, edited by Albert E. Wier, New York, Appleton, 1929. Also, see FARISH, Margaret K. *String Music in Print*, New York, R. R. Bowker Co., 1965 and ²1973.

[63]. With permission of Philippe Borer, who invented this notation.

[64]. His pupil Jean Baptiste Senaillé (1687-1730) (>Anet) apparently only wrote for solo violin and *basse*. See WALLS, Peter. 'Senaillé, Jean Baptiste', in: *Grove Music Online, op. cit.* (see note 2).

[65]. ZASLAW, Neal. 'Baptiste [Anet, Jean-Jacques-Baptiste]', in: *ibidem*.

[66]. COOPER, Jeffrey. 'Mathieu', in: *ibidem*.

[67]. KEITEL, Elizabeth – SIGNORILE, Marc. 'Aubert', in: *ibidem*.

[68]. LA LAURENCIE, Lionel de. *Op. cit.* (see note 13), vol. I, p. 211.

[69]. AUBERT, Jacques. *3 Suites pour deux violons*, Op. 15, edited by Henri Lammers, Paris-Brussels, Henry Lemoine, n.d., available at <imslp.org>.

31 (1749), Opp. 32-33 (*c*1750)[70]; Michel Corrette (1707-1795), who wrote about twenty music method books for various instruments, including the violin: *L'Art de se perfectionner sur le violon*, and *L'école d'Orphée*, which describes the French and Italian styles[71], *A viol method with lessons in 1 and 2 voices* (1750)[72], *6 Duets* Op. 23[73]; Étienne Mangean (*c*1710-*c*1756), in a style close to Leclair: *Duets* Op. 3 (1744)[74]; Nicolas Vibert (1710-1772): *Sonatas* Op. 1 (1750), which «maintain a clear delineation of melody and accompaniment, with occasional canons usually at the unison»[75], *3 Suites*, «probably intended for the upper nobility; consist of a number of short characteristic pieces, often humorous and again interestingly titled in both Italian and French»[76].

French, Early, Others (Genealogy not Known)
Several names have been detected with limited information at this time[77].

German, Others
Among the German-speaking countries, composers also wrote for treble instruments (violins, flutes, oboes, viols). Georg Philipp Telemann (1681-1767): 2 sets of *6 Sonatas for 2 flutes or violins*[78], *Intrada-Suite in D for 2 violins*[79], *XVIII Canons mélodieux ou 6 Sonates en duo*[80]; Johann Sebastian Bach (1685-1750): *2-voice canons, unspecified treble instrumentation* (BWV1075[81]; and as part of *A Musical Offering*[82] BWV1079; 3a, 3b; 3c; 3d; 3e; 4), *Fuga canonica*[83]; Christoph Förster (1693-1745): *6 Duets with optional bass* Op. 1 (Paris, n.d. engraved by Telemann before 1740, lost)[84].

---

70. KEITEL, Elizabeth – SIGNORILE, Marc. *Op. cit.* (see note 67).

71. FULLER, David – GUSTAFSON, Bruce. 'Corrette, Michel', in: *Grove Music Online, op. cit.* (see note 2).

72. CORRETTE, Michel. *Méthode pour apprendre à jouer de la vielle*, Paris, Richault, n.d., available at <imslp.org>.

73. ID. *6 Duets*, Op. 23, Paris, l'auteur-Mme Boivin, n.d., available at <imslp.org>.

74. MANGEAN, Étienne. *Sonates a duex violons egaux sans basse*, Op. 3, Paris, Le Clerc-Mme Boivin, 1744, available at <imslp.org>.

75. VIAL, Stephanie. 'Vibert, Nicolas', in: *Grove Music Online, op. cit.* (see note 2).

76. *Ibidem.*

77. The following list of duet composers requires further biographical and bibliographical research: Le Marchand (?), *6 suites of airs* (*c*1750); Jean-Baptiste Miroglio *le cadet* (1725-1785), who dedicated an earlier work to Guignon: *6 Sonates*, Op. 4 (1753) in which the second violin mostly plays an accompanying role in its lower register; Joseph-Antoine Piffer *le cadet* (?), *Sonatas*; Jean-Baptiste Dupuits (fl 1741-1757), *Suite d'amusements* Op. 2 (1760); ?Enderlé (?), *6 duets* (1762-1763); ?Guérini de Naples (?), *6 sonates* Op. 4 (*c*1760), *6 duets* Op. 5 (1761); Benoît Guillemant (fl 1746-1757), *6 sonates* Op. 2 (*c*1760); Joseph Jobert (?), *6 nocturnal duets* Op. 1 (Lyons, 1770); ?Leloup (?), book of airs with second treble accompaniment (*c*1765-1770); Pietro Leone (?), *6 duets* (1766); Franz Xaver Rambach (?), *6 sonatas* Op. 4 (1765).

78. TELEMANN, Georg Philipp. *6 Sonatas*, TWV 40:101-106, Hamburg, l'auteur, 1727, available at <imslp.org> and ID. *6. Duetto. Sonatas*, TWV 40:124-129, ms. Badische Landesbibliothek Karlsruhe, Mus Hs 274, available at <imslp.org>.

79. ID. *Intrada-Suite for 2 Violins 'Gulliver's Travels'*, TWV 40:108, in *Der getreue Music-Meister*, Hamburg, Telemann, 1728, available at <imslp.org>.

80. ID. *XIIX Canons mélodieux [...]*, TWV 40:118-123, Hamburg, L'auteur, 1738, available at <imslp.org>.

81. BACH, Johann Sebastian. *Canon in D major*, BWV 1075, available at <imslp.org>.

82. ID. *Musikalisches Opfer*, BWV 1079, (1747), rpt. Leipzig, Edition Peters, 1977, available at <imslp.org>.

83. Bach's solo violin sonatas and partitas 'without bass' were written *c*1720, apparently for Johann Georg Pisendel (1687-1755) (>Torelli), a court violinist in Dresden, colleague of Telemann and Bach. Pisendel also wrote a *Sonata in A minor for solo violin without bass* (1720-1730). See DRUMMOND, Pippa. 'Pisendel, Johann Georg', in: *Grove Music Online, op. cit.* (see note 2).

84. EAD. 'Förster, Christoph', in: *ibidem*.

Italians, Others

The Italians quickly adopted the trend of writing duets, though not every celebrated Italian violinist produced duets, notably Corelli, Vivaldi, Tartini, Locatelli, and Veracini. Many left Italy to work in foreign courts. Robert Valentine (1674; d1735-40), however represents the opposite case, as an Englishman who lived in Italy: *8 Duets* Op. 5 (1716)[85], *6 Sonatas* (c1720), a duo arrangement of his Op. 4 (1715)[86]; Francesco Geminiani (1687-1762) (>A. Scarlatti and >Corelli), who established himself in London: *L'Art du violon* (1751)[87]; Carlo Tessarini (c1690-1766) (>Vivaldi?), established himself in Amsterdam: *Il maestro e discepolo* Op. 2[88], and *Grammatica di musica* (1741)[89], one of the first violin methods, with 2-violin lessons by steps, *Trattenimento musicale: Sei duetti a due violini ò due pardessus de viole senza basso libro secondo* (c1750, in English in 1765)[90], *Pantomime for 2 violins*[91], *12 Sonatas and Canons*[92].

The School of Somis

Leclair's teacher, **Giovanni Battista Somis** (1686-1763) (>Corelli): *Ideal Trattenimenti da Camera*[93] (his brother Giovanni Lorenzo, 1688-1775, also taught and performed in Turin[94]); Leclair's rival, **Jean-Pierre Guignon** (b Turin 1702-1774) (>Somis), who appeared at the Concert spirituel[95] in 1725, toured through France with Mondonville as a performing duet[96]: *18 Duets* (Op. 3[97], Op. 7[98], Op. 8[99], Op. 9[100]), on a scale comparable to Leclair [Guignon also played duets with Gaviniès[101] (>Leclair)]; «M. Guignon et M. Gaviniès, par leurs charmans Duos, écrit le Mercure, ont satisfait également les personnes qui veulent

85. VALENTINE, Robert. *Sonates a deux dessus*, 8 Duets, Op. 5, edited by Jacques Hotteterre (1673-1763), Paris, Hotteterre-Le Sr. Boivin, 1721, available at <imslp.org>.

86. MEDFORTH, Martin. 'Valentine, Robert', in: *Grove Music Online, op. cit.* (see note 2).

87. GEMINIANI, Francesco. *L'Art du violon, […] composée primitivement par le Célèbre F. Geminiani, et nouvellement redigée, augmentée, expliquée et enrichie de nouveaux exemplar, Préludes, Airs et Duos gradués pour éclaircir et faciliter l'instruction et mettre évidement en pratique les principes de cet excellent maitre. Nouvelle édition*, Paris, Sieber, s.d., available at <imslp.org>.

88. TESSARINI, Carlo. *Il maestro e discepolo, Op. 2, 6 Divertimenti e canoni da Camera a due violini*, Urbino, Girolamo Mainardi, 1734, available at <imslp.org>.

89. ID. *Gramatica di musica*, Urbino, s.n., [c1741], available at <imslp.org>.

90. ID. *Sei duetti a due violini o pardesus de viole senza basso*, Op. 15, Paris, aux addresses ordinaires, [c1750], available at <imslp.org>.

91. ID. *Pantomine a due violini […]*, Paris, aux adresses ordinaires, [c1763], available at <imslp.org>.

92. ID. *12 Sonate a due violini con sei canoni*, Paris, Le Clerc, n.d., available at <imslp.org>.

93. SOMIS, Giovanni Battista. *Jdeali Trattenimenti da Camera a due violini, o due flauti traversieri o due pardessus di viola*, Op. 7, Paris, Mme Boivin-Mr Le Clerc-Mlle Castanerie, n.d., available at <imslp.org>.

94. BASSO, Alberto. 'Somis, Giovanni Lorenzo', in: *Grove Music Online, op. cit.* (see note 2).

95. The Concert spirituel was created following the Concert des Italiens in 1724. See COOK, Elisabeth. 'Paris. § IV. 1723-89. 2. Concert Life', in: *ibidem*.

96. ZASLAW, Neal. 'Guignon, Jean-Pierre', in: *ibidem*.

97. GUIGNON, Jean-Pierre. *Six Sonates a deux violons, flute allemande et violon, et toutes sortes d'instrumens egaux, 2 Violins*, Op. 3, Paris, Le Clerc-Castagneri, n.d., available at <imslp.org>.

98. ID. *Six Duo a deux violons*, Op. 7, Paris, Madame Boivin, [1736], available at <imslp.org>.

99. ID. *Pièces de differens Auteurs à deux violons amplifiées et doublée par J. P. Guignon*, Op. 8, Paris, Madame Boivin, [c1736], available at <imslp.org>.

100. ID. *Nouvelles variations de divers airs et les Folies d'Espagne*, Op. 9, Paris, Mme Boivin, [c1736], available at <imslp.org>.

101. COOPER, Jeffrey – GINTER, Anthony. 'Gaviniès, Pierre', in: *Grove Music Online, op. cit.* (see note 2).

admirer et celles qui ne veulent que s'amuser»[102]; <u>Louis-Gabriel Guillemain</u> (1705-1770) (>Somis), viewed as a great artist on a par with Leclair, suffered a precarious financial position that led him to suicide[103]: *6 sonates* Op. 4 (1739)[104], *Amusements* Op. 9 (1741, lost)[105]; <u>Gaspard Fritz</u> (Geneva 1716-1783) (>Somis): *Sonatas with or without bass*[106]; <u>Felice Giardini</u> (b Turin 1716-1796) (>Somis): *6 duets* Op. 2 (before 1780)[107]; <u>Edouard Du Puy</u> (c1770-1822) (>Somis >Chabran[108], or Carlo Chiabrano[109]), a Swiss-born musician who worked in Copenhagen and Stockholm from 1793[110]: *Duets*[111]; **Gaetano Pugnani** (1731-1798) (>Somis), concertmaster in Turin, at the 1754 Concert spirituel, and in London in 1767-1769 to direct the King's Theatre[112]: *6 Sonatas* Op. 5 (1763?)[113].

The School of Pugnani

<u>Luigi Borghi</u> (?1745-1806) (>Pugnani): *3 duets* Op. 10 (1790), *6 duets* (1800)[114]; **Giovanni Battista Viotti** (1755-1824) (>Pugnani), from Piedmont/Sardinia, toured with Pugnani after serving at the court in Turin: «From 1780 to 1782 [Pugnani] toured northern Europe with his illustrious pupil Viotti»[115]. Very successful debut at the Concert spirituel in 1782, then founded an opera company, the Théâtre de Monsieur (the King's brother) in 1788, presenting Cherubini. Fled Paris with the Revolution, successful in London with Salomon[116] and Haydn, director-conductor at King's Theater, until later expelled with Rode from England to Hamburg area, was a founding director of the London Philharmonic Society, at the *Académie Royale de Musique* in Paris from 1819-1821, and back to London in 1823[117]: multiple sets of *Duets* (more than any other genre)[118], often published as arrangements for other instruments, and include *L'hommage à l'Amitié*

---

102.   LA LAURENCIE, Lionel de. *Op. cit* (see note 13), vol. II, p. 280.

103.   CASTONGUAY, Gerald R. 'Guillemain, Louis-Gabriel', in: *Grove Music Online, op. cit.* (see note 2).

104.   LA LAURENCIE, Lionel de. *Op. cit* (see note 13), vol. II, p. 24 and 28: «En principe, les sonates à deux violons sont écrites pour deux instruments égaux; mais l'absence de continuo oblige l'auteur à descendre le plus possible dans le grave la partie de deuxième violon qui, pour la même raison, s'étoffe souvent de doubles cordes»; «Rien de plus juste, du reste, de plus adéquat au caractère de tels ouvrages qu'un pareil titre, car ceux-ci constituent avant tout de la musique de salon, et rappellent une fine causerie entre gens spirituels et bien élevés».

105.   CASTONGUAY, Gerald R. *Op. cit.* (see note 103).

106.   SCHANZLIN, Hans Peter. 'Fritz, Kaspar', available at <deutsche-biographie.de>.

107.   GIARDINI, Felice. *Sei Duetti a due violini*, Op. 2, London, The Author, [before 1780], available at <imslp.org>.

108.   Chabran's student, Pierre Vachon, in 1786 collaborates with Benda at the Berlin court, as concertmaster: *6 Easy Duettos*, Op. 5 (London, the author, c1775). See GARNIER-PANAFIEU, Michelle. 'Vachon, Pierre', in: *Grove Music Online, op. cit.* (see note 2).

109.   SALVETTI, Guido – MCVEIGH, Simon. 'Chiabrano, Carlo', in: *ibidem*.

110.   NEIIENDAM, Klaus. 'Du Puy, Edouard', in: *ibidem*.

111.   DU PUY, Edouard. *Duetto pour deux Violons*, Stockholm, C. T. Löwstädt, n.d., available at <imslp.org>.

112.   SCHWARZ, Boris – MCCLYMONDS, Marita P. 'Pugnani, Gaetano', in: *Grove Music Online, op. cit.* (see note 2).

113.   PUGNANI, Gaetano. *6 Sonatas for 2 Violins*, Op. 5, ms., available at <imslp.org>.

114.   PARKINSON, John A. – MCVEIGH, Simon. 'Borghi, Luigi', in: *Grove Music Online, op. cit.* (see note 2).

115.   SCHWARZ, Boris – MCCLYMONDS, Marita P. *Op. cit.* (see note 112).

116.   Viotti played a *duetto concertante* with Salomon and Libon. See LISTER, Warwick. *Amico: The Life of Giovanni Battista Viotti*, Oxford, Oxford University Press, 2009.

117.   *Ibidem*.

118.   See 'Viotti, Giovanni Battista' at <imslp.org>.

(appearing in Baillot's *Méthode de violon*[119]), *6 Serenades* (to the Duke of Cambridge)[120]; Antonio Bartolomeo Bruni (1757-1821) (>Pugnani): at least *81 Duos* (14 books), *42 Duos faciles 'pour les commençants'* (7 books)[121]; Giovanni Battista Polledro (1781-1853) (>Pugnani), worked in Bergamo, Russia, Turin, played with the young Beethoven in Carlsbad, then in Dresden for the King of Saxony (1814-1823), a friend of Paganini[122], his style bridges Pugnani to Paganini: *Duets* Op. 11 (Vienna, 1812)[123].

School of Tartini or 'School of Padua' (or 'School of Nations', 1728 onwards)

Tartini (1692-1770) (infl>Corelli, Veracini), trained many violinists who wrote duets. Antonín Kammel (b Běleč 1730; d ?London 1784): *Duets* Op. 2, Op. 5, Op. 15, Op. 18, *6 Duetti notturni*[124]; Pasquale Bini (1716-1770) (>Tartini >Nardini): *5 Duets*[125]; Tartini's devoted Pietro Nardini (1722-1793) (>Tartini), praised by Leopold Mozart and Pichl[126], now famous for a solo violin *Sonate énigmatique* (available in Cartier's *L'Art du Violon*[127]) making use of scordatura: *6 duets*[128]; Michele Stratico (1728-1783) (>Tartini), who worked in Padua: *15 Duets*[129]; Maddalena Lombardini Sirmen (or Syrmen; née Lombardini) (1745-1818) (>Tartini), to whom her teacher wrote a famous 'letter'[130]: *6 Duets* Op. 5[131]; **Bartolomeo Campagnoli** (1751-1827) (>Tartini and >Nardini in Florence), who toured Northern Europe, was concertmaster of the *Gewandhaus* in Leipzig, and visited Paris in 1801 (where he was impressed by R. Kreutzer)[132]: *Nouvelle méthode* (Leipzig, 1824; It. trans., n.d.; Eng. trans., 1856)[133], which shows a clear *'duet as diet'* foundation, *Duos for flute and violin* Op. 2[134], Op. 4, Op. 6, *3 Thèmes d'airs* [by Mozart] *connus variés* Op. 7[135], *101 easy and progressive pieces for 2 violins* Op. 20[136], *6 Duos faciles et progressives* Op. 14, *3 Thèmes d'airs étrangers variées* Op. 8, *3 Duos*

119. Baillot, Pierre(-Marie-François de Sales) – Rode, Pierre – Kreutzer, Rodolphe. *Op. cit.* (see note 53) available at <imslp.org>.

120. Viotti, Giovanni Battista. *Duos* (3 Serenades for 2 Violins, W.IV.31-33), Leipzig, C. F. Peters, [1850], rpt. in: *Collection de tous les Duos concertants pour deux violons*, London, Merton Music, n.d., available at <imslp.org>. Id. '3 Serenades for 2 Violins', W.IV.34-36, Leipzig, C. F. Peters, [1850], rpt. in: *Collection de tous les Duos concertants pour deux violon*, London, Merton Music, [1996-2010], available at <imslp.org>.

121. Fox, Leland *et al.* 'Bruni, Antonio Bartolomeo', in: *Grove Music Online, op. cit.* (see note 2).

122. Polledro's *Exercises amusants aux amateurs* (1817), are essentially duets for solo violin and may have been an inspiration to Paganini.

123. Schwarz, Boris – Senici, Emanuele. 'Polledro, Giovanni Battista', in: *Grove Music Online, op. cit.* (see note 2).

124. Pilková, Zdeńka. 'Kammel, Antonín', in: *ibidem*.

125. White, Chappell. 'Bini, Pasquale', in: *ibidem*.

126. Dellaborra, Mariateresa. 'Nardini, Pietro', in: *ibidem*.

127. Cartier, Jean-Baptiste. *L'Art du violon*, Paris, Decombe, [²1799], available at <imslp.org>.

128. Nardini, Pietro. *Six duo pour deux violons*, Paris, chez Louis [Imbault?], n.d., available at <imslp.org>.

129. Blažeković, Zdravko. 'Stratico, Michele', in: *Grove Music Online, op. cit.* (see note 2).

130. Arnold, Elsie. 'Sirmen, Maddalena Laura', in: *ibidem*.

131. Sirmen, Maddalena Laura. *Sei duetti per due violini*, Op. 5, Paris, Venier, [1775], available at <imslp.org>.

132. White, Chappell. 'Campagnoli, Bartolomeo', in: *Grove Music Online, op. cit.* (see note 2).

133. Campagnoli, Bartolomeo. *Metodo della meccanica progressiva per suonare il violino* […], Op. 21, Milan, Ricordi, n.d., available at <imslp.org>.

134. Id. *Six Duos a une flute & violon*, Op. 2, Berlin, J. J. Hummel, [early 1800s], available at <imslp.org>.

135. Id. *Trois Themes d'airs connus varies pour deux violons*, Op. 7, Leipzig, Breitkopf & Härtel, [c1790?], available at <imslp.org>.

136. Id. *101 pièces faciles et progressives pour deux violons*, Op. 20, edited by Adolf Grünwald, Braunschweig, Henry Litolff, [1881], available at <imslp.org>.

concertans Op. 9, *3 Duos* Op. 19, *3 Airs with Variations*, arr. C. Reeves (London, 1799)[137]; the enigmatic <u>Monsieur de Tremais</u> (fl *c*1728-1751) (>Tartini?), «most of his violin music demands advanced technical ability: he made considerable use of multiple stops, extremely high notes, trills, tremolos, extended staccato passages and lengthy phrases to be played in a single bow; rapid alternation between plucked and bowed notes is a technical tour de force that he may have learnt from Tartini. He often used scordatura»[138]: sets of *Sonatas* Op. 2 (1737) and Op. 8 (*c*1740)[139]; <u>Emanuele Barbella</u> (1718-1777) (>Bini>Tartini): *Sonata*[140], *Sonata Scordatura*[141], *33 Violin or Mandolin Duets*[142], which include *6 Duets* Op. 3[143], *6 Violin Sonatas (with a 2nd violin accompaniment played an octave higher than the written bass, or two octaves if needed)*[144]; <u>Gaetano Brunetti</u> (1744-1798) (>Nardini? or >Tessarini?), worked for the Spanish court[145]: *6 Duos* Op. 3 (1776), *4 Duets* (1776)[146].

Of Different Origins (Unknown Genealogy)

<u>Willem de Fesch</u> (1687; d London 1761): *6 Duets* Op. 1 (1716, lost; Paris, 1738)[147], *Musical amuzements 30 Flute Duets* Op. 11 (London, 1747)[148]; <u>Luigi Boccherini</u> (1743-1805), Rococo-style with a Spanish influence, virtuoso cellist praised by Alexandre Boucher, Pierre Rode, and Bernhard Romberg[149]: *6 Duetti* Op. 3 (1761)[150], and the dubious works *6 Duets* G 63-68 arranged from trios and quintets[151], published by Pleyel as Op. 46[152].

School of Leclair

L'abbé *le fils* [Joseph-Barnabé Saint-Sévin] (1727-1803) (>Leclair, 1740-1742), was noticed by Leclair at an orchestra audition for the Comédie-Française (Saint-Sevin was then 11 and won the post),

---

137.   WHITE, Chappell. 'Campagnoli, Bartolomeo', *op. cit.* (see note 133).

138.   COOPER, Jeffrey. 'Tremais, de', in: *Grove Music Online, op. cit.* (see note 2).

139.   *Ibidem*.

140.   BARBELLA, Emanuele. *Sonata a due violini*, in C major, manuscript, I-Nc Rari 29.5.12-14, [*c*1700-1799], available at <imslp.org>.

141.   ID. *Sérénade* (Scordatura for 2 Violins in D major), in: BAILLOT, Pierre(-Marie-François de Sales). *L'Art du violon*, Berlin, Schlesinger, [1836].

142.   WHITE, Chappell. 'Barbella, Emanuele', in: *Grove Music Online, op. cit.* (see note 2).

143.   BARBELLA, Emanuele. *Six Duets for two Violins*, Op. 3, London, Gabriel Leone, n.d., available at <imslp.org>.

144.   ID. *6 Violin Sonatas*, London, R. Bremner, n.d., available at <imslp.org>.

145.   BELGRAY, Alice B. – JENKINS, Newell. 'Brunetti, Gaetano', in: *Grove Music Online, op. cit.* (see note 2).

146.   *Ibidem*.

147.   DE FESCH, Willem. *VI Duetti a due violini*, Op. 1, Paris, Le Clerc, [1738], available at <imslp.org>.

148.   VAN DEN BREMT, Frans – RASCH, Rudolf. 'De Fesch, Willem', in: *Grove Music Online, op. cit.* (see note 2).

149.   See GALLENI LUISI, Leila. 'Boccherini, Luigi', in: *Dizionario Biografico degli Italiani*, available at <http://www.treccani.it/enciclopedia/luigi-boccherini_%28Dizionario-Biografico%29/>, accessed 11 December 2014.

150.   BOCCHERINI, Luigi. *Seis Duos à dos violines*, G. 56-61, Op. 3, Madrid, J. Fernando Palomino, [*c*1771]; available at <imslp.org> and ID. *6 Duetti per 2 violini, Opus 3, G 56-61*, critical edition edited by Rudolf Rasch, Bologna, Ut Orpheus Edizioni, 2007 (Italian National Edition of Boccherini's complete works, vol. XXIX, BCE 2).

151.   ID. *Trois duos pour deux violons*, G. 63-68, edited by Hans Sitt, Leipzig, C. F. Peters, [*c*1890], available at <imslp.org>.

152.   SPECK, Christian – SADIE, Stanley. 'Boccherini, Luigi', in: *Grove Music Online, op. cit.* (see note 2).

called Leclair's «l'élève favori»[153]: many collections of *airs with variations* Op. 3 (1756), Op. 4 (1757), Op. 5 (1758), *Recueil quatrième de duos d'opéra-comique* (1772), *Principes du violon* (1761), which includes many operatic airs for two violins[154]; **Pierre Gaviniès** (1728-1800) (>Leclair?), considered Leclair's successor and called by Viotti (or Rode?) 'The French Tartini', performed with L'abbé *le fils* at Concert spirituel in 1748, then with Blavet, Guignon, Guillaume-Pierre Dupont. He was one of the rescuing directors of the Concert spirituel (1773-1777), taught at the Conservatoire (1795-1800)[155]: *24 matinées* (1794)[156], considered unsurpassed in difficulty until Paganini, were provided a 2nd violin line[157] in 1909 by Henri Marteau (1874-1934), *6 Sonatas* similar to Leclair's; Simon Le Duc *l'aîné* (1742-1777) (>Gaviniès), trained his brother[158] Pierre Le Duc (1755-1826), a violinist, who in turn championed his new works[159]: *6 Petits duos* Op. 6 (1771); Nicolas Capron (c1740-1784) (>Gaviniès), leader of Concert spirituel[160]: *6 Duets* Op. 3 (1777), *6 Petits duos* Op. 6 (1771); Marie-Alexandre Guénin (1744-1835) (>Gaviniès and >Capron, >Gossec and >Giornovichi), founding father of the Paris Conservatoire, which was based in 1784 on the model of Italian conservatories, was however forced out in 1802 and replaced by Kreutzer[161]: *6 Duets* Op. 3 (1775), *3 Duos* Op. 13 (c1815), *Ouverture et airs du ballet Psiché* (E. L. Müller) arranged for 2 violins (c1796), *Ouverture et airs du ballet Télémaque* (Müller), arranged for 2 violins (c1796), *6 Duos à l'usage des commençants* Op. 12 (c1813/1814), *3e Livre de duos, 3 Duos* Op. 13 (c1815)[162]; François-Hippolyte Barthélemon (1741-1808) (>Gaviniès?), achieved fame when he went to London[163]: *6 Duetts* Op. 4 (1773), *6 Duettos*, 2 of which are for 2 violins (London, c1778)[164].

Others, French, Genealogy Unknown

Isidore Bertheaume (c1752-1802) (>Lemière l'aîné): *Sonate dans le style de Lolly*, violin with violin accompaniment Op. 2 (1786), *6 Duets, avec des airs variés* Op. 3 (1786)[165]; Jean-Joseph Cassanéa De Mondonville (b Narbonne 1711-1772) (>?), appears at Concert spirituel from 1734: *Duets* (c1741, lost?)[166]; Théodore-Jean Tarade (1731-1788) (>Mondonville? or >Leclair?): collection of *Duets* (1773) that includes the *Romance* by Gaviniès, *Nouveaux principes de musique et de violon* (Paris 1774; lost, however extracts appear in J.-B. Cartier, *L'Art du violon*, Paris 1798)[167], *Les amusements d'un violon seul* (includes violin duets)[168], *6*

153. Pougin, Arthur. *Op. cit.* (see note 29), p. 228.

154. Zaslaw, Neal. 'L'abbé *le fils* [Joseph-Barnabé Saint-Sévin]', in: *Grove Music Online, op. cit.* (see note 2).

155. Cooper, Jeffrey – Ginter, Anthony. 'Gaviniès, Pierre', in: *ibidem*.

156. Gaviniès, Pierre. *Les Vingt quatre matinées*, Paris, Imbault, n.d., available at <imslp.org>.

157. Id. *24 Matinées*, arranged for a second violin by Henri Marteau, Leipzig, Steingräber, 1909, available at <imslp.org>.

158. Harden, Jean – Macnutt, Richard. 'Leduc', in: *Grove Music Online, op. cit.* (see note 2).

159. *Ibidem*.

160. Zaslaw, Neal. 'Capron, Nicolas', in: *Grove Music Online, op. cit.* (see note 2).

161. Keller, Michael A. – Garnier-Panafieu, Michelle. 'Guénin, Marie-Alexandre', in: *ibidem*.

162. *Ibidem*.

163. Zaslaw, Neal – McVeigh, Simon. 'Barthélemon, François-Hippolyte', in: *Grove Music Online, op. cit.* (see note 2).

164. *Ibidem*.

165. Zaslaw, Neal. 'Bertheaume, Isidore', in: *Grove Music Online, op. cit.* (see note 2).

166. Signorile, Marc. 'Mondonville, Jean-Joseph Cassanéa de', in: *ibidem*.

167. Zaslaw, Neal – Adams, Sarah J. 'Tarade, Théodore-Jean', in: *ibidem*.

168. Tarade, Théodore-Jean. *Les amusemens d'un violon seul*, Paris, Frère, n.d.

Violin Duets Op. 3[169]; <u>Papavoine</u> (*c*1720-1793) (>?): *2 Duos 'à la grecque'* (1764), which employed quarter-tones[170]; <u>Guillaume Navoigille *l'aîné*</u> (*c*1745-1811): *6 Duets* Op. 2 (1765)[171].

Others, Genealogy not Known

<u>Giuseppe Demachi</u> (1732; d after 1791) (>?), a colleague of Gaspard Fritz, whose style shows the influence of Boccherini and Tartini: *12 Duos*, with 6 for violin/viola (or 2 violins) Op. 1 (The Hague, n.d.) and 6 for 2 violins Op. 3 (Paris, ?1774)[172]; <u>Giuseppe Maria Cambini</u> (1746-1825) (>Boccherini?): *6 Duets* Op. 4[173]; <u>Pierre Dutillieu</u> (b. Lyons 1754; d Vienna 1798): *6 Duos* Op. 1 (Vienna, 1800)[174]; **Federigo Fiorillo** (b. Germany 1755; d after 1823), mandolinist of Neapolitan origins, went to Riga and Poland, played at the Concert spirituel and in London[175]: *42 Duos*[176], including *6 Duetts concertante* Op. 14[177], *3 Duos* Op. 31[178], *Etude pour le violon formant 36 caprices* Op. 3 (with second violin added by Spohr[179]); <u>Ivan Khandoshkin</u> (1747-1804) (>Tito Porta, >Costa? >A. Rolla?), Imperial Chapel of Russia, so-called 'The Orpheus of Russian violin playing': *6 Sonates* [*c*1781][180], *Variations on a Russian Folksong* Op. 1[181], *Chansons russes variées* Op. 2 (1796)[182].

School of Lolli

Antonio Lolli (Bergamo *c*1725-1802), from 1758 to 1774 solo violinist at the Stuttgart court orchestra, presented tours across Europe, «when the Romberg brothers visited him at Naples (March 5, 1796) Lolli played solos accompanied by A. Romberg on the violin»[183]: *6 Sonatas* Op. 9 (*c*1785)[184], *36 Capriccii* for solo violin (Offenbach n.d.; doubtful); *6 Sonates* Op. 10 (Paris *c*1788), arranged as *6 Duos* (Paris *c*1777)[185]; <u>Chevalier de Saint-George</u> (Joseph Boulogne, *dit*, 1745-1799) (>Lolli? >Leclair? >Gaviniès?): *3 Sonatas for violin accompanied by a second violin* Op. post. 1800[186]; <u>Giovanni Mane Giornovichi</u> (1747-1804)

169. ID. *Six Duo pour deux violons*, Op. 3, Paris, l'auteur, n.d., available at <imslp.org>.

170. BROOK, Barry S. *et al.* 'Papavoine (i)', in: *Grove Music Online*, *op. cit.* (see note 2).

171. NAVOIGILLE, Guillaume. *VI Duetti a due violini*, Op. 2, Paris, aux adresses ordinaires de musique, [1765], available at <imslp.org>.

172. MARTINOTTI, Sergio. 'Demachi, Giuseppe', in: *Grove Music Online*, *op. cit.* (see note 2).

173. CAMBINI, Giuseppe Maria. *Six Duos à deux violons*, Op. 4, Paris, Sieber, n.d., available at <imslp.org>.

174. GRUBER, Gernot. 'Dutillieu, Pierre', in: *Grove Music Online*, *op. cit.* (see note 2).

175. WHITE, Chappell. 'Fiorillo, Federigo', in: *ibidem*.

176. *Ibidem.*

177. FIORILLO, Federigo. *6 Duetts Concertante for Two Violins*, Op. 14, London, J. Bland, [*c*1790-1800?], available at <imslp.org>.

178. ID. *Duet*, Op. 31 Nos. 1-3, edited by Wilhelm Altmann, Leipzig, Robert Forberg, n.d. (reprinted New York, International Music Co., n.d.), available at <imslp.org>.

179. ID. *36 Violinstudien*, arranged by Louis Spohr, Leipzig, C. F. Peters, [1855], available at <imslp.org>.

180. KHANDOSHKIN, Ivan Y. *Variationen über ein russisches Volkslied: für zwei Violinen = Variations on a Russian Folksong: for Two Violins: Op. 1*, Munich-Gräfelfing, W. Wollenweber, 1995 (Unbekannte Werke der Klassik und Romantik, 176).

181. ID. *Chansons Russes variées: pour deux violons*, Op. 2, 1796, Courlay, Fuzeau, 2006 (Collection Dominantes; fac-similé Jean-Marc Fuzeau).

182. ID. *Six Sonates*, Amsterdam, Jean Julien Hummel, [*c*1781]; NORRIS, Geoffrey. 'Khandoshkin, Ivan Yevstafyevich', in: *Grove Music Online*, *op. cit.* (see note 2).

183. MELL, Albert. 'Lolli, Antonio', in: *ibidem*.

184. LOLLI, Antonio. *Six Sonates pour violons*, Op. 9, Paris, Sieber, n.d., available at <imslp.org>.

185. MELL, Albert. 'Lolli, Antonio', in: *Grove Music Online*, *op. cit.* (see note 2).

186. BANAT, Gabriel. 'Saint-Georges, Joseph Bologne, Chevalier de', in: *ibidem*.

(>Lolli), an acquaintance of Haydn, Dussek and Viotti in London, however often involved in quarrels: *Duet for violin and cello or two violins* (c1786), *6 Duos dialogués* (n.d.), *6 Duets concertans* Book 2 (c1793), *Duet* (c1796), *6 Sonates*[187]; <u>Feliks Janiewicz</u> (b Vilnius 1762; d Edinburgh 1848) (>Giornovichi), Polish in exile: *6 Divertimenti* (c1805)[188].

School of Rolla

Alessandro Rolla[189] (1757-1841): leader of the ducal orchestra in Parma, then La Scala in Milan, was approached to teach the young Paganini[190] in 1795[191], many first performances by Mozart, Beethoven, Rossini, Donizetti, Bellini, from 1808 professor at Conservatoire in Milan[192]: didactic works for his own pupils, graded in difficulty, many of which were published by newly-established Ricordi, such as *3 Concertant duos* Op. 3, Op. 17, multiple sets of *3* and *6 Duos, 3 Easy duos, 3 Grand concertant duos* Op. 28, *3 Grand duos*, BI 155, 212, 201, *2 Studies, 10 Studies*[193]; <u>Nicolò Paganini</u> (1782-1840) (>A. Rolla?): *Sonata a violino scordato* (MS 118, c1802, with one violin scordatura or 'detuned')[194], a second violin line was added to his *24 Caprices* Op. 1 by <u>Alberto Bachmann</u> (1875-1963) in 1921[195]; <u>Antonio Rolla</u> (1798-1837) (>Rolla), in a letter written in 1820, Paganini praised Rolla's ability «after they had played violin duets at the request of his father»[196], performed with his father at La Scala in 1823, and became opera concertmaster in Dresden on the recommendation of Paganini[197]: many *Duets* for violins[198], and *24 Cadenzas for solo violin*[199].

The German School

Franz Benda (1709-1786) (Tartini>Graun, knew Pisendel and C. P. E. Bach), from Prague to Berlin, so-called founder of the 'German school of violin playing': *31 Duets*[200]; <u>C. P. E. Bach</u> (1714-1788): *Duet for flute and violin* (1770)[201], *Duet* (1752, lost)[202];

---

[187]. WHITE, Chappell. 'Giornovichi, Giovanni', in: *ibidem*.

[188]. BERWALDT, Jacek – MIKULSKA, Margaret. 'Janiewicz, Feliks', in: *ibidem*.

[189]. Rolla used left-hand pizzicato, chromatic ascending and descending scales, very high positions, and octave passages. See ROSTAGNO, Antonio. 'Rolla, Antonio', in: *ibidem*.

[190]. But apparently Rolla «had nothing to teach [Paganini] and recommended him to study composition with Ferdinando Paer»; see NEILL, Edward. 'Paganini, Nicolò', in: *ibidem*.

[191]. The style of Rolla is technically similar to Paganini's.

[192]. ROSTAGNO, Antonio. *Op. cit.* (see note 189).

[193]. See 'Rolla, Alessandro', <imslp.org>.

[194]. See 'List of works by Niccolò Paganini' at <imslp.org>.

[195]. Structurally, Paganini's caprices could be reduced to duets. Many performers in the 19th century developed many piano accompaniments to these works. See STOWELL, Robin. 'Paganini: 24 Capricci per il Violino solo, dedicati agli Artisti Op. 1', at <http://chase.leeds.ac.uk/article/paganini-24-capricci-per-il-violino-solo-dedicati-agli-artisti-op-1-robin-stowell/>, accessed on 11 December 2014.

[196]. See <http://biblioteche2.comune.parma.it/dm/1901.htm>, accessed on 11 December 2014.

[197]. *Ibidem*.

[198]. *Alessandro Rolla: un caposcuola dell'arte violonistica lombarda*, edited by Mariateresa Dellaborra, Lucca, LIM, 2010 (Strumenti della ricerca musicale, 15); ZAPPALÀ, Pietro – GIORGI, Paolo. 'Verso un nuovo catalogo tematico di Alessandro Rolla', in: *ibidem*, pp. 357ff.

[199]. ROLLA, Antonio. *24 Cadenze per il violino*, Milan, G. Ricordi, n.d., available at <imslp.org>.

[200]. DRAKE, John D. *et al.* 'Benda', in: *Grove Music Online, op. cit.* (see note 2).

[201]. BACH, Carl Philipp Emanuel. *1 Flöyte Duette*, H.598, ms. in DK-Kk, Gieddes Samling II,17, available at <imslp.org>.

[202]. WOLFF, Christoph *et al.* 'Bach', in: *Grove Music Online, op. cit.* (see note 2).

Antonio Rossetti (b. Anton Rösler, *c*1750-1792), Czech-born, worked in Germany, was played in Paris[203], likely influenced Mozart[204]: *6 Easy duets D43-D48*[205].

The Mannheim School

Johann Stamitz (1717-1757): appeared in 1754 at the Concert spirituel: *6 Duets for flute or violin* (*c*1775)[206]; Christian Cannabich (1731-1798) (>J. Stamitz): *6 Duettos* (London, n.d.)[207]; Thomas Alexander Erskine (1732-1781) (>J. Stamitz): *Duo*[208]; **Carl Philipp Stamitz** (1745-1801) (>J. Stamitz), in Paris and Versailles from 1770, then to The Hague[209]: multiple sets of *3* and *6 Duos for violin and viola,* or *two violas*[210]; Anton Stamitz (1750; d between 1796 and 1809) (>J. and C. Stamitz), member of the *musique du roi* at Versailles from 1782 to 1789, where he trained R. Kreutzer: *12 Duos* (published in sets of 6) Op. 8 (1777) and Op. 9 (1777)[211]; **Louis Spohr** (1784-1859) (>Eck, Mannheim-trained): *3 Concertant duos* Op. 3[212], *2 Concertant duos* Op. 9[213] (dedicated to two of his students), *3 Grand duos* Op. 39[214], *3 Concertant duos* Op. 67[215], *Duo concertant* Op. 95[216], *Duet* Op. 148[217], *Duet* Op. 150 (1856)[218], *Duet* Op. 153[219], all three last duos dedicated to Alfred (1837-1876) and Henry (1839-1905) Holmes, violinists who trained at Spohr's Violin School (?). The brothers made their professional debut together when Alfred was just 10 years old, performing in concert as duettists at the Haymarket Theatre on July 13, 1847, then toured throughout Europe[220].

203. MURRAY, Sterling E. 'Rosetti, Antonio', in: *ibidem.*

204. LANDON, Howard C. Robbins 'The Concertos: (2) Their Musical Origin and Development', in: *The Mozart Companion*, edited by Howard C. Robbins Landon and Donald Mitchell, New York, Norton, 1956.

205. ROSETTI, Antonio. *Six Duos facile pour violon*, Paris, Naderman, n.d., available at <imslp.org>.

206. WOLF, Eugene K. 'Stamitz [Stamic], Johann (Wenzel Anton)', in: *Grove Music Online, op. cit.* (see note 2).

207. WOLF, Jean K. 'Cannabich, (Johann) Christian (Innocenz Bonaventura)', in: *ibidem.*

208. JOHNSON, David. 'Kelly [Kellie], 6ᵗʰ Earl of [Erskine, Thomas Alexander]', in: *ibidem.*

209. SMACZNY, Jan. 'Stamitz [Stamic], Carl (Philipp)', in: *The Oxford Companion to Music*, edited by Alison Latham, Oxford-New York, Oxford University Press, 2002.

210. See 'Stamitz, Carl Philipp', at <imslp.org>.

211. WOLF, Eugene K. – WOLF, Jean K. 'Stamitz [Stamic], Anton (Thadäus Johann Nepomuk)', in: *Grove Music Online, op. cit.* (see note 2).

212. SPOHR, Louis. *Trois Duos concertants pour deux violons*, Op. 3, Leipzig, Bureau de Musique de C. F. Peters, [*c*1815], available at <imslp.org>.

213. ID. *Deux Duos concertants pour deux violons*, Op. 9, Leipzig, C. F. Peters, [1808?], available at <imslp.org>.

214. ID. *Grands Duos pour deux violons*, Op. 39, Leipzig, C. F. Peters, [before 1820], available at <imslp.org>.

215. ID. *Trois Duos concertant pour deux violons*, Op. 67, Leipzig, Bureau de Musique de C. F. Peters, [*c*1828], available at <imslp.org>.

216. ID. *Duo concertant pour pianoforte et violon*, Op. 95, Leipzig, Breitkopf & Härtel, [1837], available at <imslp.org>.

217. ID. *3 Grosse Duette für zwei Violinen*, Opp. 148, 150, 153, Leipzig, C. F. Peters, [1856], available at <imslp.org>.

218. *Ibidem*, available at <imslp.org>.

219. *Ibidem*, available at <imslp.org>.

220. HUSK, W. H. – MELL, Albert. 'Holmes, Alfred', in: *Grove Music Online, op. cit.* (see note 2).

The Austrian/Viennese School

Characteristically it produced violin-viola duets; however only violin are listed. Joseph Haydn (1732-1809): *6 Sonatas* Op. 6[221]; Wolfgang Amadeus Mozart (1756-1791) [222], taught by his father Leopold Mozart (1719-1787): *12 Duets* Op. 70[223]; **Paul Wranitzky** (1756-1808), Czech, moved to Vienna, regarded as being on the same level as Haydn and Mozart in his time: *Duos concertants for 2 flutes* Op. 13[224], Op. 42[225], *6 Duos for 2 flutes* Op. 2 (Berlin, 1798)[226]; Antonin Wranitzky (1761-1820), (half?) brother of Paul Wranitzky: *Duos* Op. 9 (c1802), Op. 12 (1804), Op. 20 (c1809), *Variations* for 2 violins (some published)[227]; Carl Ditters von Dittersdorf (1739-1799), Austrian: *Duet in D*[228]; Franz Anton von Hoffmeister (1754-1812), German, moved to Vienna at 14: multiple sets of *Duets*[229]; **Ignace Pleyel** (1757-1831), Austrian, went to London in 1791, collaborated with Wilhelm Cramer, who ran a rival series to Johann Peter Salomon and Haydn: multiple sets of *3* and *6 Duets*[230]; **Frantisek Krommer** (1759-1831), Czech[231], lived in Vienna and Hungary[232]: *27 Duos* published in sets of 3, Op. 2 (1793), Op. 6 (1796), Op. 20 (c1810), Op. 22 (?1800), Op. 33 (1802), Op. 35 (?1805), Op. 51 (?1805), Op. 94 (1816), Op. 110 (1829)[233]; Leopold Jansa (1795-1875), succeeded Schuppanzigh in his quartet in 1830[234]: *Concert Duets*, including Op. 16, Op. 36, Op. 46, Op. 74, Op. 81[235].

Pupils of Viotti

Jean-Baptiste Cartier (1765-1841) (>Viotti), hired by the court, assistant leader at the Paris Opera until 1821, from 1804 to 1830 was musician to Napoleon, Louis XVIII, and Charles X: *L'Art du violon* (1798)[236], which contains duets, such as *Sonate dans le style de Mr. Lolly* Op. 7, *3 Grands duos dialogués concertans* Op. 14, *6 Airs variés, 6 Duos méthodiques* Op. 11, *6 Duos* Op. 9[237]; August Duranowski (c1770-1834) (>Viotti), Polish-born Frenchman (Durand), leader of the Brussels Opera orchestra, settled in Strasbourg, apparently

---

[221]. HAYDN, Joseph. *Six Sonates à deux violons*, Op. 6, Amsterdam, J. J. Hummel, [c1796], available at <imslp.org>.

[222]. Michael Haydn (1737-1806), brother of Joseph, wrote *6 duos* for violin and viola in 1783 (pub. Vienna, 1788), however the two last ones were written by Mozart (K. 423, 424; 1783; Mozart did not take credit). See BLAZIN, Dwight. 'Haydn, Michael', in: *Grove Music Online, op. cit.* (see note 2).

[223]. MOZART, Wolfgang Amadeus. *12 Duos pour deux violons*, Op. 70, edited by August Schulz, Braunschweig, Litolff, [1894], available at <imslp.org>.

[224]. WRANITZKY, Paul. *Six Duo concertans pour deux flûtes*, Op. 13, Paris, Boyer, [1790s?], available at <imslp.org>.

[225]. ID. *Trois Duos pour deux flûtes*, Op. 42, Offenbach am Main, J. André, [c1820], available at <imslp.org>.

[226]. POŠTOLKA, Milan – HICKMAN, Roger. 'Wranitzky, Paul', in: *Grove Music Online, op. cit.* (see note 2).

[227]. *Ibidem.*

[228]. GRAVE, Margaret – LANE, Jay. 'Dittersdorf, Carl Ditters von', in: *Grove Music Online, op. cit.* (see note 2).

[229]. WEINMANN, Alexander. 'Hoffmeister, Franz Anton', in: *ibidem.*

[230]. BENTON, Rita. 'Pleyel, Ignace Joseph [Ignaz Josef]', in: *ibidem.*

[231]. Václav Pichl (1741-1805), also Czech, worked in Vienna, wrote 15 duets for 2 violins and 18 for violin and viola. See POŠTOLKA, Milan. 'Pichl [Pichel], Václav', in: *ibidem.*

[232]. WESSELY, Othmar. 'Krommer, Franz', in: *ibidem.*

[233]. See 'Krommer, Franz', at <imslp.org>.

[234]. NĚMCOVÁ, Alena. 'Jansa, Leopold', in: *ibidem.*

[235]. See 'Jansa, Leopold' at <imslp.org>.

[236]. CARTIER, Jean-Baptiste. *L'Art du violon*, second edition, Paris, Decombe, [1799], available at <imslp.org>.

[237]. SCHWARZ, Boris – GARNIER-BUTE, Michelle. 'Cartier, Jean Baptiste', in: *Grove Music Online, op. cit.* (see note 2).

impressed the young Paganini[238]: *3 Airs variés* Op. 5[239]; **Rodolphe Kreutzer** (b Versailles 1766-1831) (>his father and A. Stamitz), strongly influenced by Viotti, professor at the Paris Conservatoire from its founding in 1795 to 1826, collaborator in the *Méthode du Conservatoire* with Baillot and Rode, solo violin and later director of the Opera: *3 Duos* Op. 11, pt. 2 (*c*1800), *3 Duos* Op. 3 (between 1800 and 1809), *3 Duos concertans* Op. B (*c*1820)[240], Adolf Grünwald (1826-1901), professor at the Berlin Academy, provided a second violin to Kreutzer's *42 Études*[241]; Andreas Jacob Romberg (1767-1821) (>Viotti and Philidor), appeared at Concert spirituel[242]: *Duets* Op. 4[243], Op. 18[244], Op. 56[245]; Philippe Libon (b Cadiz 1775; d Paris 1838) (>Viotti in London), involved in London premieres of Haydn Quartets, to Paris in 1800 to the service of Joséphine, and later Marie-Louise of Austria[246]: *3 Duets* Op. 4[247]; Johann Wenzel Kalliwoda (1801-1886) (>Pixis)[248]: *Duets*, including *2 Duos* Op. 70, *3 Duos* Op. 116, *3 Duets* Op. 181, *3 Easy Duos* Op. 178, Op. 179, Op. 180, *3 Duos faciles et brillants* Op. 243[249]; **Pierre Rode** (1774-1830) (>Viotti from 13yrs of age), in 1802 collaborated on the *Méthode* with Baillot and Kreutzer, violin soloist to Napoleon, visited many countries, Tsar's solo violinist in Saint Petersburg[250]: *Duos* Op. 1, Op. 2[251], Op. 18, Op. 22, Op. 41[252], *Exercices pour le Violon* [duets] *dans toutes les positions et 50 Variations sur la Gamme. Supplément de la Méthode du violon (Violinschule) par Rode, Kreutzer et Baillot*[253]; **Pierre(-Marie-François de Sales) Baillot** (1771-1842) (>Viotti), colleague of Rode (first playing alongside him in Viotti's orchestra at the Theatre Feydeau, then replacing him during his absences) and Kreutzer at the Conservatoire (full-time from 1799), leader of the Paris Opéra, gave solo recitals and was a notable performer of chamber music (many Paris

[238]. CHMARA-ŻACKIEWICZ, Barbara. 'Duranowski, August', in: *ibidem*. Paganini could be said to have perfected the integration of 'solo duetting' techniques, using many 'dialoguing' effects that held audiences spellbound.

[239]. DURANOWSKI, August Fryderyk. *Trois Airs variés pour le violon avec accompagnement de basse*, Op. 5, Paris, Momigny, [1800], available at <imslp.org>.

[240]. CHARLTON, David. 'Kreutzer, Rodolphe', in: *Grove Music Online, op. cit.* (see note 2).

[241]. KREUTZER, Rodolphe. *40 Études ou Caprices pour le violon de Kreutzer*, arranged by Adolf Grünwald, Braunschweig, Henry Litolff, [*c*1912], available at <imslp.org>.

[242]. STEPHENSON, Kurt – WALDEN, Valerie. 'Romberg, Andreas Jakob', in: *Grove Music Online, op. cit.* (see note 2).

[243]. ROMBERG, Andreas Jacob. *Trois duos concertans pour deux violons*, Op. 4, Hamburg, Jean Auguste Böhme, n.d., available at <imslp.org>.

[244]. ID. *Trois duos concertans pour deux violons*, Op. 18, Hamburg, Jean Auguste Böhme, [*c*1810], available at <imslp.org>.

[245]. ID. *Trois duos concertans pour deux violons*, Op. 56, Copenhagen, C. C. Lose, n.d., available at <imslp.org>.

[246]. BOURLIGUEUX, Guy. 'Libon, Philippe', in: *Grove Music Online, op. cit.* (see note 2).

[247]. LIBON, Felipe. *Trois Grands duos concertans pour deux violons*, Op. 4, Milan, Ricordi, [1824], available at <imslp.org>.

[248]. *Prague School* – Friedrich Wilhelm Pixis (1785-1842) (>Viotti), worked at Mannheim in the orchestra and then in Prague as violin professor, so-called «founder of the Prague school of violin»: no known duet. See JONES, Gaynor G. – SCHIWIETX, Lucian – LINDEMAN, Stephan D. 'Pixis, Friedrich Wilhelm (ii)', in: *Grove Music Online, op. cit.* (see note 2).

[249]. See 'Kalliwoda, Johann Wenzel', available at <imslp.org>.

[250]. SCHWARZ, Boris – BROWN, Clive. 'Rode, Pierre', in: *Grove Music Online, op. cit.* (see note 2).

[251]. RODE, Pierre. *Trois duos pour deux violons*, Opp. 1, 2, 2 vols. respectively, Copenhagen, C. C. Lose, n.d., available at <imslp.org>.

[252]. SCHWARZ, Boris – BROWN, Clive. *Op. cit.* (see note 150).

[253]. RODE, Pierre. *Exercices pour le violon dans toutes les positions et 50 Variations sur la gamme: supplément de la Méthode du violon* [...] *par Rode, Kreutzer & Baillot*, Prague, Marco Berra, n.d., available at <imslp.org>.

premieres of Beethoven's string quartets)[254], after the time of Baillot and his contemporaries, Paganini's style became predominant in Paris, but the influence of the Paris school extended to Germany[255]: *L'Art du violon*[256] (1834, in which he quotes two Viotti *Duets* G94-95 both called '*Hommage à l'Amitié*'), *24 Études pour 2 violons* to add to *L'Art du violon* dedicated to his students Op. posth. (1851)[257], *3 Duets* Op. 8 1ˢᵗ book (1805), *3 Duos* Op. 16 (1806)[258], *6 Airs variés ou études* with a 2ⁿᵈ violin Op. 12 (c1811)[259]; **Jacques Féréol Mazas** (1782-1849) (>Baillot), toured Europe, school appointment in Cambrai[260]: *3 Duos concertans* from *Méthode de violon* Op. 34, *18 Duos* Op. 38, *6 Duos* Op. 39, *6 Duos brillants* Op. 40 (1834), *6 Grand duos* Op. 41 (1834), *6 Easy Duets* dedicated to his students Op. 61 (1838), *3 Duos progressifs* Op. 62 (1840), *3 Duos brillants* Op. 66 (1838), *3 Duos brillants* Op. 67 (1839), *6 Petits duos progressifs* Op. 70 (1839), *2 Duos concertans* Op. 71, *L'École du violoniste* Op. 72 (1841), which includes *6 Duos brillants*, *6 Duos faciles et brillans* Op. 82 (1841), *Collection des duos de salon* Op. 83, which includes *6 Duos brillants* (1845), *15 duos Abécédaires* Op. 85 posth. (1854), *Le Lycée du violoniste* Op. 86 includes *9 duos élémentaires* (1858), *Duos d'émulation* Op. 87 posth. (1861), and *Duos de salon* Op. 88 posth. (1861)[261]; **(Jean-)Delphin Alard** (1815-1888) (>Habeneck), succeeded Baillot[262]: *10 Études* with the accompaniment of a 2ⁿᵈ violin Op. 10, *3 Duos brillants* Op. 27, *École du violon* (adopted by the Conservatoire), *3 Duos faciles* Op. 23, *4 Duos élémentaires* Op. 22, *Les Maîtres classiques du violon* (incl. Stamitz *2 Duos for solo violin* from *Divertimenti*, Campagnoli *2 Fugues for solo violin* Op. 10, Lolli *Sonata* VI *for 2 violins*)[263]; **Charles Dancla** (1817-1907) (>Baillot) influenced by Paganini and Vieuxtemps, solo violinist at the Opera, then professor at the Conservatoire[264]: *3 Duos* Op. 15, Op. 23, Op. 24, Op. 25, Op. 32, Op. 33, Op. 34, Op. 35, Op. 60, Op. 61, Op. 62, *15 Studies* Op. 68, *2 Duos* Op. 19, Op. 20[265].

The Franco-Belgian School

Charles de Bériot (1802-1870) (>Tiby, Robberechts)[266], Belgian encouraged by Viotti, influenced by Paganini, chamber violinist to Charles X and to William I of the Netherlands, then rejected the offer to replace Baillot at the Conservatoire in 1842 (Massart accepted it), instead in 1843 became head of violin instruction at the Brussels Conservatory[267] thereby starting the Franco-Belgian

---

254. DAVID, Paul *et al.* 'Baillot, Pierre', in: *Grove Music Online, op. cit.* (see note 2).

255. Where Spohr must be considered artistically linked to Viotti and Rode.

256. BAILLOT, Pierre(-Marie-François de Sales). *L'Art du violon: nouvelle méthode*, Paris, Dépôt central de la musique, [1835], available at <imslp.org>.

257. ID. *24 Études pour violon principal avec acc.ᵗ d'un second violon*, Op. posth., Mainz, Schott, [1852], available at <imslp.org>.

258. ID. *Trois Duos pour deux Violons*, Op. 16, Paris, Typographie de la Syrene, [before 1820], available at <imslp.org>.

259. DAVID, Paul – PARIKIAN, Manoug – GARNIER-BUTE, Michelle. 'Baillot, Pierre (Marie François de Sales)', in: *Grove Music Online, op. cit.* (see note 2).

260. CHARLTON, David. 'Mazas, Jacques-Féréol', in: *ibidem*.

261. See 'List of works by Jacques Féréol Mazas', available at <imslp.org>.

262. SCHWARZ, Boris – NEWARK, Cormac. 'Alard, (Jean-)Delphin', in: *Grove Music Online, op. cit.* (see note 2).

263. See 'Alard, Jean Delphin', available at <imslp.org>.

264. MELL, Albert – NEWARK, Cormac. 'Dancla, (Jean Baptiste) Charles', in: *Grove Music Online, op. cit.* (see note 2).

265. See 'Dancla, Charles', available at <imslp.org>.

266. André Robberechts (>Viotti and Baillot). See SCHWARZ, Boris. 'Bériot, Charles-Auguste de', in: *Grove Music Online, op. cit.* (see note 2).

267. See *ibidem*.

school[268]: *3 Duos concertants* Op. 57[269], *3 Grand Studies* Op. 43[270], *Douze petits duos faciles pour 2 violons*, Op. 87[271], *Méthode de violon* Op. 102[272], in three parts containing a full accompaniment of 2nd violin (instructor); François Prume (1816-1849) (>Habeneck) taught the father of Ysaÿe[273]: *2 Duos concertants* Op. 18[274]; Hubert Léonard (1819-1890) (> Habeneck and Prume), succeeded de Bériot[275]: *Duo de concert* Op. 25 'La Bataille'[276]; Julius Eichberg (1824-1893) (>de Bériot), professor in Geneva for 11 years, became director of the Boston Conservatory of Music[277]: *Complete Method of the Violin* (1879)[278]; **Henryk Wieniawski** (1835-1880) (>Massart[279], Vieuxtemps), Polish virtuoso: *8 Études-caprices* Op. 18 (1862)[280], a 2nd violin accompaniment to his concerti was provided by Philippe Borer (*no. 1*) and Otakar Ševčik (1852-1934), *no. 2*[281]; Émile Sauret (1852-1920) (>de Bériot, Vieuxtemps, Wieniawski): *Adagio and Rondo* Op. 44[282], and duo accompaniments to standard concerti (Mozart)[283]; **Eugène Ysaÿe** (1858-1931) (>Antoine Ysaÿe, Vieuxtemps, Wieniawsky, Massart): *Sonata for 2 violins* (1915)[284], *Poème no. 4 'l'Extase'* Op. 21 (arrangement with second violin by Ysaÿe)[285].

---

268.   His most illustrious disciples were Hubert Léonard, Henry Vieuxtemps and Heinrich Wilhelm Ernst.

269.   BÉRIOT, Charles-Auguste de. *Trois Duos concertants pour deux violon*, Op. 57, Milan, Ricordi, [1847], available at <imslp.org>.

270.   ID. *Tre Grandi studi per due violini*, Op. 43, Milan, Ricordi, [1843], available at <imslp.org>.

271.   ID. *Douze petits duos faciles pour 2 violons*, Op. 87, edited by József Bloch (1862-1922), Budapest, Charles Rozsnyai, [c1908], available at <imslp.org>.

272.   ID. *Méthode de Violon*, Op. 102, in three parts containing a full accompaniment of 2nd violin (instructor), Paris, L'Auteur, [c1870], available at <imslp.org>.

273.   YSAÿE, Antoine – RATCLIFFE, Bertram. *Ysaÿe: His Life, Work, and Influence*, St. Clair Shores (MI), Scholarly Press, 1978.

274.   *Cfr. Musikalisches Wochenblatt*, V (1874).

275.   MELL, Albert. 'Léonard, Hubert', in: *Grove Music Online, op. cit.* (see note 2).

276.   See 'List of works by Hubert Léonard' at <imslp.org>.

277.   JENKS, F. H. – MORAN, John. 'Eichberg, Julius', in: *Grove Music Online, op. cit.* (see note 2).

278.   EICHBERG, Julius. *Complete Method for the Violin* (1879), revised and enlarged edition, Boston, White, Smith & Co., 1879, available at <imslp.org>.

279.   Joseph Lambert Massart (1811-1892), (>Kreutzer) a Belgian violinist, pupil of Kreutzer (annotations and revisions to the *42 Études*), replaced Baillot, taught Wieniawski, Lotto and Kreisler, among others: no known duets. See MELL, Albert. 'Massart, (Joseph) Lambert', in: *Grove Music Online, op. cit.* (see note 2).

280.   WIENIAWSKI, Henryk. *Etudes-Caprices: For Violin with a Second Violin*, Op. 18, edited by Leopold Lichtenberg, New York, G. Schirmer, 1903 (Schirmer's library of musical classics, 184-185).

281.   ŠEVČÍK, Otakar. *Elaborate Studies and Analysis bar by bar to H. Wieniawski 2. Concerto in D-minor with revised solo voice, complete piano score and accompanying second violin*, Op. 17, Brno, Ol. Pazdírek, 1929, available at <imslp.org>.

282.   BACHMANN, Alberto. *An Encyclopedia of the Violin*, translated by Frederick H. Martens, edited by Albert E. Wier, New York, Appleton, 1925.

283.   The extensive 'solo duetting' of Sauret is a clear predecessor to Ysaÿe's solo sonatas.

284.   YSAÿE, Eugène. *Première Sonate à deux violons*, Brussels, Éditions Ysaÿe, 1967, available at <imslp.org>.

285.   ID. *Extase: 4me Poème pour violon et orchestre*, Op. 21, arrangement with second violin by the author, manuscript, private collection, n.d., available at <imslp.org>.

Pupils of Spohr

Bernhard Molique (1802-1869) (>Spohr, Rovelli), German, succeeded Rovelli as court violinist in Munich, then in Stuttgart, praised by Berlioz[286]: *3 Duos concertants* Op. 2 (1825)[287], *3 Duets* Op. 3[288]; Moritz Hauptmann (1792-1868) (> Spohr): Duets Op. 2[289], Op. 11, Op. 16, Op. 17[290]; Pieter Hubert Ries (1802-1886), brother of Ferdinand Ries (1784-1838) (>Spohr and Hauptmann): *3 Duets* Op. 17[291], *Violinschule*[292]; Ferdinand David (1810-1873) (>Spohr and Hauptmann), teacher of Joseph Joachim (1831-1907) and colleague of Andreas Moser (1859-1925)[293]: *Duets* in *Violinschule* (1863)[294], *Violinschule* Op. 44 (1872)[295], *Violinschule* Op. 45[296].

School of Joseph Böhm[297]

Georg Hellmesberger Sr (1800-1873) (>Böhm), taught his sons Joseph (who taught Kreisler[298]; and wrote *Etudes for 2 violins* Op. 184[299]) and Georg Jr, Miska Hauser, Heinrich Wilhelm Ernst, Joseph Joachim, and Leopold Auer, succeeded Schuppanzigh as concertmaster of the Vienna Court Opera[300]: *Duets* Op. 4, Op. 14; **Joseph Mayseder** (1789-1863) (>Schuppanzigh): *Air Favori Russe* Op. 1, *3 Duets*

---

286. SCHWARZ, Boris. 'Molique, Bernhard', in: *Grove Music Online, op. cit.* (see note 2).

287. MOLIQUE, Bernhard. *3 Duos concertant pour deux violons*, Op. 2, Mainz, B. Schott's Söhne, [c1825], available at <imslp.org>.

288. BACHMANN, Alberto. *Op. cit.* (see note 282).

289. HAUPTMANN, Moritz. *Deux Duos concertans pour duex violons*, Op. 2, Leipzig, C. F. Peters, [1821], available at <imslp.org>.

290. BACHMANN, Alberto. *Op. cit.* (see note 282).

291. RIES, Hubert Pieter. *Trois Duos pour deux violons*, Op. 17, Berlin, Bote & Bock, n.d., available at <imslp.org>.

292. ID. *Violinschule*, edited by Hans Sitt, Leipzig, Friedrich Hofmeister, 1840, available at <imslp.org>.

293. MELL, Albert. 'David, Ferdinand', in: *Grove Music Online, op. cit.* (see note 2).

294. DAVID, Ferdinand. *David's Violin School*, edited by B. Listemann, Boston, Oliver Ditson, [c1880], available at <imslp.org>.

295. ID. *Zur Violinschule*, Op. 44, Leipzig, Breitkopf und Härtel, [1890], available at <imslp.org>.

296. ID. *Zur Violinschule: Supplément à la Méthode de violon*, Op. 45, edited by Manuel Dello, Braunschweig, Henry Litolff, n.d., available at <imslp.org>.

297. Joseph Böhm (1795-1876) (>Rode), professor at the Vienna Conservatory from 1819 to 1848, his many students included Jenő Hubay, Joseph Joachim, Edouard Reményi, Heinrich Wilhelm Ernst, Jakob Dont, Georg Hellmesberger Sr, Jakob Grün and Sigismund Bachrich, involved in championing the string quartets of Beethoven (premiered no. 12) and Joseph Haydn: no known duet. «Supervised practice was a critical element in Joseph's success. "For a long time, I [...] was not allowed to practice alone", Joachim wrote to Clara Schumann in 1861. Böhm employed a different approach to supervision with his conservatory pupils: an adaptation of the Lancasterian Monitorial System, a method developed by the British pioneer of mass education, Joseph Lancaster (1778-1838). Following Seneca's motto, Qui docet, discit ("He who teaches, learns"), Lancaster's system employed advanced students as peer tutors to help the less experienced members of the class. According to one of Joachim's fellow students, Adolf Grünwald, Böhm had his students play duets "for months together, so that the pupils became perfectly familiar with this form of music, indeed thoroughly tired of it"»; ESHBACH, Robert W. 'Study with Joseph Böhm', at <josephjoachim.com>, accessed 4 March 2014.

298. SCHWARZ, Boris. 'Kreisler, Fritz', in: *Grove Music Online, op. cit.* (see note 2).

299. BACHMANN, Alberto. *Op. cit.* (see note 282).

300. EVIDON, Richard. 'Hellmesberger', in: *Grove Music Online, op. cit.* (see note 2).

Opp. 30-32[301]; **Jakob Dont** (1815-1888) (>Böhm and G. Hellmsberger Sr), taught Leopold Auer[302]: *Duets* Op. 43 (1869), Op. 48 (1870), *Easy Exercises in All Major and Minor Keys with accompaniment of a second violin* Op. 17 (1854), *Exercises in the Art of Bowing with Shifting in the First Three Positions for 2 violins* Op. 62; Hans Sitt (1850-1922), Czech, professor at the Leipzig Conservatory: *6 Easy Instructive Duets* Op. 42 (1892), *3 Duets in the First Position for Beginners* Op. 91 (1905), *3 Short Easy Duets in the First 3 Positions* Op. 117 (1913), *3 Short Easy Duets in the First 3 Positions* Op. 118 (1913), *20 Short Concert Pieces in Progressive Difficulty for violin and piano or for 2 violins* Op. 73 (1900), *20 Duette* Op. 73b[303].

301. BACHMANN, Alberto. *Op. cit.* (see note 282).
302. MORAN, John. 'Dont, Jakob', in: *Grove Music Online, op. cit.* (see note 2).
303. See 'List of works by Hans Sitt' at <imslp.org>.

THE ROOTS OF THE VIOLIN BRAVURA TRADITION

AH!, VOUS DIRAI-JE TARTINI!
PER LA DEFINIZIONE DI UN CONTESTO EUROPEO DELLE 'PICCOLE SONATE' DI GIUSEPPE TARTINI (I-PCA 1888/1)

Gregorio Carraro

(PADOVA)

NELL'AUTOGRAFO I-Pca 1888/1[1], quello con le cosiddette 'piccole sonate'[2] di Giuseppe Tartini (Pirano d'Istria, 8 aprile 1692 - Padova, 26 febbraio 1770), si incontrano due movimenti[3] che altro non sono se non variazioni per violino solo sul tema della canzone francese *Ah!, vous dirai-je maman*.

La semplicità e il tratto particolarmente orecchiabile hanno reso questa melodia protagonista di un vasto fenomeno di diffusione[4] che, praticamente fino ai giorni nostri, non si è mai arrestato.

A parità di intonazione melodica, a oggi ne esistono diverse varianti testuali, più o meno letterarie: alcune di ambito celeste, come *Twinkle twinkle little star*[5]; di ambito infantil-ovino, come *Baa baa black sheep have you any wood?*; di ambito natalizio, come *Morgen kommt der Weihnachtsmann*[6]; di ambito aviario-agreste, come *Três galinhas a cantar*.

---

[1]. Conservato a Padova, presso la Biblioteca Antoniana.

[2]. Per una inquadratura generale delle cosiddette 'piccole sonate' *cfr.* BRAINARD, Paul. *Die Violinsonaten Giuseppe Tartinis*, tesi di dottorato, Göttingen, Georg-August-Universität Göttingen, 1959.

[3]. Si tratta di due sonate che si indicano qui di seguito con la numerazione che si legge nell'autografo, e la sigla di cui in ID. *Le sonate per violino di Giuseppe Tartini: catalogo tematico*, traduzione italiana di Claudio Scimone, Milano, Carisch, 1975 (Studi e ricerche dell'Accademia Tartiniana di Padova; Le opere di Giuseppe Tartini, III/2): Sonata V F1 (autografo, p. 13 - catalogo, p. 54), Sonata XVI C2 (autografo p. 54, catalogo p. 6). Si segnala infine un movimento alternativo della Sonata XVIII C3 (autografo p. 58, catalogo, p. 7). Il movimento con variazioni riscontrato nella C2, è indicato da Tartini nella C3 come movimento alternativo (Brainard, Catalogo, p. 7).

[4]. *Cfr.* LIST, George. 'The Distribution of a Melodic Formula: Diffusion or Polygenesis?', in: *Yearbook of the International Folk Music Council*, X (1978), pp. 33-52.

[5]. TAYLOR, Jane. 'The Star', in: *Rhymes for the Nursery*, Londra, Darton and Harvey, 1806.

[6]. FALLERSLEBEN, August Heinrich Hoffmann von. *Siebengestirn gevatterliches Wiegen-Lieder für Frau Minna von Winterfeld*, Polwisch Neudorf [Polska Nowa Wieś], Forster, Hochheimer & Co., 1827.

Tra le varianti francesi di ambito popolare si citano anche *À la pêche aux moules*, oppure *Le Palais-Royal est un beau quartier*, oppure *Quand trois poules s'en vont aux champs*.

Una particolare versione di *Ah!, vous dirai-je maman* si è individuata anche in una canzone degli anni Venti del xx secolo, *La vigne aux moineaux*, nel repertorio di Charles Armand Ménard in arte Dranem (Parigi, 1869 - 13 ottobre 1935), cantante e fantasista francese.

La melodia in questione si trova anche tra le canzoni per l'infanzia più cliccate su YouTube. Talmente semplice e suadente da commuovere non solo il cuore delle mamme, ma, a quanto pare, anche quello dei pubblicitari che l'hanno utilizzata (in una delle due varianti inglesi) per la campagna di SKY del 2011 — forse la versione più recente che si possa rintracciare, oltre alle altre (numerosissime) riconducibili più direttamente ad un ambito infantile (con veste prevalentemente di ninna nanna).

Ma si proceda con ordine alle origini della tradizione di *Ah!, vous dirai-je maman* al Settecento, che è il focus cronologico di questo breve studio.

La sua linea melodica è compresa nell'ambito di un esacordo, sul modello di una melodia del quinto modo salmodico. Con Wilhelm Tappert[7], da questa struttura salmodica derivano intere famiglie di melodie, tra cui uno degli esempi più antichi è *Presulem sanctissimum veneremur*, tratto dalla seconda parte del *Teutsche Liedlein* di Georg Forster (Norimberga 1540).

Altra possibile derivazione melodica cinquecentesca di ambito nord europeo è proposta da Hartmut Braun[8] il quale, citando gli studi del Böhme[9], ne individua l'origine in un'*Allemande* tedesca del xvi secolo.

Si prendano ora in considerazione alcuni aspetti della tradizione settecentesca della formula melodica e delle variazioni che su questa sono state composte.

Una prima versione variata di *Ah!, vous dirai-je maman* risale a François Bouin, *Amusements d'une heure et demi*, 1761[10]. Con Weckerlin[11], il tema circolerebbe già vent'anni prima, a partire cioè dal 1740, nell'ambito del repertorio del *vaudeville* dell'Opéra-Comique[12].

---

7. TAPPERT, Wilhelm. *Wandernde Melodien: Eine musikalische Studie*, Berlino, Brachvogel & Ranft, 1889.

8. BRAUN, Hartmut. *Tänze und Gebrauchmusik in Musikhandschriften des 18. und frühen 19. Jahrhunderts aus dem Artland*, Cloppenburg, Museum Cloppenburg, 1984, p. 71.

9. BÖHME, Franz Magnus. *Geschichte des Tanzes in Deutschland: Beitrag zur deutschen Sitten-, Litteratur- und Musikgeschichte nach den Quellen zum erstenmal bearb. und mit alten Tanzliedern und Musikproben*, 2 voll., Lipsia, Breitkopf & Härtel, 1886, vol. II: *Musikbeilagen: Tanzlieder und Tanzmelodien von der älteren Zeit bis zur Gegenwart*, esempi nn. 22a-b, p. 13.

10. *Cfr.* WALLON, Simon. 'Romances et Vaudevilles français dans le variations pour piano et pour piano et violon de Mozart', in: *Bericht über den Internationalen Musikwissenschaftlichen Kongress: Wien, Mozartjahr 1956, 3. bis 9. Juni*, a cura di Erich Schenk, Graz-Colonia, Böhlau, 1958, p. 668.

11. WECKERLIN, Jean-Baptiste. *Chansons populaires du pays de France avec notices et accompagnements de piano*, 2 voll., Parigi, Heugel, 1903, vol. II, p. 36.

12. *Cfr.* WALLON, Simon. *Op. cit.* (si veda nota 10).

Ulrich Konrad[13] segnala una intonazione musicale del 1765[14] e un testo poetico non datato — che pure ha una intonazione — tratto da un poemetto amoroso dal titolo *Les Amours de Silvandre*[15]. Sempre Konrad segnala due attribuzioni prive di basi documentali a Nicolas Dezède[16] (Lione 1740 - Parigi 1792) e a Jean-Philippe Rameau (Digione 1683 - Parigi 1764). Una sistemazione definitiva della melodia potrebbe arrivare intorno agli anni Settanta. A questo proposito Wallon osserva che «De Lusse pubblicò la chanson completa nel 1774, nella sua *Recueil de romances* (vol. II, p. 75)»; e ancora

> […] è soprattutto tra la musica strumentale dell'epoca che bisogna cercare [la melodia di *Ah vous dirai*]. Ella diviene effettivamente, dopo il 1770, il tema per variazioni favorito e quasi obbligatorio per i compositori francesi e per quelli stranieri residenti in Francia[17].

Tra i compositori di medio Settecento che Wallon cita, se ne riportano tre che hanno scritto variazioni per il violino: Franz Lamotte (violino e basso, 1775), Anton Stamitz (violino e basso, 1776), Barrière (due violini, 1778).

Tra le versioni violinistiche sopra indicate, salta agli occhi quella di La Motte, musicista itinerante la cui vita intercetta quella del Campagnoli, violinista allievo del Guastarobba (a sua volta allievo di Tartini). Si sottolinea il dato interessante, che negli anni Sessanta del Settecento Campagnoli è presente a Venezia e a Padova insieme al «collega Lamotta [*sic*]»[18].

Altra cosa è la tradizione di variazioni su *Ah!, vous dirai-je maman* per tastiera[19].

---

[13]. KONRAD, Ulrich. *Zwölf Variationen in C für Klavier über das franzoesische Lied «Ah!, vous dirai-je maman», KV 265 (300ₑ): Faksimile nach den autographen Fragmenten und Reproduktion des Erstdrucks*, Augusta, Deutsche Mozart-Gesellschaft, 2001. Nella prefazione all'edizione in facsimile, a p. 7 il Konrad segnala anche una fonte degli anni Settanta del XVIII secolo, *Recueil de Romances*, vol. II, Parigi, 1774 (RISM L 3093).

[14]. In: *Recueil de chansons choisies*, ms., Parigi, Bibliothéque nationale de France, Vm⁷ 3640.

[15]. La fonte è conservata presso la British Library; per una edizione moderna si veda CHARPENTREAU, Simonne. *Le livre d'or de la chanson française*, 3 voll., Parigi, Les Éditions ouvrières, 1971-1975.

[16]. L'attribuzione a Dezède è di Einstein nell'edizione del catalogo mozartiano del 1947.

[17]. WALLON, Simon. *Op. cit.* (si veda nota 10), traduzione dell'autore.

[18]. BRAGANTINI, Renzo. 'Campagnoli, Bartolomeo', in: *Dizionario Biografico degli Italiani* (Treccani, Roma, vol. XVII, 1974). Per la bibliografia delle fonti su Campagnoli, si rinvia al dizionario biografico on line <http://www.treccani.it/enciclopedia/bartolomeo-campagnoli_(Dizionario-Biografico)/>.

[19]. Si segnalano anche variazioni per altri strumenti, come quelle per cetra (ovvero pandora, ovvero orpharion, in francese cythre) (Demesse, 1776), per flauto e basso (Bordet, 1778), per viola da orbi ossia ghironda (Michel Corrette, 1783). Alle variazioni per tastiera, di cui sopra, si aggiungano alcune altre versioni che giungono fino a tempi molto recenti: per arpa (Jean-Baptiste Cardon, 1760-1803), per piano (Franz Liszt, *Albumblatt*, 1833), per clarinetto (Concerto in Si bemolle di Theodor von Schacht, 1748-1823), per orchestra (Camille Saint-Saëns, *Fossiles*, *Le Carnaval des animaux*, 1886), per organo (Johann Christian Heinrich Rinck, 1770-1846), per pianoforte e orchestra (Ernst van Dohnány, 1914), per due

Rinviando l'analisi comparata dei vari testimoni alle interessanti pagine di Van Reijen[20], si elencheranno qui di seguito i nomi di alcuni compositori di medio Settecento.

Fonti per tastiera di metà Settecento sono i compositori Montaut, George Neuman, e Neveu. Dal frontespizio dell'edizione delle sue variazioni, Montaut risulta «Organiste et Maitre de Clavecin de la ville du Man»: questa è l'unica informazione che si ha sul compositore[21]. Oltre a questa edizione, databile circa alla metà del secolo, van Reijen ne segnala un'altra, successiva di circa 20 anni, del 1788, che «purtroppo non fornisce né il cognome di Montaut né la sua attività».

George Neuman è attestato in una stampa di Amsterdam, con la dicitura «Chanson François / variée pour le / Clavecin»[22].

Quanto a Neveu, compositore — si suppone — di metà Settecento, sarebbe nato a Bruxelles intorno al 1750. Dal 1775 fino all'inizio della rivoluzione francese è attestato come clavicembalista del conte di Artois. Sul frontespizio si legge «Variations / ajoutées a plusieurs airs d'opera comique / Pour le Piano Forte et le Clavecin [...]». Le Variazioni di Neveu hanno una datazione tra la fine degli anni Settanta e i primi anni Ottanta[23].

Altro compositore della seconda metà del Settecento che ha usato *Ah!, vous dirai-je maman* come tema per variazioni è Wolfgang Amadeus Mozart[24] (KV 265-300e). Per una descrizione della fonte e ogni dettaglio su questa composizione si rinvia al già citato Konrad, e al suo lavoro editoriale del facsimile per la Deutsche Mozart-Gesellschaft (Augusta, 2001). Qui, conta sottolineare l'anno di edizione e il luogo, che oscillano tra Salisburgo 1776 (secondo la versione del catalogo 1862) e Parigi 1778 (secondo l'analisi stilistica di Théodore de Wyzewa e Georges de Saint-Foix, che è stata ripresa dal catalogo Köchel del 1937, a cura di Alfred Einstein).

Continuando la lista di compositori proposta da Van Reijen, si incontrano Louis Félix Despréaux (1746-1813), John Christian Luther (seconda metà del Settecento), Johann Christoph Friedrich Bach (1732-1795), John Hewitt (seconda metà del Settecento), Johann Gottfried Wilhelm Palschau (1742-1813), C. H. Mueller (seconda metà del Settecento), Georg Joseph Vogler (1749-1814), Johann Anton André (1775-1842).

---

pianoforti (Alessandro Longo, Op. 39 N. 1, 1922), per organo (Johannes-Matthias Michel, ★1962), per arpa (Bernet, 2002).

[20]. VAN REIJEN, Paul Wilhelm. *Vergleichende Studien zur Klaviervariationstechnik von Mozart und seinen Zeitgenossen*, Buren, F. Knuf, 1988, pp. 154-175.

[21]. *Ibidem*, p. 131.

[22]. *Ibidem*, p. 132.

[23]. *Ibidem*, p. 133.

[24]. *Ibidem*, p. 134.

Dunque, escludendo i due anonimi che Van Reijen cita[25], risultano tre compositori di variazioni per violino, e dodici per tastiera. Tartini non compare tra i violinisti, anche se, a questo punto, può essere a buon diritto collocato tra quei compositori che prima di Mozart (a partire dagli anni Cinquanta-Sessanta del Settecento) hanno dato inizio alla tradizione delle variazioni sul tema della chanson *Ah!, vous dirai-je maman*. Su questo si tornerà più avanti.

Seguendo un'altra direzione, si cerchi ora di isolare la fonte tartiniana in oggetto, riconducendo il discorso al *milieu* nel quale le 'piccole sonate' sono state composte, cioè quello del veneto storico. Un mondo spesso parallelo a quel contesto europeo sin qui descritto.

Dovendo indicare brevemente un tratto saliente di scrittura violinistica riscontrato nei movimenti sopra citati (quelli dell'autografo I-Pca1888-1, rispettivamente: Sonata V, Brainard F1, con il basso, p. 13; Sonata XVI, Brainard C2, senza basso, p. 54), ciò che salta subito agli occhi è l'utilizzo delle corde doppie. Nonostante esso sia un espediente tecnico non privo di difficoltà, pur normale nell'ambito delle variazioni su un tema, si tratta di un dettaglio tecnico che sembra riconnettere Tartini a uno stile tutto suo, riconducibile a una sensibilità musicale maturata durante l'infanzia istro-veneta. È come se, grazie a questa melodia così semplice e infantile — come quella di *Ah!, vous dirai-je maman* —, il compositore tornasse alle musiche istriane che tanto avevano influenzato la sua esperienza di ascoltatore nella prima giovinezza. Non sembra un caso se Polzonetti colloca la melodia in oggetto tra gli esempi (precisamente, il n. 6) nel capitolo dedicato alla musica istriana:

> Molti anni dopo [il 1716, quando incontra Veracini], e affermatosi come violinista di fama mondiale, il Maestro delle nazioni volle pagare anche un altro tributo al violinismo di tradizione orale. Recuperò allora qualcosa della sonorità e degli effetti caratteristici della musica istriana per violino e bassetto[26]: riminiscenze delle sue prime esperienze di ascolto. Un chiaro esempio sono quelli che potremmo definire 'effetti cornamusa' (gli stessi osservati da Pavle Merkù per i violinisti resiani [della Val di Resia, in Slovenia]), i quali si presentano abbastanza numerosi nelle "piccole sonate" del Ms. I-Pca 1888 [...][27].

Questa prospettiva potrebbe spostare la nostra mira dall'epicentro francese a una tradizione di canti popolari non dissimili da quelli descritti negli studi di Roberto Starec

---

[25]. *Ibidem*, pp. 133, 139. Van Reijen fa riferimento alla tradizione a stampa. Per avere una prima idea della tradizione manoscritta, si inserisca l'incipit del testo *Ah!, vous dirai-je maman* sul RISM online. Compaiono 70 voci di compositori, di cui 34 anonimi. Anche in questa direzione si dovrà procedere, al fine di dare una panoramica quanto più completa su questa tradizione.

[26]. Per una lettura e alcune ipotesi intorno all'uso del bassetto nelle 'piccole sonate': CARRARO, Gregorio. 'Hidden Affinities. Accompanied Solo, Tartini and Germany', in: *Ad Parnassum: A Journal of Eighteenth- and Nineteenth-Century Instrumental Music*, XI/22 (ottobre 2013), pp. 113-126.

[27]. POLZONETTI, Pierpaolo. *Tartini e la musica secondo natura*, Lucca, LIM, 2001, p. 74.

e Giuseppe Radole, in cui Polzonetti rintraccia, tra le varie tipologie, un gruppo di *canti infantili* descritti come «Ninne nanne, filastrocche, formule e giochi. Canto su scale di tre o quattro note [...] ritmo semplice, sillabico e cadenzato»[28]. Descrizione che, in vero, corrisponde perfettamente alla intonazione di *Ah!, vous dirai-je maman*.

Purtroppo al momento non si è avuto modo di rintracciare canti popolari istriani da poter sovrapporre all'intonazione della nostra chanson. Tuttavia, la natura archetipica della melodia è tale che non esclude un trattamento 'istriano' di una melodia francese, non inverosimilmente arrivata al Maestro delle Nazioni per il tramite di qualche allievo d'oltralpe[29].

Di qualche interesse può risultare a questo punto una considerazione estetica sul motivo per cui questa semplice melodia abbia incontrato il gusto di Tartini. La motivazione più semplice, e forse più efficace, è da individuarsi in una perfetta corrispondenza con l'estetica del *Trattato*, dove si legge un passo che sembra descrivere la nostra melodia:

> L'altra mia osservazione è comune a tutte le nazioni, appresso le quali sia in uso la nostra musica moderna. Ciascuna di queste nazioni ha le sue canzoni popolari, molte delle quali sono di antica tradizione, molte prodotte di nuove, e adottate dal genio comune. Per lo più sono semplicissime, anzi si osservi, che le più semplici, e naturali sono le più ricevute. È certo che in esse né vi è, né vi può esser molta modulazione, al più vi sarà nella quinta del tuono. Che il popolo ascolti più volentieri una di queste canzoni di qualunque *esquisita* cantilena modulata per tutto il suo giro, è osservazione quanto facile a farsi, altrettanto sicura nel verificarsi. Ma si dirà che l'effetto è equivoco, perché potrà egualmente procedere, e procederà forse più dalle parole delle canzoni, nelle quali il popolo prende interesse, che dalla musica delle canzoni. Ed io rispondo, che date le stesse parole congiunte alla cantilena semplice della canzone, e alla cantilena *esquisitamente* modulata secondo l'arte nostra, e dato lo stesso musico, che canti l'una e l'altra, il giudicio favorevole del popolo sarà sicuramente per la prima. Replico quanto ho detto altrove: la natura ha più forza dell'arte, ed il maggiore e miglior genere è il diatonico, ma è difficilissimo a ben trattarsi [...][30].

Alla luce di quanto sin qui osservato, rimane difficile dimostrare quale ruolo il compositore abbia giocato in questa tradizione così viva e ricca di suggestioni. Che Padova fosse un luogo visitato da numerosi musicisti è un dato risaputo: sia che Tartini fosse vivo (insegna fino alla fine dei suoi giorni a numerosi allievi, e su questo non ci si soffermi ora)

---

[28]. *Ibidem*, pp. 81-82.

[29]. Per una inquadratura dei rapporti tra Tartini e la Francia: FELICI, Candida. 'La disseminazione della musica di Giuseppe Tartini in Francia: le edizioni settecentesche di sonate per violino e basso', in: *De musica disserenda*, X/1 (2014), pp. 57-75.

[30]. TARTINI, Giuseppe. *Trattato di musica secondo la vera scienza dell'armonia*, Padova, G. Manfré, 1754, p. 148.

sia che Tartini fosse morto. Si è già citata la visita dei due violinisti Campagnoli e Lamotte (o La Motte, autore di variazioni sulla predetta chanson) negli anni Sessanta. Negli anni Settanta, dopo la morte del Maestro, si annoverano due visite illustri: quella di Charles Burney (30 luglio e 2 agosto 1770)[31] e quella del giovane Mozart (14 marzo 1771)[32].

In conclusione, restano più domande che risposte: che rapporto c'è tra le variazioni di Tartini e la fonte del Bouin (1761), citata all'inizio come uno dei primi esempi di variazioni su *Ah! vous dirai-je maman*? Come è venuto a contatto Tartini con questo tema, con questa fonte francese? Ovvero, se ha avuto un ruolo nella tradizione sin qui descritta, quale è stato?

Il punto di vista e di partenza scelto per iniziare a cercare qualche risposta è stata la puntualizzazione del contesto europeo che gravita intorno alle variazioni di Tartini. Non solo si è cercato di fornire a questo contesto una definizione testuale, ma anche estetica.

In altre parole, lo scopo del presente lavoro è di gettare una base per un successivo studio stilistico che metta a confronto la versione di Tartini con le altre variazioni per violino che circolavano intorno agli anni Cinquanta/Sessanta del Settecento.

Infine, rimane un'ultima domanda la cui risposta esula dai limiti del presente studio: fino a che punto si può allargare il contesto europeo di cui sin qui si è scritto? Quale contatto si può ipotizzare tra l'opera di Tartini (conosciuta per certo da Leopold Mozart, che nella sua scuola del violino fa copiosamente uso di esempi di abbellimenti tartiniani[33]) e le manifestazioni stilistiche di medio Settecento?

---

[31]. BURNEY, Charles. *Viaggio musicale in Italia*, a cura di Enrico Fubini, Torino, EdT, 1987 (Biblioteca di cultura musicale. Documenti), pp. 121-132.

[32]. CATTELAN, Paolo. *Mozart. Un mese a Venezia*, Venezia, Marsilio, 2000 (Saggi Marsilio. Musica critica), pp. 115-119.

[33]. *Ibidem*, pp. 119-120. Ancora intorno al legame tra Tartini e la citata *Gründliche Violinschule* di Leopold Mozart: «La *Violinschule* di Leopold Mozart è il più importante trattato per violino del Settecento, ed è anche uno degli scritti più straordinari per organizzazione e per contenuto. La cosa più sorprendente è che la parte dedicata agli abbellimenti (trillo, tremolo, mordente, vibrato, messa di voce ecc.) è quasi completamente ricalcata sullo scritto di Tartini dedicato allo stesso argomento, senza naturalmente che Leopold Mozart citi la fonte. Quindi, l'influenza che Tartini ha avuto in Germania attraverso Leopold, ma anche attraverso la presenza dei suoi allievi nelle principali corti tedesche, è un'influenza accertata e carica di conseguenze per la storia della musica: Tartini diventa il punto di riferimento per la musica strumentale violinistica dell'Europa intera [...]»; PETROBELLI, Pierluigi. 'Gli studi e le ricerche su Giuseppe Tartini dal 1935 a oggi', in: *Giuseppe Tartini in njegov čas / Tartini e il suo tempo*, a cura di Metoda Kokole, Lubiana, ZRC-SAZU, 1997, pp. 14-15. Su questo rapporto si veda anche NEUMANN, Frederick. *Ornamentation in Baroque and post-Baroque Music: With Special Emphasis on J. S. Bach*, Princeton (NJ), Princeton University Press, 1983; ID. *Ornamentation and Improvisation in Mozart*, Princeton (NJ), Princeton University Press, 1986. Per il manoscritto sugli abbellimenti, *cfr.* TARTINI, Giuseppe. *Traité des agréments de la musique*, a cura di Erwin R. Jacobi, Celle-New York, Moeck Verlag, 1961. Questa edizione riporta anche, come supplemento, il facsimile del manoscritto delle *Regole per arrivare a saper ben suonar il violino, col vero fondamento di saper sicuramente tutto quello, che si fa; buono ancora a tutti quelli, ch'esercitano la musica del Nicolai*; vedi anche GRASSO CAPRIOLI, Leonella. 'Lessico tecnico e strutture linguistiche di Tartini didatta nelle *Regole per ben suonar il violino*', in: *Tartini. Il tempo e le opere*, a cura di Andrea Bombi e Maria Nevilla Massaro, Bologna, Il Mulino, 1994 (Temi e discussioni), pp. 395-400 e 281-298. Infine, si segnala

Certamente, la semplice melodia di *Ah!, vous dirai-je maman* può essere un buon punto di partenza per aggiungere un tassello al puzzle della tradizione tartiniana, con il duplice scopo da un lato di restituire all'opera di Tartini il respiro e la dignità storico-stilistica che merita, dall'altro di porre le basi per indagare in che modo la coscienza di uno stile francese sopravviva nel gusto pan europeo di quegli anni.

una versione in tedesco moderno del trattato mozartiano: Mozart, Leopold. *Versuch einer gründlichen Violinschule*, a cura di Matthias Michael Beckmann, Salisburgo, Kulturverlag Polzer, 2008.

On the Way to France, Trade and Stylistic Awareness: Carlo Tessarini[*]

Paola Besutti

(Teramo)

A CONTEMPORARY OF PIETRO ANTONIO LOCATELLI and Jean-Marie Leclair, Carlo Tessarini da Rimini (Rimini, c1690 – Holland?, after 12 March 1767) experimented with, and made his own, the most advanced forms of commercial distribution available between Paris and other major European markets. Having left his position as violinist in the ensemble of St. Mark's in Venice, he found a flexible contractual arrangement with the chapel of the SS. Sacramento in the cathedral of Urbino (1732-1733, 1738-1740). Well aware of the marketing opportunities available beyond the Alps, he travelled to Paris (1744), where he was able to give new impetus to the marketing of his works, realizing significant financial gains in the process.

The catalogue of Tessarini's works includes (until to date) 279 instrumental compositions (sonatas, instrumental arias, duets, trio sonatas, concertos, symphonies, overtures, introductions, didactical pieces), of which 254 printed and 25 in manuscripts (*unica*), preserved in 80 libraries and archives, distributed in 13 different European countries, as well as in United States and in Canada[1]. This quantity of production is more than respectable. To provide a comparison with some contemporaries who had international careers comparable to his[2]: the catalogue of Francesco Geminiani has just over 150 compositions[3], that of Locatelli, approximately 140[4]. Moreover, with over 43

---

[*]. I wish to thank Warren Kirkendale for reading an earlier version of this article and discussing the issues with me.

[1]. For Tessarini's catalogue, see BESUTTI, Paola. 'Catalogo tematico' (henceforth BCT), in: EAD. – GIULIANI, Roberto – POLAZZI, Gianandrea. *Carlo Tessarini. Violinista, compositore, editore nell'Europa del Settecento*, Lucca, LIM, 2012 (Strumenti della ricerca musicale, 13), pp. 325-627.

[2]. For the classification of musical careers, see RASCH, Rudolf. 'Leclair, Locatelli and the Musical Geography of Europe', in the present volume.

[3]. For Geminiani's catalogue, see CARERI, Enrico. *Francesco Geminiani*, Oxford, Clarendon Press, 1993; Italian edition, Lucca, LIM, 1999 (Musica ragionata, 13).

[4]. For Locatelli's catalogue, see DUNNING, Albert. *Pietro Antonio Locatelli. Il virtuoso, il compositore e il suo tempo*, Italian translation by Oddo Piero Bertini, Turin, Fogola, 1983, pp. 325-420.

solo concertos, Tessarini ranks among the most prolific musicians cultivating this musical form. However, the quantitative data, although significant, do not express an absolute value but a parameter that must be contextualized and related to the professional choices of each musician, especially in the case of violinist-composers of Locatelli's generation.

The destiny of Tessarini's publications was troubled, but not too different from that of many of his contemporaries who lived, like him, in a new lively phase of the European music market, against which the Italian context was distinguished by inaction. Compositions published without the knowledge of the author from manuscripts found in the bustling free market of Venice, simple reprints of issues, trade agreements, publishing and commerce by the composers themselves, as well as printing privileges, are variables encountered in the diffusion of Tessarini's works. For the scholar, the difficulty is the bibliographic reordering of the music sources. Indeed, in the absence of documentation or direct administrative correspondence one should proceed by circumstantial, speculative and philological evaluation of the prints and manuscripts, comparatively reinterpreted on the basis of the most documented and updated studies on European music publishing and marketing[5]. In the case of Tessarini, the mapping of his musical sources paints the profile

---

5.   See especially: DEVRIÈS-LESURE, Anik. *Édition et commerce de la musique gravée à Paris dans la première moitié du XVIIIᵉ siècle: Les Boivin, Les Leclerc*, Geneva, Minkoff, 1976 (Archives de l'édition musicale française, 1); EAD. – LESURE, François. *Dictionnaire des éditeurs de musique français. 1: Des origines à environ 1820*, Geneva, Minkoff, 1979 (Archives de l'édition musicale française, 4); RASCH, Rudolf. 'Estienne Roger en Michel-Charles le Cène: Europese muziekuitgevers te Amsterdam 1696-1743', in: *Holland, Regionaal-Historisch Tijdschrift*, XXVI (1994), pp. 292-313; ADAMS, Sarah. 'International Dissemination of Printed Music during the Second Half of the Eighteenth Century', in: *The Dissemination of Music: Studies in the History of Music Publishing*, edited by Hans Lenneberg, Lausanne, Gordon and Breach, 1994 (Musicology, 14), pp. 21-42; RASCH, Rudolf. 'I manoscritti musicali nel lascito di Michel-Charles le Cène (1743)', in: *Intorno a Locatelli. Studi in occasione del trecentenario della nascita di Pietro Antonio Locatelli (1695-1764)*, edited by Albert Dunning, 2 vols., Lucca, LIM, 1995 (Speculum Musicae, I/1-2), vol. II, pp. 1039-1070; ID. 'Corelli's Contract: Notes on the Publication History of the Concerti grossi [...] Opera Sesta [1714]', in: *Tijdschrift van de Koninkliging Vereniging voor Nederlandse Muziekgeschiedenis*, XLVI/2 (1996), pp. 83-136; ID. 'Estienne Roger and John Walsh: Patterns of Competition between Early-18th-Century Dutch and English Music Publishing', in: *The Nord Sea and Culture (1550-1800): Proceedings of the International Conference Held at Leiden, 21-22 April 1995*, edited by Juliette Roding and Lex Heerma van Voss, Hilversum, Verloren, 1996, pp. 396-407; CORNAZ, Marie. *L'édition et la diffusion de la musique à Bruxelles au XVIIIᵉ siècle*, Bruxelles, Académie Royale de Belgique, 2001 (Mémoire de la Classe des Beaux-Arts, 3ᵉ série, 18); RASCH, Rudolf. '«Il cielo batavo». I compositori italiani e le edizioni olandesi delle loro opere strumentali nel primo Settecento', in: *Italienische Instrumentalmusik des 18. Jahrhunderts. Alte und neue Protagonisten*, edited by Enrico Careri and Markus Engelhardt, Laaber, Laaber-Verlag, 2002, pp. 237-266 (Analecta musicologica, 32); ID. 'The Dutch Republic in the Eighteenth Century as a Place of Publication for Travelling Musicians', in: *Le musicien et ses voyages. Pratiques, réseaux et représentations*, edited by Christian Meyer, Berlin, Berliner Wissenshafts-Verlag, 2003 (Music life in Europe 1600-1900: circulation, institutions, representations, 1), pp. 97-111; DEVRIÈS-LESURE, Anik. 'Technical Aspects', in: *Music Publishing in Europe 1600-1900: Concepts and Issues Bibliography*, edited by Rudolf Rasch, Berlin, Berliner Wissenschaft Verlag, 2005 (Musical life in Europe 1600-1900: circulation, institutions,

of a pugnacious artist seeking to seize the opportunities offered by different contexts, making drastic choices, trying repeatedly to find or to recreate in Italy the living conditions experienced elsewhere, until he finally abandoned his homeland. In speaking of Tessarini's relations with France it is essential to deal with the publishing history of his works, since his relationship with this nation is motivated primarily by editorial and commercial interests. However, as we shall see, in his works are not lacking in traces of French stylistic influences and clues of a conscious knowledge of the French musical world.

Towards New Markets

Born in Rimini around 1690, Tessarini may have received his musical training in the same city[6]. In 1716, at least, he was in Venice as «maestro dei concerti» at the services of the Pio Ospedaletto to SS. Giovanni e Paolo (Derelitti), and then as violinist at St. Mark's cathedral. In Venice, where he published (at the mature age of 39) his first work, he became aware of the circulation in the European market of his works, almost certainly published without the knowledge of the author. These works were, at least: the twelve *Concerti a cinque* Op. 1 (BCT 30-31), the twelve *Sonate per flauto traversie* Op. 2 (BCT 32), the ten *Concerti a più Istrumenti* Op. 3 (BCT 33), published (between 1724 and 1732) by Le Cène (Amsterdam), and shortly after (1727) reprinted in London by John Walsh (BCT 30-31a, 30-31b), the same publisher who in 1728 included a Tessarini's concerto in the anthology *Harmonia mundi* (BCT 39). To the same period belong the six *Sonate a tré* Op. 1 (BCT 32), published in Amsterdam by Gerhard Fredrik Witvogel around 1732. These Dutch and English issues were severely condemned in 1734 by Tessarini in the preface of his duets *Il Maestro, e discepolo* Op. 2 (BCT 2) for their lack of editorial care: «[…] although I know that in Holland and in England came out many other [of my works], among which, if I had to present myself conscientiously, few would have achieved my approval» (Ill. 1)[7].

Perhaps it was merely the awareness of potential profits derivable from the free publishing market, the possible theatrical engagements, and the concert activities that induced Tessarini to leave Venice and agree to a flexible contract with the chapel of the

---

representation, 2), pp. 63-88; Ead. – Lesure, François. *L'édition musical dans la presse parisienne au XVIIIe siècle. Catalogue des annonces*, Paris, CNRS, 2005 (Sciences de la musique).

6. For Tessarini's biography and related documentation, see Besutti, Paola – Polazzi, Gianandrea. 'La vita', in: Besutti, Paola – Giuliani, Roberto – Polazzi, Gianandrea. *Op. cit.* (see note 1), pp. 3-147.

7. Tessarini, Carlo. *Il maestro, e discepolo. Divertimenti da camera a due Violini […] Opera seconda*, Urbino, Stamperia della Ven. Capella del Santissimo Sacramento presso Girolamo Mainardi, 1734 (BCT 2): «Amico lettore: […] sebbene so esserne state mandate fori in Olanda, ed in Inghilterra molte altre [mie opere], trá le quali, se mi avessi dovuto presentare con sentimento, poche averebbero conseguita la mia approvazione».

Amico Lettore

Si presenta al tuo sguardo questa mia seconda opera musicale intitolata *Maestro, e Discepolo* con sicura speranza d'incontrare appresso di te gradimento migliore, che non poteua meritarsi la prima uscita alla luce assai difettosa per l'imperizia dell'Incisore, sappi, che io non tengo in conto di mio se non queste due sole opere impresse l'una in Venezia, l'altra in Urbino, seb: bene sò esserne state mandate fori in Olanda, ed in Inghiltera molte altre, trà le quali, se mi auessi dovuto presentare con sentimento, poche auerebbero conseguita la mia approuazione, nondimeno perche in ciò ben rauiso quella bontà con la quale risguardi, ed accogli le pouere mie fatiche ti assicuro non meno della mia obligazione, che di una costante premura di seruirti, e uiui felice

ILL. 1: Carlo Tessarini, *Il maestro, e discepolo. Divertimenti da camera a due violini* […] *Opera seconda*, Urbino, Stamperia della Cappella del SS. Sacramento presso Girolamo Mainardi, 1734 (BCT 2), 'Amico lettore'.

SS. Sacramento at the cathedral of Urbino[8]. Together with his wife and three daughters[9], he then moved from Venice to Pesaro. Like other similar institutions, the cathedral of Urbino entered into contracts based on the number of ceremonies and festivities to which the musicians had to contribute. The contract had to be renewed every year. With some difficulty, Tessarini obtained consent to be replaced, in case of absence, by external colleagues or by his students. The relationship with Urbino lasted more than 20 years (1733-1757). During this time he was repeatedly absent for prolonged periods. Initially, among other positions which took him away from Urbino for more or less long periods, he assumed the post of «direttore della musica instrumentale» and «primo violinista di camera» in distant Brno (Moravia), in the service of Cardinal Wolfgang Hannibal von

---

[8]. For the archival documents, see BESUTTI, Paola. 'Urbino e Roma', in: EAD. – GIULIANI, Roberto – POLAZZI, Gianandrea. *Op. cit.* (see note 1), pp. 39-113.

[9]. Urbino, Archivio di Stato, *Atti notarili*, vol. 3270, notary Carlo Giuseppe Minoli, 1750, 30 September, act of marriage between Pasqua Tessarini (Carlo Tessarini's daughter) and Giovanni Donati; Urbino, Archivio Diocesano, *Libro delli Matrimonij della Cura di S. Sergio 1664 usque ad 1751*, c. 91, 1750, 28 October, registration of the marriage between Pasqua Tessarini and Giovanni Donati; Urbino, Archivio Diocesano, *Stato delle Anime della Parrocchiale di S. Sergio per l'anno 1757*, c. 21: «n° 563 signora Elisabetta Tessarini anni 60; n° 564 signora Francesca Tessarini anni 31; n° 565 signora Catterina figlia minore anni 29». I should like to thank Paolo Righini for drawing my attention to these documents.

Schrattenbach (1660 - 22 July 1738). During his service in Moravia (c1736 - May 1738) Tessarini signed, with the publisher Le Cène, the undated dedication of an important collection of concertos, *La Stravaganza* (BCT 34; 1735-c1737). The personal signature from the author would seem to confirm an agreement between the composer and the Dutch publisher. However, that fact may also have influenced indirectly Tessarini's subsequent relationship with France. In what sense?

Back in Italy, Tessarini returned to his position in the chapel of Urbino (1738), but not without opposition. However, the year 1743 marks a turning point. On April 20, Le Cène, who had perhaps become his publisher abroad, died. This event may have led Tessarini to become more involved in the printing of his own music, up to the creation, in 1743, of his own musical printing business in Fano, together with Giovanni Francesco Tessarini, probably a relative of Carlo. Just at that moment he made the decision to leave for Paris, at that time the most active centre for the production and distribution of printed music. As we shall see, the Paris market was already interested in him, and perhaps he had already initiated some contacts there. The administrative documents of the cathedral of Urbino state: once concluded «all the functions of the Epiphany» of the year 1744, Tessarini «left for Paris in function of the Sacred Majesty [Louis xv of Bourbon]»[10]. Despite this annotation, there is no trace of any musical activity carried out by Tessarini for the court of France, while there exists his request for a royal permission («Privilège Royal») to print his works; the *privilège* was then actually obtained in 1746. Since his principal purpose for the journey was to print his music, the reference to the King of France may have been merely to secure the much desired 'Royal Privilege'.

In the autumn of 1744 he was in Paris, where he signed, on 15 November, the dedication of the *Sinfonie a due violini e basso* Op. 7 (BCT 7) to the Genoese Count Giacomo Durazzo (Genoa 1717 - Venice 1794), a famous diplomat, collector and patron of the arts. At the same time, also in Paris, another collection, the *Sei trio a due violini e basso* Op. 6 (BCT 6), was published, dedicated to Pierre Philibert de Blancheton, but without a date. Both editions, Op. 6 and Op. 7, exhibited on the title page a royal privilege for printing and a distribution in the best stores of the city («adresses ordinaires»). From this time onwards, commercial relations with France did not stop, but proved to be very rich and even accentuated. The period in which Tessarini entered fully into the Parisian

---

[10]. Urbino, Archivio della Cappella del SS. Sacramento, *Libri mastri*, vol. 4.ix, 1737-1750, c. 11: «1744 / 31 dicembre per spesa sudetta scudi due, baiocchi 91.3 sono di sua provisione a tutte le funzioni dell'epifania 1744, essendo che dopo partì per Parigi per una funzione di quella Sacrà Maestà, di dove per anche non è ritornato»; *ibidem*, c. 166: «31 dicembre 1750. Al Sig.ʳ Carlo Tessarini primo professore di violino ritornato da Parigi dopo esservi stato anni 6 ½, e girato l'Olanda, Inghilterra, Fiandra, Lingua d'oca, e varij altri stati, con aver in quelle parti dato alle stampe molte opere di musica, e finalmente sano, e salvo, d.d. a 31 dicembre 1750 per spesa di musica scudi 15, baiocchi 83:1, sono per sua provisione dalle funzioni della sacra a tutte quelle del rendimento di grazie 31 dicembre suddetto 1750, c. 187 = 15.83.1»; the documents are published in BESUTTI, Paola. 'Urbino e Roma', *op. cit.* (see note 8), pp. 87, 94.

publishing market coincides with the moment in which the production of the Italian violin music was experiencing its greatest commercial fortune in Europe. Between the beginning of the thirties and early fifties of the eighteenth century, the editions of sonatas for violin and bass, duets, trio sonatas, compositions for four parts and solo concertos increased in France by more than 300%[11]. Starting in the1740s, Parisian catalogues were to include an ever increasing number of Italian authors, the presence of whom was to surpass that of the French. These publishers, to meet growing the demand of the market, began to publish directly Italian and foreign music, and no longer distributed only editions of others, produced for example in the Netherlands and England. In the J.-P. Le Clerc catalogue, the collections of music for violin numbered more than 400, second only to the production of cantatas and music for flute. This phenomenon was also due to the great success of the music of Corelli and the popularity of works by Jean-Marie Leclair.

Between 1744 and the early 1750s, at least 21 new editions of music by Tessarini came out in Paris: *Sei trio a due violino e basso* Op. 6 (BCT 6), *Sinfonie a due violini e basso continuo* Op. 7 (BCT 7), *Sonate a violino e violoncello o cembalo* Op. 8 (BCT 8), *Sonate da camera e da chiesa a due violini e basso* Op. 9 (BCT 9), *Contrasto armonico a tre violini e basso con suoi rinforzi* Op. 10 (BCT 10), *Introducioni a quattro* Op. 11 in four books (BCT 11, 12, 13, 14), *Sonate a due flauti traversieri e basso* Op. 12 (BCT 15), *Allettamenti armonici a quattro* Op. 13 (BCT 16), *Sonate a violino o flauto e cembalo* Op. 17 (BCT 17), *Trattenimento musicale* Op. 15 for two violins (BCT 18), *Sei duetti* without thorough bass Op. 15, book second (BCT 19), twelve *Concerti a cinque* without opus number in four books (BCT 23, 24, 72, 73), twelve instrumental airs *Il piacer delle dame* (BCT 25), the concerto *L'arte di nuova modulacione* (BCT 26), the symphonies *Récreation armonique* (BCT 77). This is the largest group of editions in his catalogue.

Compared to Italy, the Parisian market was very much faster, and imposed other production standards. While in Italy the oblong format was still used, in France the vertical format was generally preferred and the cover pages were rarely decorated, usually only when the edition had the support of a dedicatee. An example of different sizes and printing styles can be supplied by the Parisian edition of the *L'arte di nuova modulacione* (BCT 26; ILL. 2): it is very spartan compared to those previously published in Italy, for example the *Sonate à tre dà camera* Op. 5 (BCT 5, ILL. 3).

As was usually the case, in France the prints were also almost always undated. A fundamental document for the interpretation of the bibliographic data is the sale catalogue, included by Tessarini in *L'arte di nuova modulacione* (ILL. 4). By comparing the list of publications contained in this advertising page with the few dedications dated (BCT 7 and 9), the commercial advertising (BCT 15), and the only dated title page (BCT 17), it is possible to reconstruct conjecturally the impressive production rate of those years and to hypothesize on the editorial strategies of the author.

---

11.   DEVRIÈS-LESURE, Anik. *Édition et commerce* [...], *op. cit.* (see note 5), pp. 72-84.

L'ARTE DI NUOVA
MODULACIONE
CAPRICIO MUSICALE
A VII Partie
DA
CARLO TESSARINI
Da Rimini
Prix 3.ᵗᵗ

A PARIS

Chez
Madame Boivin, rüe St Honoré, à la Regle d'or.
Mr. le Clerc, rüe du Roule, à la Croix d'or.
Mlle Castagneri, rüe des Prouvaires, à la Musique Roijal

A Lion
Monsieur Givry.
A Marseille
Monsieur Beltram.
A Vignon
Monsieur Iulian.

A.P.D.R.   Gravé par Mlle Vendôme.

ILL. 2: Carlo Tessarini, *L'arte di nuova modulacione. Capricio musicale a VII partie*, Paris, M.ᵐᵉ Boivin *et al.*, *c*1750-1751 (BCT 26): title page.

137

ILL. 3: Carlo Tessarini, *Sonate à tre dà camera con due violini e basso con canone al fine*, Op. 5, Fano, Stamperia di Carlo e Giovanni Francesco Tessarini, *c*1743 (BCT 5): title page.

PUBLISHING STRATEGIES IN PARIS

As documented by the aforementioned advertising page included in *L'arte di nuova modulacione* (BCT 26), Tessarini paid personally for the engraving on copper plates of the majority of the works published in Paris. It is possible to conceive a publishing agreement similar to those used by other contemporary composers: the author took care of the engraving of the plates, the Parisian traders ensured the printing and the distribution in France, leaving the author the rights of release in other markets, such as the Italian one. This production system is confirmed by some frontispieces which declared the printing house («stamperia») of Carlo and Giovanni Francesco Tessarini in Urbino, as a selling point in Italy, along with the main distributors in Paris (Élisabeth-Catherine Ballard widow Boivin,

Catalogo delle Opere di Musica Stampate in Rame del Sig.r Carlo Tessarini á Spese del Autore

Gramatica di Musica ò sia dueti a due Violini senza basso Libro Primo Opera Primo . . . . prix. 4tt

Gramatica di Musica ò sia dueti à due Violini senza basso Libro 2 . . . . 4tt

Maestro è discepolo, dueti à due Violini, senza basso Opera 2 . . . . 4tt

Aletamenti à violino solo è basso Opera 3 . . . . 4tt

Tratenimenti à violino Solo è basso Opera 4 . . . . 4tt

Sonate da camera à due Violini e Basso, con Canone Opera 5 . . . . . . 4tt

Trio a due Violini e basso Opera 6 . . . 6tt

Sinfonie à due Violini è basso Op. 7 . 6tt

Sonate à Violino solo e Basso Op. 8 . 6tt

Sonate da Camera è Chiesa a due Violini è basso con Pastoralle Op. 9 . 6tt

Contrasto Armonico à tre Violini è Basso con susi Rinforzi Opera 10 . 8tt

Introducion à due Violini Alto Viola è Basso Opera 11° Libro primo 4tt

Introducioni à due Violini Alto Viola è Basso Libro 2° 4tt

Sonate à due Flauti Traversier ò pur Due Violini e basso Opera 12° . . . 6tt

3 Concerti à 5. con Violino Obbligato Libro Primo 7tt

3 Concerti à 5. con Violino Obbligato Libro 2° 7tt

3 Concerti a 5. con Violino obbli.to Libro 3° 7tt

3 Concerti a 5. con Violino Obbli.to Libro 4 . . . . 7tt

Introducioni a due Violini Alto Viola e Basso libro 3° 4tt

Introducioni a due Violini Alto Viola e Basso libro 4° 4tt

Aletamenti Armonici a due Violini, Alto Viola et Basso Opera 13. 8tt

6 Solo per flauto travercier opera 14. 4tt

Dueti a 2. Violini opera 15 4tt

Il piacier delle Dame 12 facile Ariete Istrumentalli per Violini flauto per desus è Basso 2tt

Sonate a due Violonzelli Oper Violino del Sig.r Pasquali 4tt

Pasquali Sonate a Violino Solo e Basso 4tt

3. Concerti Tartini a 6 con Violino Oblig.to Lib.o P.mo 8

Sonate pour le Clavecin 2.tt

L'Arte di nuova Modulacione Caprizio Musicale a 7 parti 3.tt

Il Piacier delle Dame, facile ariete Instrumentali con Violino, Flauto Travercier pardesu de Viola e Basso 2tt

Si Vendono in molte Città d'Italia e fuori Principalmente in fiera di Sinigalia

ILL. 4: Carlo Tessarini, *L'arte di nuova modulacione. Capricio musicale a VII partie*, Paris, Mme Boivin *et al.*, c1750-1751 (BCT 26): promotional catalogue.

rue St. Honoré à la Règle d'Or; Jean-Pantaléon Le Clerc, rue du Roulle à la Croix d'Or). For the moment it is not possible to document whether, on his return to Italy, Tessarini had brought with him the engraved plates. This possibility seems likely because he aimed to adopt in Italy the methods of production and trade known abroad. Furthermore, some debts of his are recorded (1750) with the paper mill of SS. Sacramento in Urbino for the purchase of paper, almost certainly used to produce new editions of the music engraved first in Italy and then in France[12]. To resolve this issue, however, it will be necessary to continue to compare watermarks and paper types of the musical sources still extant.

In this context we must always remember that an edition based on plates previously engraved is not to be considered a 'new' edition, but a new print run, even when it is accompanied by a different frontispiece, for example with new addresses of the places of sale. Although a new print run does not present substantial information about the musical content of the collection, it can tell much about its publishing history, among other things about its progress. For example, one can evaluate the persistence of the sonatas for two violins, published by Ch.-N. Le Clerc (BCT 38; 1737 ca.), which had a new print run after 1760 (BCT 38a); likewise for the Parisian edition, produced by the same Le Clerc (BCT 2b; 1745-1750 ca.), of duets *Il maestro e discepolo* (BCT 2; 1734). The same plates, used for multiple print runs, are not always immediately recognizable. For example, in the case of *Introducioni* book second (BCT 12; 1745 ca.), the existence of a new print run (BCT 12a) is revealed only by the correction of small misprints in the title page («Libro II» instead of «Libero II»).

Most of the collections marketed in Paris were engraved in the beautiful hand of Marie-Charlotte Vendôme; this fact confirms that Tessarini left Italy with many handwritten scores, perhaps ready for printing, but not with plates already engraved. Mademoiselle Vendôme was one of the best engravers active in Paris in those years. She engraved also the first edition (1764) of Mozart's sonatas for violin and harpsichord Op. 1 (KV 6, KV 7)[13]. The title pages and the music also report the names of Robert (BCT 6, 11 and 18), the engraver preferred by Pierre Philibert de Blancheton, of Labassée (BCT 2a), of Mademoiselle Michelon (BCT 37) and of Joseph Renou (BCT 3a). These last three were paid by the publisher Ch.-N. Le Clerc for engraving works that he selected and included in his exclusive catalogue.

Tessarini's name was known in the Parisian publishing market even before his arrival in France. For at least ten years (from c1734), his concertos and sonatas, already published in Amsterdam by Le Cène (BCT 30, 31, 32, 33), were available at leading shops. In addition, about seven years before his arrival in France (c1737), Charles-Nicolas Le Clerc had published (perhaps without the authorization of the author) and included in his catalogue two collections of duets for two violins without thorough bass (BCT 37, 2a). In 1741 widow Boivin also distributed an edition (perhaps unauthorized) of a collection of sonatas for violin and bass, numbered as Op. 5 (BCT 3a). It may have been this proliferation of editions that led to the author's decision to establish personal contact with Boivin and Le Clerc.

---

12.   See BESUTTI, Paola. 'Urbino e Roma', *op. cit.* (see note 8), p. 95.
13.   DEVRIÈS-LESURE, Anik. 'Technical Aspects', *op. cit.* (see note 5), p. 82.

Like the Dutch publishers, even these Parisians in some cases started their own publishing series. For the moment, it is possible to reconstruct at least seven different sets of opus numbers in Tessarini's catalogue[14]:

1) the one created by Tessarini himself;

2) the one started by Le Cène;

3) the one perhaps initiated by Jean-Pantaléon Le Clerc (shop with the signboard «à la croix d'Or»);

4) the one created by the English publisher John Walsh (BCT 30-31a, 32a, 15a), partly corresponding to that of Le Cène; 5) the one inaugurated by the Dutchman Fredrik Witvogel (BCT 36, 37, 67, 68, 71), known for his lack of scruples[15];

6) the one inaugurated by Charles-Nicolas Le Clerc, «Ordinaire de la Chambre du Roy, et de l'Academie Royalle de Musique» (BCT 37, 2a)[16];

7) the one initiated, for a single work, by renowned Scottish composer and publisher James Oswald (BCT 38b)[17].

The two series initiated by the French publishers are based on two very different production models. The one by Jean-Pantaléon Le Clerc, not yet fully documented, seems to fit into a distribution system that could be defined as having escaped from the author's control. The opus number 5 and 4, respectively, used to denote a new edition of the *Allettamenti da Camera a violino solo, e violoncello* Op. 3 (BCT 3a) and the *Caprice* for violin (perhaps BCT 3/vi)[18], may well have continued the numbering of the only three Tessarini's works known in France up to that time: those published by Le Cène in twenties and early thirties[19]. The sequence inaugurated by Charles-Nicolas Le Clerc identified, however, a

[14]. Besutti, Paola. 'Catalogazione e dubbi attributivi', in: Ead. – Giuliani, Roberto – Polazzi, Gianandrea. *Op. cit.* (see note 1), pp. 253-275: 254-263.

[15]. On Witvogel see Dunning, Albert. *De muziekuitgever Gerhard Fredrik Witvogel zijn fonds. Een bijdrage tot geschedenis van de Nederlandse muziekuitgeverij in de achttiende eeuw*, Utrecht, Oosthoek, 1966 (Muziekhistorische monografieën, 2). About the unclear history of the Tessarini's works published by Witvogel, see Besutti, Paola. 'Catalogazione e dubbi attributivi', *op. cit.* (see note 14), p. 267; Ead. 'Il flauto traverso', in: Ead. – Giuliani, Roberto – Polazzi, Gianandrea. *Op. cit.* (see note 1), pp. 175-185; Ead. 'Le prime stampe non autorizzate: Le Cène, Walsh, Witvogel', in: *ibidem*, pp. 278-286.

[16]. Besutti, Paola. 'Produzione in esclusiva di un editore', in: Ead. – Giuliani, Roberto – Polazzi, Gianandrea. *Op. cit.* (see note 1), pp. 296-303.

[17]. On James Oswald (Crail 1710 - Knebworth 1769) see Johnson, David – Melvill, Heather. 'Oswald, James', in: *Grove Music Online*, <http://www. oxfordmusiconline.com> (accessed 19 February 2015). About the cataloguing errors regarding the collection *Six Sonatas or Duetts and Canone's. Book 2.*[d], published by Oswald (BCT 38b), see Besutti, Paola. 'Catalogazione e dubbi attributivi', *op. cit.* (see note 14), pp. 262-263.

[18]. About the Le Clerc's catalogue (à la Croix d'Or, 1742-1751), see Devriès-Lesure, Anik. *Édition et commerce* […], *op. cit.* (see note 5), p. 259.

[19]. About this publishing numeration, see Besutti, Paola. 'Catalogazione e dubbi attributivi', *op. cit.* (see note 14), p. 261.

production system based on direct engagement of the publisher. The edition was published at his expense, distributed with 'exclusive rights' and inserted in a catalogue, containing only works produced by that publisher, but not necessarily hitherto unpublished[20].

Charles-Nicolas Le Clerc was the first to choose the latter system. From 1736 he continued in fact to propose works exclusively, without however prohibiting their distribution by other traders. As I have mentioned, from the start of his publishing career, he included two of Tessarini's collections (BCT 37, 2a) among those published at his own expense and exclusively distributed by him. Lacking direct documentation on the relationship between Ch.-N. Le Clerc and Tessarini, we do not know whether there was an agreement between them. The editorial strategy implemented by Ch.-N. Le Clerc could allow variants: the purchase of all the repertoire of an author, or some of his works; sharing with the author of both the printing costs and the subsequent profits; or the use of subscribers to bear the cost of engraving and printing. The purchase of one or more works by the publisher was the most common practice: he could pay a lump sum for the work[21]; he also could ask for the privilege of printing and then enjoy the profits. Also the practice of the transfer of the rights from one to another publisher could fit into this production chain, as it did by J.-P. Le Clerc in favour of his brother Ch.-N. Le Clerc (1752)[22]. Ch.-N. Le Clerc took advantage of this possibility several times; in fact, it was permitted by the lack of regulations. He did so legally, certainly for the publication of works by Locatelli. The engraver Louis-Hector Hue (Hüe) even produced a catalogue of his own engravings. The payment of the engraving by a publisher was not so frequent in those years. This situation changed in the second half of the century, when the commitment of the publishers in the selection and the publication of the works became prevalent, but Tessarini could not enjoy these changes.

Thanks to the reputation that had preceded him, 'Carlo da Rimini' created a network of relationships with leading personalities of Parisian society that likely contributed to the costs of engraving plates. Their names are immortalized by the dedications: Pierre Philibert de Blancheton (BCT 6), the Genoese Count Giacomo Durazzo (BCT 7), the Marquis Paul Hyppolite Beauvillier (BCT 8), the Marchioness Vidam de Vasse perhaps from Holland (BCT 9), the not clearly identified treasurer of the city of Paris Rousseau (BCT 10), the Marquis Giorgio Maria Louizzi (BCT 11), the Marchioness Monbason (BCT 15), the Marchioness Jeanne-Marguerite de la Baume-Montrevel (BCT 16), the ministers of the Congress of Aix-la-Chapelle (BCT 17), the official of the royal finances Claude-Henri Watelet (BCT 18). Often, after a first edition with a dedication, a work was given a new

---

[20].   See note 16.

[21].   See, for example, the case of François Boivin who paid 200 livres to buy two works by Jean-Baptiste Loeillet: DEVRIÈS-LESURE, Anik. *Édition et commerce* [...], *op. cit.* (see note 5), p. 58.

[22].   *Ibidem*, pp. 33-34, 59.

title page, reprinted without the dedication (from the same plates), and newly distributed. An example is the collection of the sonatas Op. 8 (BCT 8), first dedicated to the Marquis Beauvillier and then, shortly after, printed without dedication (BCT 8a). Often a work was dedicated to a personage who was not only wealthy and socially well-placed, but also very close to the Court: for example, the official of the royal finances Claude-Henri Watelet (Paris, 1718 - ivi, 1786), «knowledgeable of music, no less than excellent in painting» («intendente nella musica, non meno che eccellente nella pittura»)[23]. He was a well-known collector, and probably contributed to the engraving of Op. 15 (BCT 18), the title page of which was finely engraved by the renowned designer Hubert (?) Robert, who also decorated the cover of the *Sonate a tre* Op. 6 (BCT 6), dedicated to the famous Pierre Philibert de Blancheton, creator of a very important manuscript collection of instrumental music, in which also two of Tessarini's concertos were included (BCT 53, 54). Likewise in Paris, Tessarini may have met Giuseppe Canavasso (1714 - *post* 1767), whose *Sei sonate per violino e basso* Op. 1 he published at his own expense[24].

In Paris, Tessarini began the process of requesting the royal privilege of printing[25]. It was no easy feat, but he may have been helped by Giovanni Francesco Tessarini who, shortly before 1746, was in Paris[26]. Also the printing privileges present problems of interpretation. A royal privilege can be seen already in the early works published in Paris, when the privilege had not yet been obtained by the author. He received it only

---

[23]. About Watelet, see HOWARD, William Adams. *The French Garden, 1500-1800*, New York, Braziller, 1979 (World landscape art & architecture series), pp. 115ff; BAILEY, Colin B. *Patriotic Taste: Collecting Modern Art in Pre-Revolutionary Paris*, New Haven-London, Yale University Press, 2002, pp. 65ff. Watelet published: WATELET, Claude-Henri. *Essai sur les jardins*, Paris, s.n., 1774; ID. *L'arte de peindre: poème avec des réflexions sur les différentes parties de la peinture*, Paris, H. L Guérin et L. F. Delatour, 1760. The second trip to Italy of Watelet (1763-1764) was described by the incisions of Hubert Robert.

[24]. DUNNING, Albert. 'Some Notes on the Biography of Carlo Tessarini and his Musical Grammar', in: *Festschrift für Erich Schenk: zum 60. Geburtstage gewidmet von Kollegen, Freunden und Schülern*, Graz-Vienna-Cologne, Böhlau, 1962 (Studien zur Musikwissenschaft, 25), pp. 115-122: 120. Dunning mentions the link between Tessarini and Giuseppe Canavasso (Canavas).

[25]. About Tessarini and the royal privileges, see BESUTTI, Paola. 'Il viaggio a Parigi: nuove edizioni e privilegi reali', in: EAD. – GIULIANI, Roberto – POLAZZI, Gianandrea. *Op. cit.* (see note 1), pp. 306-311.

[26]. The information is written on the emblem of the Accademia degli Anarconti (Fano); see Fano, Biblioteca Federiciana, B.10.40, *Quadro storico-topografico della città di Fano*, Fano, s.n., 1763, table III.5: *Principali comunità secolari, ed ecclesiastiche, esistenti in detta città di Fano*: «Academia philarmonica / Anarconton / ab exiguis initiis / A. 1742 profecta, / celebris Francisci Tessarini / annis 1746. 1757. Fanum / modo parisium incolentis, / excellentia oblatis scriptis / magnum incrementum / promerita, nobilibus praecipue alumnorum / non raris studiis suffulta, sui principatum / nemini committens / binae concordi discordiae / innixa». The emblem is reproduced in BESUTTI, Paola. 'Urbino e il nuovo contratto (1741-44)', in: EAD. – GIULIANI, Roberto – POLAZZI, Gianandrea. *Op. cit.* (see note 1), pp. 73-87: 80. The possibly relationship with Carlo is unknown.

in autumn 1746[27]. However, the rules of royal privileges in those years were not yet seriously properly regulated for musical works, and sometimes these appeared even when acquired indirectly. To protect the commercial rights of the French booksellers, the request for a royal privilege to print a non-musical book was made obligatory in France from the mid-seventeenth century, as well as its recording in the books «de la communauté des libraires», still preserved in the Bibliotheque nationale of Paris[28]. The instrumental works, since they did not have a text under the music, initially were not included in this regulation. Thus an author, at his own risk, could ignore this law. However, it did involve the payment of fees by the applicant. As already mentioned, there were no rules which could prevent someone from taking possession of any music, manuscript or published, then engraving it, printing it, and placing it on the market. In this jungle the royal privileges were the only partial defence. The most astute writers, engravers, retailers, and publishers, while not requiring privileges, obtained them to protect their investments from possible abuses. If a work was protected by privilege, any counterfeiter could be punished. In 1786, given the increasing activity of the music market, the application of the royal privilege was extended to musical editions[29].

In case of Tessarini, the printing privileges stated on his works can be traced to those possessed by J.-P. Le Clerc, widow Boivin, François Dufresne, Charles-Nicolas Le Clerc, or Nicolas Chédeville[30] before he obtained a similar right (*ante* 1746). For the moment

---

[27]. Paris, Bibliothèque nationale de France, ms. fr. 21997, 1746, 29 July and 17 November, no. 2361 and no. 2469: «P.G. pour 12 ans à Tessarini pour Sonate à Violon Solo de Pasquali, Concerti de Tartini, Sonates à Violon Solo, Simphonies, Introduction, Contrasto armonico de Tessarini»; the document is published in CUCUEL, George. 'Quelques documents sur la librairie musicale au XVIIIe siècle', in: *Sammelbände der Internationalen Musikgesellschaft*, XIII/2 (1912), pp. 385-392: 388. *Ibidem*, ms. fr. 21958, 1747, 22 January: «P.G. pour 12 ans, du 9 décembre, au Sr Tessarini pour des sonates, trios et autres pièces de musique instrumentale de la composition de Sr Tessarini, une sonate de Pasquali et un concerto de Tartini»; the document is published in BRENET, Michel. 'La librairie musicale en France de 1653 à 1790 d'après les Registres de privilèges', in: *Sammelbände der Internationalen Musikgesellschaft*, VIII/3 (1907), pp. 401-466: 444.

[28]. A census of privileges included in «Registres des privilèges» of «Chambre royale des libraires et imprimeurs de Paris», is published in BRENET, Michel. *Op. cit.* (see note 27), and in CUCUEL, George. *Op. cit.* (see note 27). About the privileges, see also: DEVRIÈS-LESURE, Anik. *Édition et commerce* [...], *op. cit.* (see note 5), pp. 62-63.

[29]. BRENET, Michel. *Op. cit.* (see note 27), p. 411.

[30]. Paris, Bibliothèque nationale de France, ms. fr. 21957, 1739, 12 October: «P.G. pour 9 ans, du 7 août. [...] Le sieur Nicolas Chédeville, l'un des hautbois de notre chambre, nous ayant fait remontrer qu'il souhaiteroit faire imprimer, graver et donner au public plusieurs ouvrages intitulés le *Printemps* de Vivaldy, Concerto, et autres concerto et sonates Choisies de tous les auteurs italiens, et même d'extraire dans les quatorze œuvres de Vivaldy, le dix d'Albinony, le dix de Valentiny, le six de Corelly, le deux de Veraciny, les trois de Tessariny, les trois de Locatelly, les quatres de Quantz, les deux de Brevio, le deux de Mahault, les trois de Tartiny, les deux de Scarlaty [Domenico], pour accomoder, transporter et les ajuster d'une manière facile à pouvoir être exécutée sur la Musette, Viele ou flutte avec accompagnement de violons et de basse, et toutes les musiques instrumentales de sa composition. Mais comme il craint que

neither J.-P. Le Clerc *aîné* (shop in rue du Roule à la Croix d'Or) nor E.-C. Ballard widow Boivin (shop in rue St. Honoré à la Règle d'Or) seem to have been explicitly holders of a privilege for works by Tessarini. We know, however, that the documentation concerning the royal privileges is incomplete. As mentioned above, from the 1730s J.-P. Le Clerc had obtained privileges for the edition of Italian instrumental music (in 1730, 1737). This privilege could have also tacitly included works by Tessarini. Furthermore, one cannot exclude the possibility that the widow Boivin or the same Le Clerc[31] had acquired the privilege obtained by François Dufresne (31 December 1736) for unidentified concertos, trios and sonatas by Tessarini and by other authors[32].

---

quelques copistes et gens mal intentionnez ne s'avisassent de les copier ou faire copier ou contrefaire, ce qui lui feroit un tort considéreble, étant un travail immense tant pour la depense que par les recherches qu'il faut qu'il fasse sur la Musette pour la pousser au plus haut point de sa perfection, s'il nous plaisait de luy accorder nos lettres de privilège sur ce nécessaires, à ces causes voulant traiter favorablement le dit S^r exposant et lui donner des marques de la satisfaction que nous avons des services qu'il nous a rendus et ceux qu'il nous rend actuellement près de notre personne, nous lui avons permis et permettons, […] à condition neanmoins que ledit privilège ne pourra préjudicier aux privilèges que nous avons cy devant accordés pour des musiques étrangères et qu'il n'aura lieu que pour les pieces que le dit Sr Chedeville aura accomodées à la musette et à la Viele et dont il aura dèposé une copie signée de lui à la chambre syndicale»; the document is published in: *ibidem*, p. 440. Chédeville published works facilitated for musette. He never took advantage of the privilege for Tessarini's works, but actually published the 'four seasons' of Vivaldi: *Le printemps, ou Les saisons amusantes* (*Le printemps / ou / Les saisons / amusantes / concertos / D'Antonio Vivaldy / mis pour les Musettes et Vielles / avec accompagnement de Violon / Flute et Basse continue. / Par Mr Chedeville Del Cadet / Hautbois De la Chambre du Roy / et Musette ordinaire De l'Academie Royalle / De Musique. Opera ottava*, 1739); EVERETT, Paul. *Vivaldi: The Four Seasons and Other Concertos Op. 8*, Cambridge, Cambridge University Press, 1996 (Cambridge music handbooks), p. 4.

^{31}.   Paris, Bibliothèque nationale de France, ms. fr. 21959: «12 janvier 1751. P.G. pour 20 ans, du 18 novembre 1750, au Sr Charles Nicolas Le Clerc, l'un des vingt-quatre violons de notre chambre […] pour donner au public des cantates et cantatilles mises en musique par le Sieur Bourgeois intitulées *L'amante volage, Minerve et l'amour, L'incostance, Les souhaits de l'amour, Télémaque et Eucharisi, Bacchus, La simphonie italienne, Céphale et l'Aurore, Zéphire et la rose, Le concert, Les amours mutuels, Le dépit de l'amour, Calypso, et L'aveu sincère*; et les œuvres instrumentales composées par Abaco père et fils [dall'Abaco], Albinoni, Angelini, Alberto Gallo, Bezzossi [Besozzi], Boni, Baptista Briouschi [Brioschi], Brevio [Brivio], Corelli, Kamerloquer [Camerlocher], Servetto [G. Bassevi, detto Cervetto], Canabi [Cannabich], Cavalari [Cavallari], Costanzi, Desplanes, Daniello [Aniello Sant'Angelo], dall'Oglio, Du Tartre, De Monceaux, Forceter [Forster], Ferlingue [Ferling], Fech [Fesch], Fritz, Forni, Gronemai [Groneman], Guerini, Gray, Guillemain, Geminiani, Gottwalt, Handel, Hasse, Hamal, Hevard, Hanot, Klein, Kennis, L'ami du clavier, Locatelli, Lanzetto [Lanzetti], Loeillet, Lavalliere, Le Maire, Maho [Mahault], Madonis, Melanco, Martini [Gioseffo San Martini], Marcello, Mangan [Mangean], Masse, Miroglio, Paganelli, Porpora, Pichler, Perez, Quantz, Quinari [Quignard], Repel per [Rebel padre], Santio [de Santis], Smalle, Spourni, Schmitz, Somis l'aîné, Somis cadet, Scarlatti [Domenico Scarlatti], Soullalez [?], Thelleman [Telemann], Tartini, Themanza [Temanza], Thessarini [Tessarini], Thriermeo [Triemer?], Tortoriti, Tremais, Vivaldi, Wermand [?], Valentini, Valentine, Veracini, Zani»; the document is puplished in BRENET, Michel. *Op. cit.* (see note 27), p. 446.

^{32}.   Paris, Bibliotèque nationale de France, ms. fr. 21956; 1737, 4 February: «P.G. [privilège général] pour 8 ans, du 31 décembre 1736, au Sr François Dufresne pour «plusieurs Sonates, solo, trio et concerto des Sieurs★★★,

In the 1730s and 40s only a few Italian composers obtained a privilege to print their own music in Paris: Michele Mascitti (1731)[33], Luigi Madonis, music teacher of the ambassador of Venice (1731)[34], Giovanni Bononcini (1733)[35], and Piero Gianotti for trio sonatas and sonatas for violin (1736, 1746)[36]. The request for a privilege by Tessarini includes works by Tartini and Pasquali, but not the name of Giuseppe Canavasso, whose work *Sei sonate per violino e basso* Op. 1 Tessarini published in Italy (Urbino, undated).

It is clear that, in this period, even in the case of the printing privileges, the relationship between cause and effect is not always a straight line. Commercial relations of such intensity had to have an effect on Tessarini's musical activities: both didactically and stylistically. Albeit very briefly, some points for reflection will also offered in this perspective.

RELATIONSHIPS WITH THE FRENCH MUSIC WORLD

As already stated, Tessarini was in Paris for the first time between 1744 and 1746, and perhaps a second time (1752-1753) with the brothers Giuseppe Bernardo Merchi and Giacomo Merchi, renowned theorbo, lute, mandolin, and colascione players, present at the Concert spirituel in Paris, and founders of the modern didactics of the guitar. With them Tessarini presented concerts in Frankfurt in September 1752; he was then in Brussels with Berlati, a unknown musician. Clues obtainable once again from musical sources indicate a possible visit of Tessarini to Paris, before or after Brussels[37]. Once again this second trip could have been for publishing reasons: in fact, in those months the shop in rue St. Honoré (à la Règle d'Or), long managed by Élisabeth-Catherine Ballard widow Boivin — head of the group of publishers and booksellers in contact with Tessarini — passed to Marc Bayard (until 19 May 1762)[38]. The composer may have felt the need to take stock of business relationships. In addition, the handover from the widow Boivin to Bayard may also have released Tessarini from the previous constraints, fostering new collaborations, for example,

Nicolo Porpora, Carlo Tessarini, Pichler [Placidus], Brevio [Giuseppe Ferdinando Brivio della Tromba], Albert Gallo et autres»; the document is published in: *ibidem*, p. 437. About Dufresne and Tessarini, see also: BESUTTI, Paola. 'Produzione in esclusiva [...]', *op. cit.* (see note 16), pp. 298-299.

[33]. «Un recueil de Sonates et autres pièces de musique tant vocale qu'instrumentale» (1731, 26 January); see, BRENET, Michel. *Op. cit.* (see note 27), p. 433.

[34]. *Ibidem*, p. 434.

[35]. *Ibidem*, pp. 435-436.

[36]. *Ibidem*, pp. 437, 444.

[37]. For the documentation on this trip and previous errors concerning its dating, see BESUTTI, Paola – POLAZZI, Gianandrea. 'Mete europee', in: EAD. – GIULIANI, Roberto – POLAZZI, Gianandrea. *Op. cit.* (see note 1), pp. 115-147: 131-136.

[38]. On the business of the widow Boivin see DEVRIÈS-LESURE, Anik. *Édition et commerce* [...], *op. cit.* (see note 5), pp. 41-42.

with Louis-Hector Hue (Hüe), who around 1753 financed the edition of the violin sonatas Op. 16 (BCT 69, 20), now incompletely preserved[39].

Despite repeated appearances of Tessarini in France, we have, to this day, no information about his concerts, which certainly took place. He surely listened to music and made himself heard. It is not possible to summarize here the series of musical clues that seem to confirm his gradual approach toward writing music in a more brilliant and urbane violin style, which we now perceive as 'French'. Here we will focus on two aspects, macroscopic and objective.

His well-known *Gramatica di musica* (BCT 40), published many times between 1740 and 1791, was also translated into French and published in Belgium in Liège (*c*1760). After the first edition, engraved in Urbino and printed in Urbino or in Rome by Girolamo Mainardi, the *Gramatica* had at least six other editions in different languages, reworked, with no editorial notes, but conjecturally datable by external sources: a Belgian edition (BCT 40a, Liège *c*1760) and two French-Dutch in French language (BCT 40b and BCT 40c, Paris-Amsterdam, *c*1762), two in English (BCT 40d, Edinburgh *c*1765; BCT 40e, London *c*1765), and another in Italian edition, much later (BCT 40f, Pilucchi-Cracas, Rome 1791). The various editions can be related essentially to two different traditions[40].

From the first Italian edition comes the very faithful English translation, *A musical grammar* (BCT 40d, Edinburgh *c*1765), which retains on the title page the dedication to the Marquis Angelo Gabrielli[41]. From the Belgian edition, *Nouvelle méthode pour apprendre* [...] *à jouer du violon* (BCT 40a, *c*1760), derive, on the other hand, the editions in French, Paris-Amsterdam, *c*1762 (BCT 40b, 40c) and London *c*1765 (BCT 40e BCT). These four French-language editions are a kind of alternative version, radically changed in the practical section. However, contrary to what has been suggested elsewhere[42], it seems unlikely that this alternative tradition could have derived from a source outside of the control of the author. Some elements could suggest a conscious adaptation from a manual,

---

[39]. For the interest in Tessarini's music of Louis-Hector Hue (Hüe), «l'un des meilleurs graveurs de Paris», see BESUTTI, Paola. 'Produzione in esclusiva [...]', *op. cit.* (see note 16), p. 300.

[40]. On the publishing history of *Gramatica di musica*, see ROVIGHI, Luigi. 'Prefazione', in: *Tessarini Carlo, Gramatica di musica. Insegna il modo facile, e breve per bene imparare di sonare il violino su la parte (Urbino, 1741)*, edited by Luigi Rovighi, Lucca, LIM, 1988 (Esercizi di musica, 1), pp. vii-xvii. Some errors of dating are discussed and corrected in BESUTTI, Paola. 'La Gramatica di musica: fonti e fortuna', in: EAD. – GIULIANI, Roberto – POLAZZI, Gianandrea. *Op. cit.* (see note 1), pp. 151-157.

[41]. The Edinburgh edition has a few variants and includes the duet BCT 40 XXVIII (*Lezione in tempo diverso*), that on copy of *Gramatica di musica*, preserved in the Museo della musica of Bologna, and used for the facsimile edition *Tessarini Carlo, Gramatica di musica, op. cit.* (see note 40), is absent for a misprint. This duet is absent even in a more recent facsimile that reproduces only the first book: *Violon: méthodes, traités, ouvrages généraux*, edited by Alessandro Moccia, 3 vols., Corlay, Fuzeau, 2002 (Méthodes et traités, 13. Serie IV, Italie 1600-1800), vol. I, pp. 189-200.

[42]. DUNNING, Albert. 'Some Notes [...]', *op. cit.* (see note 24), pp. 120-121.

originally conceived for beginners, to a method for amateurs, who were more in need of improving than of basic training. This revision is attributable, until proven otherwise, to the author himself, who signed the dedication (undated) of the Liège edition to «Monsieur de Percevale, conseiller receveur general de sa Imperial Majesty, lieutenant de la cour feudal [*sic*] de la Ville et de Malines provinces». Moreover, at that time Tessarini was in the Netherlands and was beginning to establish close relations with Parisian distributors, who later spread the *Gramatica* «aux adresses ordinaires».

Further confirmation that Parisian editions, reproducing that of Liège, were the result of a new didactic and commercial strategy, agreed upon by the author and the publisher, comes from the advertising, in the *Nouvelle méthode* (BCT 40c), of some collections such as the lost *Nouvelle récréation armonique* (BCT 77), the concerto *L'arte di nuova modulacione* (BCT 26), and the duets Op. 15 (BCT 18). Tessarini caters to this new audience by promoting his own innovative method in the following manner:

> The works from the Nouvelle Methode are / A *Nouvelle Récréation Armonique* mixed of Pantomimes for two Violins, Contrabass, and Hunting Horns *ad Llibitum*. Price 5 Liv. / The *Art* d'une *Nouvelle Modulation* or *Methode de Composition* absolutely different from those of the Old and Modern composers. Demonstrated in a concerto for 4 parts through seven different tones without having to stop, and finally ending with the same Tone from what started with? [...][43].

This eloquent notice, published after the index of the *Nouvelle Méthode* (BCT 40c), as well as offering interesting elements on the meaning of *Arte di nuova modulacione*[44], confirms that the aptness of the new method derived mainly from the wish to include references to other separately published compositions which were useful to the user's musical practice but, above all, were promoted commercially as the basic manual.

Tessarini, therefore, an author sensitive to the trends of the lively transalpine musical life, firmly tied to his musical tradition, yet inspired by a desire for a continuous improvement (not so usual in the contemporary production) perhaps did not recognize himself in the widespread criticism toward the 'Italian' composers, circulating in France, Holland and England. In this sense, *L'arte di nuova modulacione* (BCT 26) can appear also

---

43. TESSARINI, Carlo. *Nouvelle methode pour apprendre par théorie dans un mois de tems á jouer du violon*, Amsterdam, Olofsen, *c*1762 (BCT 40c): «Les Ouvrages Appartenants à la Nouvelle Methode sont / Une *Nouvelle Récréation Armonique* mellée de Pantomines à deux Violons, Basses, & Cors de Chasse *ad Libitum*. Prix 5 Liv. / L'*Art* d'une *Nouvelle Modulation* où *Methode de Composition* absolument différent de celles des Compositeurs Anciens & Modernes. Démontrée dans un Concert à 4 Parties, qui en passant sept Tons differents sans devoir s'arrèter, finit enfin par le même Ton par le quel il a commencé [...]».

44. See BESUTTI, Paola. 'L'arte di nuova modulacione', in: EAD. – GIULIANI, Roberto – POLAZZI, Gianandrea. *Op. cit.* (see note 1), pp. 241-245.

as the proud answer of one who was joined, for example by Charles Avison (1752), to the ranks of Italian composers (Vivaldi, Alberti, Locatelli) accused of a poor sense of harmonic variety and true invention and defined as authors of little entertainments for children[45]. Although we have no letters or theoretical proclamations by Tessarini, *L'arte di nuova modulacione* appears today as a kind of musical response to his detractors. This «capricio» pursues the aim of a harmonic demonstration, evoked by the title, made explicit in the aforementioned advertising and realized in the composition.

Seventy years old, Tessarini moved to the Netherlands permanently after having been there several times for more or less long periods. In Holland he was active until 1767. No death certificate has yet been found[46]. During this last period he resumed his publishing activities, distributing his editions mainly in France. Several works were published: in France, the French version of his manual for violin (BCT 40c), the *Sei grand overture a quattro* Op. 19 (BCT 21), the *Sei grand sinfonie* Op. 20 (BCT 22), and the duets *Pantomime* (BCT 27); in the Netherlands (Covens), six sonatas for solo violin and bass, with a dedication dated 15 September 1763 (BCT 28) and six symphonies *Recueil harmonique* (BCT 29), with a subscription dated 1764. The method of publishing more frequently practiced by the author was a subscription. In this period he devoted himself mainly to symphonies in four parts (BCT 22, 29), which could be named 'overture' (BCT 21) — compositions suitable for large academic gatherings or public concerts, such as those then frequented by Tessarini in Arnhem and in other centres of the Netherlands[47].

Although Tessarini was to leave few biographical traces, hidden in his last *Sei grand sinfonie* Op. 20 (BCT 22) is a marvellous musical cosmopolitanism and stylistic awareness. He named the last symphony (BCT 22/VI) *Les trois nations*, articulated in this manner: *Presto Allemand* (BCT 22/VI/i), *Andante grazioso François* (BCT 22/VI/ii) and *Allegro assai Italien* (BCT 22/VI/iii). The initial *Presto* (Ex. 1), evoking the German style, is based on very clean chordal blocks, on quick and squared phrasing constructed upon the degrees of the principal tonality, the trend for third-overlapping, rarely present in Tessarini's style, is frequently adopted here. The overall effect is a kind of Tessarini devoid of nuances. To interpret the French softness, the *Andante grazioso* has a ternary rhythm (Ex. 2). He chooses the form of theme and variations. Each variation has a refrain, with the main theme repeated at the end. Very frequent are slipping rhythmic figures, as the triplet

---

[45]. AVISON, Charles. *An Essay in Musical Expression*, London, Davis, 1752, p. 42: «Of the first and lowest Class are Vivaldi, Tessarini, Alberti, and Locatelli, whose Compositions being equally defective in various Harmony and true Invention, are only a fit Amusement for Children».

[46]. The last biographical information is concerned, once again, with a concert (Gröningen, John Philip Riedel's Concert Hall, 1767, 12 March), advertised in the newspaper *Opregte Groninger Courant* (1767, 6 March). I would like to thank Paolo Righini for giving me this information.

[47]. About the Tessarini's several journeys in Holland, see BESUTTI, Paola – POLAZZI, Gianandrea. 'Mete europee', *op. cit.* (see note 37), pp. 123-127, 136-147.

Ex. 1: Carlo Tessarini, Sinfonia VI, *Les trois nations*, *Presto Allemand*, bb. 1-15.

Ex. 2: Carlo Tessarini, Sinfonia VI, *Les trois nations*, *Andante grazioso François*, bb. 1-9.

Ex. 3: Carlo Tessarini, Sinfonia VI, *Les trois nations*, *Allegro assai Italien*, bb. 1–15.

ITALIEN
ALLEGRO ASSAI

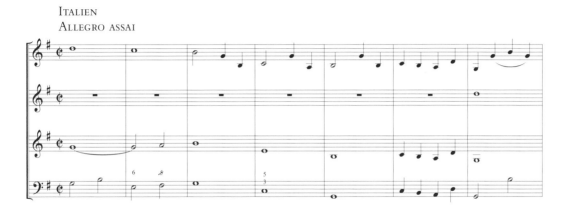

against two, embellishments and chromaticism. To denote the Italian style, in the final *Allegro assai* (Ex. 3), Tessarini opts for the element of sequences, especially on the pedal point. He then creates a very simple and schematic theme that launches into a series of sequences that overwhelms all the entries, and which are based mainly on very long pedal points, supported also by the «single key» («tasto solo») or single musical note. This movement gives the impression of a caricature effect, perhaps sought by Tessarini, which does not detract from the fact that, even with humorous intent, he had keenly grasped what his listeners would have immediately recognized as typical of the different styles. It is interesting to note, however, that in the other edition, presented shortly after in Paris (BCT 22a), the same symphony does not bear a title. Perhaps the author was not able to replace this piece or at least to provide it with the appropriate title. It is also possible that the Parisian publishers feared that the titles could harm the reception of the piece. Certainly, if someone had to base an assessment about the author only on this composition, with no indication of its title, he would have a partial and distorted image. This latter case confirms how in this period the evaluation of music should not be separated from the study of the strategies of publication.

Bridging the Baroque and Classical Periods
The Role, Lives and Innovations of French Violinist-Composers
Leclair, Guignon, Guillemain, and Mondonville

Sallynee Amawat
(Montréal, QC)

This study will examine and discuss a group of French violinist-composers whose repertoire contributed to the foundation of the French violin school. Typically, this school is associated with the influence of the Italian violinist Giovanni Battista Viotti (1755-1824) on Paris Conservatoire professors Pierre Rode (1774-1830), Rodolphe Kreutzer (1766-1831), and Pierre Baillot (1771-1842). However, a generation before Viotti, new innovations in violin technique and composition were already emerging in publications and performances in France. While many influential composers in France during the eighteenth-century made significant contributions to violin playing during the High Baroque period, this study will focus on Jean-Marie Leclair (1697-1764), Jean-Pierre Guignon (1702-1774), Louis-Gabriel Guillemain (1705-1770), and Jean-Joseph Cassanéa de Mondonville (1711-1772). Through an analysis of their biographical history, I have drawn fresh insights into their shared time and activities in both Paris and Lyons and the musical influences to which they were exposed. My theoretical framework is built around three essential questions: 1) What were the precise biographical links between them that can be firmly identified (i.e. origins, location, studies — musical and other — and intersections in time that point to personal encounters between them); 2) In what ways are these biographical links reflected in their compositional output, and what we can trace to their performance legacy? 3) How have their compositional output and performing practice contributed to what was later identified as a French violin school? Once these intersecting biographical factors elucidated, I will proceed to analyze a representative selection of musical sources from each of these three composers and apply techniques of close reading to internal (to the music) and external evidence (treatises) about their innovative and contextualized use of violin techniques. The works I have chosen for my close study were all published either in the same year, or less than five years apart. The results of my study indicate that these violinist-composers may effectively have acted as a bridge between the baroque and Classical periods of violin composition, and the transition to increasingly higher technical demands on the instrument that would continue to develop in the Classical era.

THE COMPOSERS AND THEIR CONNECTIONS

The son of a master lacemaker, Jean-Marie Leclair was born on May 10, 1697 in Lyons. The eldest of eight children, his brothers Jean-Marie *le cadet*, Pierre, and Jean-Benoît were also violinist-composers, though not as famous as their eldest brother. Neal Zaslaw has shown that the earliest documentation in Leclair's career lists him among the dancers of the Lyons opera in 1716, where he also met his first wife[1]. In 1722, Leclair made his first trip to Turin, possibly as one of the many free-lance actors, dancers and musicians who traveled there to participate in the festivities celebrating the marriage between Prince Carlo Emanuele of Piedmont to Princess Anna Cristina of Sulzback[2]. It was in Turin that Leclair came under the tutelage of Giovanni Battista Somis, one of the central figures of the Piedmontese school of violin playing, and whose Italian influence can be traced in the bulk of Leclair's violin sonatas. In 1723, Leclair traveled to Paris and came under the patronage of Joseph Bonnier, one of the richest men in France, to whom he dedicated his Op. 1 book of Sonatas for violin and basso continuo[3]. His Op. 2 book of Sonatas for violin and basso continuo was published in 1728. That same year he made his debut at the Concert spirituel with twelve concerts featuring his own sonatas and concertos. His debut was met with critical acclaim, and he enjoyed great success over the next few years, with additional performances at the Concert spirituel and in Kassel[4]. Leclair was appointed *ordinaire de la musique du roi* in 1733 by King Louis XV, to whom he dedicated is third book of Sonatas, Op. 5 (1734). He remained in service of the King until 1737, in which a dispute with Jean-Pierre Guignon over leadership of the orchestra led him to resign and leave Paris[5].

Leclair's years outside of Paris took him to the Netherlands and The Hague, where he spent three months, and eventually nine months out of the year in service at the Court

[1]. ZASLAW, Neal. *Materials for the Life and Works of Jean-Marie Leclair l'aîne*, unpublished Ph.D. Diss., New York (NY), Columbia University, 1970, pp. 9-10.

[2]. *Ibidem*, pp. 10-11. Leclair's name is not included in the list of regular musicians employed at the Court of Piedmont; it is possible he was in Turin as a free-lance musician and dancer.

[3]. ID. 'Leclair, Jean-Marie', in: *Grove Music Online*, <www.oxfordmusiconline.com>, (accessed 13 January 2014).

[4]. *Ibidem*. It was in Kassel that Leclair and Locatelli performed together at court, and were observed by J. W. Lustig as playing «like an angel» (Leclair), and «like a devil» (Locatelli).

[5]. LA LAURENCIE, Lionel de. *L'école française de violon de Lully à Viotti: études d'histoire et d'esthétique*, 3 vols., Paris, Delagrave, 1922-1924, Rpt. Geneva, Minkoff, 1971, vol. I, p. 282.

of Orange. He returned to Paris in 1743 to publish his fourth and final book of violin Sonatas, Op. 9, and went into semi-retirement for the next few years. His first and only opera, *Scylla et Glaucus*, was premiered at the Académie Royale de Musique in 1746. In subsequent years, Leclair published his remaining works, which included chamber music for two violins and trio sonatas, but in 1758 he separated from his second wife and bought a small house in a dangerous part of Paris. On the morning of October 23, 1764, Leclair was found stabbed to death in his home. His murder remains unsolved to this day[6].

One of Leclair's most formidable rivals and a violinist of considerable virtuosity, Jean-Pierre Guignon was Italian by birth but made his career mostly in France. Born in Turin in 1702, Guignon was also a pupil of Somis. He made his debut at the Concert spirituel in 1725, three years previous to Leclair. He appeared with violinist (Jean-Jacques-)Baptiste Anet (1676-1755) in three concerts presented as a competition between the French and Italian styles. In 1730, Guignon performed his own concerto and sonatas for the French king, which led to his appointment as *musicien ordinaire de la musique du Roy* in 1733, the same year as Leclair[7]. It was in this year that the most famous account of the rivalry between Leclair and Guignon takes place. Both musicians vied for the position of first violin, and eventually an arrangement was made in which both violinists would rotate on a monthly basis. After Leclair's month as first violin was up, rather than accept a lower rank to Guignon, Leclair resigned and left Paris[8]. Guignon, however, retained the position until 1762.

In 1736 Guignon travelled to Lyons, where he performed for the Duke de Villeroy and dedicated his Op. 2. Two years later, he performed in Telemann's Paris quartets and travelled to Italy with another violinist-composer, Louis-Gabriel Guillemain. Guignon became a naturalized French citizen in 1741, the same year the king also granted him the long-vacant position of *Roy et maître des ménétriers et joueurs d'instruments tant hauts que bas et communauté des maîtres à dancer*. Guignon sought to use his new position to revive the guild system, which would have required all musicians to join and pay membership dues that he would have benefited from, but his attempts failed and eventually his position was permanently abolished[9].

In the summer of 1744, Guignon traveled once again to perform in Lyons, this time with Jean-Joseph Cassanéa de Mondonville, another violinist-composer. The pair also toured other parts of France, including Dunkirk [Dunkerque]. Their concerts in Lyons were met with critical acclaim by the general public and progressive musicians,

---

[6]. For a detailed description surrounding the death of Leclair, see BOROWITZ, Albert. 'Finale Marked Presto: The Killing of Leclair', in: *Musical Quarterly*, LXXII/2 (1986), pp. 228-238.

[7]. ZASLAW, Neal. 'Guignon, Jean-Pierre [Guignone, Giovanni Pietro]', in: *Grove Music Online, op. cit.* (see note 3).

[8]. LA LAURENCIE, Lionel de. *Op. cit.* (see note 5), vol. I, pp. 269-275.

[9]. *Ibidem*, vol. II, pp. 40-76.

but were criticized by the more conservative academics[10]. Guignon and Mondonville returned to Lyons once again the following summer to give another series of successful performances. After 1750, Guignon no longer appeared in public, but still performed at court and in the salons.

French violinist-composer Louis-Gabriel Guillemain was born in Paris in 1705 and was raised by the Count of Rochechouart[11]. The circumstances which brought him there are unknown, but Luynes claims that the Count saw to it that the young Guillemain received musical instruction after observing that the boy had taken «a liking [to] the violin»[12]. Later in his life, Guillemain also studied with Somis in Italy, although the exact time and length of his stay in Italy are unknown[13].

Upon his return from Italy, Guillemain moved to Lyons where he performed with the opera orchestra and held the position of «symphoniste»[14]. After 1729, Guillemain became the first violinist of the Dijon Académie de Musique and in 1734 published his Op. 1 Sonatas for violin and basso continuo, a collection that makes highly virtuosic demands on the performer[15]. In 1738 he entered the service of Louis XV as a *musicien ordinaire*, just a few years after Guignon and a year after Leclair had left. Was he hired as a replacement for Leclair? Also around these years, he traveled to Italy with Guignon, most likely to give concerts[16]. Early into his career at court he became one of the most highly paid court musicians, with a salary on par with Guignon. That year, music thrived at court, and both violinists performed almost one hundred concerts together[17].

The remainder of Guillemain's career centered around Paris and the musical life at court. All eighteen of his published works consisted of instrumental music. While his symphonies were often performed at the Concert spirituel in the 1750's, it is likely that Guillemain himself never appeared as a soloist, possibly due to stage fright[18]. His taste for exquisite decorations, in keeping with the fashions of high society at the time, far surpassed his means to acquire them and he was constantly in debt. Guillemain sought to improve his financial situation by publishing some of his later works which, compared with the Op. 1 Sonatas, were much more accessible to the growing number

---

[10]. ZASLAW, Neal. 'Guignon, Jean-Pierre [Guignone, Giovanni Pietro]', *op. cit.* (see note 7).

[11]. LUYNES, Charles-Philippe d'Albert de. *Mémoires du Duc de Luynes sur la cour de Louis XV: 1735-1758*, 17 vols., Paris, Firmin-Didot frères, 1860-1865, vol. II, p. 109.

[12]. *Ibidem.*

[13]. *Ibidem*, p. 109: (18 April 1738) «il a été en Italie, où il a joué avec Somis pendant longtemps».

[14]. LA LAURENCIE, Lionel de. *Op. cit.* (see note 5), vol. II, p. 2.

[15]. His last publication, the Op. 18 *Amusement pour le violon seul... avec douze caprices*, also demand the same level of technical virtuosity as the Op. 1 collection.

[16]. CASTONGUAY, Gerald Richard. 'Guillemain, Louis-Gabriel', in: *Grove Music Online, op. cit.* (see note 3).

[17]. ID. *The Orchestral Music of Louis-Gabriel Guillemain*, Ph.D. Diss., New Brunswick (NJ), Rutgers University, 1975, p. 43.

[18]. ID. 'Guillemain, Louis-Gabriel', *op. cit.* (see note 16).

of amateurs and connoisseurs of music in Paris. His publications between 1739 and 1745 included duets and trio sonatas for a wider range of instruments, but violinistic idioms still remained a significant feature of his works and his more difficult compositions remained technically demanding, particularly the Op. 4 Duos for two violins[19].

Despite his efforts to appeal to a broader market for his publications and a seemingly successful and long-running career at court, Guillemain's self-indulgences kept him in debt to the end of his life. Sadly, in his later years he turned to excessive drinking until his death on October 1, 1770. Although there is no official mention of suicide, the unorthodox, hasty conditions of his burial on the same day of his death indicate that he most likely took his own life[20].

While it is significant that the composers Leclair, Guignon, and Guillemain were all former students of G. B. Somis, there is one other composer worth mentioning who, while not sharing the same pedagogical background, was also a successful violinist composer whose compositions made a significant contribution to the pre-classical French violin school. Jean-Joseph Cassanéa de Mondonville was born in 1711 in Narbonne, and most likely received his early musical education from his father, who was organist at the Narbonne Cathedral. In 1731 Mondonville settled in Paris, and went on to publish his first set of Sonatas for violin (Op. 1) and *Sonates en trio* (Op. 2) in 1733 and 1734, respectively. He made his debut at the Concert spirituels in 1734, after which the *Mercure de France* praised his virtuosity[21].

Mondonville held the position of first violin in the Concert de Lille in 1738, the same year his Op. 4, *Les son harmoniques*, was published. This work was among the first to introduce the technique of playing natural harmonics on the violin by lightly touching the finger to the string. He returned to Paris and in 1739 was appointed violinist of the royal chamber and chapel[22]. Mondonville toured and performed in Lyons with Guignon in the summer of 1744 and 1745, and in that same year, performed with Guillemain at the Concert spirituels[23]. The peak of his career culminated in 1747 when he performed *seul* at the Concert spirituels, and was also appointed associate director the following year. His Op. 5 collection was also published in 1748[24].

Mondonville's success continued until his death in 1772. Throughout his lifetime he was well-liked and respected by those who lived and worked with him, and upon

---

[19]. Id. *The Orchestral Music* [...], *op. cit.* (see note 17), p. 51.

[20]. *Ibidem*, pp. 107-108.

[21]. Signorile, Marc. 'Mondonville, Jean-Joseph Cassanéa de', in: *Grove Music Online*, *op. cit.* (see note 3).

[22]. *Ibidem*.

[23]. Borroff, Edith. *The Instrumental Works of Jean-Joseph Cassanéa de Mondonville*, Ph.D. Diss., Ann Arbour (MI), University of Michigan, 1958, p. 8.

[24]. *Ibidem*, p. 9.

his death, the *Mercure de France* published a long obituary dedicated to the composer, describing him as a «bon mari, bon pere, bon ami»[25].

Their Compositions: Ushering in the Classical Era

The works composed for solo violin and basso continuo by all four composers can be described as virtuosic and technically demanding. Multiple and double stops, trills, and varied bow articulations are some examples of left and right-hand technique frequented in these pieces. The discussion and instructions for execution of such techniques can be found in the treatises published in the pre-classical and classical period, namely that of L'abbé *le fils*[26] (1761), and Jean-Baptiste Cartier (1798). In the nineteenth century, the treatise of Pierre Baillot (1834) takes the discussion further, indicating that these elements have become firmly rooted in the pedagogy of the French violin school[27].

The use of double and multiple stops are characteristic of the violin sonatas of all four composers, most likely inherited from the Italian tradition and their teacher G. B. Somis, whose Op. 2 Sonatas for violin and bass feature extensive double and multiple stop passages in nearly every fast movement. In Leclair's third book of Sonatas, Op. 5, several sonatas in the collection feature movements which involve similar passagework. Some movements, such as the *Gavotta* in Sonata No. 6 in C minor (Ex. 1), involve executing double stops for virtually the entire length o the movement. Like Sonata No. 6, Sonatas Nos. 9, 10, 11, and 12 each feature at least one movement comprised almost entirely of double and multiple stops. The collection culminates with Sonata No. 12, featuring three movements (*Adagio*, *Allegro ma non troppo*, and *Ciaccona*) that involve highly technical multiple stops throughout the entirety of the movement. Trills and double trills are also added to both the double and multiple stops as ornamentation. In Guillemain's first book of *Sonatas à violon seul avec la basse continue*, published the same year as Leclair's Op. 5, we see similar technical demands in his use of double/multiple stops and double trills (Ex. 2). His use of these techniques eclipses that of Leclair's. Over half of the sonatas in this collection involve executing double/multiple stops for large portions of the inner movements, and several of those have multiple movements involving this highly virtuosic technique.

---

25. *Mercure de France*, December 1772, pp. 196-197.
26. L'abbé *le fils* (Joseph-Barnabé Saint-Sévin, 1727-1803) was also a student of Leclair.
27. For a complete list of treatises published in France between *c*1760-*c*1840, see Stowell, Robin. *Violin Technique and Performance Practice in the late Eighteenth and early Nineteenth Centuries*, Cambridge, Cambridge University Press, 1985 (Cambridge musical text and monographs), Appendix, pp. 368-370.

Ex. 1: Jean-Marie Leclair, Sonata No. 6, Op. 5, III mov., *Gavotta*[28].

Ex. 2: Louis-Gabriel Guillemain, Sonata No. 2, Op. 1, I mov., *Andante*[29].

[28]. LECLAIR, Jean-Marie. *Troisième livre de sonates à violon seul avec la basse continue*, Paris, l'Auteur, la veuve Boivin, Le Clerc, [1734].

[29]. GUILLEMAIN, Louis-Gabriel. *Sonates, à violon seul avec la basse continue, premier livre (nouvelle édition revue par l'auteur)*, (1739-1740), introduction by Philippe Lescat et Jean Saint-Arroman, Courlay, J. M. Fuzeau, 1987 (Fac-similé Jean-Marc Fuzeau; Musique française classique de 1650 à 1800, 16).

Mondonville advanced this technique in his *Les son harmoniques*, Op. 4, by utilizing harmonic double stops, as well as double trills. Approximately twenty-five years after Mondonville, L'abbé *le fils* not only includes all of the natural and artificial harmonics in his *Principes du violon*, but expanded further to include diatonic and chromatic scales, trills, and whole pieces in harmonics[30]. He describes the role of both the left and right hand in the execution of double stops, and discusses and includes exercises for practicing double stops in thirds, fourths, fifths, sixths and octaves, and cadential trills[31]. Cartier's treatise, *L'art du violon*, also includes exercises for practicing double and multiple stops in scales, and the same cadential double cadential trill exercise that was published in *Principes* […] by L'abbé *le fils*[32]. The same techniques are discussed by Baillot well in to the 19th century, although he deals with the broader issues such as how to practice intonation with relevant exercises[33].

Guignon's Op. 1 Sonatas for violin and bass were published in 1737. While his virtuosity undoubtedly rivalled that of his contemporaries by reputation of his public performances, his compositions were relatively less demanding. Similar technical demands are made upon the player, although his use of multiple stops is in this collection, published a few years after that of Leclair's Op. 5 and Guillemain's Op. 1, are considerably less than his contemporaries. However, Guignon's Sonatas demand a mastery of precise bow articulations, as his meticulous use of dots and strokes can be found throughout the bulk of his writing[34].

Characteristic of works for violin from this transitional era are the appearance of more specific right-hand articulation markings and use of varied bow strokes. Slurred bowings, such as slurred *tremolo*, slurred *staccato*, or *roulades*[35], are examples of the types of articulation utilized and discussed in both the repertoire for violin and treatises on violin playing. The ambiguity of eighteenth century notation makes it difficult to realize exactly how these articulations were realized. However, tempo and character of the movement formed the basic ground rules for execution[36].

In the first movement of Leclair's Sonata No. 2, Op. 5, both the violin and bowed bass instruments have repeated notes under one slur, indicating the use of slurred *tremolo*.

---

[30]. L'ABBÉ LE FILS [Joseph-Barnabé Saint-Sévin]. *Principes du violon*, Paris, l'Auteur, 1722; Rpt. Geneva, Minkoff, 1976, pp. 72-73.

[31]. *Ibidem*, pp. 64-65.

[32]. CARTIER, Jean-Baptiste. *L'art du violon*, Paris, Decombe, c1796; Rpt. of the third edition (1803), New York, Broude Bros, 1973, pp. 30-33.

[33]. BAILLOT, Pierre(-Marie-François de Sales). *The Art of the Violin*, edited and translated by Louise Goldberg, Evanston (IL), Northwestern University Press, 1991, pp. 145-157.

[34]. Guignon's notable use of the term *Staccato* included in the title of particular movements, such as in Sonata No. 6 (II mov., *Largo-Staccato*), may indicate his instructions for a particular type of bow stroke or character.

[35]. L'ABBÉ LE FILS [Joseph-Barnabé Saint-Sévin]. *Op. cit.* (see note 30), p. 54.

[36]. STOWELL, Robin. *Op. cit.* (see note 27), p. 172.

As Robin Stowell indicates, this type of articulation «can be played either *staccato* or *legato*, according to the context or notation. Dots or strokes under a slur generally indicate the use of the *staccato* version, whereas a slur alone implies a *legato* interpretation»[37]. The passage by Leclair (Ex. 3), is an example of a *legato*-style slurred *staccato*, given the *Andante* indication at the beginning of the movement. In contrast, the same articulation marking would have been interpreted as *staccato* in the *Allegro* from Guillemain's Sonata No. 1 (Ex. 4).

Ex. 3: Jean-Marie Leclair, Sonata No. 2, Op. 5, 1 mov., *Andante*.

Ex. 4: Louis-Gabriel Guillemain, Sonata No. 1, Op. 1, II mov., *Allegro*.

Another type of slurred *staccato*, as seen in Guignon's Op. 1 (Ex. 5), is a *roulade*. L'abbé *le fils* describes the execution of a *roulade* as: «When the notes of a roulade are slurred, one should begin playing it at half strength and swell the tone as one approaches the last note, which must have the brightest tone; if the roulade is not slurred, its tone must be increased, observing the same gradation […]»[38].

---

37. *Ibidem*, p. 176.
38. L'ABBÉ *LE FILS* [Joseph-Barnabé Saint-Sévin]. *Op. cit.* (see note 30), 54.

Ex. 5: Jean-Pierre Guignon, Sonata No. 2, Op. 1, iv mov., *Allegro molto*.

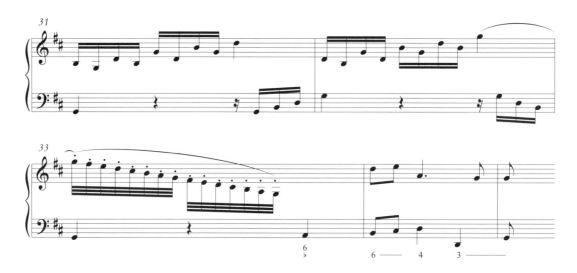

In the nineteenth century, Baillot describes these techniques as *staccato*, but also describes it as a series of little *martelés* and *articulated détaché*. He also gives detailed instruction on the proper execution, along with many examples of the slurred *staccato*, as well as using varied bowings[39].

Rapid passagework was a common characteristic of the eighteenth-century violin sonata, and an opportunity for the composer/performer to demonstrate agility in both the left and right hands. Its appearance in France, particularly among the composers in this study, was clearly due to the strong Italian influence. Somis, along with Corelli and Vivaldi, are a few examples of Italian composers whose compositions often demand this particular skill. *Batterie* involved rapid string crossings between adjacent strings, and *brisure* involved string crossings between non-adjacent strings. Both were particularly common within the eighteenth century. Similarly, when using slurred bowings, they were referred to as *bariolage* and *ondeggiando*, respectively[40].

Leclair's Sonata No. 1 (Ex. 6) shows an example of *batterie*, in which the string crossings alternate between a fingered note on the A string with an open E. Mondonville employs the same technique, but with slurs, in his Sonata No. 6. Guignon expands further by requiring the performer to cross non-adjacent strings (G to A) at the bottom of the scaler passage (Ex. 7). Similarly, Guillmain's Sonata No. 8 (iii mov. *Allegro ma non presto*) demands the performer cross over two non-adjacent strings, from E to G.

---

39. BAILLOT, Pierre(-Marie-François de Sales). *Op. cit.* (see note 33), pp. 175-185.

40. Stowell defines *bariolage* as an «essentially nineteenth-century term to describe the alternation of notes on adjacent strings, one of which is usually open [...]»; STOWELL, Robin. *Op. cit.* (see note 27), p. 172.

Ex. 6: Jean-Marie Leclair, Sonata No. 1, Op. 5, II mov., *Allegro*.

Ex. 7: Jean-Pierre Guignon, Sonata No. 6, Op. 1, IV mov., *Allegro*.

While these types of passages can be found frequented throughout the sonatas of each of the composers in this study, and certainly that of others, Stowell says they are all but neglected in the treatises of the eighteenth-century[41]. Since they can be found readily throughout the compositions of the violinist composers in this study and beyond, their absence from the treatises of the time may indicate that these techniques were still considered experimental in the eighteenth-century. They eventually find their way into later treatises of the French violin school. Baillot mentions the use of *bariolage*, and defines it as thus: «The name bariolage is given to a type of passage which presents an appearance of disorder and bizarreness because the notes are not played one after the other on the same string […] but alternately with one stopped note and one on an open string»[42].

Based on the historical background of each of these composers, one could easily imagine the influences that each would have had upon each other. Being active musicians in France at the same time and each having their own works publicly performed and published within a few years of each other, all of these composers would have been worthy adversaries of each other in a highly competitive environment. In a time when public and private performances were rapidly gaining popular favor, the most effective means to

---

[41]. *Ibidem.*

[42]. BAILLOT, Pierre(-Marie-François de Sales). *Op. cit.* (see note 33), p. 219.

promote oneself as a violinist was to compose and perform their own works. It would have been to the personal advantage of each of these violinists to try and 'outplay' the other, and the rivalry between certain composers, such as Leclair and Guignon, were well known. This kind of competitive strategy would have encouraged performers to push themselves to the very edge of their technical ability and the capability of their instruments. The strong Italian compositional influences, inspired by the great masters such as G. B. Somis, allowed for violinist-composers such as Leclair, Guignon, and Guillemain to utilize the sonata and concerto form to exploit their pyrotechnics. Other violinists were able to take advantage of these influences and use them to develop violin technique even further, such as Mondonville's use of harmonics. All of these advancements served to firmly establish these genres and their respective technical aspects in the French violin school by the later half of the eighteenth century.

Pierre Pagin's Capriccios for Antonio Vivaldi's Violin Concerto *La primavera*, RV 269

Michael Talbot
(Liverpool)

Tartini and Vivaldi

T HIS ARTICLE IS ABOUT THE CAPRICCIOS written by one of Giuseppe Tartini's favourite pupils for one of Antonio Vivaldi's favourite concertos, the 'Spring' concerto from the cycle *Le quattro stagioni*, which stands at the head of the collection *Il cimento dell'armonia e dell'inventione*, Op. 8 (1725). At one remove, therefore, it is also about the relationship between Vivaldi and Tartini themselves. This relationship is complex, ambiguous and poorly documented at a biographical level. Although their birth dates (1678 and 1692, respectively) were similar enough to make the second half of Vivaldi's career (1720-1741) coincide with the whole of Tartini's 'first' creative period (*c*1721-1735) and the start of his second (*c*1735-1750), the two men seem almost to have been two ships passing in the night[1]. This apparent paucity of personal interaction may partly be due to the fact that by the time Tartini became most active as a touring virtuoso of the violin, in the 1720s, Vivaldi had already largely abandoned this role on account of his major involvement and overriding interest in operatic composition and management, and perhaps also to conserve his frail health.

Indeed, it is this very turn to opera on Vivaldi's part that gave rise to Tartini's tart remark, as reported by Charles de Brosses, to the effect that Vivaldi was unwise to exchange violin composition for vocal composition since he was successful in the first but hissed in the second[2]. Elsewhere, I have described this comment as smacking of sour grapes[3], but it

---

[1]. On Tartini's three creative periods, see Dounias, Minos. *Die Violinkonzerte Giuseppe Tartinis als Ausdruck einer Künstlerpersönlichkeit und einer Kulturepoche*, Wolfenbüttel, Kallmeyer, 1935. The Vivaldi-Tartini relationship is summarized in Talbot, Michael. *The Vivaldi Compendium*, Woodbridge, The Boydell Press, 2011, p. 180.

[2]. Brosses, Charles de. *Lettres historiques et critiques sur l'Italie*, 3 vols., Paris, Ponthieu, an VII [1799], vol. II, p. 316: «Vivaldi, qui a voulu s'exercer dans les deux genres, s'est toujours fait siffler dans l'un, tandis qu'il réussirait fort bien dans l'autre».

[3]. Talbot, Michael. *Vivaldi*, London, J. M. Dent, ²1993 (Dent master musicians series), p. 130.

needs also to be viewed against the background of a widespread feeling in the earlier part of the eighteenth century, arising from a guild mentality among professional musicians, that it was somehow improper, even presumptuous, to disconnect one's activity as a composer from one's activity as a performer in public[4]. There are tantalizing hints of a personal connection between the two composers during the 1720s. In 1720-1721 Tartini taught violin to the Venetian patrician Girolamo Ascanio Giustiniani and in 1734 dedicated his Op. 1 violin sonatas to him; in 1726s Vivaldi, in his role as impresario at the S. Angelo theatre, sold a block of tickets to Giustiniani, and in 1736 the latter purchased from him a manuscript containing violin sonatas[5]. Then there is the intriguing fact that the surviving partbook for principal violin copied for Anna Maria of the Pietà in 1723-1726 contains a concerto by Tartini (D. 85), apparently the original version of a concerto published by Le Cène in 1728 (in the so-called Op. 1 set). Unless one of the Pietà's governors or benefactors forced this item on its *coro*, one has to conclude that it was admitted to its repertory with Vivaldi's concurrence[6]. Finally, there is the indirect evidence of reciprocal musical influence. In his concertos Tartini took as his starting point Vivaldian ritornello form (although he quickly developed his own distinctive variant of this structure), while Vivaldi, at the end of his career, started increasingly to employ a form of accompaniment to the principal violin popularized by Tartini but little used by him previously; this consisted of a simple two-strand texture assigned to first and second violins[7]. One infers that at least within the genre of the violin concerto there was some degree of mutual respect between the two composers.

---

4.   The apologetic comments of the Milanese violinist-composer Carlo Zuccari (1704-1792) to Giovanni Battista Martini, to whom, in 1755, he had sent a vocal canon of his own composition, reveal the depth of this mentality, which was firmly anchored in social reality. Zuccari writes: «Già capisco che il mio impegno è stato troppo ardito in accingermi a così ardua impresa che oltrepassa gli limiti dell'obligo di un povero professore di violino» («I readily accept that I have been too bold in taking on such a demanding task, which goes beyond the boundaries of a poor professional violinist's obligations»). On this subject, see ID. 'Eight «Double-Stopped» Fugues in A Major: Essays in the Union of Counterpoint and Violinistic Virtuosity by Corelli, Bitti, Albinoni, Carbonelli and Zuccari', in: *Ad Parnassum: A Journal of Eighteenth- and Nineteenth-Century Instrumental Music*, XII/24 (October 2014), pp. 1-30.

5.   ID. *The Vivaldi Compendium, op. cit.* (see note 1), pp. 89-90.

6.   On this concerto and the volume of which it forms part, see ID. 'Anna Maria's Partbook', in: *Musik an den venezianischen Ospedali/Konservatorien vom 17. bis zum frühen 19. Jahrhundert – La musica negli ospedali/conservatori veneziani fra Seicento e inizio Ottocento*, edited by Helen Geyer and Wolfgang Osthoff, Rome, Edizioni di Storia e Letteratura, 2004 (Ricerche [Deutsches Studienzentrum in Venedig / Centro Tedesco di studi veneziani], 1), pp. 23-81. At a much later date Tartini's concertos D. 7, D. 65 and D. 99 are known to have been taken into the Pietà's repertory.

7.   Vivaldi's A major concerto RV 552 (1740), with its 'echo group' comprising a second principal violin and two accompanying violins, is the best-known instance. The form of accompaniment is illustrated in Ex. 1b, below.

Rather unexpectedly, Tartini and Vivaldi also interacted by proxy. That proxy was Tartini's beloved pupil and, so to speak, personal representative in the French capital: Pierre Pagin.

PIERRE PAGIN (1723-1799)

Until the recent appearance of a long article by Beverly Wilcox describing in considerable detail Pagin's life and career[8], knowledge about this important, and in his day much-lauded, French violinist-composer was patchy, dispersed and in some particulars inaccurate. The condensed account I shall give here largely follows Wilcox, and to avoid excessive use of footnotes I shall leave unreferenced all simple factual information presented in her article with full identification of the primary sources. On the other hand, I shall reference in the ordinary way anything that supplements, corrects or interprets differently the biographical data.

Pagin, whose baptismal forenames appear to have been Pierre Jean Baptiste (but who during his lifetime was generally known as 'Pierre' or 'Jean-Pierre'), was born in Paris in July 1723[9]. His father was a dancing master, also named Pierre Pagin, who is described in the register recording his son's wedding as a «bourgeois de la ville de Châlons-en-Champagne». The family lived in rue Sainte-Anne in the parish of Saint-Roch. Pagin's mother, Marguerite Maillard, died while he was still young. On 22 January 1728, when his father was on the point of remarrying, his maternal grandfather, Pierre Maillard, was appointed official guardian (*tuteur*) to Pagin and his three sisters[10]; it is uncertain how closely Pagin maintained contact with his father thereafter, although one would imagine that in his boyhood he was instructed in the rudiments of violin-playing by him.

It is similarly unclear from whom (if anyone) Pagin received more advanced tuition in Paris. The physicist Jacques-Alexandre-César Charles, in his manuscript notes entitled *Acoustique*, completed in 1802, claimed that the teacher in question was Pierre Gaviniès, but this is virtually ruled out by the simple fact that Gaviniès (1728-1800) was five years Pagin's junior[11].

---

[8]. WILCOX, Beverly. 'The Hissing of Jean-Pierre Pagin: Diderot's Violinist Meets the Cabal at the Concert Spirituel', in: *Studies in Eighteenth-Century Culture*, XL (2011), pp. 103-132.

[9]. The birth date of 1721 given in the entry for Pagin in FÉTIS, François-Joseph. *Biographie universelle des musiciens et bibliographie générale de la musique*, second edition, 8 vols., Paris, Firmin Didot, 1860-1865, vol. VI, p. 419, is therefore incorrect. Equally incorrect is the forename 'André-Noël' given by Fétis and repeated in countless later writings. The full version of Pagin's name with all three forenames appears in a document of 13 April 1749 recording the wedding of his sister Isabelle Charlotte, for which he acted as a witness.

[10]. Paris, Archives Nationales, Registre de Clôture d'inventaires après décès fait au Châtelet de Paris, 1725-1736, AN Y5283 (not cited by Wilcox).

[11]. On Charles and his writings, see BARBIERI, Patrizio. 'Musical Instruments and Players in J.-A.-C. Charles's *Acoustique* (Paris, c. 1787-1802) and Other French Technical Sources', in: *Journal of the American Musical Instrument Society*, XXIII (1997), pp. 94-120.

Another point needing clarification is whether Pagin had already begun to appear in public as a violinist at the point when, probably not long after 1740, he went to Padua to become a pupil at Tartini's aptly described École des Nations, which had come into formal being in 1728. Wilcox mentions in passing[12], but does not discuss in detail, Pagin's service to the wayward Charles-Emmanuel de Crussol (1707-1762), who became 8th duc d'Uzès in 1739. Crussol, who was both a soldier — a serious injury at the Battle of Parma in 1734 left him with a permanent deformity that earned him the nickname 'Le Bossu' ('The Hunchback') — and a wit and littérateur who corresponded with Voltaire in later life, was also something of a libertine. Between c1739 and c1742 Crussol had a scandalous extra-marital liaison with Jeanne Tronchet *dite* de Mainville (1724-1791), a singer-actress at the Opéra-comique, as emerges from a copious police file on her compiled between 1749 and 1757[13]. Tronchet, whose amours were multiple (her lovers included Pagin's future employer, the comte de Clermont), and who ended her colourful career by marrying the violinist Joseph-Barnabé Saint-Sevin (known as L'abbé *le fils*) in 1762, masqueraded as the count's wife in an unsuccessful attempt by him to obtain a large loan. Threatened with public disgrace when this fact was uncovered, the duke, according to the police report, married her off to his *domestique* Pagin, the wedding (or apparent wedding) taking place in Avignon towards 1742. Pagin is not an uncommon surname in France, but there seems no doubt in the context of other information in the reports that this was 'our' Pagin. His description as a 'domestic' needs to be interpreted according to the usage of the time, in which the term denotes a rank within the household rather than a specific job within it. Seeing that at the time Pagin had not yet reached the age of twenty, this has the appearance of an 'entry-level' post that may well have required him to act full-time or part-time as a violinist — Crussol was, after all, an enthusiast for music and *fêtes* in general. As a musician of similar age to Tronchet, Pagin may have appeared the most suitable candidate to become (or pass as) her husband.

It has been mooted that Pagin was introduced to Freemasonry already while in the service of Crussol, who belonged to the Brotherhood[14]. No hard evidence has been adduced in support of the claim, but whether it is true or not, Pagin could scarcely have avoided Masonic contact at some point, seeing that the order was so fashionable at the higher levels of society precisely during this period — and especially when his next employer, the comte de Clermont, was Grand Master of the Grand Masonic Lodge of France[15].

---

[12]. WILCOX, Beverly. *Op. cit.* (see note 8), p. 130 (note 54).

[13]. The dossier was compiled by the newly formed Bureau de la Discipline des Mœurs, a kind of vice squad whose activity in reality focused less on the regulation or limitation of prostitution than on gathering intelligence on persons of interest who frequented prostitutes and *demi-mondaines*. The dossier on Tronchet (identified as 'Demoiselle Mainville dite Rozette') is preserved in Paris, Bibliothèque de l'Arsenal, Ms. 10238. Among the depositions is one made on 22 April 1751 jointly by Pagin and Tronchet, on the content of which precise information is lacking.

[14]. KERVELLA, André. *Réseaux maçonniques et mondains au siècle des Lumières*, Paris, Éditions Véga, 2008, p. 113.

[15]. That Pagin (appearing in apparently garbled guise as «André Pagni»), his colleague Michel Blavet, who was Clermont's *Surintendant de musique*, and Clermont's secretary Pierre Laujon all became Masons is

Determining the year when Pagin went to Italy is difficult on account of the contradictory nature of the evidence. Charles writes, in the anecdotal style of the day: «Sorti de France à l'âge de 20 ans […] il fut faire un tour en Italie pour entendre Tartini: il fut si effrayé du jeu de Tartini, qu'il se mit à son école»[16] («Leaving France at the age of twenty, he undertook a trip to Italy in order to hear Tartini: he was so stunned by Tartini's playing that he enrolled in his school»). The suggestion that it was not part of Pagin's original plan to remain in Padua lacks corroboration from other accounts but is at least plausible. That he was aged 20 at the time — which would make the year 1743 or even 1744 — could also be true: the amount of detail in Charles's account suggests that his information came directly from the musician. But in that case, the inference drawn by Barbieri from Charles's statement that Pagin was the recipient of a violin made by the ninety-year-old Girolamo II Amati (1649-1740) at Tartini's request for «un jeune homme qu'il avait adopté» («a young man whom he had adopted») cannot be correct, even if Charles's earlier remark that this violin was «celui que possédait le célèbre Pagin» («the one owned by the famous Pagin») may nevertheless hold water[17]. Moreover, it defies reason that Tartini would order such a fine, and one imagines expensive, instrument for an absolute novice, whereas it is just possible that the unnamed «young man» for some reason did not keep the instrument, which Pagin was then able to take back to Paris, perhaps even as a leaving present from the master.

As Wilcox was the first to point out, the year of Pagin's return home from Padua cannot be later than 1745, if we assume that he was in Paris to receive the homage of the dedication that Louis Hue, the engraver-cum-publisher of Tartini's Op. 4 and Op. 5 violin sonatas, both datable from catalogues to that year, inscribed to him[18]. True, the genuineness of these two collections has been called into question[19], but for no good reason, since only

---

asserted in BORD, Gustave. *La Franc-maçonnerie en France des origines à 1815*, Paris, Nouvelle Librarie Nationale, 1908 (Bibliothèque d'histoire nationale. Période révolutionnaire), vol. I [only one volume published], *Les ouvriers de l'idée révolutionnaire (1688-1771)*, p. 170 (but citing no primary sources). It is possible, however, that Pagin on occasion encouraged, or at least sanctioned, the Italianization of his surname to «Pagni», since this is the form in which it is found in a letter from François Fayolle to the editor of *The Harmonicon* (V [1827], p. 46) claiming that «all the pupils of Tartini, from Pagni down to La Houssaye» credited the discovery of the *terzo suono* to their master. An equation of «Pagni» with «Pagin» is in fact made explicit in SCHILLING, Gustav. *Encyclopädie der gesammten musikalischen Wissenschaften, oder Universal-Lexicon der Tonkunst*, second edition, edited by Gustav Schilling and Gottfried Wilhelm Fink, 7 vols., Stuttgart, Köhler, 1840-1842, vol. V, p. 351.

[16]. BARBIERI, Patrizio. *Op. cit.* (see note 11), p. 97.

[17]. *Ibidem.* Fétis (*Op. cit.* [see note 9], vol. VIII, p. 300) muddies the waters by claiming that Antonio Stradivari (c1644-1737) sold Pagin a violin he had made at the age of eighty-two (i.e., c1746, on the basis that the Belgian scholar wrongly believed Stradivari's date of birth to be 1664). This account is obviously untrue, but could conceivably be a heavily garbled version of the Amati story.

[18]. The two opus numbers in fact represent a single collection divided into two volumes, which explains why their dedications and title pages (except for the removal of the numeral 'I' before 'V' in the second volume) are identical.

[19]. In SCHWARZ, Boris. *Great Masters of the Violin: from Corelli and Vivaldi to Stern, Zukerman and Perlman*, New York, Simon & Schuster, 1983, p. 74.

one sonata in Op. 4 and two in Op. 5 lack authenticated concordances[20]. If the forgery was Hue's, Tartini's faithful acolyte Pagin would be the last person to choose as a dedicatee; if it was Pagin's, one has to explain how he remained a favourite of Tartini to the very last. It is much more likely that Pagin, in return for so many favours received from Tartini, acted by arrangement as an intermediary, passing on the manuscripts to the publisher and seeing the two collections through the press. The dedications could well have been a reward for this service — one with obvious publicity value for a young musician just about to embark on a public career.

Nothing specific is known of Pagin's activities in 1746, but by 1747 he had joined the musical establishment of Louis de Bourbon-Condé, comte de Clermont (1709-1771), third son of Louis III, duc de Bourbon, and Louise-Françoise de Bourbon, a natural daughter of Louis XIV. Clermont pursued an ecclesiastical career, quickly being entrusted with six abbeys. But he was also drawn to soldiering, participating in the Wars of the Polish Succession and the Austrian Succession and, after a longer interval, the Seven Years' War. In 1737, between the first two campaigns, he became abbot at Saint-Germain-des-Prés, giving up four of his existing abbotships for the privilege. Strongly inclined towards female opera singers, literature and the arts, Clermont established in 1747 a rural court at Berny, reminiscent of the earlier court at Sceaux of the duchesse du Maine, which became a centre for dramatic and musical entertainments. The flautist Michel Blavet led the musicians, and Pagin, as first violinist, was his deputy. In 1755 the theatre at Berny closed permanently, but before that event, in 1751, Clermont had been made governor of the province of Champagne et Brie, a post that enabled him to support his protégés in new ways[21].

Meanwhile, Pagin was establishing himself under Clermont's protection in Paris. On 16 March 1748 he applied for a *privilège général* for twelve years to publish «Sonates et autres pièces instrumentales», which was registered on 9 April 1748[22]. A set of six *Sonates à violon seul avec basse-continue [...] composées par M.ʳ Pagin, Pᵉʳ œuvre*, engraved privately by Louis Hue, soon duly appeared, being advertised in the *Mercure de France* for June 1748. The «autres pièces instrumentales» seem never to have materialized, however. Pagin apparently had no long-term ambitions as a composer: he marked his entry into the public sphere with a publication proving his competence as a composer and providing him with useful repertory material — and left it at that.

Pagin's choice of dedicatee is interesting. He was Louis Joseph d'Albert, comte de Luynes (1672-1758), from 1742 prince de Grimberghen. D'Albert was a soldier in Bavarian

20. As detailed in FELICI, Candida. 'La disseminazione della musica di Giuseppe Tartini in Francia', in: *De Musica Disserenda*, X/1 (2014), pp. 55-72: 69.

21. On Clermont, see CLERMONT, Louis de Bourbon de. *Le comte de Clermont, sa cour et ses maîtresses. Lettres familières, recherches et documents inédits*, edited by Jules Cousin, 2 vols., Paris, Académie des Bibliophiles, 1867.

22. BRENET, Michel. 'La Librairie musicale en France de 1653 à 1790, d'après les registres de privilèges', in: *Sammelbände der Internationalen Musik-Gesellschaft*, VIII (1906-1907), pp. 401-466: 444.

service who between 1742 and 1745 was Ambassador Extraordinary of the Wittelsbach emperor Charles VII to the allied French court. A literary figure of some note, D'Albert belonged to Clermont's circle, and may first have been encountered there by Pagin. Interestingly, the list of designated sellers engraved on the title page of the sonatas includes, besides the expected Boivin and Le Clerc, the name of the author himself, at the address of «Ruë de Grenelle chez M. le Prince de Grimberghen, fauxb.ᵍ S.ᵗ Germain». It may well have been by agreement with Clermont, resident at the Abbey of Saint-Germain-des-Prés (where Pagin was later accommodated), that the musician obtained this temporary lodging.

Meanwhile, Pagin had made his début at the Concert spirituel. On 8 December 1747 he appeared with one of his own solo sonatas, following this on 24 December with a concerto by Tartini, whose music was new to Parisian audiences. Between then and the fateful day of Easter Sunday, 29 March 1750, twenty-two further solo appearances followed, and it also appears from annotations on performing material from this time that Pagin often acted as leader of the orchestra[23]. His choice of repertory is rarely evident from the written record (consisting largely of *affiches* and reports in the *Mercure*): more often than not, we find only the laconic phrase «Pagin joue seul» («Pagin plays a solo»)[24]. However, we know for certain that he played a Tartini concerto again on 1 November 1748; Vivaldi's Concerto *La tempesta di mare* (RV 253, immediately following *Le quattro stagioni* in the Op. 8 collection), on 15 May 1749; an unspecified concerto by Locatelli (presumably taken from *L'arte del violino*, Op. 3) on 1 November 1749; and Vivaldi's 'Spring' Concerto, *La primavera* (RV 269), on 15 March 1750. By implication, Pagin played Tartini on most other occasions, as the content of his surviving capriccios and cadenzas seems to confirm. One has almost the impression that the insertion of concertos by Locatelli and Vivaldi into his programmes was a calculated novelty aimed at mollifying critics who reproached him for playing only concertos by his master[25].

On 29 March 1750 there occurred the famous, and in the annals of the Concert spirituel previously unparalleled, 'hissing' of Pagin. Even if one does not necessarily lend full credence to a statement by the first editor of Charles de Brosses's correspondence that the reaction of the indignant Pagin was break his bow[26], there is no doubt that the violinist was shaken and humiliated enough to retire for good from the public arena. Wilcox has examined in great depth the background to this sorry event and its aftermath[27]. Its causes

---

[23]. For example, in a *Laudate pueri Dominum* by Fiocco (F-Pn, VM1 - 1456) and a *Nisi Dominus* by Adolfati (F-Pn, VM1 - 1314).

[24]. The fullest record of Pagin's appearances is found in PIERRE, Constant. *Histoire du Concert spirituel 1725-1790*, Paris, Société française de musicologie, 1975 (Publications de la Société française de musicologie, 3ᵉ série, 3).

[25]. As will be shown, musical material once in Pagin's possession, including a specially written capriccio, suggests that he also played at least one concerto attributed to Pergolesi at the Concert spirituel.

[26]. BROSSES, Charles de. *Op. cit.* (see note 2), vol. 1, p. 205, n. 1.

[27]. WILCOX, Beverly. *Op. cit.* (see note 8), pp. 110-123.

seem to have been complex: one factor was undoubtedly a general anti-Italian current among part of the audience, aggravated by the fact that Pagin himself was French by birth and therefore could appear as an ominous portent of the future direction of French music. There may even have been some animus directed at Tartini on account of his disagreements with Rameau on the theoretical terrain. More than anything else, perhaps, Tartini's at the time novel musical language and the manner of playing that Pagin had imbibed from his master, which entailed, for instance, a freer approach to tempo than was normal for Italian music, may have disconcerted the audience. The consensus among French commentators in the succeeding decades was that Pagin's treatment was shameful and undeserved, and any further criticism of his playing was very muted in comparison with the plaudits that he continued to win.

Subsequent events showed the débâcle at the Concert spirituel to have been, in career terms at least, a blessing in disguise for Pagin. An immediate consequence was that Clermont, known for generosity towards his favourites, made him his *trésorier général* with an annual salary equivalent to £250, as reported by Burney[28]. This secure post, held until Clermont's death in 1771, became the foundation of his future wealth. Other lucrative positions followed. In 1757 Pagin purchased the office of alternate tax collector (*receveur alternatif des tailles*) for the district (élection) of Vézelay, to which a similar office pertaining to Coulommiers-en-Brie was later added. In 1783 he purchased from the French crown an even more prestigious office, becoming one of four *audienciers en la Chancellerie établie près la cour du Parlement de Paris*, a post he held until the Revolution. The professional musician had metamorphosized first into a gentleman and finally (via the last office) into a nobleman with a coat of arms. Such a transition, surprisingly common in the eighteenth century, was regarded at the time not at all as a dereliction of artistic duty, but rather as a desirable improvement in status as a result of personal merit and/or good fortune.

Pagin did not, of course, abandon music, although he now channelled his musical activities in two particular directions. First, there was teaching. His most notable pupil was Pierre-Nicolas La Houssaye (1735-1818), who studied first with him and then with Tartini in Padua, after a brief service with Clermont. Another was Étienne-Bernard-Joseph Barrière (1748-1816 or 1818), who in 1776 dedicated his Op. 1 (*Six Quatuors concertans*) to his master[29]. Second, there was participation in private music-making. Pagin's best-known appearances in this domain, dating from the 1770s, are those where

---

28. BURNEY, Charles. *The Present State of Music in France and Italy, or the Journal of a Tour through Those Countries Undertaken to Collect Materials for a General History of Music*, London, Becket, 1771, p. 43.

29. One wonders whether a certain «M. de L...», described as «un homme de condition, de Monteuil-sur-mer», who in 1760 dedicated to Pagin a set of six sonatas for two violins engraved by Hue, was an amateur pupil of his.

he accompanied the gifted harpsichordist and *salonnière* Anne-Louise Brillon de Jouy: the advent of the 'accompanied' sonata in the second half of the century was indeed heaven-sent for Pagin in his newly acquired status[30].

Around 1750 Pagin began to court the young Marie-Marguerite Camus, only surviving daughter of Charles-Étienne-Louis Camus (1669-1768), a celebrated architect, mathematician and member of the Académie Royale des Sciences (and of the Royal Society in London). Already informed of Pagin's alleged marriage to Jeanne Tronchet by an anonymous letter dated 22 April 1751, Charles Camus took fright and on 13 October 1752 entrusted his daughter to the protection of the convent of the Blue Nuns in Paris[31]. He later relented, and compensated for his previous disapproval not merely by allowing the marriage to take place on 27 August 1757 but also by treating his son-in-law with exceptional amity (duly reciprocated), inviting the couple to share his academician's apartment at the Louvre and making handsome presents to them[32]. In 1761 the Pagins had a first son, Gaspard, who died in 1769[33]. A second son, Jean, was born on 4 January 1762. He became a lawyer (*avocat*) and in time succeeded to the considerable pension (400 livres p.a.) accorded by the state to Camus's widow[34]. Marie-Marguerite died on 4 December 1767, and her grief-stricken father followed on 2 February 1768. The inheritance was considerable: Pagin was left a harpsichord, two violins, tableware worth 2,000 livres, miniature portraits of him and his wife and additional real estate. He never remarried: in 1776 the German historian and polymath Christoph Gottlieb von Murr succinctly observed: «Herr Pagin lebt jetzt für sich» («Monsieur Pagin now lives alone»)[35]. Not long after Camus's death Pagin moved into the fashionable rue Culture Sainte-Catherine, his last Parisian address.

During all this time, Pagin remained in friendly contact with his teacher. Murr was in fact the bearer of a letter of recommendation to Pagin written by Tartini in 1760 on behalf of his German pupil Johann Georg Holzbogen, who was visiting Paris. This letter,

---

[30]. Burney, Charles. *Op. cit.* (see note 28), pp. 42-43, reports on the playing of the Brillon-Pagin duo in July 1770. Pagin later also played chamber music with Benjamin Franklin, a member of Brillon's circle.

[31]. *The Diary of the 'Blue Nuns' or Order of the Immaculate Conception of Our Lady at Paris, 1658-1810*, edited by Joseph Gillow and Richard Trappes-Lomax, London, Catholic Record Society, 1910 (Publications of the Catholic Record Society, 8), p. 333. The so-called Blue Nuns were an English-speaking community. Marie-Marguerite's anonymity was safeguarded by giving her a private room and the cover-name of 'Mademoiselle Clément'. She returned to her father on 6 May 1756.

[32]. Wilcox, Beverly. *Op. cit.* (see note 8), p. 109, mentions 40,000 livres in cash, and a part-interest in two houses that were rented out.

[33]. Gaspard's year of birth, not given by Wilcox, is reported in Sturdy, David J. *Science and Social Status: The Members of the Académie des Sciences, 1666-1750*, Woodbridge, The Boydell Press, 1995, p. 384.

[34]. As published in *État nominatif des pensions sur le trésor royal: imprimé par ordre de l'Assemblée nationale*, 4 vols., Paris, Imprimerie Nationale, 1789-1791, vol. IV, p. 454.

[35]. Murr, Christoph Gottlieb von. 'Entwurf eines Verzeichnisses der besten jetztlebenden Tonkünstler in Europa', in: *Journal der Kunstgeschichte und zur allgemeinen Litteratur*, II (1776), pp. 3-28: 21.

rather than talking up Holzbogen's merits, is instead full of compliments to, and expressions of endearment towards, Pagin, describing him as «uno, anzi il principale di quelli che io ho avuto la sorte d'istruire nel Violino («one, indeed the most important, among those to whom fate has led me to teach the violin»)[36]. At some point no earlier than 1748 (the date of the first edition) Pagin had done Tartini, presumably by agreement, the favour of supervising a second edition of his Op. 7 Sonatas, in which the central movement of the third sonata was given new ornamentation and the fourth and sixth sonatas were replaced by different ones[37]. Count Benvenuto di San Raffaele, Director of Education at the court of Savoy in Turin and a former pupil of Tartini (who penned an astute and by no means wholly uncritical assessment of his teacher), confirms that Pietro Nardini (1722-1793) and Pagin were the master's two favourite students[38], while we learn from Charles's *Acoustique* that in his old age Tartini used to say: «allez entendre Pagin, vous m'entendrez encore» («go and hear Pagin, you will still hear me»)[39].

The Revolution deprived Pagin of his royal sources of income but left him otherwise unscathed. Nevertheless, on 21 March, towards the end of the Terror, he and his son opted for a quieter life and jointly purchased for 85,000 livres a farm at Coulommiers, his former centre of operations as a tax collector. He died there on 12 November 1799. In the year of his death (or, more exactly, the revolutionary 'an VIII' partly coinciding with it) the portraitist François Dumont (1751-1831) executed miniature portraits of both him and his son, having painted an unidentified «Mademoiselle Pagin» (who might be an unmarried sister or an unknown daughter or granddaughter) three years previously. Information in Dumont's fee book informs us that the portrait of Pierre was a copy of one already existing, something that one might already have suspected from the middle-aged rather than elderly appearance of the subject, who is depicted in the act of momentarily breaking off from performing on his rather oversized violin (unless this instrument is in fact a viola) in order to contemplate a statue of Apollo[40]. Perhaps the portrait was copied soon after Pagin's death as a keepsake for a family member, and the original was possibly the very one inherited from Camus.

---

36. *Ibidem*, p. 20.
37. It is significant that all the sonatas of the modified Op. 7 were in Pagin's own collection of Tartini sonatas, listed by incipit in D-B, Mus. ms. Kat 805,5 (to be discussed shortly), except the second (Brainard B7), which could, however, have been taken from the so-called 'Op. 1' brought out in 1732 by G. F. Witvogel in Amsterdam. Tartini's Op. 6 (*c*1748), similarly, may have been assembled by Pagin for publication in Paris, since five out of six of its sonatas were in his collection, and the exception (Brainard A19) is not known from other sources.
38. ROBBIO DI SAN RAFFAELE, Benvenuto. 'Lettere due sopra l'arte del suono', Vicenza, Veronese, 1778, as republished in: *Scelta di opuscoli interessanti*, III (1784), pp. 180-187: 185.
39. BARBIERI, Patrizio. *Op. cit.* (see note 11), p. 96.
40. Information on the portrait, together with a reproduction of it, can be found in the catalogue for Christie's Sale 6439, held in London on 22 May 2001. I have not been able to trace the portrait's purchaser.

Jean Pagin prospered. Later on, he moved to the village of Aulnoy outside Coulommiers, occupying the imposing residence known as the Château du Rû[41]. Five months after his death, in August 1844, his large collection of paintings, drawings, engravings and books of all descriptions, of which the published sale catalogue survives, was auctioned over four days[42]. The catalogue includes, however, no editions or manuscripts of music, and no portraits of Pagin family members. The reason for the absence of any music, which Jean, as the sole surviving son, presumably inherited from his father, must remain conjectural, but there is a good chance that it was sold separately to one or more persons either before or after his death. As for the missing portraits, they may well have remained for a longer time in the family.

Pagin's Collection of Music

A vital step forward in the identification of Pagin's musical collection has been taken in a very recent article by Ada Beate Gehann[43]. Its starting point was the unexpected presence in the Staatsbibliothek zu Berlin - PK of an unusually large collection of eighteenth-century manuscript sources of sonatas and concertos by Tartini together with a heterogeneous group of associated manuscript thematic catalogues. Via painstaking analysis of this dauntingly complex assortment of materials Gehann established some important facts about the provenance of the collection. Proceeding backwards in time, these are:

1. that the bulk of the collection was purchased for the library from the Berlin firm of Leo Liepmannssohn Antiquariat in 1921[44];

2. that a smaller number of items from it were purchased from the same dealer in the same year by the Library of Congress[45];

---

[41]. See *Dictionnaire topographique des environs de Paris jusqu'à 20 lieues à la ronde de cette capitale*, edited by Charles Oudiette, Paris, the Author, ²1817, p. 29. The text mentions Pagin by name as the current occupant of the Château du Rû, adding that he was at the time serving as mayor of the village.

[42]. *Cabinet et bibliothèque de feu Jean Pagin, tableaux, dessins, estampes, curiosités, dont la vente aura lieu le lundi 13 janvier et jours suivants*, Paris, Husson-Ducroquet-Techener-Defer, 1844. The catalogue is introduced, on pp. 1-2, by a short biographical note on Jean Pagin that emphasizes his debt, as a connoisseur of the fine arts, to his father, whom one suspects of being the previous owner of many items.

[43]. GEHANN, Ada Beate. 'A Collection of Concertos by Giuseppe Tartini in the Staatsbibliothek zu Berlin - Preussischer Kulturbesitz', in: *De Musica Disserenda*, X/1 (2014), pp. 91-116. I am immensely grateful to the author for letting me have sight of her article in advance of publication and for sharing various thoughts about the matters discussed in it.

[44]. *Ibidem*, p. 98.

[45]. *Ibidem*, pp. 105-106. The manuscript items comprise four concertos, respectively by (or at any rate attributed to) Pergolesi, La Houssaye (see earlier) and another Tartini pupil, Joseph Touchemoulin (two concertos). In all probability, the Library of Congress also acquired printed items from the collection on the same occasion.

3. that the full collection was sold by auction in Leuven (Louvain) in 1879, immediately after the death of its previous owner, the Belgian violinist and conductor Joseph Terby Jr (1808-1879), a native of the same city who had resided in Paris between c1825 and 1859 or 1860[46]. Most of its items are identifiable as lots in the published sale catalogue[47];

4. That Terby had acquired the basis of the Tartini collection, later augmented by copies made by himself or relatives — his father Joseph Sr (1780-1860) and brother François (1812-1884) were likewise musicians — and through a few extra acquisitions, by 1849 at the latest[48].

The sale catalogue contains (on page 13) an annotation regarding the Tartini works of great importance for two separate reasons. This note reads: «Tartini les légua à son élève favori Pagin et M. Terby eut la bonne fortune de les acquérir après le décès de l'un des descendants de ce dernier» («Tartini bequeathed them to his favourite pupil Pagin, and M. Terby had the good fortune to acquire them after the death of one of the latter's descendants»[49]). The statement that the Tartini collection was a bequest (a misleading form of description, as we will shortly see) must derive from a heading on the oldest of the thematic catalogues[50], thereby establishing that this catalogue and the others formed part of the collection as sold in 1879, even though they cannot be matched to any precise lot number[51]. Even more revealing is the statement that the Tartinian items were acquired from a descendant of Pagin, since Jean Pagin's death in 1844 and the fact the rest of his diverse collection was auctioned off soon afterwards make it entirely plausible that Terby purchased the music from his heirs by private arrangement. But whether or not this music passed directly from Pierre Pagin to Jean Pagin, and then equally directly to Joseph Terby, its ultimate source is not in doubt: the collection, with Tartini's works at its heart, initiated by the violinist in Padua and continued in Paris.

---

[46]. *Ibidem*, pp. 98-106, *passim*.

[47]. *Catalogue de la belle collection de violons italiens, archets de Tourte, musique de chambre et manuscrits précieux de grands maîtres anciens et modernes délaissée par feu M' Joseph Terby ancien violon-solo du Théâtre impérial Italien de Paris et maître de chapelle de l'église de St-Pierre à Louvain […]*, [Louvain], s.n., [1879].

[48]. GEHANN, Ada Beate. *Op. cit.* (see note 43), p. 99. Gehann mentions the contribution to the collection of François Terby but not the possible one of Joseph's homonymous and remarkably long-lived father in Leuven, who may have been responsible for the inscription «Lovani 1849» on copied parts for one concerto (D. 119) and other material.

[49]. As cited *ibidem*, p. 101.

[50]. D-B, Mus. ms. theor. Kat. 805,5. For convenience, I will refer to this source in later references as 'Kat. 805,5' and abbreviate similarly for the companion catalogues. All seven catalogues in Mus. ms. theor. Kat. 805 (*Thematische Verzeichnisse der Konzerte und Sonaten Giuseppe Tartinis*) are consultable online via the link <http://digital.staatsbibliothek-berlin.de/werkansicht/?PPN=PPN641727615>.

[51]. Perhaps the catalogues were listed under Lot 245, a «Paquet de hasard» («Parcel of oddments»).

Evidence from the Inventories

Two Berlin catalogues in particular are relevant to the present argument. The first, Kat. 4/5, which comprises a single folio with 48 sonatas listed with first-movement incipits on the first side (Kat. 5) and 63 concertos on the second (Kat. 4), is written on 'three crescent moons' paper from the Veneto. It is penned throughout in Pagin's own hand (this can easily be verified by comparison with his composition manuscripts, such as those transmitting his capriccios and cadenzas) and must therefore have been initiated in Padua or shortly after his return to Paris. The second catalogue, Kat. 1, written on paper of indeterminate provenance but probably French, lists by first-movement incipit 97 concertos, one of which is entered twice under the respective numbers 61 and 84. As Gehann rightly surmises, this duplication may have been no accident if the catalogue served as an inventory of music by Tartini present in the collection rather than as a mere list of compositions by him known to exist[52].

Where my analysis of these catalogues parts company with that of Gehann, however, is in its conclusion that (a) a single hand, operating over several decades, was responsible for the whole of both inventories (treating Kat. 4 and Kat. 5 as a single item, Kat. 4/5) and (b) that this hand was unquestionably Pagin's own[53]. In Kat. 4/5 three discrete chronological layers can be distinguished:

Layer	Concertos Numbered	Sonatas Numbered
1 (early)	1-21	1-37
2 (middle)	22-47	38-40
3 (late)	48-63	41-48

Note: Sonatas 41-48 abandon the progressive numbering and adopt instead (obviously to facilitate their location) the number occupied by the respective sonata in Tartini's manuscript collection of *Piccole sonate* (I-Pca, 1888): respectively, 9, 2, 8, 5, 10, 4, 1, 3. Additional sonatas for which no incipit is given are indicated by an annotation in the upper left-hand corner of the page: «Oltre — le 12. sonate stampate con la Pastorale.» («Plus — the 12 printed sonatas with the Pastorale» [i.e., the set published as Op. 1 in 1734 by Michel-Charles le Cène]).

The 'early' layer is the one coinciding chronologically with the centred heading on the page with sonatas (Kat. 5), which originally read «Del S.ᵍʳ Giuseppe tartini». At some undetermined point after the original heading was written, it was amended to read: «Inventaire General de touts mes Biens | herités Dal [altered from 'Del'] S.ᵍʳ Giuseppe

---

[52].   Gehann, Ada Beate. *Op. cit.* (see note 43), p. 92.

[53].   *Ibidem*, especially pp. 92-93. Gehann regards the scribe who created Kat. 4/5 as an Italian with imperfect French rather than as a Frenchman (i.e., Pagin) with good Italian — and keen to show off the fact — but sloppy handwriting: hence her transcription of «mes Biens» as «men Biem».

tartini» («General Inventory of all my Property inherited from Signor Giuseppe Tartini»). Since Layer 1 comprises sonatas and concertos taken home from Padua *c*1745, this is clearly not an 'inheritance' from Tartini following his death, although it could well have been a parting gift with a comparable significance.

Two notational features in particular mark out Layer 1: the use of an unusual form of treble clef in which the descender loops to the right instead of to the left. This is a specifically Italian form employed by Tartini[54], which Pagin is perhaps consciously imitating. The second feature is the placement of the separate flag for a quaver with a descending stem on the left, not the right, of the stem. This not Tartini's way, but it is found, for instance, in Le Cène's engraved editions, such as that of Locatelli's *L'arte del violino*, Op. 3.

In the 'middle' layer these two notational features assume a more conventional — one might say, more typically French — form. The treble clef has a straight descender with just a hint of a tight curl to the left at its tip, and the quaver flag moves to the right side of the descending stem. That the scribe is nevertheless the same is evident from scrutiny of the collection of capriccios and cadenzas (D-B, Mus. ms. autogr. Pagin, P. 1 M), where, on p. 23, staves 1-6 feature the 'ordinary' treble clef and the continuation on staves 7-10 the 'Tartinian' one; or, on p. 22, where a 'backward-facing' flag suddenly pops up from nowhere at the start of the fourth staff.

The 'late' layers of the two inventories employ the same notational forms as the respective 'middle' layers, but are distinguished by ink colour and tiny graphical variations arising from the use of a different nib. There is a clue to the approximate date of Layer 3 in an annotation scribbled by Pagin in the margin before Concerto 55 on the penultimate staff. This reads: «envoye a Lyon | pour Mr Guillon» («sent to Lyon for M. Guillon»). This Guillon (in full: Guillon de Loïse), who died in 1794, was a former officer in a regiment of German infantry in French service who turned to music both as a performer on the violin and bassoon and as a composer, his works ranging from a set of six duets for violin and viola published in 1776 to the music and words of an opera, *Lausus et Lydie*, performed in 1787 in Lyon, where he was active as a concert organizer. It would appear, therefore, that Layer 3 of the concertos dates from the last quarter of the century[55].

Kat. 1 occupies the first two pages of a bifolio. Its heading, «Concerti del S.gr tartini», matches the handwriting and orthographic style of that for Kat. 5 (before the additions were made) very closely. Its 97 concerto incipits are written throughout in Pagin's later, 'French-style' hand. Nos. 1-73 (where 1-63 correspond exactly to the numbering of Kat. 5, although the new incipits contain sometimes more, sometimes less, music than those of the earlier catalogue) constitute the initial layer, which must postdate the completion of

---

[54]. It can be seen, for example, in the facsimile (the opening of the concerto D. 117) facing the title page of Dounias's book.

[55]. The fact that Pagin was apparently willing to loan out musical material in his possession may partly account for the 'missing' concertos listed in the inventories but not preserved in the Berlin collection.

Kat. 4/5. A second layer, clearly distinguishable by the use of a finer nib, comprises nos. 74-94, and the last three Concertos, Nos. 95-97, for which the incipits are written in a distinct brown ink, constitute a final layer. This inventory must date from the period of Pagin's retirement from the concert stage, its final three entries perhaps made not long before his death[56].

It is interesting that there is a degree of parallelism between the date of composition of the Tartini concertos preserved in Berlin (insofar as Dounias was able to establish it by applying stylistic criteria) and their numbering. Significantly, the last concerto from Tartini's style period I (dated by Dounias 1721-1735) arrives in Kat. I at No. 30, while the first concerto from style period III (1750-1770) arrives at No. 74. Pagin clearly made some effort to keep his Tartini collection up to date, whether through contact with his teacher or by independent effort, long after he had retired from public view as a performer.

Cadenzas and Capriccios

Before we study the composite manuscript D-B, Mus. ms. autogr. Pagin, P. 1 M and more especially its three Vivaldi-related items, it will be useful to sketch the history and nature of instrumental cadenzas and capriccios.

In vocal music, decoration of the final cadence for the singer by means of a short, intercalated, improvised passage had become a common feature by the end of the seventeenth century. Such passages were typically unmeasured, variable in speed and (obviously) single-line, remaining firmly within the key of the cadence[57]. Shortly after 1710[58], a more elaborate, often precisely notated version of the same device began to gain

---

[56]. In this connection, it is interesting that Felici (Op. cit. [see note 20], p. 62, n. 40) mentions that during the French occupation of Padua (1797-1799) a collection of Tartini's works assembled by his former pupil and successor as primo violino at the Basilica del Santo, Giulio Meneghini (1741-1824), was dispatched to France. These manuscripts were sent partly to a certain «Cittadin Pagnini» and partly to the commissary Claude-Louis Berthollet, who had special responsibility for requisitioning objets d'art. Could «Pagnini» possibly be an elaboration of the «Pagni» identified earlier (see note 15) as an Italianized form of Pagin's surname? If so, the fact that manuscripts of the same nos. 95-97 (respectively, D. 36, 37 and 35) are held today by the Paris Conservatoire would lend support to a hypothesis that the three works came as a group into Pagin's possession via this route. It would also explain an anomaly noticed by Gehann (Op. cit. [see note 43], p. 104): that uniquely these three scores in the Berlin collection, all copied by the well-known Paduan scribe known as «Berkeley A», carry numbers matching those allotted to them in Kat. 805,1.

[57]. Sometimes, the dominant remained as a pedal-note during the cadenza, although in fully developed examples the bass was made to pause.

[58]. The advent of the unaccompanied instrumental cadenza is dated to «around 1710-1716» («ohngefähr zwischen 1710 und 1716») in Quantz, Johann Joachim. Versuch einer Anweisung die Flöte traversiere zu spielen, Berlin, Voss, 1752, p. 152.

currency in movements with a solo violin, whether concerto movements or arias[59]. Two complementary 'species' of instrumental cadenza evolved. The first was closely modelled on the vocal cadenza as described and strictly monophonic. The second was more extended, in regular (albeit sometimes shifting) metre and often multi-sectional; it employed regular, repetitive figurations (formed from broken chords, scales etc.) and admitted modulation as well as multiple stopping, echo effects, imitations and other devices from the violin virtuoso's toolbox[60]. Olivier Fourés, author of an important study of Vivaldi's violin concertos, aptly observes apropos of these cadenzas of the second type (which he classifies under the generic name 'fantaisies'): «L'essence de la fantaisie est celui de rendre compte d'une prise de risque extrême» («The essence of the fantasia is to give evidence of extreme risk-taking»)[61].

The first species, which I will call the 'simple cadenza', invariably begins on dominant harmony, in keeping with its historical origin. The second species, the 'patterned cadenza', more commonly begins on tonic harmony, although a few examples beginning on the dominant also exist[62]. The two species may be inserted either on their own or in tandem (always in the sequence: patterned cadenza → simple cadenza). Opening on the dominant implies insertion at the end of the final solo episode, while opening on the tonic implies that the cadenza (of the patterned type) follows on from what would otherwise have been a normal concluding orchestral ritornello, and is in turn succeeded by an abbreviated, often rather tokenistic, 'second' closing ritornello. Patterned cadenzas occur mostly in final movements but sometimes also in first movements. Simple cadenzas include in addition a few for central slow movements.

Vivaldi uses the undifferentiated term 'cadenza' for both improvisatory species. However, in the next generation (that of Locatelli and Tartini) 'cadenza' tends to be reserved for simple cadenzas, while 'capriccio' is preferred for patterned ones[63]. Finally, in

[59]. Full-scale, unaccompanied cadenzas for violin within operatic arias, which Vivaldi appears to have pioneered, do not seem, however, to have outlasted the decade.

[60]. In MARCELLO, Benedetto. *Il teatro alla moda*, Venice, Pinelli, [1720], p. 43, we read: «in fine [il maestro] farà *Cadenza lunghissima*, quale porterà seco già preparata, con *Arpeggi, soggetti a più chorde &c. &c. &c*» («at the end [the maestro] will make a very long cadenza, which he will bring along ready-prepared, with arpeggios, multiple-stopped themes etc. etc. etc.»). Marcello evidently recognized clearly the peculiar nature of the cadenza as (to use an oxymoronic description) a 'rehearsed improvisation'.

[61]. FOURÉS, Olivier. *L'Œuvre pour violon d'Antonio Vivaldi, ossia il violino in maschera*, 2 vols., Ph.D. Diss., Lyon, Université Lumière Lyon II, 2007, vol. I, pp. 416-427 (discussion) and vol. II, pp. 3-16 (transcriptions). See also GRATTONI, Maurizio. '«Qui si ferma à piacimento»: Struttura e funzione della cadenza nei concerti di Vivaldi', in: *Nuovi studi vivaldiani. Edizione e cronologia critica delle opere*, edited by Antonio Fanna and Giovanni Morelli, 2 vols., Florence, Olschki, 1988 (Quaderni vivaldiani, 4/1-2), vol. I, pp. 479-492.

[62]. In Vivaldi's concertos these occur only in the first movement of the concerto RV 208 and the last movement of RV 583.

[63]. See the extended discussion in WHITMORE, Philip. 'Towards an Understanding of the Capriccio', in: *Journal of the Royal Musical Association*, CXIII/1 (1988), pp. 47-56.

the second half of the eighteenth century, the adoption of the term 'capriccio' (in French, 'caprice') for an independent, étude-like unaccompanied piece (which will receive its classic definition in Paganini's Op. 1) inevitably leads to a cessation of this short-lived nomenclature and the restoration of undifferentiated 'cadenza' for all improvised (or improvised-sounding) insertions for unaccompanied soloist in concerto movements[64].

Terminology aside, Vivaldi's patterned cadenzas differ from the capriccios of Tartini and Locatelli in one important respect. They employ almost exclusively 'passe-partout' musical ideas unrelated to the thematic substance of the host movement[65]. In Locatelli's Op. 3 (1733), a change of approach is clearly underway, since the capriccio for the first movement of the ninth concerto and, in a less overt way, that for the third movement of the fifth concerto refer back to the main thematic material. Such back-reference becomes almost automatic in the capriccios of Tartini's concertos — with one important proviso. Tartini's particular brand of ritornello form favours the use of a 'lyrical' version of the opening phrase of the ritornello as a head-motive to introduce all the solo episodes in the appropriate key. This is the probable reason why his (and Pagin's) capriccios are usually launched with a paraphrase, rather than a straightforward requotation, of the ritornello opening or the related head-motive for the episodes, which between them have already been heard so many times. This three-way relationship is illustrated by Ex. 1, taken from the third movement of D. 21, which shows in turn (a) the opening of the first orchestral ritornello, (b) the opening of the first solo episode and (c) the start of Pagin's capriccio for this movement[66].

Ex. 1(a): Giuseppe Tartini, Violin Concerto D. 21, third movement, bars 1–5.

[64]. Louis-Gabriel Guillemain's *Caprices*, Op. 18, of 1762 are early examples of independent pieces with this name.

[65]. As a result of this lack of thematic connection, Vivaldi is able to use identical material in the fully notated cadenzas in RV 208 and RV 212a. His preference for 'neutral' thematic material was perhaps a calculated decision designed to facilitate recycling.

[66]. The transcriptions for (a) and (b) follow the text of the manuscript parts in D-B, Mus. ms. 21635/44 (ignoring the added horn parts); that for (c) is taken from Pagin's autograph manuscript in D-B, Mus. ms. autogr. Pagin, P. 1 M, p. 5 (see note 67).

181

Ex. 1(b): Giuseppe Tartini, Violin Concerto D. 21, third movement, bars 31-35.

Ex. 1(c): Giuseppe Tartini, Violin Concerto D. 21, third movement, bars 1-5 of Pagin's cadenza.

THE COLLECTION OF CAPRICCIOS AND CADENZAS BY PIERRE PAGIN IN BERLIN

D-B, Mus. ms. autogr. Pagin, P. 1 M is a collection of capriccios and cadenzas (plus miscellaneous sketches and jottings), preserved mostly on loose folios and visibly belonging to several different periods and contexts[67]. A similar capriccio written by Pagin for the B-flat Concerto by Tartini D. 119 is not included with the others, but has instead been united (or perhaps reunited) with the Berlin parts for the host work[68]. TABLE 1 summarizes the folder's contents. It is interesting that several of the works it contains (not, however, the Vivaldian items) are preserved in Berlin with added parts for horns, a probable pointer to performance with a large orchestra at the Concert spirituel[69].

[67]. Consultable at <http://digital.staatsbibliothek-berlin.de/werkansicht/?PPN=PPN756788838>.

[68]. D-B, Mus. ms. 21635/133, consultable at <http://digital.staatsbibliothek-berlin.de/werkansicht/?PPN=PPN756790727>.

[69]. Details regarding instrumentation are given in GEHANN, Ada Beate. Op. cit. (see note 43), pp. 108-112 and passim.

Table 1
The Contents of Staatsbibliothek zu Berlin – PK, Mus. ms. autogr. Pagin, P. 1 M

Page	Content	Annotations	Comments
1	Capriccio + cadenza for a movement in E major [= Tartini, D. 49/3]	Heading: «Capricio Del Concerto in elami Di pietro Pagin»	
2	Two brief sketches from unidentified Capriccios or other music		
3	Cadenzas for movements in A major and E major) [= Tartini, D. 98/1, 2]		
4	Untitled preliminary sketch for the second capriccio on p. 5		
5	(a) Capriccio for a movement in D major [= Tartini, D. 21/3] (b) Capriccio for a movement in A major [= Tartini, D. 98/3]	(a) «Capricio» (b) «Capricio»; cue at end for «Cadenza»	
6	Capriccio + cadenza for a movement in D major [= Tartini, D. 21/1]. Lower down: two brief sketches	«Cadenza del Concerto in elamire magiore»	
7	Preliminary sketch for a capriccio in C major	«pasqua»	A reference to Easter Sunday 1750, date of Pagin's last performance at the Concert spirituel?
8	Void of music	«Sonata a Violino Solo e Basso»	See entry for p. 11
9	(a) Capriccio for a movement in E major of which only the clef and key signature are entered, leaving the first four staves otherwise void of notation [probably Vivaldi, RV 269/1] (b) Capriccio for a movement ostensibly in E minor [= Vivaldi, RV 269/3]	(a) «Capricio» (b) «Capricio»; cue at end for «Cadenza»	See entry for p. 17
10	Void of music		
11	(a) First section of an unidentified binary-form movement in F major for violin and bass (by Pagin?) in two-stave score (b) Sketch of what appears to be the opening of a movement in E flat major	(a) No textual annotations (b) Marginal note: «8 aoust 1780»	(a) Apparently the start of the first movement of a projected violin sonata
12	Void of music		

13	Pen trials (?), followed by preliminary sketches for two cadenzas for a movement or movements in D major [probably, for both, Tartini, D. 28/1]	First cadenza headed «Cadenza p.ᵐᵃ»	
14	(a) Capriccio for a movement in D major [= Tartini, D. 28/3] (b) A three-bar sketch, possibly relating to the same movement	(a) «Capricio»; cue at end for «Cad.ᶻᵃ»	
15	Two cadenzas for a movement or movements in A major	Headed respectively «Cadenza» and «Cadenza prima»	
16	Void of music		
17	(a) Capriccio for a movement in E major [= Vivaldi, RV 269/1] (b) Preliminary sketch for a capriccio + cadenza (partially) ostensibly in E minor [= Vivaldi, RV 269/3]	(a) «Capricio»; cue at end for «Cadenza» (b) «Caprici[o]»	See entry for p. 9
18	Capriccio for a movement in F major [= Pergolesi (attr.), Violin Concerto in F major, 4ᵗʰ movement]	«Capricio»	See parts for this concerto (originating from Pagin's collection) in US-Wc, M 1012 P45P Case
19	(a) Cadenza for a sonata movement in E flat major, followed by the start of an alternative cadenza for the same movement (b) An unrelated sketch in A major	(a) «Cadenza per la sonata in elami»; preceding the alternative cadenza: «altra»	(a) Very possibly for the third movement of Tartini's Sonata Brainard Ex. 1
20	Void of music		
21	(a) Sketch for a capriccio (?) + cadenza in A major (b) Sketch for a cadenza in G major	(a) «Acordatura»; cue at end for «Cadenza» (b) «Cadenza»	(a) 'Accordatura' normally means 'tuning (system)'. Its significance here is elusive (b) Possibly for Tartini, D. 78/1: see entry for p. 22
22	Capriccio (+ cadenza) for a movement in G major [= Tartini, D. 78/3]	«Capricio»	
23	Capriccio for a movement in C major, followed by fragmentary sketches	«Capricio»	
24	Void of music		

Note: The collection consists of loose folios (pp. 1-2, 3-4 etc.) except for pp. 5-8, which are a bifolio. Annotations can be assumed to be headings unless otherwise indicated. Music can be assumed to be notated in the treble clef on a single staff unless otherwise indicated. A digit following a forward slash identifies the movement within a work.

The capriccios and cadenzas exist in a variety of states, ranging from rough sketches to more or less finalized, though never entirely neat, versions[70]. It must always be remembered that these pages were for Pagin's private use, not for wider circulation. They served their purpose adequately by reminding him of what he had already worked out by trial and error (and doubtless largely memorized) on his instrument, and none of them is free from compositional corrections or modifications made either in the course of their initial writing down or at any point subsequently. Their notation is often simplified and even incorrect by normal standards (as when note values or bar lengths are mathematically inexact or required accidentals are omitted). What is true of the capriccios is even truer of the cadenzas, many of which are incomplete, petering out after a few notes, or indecipherable in places. Here and there, Pagin has used void staves for sketches and jottings of various kinds, at least one of which (on p. 11) was made as late as 1780.

The fact that capriccios by Tartini and others following in his tradition quote or paraphrase primary thematic material from the work to which they belong has made it easy to identify for which concerto and movement most of the present group were designed[71]. In a few instances, the association is confirmed by indications within the corresponding scores once possessed by Pagin.

PAGIN'S CAPRICCIOS FOR *LA PRIMAVERA*

Before we examine the capriccios for *La primavera*, it will be useful to summarize the history of the reception of this concerto in France up to the point, on 15 May 1749, when Pagin stepped forward to play it[72]. The late arrival of the concerto genre in France meant that the country did not experience the publication in 1711 of Vivaldi's first concerto collection (*L'estro armonico*, Op. 3) as a seminal moment. For most French musicians and audiences, his fifth such collection (*Il cimento dell'armonia e dell'inventione*, Op. 8), published in 1725 by Le Cène in Amsterdam and in 1739 by Le Clerc in Paris, was the one via which they first made acquaintance with his concertos. Fortuitously, but also fortunately, this was the Vivaldian opus most heavily laden with programmatic and descriptive concertos, which struck a particular chord in France in view of the national aesthetic preference for the 'imitation of nature'. Of the four concertos belonging to the 'Four Seasons' cycle, *La*

[70]. In two instances (see pp. 4-5 and 9, 17), a capriccio is preserved in two versions: one a preliminary sketch and the other a more finished version.

[71]. All the identifications made in the table, except those of the sonata movement (p. 19) and — more speculatively — the concerto by an unknown composer performed on Easter Sunday in 1750 (p. 7), have already been proposed in GEHANN, Ada Beate. *Op. cit.* (see note 43), pp. 102 and 105.

[72]. On Vivaldi reception in France, see TALBOT, Michael. '«Le plus habile compositeur qui soit à Venise»: Vivaldi's Reputation in Eighteenth-Century France', in: *Mélanges en l'honneur de Frank Dobbins*, edited by Marie-Alexis Colin, Turnhout, Brepols, forthcoming.

primavera (Op. 8 No. 1) was by far the most popular and most frequently programmed. It was first performed at the Concert spirituel on 7 February 1728 and from that year until April 1749 became a 'warhorse' of the Piedmontese violinist Jean-Pierre Guignon, who on one famous occasion (25 November 1730) led an impromptu performance of it at court, given by noble amateurs at Louis XV's behest. Pierre Gaviniès also played it at least once (on 1 November 1741) at the Concert spirituel. After Pagin's final appearance in 1750 it was taken up by further leading violinists (Canavas, Ferrari, Vachon, Capron, Leduc), receiving its last-known performance there in 1763. Seen in this perspective, *La primavera* was an obvious choice for Pagin, especially if he was already under pressure to widen his repertory.

The Capriccio for the First Movement

No preliminary sketch is preserved for the capriccio notated on the first four staves of p. 17, although one may well have existed once. The tonic harmony implied by the upbeat to the first of its sixteen bars makes its logical point of insertion the end of the final bar of the movement, with the expectation that in order to round off the movement the appended cadenza (indicated but not notated) has to be followed by a restatement either of the complete final ritornello (bars 76-82) or of its second half.

Ex. 2 is a transcription of the capriccio. 'Reconstruction' would perhaps be a better term, since many details in the source, especially Pagin's intentions regarding accidentals, are unclear: the difference between an error or omission in the notation and a deliberate musical 'licence' (such as a transient change of metre) is often hard to determine with confidence, and, to complicate matters, the manuscript has undergone numerous small changes whose chronological sequence is uncertain. Fortunately, the online digitized reproduction of the source allows the reader to compare my version directly with the original and, where desired, adopt different solutions.

The iconic opening phrase of the movement, amplified through triple stopping, blazes forth at the start. This phrase is then freely developed in bars 2-4, with a bold modulation to the supertonic major (F sharp) that appears, from the untidy positioning of the extra sharps required, not to have formed part of the original plan. Bars 6-9 are sequential *Fortspinnung* taking the music to the 'tonicized' dominant of B major, in which key the initial phrase is briefly heard again (bar 10). A transition (bar 11) prefaces a reprise of the same phrase in its original key (bar 12), which is continued with new sequential material to the imperfect cadence and fermata for a cadenza in bar 16.

This brief passage exemplifies to perfection the characteristics of Pagin's violinistic style as described in contemporary testimony and illustrated by his six sonatas. Pyrotechnics, rapidity of execution and the abundant use of the ultra-high register were not the features that brought him fame. Rather, it was the beautiful sound he produced, the lightness of his bow and the neatness of his execution that stood out[73]. His expression in Adagio movements was particularly commended[74]. On the technical side, La Laurencie draws attention to his fondness for successions of trilled notes, pedals (including inverted pedals), wide leaps and multiple stopping (for the sake of chordal reinforcement or bass support rather than polyphony)[75].

Pagin's apparent intention to copy out again (or produce a new version of?) this capriccio at the top of p. 9 proceeded no further than the opening key signature. However, this key signature has a puzzling detail. After writing the fourth sharp (for the note D) Pagin smudged it out, leaving only three sharps. That this was his deliberate intention is clear from the key signature at the start of the third-movement capriccio (in E minor throughout), which has no natural cancelling the customary sharp for D. Why Pagin, as late as 1750, should have reverted to an obsolete three-sharp key signature for E major is mystifying.

Ex. 2: Pierre Pagin, Capriccio for the first movement of Vivaldi's *La primavera*, RV 269.

CAPRIC[C]IO

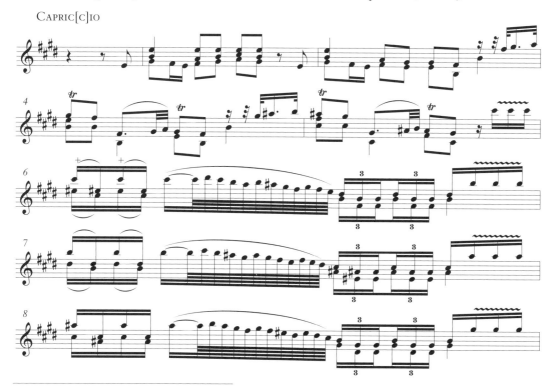

---

[73]. See FÉTIS, François-Joseph. *Op. cit.* (see note 9), and LA DIXMERIE, Nicolas Bricaire de. *Les deux âges du goût et du génie français sous Louis XIV et sous Louis XV*, Paris, Lacombe, 1769, pp. 498-499.

[74]. BURNEY, Charles. *Op. cit.* (see note 28) observes: «he [Pagin] has a great deal of expression and facility of executing difficulties».

[75]. LA LAURENCIE, Lionel de. *L'école française de violon de Lully à Viotti: études d'histoire et d'esthétique*, 3 vols., Paris, Delagrave, 1922-1924, vol. II, pp. 184-185.

The Capriccio for the Third Movement

The first draft for this capriccio of 45 bars in 6/8 metre (equivalent to 22 bars in the 12/8 metre of Vivaldi's movement), transcribed as Ex. 3a, is notated extremely untidily, with many omissions (of dots, accidentals, articulations etc.). Its likely point of insertion is half-way through bar 79. It effectively acts as a prolongation of the final episode, which begins in bar 72 and takes the form of a short, rhapsodic passage over a *tasto solo* dominant pedal in the parallel key, E minor, which eventually cadences into a reprise of the opening orchestral ritornello in the major mode.

Pagin starts by playing with a four-note snippet taken from the movement's opening, but half-way through bar 8 reintroduces in literal form the figure heard in bars 76 and (repeated) 77 in the concerto movement. This is immediately followed by a paraphrase employing double stopping that leads to a half-close. Then, half-way through bar 12, Pagin unexpectedly introduces a figure (based on the ascending form of the *passus duriusculus* connecting the dominant to the tonic via chromatic steps) inspired by the concerto's first movement, where (in bars 59-62) it represents the gradual reanimation of the birds after a thunderstorm[76]. Up to the half-close in bar 35 (marked by a fermata) Pagin develops several variants of this chromatic idea. He then rounds off the capriccio with a feast of trills and wide leaps (the latter calling for either prodigious extension of the hand or exceptionally

---

[76]. The relevant lines of the accompanying *Sonetto dimostrativo* read: «Indi tacendo questi [lampi e tuoni] gl'augelletti / Tornan di nuovo al lor canoro incanto» («Once they [thunder and lightning] have fallen silent, the little birds / Return anew to their melodious incantation»).

nimble string-crossing), ending with a flourish ascending to a dominant seventh. The opening of a cadenza is sketched. Surprisingly, this immediately wanders off towards tonal regions to the 'flat' side of C major, and one wonders by what devious route Pagin would eventually have regained E major.

Ex. 3a: Pierre Pagin, Capriccio for the third movement of Vivaldi's *La primavera*, RV 269 (first draft).

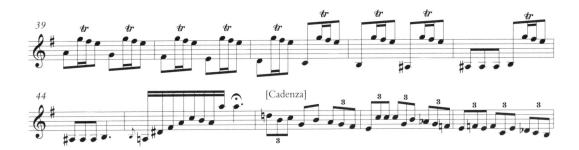

Ex. 3b: Pierre Pagin, Capriccio for the third movement of Vivaldi's *La primavera*, RV 269 (second draft).

Pagin's second version of the same capriccio 'tidies up' and slightly improves it, albeit more in visual appearance than genuine substance. With only 31 bars, it is more concentrated, but also blander. Its ingredients are sufficiently similar not to need separate comment here.

PAGIN'S CAPRICCIOS FOR *LA PRIMAVERA*: A MISMATCH?

In his *Trattato di musica* of 1754 Tartini observes: «Quell'uditorio, il quale molte volte niuno, o poco attenzione ha prestato alla composizione, l'ho veduto sempre attento all'armonia del tasto fermo» («An audience that has paid little or no attention to the composition is always attentive to harmony over a bass pedal, as I have witnessed many times»)[77]. This is not an ironic statement, but rather a special commendation of *tasto solo* textures. Always searching, via mathematics or aesthetics, for musical universals not specific to a single age, style, milieu or nation, Tartini harboured a particular fondness for ultra-simple accompaniments consonant with his idealized vision of the 'natural', whether these took the form of pedal basses, *bassetti* on violins or rudimentary self-accompaniment, as in his *Piccole sonate*. The unaccompanied capriccio or cadenza represents the *nec plus ultra* of the same orientation. Within Tartini's violin concertos, his own capriccios — and the ones written for them by his disciple Pagin — form a well-integrated element, both structurally and aesthetically, becoming, so to speak, the climax and apotheosis of the soloist's contribution. We may today share Benvenuto di San Raffaele's regret at what he termed Tartini's «parsimonia negli accompagnamenti» («parsimoniousness in accompaniments»)[78], but the validity of the capriccio's role within the general plan of the concerto is never in question.

---

77.   TARTINI, Giuseppe. *Trattato di musica secondo la vera scienza dell'armonia*, Padua, Manfrè, 1754, p. 148.
78.   ROBBIO DI SAN RAFFAELE, Benvenuto. *Op. cit.* (see note 38), p. 184.

In contrast, Vivaldi's capriccios (always called 'cadenzas', as we saw) have a much more specialized role and ambition. Their task is not to represent a cherished aesthetic in a particularly pure, pristine manner, but to astonish the listener and glorify the protagonist. Consequently, they find their place in the small minority of his violin concertos in which the technical challenge becomes the main *raison d'être*[79]. Not surprisingly, most of these concertos, numbering two dozen or slightly more, are in either D major or A major, the two keys that best suit the violin at its most exhibitionistic. Where a Vivaldi concerto is intended for more everyday purposes, such as the recreational music-making of music clubs, no capriccio is indicated; nor is there ever one in the many concertos whose prime concern is expression, as exemplified in the highest degree by his programmatic and descriptive works.

Viewed in this light, the addition by Pagin of capriccios to the outer movements of *La primavera*, however well this feature had earlier been received in his Parisian performances of Tartini concertos, was an ill-considered act completely at variance with the poetic nature of this concerto. (Perhaps he had been tempted into indiscretion by the success of a capriccio previously written for the finale of Vivaldi's *Tempesta di mare* concerto, where the incongruity would have been less apparent, given the highly conventional nature of the pictorialism in this movement.) By the time the French virtuoso presented the concerto at the Concert spirituel it had become Vivaldi's 'signature' work: a prime example of the kind of recent Italian music with which French audiences felt most comfortable, and for that reason alone a dangerous composition to tamper with. We do not know the full reason, or combination of reasons, why Pagin was hissed off the stage on 29 March 1750, but it is safe to surmise that his surviving capriccios for RV 269 are more likely to have harmed than to have enhanced his standing.

IN CONCLUSION

As yet, no comprehensive study exists of Tartini's pupils and of their collective and individual achievements as performers and composers. If and when one comes to be written, Pagin will achieve a prominent position as a vital link between the Tartinian and French violin schools and also as a propagator of his master's music and compositional approach. His role in the Parisian publication of Tartini's music certainly deserves re-examination. He will be equally central to a history of the cadenza in the violin concerto, if only because of the convenient preservation of so many of his capriccios and cadenzas

---

[79]. Olivier Fourés has coined the apt expression 'concerto di sfida' ('test-piece concerto') for this kind of work.

in a single location[80]. It may even be possible one day to extend the search for Pagin's musical library beyond the confines of the Staatsbibliothek zu Berlin and to attempt a reconstruction of his personal collection of published as well as manuscript music, tracing its passage during the 'lost' years between 1879 and 1921.

Pagin's significance for Vivaldian studies and performance is less certain. The uniqueness of his capriccios in the rich, complex history of the performance and reception of RV 269 ensures them at least a footnote in the historical record, but it is hard to see them taken up seriously by present-day performers unless in a spirit of sheer novelty for novelty's sake.

As a violinist, Pagin was clearly remarkable, even though he paid a heavy price for his unquestioning fidelity to his master's style. As a composer, in contrast, he was at best mediocre, and the total silence of contemporaries with regard to his achievement in this realm tells its own story. Perhaps we should admire him most for his activity behind the scenes: as Tartini's unofficial agent in Paris; as a gentle ambassador for Italian music within France; as a formative influence, through teaching and personal example, on the illustrious French violin school; and, not least, as a man who won the friendship of others easily, steered clear of *querelles* and ended his long life in security and provincial calm.

---

[80]. For the keyboard concerto, there is already Whitmore, Philip. *Unpremeditated Art: The Cadenza in the Classical Keyboard Concerto*, Oxford–New York, Clarendon Press–Oxford University Press, 1991 (Oxford monographs on music).

Italian Violin School in Mid-Eighteenth-Century France: From the Concert Spirituel to Literary Pamphlets

Candida Felici
(Milano)

L E Violon, cet instrument si beau & si nécessaire, est cultivé, Monsieur, par les personnes de la plus haute distinction, & l'on accorde beaucoup de gloire & d'estime aux Artistes qui y excellent. Les plaisirs que nous procurent les Arts aimables, ne sauroient être trop payés.

On a fait un si grand progrès dans l'Art de jouer du Violon, qu'on peut avancer, sans risquer de se méprendre, que les François à présent égalent les Italiens. Il ne reste donc plus à ceux-ci que l'avantage d'avoir brillé les premiers.

Les Sonates nous viennent d'Italie, ainsi que les Cantates, & il seroit ridicule de ne pas avouer que les Italiens sont nos maîtres en ce genre, sans parler de beaucoup d'autres connoissances dont nous leur sommes redevables[1].

With these words Pierre-Louis d'Aquin de Chateau-Lyon, son of the famous organist and composer Louis-Claude, introduces the sixth of his *Lettres sur les hommes célèbres*, which is devoted to the violin and other string and wind instruments; his statement not only shows how the presence of the violin was already strongly affirmed in France by the mid-eighteenth century, but also how equally strong was the opposition between Italian and French music. Already in the 1720s the viola da gamba was beginning to give way to the violin, especially in public concerts, where the penetrating sound of the latter was better perceived than the softer timbre of the viol.

---

[1]. Aquin de Chateau-Lyon, Pierre-Louis d'. *Lettres sur les hommes célèbres dans les sciences, la littérature & les beaux arts, sous le regne de Louis xv. Premiere partie*, Paris, Duchesne, 1752, second edition as *Siècle littéraire de Louis xv, ou lettres sur les hommes célèbres. Premiere partie*, Paris, Duchesne, 1754, *Lettre vi. Sur le violon, la basse de viole, & les autres instrumens*, p. 128.

In 1725, the first year of activity of the Concert spirituel[2], Anne Danican Philidor[3], who had conceived this concert series, contraposes two violinists, one French and the other Italian — Jean-Jacques-Baptiste Anet, *dit* Baptiste, and Pietro Ghignone[4] (*alias* Pierre Guignon) — even if the two were not truly representative of the French style on the one hand and of the Italian style on the other, given that Anet had studied in Rome with Corelli and Ghignone with the Turin violinist and composer Giovanni Battista Somis, also a pupil of Corelli. The contest was evidently intended to draw the public's attention to the newly founded institution.

Interestingly, Noël-Antoine Pluche, author of *Le spectacle de la nature*[5], in the seventh volume of his monumental work issued in 1746, contrasts the two violinists Guignon and Baptiste, just as Philidor had done in 1725: even though he denies any intention to repeat the usual comparison between Italian and French music, Pluche actually describes their repertoires and performance styles as paradigms of two opposing musical ideals:

> M. Guignon, persuadé que la musique est faite pour tirer l'homme de l'ennui, a choisi la méthode la plus propre à l'amuser & à le surprendre. Le jeu de cet habile artiste est d'une légèreté admirable; & il prétend que l'agilité de son archèt rend au Public un double service, qui est de tirer les Auditeurs de l'assoupissement par son feu, & de former, par le travail de l'exécution, des concertans qu'aucune difficulté n'arrête. […]
>
> M. Baptiste au contraire n'approuve point cette ambition de dévorer toute sorte de difficultés, ou s'il la croit utile à quelque chose, il est bien éloigné de la regarder comme la route de la perfection. C'est, selon lui, aller arracher péniblement quelques perles baroques au fond de la mer; pendant qu'on peut trouver des diamans à la surface des terres. […] Baptiste applique à sa musique ce qu'on a dit de la poésie; que c'est peu de chose de causer la surprise à quelques amateurs par une vivacité brillante, mais que le grand art étoit de plaire à la multitude par des émotions douces & variées. Il exige dans cette vûe que le son instrumental soit suivi, soutenu, moelleux, passionné & conforme aux accens de la voix humaine, dont il n'est que l'imitation & l'appui, comme la voix elle même est l'imitation de la pensée & du sentiment[6].

---

[2]. See PIERRE, Constant. *Histoire du Concert spirituel: 1725-1790*, Paris, Société française de musicologie, 1975 (Publications de la Société française de musicologie, 3ᵉ série, 3); see also FAVIER, Thierry. 'Nouvelles sociabilités, nouvelles pratiques: les concerts sous le règne de Louis xv', in: *Regards sur la musique au temps de Louis xv*, edited by Jean Duron, Wavre, Mardaga, 2007 (Regards sur la musique), pp. 107-140.

[3]. Anne Danican Philidor, 1681-1728.

[4]. See PELAGALLI, Rossella. 'Ghignone, Giovanni Pietro', in: *Dizionario Biografico degli Italiani*, <www.treccani.it/enciclopedia/giovanni-pietro-ghignone_(Dizionario-Biografico)/> (accessed 13 December 2014), and ZASLAW, Neal. 'Guignon, Jean-Pierre [Ghignone, Giovanni Pietro]', in: *Grove Music Online*, <www.oxfordmusiconline.com>, accessed 13 December 2014.

[5]. PLUCHE, Noël-Antoine. *Le spectacle de la nature, ou entretiens sur les particularités de l'histoire naturelle* […], 8 vols., Paris, veuve Estienne, 1732-1750, vol. VII: *Ce qui regarde l'Homme en Société*, 1746.

[6]. *Ibidem*, pp. 103-104. On the comparison between Italian and French music in *Le spectacle de la nature* see PALISCA, Claude V. '"Baroque" as a Music-Critical Term', in: *French Musical Thought 1600-1800*, edited by Georgia Cowart, Ann Arbor (MI), UMI Research press, 1989 (Studies in music, 105), pp. 7-21.

Pluche claims that he does not prefer one or the other, but it is evident that his favour goes to Anet's cantabile style and not to Guignon's virtuosity. On the contrary d'Aquin considers the latter a representative of both Italian and French styles:

> Mr. *Guignon* Piémontois, [...] après avoir passé quelque-tems à Paris, se perfectionna dans notre Musique. Il a encore aujourd'hui le double avantage de jouer également bien, la Musique Françoise & Italienne[7].

In the anonymous — but strongly resembling d'Aquin's previously mentioned 6th letter — *Mémoires pour servir à l'histoire de la musique vocale et instrumentale*, published in the *Mercure de France* of June 1738, the concern to place French violinists on the same level as their Italian contemporaries emerges once again:

> Comme on l'a déja dit, la France peut se mettre au moins au pair avec l'Italie pour le Violon; Mrs. *Guignon* et *le Clerc* sont très renommés; M. *Cupi*, frere de Mlle *Camargo*, célèbre Danseuse, vient de faire paroître un talent pour le Violon, capable de le faire placer au même niveau; et comme il est plus jeune, il peut faire encore de grands progrès et les égaler au moins. Les Connoisseurs assûrent, qu'il est très capable de réunir en lui le sentiment, le tendre et le doux de le Clerc, avec le feu, le brillant et le surprenant de Guignon[8].

The author of the *Mémoires* depicts the performance styles of three important violinists active in France; significantly, the Italian Guignon is included in the French school alongside Jean-Marie Leclair.

That Guignon came to be considered a French composer (and indeed in 1741 he became a naturalized French citizen) emerges even more convincingly from the fact that at the end of the century, when Jean-Baptiste Cartier wrote his fundamental *L'Art du violon*, he placed Guignon's works under the label of the French school[9] (see ILL. 1).

The first step for every musician wishing to achieve success in Paris was to perform at one or more of the concert series in the capital, above all at the Concert spirituel, the ideal place to display one's instrumental and compositional skills. At an early stage it took place in the Tuileries Palace on religious feast days, when the Opéra was closed, realizing 20 to 30 concerts per year. Because of the monopoly on public performance of music held by the Académie royale de musique[10], the Concert spirituel could not include vocal music

---

7.   AQUIN DE CHATEAU-LYON, Pierre-Louis d'. *Op. cit.* (see note 1), p. 134.

8.   *Mercure de France*, June 1738, pp. 1110-1118: 1116.

9.   CARTIER, Jean-Baptiste. *L'Art du violon, ou Collection choisie dans les sonates des écoles italienne, françoise et allemande, précédée d'un abrégé de principes pour cet intrument; dédié au Conservatoire de Musique*, Paris, Decombe, [1798].

10.   This monopoly obliged the organizers of the Concert spirituel to pay a high licence fee to the Académie.

ILL. 1: Jean-Baptiste Cartier, *L'Art du violon*, [1798], p. 34.

in French, so motets with Latin texts by French composers represented the most important part of these *soirées*; later in the century, however, things changed and also sacred and secular music with French and Italian texts was allowed. The concert programs in the mid-eighteenth century, often described in the *Mercure de France*, give us a clear idea of the role held by the violin: the concert began with a *symphonie* (whose author is rarely revealed), followed by a *motet à grand chœur* (usually by Lalande[11] or, later, by Mondonville[12]), a sonata

---

11. Michel-Richard de Lalande (or Delalande), 1657-1726.
12. Jean-Joseph Cassanéa de Mondonville, 1711-1772.

for a solo instrument (usually violin or flute, but also bassoon, oboe or other instruments) or for a duet, followed by a small motet for one or two voices, a concerto or sonata preferably for violin and lastly a *grand motet* for soloists, choir and orchestra.

Naturally the Concert spirituel is not the only concert series where the violin enjoyed great favour; many other concerts took place in the *hotels particuliers* of the Parisian nobility, particularly those of Madame de Pompadour, Le Riche de La Pouplinière or the count of Clermont, and in the second half of the century there were subscription concerts like the Concert des amateurs (1769-1780) — successively replaced by the Concert de la Loge Olympique (1786-1789) — not to mention the musical performances at court[13].

At the beginning of the century the Neapolitans Michele Mascitti and Giovanni Antonio Piani — known as Des Planes — introduced the Italian violin repertoire into France[14].

Many Italian musicians who won a reputation on the French musical scene came, for obvious geographic reasons, from the Piedmont; they were usually pupils of Giovanni Battista Somis (1686-1763), whose exhibition of 1733 at the Concert spirituel left a strong impression on the Parisian public. He taught many Italian and French violinists and composers, leaving a lasting mark on eighteenth-century instrumental music; we can name Giovanni Battista and Pietro Miroglio (who settled in Paris), Giuseppe Canavasso (*alias* Canavas, who settled in Paris with his brother Giovanni Battista, a cellist), Carlo Chiabrano (Somis's nephew, who after performing in Paris went to London[15]), the already mentioned Pietro Ghignone, Gaetano Pugnani, Felice Giardini, Jean-Marie Leclair, Louis-Gabriel Guillemain and many others.

To these we must add the violinists and composers who, like Somis, studied with Corelli and played a significant role in France, namely Geminiani and the Parisian Jean-Jacques-Baptiste Anet.

---

[13]. On the concerts in France during the eighteenth century see BRENET, Michel. *Les Concerts en France sous l'ancien régime*, Paris, Fischbacher, 1900; on the eighteenth-century French orchestra see SPITZER, John – ZASLAW, Neal. *The Birth of the Orchestra. History of an Institution, 1650-1815*, Oxford-New York, Oxford University Press, 2004, chapter 6, 'The Orchestra in France'.

[14]. We find Mascitti quoted for the first time in the *Mercure de France* of November 1704, p. 272, where the publication of his first set of sonatas for one or two violins is announced; during his long life Mascitti published nine sonata collections in France, the last in 1738; see LA LAURENCIE, Lionel de. *L'école française de violon de Lully à Viotti: études d'histoire et d'esthétique*, 3 vols., Paris, Delagrave, 1922-1924, vol. I, pp. 132-143, and TALBOT, Michael. 'Mascitti, Michele [Michel, Miquel]', in: *Grove Music Online, op. cit.* (see note 4), accessed 13 December 2014. Piani, or Des Planes, published his first set of sonatas in 1712; see ZASLAW, Neal. 'Piani [Piana, Piano], Giovanni Antonio [Desplanes, Jean-Antoine]', in: *ibidem*, accessed 13 December 2014. Corelli's sonatas for violin were first published in France in 1708.

[15]. We know that, after enjoying great success at the Concert spirituel in 1751, Chiabrano performed several times in London from January 1752 until April 1754, then there is no evidence of other exhibitions by him in England; see MCVEIGH, Simon. *Calendar of London Concerts 1750-1800*, London, Goldsmiths College, University of London, <http://research.gold.ac.uk/10342/>, accessed 13 December 2014.

Another Italian school of great importance for French musical development is that of Giuseppe Tartini in Padua, the so-called 'Scuola delle nazioni'. He never performed in France and, except for a three-year sojourn in Prague, he never moved from Italy but had several pupils from all over Europe: some of them were active in France, like the Italian Lorenzo Carminati (who settled in Lyon and played at the Concert spirituel in April 1753[16]), Domenico Ferrari and the French Pierre (or Jean-Pierre) Pagin[17], Petit[18], de Tremais[19], Pierre-Nicolas La Houssaye[20], Joseph Touchemoulin and Maddalena Lombardini Sirmen (who performed several times at the Concert spirituel in 1768, 1769 and 1785[21]).

[16]. On 8, 13, 17, 19, 23 and 24 April 1753; see *Mercure de France*, June 1753, pp. 163-171, where on p. 164 we read: «M. Carminati, Venitien, établi à Lyon, joua un Concerto de violon, & a joué plusieurs fois depuis. Les Connoisseurs l'ont fort goûté, & le Public a trouvé son jeu fort précis & fort sage». In the same days as Carminati's exhibitions, Pergolesi's *Stabat Mater* was performed for the first time at the Concert spirituel; afterwards it became an established institution of the Concert spirituel receiving 82 performances until 1790.

[17]. The first name André-Noël attributed to Pagin in the *New Grove* — FAY, Laurel – BARBIERI, Patrizio. 'Pagin, André-Noël', in: *Grove Music Online, op. cit.* (see note 4), accessed 13 December 2014 —, in *MGG* — WIRSTA, Aristide. 'Pagin, André-Noël', in: *Die Musik in Geschichte und Gegenwart. Allgemeine Enzyklopädie der Musik, begründet von Friedrich Blume. Zweite, neubearbeitete Ausgabe*, edited by Ludwig Finscher, 29 vols., Kassel [...], Bärenreiter; Stuttgart-Weimar, Metzler, 1994-2008, *Personenteil*, vol. XII (2004), cols. 1555-1556 — and in the present writer's article 'La disseminazione della musica di Giuseppe Tartini in Francia: le edizioni settecentesche di sonate per violino e basso', in: *De musica disserenda*, X/1 (2014), pp. 57-75, seems to be incorrect on the basis of the following facts: a letter by Tartini to a certain Pietro (whose autograph was sold by Sotheby's in London in 2010) was copied by Christoph Gottlieb von Murr in *Journal zur Kunstgeschichte und zur allgemeinen Litteratur*, part II (1776), p. 20; here Murr writes that, having met Tartini together with Johann Georg Holzbogen in Padua, where the latter received violin lessons from the *Maestro delle Nazioni*, Tartini, knowing that afterwards they intended to go to Paris, had given them a letter addressed to Pagin. Further evidence that Pagin's first name was Pierre also comes from a manuscript now kept in the Staatsbibliothek zu Berlin, which contains a sketch titled *Capricio Del Concerto in elami Di pietro Pagin* and is possibly an autograph (D-B, Mus. ms.autogr. Pagin, P. 1 M). Lastly, in 1844 after the death of Jean Pagin, Pierre's son, his library was sold and in the published catalogue we read: «M. Jean Pagin, né à Paris, au palais du Louvre, le 4 janvier 1762, est mort en août 1844. Il était fils de Jean-Pierre Pagin, artiste très distingué de son temps, conseiller du roi, trésorier de S. A. S. Monseigneur le comte de Clermont, et petit-fils de M. Camus, célèbre mathématicien et membre de l'Académie des sciences»; *Cabinet et bibliothèque du feu Jean Pagin* [...], Paris, Mᶜ Husson, Mᶜ Ducroquet, Techener, Defer, 1844, p. 1. On the subject see PINCHERLE, Marc. *Tartiniana*, Padova, CEDAM, 1972 (I quaderni dell'Accademia tartiniana, 1), p. 9; see also WILCOX, Beverly. 'The Hissing of Jean-Pierre Pagin: Diderot's Violinist Meets the Cabal at the Concert Spirituel', in: *Studies in Eighteenth-Century Culture, Volume 40*, edited by Downing A. Thomas and Lisa Forman Cody, Baltimore-London, The Johns Hopkins University Press, 2011 (Studies in eighteenth-century culture, 40), pp. 103-132, GEHANN, Ada Beate. 'A Collection of Concertos by Giuseppe Tartini in the Staatsbibliothek zu Berlin - Preussischer Kulturbesitz', in: *De musica disserenda*, X/1 (2014), pp. 95-119, and Michael Talbot's article in the present volume.

[18]. First name unknown.

[19]. First name unknown.

[20]. See COOPER, Jeffrey. 'La Houssaye [Housset], Pierre(-Nicolas)', in: *Grove Music Online, op. cit.* (see note 4), accessed 13 December 2014.

[21]. *Mercure de France*, September 1768, pp. 117-118; April 1769, pp. 143-144; May 1785, pp. 76-77.

Over and above any ideological contrasts, Italian composers and violinists (first of all Corelli, successively Somis, Tartini, Locatelli, Pugnani and lastly Viotti) acted as fundamental stylistic references in France in the two intermingled aspects of compositional procedures and performance practices. This stylistic primacy, already evident in Pierre-Louis d'Aquin's words, does not exclude an opposite influence of French musical language on Italian composers, above all those who lived in France for long periods or for the rest of their lives.

The descriptions in the *Mercure de France* and in contemporary writings inform us of the performance characteristics particularly appreciated in Parisian concerts and highlight specific aspects of French and Italian music.

The *Mercure de France* describes with emphasis the performance style of a violinist who appeared fleetingly at the Concert spirituel in 1751 and was enormously appreciated, Carlo Chiabrano[22]:

> Les applaudissemens que M. Chiabran, neveu du fameux M. Somis, & Ordinaire de la musique du Roi de Sardaigne, a reçûs la premiere & la seconde fois qu'il a parû, ont été poussés dans la suite jusqu'à une espece d'enthousiasme. L'exécution la plus aisée & la plus brillante, une légereté, une justesse, une précision étonnante, un jeu neuf & unique, plein de traits vifs et saillans, caractérisent ce talent, aussi grand que singulier. L'agrément de la Musique qu'il joue & dont il est l'Auteur, ajoûte aux charmes de son exécution[23].

In general, the performance of Italian violinists was characterized by the brilliance and rapidity of passages in the allegros, the expressiveness in the adagios, the rich ornamentation, the agility in the use of the bow, the melodic skips of more than two octaves and the improvisation of cadenzas; to these we must add new techniques, like double stopping or the use of natural harmonics (see ILLS. 2 and 3). D'Aquin, in the *Lettres sur les hommes célèbres*, informs us that Leclair was one of the first French composers to adopt double stops, inspired by his Italian contemporaries. The use of this device is also described in a passage of Diderot's *Neveu de Rameau*[24], where he (*Lui* in the dialogue) mimics the performance of an Italian violinist playing an *Allegro* by Locatelli:

> En même temps, il se met dans l'attitude d'un joueur de violon; il fredonne de la voix un allegro de Locatelli, son bras droit imite le mouvement de l'archet; sa main gauche et ses doigts semblent se promener sur la longueur

[22]. See SALVETTI, Guido – McVEIGH, Simon. 'Chiabrano [Cianbran, Ciabrano], Carlo (Giuseppe Valentino) [Chabran, Charles]', in: *Grove Music Online*, *op. cit.* (see note 4), accessed 13 December 2014. See also McVEIGH, Simon. *Calendar of London Concerts 1750-1800*, *op. cit.* (see note 15).

[23]. *Mercure de France*, May 1751, pp. 187-188; see also *Mercure de France*, June 1751, pp. 163-166.

[24]. DIDEROT, Denis. *Le neveu de Rameau*, edited by Jean Fabre, Geneva, Droz and Lille, 1950 (Textes littéraires français).

du manche [...]. Comme vous avez vu quelquefois au concert spirituel, Ferrari ou Chiabran, ou quelque autre virtuose, dans les mêmes convulsions, m'offrant l'image du même supplice, et me causant à peu près la même peine [...]. Au milieu de ses agitations et de ses cris, s'il se présentait une tenue, un de ces endroits harmonieux où l'archet se meut lentement sur plusieurs cordes à la fois, son visage prenait l'air de l'extase; sa voix s'adoucissait, il s'écoutait avec ravissement[25].

Diderot mentions, along with Locatelli, two musicians who enjoyed an enormous success at the Concert spirituel, Carlo Chiabrano and Domenico Ferrari. The latter performed during Easter 1754, alternating in the same days with Gaetano Pugnani; he played concertos and sonatas of his own composition finishing on the Sunday after Easter with Vivaldi's *La primavera*. This is the comment published in the *Mercure de France* concerning his first exhibition on 31 March: «Ce virtuose Italien a des graces, un fini, un savoir, une sagesse, un goût au dessus de tous les éloges, son jeu est la perfection même»[26].

ILL. 2: Felice Giardini, *Sei sonate a violino e basso*, [1751], Sonata No. 6, last movement, *Giga*, extract.

[25]. *Ibidem*, pp. 26-27. On the subject see HEARTZ, Daniel. 'Locatelli and the Pantomime of the Violinist in *Le neveu de Rameau*', in: *Diderot Studies XXVII*, edited by Diana Guiragossian Carr, Geneva, Droz, 1998, pp. 115-127. Diderot was possibly referring to Locatelli's Sonata Op. 6 No. 4, issued in Amsterdam in 1737 and printed again in Paris in 1740 (*XII Sonate a violino solo e basso da camera* [...] *opera sesta*, Paris, Le Clerc, [1740]); the second movement, *Allegro*, has an ABA form, where B is characterized by a series of chords played *piano* in static harmonies.

[26]. *Mercure de France*, May 1754, pp. 182-187.

ILL. 3: Domenico Ferrari, *Sei sonate a violino solo e basso* […] *Opera 1.ª*, c1758, Sonata No. 5, last movement, *Minuetto*, extract.

The dissemination of the Italian repertoire in France occurred not only through the performance of Italian and French virtuosos; musicians like Locatelli and Tartini had a great influence on instrumental music of the period even if they never performed in France. The flourishing Parisian publishing industry also contributed to the spreading of the Italian style through the printing of several sets of sonatas and concertos by Italian masters. French publishers sold music scores coming from Amsterdam or London, or printed editions already issued in these cities; but from the mid-eighteenth century they published more and more compositions that had been appreciated by the Parisian audience at the Concert spirituel and at the other concert series held in the French capital.

The printing of a set of sonatas could be either the cause or the effect of an exhibition at the Concert spirituel; on the one hand a new music edition could inspire the concert organizers to invite a virtuoso, on the other the success obtained in one or more public exhibitions could encourage the musician to print his own music in order to advance his career.

There are many cases of temporal proximity between the issuing of music editions and the playing of the same pieces at the Concert spirituel. Here I will give just some examples from the mid-eighteenth century:

• Jean-Baptiste Cupis publishes his *Sonates a violon seul avec la basse continue* Op. 1 in 1738, the same year as his first exhibition at the Concert spirituel[27];

• Pierre Pagin publishes his *Sonates a violon seul et basse-continue* Op. 1 in 1748 and he plays at the Concert spirituel in the years 1747-1750[28];

• Felice Giardini publishes his Op. 1, *Sei sonate a violino e basso*, in 1751; the previous year he had played at the Concert spirituel[29];

• Carlo Chiabrano publishes his *Six sonates à violon seul et basse continue*[30] Op. 1 in 1751 (two of which will be included in *L'Art du violon* by Cartier in order to demonstrate the use of natural harmonics and of the hunting style, see ILL. 4); his first exhibition at the Concert spirituel takes place in the same year.

Certainly, there are also instances in which sonata and concerto collections were issued only some years after the first public performance of a virtuoso-composer, as in the case of Gaetano Pugnani and Domenico Ferrari, whose exhibitions at the Concert spirituel had taken place in 1754, as we have seen, but their Sonatas Op. 1 were issued in 1761[31] and in 1758[32] respectively.

As with Chiabrano, a sonata from Ferrari's Op. 1 — the first movement of No. 6 — will be included in Cartier's *L'art du violon* at the end of the century.

Also the publishing of Tartini sets of violin sonatas, issued in Paris between 1744 and 1757, but especially in the years 1747 to 1750[33], seems partly due to the favour that his music enjoyed at the Concert spirituel. The *Affiches de Paris* report that on 24 December 1741

---

[27]. CUPIS, Jean-Baptiste. *Sonates a violon seul avec la basse continue* [...] *1.*^{re} *œuvre*, Paris, l'Auteur-veuve Boivin-Le Clerc, 1738. On Cupis's exhibitions at the Concert spirituel see SADIE, Julie Anne. 'Cupis [De Cupis, Cuppis, Cuppi, Capi, Cappi] de Camargo', in: *Grove Music Online, op. cit.* (see note 4), accessed 13 December 2014.

[28]. PAGIN, Pierre. *Sonates a violon seul et basse-continue dediées a Monseigneur le Prince de Grimberghen. P.*^{er} *œuvre*, Paris, Chez l'auteur-Mme Boivin-Le Clerc, [1748].

[29]. GIARDINI, Felice. *Sei sonate a violino e basso* [...] *opera 1.*^a, London, the Author, 1751, 2nd edition Paris, Moria, s.d.; *Sei duetti a due violini* [...] *opera seconda*, London, the Author, 1751, 2nd edition Paris, Vandôme, 1756. *Mercure de France*, April 1750, p. 185: Easter Tuesday, 24 March, «M. *Felice del Giardino*, a joué seul sur le violon un Concerto de sa composition, fort applaudi»; Thursday, 26 March «*Il Signor Felice del Giardino* a joué avec M. *Venier* des Duo de sa composition, qui ont fort réussi, tant pour leur propre beauté, que par la perfection de l'exécution».

[30]. CHIABRANO, Carlo. *Six sonates à violon seul et basse continüe* [...] *1*^{er} *œuvre*, Paris, l'Auteur, [1751].

[31]. PUGNANI, Gaetano. *Sei trio a due violini, e basso* [...] *opera prima*, Paris, La Chevardière, [1761]. On Pugnani's exhibitions at the Concert spirituel see the *Mercure de France*, Mars 1754, p. 193: «M. Pugnani, Ordinaire de la Musique du Roi de Sardaigne, joua un concerto de violon de sa composition. Les Connoisseurs qui étoient au Concert prétendent qu'ils n'ont point entendu de violon supérieur à ce *virtuose*».

[32]. FERRARI, Domenico. *Sei sonate a violino solo e basso* [...] *gravée par M.elle Vendôme. Opera 1.*^a, Paris, aux adresses ordinaires, *c*1758.

[33]. On the subject see FELICI, Candida. *Op. cit.* (see note 17).

Ill. 4: Carlo Chiabrano, Sonata Op. 1 No. 5, in: Jean-Baptiste Cartier, *L'Art du violon*, [1798], p. 94.

Petit played a violin sonata by Tartini[34]; the *Mercure* tells us that Pagin played a concerto by Tartini in December 1747 and again in November 1748, on the feast of All Saints[35]; even Gaviniès[36], not a pupil of the Italian master, played a sonata by him in February 1751[37].

---

34. Petit played again a sonata by Tartini at the Concert spirituel in 1747; see *Mercure de France*, November 1747, p. 123.
35. *Mercure de France*, December 1747, p. 123; November 1748, p. 168.
36. Pierre Gaviniès, 1728–1800.
37. *Mercure de France*, March 1751, p. 171.

Tartini was particularly appreciated in France for his cantabile style and for the expressiveness in the adagios; the Parisian audiences, but also the *philosophes* — often unfavourable to instrumental music —, liked the presence of literary references in some of his pieces. In their opinion such literary quotations could free sonatas and concertos from the lack of meaning that Fontenelle had well expressed with the famous words «sonate que me veux-tu?». This is at least what d'Alembert says in his booklet *De la liberté de la musique*, published in 1759 as an echo of the *querelle des bouffons*, which had held the attention of the French public from 1752:

> Les auteurs qui composent de la musique instrumentale ne feront qu'un vain bruit, tant qu'ils n'auront pas dans la tête, à l'exemple, dit-on, du célèbre Tartini, une action ou une expression à peindre. Quelques sonates, mais en assez petit nombre, ont cet avantage si désirable, et si nécessaire pour les rendre agréables aux gens de goût. Nous en citerons une qui a pour titre *Didone abbandonata*. C'est un très-beau monologue; on y voit se succéder rapidement et d'une manière très-marquée, *la douleur, l'espérance, le désespoir*, avec des degrés et suivant des nuances différentes; et on pourrait de cette sonate faire aisément une scène très-animée et très-pathétique[38].

According to D'Alembert the possibility to transform Tartini's famous sonata known as *Didone abbandonata*[39] into a theatrical scene is what makes it a piece of real music, not only useless noise.

As we have seen from the quoted comments, the admiration for Italian music and performers went hand in hand with the nationalistic protectionism towards French music. So, while Tartini was greatly appreciated, the fact that his pupil Pierre Pagin, a Frenchman, refused to play any other music than Italian was nevertheless seen as extremely dangerous. At least this could be an explanation for the fact that, after playing there for three years from 1747 to 1750, Pagin was hissed during the Concert spirituel and successively refused to perform in public venues[40].

Echoes of this episode appear in the exchange of writings following the issuing of Friedrich Melchior Grimm's pamphlet against the tragédie lyrique *Omphale* by Destouches

---

[38]. ALEMBERT, Jean Le Rond d'. *Mélanges de littérature, d'histoire, et de philosophie*, 5 vols., Amsterdam, Zacharie Chatelain, 1759, vol. IV; Rpt. in *La Querelle des Bouffons: texte des pamphlets*, edited by Denise Launay, 3 vols., Geneva, Minkoff, 1973, vol. III, pp. 2199-2284.

[39]. The sonata known as *Didone abbandonata* is Op. 1 No. 10, B g10 in the Brainard Catalogue; BRAINARD, Paul. *Le sonate per violino di Giuseppe Tartini: catalogo tematico*, traduzione italiana di Claudio Scimone, Milan, Carisch, 1975 (Studi e ricerche dell'Accademia Tartiniana di Padova; Le opere di Giuseppe Tartini, III/2).

[40]. On the subject see FELICI, Candida. *Op. cit.* (see note 17), WILCOX, Beverly. *Op. cit.* (see note 17) and also TALBOT, Michael. 'Pierre Pagin's Capriccios for Antonio Vivaldi's Violin Concerto *La primavera*, RV 269', in the present volume.

and in general against French musical theatre[41]. This happened during the winter and spring of 1752, just a few months before the arisal of the *querelle des bouffons*, when Pergolesi's *Serva padrona* was performed at the *Opéra*. The anonymous author of the *Remarques au sujet de la Lettre de M. Grimm sur Omphale* described the hissing of Pagin at the Concert spirituel, accusing Grimm of having avoided standing up for him:

> J'aurois eu du plaisir à lire dans votre Lettre jusqu'à quel point la nation ingrate envers un talent si sublime, a osé l'humilier publiquement. C'est-là qu'il falloit prendre le ton de vos Philosophes, & dire que l'amour de son talent lui a fait passer les Alpes, pour chercher un maître digne de lui. C'est la Musique de ce Maître qui inspire de nobles sensations. Original en tout, il n'a reçu de loix que celles de son génie. La sublimité de ses Ouvrages le fait estimer de tout homme capable de sentir la vérité. Il a su bannir le fard de la Musique pour servir la nature. Il est connu dans toute Europe, mais chéri de peu de gens, comme aussi peu de gens ont le bonheur de distinguer le bruit, d'avec le sentiment et l'expression. Tel est le maître que M. Pagin a fidèllement suivi dans ses études[42].

While in polemics with Grimm, the unknown author gives us a list of the reasons for which the *philosophes* appreciated Tartini's style: his quest for nature, truth, feeling, expression. Grimm answered the *Remarques* in his *Lettre de M. Grimm à l'Abbé Raynal sur les remarques au sujet de sa lettre d'Omphale*[43], saying that he esteemed Pagin and that he found the hissing of his performance more humiliating for the Parisian public than for the actual violinist. Rousseau in his *Lettre à M. Grimm, au sujet des remarques ajoutées à sa lettre sur Omphale* was even clearer:

> Le Commentateur s'étend sur l'éloge de Pagin et de son illustre maître, et nous y applaudissons vous et moi de très bon cœur. Il voudrait que vous eussiez dit jusqu'à quel point la nation ingrate envers un talent si sublime, a osé l'humilier publiquement. Il fallait dire, *s'humilier publiquement*. Midas n'humilia point Apollon, et un cygne peut être hué par des oies sans en être humilié[44].

The 'swan' Pagin and his teacher Tartini were admired precisely for those qualities of *cantabilità*, expressiveness and naturalness that the abbé Pluche had ascribed to the French school represented for him by Jean-Jacques-Baptiste Anet, in contrast to pure virtuosity. But for many Italian musicians active in France expressiveness meant not only a cantabile

---

[41]. GRIMM, Friedrich Melchior, Freiherr von. *Lettre de M. Grimm sur Omphale*, [Paris], s.n., 1752. All the quoted texts relating to this subject can be read in *La Querelle des Bouffons* […], *op. cit.* (see note 38).

[42]. D.***. *Remarques au sujet de la Lettre de M. Grimm sur Omphale*, Paris, s.n., 1752, pp. 25-26.

[43]. *Mercure de France*, May 1752, pp. 187-192.

[44]. [ROUSSEAU, Jean-Jacques]. *Lettre à M. Grimm, au sujet des remarques ajoutées à sa lettre sur Omphale*, [Paris], s.n., 1752, pp. 11-12.

style, it also implied exploring new technical possibilities in articulation, bow technique, range, polyphonic writing; in a word it implied virtuosity.

To conclude this brief survey, in spite of the ideological controversies between *philosophes* and *conservateurs*, supporters of Italian or of French music, partisans of the primacy of melody and of that of harmony, oppositions that were typical during the eighteenth century, these aesthetic paradigms seem to surmount the ideological barriers; the wide circulation of musicians, the spreading of their music through print, were to create that common musical language (even in nationalistic France), that humus which was destined to feed the diverse musical experiences of the late eighteenth century.

«Son razzi matti, son rocchetti che girano»: sulle 'stravaganze' dei violinisti virtuosi

Simone Laghi
(Cardiff)

L'EVOLUZIONE DI UN LINGUAGGIO idiomatico nell'ambito della tecnica violinistica del XVIII secolo e l'affermarsi di una letteratura dedicata in maniera esclusiva a questo strumento portarono alla definizione di standard tecnici ancora oggi ritenuti altissimi. Le esecuzioni e le composizioni di virtuosi fra i quali Pietro Antonio Locatelli, Antonio Vivaldi e Antonio Lolli suscitarono senza dubbio ammirazione, ma anche severe critiche da parte di un pubblico più interessato alla delicatezza del suono e a una corretta semplicità compositiva legata alla tradizione.

In questa sede il fenomeno sarà contestualizzato nell'ambiente anglosassone, alla luce delle numerose testimonianze pervenuteci, contenute nelle lettere e nei diari della famiglia Burney, nei manuali di storia della musica (John Hawkins, Charles Burney), nei trattati dedicati alla prassi compositiva esecutiva (Charles Avison, Francesco Geminiani) e nei giornali dell'epoca.

Pietro Antonio Locatelli

I commenti relativi alle composizioni di Pietro Antonio Locatelli in Gran Bretagna riconoscono al violinista solide doti compositive corredate da un virtuosismo che pare essere tollerato, più che apertamente lodato.

Charles Avison (1709-1770) pone Vivaldi, Tessarini e Locatelli (aggiungendo anche Alberti) nella categoria degli «adventurers in Music [...] whose Compositions being equally defective in various Harmony, and true Invention, are only a fit Amusement for Children; nor indeed for these, if ever they are intended to be led to a just Taste in Music»[1].

---

[1]. Avison, Charles. *An Essay on Musical Expression*, Holborn, C. Davis, 1753, pp. 37-39: «Avventurieri della musica [...] le composizioni dei quali sono parimenti manchevoli in varietà di armonia, vera intuizione, e sono solamente una forma di passatempo per i bambini; e nemmeno per loro, se si ha l'intenzione di

Quando Charles Burney giunse ad Amsterdam nel 1772 durante il suo viaggio attraverso l'Olanda e la Germania, Locatelli era già morto da otto anni, ma ebbe comunque modo di conoscere un suo allievo, Jacob Potholt (1720-1782). Quest'ultimo (cui Burney si riferisce ripetutamente chiamandolo Pothof) fu organista della Westerkerk di Amsterdam dal 1743 al 1766, anno dal quale ricoprì il medesimo incarico alla Oude Kerk. Ascoltando l'esecuzione di Potholt, Burney ritenne di cogliere l'essenza del lascito musicale del violinista bergamasco:

> Locatelli […] used to give him instructions, and to encourage his musical studies by allowing him the advantage of being always a hearer at his public concerts, as well as private performances. This, in some measure, helped me to account for his taste and fancy, for Locatelli was possessed of a great deal of both: and though he delighted in capricious difficulties, which his hand could as easily execute as his head conceive, yet he had a fund of knowledge, in the principles of harmony, that rendered such wild flights agreeable, as in less skillful hands, would have been insupportable[2].

In una ulteriore testimonianza, Burney precisa che «Locatelli […] had more hand caprice and fancy than any violinist of his time. He was a voluminous composer of music that excites more surprise than pleasure»[3].

Le 'stravaganze' di Antonio Vivaldi e Carlo Tessarini

La parola 'stravaganza' in ambito violinistico è stata spesso usata per caratterizzare brani con marcati connotati virtuosistici o un intento programmatico. All'inizio del XVII secolo, Carlo Farina compose un *Capriccio stravagante*, utilizzando un violino, due viole e un violone per imitare altri strumenti come la tromba, l'organo, la chitarra e i versi

---

indirizzarli verso un corretto Gusto per la musica». Qui e laddove non diversamente indicato, le traduzioni sono dell'autore.

[2]. Burney, Charles. *The Present State of Music in Germany, the Netherlands, and United Provinces*, 2 voll., Londra, T. Becket-J. Robson-G. Robinson, ²1775, vol. II, pp. 290-291: «Locatelli […] lo istruì e lo incoraggiò nei suoi studi musicali permettendogli di avere l'occasione di essere sempre presente come uditore ai suoi concerti pubblici, come anche alle esibizioni private. Questo, in qualche misura, mi aiutò a farmi una idea del gusto e della fantasia che Locatelli possedeva in notevole quantità: sebbene deliziasse con difficoltà capricciose, che la sua mano poteva eseguire non appena la sua mente le avesse concepite, egli possedeva un solido bagaglio di conoscenza dei principi dell'armonia che rendevano quelle selvagge volate accettabili, mentre sarebbero state insopportabili in mani meno abili».

[3]. Id. *A General History of Music from the Earliest Ages to the Present Period. To which is prefixed a Dissertation on the Music of the Ancients*, 4 voll., Londra, The Author, 1776-1789; vol. III, p. 573: «Locatelli […] ebbe più capriccio di mano e fantasia di qualsiasi violinista del suo tempo. Fu un prolifico compositore di musica che provoca più stupore che piacere».

di alcuni animali come la gallina, il gatto e il cane. Una *Stravagance* di Nicola Matteis il vecchio, scritta verso la fine del medesimo secolo, è caratterizzata da ampi salti fra le corde. La *Stravaganza* divenne una sorta di dichiarazione poetica con Antonio Vivaldi (1678-1741), che scelse appunto questo titolo per la sua Op. 4⁴. La raccolta, pubblicata inizialmente da Roger ad Amsterdam nel 1716, venne ristampata nel 1728 in una seconda edizione, leggermente modificata, per i tipi di Walsh.

Lo stesso titolo venne scelto circa vent'anni dopo anche dal riminese Carlo Tessarini (*c*1690-1766) per la sua raccolta di concerti Op. 4, pubblicata ad Amsterdam a partire dal 1736: originariamente l'opera doveva essere strutturata in quattro volumi, ma solo due di questi videro la luce prima della morte dell'editore, Le Cène, avvenuta nel 1743. Il violinista riminese soggiornò in Inghilterra nel 1747, quando si esibì a Londra come primo violino nell'orchestra della Ruckholt House, in Essex. In questa sala, durante l'estate, ciascun lunedì mattina si teneva un concerto seguito da un ballo. La stagione cominciò il 24 aprile e Tessarini vi partecipò regolarmente fino a ottobre⁵.

Il 9 marzo 1748 Tessarini iniziò una sottoscrizione per la pubblicazione dei suoi *Allettamenti armonici a quattro* Op. 13 e per le Sei Sonate Op. 14. Negli annunci relativi si precisa che si sarebbe potuto assistere alle sue esibizioni ogni venerdì mattina presso l'alloggio che condivideva con Mr. Roure, un parrucchiere, vicino a Haymarket. Il 18 aprile dello stesso anno eseguì alcune sue composizioni per violino nella Hickford's Room, durante il nono appuntamento di una serie di concerti per sottoscrizione organizzati dal cantante Filippo Palma.

Avison cita il «deluge of unbounded Extravaganzi, which the unskillful call Invention, and which are merely calculated to shew an Execution, without either Propriety or Grace»⁶ per definire un insieme di composizioni che, invece che dare piacere, hanno il solo scopo di sorprendere ed accattivarsi l'attenzione dell'orecchio incompetente⁷. Le imitazioni di strumenti come il flautino, i corni e la cornamusa sul violino vengono considerate da Avison un «low Device», un mezzuccio per creare sorpresa: a suo parere, tutti questi espedienti non avrebbero potuto prevalere per lungo tempo sul naturale «Love of Harmony» («amore per l'armonia»). Il compositore si sarebbe dovuto astenere dal fornire all'esecutore dei pretesti per esibirsi in espressioni di «low Buffoonery»; secondo Avison, anche l'utilizzo di corde doppie era da evitare, poiché avrebbe ottenuto il solo risultato di rendere l'esecuzione

---

4. Considerato il contesto editoriale dell'epoca, sussiste la possibilità che il titolo alla raccolta sia stato assegnato da Roger, ma la presenza della dedica dell'autore a Vettor Delfino sul frontespizio fa ritenere che Vivaldi abbia seguito personalmente il processo di stampa, assegnando il titolo in prima persona.

5. Koole, Arend – Dunning, Albert. 'Tessarini, Carlo', in: *Grove Music Online*, <http://www.oxfordmusiconline.com> (consultato il 5 novembre 2014).

6. Avison, Charles. *Op. cit.* (si veda nota 1), p. 31: «profluvio di interminabili Stravaganze, che gli incapaci chiamano Invenzione, e che sono solamente calcolate per mettersi in luce durante l'esecuzione, senza alcuna Eleganza o Grazia».

7. *Ibidem*, p. 33.

più difficile, compromettendo l'espressività e costringendo uno strumento nobile come il violino a imitare due strumenti mediocri[8].

William Hayes (1708-1777), professore di musica ad Oxford, replicò alle affermazioni di Avison all'interno del pamphlet *Remarks on Mr. Avison's Essay on Musical Expression*, ponendo Vivaldi in maggior rilievo rispetto ai colleghi:

> I think Vivaldi has so much greater merit than the rest that he is worthy of some distinction. Admitting therefore the same kind of levity and manner to be in his compositions with those of Tessarini, etc., yet an essential difference must still be allowed between the former and the latter, inasmuch as an original is certainly preferable to a servile, mean copy[9].

Lo stesso Burney, nella sua *General History of Music*, pone Tessarini e Vivaldi, insieme a Tomaso Albinoni (1671-1750) e Domenico Alberti (1710-1746), in un insieme di compositori che definisce «light and irregular troops»[10], all'interno di un ideale esercito formato dai musicisti italiani. Il minimo comune denominatore che caratterizza questi quattro autori è quello di essersi formati a Venezia, e non all'interno della scuola romana di matrice corelliana: secondo lo storico inglese, Roma fu l'unica vera fucina dei compositori che permisero alla fama della musica italiana di esplodere in modo inarrestabile durante la prima metà del XVIII secolo[11]. Lo stesso Händel, in virtù del periodo trascorso a Roma, veniva considerato un paladino della musica italiana, se non altro per quanto riguarda il melodramma.

Proprio i nomi dei quattro compositori citati da Burney compaiono in una raccolta di concerti pubblicata dal Walsh e Hare nel 1728 e intitolata *Harmonia Mundi*[12]. In questa raccolta troviamo quattro concerti per violino (uno anonimo, uno di Alberti, uno di Tessarini e uno di Albinoni) e due concerti per oboe (uno di Albinoni e uno di Vivaldi [RV 456]). Le opere di Albinoni in questa raccolta sono oggi considerate spurie, e anche il concerto per oboe di Vivaldi è di dubbia attribuzione[13]. L'esistenza di questa collezione

---

8. *Ibidem*, p. 110.

9. HAYES, William. *Remarks on Mr. Avison's Essay on Musical Expression: wherein the characters of several great masters, both ancient and modern, are rescued from the misrepresentations of the above author; and their real merit asserted and vindicated. In a letter from a gentleman in London to his friend in the country*, Londra, J. Robinson, 1753, p. 39: «Penso che Vivaldi abbia un merito molto più grande degli altri e ha diritto a una certa considerazione. Pur riconoscendo che le sue composizioni sono caratterizzate dalla stessa leggerezza e dal medesimo manierismo delle composizioni di Tessarini ecc., tuttavia vi è una differenza essenziale fra il primo e il secondo, se non altro perché un originale è preferibile a una banale, brutta copia».

10. «Truppe leggere e irregolari»; la terminologia si riferisce, in gergo militare, alla fanteria leggera composta da mercenari.

11. BURNEY, Charles. *A General History of Music*, op. cit. (si veda nota 3), vol. III, p. 561.

12. Titolo completo: *Harmonia Mundi, The 2d Collection. Being VI. Concertos in Six Parts for Violins and other Instruments. Collected out of the choicest Works of* […] *Vivaldi, Tessarini, Albinoni, Alberti, never before Printed*.

13. A tale proposito cfr. le voci 'Vivaldi, Antonio' e 'Albinoni, Tomaso Giovanni' a cura di Michael Talbot in: *Grove Music Online*, op. cit. (si veda nota 5), consultate il 5 novembre 2014.

ci pone dunque di fronte al problema relativo all'autenticità delle edizioni. La coincidenza fra gli autori citati dallo storico e quelli inclusi nella raccolta può essere fortuita: è tuttavia verosimile che il giudizio della critica dell'epoca si sia formato sull'analisi di opere spurie.

Francesco Maria Veracini e Francesco Geminiani

Francesco Maria Veracini (1690-1768) e Francesco Geminiani (1687-1762) approdarono a Londra nello stesso anno. Veracini vi arrivò per la prima volta fra il 9 e il 27 gennaio 1714. La sua formazione affondava le radici nell'ambiente fiorentino, e venne principalmente curata dallo zio Antonio Veracini (1659-1733), violinista e compositore; l'ipotesi che Veracini abbia frequentato la scuola di Corelli non è suffragata da alcuna prova.

Dopo aver soggiornato a Londra per tutto il 1714, Veracini lasciò le isole britanniche. Vi fece ritorno nel 1733, probabilmente con l'intenzione di trovare un incarico come compositore. Nel 1738, dopo aver presentato al pubblico londinese le opere *Adriano in Siria*, *La Clemenza di Tito* e *Partenio*, ripartì nuovamente per Firenze. Fece ritorno in Inghilterra nel febbraio del 1741.

La musica di Veracini venne definita da Burney troppo «wild and flighty» (selvaggia e volubile), in quanto latrice di notevoli elementi di rottura con la tradizione corelliana, ritenuta un modello di «simplicity, grace, and elegance in melody, and of correctness and purity in harmony»[14]. Il pubblico inglese dimostrò però di non essere sempre d'accordo con le opinioni dello storico: le prime tre opere di Veracini in Inghilterra non ottennero consensi clamorosi (*La Clemenza di Tito* fu probabilmente un fiasco e scomparve dalle scene dopo quattro serate senza lasciare traccia[15]), ma *Rosalinda*, presentata nel 1744, ebbe un discreto successo e numerose repliche. Ecco il racconto di un incredulo Burney relativo alla messa in scena di quest'opera:

> After eight representations of this opera [*Alfonso*, di Lampugnani], it gave
> way, January 31st [1744], to another called ROSELINDA, set by Veracini, at that

---

[14]. Burney, Charles. *A General History of Music*, op. cit. (si veda nota 3), vol. IV, p. 640. «VERACINI, who was now [1714] regarded as the greatest violinist in Europe performed *symphonies* between the acts, at the opera, immediately after his arrival, and in April had a benefit concert at Hickford's room. His compositions, however, were too wild and flighty for the taste of the English at this time, when they regarded the sonatas of Corelli as the models of simplicity, grace, and elegance in melody, and of correctness and purity in harmony» («VERACINI, che all'epoca [nel 1714] era considerato come il più grande violinista in Europa, eseguì delle *sinfonie* fra gli atti, all'opera, immediatamente dopo il suo arrivo, e in aprile tenne un concerto a proprio beneficio alla Hickford Room. Le sue composizioni, tuttavia, erano troppo selvagge e volubili per il gusto inglese dell'epoca, che considerava le sonate di Corelli come modelli di semplicità, grazie ed eleganza nella melodia, e di correttezza e purezza nell'armonia»).

[15]. Hill, John Walter. *The Life and Works of Francesco Maria Veracini*, Ann Arbor (MI), UMI Research Press, 1979 (Studies in musicology), p. 42.

time the leader of the opera band. The first air that presents itself in the printed copy of the favourite songs is "The lass of Patie's mill", which Mont[i]celli condescended to sing, and Veracini to set parts and ritornels to, in order, as they imagined, to flatter the English. But as few of the North Britons, or admirers of this national and natural Music, frequent the opera, or mean to give half a guinea to hear a Scots tune, which perhaps their cook-maid Peggy can sing better than any foreigner, this expedient failed of its intended effect. Veracini's own Music in this opera is wild, aukward, and unpleasant; manifestely produced by a man unaccustomed to write for the voice, and one possessed of a *capo pazzo*. This opera, to my great astonishment when I examined the Music, ran twelve nights[16].

Geminiani fu invece certamente allievo di Corelli. Dopo un periodo di studi a Roma si trasferì a Napoli dove, grazie alla reputazione acquisita nelle sue esibizioni romane, venne immediatamente impiegato come violino principale. Avendo però mostrato un'eccessiva predilezione per l'uso del rubato, creando notevole confusione tra i ranghi dell'orchestra, venne retrocesso al ruolo di violista[17]. Nel suo *Treatise of Good Taste in the Art of Musick*, Geminiani espresse il proprio disappunto riguardo alla situazione musicale londinese che, a suo parere, non aveva fatto alcun progresso dal giorno del suo arrivo sull'isola: «The hand was more considered than the Head; the Performance than the Composition; and hence it followed, that instead of labouring to cultivate a Taste, which seem'd to be all that was wanting, the Publick was content to nourish Insipidity»[18].

---

[16]. BURNEY, Charles. *A General History of Music*, op. cit. (si veda nota 3), vol. IV, p. 451: «Dopo otto rappresentazioni di quest'opera [*Alfonso*, di Lampugnani], essa lasciò il posto, il 31 gennaio [1744], a un'altra chiamata ROSELINDA, messa in musica da Veracini, a quell'epoca direttore dell'orchestra dell'opera. La prima aria che venne proposta nella collezione delle arie predilette è 'The lass of Patie's mill', che Monticelli accettò di cantare e Veracini di orchestrare e dotare di ritornelli, immaginando di ottenere lo scopo di accattivarsi gli inglesi. Ma dato che pochi fra gli scozzesi, o fra gli ammiratori di questa musica nazionale e naturale, frequentano l'opera, o sono intenzionati a pagare una mezza ghinea per ascoltare una canzoncina scozzese, che probabilmente la loro cameriera Peggy sa cantare meglio di qualunque straniero, questo espediente si rivelò inefficace nel suo intento. La musica di Veracini in quest'opera è selvaggia, strana e sgradevole; chiaramente composta da un uomo non abituato a scrivere per la voce, da un *capo pazzo*. Questa opera, con mia grande sorpresa quando ne analizzai la musica, venne ripresa per dodici serate».

[17]. Testimonianza riferita a Burney da Emanuele Barbella (1718-1777), che a sua volta l'aveva appresa dal padre Francesco Barbella, compositore e maestro di violino al Conservatorio di S. Maria di Loreto, in Napoli. Riportata in BURNEY, Charles. *The Letters of Dr Charles Burney. Volume 1: 1751-1784*, a cura di Alvaro Ribeiro Jr, Oxford-New York, Clarendon Press-Oxford University Press, 1991, p. 146.

[18]. GEMINIANI, Francesco. *A Treatise of Good Taste in the Art of Musick*, Londra, s.n., 1749, p. 4: «La mano era più considerata del cervello; l'esecuzione più della composizione; e pertanto ne conseguì che, invece di impegnarsi per coltivare il gusto, che pareva la sola cosa mancante, il pubblico si accontentò di incoraggiare le Insulsaggini». Recentemente è stata pubblicata l'edizione critica di questo trattato, edita da Peter Walls, Bologna, Ut Orpheus Edizioni, 2012 (Francesco Geminiani, Opera omnia, 12).

IL 'CUCÙ' DI VIVALDI

Nel trattato *The True Art of Playing on the Violin* (Londra, 1751) Geminani dimostra di aderire, se non altro formalmente, ad un ideale di sobrietà e purezza esecutiva sicuramente condiviso da Burney. Dall'introduzione del trattato:

> The Intention of Musick is not to please the Ear, but to express Sentiments, strike the Imagination, affect the Mind, and command the Passions. The Art of playing the Violin consists in giving that Instrument a Tone that shall in a Manner rival the most perfect human Voice; and in executing every Piece with Exacteness, Propriety, and Delicacy of Expression according to the true Intention of Musick. But as the imitating the Cock, Cuckoo, Owl, and other Birds; or the Drum, French Horn, Tromba-Marina, and the like; and also sudden Shifts of the Hand from one Extremity of the Finger-board to the other, accompanied with Contortions of the Head and Body, and all other such Tricks rather belong to the Professors of Legerdemain and Posture-masters than to the Art of Musick, the Lovers of that Art are not to expect to find any thing of that Sort in this Book[19].

Che Geminiani intendesse riferirsi anche a Vivaldi vi sono pochi dubbi. Il 1720 vide la pubblicazione londinese di una raccolta di due concerti vivaldiani, dapprima per i torchi di John Jones e, poco dopo, per quelli di John Walsh: si tratta dei Concerti RV 335 *The Cuckow* e RV 347 Op. 4 n. 5, definito *Extravaganza*[20]. Detta raccolta, che precedeva dunque la stampa di Walsh dell'intera Op. 4 (datata 1728), venne pubblicizzata sul *Post Boy* del 21 Aprile 1720: «Two celebrated Concerto's the one commonly call'd the Cuckow, and the other Extravaganza, compos'd by Signor Antonio Vivaldi, and perform'd by Monsieur Duburge, at his late Consort; pr 3 s.» — Matthew Dubourg (1703-1767) fu un violinista inglese, concertista già all'età di 11 anni e abituale interprete di Vivaldi in Inghilterra e Irlanda. Peraltro, Dubourg non disdegnava la più sobria musica corelliana, come dimostrano i suoi abbellimenti alle Sonate Op. 5[21].

---

[19]. ID. *The Art of Playing on the Violin* […], Londra, s.n., 1751, p. 2: «Il fine della musica non è quello di appagare l'orecchio, ma di esprimere sentimenti, colpire l'immaginazione, influenzare la mente, e condizionare le passioni. L'arte del suonare il violino consiste nel dare allo strumento un suono che possa in qualche modo corrispondere a quello della più perfetta voce umana: e [lo deve fare] eseguendo ogni brano con precisione, appropriatezza e delicatezza di espressione secondo le vere intenzioni della musica. Ma l'imitazione del gallo, del cucù, del gufo e di altri uccelli; o del tamburo, del corno, della tromba marina e simili; come anche improvvisi cambi di posizione da una estremità della tastiera all'altra, accompagnati da contorsioni della testa e del corpo, e tutti gli altri trucchetti simili appartengono più ai professori di giocoleria e agli insegnanti di portamento che all'arte della musica, e gli amanti di quest'arte non si devono aspettare di trovare alcuna di queste cose in questo libro».

[20]. VIVALDI, Antonio. *Two Celebrated Concertos the One Commonly Called the Cuckow and the Other Extravaganza*, Londra, I. Walsh and I. Hare, 1720.

[21]. Duburg aggiunse diminuzioni all'*Adagio* della Sonata n. 5 e a tutti i movimenti delle Sonate nn. 7-11. Citato da BOYDEN, David D. *The History of Violin Playing from Its Origins to 1761, and Its Relationship to the*

L'imitazione dei versi degli uccelli nella prassi esecutiva è stata già citata in precedenza discutendo il *Capriccio stravagante* di Farina. Ma non sono solo le reazioni provocate dalle composizioni di Vivaldi a evidenziare l'interesse per tale tradizione, che pare ben radicata nell'ambiente musicale londinese: nel 1717 l'editore Richard Meare pubblicò un trattato per flauto e flautino intitolato *The Bird Fancyer's Delight*[22], contenente le istruzioni necessarie per imitare i versi di vari uccelli. Ancora, nel 1775, veniva pubblicato un annuncio relativo all'esibizione di un certo «Sieur Gaetano», specializzato nell'imitazione dei versi degli uccelli[23].

A dispetto della critica, i concerti vivaldiani e le imitazioni in essi contenute mietevano un notevole successo di pubblico, e non solo a Londra. Lo si evince da una testimonianza di Burney che, proprio in riferimento al Concerto RV 335, afferma:

> [Vivaldi's] Cuckoo Concerto, during my youth, was the wonder and delight of all frequenters of country concerts; and Woodcock, one of the Hereford waits, was sent far and near to perform it. If acute and rapid tones are evil, Vivaldi has much of the sin to answer for[24].

L'esecutore del Concerto di Vivaldi in questo caso viene identificato in Thomas Woodcock, fratello del più celebre flautista Robert Woodcock. Thomas era proprietario di un caffè a Hereford, ai confini fra Inghilterra e Galles. Come Dubourg, anche Woodcock aveva la fama di essere un violinista particolarmente raffinato nell'esecuzione delle sonate di Corelli[25].

Violin and Violin Music, Oxford, Oxford University Press, 2002, p. 222.

[22]. *The Bird Fancyer's Delight, or Choice Observations And Directions Concerning the Teaching of all sorts of Singing birds after the Flagelet & Flute if rightly made as to Size & tone, with a Method of fixing the wett Air in a Spung or Cotton, with Lessons properly Composed, within the Compass & faculty of each Bird, viz. for the Wood-Lark, House-sparrow, Canary-Bird, Black-thorn-Linnet, Garden-Bull-Finch, and Starling*, Londra, Richard Meare, 1717.

[23]. *Public Advertiser*, 28 marzo 1775: «SIEUR GAETANO's imitation of all Kinds of Birds, and BRESLAW with his Italians amazing Performances [...] Sieur Gaetano will imitate the Blackbird, Canary-bird, Linnet, [...] Skylark, Nightingale, and Crow, in the same Manner as he had the Honour of perform'ng before their Majesties and the Royal Family. [...] Breslaw and his Italians will wait on private Companies for Three Guineas».

[24]. BURNEY, Charles. *A General History of Music*, op. cit. (si veda nota 3), vol. III, p. 561. «Il Concerto del Cucù [di Vivaldi], durante la mia giovinezza, è stato la meraviglia e il diletto di tutti i frequentatori dei concerti di campagna; Woodcock, uno dei musicisti della città di Hereford, veniva mandato vicino e lontano a eseguirlo. Se i suoni acuti e veloci sono malefici, Vivaldi ha molti peccati di cui rispondere». Una parafrasi di questa frase di Burney è riportata in 'On the rise and progress of the violin' sul *Quarterly Musical Magazine*, pubblicato a Londra ed edito da Richard Mackenzie Bacon (l'autore dell'articolo non è specificato, ma probabilmente si tratta dell'editore stesso), IV (1822), p. 54: «Don Antonio Vivaldi [...], between 1714 and 1737, published eleven different instrumental pieces, besides his pieces called Stravaganze, the chief merit of which was rapid execution. His cuckoo concerto was for years the wonder and delight of all frequenters of country concerts».

[25]. HAWKINS, John. *A General History of the Science and Practice of Music*, 5 voll., Londra, T. Payne, 1776, vol. V, pp. 213-214.

Il favore riservato ai lavori vivaldiani è avallato dalle numerose edizioni inglesi, come schematizzato in Tavola 1 e 2.

Tavola 1
Le opere strumentali di Vivaldi stampate a Londra

Opus	Titolo	Prima edizione	Edizione londinese	Titolo dell'edizione londinese
2	*12 Sonate per violino, e basso per il cembalo*	Venezia, A. Bortoli, 1708	Walsh and Hare, 1721	*XII. Solos for a Violin with a Thorough Bass for the Harpsicord or Bass Violin*
3	*L'estro armonico*	Amsterdam, E. Roger, 1711	nn. 1-7: Walsh and Hare, 1715	*Vivaldi's most Celebrated Concertos in all their parts for Violins or other Instruments With a Thorough Bass for the Harpsicord*
			nn. 8-12: Walsh and Hare, 1717	*The Second Part of Vivaldi's most celebrated Concertos in all their Parts for Violins and other Instruments with a Thorough Bass for the Harpsicord*
4	*La stravaganza*	Amsterdam, E. Roger, 1716	Walsh and Hare, 1728	*La Stravaganza. Concerti Opera Quarta. Vivaldi's Extravaganzas in Six Parts for Violins and other Instruments, being the choicest of that Author's Work*
8	*Il cimento dell'armonia e dell'inventione*	Amsterdam, M.-C. Le Cène, 1725	n.d.	n.d.

Tavola 2
I concerti di Vivaldi stampati a Londra in collezioni miscellanee

Titolo	Concerti	Editore e data
Two Celebrated Concertos the one Commonly called the Cuckow and the other Extravaganza	RV 335 RV 347 Op. 4 n. 5	Walsh and Hare, 1720
Harmonia Mundi. The 2d Collection. Being VI. Concertos in Six Parts for Violins and other Instruments. Collected out of the choicest Works of [...] Vivaldi, Tessarini, Albinoni, Alberti, never before Printed	RV 456 (per oboe, dubbio)	Walsh and Hare, 1728

Select Harmony: being XII concertos in six parts, for violins and other instruments	Concerto I, Op. 8 [n. 7 in Re min., RV 242]	Walsh and Hare, 1730
	Concerto II, Op. 8 [n. 8 in Sol min., RV 332]	
	Concerto III, Op. 9 [n. 1 in Do magg., RV 181a]	
	Concerto IV, Op. 9 [n. 2 in La magg., RV 345]	
	Concerto V, Op. 6 [n. 2 in Mi♭ magg., RV 259]	
	Concerto VI, Op. 7 [I, n. 3 in Sol min., RV 326]	
	Concerto VII, Op. 7 [in La magg., RV Anh. 65; precedentemente RV. 338, attribuito a J. Meck]	
	Concerto VIII, Op. 7 [II, n. 4 in Fa magg., RV 294a]	
	Concerto IX, Op. 6 [n. 1 in Sol min., RV 324]	
	Concerto X, Op. 7 [II, n. 2 in Sol magg., RV 299=BWV 973]	
	Concerto XI, Op. 7 [II, n. 5 in Re magg., RV 208a]	
	Concerto XII, Op. 7 [II, no. 6 in Re magg., RV 214]	

Il primo Concerto de *Le quattro stagioni*, ossia *La primavera* (RV 269), è contenuto nell'Op. 8 *Il cimento dell'armonia e dell'inventione*, pubblicata ad Amsterdam da Le Cène nel 1727: di questa collezione non risultano edizioni londinesi. Il Concerto RV 269 risulta eseguito in soli due concerti pubblici a Londra (nel 1755 e nel 1757) e in entrambe le occasioni il solista fu Giovanni Battista Marella (1746-1777)[26]. Anche *La primavera* è caratterizzata dalle imitazioni dei versi degli animali e dei suoni della natura. Avison critica Vivaldi disapprovando, in particolare, l'imitazione del latrato di un cane, presente nel *Largo* ed eseguito dalla viola che deve suonare «sempre molto forte e strappato» mentre i violini riproducono il mormorio delle foglie suonando «pianissimo»:

> The singing of a Cuckoo, and the cackling of a Hen, have, in fact, been often introduced into musical Performances. Vivaldi, in his Seasons, or Concertos, so called, has imitated the barking of a Dog; besides many other strange Contrivances; attempting even to describe, as well as imitate, the various Changes of the Elements. If those Composers, who take such pleasure in their musical Imitations of the Noise of Animals, will shew their Ingenuity in that Way, I would advise them rather to follow the much more effectual Method of introducing the Creatures themselves[27].

---

[26]. Le date sono tratte da McVeigh, Simon. *Calendar of London Concerts 1750-1800*, Londra, Goldsmiths College, University of London, reperibile online <http://research.gold.ac.uk/10342/> (consultato in data 1 ottobre 2014). Dato che il *Calendar* si riferisce solo a Londra e parte dal 1750 non è significativo per quanto concerne le esecuzioni di musiche vivaldiane nel periodo precedente; tuttavia da un'analisi dei giornali a partire dalla pubblicazione dell'Op. 8 non risultano esecuzioni del concerto in questione, mentre l'RV 335 viene menzionato in diverse occasioni. È auspicabile un'ulteriore ricerca per definire l'effettivo impatto della musica di Vivaldi sui programmi da concerto nelle aree periferiche delle isole britanniche.

[27]. Avison, Charles. *Op. cit.* (si veda nota 1), p. 109: «Il canto del Cucù e il verso della gallina sono infatti stati spesso introdotti nelle esecuzioni musicali. Vivaldi, nelle sue Stagioni, dette anche concerti, ha imitato l'abbaiare di un cane; accanto a molti altri bizzarri espedienti; tentando addirittura di descrivere, oltre che di

John Hawkins (1719-1789) dedica a Vivaldi una voce di *A General History of the Science and Practice of Music* (1776)[28]. Citando l'Op. 8 di Vivaldi l'autore sente la necessità di chiarire subito che «The plan of this work must appear very ridiculous», con riferimento al programma poetico dei concerti delle *Stagioni*. Prosegue poi con una certa obiettività:

> Whether it be that the attempt was new and singular, or that these compositions are distinguished for their peculiar force and energy, certain it is that the Opera VIII is the most applauded of Vivaldi's works. Indeed the peculiar characteristic of Vivaldi's music, speaking of his Concertos — for as to his Solos and Sonatas they are tame enough — is that it is wild and irregular; and in some instances it seems to have been his study that it should be so; some of his compositions are expressly entitled Extravaganzas, as transgressing the bounds of melody and modulation; as does also that concerto of his in which the notes of the cuckoo's song are frittered into such minute divisions as in the author's time few but himself could express on any instrument whatsoever[29].

Hawkins infine tenta quasi di giustificare le 'stravaganze' di Vivaldi, facendo un paragone con Corelli e i suoi allievi (Geminiani, *in primis*):

> For these his singularities, no better reason can be given than this: Corelli, who lived a few years before him, had introduced a style which all the composers of Italy affected to imitate: as Corelli formed it, it was chaste, sober, and elegant, but with his imitators it degenerated into dullness; this Vivaldi seemed to be aware of, and for the sake of variety, gave into a style which had little but novelty to reccomend it[30].

---

imitare, il susseguirsi degli elementi [della natura]. Se questi compositori, che si compiacciono di introdurre nelle loro imitazioni musicali i versi degli animali, vorranno mostrare la loro ingenuità in questo modo, io suggerirei loro di perseguire un metodo molto più efficace, introducendo [nell'esecuzione] gli animali stessi».

28. HAWKINS, John. *Op. cit.* (si veda nota 25), vol. V, p. 213.

29. «Sia perché il tentativo fosse nuovo e originale, o sia perché queste composizioni si distinsero per la loro particolare forza ed energia, certo è che l'Opera VIII risulta il più apprezzato fra i lavori di Vivaldi. Certamente la caratteristica della musica di Vivaldi, in riferimento ai concerti — dato che le sonate a solo e i trii sono abbastanza scialbi — è di essere selvaggia e irregolare; e in alcuni casi sembra che fosse proprio nelle sue intenzioni di renderla tale; alcune delle sue composizioni sono espressamente chiamate Stravaganze, dato che infrangono i limiti della melodia e della modulazione; come accade anche in uno dei suoi concerti dove le note del verso del cucù sono frammentate in valori così piccoli che ai tempi dell'autore pochi le potevano eseguire su qualsivoglia strumento, tranne lui stesso».

30. «Per queste sue particolarità, non ci può essere una ragione migliore di questa: Corelli, che visse pochi anni prima di lui, aveva introdotto uno stile che tutti i compositori italiani tentarono di imitare: Corelli lo concepì casto, sobrio ed elegante, ma con i suoi emuli scadde nell'apatia; Vivaldi sembrò consapevole di questo e, al fine di introdurre qualche differenza, si abbandonò a uno stile che aveva poco da offrire a parte la novità».

George Dubourg (1799-1882), nipote di Matthew, pubblicò nel 1836 un libro intitolato *The Violin, being an Account of that Leading Instrument and Its Most Eminent Professors &c.* che contiene osservazioni sui violinisti del passato. Vivaldi subisce il solito trattamento, venendo accusato di essere un compositore inconsistente, irregolare, disordinato; si osserva, parafrasando Hawkins ma in tono meno accondiscendente, che Vivaldi voleva solo generare stupore e creare consenso introducendo bizzarre novità:

> To account for the singularity of Vivaldi's style, it should be observed that he had been witness to the dull imitations of Corelli that prevailed among the masters of his time; and that, for the sake of variety, he unfortunately adopted a style which had little but novelty to reccomend it, and could serve for little else but "to please the itching vein of idle-headed fashionists"[31].

ANTONIO LOLLI

Un'importante testimonianza sull'attività di Antonio Lolli (1725-1802) è data dal libello *Essai sur le gôut de la musique* del marchese Giovanni Battista Rangoni[32]. Nel trattato, stampato in francese con testo italiano a fronte, vengono messi a confronto tre dei più importanti protagonisti della scuola italiana del violino nel XVIII secolo: i primi due sono Nardini e Pugnani, considerati iniziatori di importanti tradizioni che vedranno l'affermazione di grandi campioni dello strumento come Campagnoli (allievo di Nardini) e Viotti (scuola Pugnani); il terzo è appunto Lolli.

Rangoni riconosce a Lolli notevoli abilità strumentali, tuttavia non supportate da altrettanta perizia compositiva:

> Molta velocità, e poca dolcezza; molta leggierezza e poca espressione, e poco fondo; molta di quella difficoltà stravagante e bizzarra che sorprende senza muovere, e niente di quella che è legata alle regole fondamentali del contrappunto, e buon gusto che ammirasi nelle sonate scritte con rigore geometrico dal Corelli, dal Tartini, ed in quelle d'un gusto più raffinato, benché

---

[31]. DUBOURG, George. *The Violin: Being on Account of That Leading Instrument, and Its Most Eminent Professors, from Its Earliest Date to the Present Time; [with] Hints to Amateurs & Anecdotes*, Londra, R. Cocks and Co., ⁴1852, p. 55: «Per dare una testimonianza della particolarità dello stile di Vivaldi, si deve considerare che egli fu testimone delle opache imitazioni di Corelli che prevalsero fra i maestri del suo tempo; e che sfortunatamente, per il gusto della varietà, adottò uno stile che aveva poco da offrire a parte la novità, e non serviva ad altro che a "soddisfare i pruriti di stupidi modaioli"». George Dubourg qui cita l'incipit della prefazione del *Musick's Monument* di Thomas Mace (1613-1706): pubblicato a Londra nel 1676, il *Monument* rappresenta una difesa della tradizione musicale inglese e un tentativo di reazione alle influenze straniere.

[32]. RANGONI, Giovanni Battista. *Saggio sul gusto della musica col carattere de' tre celebri sonatori di violino i signori Nardini, Lolli, e Pugnani / Essai sur le gôut de la musique avec le caractére te trois célébres joueurs de violon, Messieurs Nardini, Lolli & Pugnani*, Livorno, Masi, 1790.

meno profonde, del Pugnani, Giardini, e d'altri. In oggi si corre molto, perché s'ha timore di fermarsi. Son razzi matti, son rocchetti che girano.

Le doti tecniche sono quindi indiscutibili, ma vengono contestate la mancanza di sentimento e la predilezione per il tecnicismo fine a se stesso, a discapito della cantabilità. Giuseppe Bertini (1759-1852), che probabilmente ebbe occasione di ascoltare le ultime esibizioni di Lolli a Palermo, riporta quanto segue:

> Egli saliva più al di là di qualunque altro suonatore; i suoi capricci talmente lo trasportavano negli a solo, che il più esercitato accompagnatore poteva appena seguirlo: egli medesimo non poteva accompagnare il canto, perché difficilmente andava in misura[33].

Dall'affermazione del Bertini possiamo desumere che Lolli, come anche Geminiani nel suo debutto napoletano, sia stato solito fare un uso decisamente generoso del rubato. Il Bertini prosegue citando un aneddoto significativo che lascia intendere il disinteresse di Lolli nei confronti delle forme musicali cantabili:

> Essendo stato [Lolli] pregato un giorno di sonar un adagio, ricusò di farlo: Io son di Bergamo, ei soggiunse, i cittadini di questo paese son troppo matti per poter sonare l'adagio.

In un contesto storico ove l'espressività e il sentimento erano requisiti fondamentali per un musicista, Lolli trascurò esplicitamente gli adagi, anzi «raccorciolli assai ne' suoi concerti, e vi mise in oltre si poca espressione e melodia che di raro diè da lagnarsi della loro breve durata»[34].

Durante il suo breve soggiorno in Gran Bretagna, Lolli fu soggetto ad aspre critiche. Di seguito vengono elencati, in ordine cronologico, alcuni articoli relativi alle sue apparizioni londinesi. La prima esibizione venne così commentata dal *Public Advertiser* (venerdì, 14 gennaio 1785)[35]:

> [...] Lolli is of the right origination for a musician; that is, as his name indicates, he is a native of Italy. He has been for some time since settled at Petersburgh — tempted by that settled Viaticum with such prudent liberality held out by the different Courts on the Continent, and the hope probably of something more. —

---

33. BERTINI, Giuseppe. *Dizionario storico-critico degli scrittori di musica e de' più celebri artisti di tutte le nazioni sì antiche che moderne*, 4 voll., Palermo, Tipografia Reale di Guerra, 1815, vol. III, p. 32.

34. In *ibidem*, con riferimento alla testimonianza contenuta alla voce 'Concerto' in FRAMERY, Nicolas-Étienne – GINGUENÉ, Pierre-Louis. *Encyclopédie méthodique ou par ordre de matières* [...] *musique*, Parigi, Panckoucke, 1791, p. 301: «Lolli, qui avoit des raisons pour ne pas aimer les adagios, les abrègea beaucoup dans ses *concertos*, & y mit encore si peu d'expression & de mélodie, qu'on fut rarement tenté de se plaindre de leur peu de durée, & qu'on s'habitua peu à peu à ne les regader que comme une sorte de repos & de transition d'un allegro à l'autre».

35. Lo stesso articolo si trova sul *Gazetteer and New Daily Advertiser*, sabato, 15 gennaio 1785.

He has of late been travelling through many parts of Germany, &c. There he
was found by the Prince of Osnaburgh, and a little patronized by him; and with
letters from him to the Prince of Wales, &c. Mr. Lolli came to London. So
much for the *D'ou vient il?* respecting Lolli. His professional performance will
be dispatched in fewer words. His taste — his feeling — his tone — the great
accompanyments of a violinist — do not detain us a moment. These he has
much to learn in — indeed so much, as, considering his age, which appears the
full confirmed maturity of fifty years, leaves little hope of its ever being learnt
at least on this side of the grave. As to his execution, that is indeed a wonder.
The ease with which he vanquishes difficulties — the rapidity and enormous
distance of his shifts on the instrument — and in general the art he has achieved
in enlarging the limits of that instrument — all are most astonishing! — But are
they pleasing? Are they even intelligible? If not, they may be astonishing, and
astonishingly to his credit as a man of ingenuity, industry, and a mechanic, but
not as a musician! Agility, however, will do for once — and therefore perhaps
it might answer as an excitement of curiosity to have him for a night at the
Pantheon, the Festino, the Anacreontic, or anywhere else[36].

Seguono altre testimonianze dal *Gazetteer and New Daily Advertiser* (lunedì 17 gennaio
1785)[37]:

Last Friday night [14 gennaio] there was a grand Concert at Lord
Brudenell's, at which were present his Royal Highness the Prince of Wales, the
Foreign Ambassadors, and many of the Nobility. [...] Lolli played a concerto
and a solo; [...] he performed in a style more pleasing than usual[38].

---

[36]. «Lolli proviene dal posto giusto per un musicista; ossia, come suggerito dal nome, è nato in Italia. Egli
è stato per qualche tempo a San Pietroburgo — tentato dai compensi elargiti con saggia generosità dalle diverse
Corti del continente, e probabilmente con la speranza di qualcosa di più. — Recentemente ha viaggiato in
diverse parti della Germania, ecc. Lì venne scoperto dal Principe di Osnaburgh, che lo sostenne un po'; grazie
alle sue lettere, si presentò al Principe di Galles, ecc., e infine Lolli arrivò a Londra. Questo per quanto riguarda
il *D'ou vient il?* Il suo profilo professionale verrà discusso in poche parole. Il suo gusto — il suo sentimento — il
suo suono — le principali caratteristiche di un violinista — non ci hanno toccato affatto. Ha ancora molto da
imparare in questo campo — davvero molto dato che, considerata la sua età, che sembra aver raggiunto la piena
maturità dei cinquant'anni, vi sono poche speranze che egli possa imparare prima di mettere il piede nella fossa.
Riguardo la sua esecuzione, questa è davvero una meraviglia. La facilità con la quale egli domina le difficoltà —
la velocità e l'enorme distanza coperta dai sui cambi di posizione sullo strumento — e in generale l'abilità che
egli ha acquisito nell'ampliare i limiti dello strumento — sono tutte estremamente affascinanti! — Ma sono
piacevoli? Sono se non altro comprensibili? Se non lo sono, possono essere considerate sorprendenti e possono
contribuire a rendere stupefacente la sua fama di uomo ingenuo, diligente e meccanico, ma non di musicista!
L'agilità tuttavia sarà interessante per una volta e forse potrà soddisfare l'eccitazione della curiosità di averlo per
una serata al Pantheon, al Festino, alla Anacreontic [Society], o in qualunque altro posto».

[37]. Anche nel *Morning Herald and Daily Advertiser*, lunedì, 17 gennaio 1785.

[38]. «Venerdì sera scorso [14 gennaio] si tenne un gran concerto nella residenza di Lord Brudenell, al
quale erano presenti Sua Altezza Reale il Principe di Galles, gli ambasciatori stranieri, e molta della nobiltà.
[...] Lolli suonò un concerto e un solo; [...] si esibì in uno stile più piacevole del solito».

Infine, nuovamente dal *Public Advertiser* (venerdì, 18 febbraio 1785):

> Lolli, as far outdone by Cramer and Giardini in the superior excellencies
> of the violin, *taste* and *pathos*, as he outdoes them in excentric oddity, trick, and
> voluble execution, is esteemed at the highest rate in some foreign countries, —
> many parts of Germany, with the Dutch, and in some towns in France! — But
> not in Italy, nor, to the credit of our musical judgement, in England! In Russia
> particularly so far carried is this *Lolli Mania*, that he is the musician of renown,
> and has actually a pension from the Empress of no less than four thousand
> roubles a year[39]!

Il 23 febbraio 1785 Lolli si esibì suonando un solo per violino al termine del primo
atto della rappresentazione de *L'Allegro, il Penseroso e il Moderato* di Händel, al King's
Theatre. Il *Gazetteer and New Daily Advertiser* dello stesso giorno annunciò così la serata:

> The immediate departure of Signor Lolli from England, must be regretted
> by all lovers of the violin; his astonishing execution upon that instrument
> surpasses every thing that has been heard before. We are sorry to add, that we
> fear his performance this evening will be one of the last he will treat the public
> with in this kingdom[40].

Il *Morning Chronicle and London Advertiser* dello stesso giorno si spinse oltre, definendo
Lolli il miglior violinista d'Europa e sottolineando che una delle sue principali abilità era
quella di riprodurre con il violino il verso dell'usignolo:

> Sig. Lolli, who is allowed by all who have heard him, to be the most
> capital performer upon the violin in Europe, will this Evening give the publick
> an opportunity to gratify their curiosity: his wonderful execution upon that
> instrument, has excited the astonishment of the greatest cricks in musick.
> We are only sorry, that his engagements will, in a few days, oblige him to
> leave the kingdom. It is said, that Sig. Lolli introduces, in his Preludios, some
> passages of sounds and rythms, so accurately, taken from the nigthingale's
> song, that is impossible not to imagine we are really listening to the strains of
> the enchanting bird[41].

---

[39]. «Lolli, superato di gran lunga da Cramer e Giardini nelle qualità superiori del violino, in *gusto* e *pathos*,
così come lui li supera in stranezze eccentriche, trucchetti e nell'esecuzione imprevedibile, è sommamente
stimato in alcuni paesi stranieri, — in molte parti della Germania, dagli olandesi, e in alcune città della
Francia! — Ma non in Italia e nemmeno, a conferma del nostro gusto musicale, in Inghilterra! In Russia
questa *Lolli-mania* si è diffusa così tanto che egli è un musicista famoso e, al momento, riceve una pensione
dalla Imperatrice di non meno di quattromila rubli all'anno!».

[40]. «L'immediata partenza del Signor Lolli dall'Inghilterra sarà considerata con rammarico da tutti
gli appassionati di violino; la sua stupefacente esecuzione su questo strumento supera ogni cosa udita in
precedenza. Siamo dispiaciuti di aggiungere che temiamo che questa esibizione sarà una delle ultime occasioni
nelle quali egli intratterrà il pubblico di questo regno».

[41]. «Il Sig. Lolli, che a detta di tutto coloro che lo hanno ascoltato, viene definito il più grande violinista
d'Europa, questa sera darà al pubblico la possibilità di soddisfare la propria curiosità: la sua meravigliosa abilità

Il *Public Advertiser* (sempre del 23 febbraio 1785) rilanciò con ulteriori elogi, conferendo a Lolli la palma di miglior violinista del mondo. L'attesissima esibizione ebbe però esito sfavorevole: un articolo sdegnato, apparso sul *Public Advertiser* del 9 marzo, così commenta:

> Poor Lolli's reception in England has been very much worse than he expected — but the truth is, the national taste in England is far above the low state now subsisting almost every where but in Italy. Laughter is a strange and rather disreputable emotion at solo playing — and yet was this the only peculiar mark of popular attention received by Lolli. His _____[42] laughed most immoderately — So did the rest of the audience[43].

Burney ci fornisce maggiori delucidazioni in merito all'accaduto, biasimando il comportamento irrispettoso del solista:

> The celebrated performer on the violin, Lolli, came into England in the beginning of 1785; but by a caprice in his conduct equal to his performance, he was seldom heard. And then so eccentric was his style of composition and execution, that he was regarded as a madman by most of his hearers. Yet I am convinced that in his lucid intervals he was, in a serious style, a very great, expressive, and admirable performer. In his freaks nothing can be imagined so wild, difficult, grotesque, and even ridiculous as his compositions and performance. After playing at the oratorio, and making the grave and ignorant laugh at very serious difficulties upon which he had perhaps but ill bestowed his time, he suddenly left the kingdom, à la sourdine; perhaps, at last, to shun difficulties of another kind[44].

---

sullo strumento ha suscitato lo stupore dei più grandi critici musicali. Siamo solamente dispiaciuti che i suoi impegni lo obblighino a lasciare il regno fra pochi giorni. Si dice che il Sig. Lolli introduca nei suoi Preludi alcuni passaggi di suoni e di ritmi così accuratamente tratti dal verso dell'usignolo, che è impossibile non immaginare di star davvero ascoltando il canto di quest'uccello ammaliatore».

42. Probabilmente la parola 'Majesty' o 'Highness', con riferimento a qualche membro della famiglia reale, è censurata nel testo originale.

43. «La ricezione del povero Lolli in Inghilterra è stata molto peggiore di quanto egli si aspettasse — ma la verità è che il gusto nazionale in Inghiterra è di molto superiore alla misera condizione nel quale versa in ogni dove eccetto l'Italia. La risata è una bizzarra e discutibile manifestazione se applicata al solismo — e tuttavia questo è stato l'unico specifico segnale di riconoscimento popolare ricevuto da Lolli. Sua_____ rise smodatamente — Lo stesso fece il resto della platea».

44. Burney, Charles. *A General History of Music*, *op. cit.* (si veda nota 3), vol. III, pp. 680-681: «Il celebre violinista, Lolli, arrivò in Inghilterra all'inizio del 1785; ma a causa della bizzarria della sua condotta paragonabile a quella delle sue esecuzioni, fu udito raramente. Il suo stile di composizione e di esecuzione era così eccentrico che egli veniva considerato come un pazzo dalla maggior parte degli ascoltatori. Tuttavia io sono convinto che nei suoi intervalli di lucidità egli fu, nello stile serio, un esecutore davvero grandioso, espressivo e ammirevole. Nei suoi momenti di pazzia non si può immaginare niente di più selvaggio, difficile, grottesco e addirittura ridicolo come le sue composizioni ed esecuzioni. Dopo aver suonato a un oratorio,

Dalla successione di questi articoli è possibile trarre alcune conclusioni. La prima è che alcuni avvisi (con riferimento a quelli apparsi simultaneamente su diverse testate in data 23 febbraio) avevano un evidente scopo pubblicitario e venivano divulgati per attirare il pubblico agli spettacoli. Gli interessi commerciali producevano articoli che alimentavano aspettative altissime, salvo poi, nei giorni successivi all'evento, tradursi in resoconti ben più ridimensionati. La seconda è che al musicista veniva richiesto un sobrio contegno pubblico e una certa eleganza nei modi; il *decus* era un requisito fondamentale, al pari delle doti artistiche. Un comportamento irrispettoso o volgare poteva influire seriamente su una carriera, specialmente nell'ambiente londinese, e ciò valeva sia all'interno di un contesto pubblico che nelle relazioni private: il rifiuto di un invito da parte di una personalità equivaleva infatti a un'offesa. Charlotte Burney racconta in una lettera alla sorella Susan[45] di come Lolli si fosse palesemente inventato una scusa per defilarsi da un invito precedentemente accettato a casa Burney, cosa che offese gravemente il padrone di casa. Inimicarsi Charles Burney nella Londra di fine Settecento significava condannarsi ai margini dell'attività musicale[46]. In seguito allo spiacevole evento del 23 febbraio, Lolli cercò di organizzare un ulteriore concerto a Londra, inizialmente annunciato per il 2 maggio, poi rimandato al 9, poi ancora al 13 e infine al 16 a causa di «unforeseen accidents [eventi imprevisti]». Tutti i posticipi sono documentati dai trafiletti dei giornali che, di volta in volta, annunciavano la data alla quale il concerto veniva rinviato[47]. Il motivo dei ripetuti spostamenti è presto detto: Lolli era fuggito dall'Inghilterra. A causa di un debito contratto precedentemente in Russia, il virtuoso venne arrestato durante il soggiorno londinese e fu rilasciato solo dopo che il collega violinista Salpietro ebbe firmato una lettera di garanzia, a puro titolo di amicizia. Salpietro si ritrovò quindi con il debito di Lolli da saldare e si vide costretto a organizzare un concerto a proprio beneficio, per rimediare all'incresciosa situazione[48].

Conclusioni

Le testimonianze vagliate circostanziano il *bad taste* violinistico; tra le manifestazioni più comuni:
- l'imitazione degli animali, degli uccelli in particolare;
- l'imitazione di altri strumenti musicali;

---

facendo una grassa e ignorante risata di alcune serie difficoltà, che aveva forse trascurato, lasciò il regno improvvisamente, in sordina; forse, infine, per nascondere problemi di altro tipo».

45. Lettera datata 15 gennaio 1785. British Library, Egerton MS 3700A, f. 129.

46. Per ulteriori riferimenti alla vicenda e relativamente ai rapporti fra i musicisti e la famiglia Burney: Woodfield, Ian. *Salomon and the Burneys: Private Patronage and a Public Career*, Aldershot, Ashgate, 2003 (Royal musical association monograph, 12).

47. Cfr. *Morning Herald and Daily Advertiser*, 22 aprile, 7 maggio 1785; *General Advertiser*, 9 maggio 1785; *Morning Post and Daily Advertiser*, 9 maggio 1785.

48. *Public Advertiser*, 23 maggio 1785.

- repentini cambi di posizione (con conseguente discontinuità della linea melodica);
- postura sgradevole e disarmonica dell'esecutore.

Si profilano così due correnti: un violinismo sobrio, tutto sommato scolastico, e un virtuosismo aggressivo, *flamboyant*, caratteristico di pochi virtuosi che padroneggiavano un bagaglio tecnico enorme per lo standard dell'epoca. Un paragrafo fondamentale per l'analisi di queste figure viene scritto da Burney nella *History:*

> Veracini and Vivaldi had the honour of being thought mad for attempting in their works and performance what many a sober gentleman has since done uncensured; but both these musicians happening to be gifted with more fancy and more hand than their neighbours, were thought insane; as friar Bacon, for superior science, was thought a magician, and Galileo a heretic[49].

I violinisti virtuosi venivano quindi universalmente riconosciuti come tecnicamente molto dotati; ciò che veniva loro contestato era il gusto per l'esibizionismo (salti improvvisi e frequenti che interrompevano la melodia, imitazioni, eccessi), spesso unito a comportamenti inconsueti o sgradevoli. Il pubblico era forse già pronto a subire il fascino controverso di un Paganini che suona il violino di notte in un cimitero, ma l'*ancien régime* musicale resisteva alle innovazioni, almeno fino a quando non venne travolto, alla fine del XVIII secolo, dal romanticismo, e influenzato dalle atmosfere del romanzo gotico che proprio in quegli anni andava affermandosi come genere letterario, spazzando via l'Arcadia e il sobrio stile classico.

Il violinista del periodo tardo-barocco riceveva una formazione di matrice artigianale, il cui obiettivo era di preparare l'apprendista a operare come ripienista in un contesto orchestrale o in una cappella musicale: in entrambi i casi, i datori di lavoro erano l'aristocrazia o il clero. Le rare punte di eccellenza erano spesso raggiunte grazie a capacità tecniche straordinarie, derivate dal talento personale, o agli insegnamenti delle poche celebrità che fungevano da catalizzatori per i giovani talenti di tutta Europa (Corelli, Somis, Tartini, fino a Pugnani e Rolla ecc). Se al giorno d'oggi è normale che gli studenti di violino si confrontino durante il corso degli studi con le massime espressioni del virtuosismo di tutte le epoche, nel Settecento i requisiti tecnici per poter accedere all'attività professionale erano minimi e, in una scala di valori ideale, la tecnica era subordinata al *true taste*, al bel suono, alla musicalità e alla *bella semplicità*. Nonostante l'ambiente musicale della Londra georgiana permettesse alla libera impresa musicale di svilupparsi autonomamente, i comportamenti sopra le righe degli artisti non erano ancora visti di buon grado: il musicista era ancora considerato al servizio del pubblico.

---

49. BURNEY, Charles. *A General History of Music, op. cit.* (si veda nota 3), vol. III, p. 569: «Veracini e Vivaldi ebbero l'onore di essere considerati pazzi per aver tentato nelle loro opere ed esecuzioni ciò che molti sobri gentiluomini hanno da allora fatto senza essere censurati; ma entrambi questi musicisti, essendo dotati di più fantasia e abilità dei loro colleghi, erano considerati folli; come Bacone, per la sua grande conoscenza, venne considerato un mago e Galileo un eretico».

Per inciso, fu in seguito alla spinta illuministica della Rivoluzione francese, con l'apertura dei conservatori, che la didattica musicale si è giovata di programmi di studio comprendenti autori di epoche diverse; fino a quel momento l'istruzione musicale era prevalentemente costituita dagli input di una singola figura autoritaria che imponeva uno stilema univoco agli allievi. Il mercato delle edizioni a stampa offriva un ampio assortimento di composizioni, ma si rivolgeva esclusivamente a coloro che potevano farsi carico dell'acquisto, ossia gli *amateurs* degli ambienti nobili e borghesi (se non alcuni affermati musicisti); l'accesso era pressoché precluso agli strumentisti che non si trovassero sotto l'ala protettiva di un qualche mecenate o di una qualche istituzione. Al contempo, i virtuosi non avevano nessun interesse a divulgare le proprie conoscenze tecniche e a creare della concorrenza[50]. Solo nel XX secolo gli apparecchi di registrazione e riproduzione del suono hanno reso possibile l'apprendimento per imitazione anche a distanza.

L'incomprensione generatasi fra Burney e Lolli a causa del mancato appuntamento evidenzia un'ulteriore caratteristica imprescindibile per la carriera di un violinista a Londra. Discutendo del successo che il violinista inglese Michael Christian Festing (1705-1752) aveva ottenuto nel corso della sua carriera, Burney afferma che egli non aveva una mano felice e dimostrava poco talento per la composizione. Festing possedeva tuttavia altre doti: una buona conoscenza del contrappunto, buon senso, onestà, condotta prudente, comportamento da gentleman. L'insieme di queste qualità umane, unite a un modesto bagaglio tecnico, diedero a Festing una grande notorietà: «Learn hence, ye young professors, that something else is necessary, besides musical talents, to carry you reputably and comfortably through the world!» («Imparate, dunque, o giovani professori, che è necessario qualcosa di più oltre al talento musicale, per vivere dignitosamente e confortevolmente nel mondo!»)[51].

Si può quindi desumere che titoli come *La stravaganza* (che la loro origine fosse dovuta al compositore o all'editore poco importa in questo contesto) avessero il deliberato intento di scuotere l'ascoltatore e di destarlo dall'arcadico rassicurante sopore corelliano, attirando l'attenzione del pubblico; possibilmente, anche facendo storcere qualche naso.

---

[50]. Significativo è l'aneddoto relativo a Locatelli, che impediva ai professionisti di accedere ai suoi concerti; con riferimento alla lettera di Benjamin Tate, 11 aprile 1741, in DUNNING, Albert. *Pietro Antonio Locatelli: der Virtuose und seine Welt*, 2 voll., Buren, F. Knuf, 1981, vol. I, p. 204.

[51]. BURNEY, Charles. *A General History of Music, op. cit.* (si veda nota 3), vol. IV, pp. 668-669: «This performer, with a feeble hand, little genius for composition, and but a shallow knowledge in counterpoint, by good sense, probity, prudent conduct, and a gentleman-like behaviour, acquired a weight and influence in his profession, at which hardly any musician of his class ever arrived. He led during many years at the opera, at Ranelagh, at the concert at Hicksford's room, at the Swan and Castle concerts in the city, and often at Handel's oratorios. Nor was there a benefit concert for any English professor at that time whitout solo on the violin by Mr M. C. Festing; and yet there is not a ripieno player on the violin at the opera now, whose hand and abilities are not superior to those of Festing upon that instrument».

THE GOLDEN AGE OF VIRTUOSITY

Un solismo da camera:
Baillot e il *trio brillant* parigino nell'editoria musicale d'inizio secolo XIX[*]

Alessandro Mastropietro
(Catania)

Quando Momigny pubblica nel 1800 l'Op. 1 di Pierre Baillot (Passy 1771 - Parigi, 1842), i *Six Trios pour deux violons et basse*, la musica destinata all'organico di due violini e basso aveva sostanzialmente ultimato un tragitto di graduale trasformazione, avviatosi dalle ultime propaggini della sonata a tre trans-corelliana attorno alla metà del XVIII secolo. Attraversata la fase della musica strumentale *dialoguée* e poi — con esempi meno numerosi rispetto al quartetto e ad altre formazioni cameristiche — di quella *concertant*[1], di continuo attratto nella condotta delle parti dall'influenza della sonata solistica per violino e basso cui fosse aggiunta una seconda parte interna di accompagnamento, il trio a due violini finisce col far prevalere (salvo alcuni esempi di semplici trii 'didattici') quest'ultima tendenza solistica, in una modalità sempre meno 'dialogica' e sempre più favorevole al protagonismo del violino primo.

Preannunciata dai trii di metà secolo firmati da compositori-virtuosi, quali Tartini o Barbella (i cui *Six Trios*, stampati a Londra da Welcker, Baillot possedeva)[2], la tendenza si

---

afferma, con una buona dose di mediazione col modello *concertant*, nei *Six Trios* di Federigo Fiorillo (Sieber, Op. 2, *c*1788) e poi, con più decisa evidenza, in quelli del mentore parigino di Baillot, Giovanni Battista Viotti, sin dalla prima raccolta di *Sei Trii* Op. 2, non a caso dedicati a un solista di gran nome, il suo maestro Gaetano Pugnani. La raccolta di Viotti[3] è un punto di riferimento per fissare le due caratteristiche salienti del cosiddetto *trio brillant*[4] — nonostante essa non rechi ancora nel frontespizio l'aggettivo che diverrà correlato, sin dai primi e quasi contemporanei trii con due violini di Baillot e Rodolphe Kreutzer[5], alle peculiarità seguenti:

22314), reca un timbro-firma col nome 'Baillot', da identificarsi meglio in Pierre anziché (come da catalogo online) nel figlio, pianista e compositore, René Baillot (1813-1889), essendo la segnatura più coerente con lo specifico fondo del violinista. L'impianto dei trii inclusi in questa raccolta prefigura, nella scrittura del violino II più spesso formulare/d'accompagnamento che dialogica o parallela al melos del violino I, quello del trio *brillant*, pur limitandosi la scrittura del primo strumento a un virtuosismo del canto e del gusto, senza dunque punte di virtuosismo che invece si colgono, nel medesimo autore (e con una peculiare quota di estro descrittivo), nei *Six Duos* con basso *ad libitum* stampati a Parigi nel 1772 circa da Verdone frères.

3. I *Six Trios a Deux Violons et Basse dedié [sic] au celèbre Monsieur Pugnani* [...] *Œuvre 2*, stampati a Parigi da Sieber nel 1787 circa (datazione dell'edizione a cura della Bibliothèque nationale di Parigi, ma forse composti già in precedenza), sono già fuori della condotta *dialoguée* o *concertant*, alla quale pure fa riferimento DELLABORRA, Mariateresa. *Giovanni Battista Viotti*, Palermo, L'Epos, 2006 (L'amoroso canto, 4), p. 96, per quanto la prima si possa cogliere — soprattutto nel Trio 4 in Si♭ magg. — negli agganci in terze parallele del violino II al violino I, o al rilievo figurale dell'accompagnamento di alcuni episodi; la matrice solistica è avvalorata dall'essere. Un ritorno a una maggiore compartecipazione tematica da parte dei due strumenti tradizionalmente di accompagnamento si riscontra, in Viotti, nei *Trois Trios* pubblicati nel 1796 senza numero d'opera a Londra da Corri, Dussek & Co. e — *cfr. infra* nota 17 — a Parigi da Pleyel (nonché, a seguire, a Offenbach da André, come Op. 26), dovuta forse a una destinazione meno solistico-personale e più editoriale, salvo il ritorno alla formula solistica con gli *opus* successivi (dal 16 al 19), usciti a Parigi nel corso del primo decennio del XIX secolo. Per la possibile destinazione concertistico-privata di tali opere e di quelle analoghe di Baillot, si veda *infra*. Per l'elenco, *cfr. ibidem*, pp. 214-215; WHITE, Edwin Chappell. *Giovanni Battista Viotti (1755-1824): A Thematic Catalogue of His Works*, New York, Pendragon Press, 1985 (Thematic catalogues, 12), pp. 63-77.

4. Sul trio *brillant*: UNVERRICHT, Hubert. *Op. cit.* (si veda nota 1), pp. 233-255.

5. I *Trois Trios brillans pour deux violons et basse dediés à son ami Garnier de Lyon* [...] lettre A (1 [catalogo Isola] 164-166) di Rodolphe Kreutzer (Versailles 1766 - Ginevra 1831) furono composti nel 1802, ma editi solo l'anno successivo a Parigi dal Magasin de musique. Proprio intorno al 1800, tuttavia, appare — presso Pleyel, Parigi — un *Premier Pot-pourri pour violon avec accompagnement de violon et basse* di Kreutzer, seguito a ruota da altri due *pot-pourri ou air varié* (I 132-134, che li data 1799) per la medesima formazione: nell'ambito del filone virtuosistico su temi 'alla moda', sono anch'essi punti di riferimento, solo a notare i temi variati (in forma esclusiva, nel secondo e terzo brano; l'uno dopo l'altro tra loro senza soluzione di continuità, nell'autentica formula del pot-pourri, nel primo) dal violinista-compositore francese, scelte destinate a riverberarsi ('Nel cor più non mi sento', tema del secondo *pot-pourri ou air varié*) fino a Paganini. Per i trii nell'elenco delle opere di Kreutzer, *cfr.* ISOLA, Ingrid. *Rodolphe Kreutzer: Komponist, Virtuose, Violinpädagoge: der Weg zum Erfolg 1766-1799*, Francoforte, Peter Lang, 2010 (Europäische Hochschulschriften. Reihe XXXVI, Musikwissenschaft, 263), pp. 561-569.

1) conferimento al primo violino di un ruolo da leader quasi costante nella conduzione del discorso (laddove il *trio concertant* faceva circolare tale ruolo, anche se non del tutto pariteticamente, tra gli strumenti), e con tratti di bravura tecnica assai impegnativi in alcuni episodi, prediligendo tuttavia — almeno nella prima fase della sua esistenza storica — il virtuosismo del canto e del 'bello stile';

2) adozione nel primo movimento di un impianto in forma sonata sufficientemente articolato, di modo che la presenza di episodi virtuosistici non sbilanci una certa proporzione della forma tra momenti tematici e più genericamente figurali, e poi, nei movimenti successivi (due più spesso di uno), adozione di schemi formali per lo più adatti a valorizzare — accanto alla supremazia del violino — gli elementi da 'pezzo lirico' o 'caratteristico'.

Pur non del tutto aliene da una loro applicazione al quartetto d'archi stesso o al trio con viola, tali caratteristiche vi raggiungono assai meno frequentemente la radicalità con cui sono di regola praticate nella formula *brillant* del trio a due violini; perciò, alcune di queste raccolte appaiono in una versione alternativa per violino e pianoforte nella quale le due parti di mero accompagnamento (violino II e violoncello ovvero basso) sono in sostanza assegnate rispettivamente a mano destra e sinistra del pianoforte, salvo qualche ispessimento accordale della linea originariamente al violino II[6]. La soluzione è riconoscibile confrontando, con la versione per trio, quella alternativa per violino e pianoforte dei *Trios ou Sonates* Op. 39 di Baillot: nell'Ill. I[7], la riproduzione della prima pagina dell'edizione 'pianistica' del Trio 2 (si noti in alto a sinistra il permanere di tale titolazione, nonostante gli strumenti siano quelli della versione sonata) riflette quasi perfettamente la distribuzione su tre strumenti, solo che si riduce a una/due note la densità verticale degli eventi dell'accompagnamento nella mano destra del pianoforte (alias violino II) e si eliminino i raddoppi d'ottava della mano sinistra (alias violoncello).

Gli anni in cui il grosso delle raccolte di trii a due violini di Baillot vede la luce (il primo decennio dell'Ottocento) sono quelli di nuovo più favorevoli a quest'organico che a partire dal 1780, nel panorama cameristico senza tastiera obbligata, aveva progressivamente ceduto al quartetto d'archi il primato del favore dell'editoria musicale e, con esso, della

---

6. Ma questa *non* è la soluzione riconoscibile nella versione alternativa di quattro dei *Six Trios* Op. 2 di Viotti, comparsi a stampa forse addirittura prima della loro versione per trio a due violini come *Sonates pour clavecin ou piano-forte avec accompagnement de violon* […] (Sieber, libri I e II): lì, nella tradizione della sonata tastieristica accompagnata nella seconda metà del XVIII secolo, è la mano destra della tastiera a tenere preferenzialmente il pallino del discorso, cedendolo solo provvisoriamente al violino; nella seconda sonata dal libro I (= Trio 2 dell'Op. 2) in Mi magg., le ripetizioni periodico-tematiche — come quella in apertura dell'*Allegro con moto* iniziale — sono funzionali a tale cessione, dando un carattere moderatamente *concertant* al brano, ma — e ciò è significativo — nella versione per trio il melos principale rimane costantemente appannaggio del violino I: data la medesima sostanza musicale, insomma, il trio è conforme a una condotta *brillant*, mentre la *Sonate* si accompagna a una condotta — moderatamente — *concertant*.

7. La copia riprodotta è conservata in I-Nc, segnatura Ms. Appendice B. 166.

ILL. 1: Baillot, Trio 2 Op. 39 in Fa minore, versione per violino e pianoforte (*Trios Trios ou Sonates* […] Op. 39, Lione, Nalès, 1832), prima pagina della parte pianistica con guida del violino.

fruizione di 'conoscitori e amatori'. Nel corso del decennio appaiono circa 20 opere a stampa di trii in due-tre-quattro movimenti per la formazione a due violini e violoncello, senza contare le importanti raccolte esitate nell'anno 1800 (tra cui la prima del Baillot) e le pubblicazioni di *pot-pourris* o *airs variés*[8].

---

8. Nell'osservare la distribuzione (puramente indicativa, essendo molte edizioni settecentesche non precisamente databili) di nuove opere a stampa per tale formazione è lampante — dopo la flessione di fine secolo — la ripresa d'interesse, dovuta propria alla tipologia del trio *brillant*, ma scemata definitivamente nei decenni seguenti [i dati sono stati elaborati all'interno di un proprio progetto di ricerca in fieri sul trio a due violini nella stampa musicale dal 1750 in avanti]: 1751-1760: 50; 1761-1770: 90; 1771-1780: 63; 1781-1790: 38 più 1 *pot-pourri* ecc.; 1791-1800: 17 più 1; 1801-1810: 21 più 5; 1811-1820: 11 più 6; 1821-1830: 8 più 5; 1831: 4.

La formula virtuosistica del tema con variazioni era d'altronde congeniale all'orientamento 'solistico' del trio a due violini, ma non sembra esserle associato in modo biunivoco, come accade per i trii in più movimenti: *airs variés* di tal genere sono destinate — nell'ambito cameristico — anche a formazioni a quattro o a cinque archi, nelle quali i componenti al di fuori del primo violino sono tuttavia definiti sempre (mentre nei trii ciò non accade regolarmente) come una 'aggiunta' (*avec*) con funzione 'di accompagnamento'. Non si tratta pertanto di veri quartetti per archi, ma di pezzi per violino accompagnati, sicché, quando gli archi ad accompagnare il solista sono quattro (ovvero due violini, viola e violoncello), l'organico risultante in totale — tre violini, viola e violoncello — non corrisponde ad alcuna delle formule normalmente praticate a cavallo del 1800 nel quintetto di soli archi (con due viole, con due violoncelli o con contrabbasso)[9].

La Tavola I mostra la produzione a stampa più rappresentativa — per corposità o rilevanza — dedicata al trio a due violini dal 1790 circa fino al 1830 e oltre, con l'avvertimento che la distinzione tra *concertant* e *brillant* è a volte sfumata[10] (anche laddove la titolazione riporti uno dei due epiteti), e che l'assenza della definizione *brillant* non esclude l'appartenenza del contenuto dell'edizione musicale a tale genere.

Tavola I

Trii a due violini stampati dal 1790 circa fino al 1830 (selezione)

G. B. Viotti	21 Trii in 6 *opus* (1787, 1796/7, 1801/2, 1802/3, 1802/4, 1808), sostanzialmente *brillants*, prime edizioni a Parigi (salvo forse il secondo *opus*) con numerose riedizioni
I. Pleyel	12 Trii in 3 *opus* [4 libri] (1787, 1788, 1797), *concertants*, prime edizioni a Vienna (Artaria) o a Parigi (Pleyel)
A. B. Bruni	18 Trii in 6 *opus* (tra il 1790 e il 1810), *concertants*, prime edizioni per lo più a Parigi
P. Baillot	15 Trii in 4 *opus* (tra il 1800 e il 1827 circa), *brillants* (vedi *infra* per le edizioni). Inoltre, 4 *airs variés* in 3 *opus*
R. Kreutzer	9 Trii in 3 *opus* (1803, 1812, 1830 ma composti 1802-1805), *brillants*, prime edizioni a Parigi (ma il Trio 3 del terzo *opus*, '*Lettre C*', è rimasto manoscritto). Inoltre 3 *pot-pourris*/*airs variés* (1800).

---

[9]. Gli sporadici esempi settecenteschi di quintetti per archi a tre violini, come i quintetti di Giovanni Battista Sammartini, rimontano infatti ad alcuni decenni addietro, sono complessivamente ascrivibili alla musica da camera *dialoguée* di metà secolo, e guardano per alcuni aspetti ancora più indietro, alla formula della scrittura strumentale a tre parti acute con basso, incontrabile nella scuola strumentale napoletana (Marchitelli, Alessandro Scarlatti) o nei *quatuors* delle prime due raccolte di *Musique de table* di Telemann.

[10]. Una condotta intermedia tra le due tipologie, ad esempio, mostrano i *Trois Trios* [...] Op. 48 del francese Frédéric Blasius, pubblicati a Parigi da Bochsa nel 1803. Fra gli autori 'di scuola francese' sono stati inclusi anche Libon (spagnolo di nascita) e Bindernagel (tedesco), poiché attivi prevalentemente a Parigi. Anche nel catalogo di Nicolò Paganini è presente un brano edito per quest'organico (*Sonata a violino principale con accomp.° di violino e violoncello* [o di piano]), ma si tratta di un *air varié* in edizione postuma (Schott, 1860).

Altri trii *brillants* di scuola francese: Felipe [Philippe] Libon (6 in 2 *opus*, 1797-1807); Joseph Bindernagel (3, 1798); Pierre Jean Wacher (3, 1800); Jacques-Féréol Mazas[11] (3, secondo decennio del XIX secolo).

Altri trii *brillants* di scuola non francese (selezione): Feliks Janiewicz (3, 1800); Ferdinand Fränzl (3, 1805 circa); Felice Radicati (1, 1808); Johann Martin [Jean Frédéric] Nisle (3, 1809-1817); Giovanni Battista Polledro (3, 1812-13), Karol Józef Lipiński (2, 1830 e 1833).

Risulta evidente come Parigi sia stato il luogo della prima irradiazione editoriale e, con tutta probabilità, anche esecutiva del repertorio *brillant* per trio con due violini, così come il fatto che dall'inizio dell'Ottocento — nonostante le riserve critiche emerse soprattutto in area germanofona, si veda *infra* — il modello si sia diffuso, compositivamente ed editorialmente, ad altre culture geografico-musicali, compresa (e non secondaria nella percentuale relativa) quella mitteleuropea.

La produzione per trio a due violini di Baillot edita a stampa si distribuisce dunque in 5 libri (tre trii ciascuno) per quattro numeri d'opera (i primi due libri infatti fanno entrambi parte dell'Op. 1), più tre numeri d'opera di *airs variés*:

TAVOLA 2
TRII (IN PIÙ MOVIMENTI) PER DUE VIOLINI E VIOLONCELLO, EDITI A STAMPA, DI BAILLOT[12]

OPUS	TONALITÀ	MOVIMENTI
Six Trios pour deux violons et basse [anche *violon e piano*] [...] *Œuvre 1er livre 1./2.* [...] *dédiés à sa mère*, Momigny, Parigi, 1800, riedizione André, Offenbach, 1800 (composti tra il novembre 1798 e l'ottobre 1800)[a]	I. Re min.	Introduzione. *Grave/Allegro furioso* 4/4 - *Andantino* (Re magg.) 2/4 - *Presto* 6/8
	II. Mi♭ magg.	*Allegro risoluto* 2/4 - *Andante* (Do min.) 3/4 - *Presto ma non troppo* 6/8
	III. La magg.	*Allegro* 4/4 - *Adagio* (Mi magg.) 4/4 - *Presto* 2/4
	IV. Sol min.	*Allegro moderato* 4/4 - *Adagio* (Si♭ magg.) 3/4 - *Presto ma non troppo* 3/4
	V. Fa min.	Introduzione. *Grave/Allegro agitato* 2/2 - *Largo* (Fa magg.) 4/4 - *Presto agitato* 2[/2]
	VI. Re magg.	*Allegro moderato* 4/4 - *Andantino affettuoso* (Fa magg.) 3/4 - *Allegretto* 6/8

[11]. Mazas fu peraltro allievo di Baillot presso il Conservatoire, dal 1802 al 1805 (CHARLTON, David. 'Mazas, Jacques-Férol', in: *New Grove Online*, <http:www.grovemusiconline>, accesso 4 marzo 2015).

[12]. Le date di pubblicazione qui accolte, alcune con un minimo beneficio del dubbio, sono quelle proposte alla voce 'Baillot' del *New Grove* (vedi *supra*), salvo correzioni laddove esse siano state imposte da dati acquisiti in relazione alle copie consultate (ad esempio, per la datazione dell'edizione Arnaud dei *Trois Trios* Op. 39, la cui copia di riferimento è conservata in NL-DHk con segnatura NMI 95 B 30 (7-9), appartenuta, fra gli altri, a Louis Picquot, come da timbro ex-libris).

Trois Trios pour deux violons et basse [...] *Œuvre* IV, *3.ᵉ livre dédiés à Mme Eugénie Beaumarchais Delarue*, Imprimérie du Conservatoire, Parigi, 1803?, riedizione André, Offenbach: *Trois Trios brillante* [...] (composti tra il novembre 1802 e il marzo 1803)	I. Do magg.	*Maestoso e brillante*, 4/4 - *Andante* (Fa magg.) 6/8 - *Presto militare*, 2[/4]
	II. Fa magg.	*Allegro molto vivace* 2/4 - *Romance. Andante un poco Allegretto* (Si♭ magg.) 2[/2] - *Presto ma non troppo. Scherzando*, 3[/4]
	III. La magg.	*Tempo giusto* 4/4 - *Adagio non troppo. Simplice* (Fa♯ min.) 4/4 - *Allegretto* 6/8
Trois Trios pour deux violons et basse... Œuvre IX, *4.ᵉ livre dédiés à Mme Eugénie Beaumarchais Delarue*, Imprimérie du Conservatoire, Parigi, 1805? (composti tra il gennaio 1804 e il gennaio 1805)	I. Mi magg.	*Moderato* 4/4 - *Andantino* (La min.) 3/4 - *Pastorale* 6/8
	II. La min.	*Molto vivace* 2/4 - *Andante* (Do magg.) 3/4 - *Presto. Agitato* 2/4
	III. Mi min.	*Presto ma non troppo. Agitato* 3/8 - *Minuetto. Andantino* 3/4 - *Allegro molto* 2/4
Trois Trios pour deux violons et basse ou violon et piano [...] *Œuv. 39, 5.ᵉᵐᵉ livre de Trios dédiés a Monsieur Eloi de Vicq*, Lyon, Arnaud, 1827?, ristampa Lyon, Nalès, 1832: *Trois Trios ou Sonates pour violon avec accompagnement de second violon et basse ou de piano seulement* [...] (probabilmente composti tutti prima del 1822ᵇ e forse già pubblicati da Frey nel 1821)	I. Si♭ magg.	*Allegro risoluto* 4/4 - *Adagio* (Mi♭ magg.) 4/4 - *Pastorale. Allegro non troppo* 6/8
	II. Fa min.	*Introduction Lento* 3/4/ *Allegro* 2/2 - *Un poco Adagio* (Fa magg.) 4/4 - *Allegro agitato ma non presto* 2/2
	III. La magg.	*Moderato* 2/2 - *Adagio* (Mi magg.) 3/4 - *Rondò* 2/4

ᵃ.   Le indicazioni tra parentesi quadre sugli anni di composizione sono riportate in: François-Sappey, Brigitte. 'Pierre Marie François de Sales Baillot (1771-1842) par lui-même: étude de sociologie musicale', in: *Recherches sur la musique française classique*, XVIII (1978), pp. 126-211: 207-209, e dovrebbero provenire (tra le fonti elencate dalla studiosa in apertura di saggio, p. 130) dal *Catalogue de mes œuvres de musique*, manoscritto, nel fondo appartenuto a Magdeleine Panzéra-Baillot, pronipote del violinista e compositore, ora alla BnF; si veda Reynaud, Cécile. 'Les Fonds consacrés à Baillot au Département de la Musique de la Bibliothèque nationale de France', in: *Musique, esthétique et société au XIXᵉ siècle. Liber amicorum Joël-Marie Fauquet*, a cura di Damien Colas, Florence Gétreau e Malou Haine, Wavre, Mardaga, 2007 (Musique musicologie), pp. 37-52: 47, con l'indicazione del *Catalogue* entro l'inventario del fondo, conservato sotto la segnatura Res. Vmb. Ms. 84 (2). Arrestandosi le notizie del catalogo al novembre 1821, potrebbe essere autentica l'indicazione dell'anno di composizione e di prima edizione da parte di J.-J. Frey dei *Trois Trios* Op. 39, nonostante una copia di quest'edizione non risulti localizzabile; d'altra parte, Frey fu effettivamente editore — intorno a quegli anni — di molta musica da camera di autori francesi, e una decina d'anni prima, dei *Trios Trios Brillants Lettre B* (I 171-173) di Kreutzer. L'indicazione di Ozi quale editore degli Opp. 4 e 9 non contraddice quella qui riportata (Imprimérie du Conservatoire), essendone il fagottista e compositore Étienne Ozi di fatto il direttore.

ᵇ.   Il Trio 2 in Fa min. dell'Op. 39 fu eseguito infatti, secondo l'incipit riportato dal Baillot stesso nel documento *Programmes de toutes mes séances de quatuors et quintettes, depuis l'origine (12 dicembre 1814)* (di cui *infra* alla nota 32), nel concerto di sabato 9 marzo 1822 (p. 82, quinto e ultimo pezzo, *Trio de Baillot 14ᵉ*). Per la data e l'editore, si veda nota precedente.

TAVOLA 3

AIRS VARIÉS PER DUE VIOLINI E VIOLONCELLO, EDITI A STAMPA, DI BAILLOT

Deux Airs variés pour violon avec accompagnement de second violon et basse Œuvre 5 dédiés à son Ami Roland de Caen, Imprimérie du Conservatoire, Parigi, 1803?, riedizioni Naegeli, Zurigo, 180?; la II riedita in tempi moderni da Senart (composti tra l'aprile e il luglio 1803)	I. [Air 'J'ai vu Lise…']	*Adagio* 4/4, La magg., 6 variazioni, ciascuna con carattere e agogica diversi
	II. *Air d'Handel* [The Harmonious Blacksmith],	*Adagio assai* 4/4, Mi magg., 9 variazioni, ciascuna con carattere e agogica diversi
Air de Paesiello, varié pour le violon avec accompagnement de second violon & basse [...] *Op. 19*, Pleyel, Parigi, 1810, numerose riedizioni, tra cui André, Mollo e Ricordi, anche in versione per violino e pianoforte (composto nel novembre 1810)	[Cavatina 'Saper bramate… (Io son Lindoro)']	*Andante* 4/4, Si♭ magg., 7 variazioni, con mutazioni di agogica
Air de Grétry varié en trio Op. 33, Janet et Cotelle, Parigi, 1815	[Air 'Tandis que tout sommeille']	*Andante*, 3/8, Re min.[a]

a. I dati, non essendo stata localizzato un testimone, sono attinti dall'incipit riportato dallo stesso Baillot nel documento *Programmes de toutes mes séances de quatuors et quintettes, depuis l'origine (12 décembre 1814)* (di cui *infra* alla nota 32): nelle sue 5 occorrenze — a partire dal concerto del 26 gennaio 1819 — nei programmi delle *Séances* (pp. 50, 59, 70, 79, 149), il brano è sempre nominato come *Air de Grétry, Varié – par Baillot, 28ᵉ*, senza indicazione più precisa della fonte operistica: nonostante sia assente anche il numero d'*opus*, si ritiene di poter proporre con buona certezza l'identificazione con l'Op. 33, la penultima (e unica riguardante un tema di Grétry) dedicata da Baillot al genere dell'*air varié*.

L'indicazione costante di *basse* per la parte grave non va intesa come prescrizione d'uso di un contrabbasso, la cui estensione senza la quinta corda grave non si adatterebbe a quella mostrata dalle parti (regolarmente estese fino al *do₁*): essa è piuttosto un'allusione alla funzione prevalente di basso armonico — anziché motivico-tematico — della parte, coerentemente al suo ruolo *d'accompagnement*, il che non esclude, nella prassi esecutiva del tempo, la possibilità di raddoppio del violoncello con un contrabbasso.

Quattro libri su cinque sono concentrati entro i primi 10 numeri d'opera, ma ciò non ostacola l'assenza di differenze tra i libri e i lavori al loro interno. I trii che concedono più visibilità figurale, cura contrappuntistica e compartecipazione tematica ai due strumenti non solisti, sono quelli dell'Op. 9[13]; essi appaiono anche i più compatti sotto l'aspetto espressivo e formale, e più facilmente degli altri potrebbero trovare posto oggi in un programma concertistico da camera. Passi come quello che apre la parte centrale in minore dell'*Andante* del Trio 2, col suo dialogo alternato tra i due violini e la linea del basso al violoncello profilata con una figura ritmica prominente (Es. 1), o come l'attacco del finale

---

13. Gli esempi — trascritti in partitura da chi scrive — sono stati preparati sulla base della copia consultata, conservata presso I-Nc, segnatura 49.3.34.

Es. 1: Baillot, Trio Op. 9 n. 2 in La min., *Andante*, in Do magg., prima parte della sezione centrale ('*Minore*'), batt. 38-54.

(*Allegro Molto*) del Trio 3 in Mi min. (si veda l'ILL. 2), un tema inquieto e sommesso ma anche un po' scherzoso che, grazie all'unisono e al pianissimo, parifica di fatto gli strumenti, o come la strofa-ponte in stile imitativo — tutti gli strumenti coinvolti nella circolazione del soggetto — all'interno del finale (*Presto. Agitato*) del Trio 2 in La min., sono eccezioni entro una condotta che è ben esemplificata dal veemente attacco (*Presto ma non troppo. Agitato*) del Trio 3 (Es. 2).

ILL. 2: Baillot, Trio Op. 9 n. 3 in Mi min., *Allegro molto*, batt. 1-15, riproduzione della parte di violino II. Tutti e tre gli strumenti enunciano in **p** all'unisono il tema (il violoncello un'ottava sotto), fino alla batt. 16 (così anche nella ripresa del tema, entro una forma sonata camuffata all'inizio da Rondò per via della ripetizione del tema), per poi differenziarsi gradualmente (subito il violoncello, poi il violino II dopo due battute di pausa e due di ulteriore unisono) e acquisire funzioni tematiche diversificate.

Nell'Es. 2 è evidente la stratigrafia funzionale della *texture*: il primo violino, depositario esclusivo e continuativo del tema; il secondo violino, assegnato a una figura di accompagnamento ugualmente continua, rilevante sì sotto l'aspetto ritmico (peraltro confliggente con la terzina di semicrome della testa tematica) e nel codice affettivo suggerito, ma scelta tuttavia tra quelle ordinarie a disposizione; infine, il violoncello, ancorato a funzioni di basso, seppur qui di nuovo caratterizzante per il suo ruolo di pedale di tonica,

Es. 2: Baillot, Trio Op. 9 n. 3 in Mi min., *Presto ma non troppo. Agitato*, batt. 1-18.

abbandonato solo all'esaurirsi dell'energia cinetica dello spunto iniziale al violino primo e al suo chiudersi in ripetizioni della coda tematica di crome parzialmente ribattute. Sembra emergere pertanto, nei Trii dell'Op. 9, un compromesso tra assegnazione di ruoli gerarchici tra le parti e loro investimento da parte di un lavorio motivico superiore alla media (in un genere incline più all'estroversione del concerto solistico che all'organicità sonatistica), indice forse di un tentativo di rilancio della neonata formula *brillant* oltre il perimetro convenzionale a essa connaturato. Che nel *Quatrième livre* di Baillot (libro che appare puntare in alto anche sui piani della temperatura espressiva — due trii su tre sono in minore, e caratterizzati nei tempi veloci da un tematismo sia micro-motivico sia deliberatamente drammatico, per l'acceso e 'gestuale' protendersi dei micro-motivi ritmici — e dell'eloquio nobile ed elevato dei temi, come quello che apre il *Moderato* del Trio 1, muovendosi sempre nel registro medio-grave del violino) affiorino, come nel secondo *opus* pubblicato di Viotti sicuramente noto a Baillot[14], indizi di ammorbidimento del protagonismo del primo-solista, può dipendere da fattori sia meramente artistici sia contestuali. Se Viotti, a metà decennio 1790, viveva da alcuni anni immerso nel vivace ambiente londinese, assai adatto alla conoscenza e all'emulazione della musica strumentale all'epoca più avanzata, e vi aveva pressoché debuttato (terzo concerto nella stagione di Salomon del 1793, 28 febbraio) proprio con una performance in trio a due violini accompagnato dallo stesso Salomon e dal violoncellista Jean Mara[15], Baillot si apprestava nel 1805 — anno di presunta pubblicazione dell'Op. 9 — a un cimento europeo con la tournée che avrebbe raggiunto la Russia dopo aver toccato Vienna, peraltro intrapresa con il violoncellista Lamare, suo sodale attestato in un concerto di circa 5 anni avanti annoverante un Trio in Fa minore (quasi sicuramente il Trio 5 dell'Op. 1, appena pubblicata nel 1800) suonato con Rode al secondo violino[16]. Il nuovo libro di Baillot, meno radicale nella primazia del violino 1, oltre a soddisfare un'accresciuta consapevolezza personale dei suoi mezzi creativi, avrebbe quindi potuto servire come efficace 'biglietto di presentazione' performativo all'estero, adatto al contempo come vetrina solistica e come attestato di capacità compositiva[17].

Tornando all'organizzazione della partitura per strati funzionali, è a volte problematico tracciare il confine tra processi formulari e tematicità secondaria. Tuttavia, in presenza di un comportamento non tematico ma chiaramente solistico-virtuoso del primo violino, di figure di accompagnamento ancor più stereotipe, e di una linea del violoncello rigidamente legata a un basso d'armonia privo di arricchimenti ritmici o ornamentali, si riconoscono agevolmente i tratti di scrittura che avvicinano questi trii al genere-concerto, soprattutto ai suoi episodi di bravura. Ciò non impedisce che anche negli episodi tematici, come si è

---

[14]. Lettera di Baillot all'amico François de Montbeillard, del 6 ottobre 1796, cit. in: FRANÇOIS-SAPPEY, Brigitte. 'Pierre Marie François de Sales Baillot (1771-1842) par lui-même', *op. cit.* (si veda TAVOLA 2, nota a), p. 181: «Nous avons aussi fait de nouveaux trios de Viotti, manuscrits, chez Pleyel, ainsi que des quatuors de ce dernier […]»; *cfr. supra*, nota 3.

[15]. DELLABORRA, Mariateresa. *Op. cit.* (si veda nota 3), pp. 38 e sgg.: 40.

[16]. FÉTIS, François-Joseph. 'Baillot', in: *Biographie universelle des musiciens et bibliographie générale de la musique*, 8 voll., Parigi, Firmin Didot, ²1866-1868, p. 220: «[…] une émotion d'un genre aussi neuf pour mon âme fut celle que je ressentis à la séance dont je viens de parler, lorsque j'entendis Baillot jouer un trio (c'était en *fa* mineur, je m'en souviens), accompagné par Rode et par de Lamare […]» (per la testimonianza nella sua interezza, e per il resoconto del lungo soggiorno estero di Baillot dal 1805 al 1808, si veda *ibidem*, pp. 220-221). Il ricordo rimase così impresso al giovane Fétis, da generare questa testimonianza, poiché si era appena trasferito dalla provincia a Parigi per studiare in Conservatoire, e ciò accadde proprio nel 1800 (ELLIS, Katharine [et al.]. 'Fétis, François-Joseph', in: *New Grove Online*, <http:www.grovemusiconline>, accesso 4 marzo 2015).

[17]. Questa potrebbe essere la ragione dell'assenza dei *Trios* Op. 9 tra quelli proposti nell'ambito delle parigine *Séances de quatuors et quintettes*, nel cui ambito il trio a due violini si presentava come un concerto solistico in veste da camera, e perciò sarebbe entrato in conflitto con le caratteristiche più 'sonatistiche' dell'Op. 9. Fra i trii di Kreutzer, l'unico a investire di una tematicità non del tutto secondaria gli altri strumenti, è il *Trio 2 'lettre B'* (in Fa min.), in particolare nel primo (*Agitato e con fuoco*) e nel secondo (*Andante*) movimento.

osservato, la *texture* sia semplificata in questa foggia, e che persino lì il primo violino affermi una supremazia categorica, destinata a incarnarsi nella capacità o di far cantare lo strumento o di porlo al centro di un tuttotondo drammatico.

Prima di approfondire il piano delle soluzioni formali, va premesso che tutti i trii di Baillot sono in tre movimenti, secondo la disposizione tipica del concerto solistico (allegro, a volte preceduto da introduzione lenta; moderato o lento, comunque lirico; veloce e brillante, o caratteristico, anche se in tempo più moderato), laddove lo schema in tre movimenti, soprattutto nell'ambito del trio a due violini, disponeva in precedenza di una maggior varietà di soluzioni, a partire dalla scelta di aprire con un tempo lento o di mezzo carattere: vi si può leggere uno iato proprio nei confronti del modello del trio 'galante', coi non numerosi casi in due movimenti a richiamarli alla lontana[18].

L'attrazione dei principi formali vigenti nel genere concerto è in effetti più sottile e tuttavia sensibile: essa si maschera dietro un ossequio complessivo ma generico agli schemi cameristici non-solistici, mentre alcune spie formali smascherano l'altro modello di riferimento. Di tali segnali, ne illustro e discuto soprattutto due possibili:

1) non infrequente è in Baillot l'adozione di un brevissimo siparietto condotto per lo più da violino II e violoncello per pochissime battute, sì da disegnare lo sfondo figurale sul quale si staglierà l'ingresso del primo da protagonista. Ciò accade nei movimenti centrali del Trio 4 dell'Op. 1 (*Adagio*, 4 batt. con il concorso anche del violino I), del Trio 1 (*Adagio*, 1 batt.) e del Trio 2 (*Un poco Adagio*, mezza batutta) dell'Op. 39, nei Finali del Trio 1 (*Pastorale. Allegro non troppo*, 1 batt.) e del Trio 3 (*Rondo. Allegro non troppo*, 4 batt.) dell'Op. 39, e nei primi movimenti di altri tre trii: Trio 6 dell'Op. 1 (*Allegro moderato*, 5 batt.), Trio 1 dell'Op. 4 (*Maestoso e brillante*, 3 batt.), Trio 3 dell'Op. 39 (*Moderato*, 1 batt.). Altrove, è possibile riconoscere frasi o periodi introduttivi, coinvolgenti anche il primo violino, avanti che esso esponga il vero 'primo tema' (primi movimenti del Trio 2 dell'Op. 1, *Allegro risoluto*, 6 batt. e del Trio 3 dell'Op. 4, *Tempo giusto*, 7 batt.[19]; secondo movimento del Trio 3 dell'Op. 39, *Adagio*, 8 batt.), mentre in altri tre trii — tutti in minore — si incontra una vera e propria introduzione lenta autonoma dal successivo 'primo Allegro' (si veda *supra* Tavola 2). Quale ragione — accanto alla cosiddetta *funzione fatica*, attivatrice del canale comunicativo, perciò preparatoria e creatrice di attesa — per una così consistente occorrenza di introduzioni? Formulo l'ipotesi che esse siano un gesto formale sostitutivo — e oltremodo residuale — del tutti iniziale del tempo veloce iniziale in un concerto, gesto esteso saltuariamente anche ai tempi seguenti (che pure in genere non

---

[18]. Trio *brillant* in due movimenti è quello Op. 2 n. 1 (in La magg.) di Viotti.

[19]. Il caso di questo movimento esemplifica abbastanza bene gli altri: le 7 battute di apertura vengono tralasciate alla riesposizione del tema che precedono nell'esposizione (l'autentico 'primo tema') all'interno della terza parte della forma sonata, che si tratti di 'falsa ripresa' (Fa magg.) o di 'vera ripresa' (La magg.). La prima edizione dell'Op. 4 è disponibile online sul sito della Sibley Music Library di Rochester, NY (<http://hdl.handle.net/1802/8568>), dove sono conservati anche i due libri dell'Op. 1.

presentano un tutti d'apertura[20]). I coevi *Trios brillants* di Kreutzer, peraltro, propongono occasionalmente soluzioni analoghe (Trio 3 '*lettre A*', III mov., *Polonaise*; Trio 3 '*lettre B*', III mov., *Rondo*; Trio 1 '*lettre B*', I mov., *Moderato*);

   2) un altro gesto formale allusivo alla disposizione dei tutti orchestrali riguarda l'inversione pressoché sistematica della 'riesposizione regolare', nella sezione di 'ripresa', dei due temi principali nei brani in forma sonata. Per 'riesposizione regolare nella ripresa' intendo la riesposizione nella tonalità d'impianto di un tema principale della forma, nella sua ultima parte. Il tema che per primo viene riesposto regolarmente nella tonalità d'impianto (per intero o limitatamente alla sua conclusione cadenzale-armonica) è, in questi trii di Baillot, più spesso il secondo tema, poiché il primo tema è già stato riesposto, ma in altra tonalità (la cosiddetta 'falsa ripresa'), per cui la sua ulteriore e ultima riesposizione — alla tonalità di partenza — sembra assumere due paralleli obiettivi formali: chiudere senza pendenze strutturali il percorso tonale della forma, e insieme simulare l'ultimo intervento di un tutti, nonostante esso nel concerto si appoggi a materiale tematico non imparentato direttamente al primo tema. Tale particolare conformazione interessa — con una sola eccezione — anche i trii più compatti e sonatistici dell'Op. 9, nei quali invece sono del tutto assenti i brevi episodi introduttivi rilevati in quasi tutti gli altri trii. L'inversione della 'riesposizione regolare dei temi' non si riscontra invece nei tre Trii Op. 39, pubblicati nel decennio 1820: è prevedibile che la crescente modellizzazione morfologica abbia operato contro questa soluzione, indipendentemente o meno dall'apparizione dei trattati di Reicha quali possibili fonti normative[21].

   Qualche attinenza alla disposizione formale di un primo tempo di concerto — con la sua 'doppia esposizione' (la prima del tutti, la seconda del solo) dei due temi principali — potrebbe contenere l'inusuale permanenza alla tonica dell'esposizione del primo tempo, *Moderato*, del Trio 3 Op. 1, in La magg.: dopo aver esposto la prima e alquanto mobile tonalmente idea tematica (batt. 1-12), e averla estesa fino a toccare stabilmente, con nuove figure ritmico-melodiche, la tonalità alla dominante, maggiore o minore (batt. 13-29), il melos principale transita di nuovo per la tonalità d'impianto riesponendo la prima idea tematica (batt. 33-36), prima di riposizionarsi alla dominante (stavolta indiscutibilmente Mi magg.) per l'esposizione di un 'secondo tema' in realtà non distante dalle 'estensioni'

---

[20].   Ciò vale, ad esempio, per il primo dei casi qui elencati, l'*Adagio* in Si♭ magg. dal Trio 4 dell'Op. 1: le quattro battute d'introduzione, coinvolgenti anche il violino I, ritornano alla conclusione della forma, proprio come fossero il suo siparo di apertura/chiusura, incorniciando l'usuale schema ternario A-B-A'.

[21].   Il riferimento è al *Traité de mélodie* (1814) e al *Traité de haute composition musicale* (1824-1826). Quale esemplificazione, segnalo il primo movimento (*Maestoso e brillante*) del Trio 1 Op. 4 in Do magg.: la prima, imperiosa idea tematica (violino I, batt. 3-7, risposta nella sola testa a batt. 12-13 per generare di seguito le figure del ponte modulante) verrà risposta nella ripresa solo alla fine (ultime 8 batt.) ancor meglio accomodata al *topic* della marcia, mentre la seconda idea (cantabile), presentata nell'esposizione a batt. 24 e sgg., è quella risposta per prima ad apertura della ripresa, dopo la canonica fermata alla fine dello sviluppo, su un accordo di V grado strutturale della tonalità d'impianto.

del primo poc'anzi proposte, e spostato leggermente in avanti nella proporzione tra prima e seconda area tonale (batt. 36-59). Il percorso potrebbe dunque simulare, appena accennandola, alla 'doppia esposizione' in una forma sonata da concerto, pressoché asciugata da tutti gli episodi di bravura e inquadrata in una 'normale' esposizione sonatistica con ritornello (nei trii di Baillot, nessuno degli impianti formali di primi tempi si spinge infatti ad abolire il ritornello dell'esposizione, categoricamente assente quando la forma sonata convive con la doppia esposizione tematica del concerto solistico)[22].

Al di là di questi segnali, l'operare di una logica paratattica, traslativa, a pannelli, della forma vige soprattutto nei Trii dell'Op. 1 e dell'Op. 4: nei primi movimenti, calandosi nella formula sonatistica e contribuendo spesso a differenziarla rispetto alle proporzioni e all'assetto tonale dei modelli poi invalsi, tale influenza è forse più evidente che nei Rondò finali o nelle canzoni ternarie (in schema formale A-B-A') del tempo centrale (lì i due schemi prevalenti, ma declinati nei primi trii con una libertà perfino arrischiata — e perciò peculiare — nella costruzione melodica, quale non si troverà più nella squadrata fraseologia dei Trii Op. 39). In confronto, la costruzione morfologica complessiva e fraseologica si presenta più compatta e squadrata nei trii di Kreutzer, non solo negli episodi 'tematici', ma anche in quelli di bravura tecnica o di virtuosismo del canto; il *ductus* formale dei suoi trii risulta in definitiva più prevedibile, meno sorprendente di quello di Baillot, ricorrendo di norma — nei primi due *opus* a stampa — alla riesposizione alla dominante della prima idea tematica subito all'apertura della seconda parte della forma sonata, e a un posizionamento (tonale e temporale) relativamente ortodosso della seconda idea tematica, in genere assai contrastante con le figure virtuosistiche nel cui mezzo (tra ponte modulante e codette di chiusura) si apre un varco nell'esposizione. La solidità con la quale le forme di Kreutzer si presentano è, d'altra parte, direttamente proporzionale all'aumento del grado medio di virtuosismo che esse assorbono nei passaggi violinisticamente più impegnativi: l'effetto sorpresa, il fattore-varietà, sembrerebbe lì annidato nella scrittura, prima che nella forma.

Nondimeno, sul piano della mera scrittura violinistica, i trii di Baillot mettono in luce l'arsenale virtuosistico che si incontra nella parte solistica dei concerti suoi e di autori coevi: lunghi passaggi nel registro sovracuto o su corde specifiche (espressamente indicate), condotta riccamente ornamentale (in primo piano nei tempi lenti), figure brillanti — arpeggi scale o salti alternati e veloci di corda — tipiche e codificate pure nell'*Art du violon*; figure che, in casi eccezionali e per brevi episodi confinati a un registro medio-grave, possono transitare anche al secondo violino. Le corde doppie sono impiegate, ma con parsimonia, evitando in genere i bicordi di ottava a favore di quelli di terza o di sesta (come accade peraltro anche negli assoli dei suoi concerti). La figuralità 'brillante' del violino I è insomma coerente con quanto emerge dagli analoghi brani di Viotti, dell'allievo Mazas o, ancora, di Rodolphe Kreutzer, i cui trii (almeno quelli della '*lettre A*') si presentano

---

22. Tra gli autori più vicini a Baillot, l'unico caso di esposizione 'continua' (ovvero non bipartita dal segno primo ritornello) si ravvisa in Kreutzer, *Trio 1 'lettre C'* in Si min. I 218, 1 movimento (*Moderato*).

tuttavia più impegnativi e forniti, in tutti i movimenti lenti (nonché nel *Rondeau* del Trio 3), di una vera e propria cadenza solistica; è invece leggermente differente se paragonata ai *Trios brillants* della generazione immediatamente successiva: i trii di Baillot, come quelli di Viotti e (con una densità di 'bravure' poco superiore) Kreutzer, fanno uso del campionario virtuosistico secondo un certo equilibrio distributivo, conferendo risalto alla bravura espressiva o cantabile, e disseminando con equanimità e senza ostentazione le altre arditezze tecniche. È invece evidente, ad esempio, nei trii di Giovanni Battista Polledro (un allievo di Pugnani poco più giovane di Baillot) lo sbilanciamento verso la tecnica delle doppie corde, per la quale andava famoso[23], caratteristica osservabile anche nei trii — peraltro ben curati nella condotta delle parti di accompagnamento — di Janiewicz[24]; oppure, in alcuni passaggi dei trii del franco-spagnolo Philippe Libon (allievo di Viotti ma coetaneo di Polledro[25]), verso quella delle ottave. Nei Trii di Lipiński[26] invece, ancora successivi e ormai avveduti delle soluzioni paganiniane, l'innalzamento delle difficoltà tecniche per il primo violino è, specialmente nel primo Trio Op. 8 (in Sol min.), generalizzato non solo per la loro tipologia, ma anche per la loro acquisizione entro brani estesi a dimensioni formali pressoché doppie rispetto ai trii di Baillot.

Questi ultimi, nella condotta e nell'impianto formale, sono anche ben distinguibili dai quartetti[27]: è innegabile che i quartetti *concertants* di Viotti, Baillot o Kreutzer assegnino al primo violino un frequente e prolungato primato[28], ma non in forme così assolute come

---

[23]. Di Polledro (Piovà, presso Casale Monferrato, Alessandria, 1781-1853), sono noti tre trii a due violini e basso, stampati (uno per ciascun *opus*) come Opp. 2, 4 e 9 da Breitkopf intorno al 1812. Si veda SCHWARZ, Boris – SENICI, Emanuele. 'Polledro, Giovanni Battista', in: *New Grove Online*, <http:www.grovemusiconline>, accesso 4 marzo 2015.

[24]. L'unico *opus* di *Trios Trios pour deux violons et basse* di Feliks Janiewicz (Vilnius 1762 - Edimburgo 1848), stabilitosi già dal 1792 nel Regno Unito dopo periodi a Vienna, in Italia e a Parigi (BERWALDT, Jacek – MIKULSKA, Margaret. 'Janiewicz, Feliks', in: *ibidem*), è stato stampato da Imbault appena dopo il 1801.

[25]. Di Libon (Cadice 1775 - Parigi 1838) sono stati esaminati due libri a stampa, ciascuno di tre trii, l'Op. 3 (Auguste Le Duc) e l'Op. 6 (Pleyel, dedicati all'imperatrice Josephine, al cui servizio lavorò a partire dal 1800).

[26]. A Karol Józef Lipiński (Radzyń 1790 - Urłów, presso Lviv, 1861) si devono almeno i *Trio pour deux violons et violoncelle* Opp. 8 e 12, stampati agli inizi degli anni '30 dell'Ottocento.

[27]. Recano la qualifica di *brillant* le stampe di numerosi Quartetti di Spohr, nonché altri di Andreas Romberg, Peter Hänsel, Charles Maucourt. Solo in pochissimi casi, il *quatuor brillant* è esplicitamente descritto nel frontespizio quale lavoro *pour le violon avec accompagnement d'un second violon, alto et violoncelle* (ad esempio, il *4.ᵉ Quatuor brillant* Op. 8 di Joseph Mayseder, pubblicato a Vienna intorno al 1815).

[28]. Un primato garbato e non troppo sbilanciato lo si attendeva d'altronde in un normale quartetto degli autori già (o di lì a poco) 'classici' nel *milieu* musicale parigino della monarchia di Luigi Filippo, ovvero Haydn, Mozart e il primo Beethoven. Si legga la diagnosi di Eugène Sauzay, genero e collaboratore di Baillot, alla faticosa ricezione — da parte dell'affezionato pubblico delle *Séances de quatuors et quintettes* di Baillot — di un lavoro 'moderno', quale era considerato il Quartetto in Do♯ min. Op. 131 di Beethoven: «[…] Mais, quelques belle qu'elle fût, cette musique à quatre voix également importantes, qui exige quatre exécutants de même talent, ne fut pas du tout comprise par l'auditoire des séances habitué aux formes

in un *trio brillant*, dove i passaggi dialogici sono, come si è visto, estremamente eccezionali, mentre anche nei quartetti più orientati alla formula *brillant* essi conservano circoscritte ma doverose apparizioni[29] (organiche e diffuse nella formula *concertant*)[30], e la condotta delle *Nebenstimmen* o delle parti di accompagnamento è di norma sottoposta a una minima cura contrappuntistica, non limitandosi alla mera applicazione di figure stereotipe.

Solo in un repertorio, quello degli *airs variés*, l'organico di trio, quartetto o quintetto è totalmente indifferente alla condotta: il primo violino vi è il protagonista assoluto, certificato anche dalla dizione dei titoli che sottolineano regolarmente essere gli altri strumenti ad arco (siano due, tre o quattro) *d'accompagnement*. Il novero dei brani che Baillot ha dedicato al genere eccede pertanto i quattro lavori — per tre *opus* — scritti per l'organico a tre, solista compreso: essi erano d'altronde assai richiesti per terminare il concerto, dai tradizionali sottoscrittori delle *Séances de quatuors et quintettes* organizzate da Baillot[31], evidentemente desiderosi di un lavoro di facile ed estroverso ascolto al termine di programmi devoluti al 'bello più puro e ideale' della musica da camera[32]. La scelta di

---

hiérarchiques, claires et consacrées de Haydn, Mozart et du premier Beethoven, où la voix du premier violon est prépondérante. […] Virtuose soliste hors de pair, habitué à dominer le vieux quatuor traditionnel de toute la hauteur de son génie d'exécution, Baillot n'était pas plus fait pour l'égalité et la fraternité qu'en 1814 Napoléon pour l'acte additionnel»; pubblicato in François-Sappey, Brigitte. 'La vie musicale à Paris à travers les *Mémoires* d'Eugène Sauzay (1809-1901)', in: *Revue de Musicologie*, LX/1-2 (1974), pp. 159-210: 195.

[29]. Il *Quatuor brillant* Op. 11 (1807) di Spohr, tra i più rigidi nella scrittura *brillant*, devolve a tale *texture* i brevi episodi di chiusura delle tre sezioni principali (esposizione, sviluppo, ripresa) del primo movimento in forma-sonata.

[30]. Il Quartetto I dai *Trois Quatuors* Op. 34 di Baillot, in sostanza un *quatuor concertant* con qualche venatura solistica, è attraversato spesso da relazioni dialogiche in 'stretto' tra i due violini, o tra la coppia dei violini da una parte e gli altri due strumenti dall'altra; altrove, il primo violino è deputato a parte interna (anche se motivicamente pregnante), o viene agganciato all'unisono da uno o più strumenti del quartetto. Qualora esso rivesta ruolo-guida (ampiamente nel *Larghetto* in 6/8, terzo di quattro movimenti), viene contornato — espressamente nelle riesposizioni — da figure di accompagnamento meno neutre della media. Si ringrazia per la collaborazione nell'esame di questo brano il Palazzetto Bru Zane – Centre de musique romantique française di Venezia, che ne ha propiziato un'esecuzione pubblica (curata dal Quatuor Mosaïques) il 27 settembre 2014.

[31]. La consuetudine di Baillot di concludere sempre una *Séance de quatuors et quintettes* con un pezzo solistico, più spesso un tema con variazioni che un *romance*, un trio a due violini, o un concerto (intero o un solo movimento), è confermata dallo spoglio del prezioso documento dal titolo *Programmes de toutes mes séances de quatuors et quintettes, depuis l'origine (12 décembre 1814)*, prevalentemente ms. autografo, proveniente dal fondo Baillot appartenuto a Daniel Lainé, pronipote del musicista, ora alla Bibliothèque nationale de France e da poco parzialmente disponibile online grazie alla inventariazione e digitalizzazione condotta dal Palazzetto Bru Zane. Il documento (200 pp.), con numero di serie A01, è consultabile all'indirizzo <http://bruzanemediabase.com/Fonds-d-archives/Fonds-Baillot/Programmes-des-seances-de-musique-de-chambre-Pierre-Baillot/(offset)/1>.

[32]. Così Sauzay: «Bien que les quatuors fussent composés d'artistes de talent, habitués à accompagner le célèbre violoniste, le public d'élite qui les suivait venait pour admirer le génie d Baillot plus que pour écouter une musique concertante. Aussi Baillot finissait-il chacune de ces séances par un de ses airs variés dans lesquels

temi noti e accattivanti, e tuttavia deliberatamente pescati tra autori della 'antica scuola', va di pari passo a una tecnica variativa brillante ma nitida, con figure di diminuzione o di scrittura (bicordi in due voci parallele; accordi) molto riconoscibili, arricchita da qualche tocco timbrico (alla tastiera, al ponticello) ma, soprattutto, dallo sforzo di conferire un carattere agogico, ritmico ed espressivo distinto per ciascuna variazione. La combinazione sempre mutevole di questi elementi si osserva bene nella *Air d'Handel* (seconda dall'Op. 5): evitata qualsiasi trasformazione armonica-tonale (tutte le 9 variazioni in Mi magg. e ligie allo schema armonico presente nel tema) o strutturale-fraseologica, la varietà è generata a ogni nuova variazione sia dalla figura sia dall'andamento (mai due agogiche simili di seguito), occasionalmente anche dal metro o dal *topic* (VI e VII variazione in metro ternario, dapprima un *Maestoso* con ritmi puntati alla francese, quindi un *Tempo di Minuetto*).

Contesto esecutivo e ricezione (una conclusione provvisoria)

I trii a due violini di Baillot e di altri violinisti-compositori (non solo di scuola violinistica francese) si situano dunque, per caratteristiche morfologiche e di scrittura strumentale, in un terreno intermedio tra il genere concerto e i generi da camera, nei confronti dei quali il compromesso formale rimane — con oscillazioni tra autori e singoli lavori — ossequioso ad alcuni principi strutturali a essi propri.

Le loro esecuzioni documentate, quali quelle già esaminate (un trio di Viotti nei londinesi concerti di Salomon del 1793; una lettura — ancora viottiana — presso l'editore Pleyel da parte di Baillot e sodali nel 1796; il Trio 4 dell'Op. 1 di Baillot suonato *par lui-même* — con Rode e de Lamare — in un concerto parigino del 1800...), quelle da esaminare entro le *Séances de quatuor et quintettes*, e ulteriori che verranno ora discusse, confermano tale collocazione, che rendeva possibile il proporsi di questo repertorio sia in situazioni private sia in occasioni performative pubbliche, o ancora in un dominio intermedio (analogamente al piano della morfologia-scrittura) tra i due, nel quale possono essere annoverati appunto i cicli di *concerts de musique de chambre* (o *Séances de quatuor et quintettes*) proposti da Baillot su sottoscrizione in spazi privati[33]: un elenco sommario di

---

il faisait admirer sa virtuosité»; pubblicato in FRANÇOIS-SAPPEY, Brigitte. 'La vie musicale à Paris à travers les *Mémoires* d'Eugène Sauzay (1809-1901)', *op. cit.* (si veda nota 28), p. 192.

[33].   Sulle modalità di organizzazione, localizzazione e svolgimento dei cicli (che iniziarono il 12 dicembre 1814, sulla scorta di una precedente positiva esperienza di Baillot nel corso del suo soggiorno in Russia) e la natura della partecipazione, si può ricorrere di nuovo alla testimonianza di E. Sauzay riportata in *ibidem*, pp. 191-195. Per ulteriori informazioni: FAUQUET, Joël-Marie. *Les Sociétés de musique de chambre à Paris de la Restauration à 1870*, Parigi, Aux amateurs de livres, 1986 (Domaine musicologique, 1). Per l'attività musicale in Francia in quel periodo, si veda: MONGRÉDIEN, Jean. *La musique en France des Lumières au Romantisme (1789-1930)*, Parigi, Flammarion, 1986 (Harmoniques. La musique en France). Inoltre, accanto al documento di cui alla nota 31, si possono consultare soprattutto — tra quelli disponibili online — i *Documents relatifs*

autori e brani proposti in quella sede[34] conteggia quattro trii di Baillot e tre di Viotti (tutti *trios brillant* a due violini e basso), più un numero di *airs variés* di Baillot (21) per vari organici che coprono tre quarti della sua produzione nel campo e, significativamente, tutta quella per trio.

La cronologia delle esecuzioni dei lavori (propri e di Viotti)[35] per trio a due violini nelle *Séances* è la seguente[36]:

8ᵃ e ultima della prima annata — prima serie, lunedì 30 gennaio 1815, sesto e ultimo pezzo, *Air de Païsiello | Varié par Baillot* (= Op. 19, in Si♭ magg.); p. 12.

10ᵃ - 2ᵃ della seconda serie della prima annata, lunedì 27 febbraio 1815, quinto pezzo, *Trio de Baillot | 8.ᵉ* (= Op. 4 n. 2 in Fa magg.); p. 14.

14ᵃ - 2ᵃ della seconda annata, 25 novembre 1816, quinto pezzo, *Trio de B. [Baillot] en la* (= Op. 4 n. 3); p. 19.

19ᵃ - 3ᵃ della seconda serie della seconda annata, 10 febbraio 1817, quinto e ultimo pezzo, *Trio de Baillot | 8.ᵉ* (= Op. 4 n. 2 in Fa magg.); p. 26.

20ᵃ - 4ᵃ della seconda serie della seconda annata, 24 febbraio 1817, quinto e ultimo pezzo, *Trio de Viotti | 15.ᵉ* (Op. 17 n. 3, W III:15, in Sol magg., incipit del 1 mov. in 2/4 e valori dimezzati); p. 27.

21ᵃ - 1ᵃ della terza serie della seconda annata, 3 marzo 1817, quinto e ultimo pezzo, *Air Varié par | Baillot | 1.* (= Op. 5 n. 1 in La magg.); p. 28.

24ᵃ - 4ᵃ della terza serie della seconda annata, 24 marzo 1817, quinto e ultimo pezzo, *Trio de Baillot | 5.ᵉ* (= Op. 1 n. 5 in Fa min.); p. 31.

3ᵃ della prima serie della terza annata, martedì 9 dicembre 1817, quarto pezzo, *Trio de Viotti | 8.ᵉ* (= s.n. d'Op., n. 2, W III:8, in Re min); p. 35.

2ᵃ della seconda serie della terza annata (6), martedì 10 febbraio 1818, quinto e ultimo pezzo, *Trio de Baillot | 5.ᵉ* (= Op. 1 n. 5 in Fa min.); p. 38.

3ᵃ della terza serie della terza annata (11), martedì 21 aprile 1818, terzo pezzo, *Air d'Handel, Varié | par Baillot | 2.ᵉ* (= Op. 5 n. 2, in Mi magg.) / quinto e ultimo pezzo, *Trio de Viotti | 8.ᵉ* (= s.n. d'Op., n. 2, W III:8, in Re min); p. 43.

---

au public des séances de musique de chambre (Pierre Baillot), serie A06, all'indirizzo <http://bruzanemediabase.com/Fonds-d-archives/Fonds-Baillot/Documents-relatifs-au-public-des-seances-de-musique-de-chambre-Pierre-Baillot/(offset)/6>.

34. François-Sappey, Brigitte. 'Pierre Marie François de Sales Baillot (1771-1842) par lui-même', *op. cit.* (si veda Tavola 2, nota a), p. 189. Il documento (ms. autografo), dal titolo *Relevé général de tous les morceaux de musique qui ont été exécutés dans nos séances de quatuors et quintettes commencées à Paris, rue Bergère no 16, le 12 décembre 1814 et continués sans interruption pendant 25 ans qui sont révolus au 12 décembre 1839*, è consultabile online — entro la serie A02 del fondo Baillot digitalizzato (si veda nota 31) — all'indirizzo <http://bruzanemediabase.com/Fonds-d-archives/Fonds-Baillot/Documents-de-synthese-relatifs-aux-seances-de-musique-de-chambre-Pierre-Baillot/(offset)/2>, pp. 3-5.

35. L'assenza del repertorio di genere firmato da Kreutzer (del quale, nelle *Séances*, Baillot propone solo un *air varié* per altro organico) sembra confermare quel sottile divario stilistico — centrato nel rapporto tra impianto formale e arsenale tecnico — rilevato *supra*.

36. I dati, estratti dal documento di cui a nota 31, sono presentati in questa sequenza: numero d'ordine complessivo (quando riportato) e relativo della *Séance* (con riferimenti ad annata e serie al suo interno), data, numero in ordine di apparizione del brano, titolo (in corsivo) come indicato da Baillot, equivalenza abbreviata desunta dall'incipit musicale; infine, pagina nel documento digitalizzato consultabile online.

1ª della seconda serie della quarta annata (5), martedì 26 gennaio 1819, quinto e ultimo pezzo, *Air de Grétry, Varié | par Baillot | 28.ᵉ* (= Op. 33, in Re min.); p. 50.

3ª della seconda serie della quarta annata (7), martedì 9 febbraio 1819, quinto e ultimo pezzo, *Air Varié par Baillot | 1.ᵉʳ* (= Op. 5 n. 1 in La magg.); p. 52.

4ª della terza serie della quarta annata (12), martedì 23 marzo 1819, quinto e ultimo pezzo, *Trio de Viotti | 8.ᵉ* (= s.n. d'Op., n. 2, W III:8, in Re min); p. 57.

1ª della prima serie della quinta annata, martedì 11 gennaio 1820, quinto e ultimo pezzo, *Air de Grétry, Varié | par Baillot | 28.ᵉ* (= Op. 33, in Re min.); p. 59.

4ª della prima serie della quinta annata, martedì 1 febbraio 1820 (ultima fatta presso M.ᵐᵉ Bigot), quarto pezzo, *Trio de Viotti | 15.ᵉ* (Op. 17 n. 3, W III:15, in Sol magg., incipit del 1 mov. in 2/4 e valori dimezzati); p. 62.

4ª della seconda serie della quinta annata (8), martedì 28 marzo 1820, quinto pezzo, *Trio de Viotti | 8.ᵉ* (= s.n. d'Op., n. 2, W III:8, in Re min); p. 66.

3ª della prima serie della sesta annata, sabato 24 febbraio 1821, quinto e ultimo pezzo, *Air de Grétry, | Varié par Baillot | 28.ᵉ* (= Op. 33, in Re min.); p. 70.

2ª della seconda serie della sesta annata (6), sabato 24 marzo 1821, quinto e ultimo pezzo, *Trio de Baillot | 5.ᵉ* (= Op. 1 n. 5 in Fa min.); p. 73.

3ª della prima serie della settima annata, sabato 9 febbraio 1822, quinto e ultimo pezzo, *Air de Grétry, Varié | par Baillot | 28.ᵉ* (= Op. 33, in Re min.); p. 79.

4ª della prima serie della settima annata, sabato 16 febbraio 1822, quarto pezzo, *Trio de Viotti | 16.ᵉ* (= Op. 18 n. 1, W III:16, in Si♭ magg.); p. 80.

2ª della seconda serie della settima annata (6), sabato 9 marzo 1822, quinto e ultimo pezzo, *Trio de Baillot | 14.ᵉ* (= Op. 39 n. 2 in Fa min.); p. 82.

4ª della seconda serie della settima annata (8), sabato 23 marzo 1822, quinto pezzo, *Trio de Viotti | 8.ᵉ* (= s.n. d'Op., n. 2, W III:8, in Re min); p. 84.

88ª – 2ª della dodicesima annata, sabato 4 marzo 1826, quinto e ultimo pezzo, *Air d'Handel | Varié par Baillot | 2.ᵉ* (= Op. 5 n. 2, in Mi magg.); p. 105.

112ª – 2ª della seconda serie della quindicesima annata, martedì 24 marzo 1829, quinto e ultimo pezzo, *Air d'Handel, Varié | pour le Violon, par Baillot | 2.ᵉ* (= Op. 5 n. 2, in Mi magg.); p. 132.

123ª – 2ª della prima serie della diciottesima annata, martedì 31 gennaio 1832, quarto pezzo, *8.ᵉ Trio de Viotti* (= s.n. d'Op., n. 2, W III:8, in Re min.) / quinto e ultimo pezzo, *Air de Païsiello | Varié par Baillot | 15.ᵉ* (= Op. 19, in Si♭ magg.); p. 148.

124ª – 1ª della seconda serie della diciottesima annata, martedì 7 febbraio 1832, *Air de Grétry, | Varié par Baillot | 28.ᵉ* (= Op. 33, in Re min.); p. 149.

Predilezioni e curve d'interesse nel tempo si colgono facilmente dalle statistiche: inaspettatamente, il brano più eseguito (sei apparizioni, ben distribuite nelle annate) è un Trio di Viotti (quello in Re min., secondo della raccolta Corri-Dussek / Pleyel), seguito dall'*Air Varié* 'favori' da Baillot (e forse dal suo pubblico[37]), l'Op. 33 su tema di Grétry (cinque apparizioni); gli altri brani, trii o *airs variés*, assommano tre (i propri Trio 5 dall'Op. 1 e *Air Varié* Op. 5 n. 2 su tema di Handel) o due apparizioni (il Trio Op. 17 n. 3 di Viotti,

---

37. Dallo spoglio dei *Programmes* delle *Séances*, risulta — attraverso aggiunte a matita sull'originale a penna o stampato — che alcuni brani potevano essere richiesti in anticipo (*demandé*) dal pubblico dei sottoscrittori. Ciò è accaduto soprattutto nelle ultime annate, con un singolare favore nei confronti della *Serenata* Op. 8 per trio d'archi di Beethoven.

il proprio Trio 2 dall'Op. 4, e i propri *Airs Variés* Op. 5 n. 1 e Op. 19 su tema dal *Barbiere* di Paisiello); tre brani (i Trii Op. 17 n. 3 e Op. 18 n. 1 di Viotti, e il proprio Trio Op. 39 n. 2) sono eseguiti una sola volta. La presenza in programma di questi brani è continua nelle prime sette annate (dal 1814 al 1822), con apparizioni stagionali da due a cinque (seconda annata) e una delle sue presenze 'doppie' (terza annata). Al di là della maggiore probabilità statistica, legata al numero elevato di *séances* in quelle annate (generalmente 12, mentre in seguito esse si abbasseranno a 4 o 8, o perfino a 2), spiccano le assenze in successive annate consecutive, ovvero le riapparizioni isolate nel 1826 e 1829, prima di un'apparente ripresa d'interesse nel 1832 (tre brani) e quindi della definitiva eclissi fino al termine delle iniziative nel documento (1840). Dal momento che una precisa porzione del programma era e continuerà ad esser deputata a brani solistico-brillanti, se ne evince una drastica caduta d'interesse — e d'adeguatezza coi tempi — del repertorio per questa formazione, parallela alla irregolare comparsa dei quartetti più 'moderni' e problematici (tra cui quelli del Beethoven più impegnativo — Op. 59 n. 3, Op. 74 e Op. 131 per intero, movimenti dalle Op. 59 e 135), mentre altri organici e/o generi non perderanno tale funzione. Inoltre, sono pochi i brani che attraversano le due fasi (densità - saltuarietà) delle apparizioni documentate, ovvero il Trio in Re min. di Viotti e quasi tutti i propri *airs variés*: gli altri (e in particolare i propri trii) compaiono nell'una o nell'altra fase, a seconda della loro, relativa, prossimità compositiva all'annata, per cui i trii dei primi due *opus* spariscono col 1821, e l'unica proposta dall'ultimo *opus* si situa (1822) immediatamente dopo la sua presumibile composizione e, forse, pubblicazione, entrambe probabilmente finalizzate all'occasione e ad altre analoghe.

L'elemento a mio avviso più rilevante è la posizione, in un programma di *séance*, di questi brani: il programma tipo di una serata prevedeva cinque o sei 'numeri', dei quali — dopo i lavori cameristici 'classici' eseguiti per intero — almeno l'ultimo (se non gli ultimi due, o episodicamente un numero centrale) doveva proporre gli esecutori — Baillot in testa — in una chiave solistico-brillante[38]. A parziale rettifica (o meglio integrazione) delle indicazioni di Sauzay di cui *supra*, il brano non doveva obbligatoriamente essere — anche se assai spesso lo era — un *air varié* per un qualsiasi organico (trio compreso), ma poteva essere un concerto (completamente o parzialmente), un *morceau* caratteristico o un *romance* strumentale, o appunto un trio *brillant* a due violini (8 casi di ultimo pezzo in assoluto, nessuno dei quali dopo il 1821).

Nell'immagine restituita dalle sue esecuzioni nelle *Séances*, dunque, questo specifico repertorio si pone quale anello di congiunzione tra la prevalente proposta sonatistico-

---

[38]. Nel corso della primissime annate, l'epilogo brillante fu realizzato con un movimento isolato dal repertorio cameristico ordinario, ricorrendo di solito a un tempo isolato da un quintetto di Boccherini, e più avanti — saltuariamente — a uno in forma variazioni di altro autore, mentre nelle ultime la prassi di un tempo 'cantabile' dopo un intervallo a due terzi del programma divenne alquanto frequente.

cameristica degli autori rappresentanti allora l'apice dell'elevatezza strumentale (Boccherini, Haydn, Mozart, Beethoven, Onslow) e le già evidenziate, non sporadiche esecuzioni da camera di concerti solistici (parziale — «9 fragments de concertos di Baillot» — o completa — «4 concertos de Viotti e le concerto de piano en *mi* bémol de Beethoven» [!], nonché concerti di Tartini, di Pugnani e uno per pianoforte di Mozart da parte di Felix Mendelssohn — programmato, anche se non eseguito per impedimenti non musicali)[39], funzionali alle quali esistevano, accanto alle riduzioni pianistiche, trascrizioni cameristiche della componente orchestrale appositamente realizzate da musicisti terzi per l'immissione sul mercato editoriale[40].

La congenialità per ambienti esecutivi non troppo vasti si può leggere in filigrana nelle tracce di altre performance parigine di trii a due violini (non di Baillot) a inizio Ottocento[41]: accanto a quella di un trio non meglio specificato da parte dei fratelli Rousseau (Frédéric, violoncellista e fondatore dei concerti della Rue de Clery, e il suo *ainé* violinista) e del violinista Chol per il concerto del 23 febbraio 1803 presso l'Athénée des étrangers (*annonce* in *AAA*, 22 febbraio 1803), sono documentate, a breve distanza, quelle di un trio di Viotti, con violino I (essendo l'unico strumentista citato) A.-M. Xavier, l'11 settembre 1803, e di un trio di Kreutzer, con violino I (*idem*) il giovane Georges, il 2 ottobre 1803. Entrambe le esecuzioni sono inserite nella serie dei Concert de l'Académie de Musique (rispettivamente 6ª *séance* – 2° concerto e 15ª *séance* – 5° concerto) e recensite dalla *Correspondance des amateurs musiciens*, il 17 settembre 1803 e l'8 ottobre 1803. Sorvolando sul giudizio dell'anonimo recensore (puntato sulle qualità dell'interprete, anziché sui brani) e sulla confezione complessiva dei due programmi (il dettaglio dei quali è conservato solo per il secondo, conformato all'usuale esordio — e,

---

[39].   Le informazioni provengono, quanto ai documenti citati, sia dal 'documento di sintesi' delle stagioni di *Séances* dal 1814 al 1840 (A02, *cfr.* nota 34, e FRANÇOIS-SAPPEY, Brigitte. 'Pierre Marie François de Sales Baillot […]', *op. cit.* [si veda TAVOLA 2, nota a], p. 189), sia dai programmi dettagliati (A01, *cfr.* nota 31). La *Séance extraordinaire de musique instrumentale* (con orchestra) che avrebbe dovuto ospitare Mendelssohn (nonché l'esecuzione del Concerto per violino e orchestra di Beethoven) si sarebbe tenuta sabato 7 aprile 1832, ma — dal documento — non si poté effettuare per un'epidemia di colera. Quella (sempre con orchestra) con l'esecuzione del Concerto n. 5 in Mi♭ magg. di Beethoven (solista Ferdinand Hiller) si svolse il 19 aprile 1836, ma il brano non è posizionato alla fine, bensì al centro del programma, essendo probabilmente ritenuto un lavoro denso più che brillante.

[40].   Si segnala qui il *Quatuor brillant pour deux violons, alto et violoncelle arrangé d'après l'onzième concerto pour le violon de L. Spohr, par Othon Gerke*, Lipsia, senza indicazione d'editore (ma probabilmente Breitkopf), s.d. (secondo quarto del XIX secolo). L'utilizzo di un'orchestra con fiati e timpani per accompagnare il solista è eccezionale, nelle *Séances* di Baillot, e limitato a singoli concerti extra-ordinari (negli anni 1832-1833 e 1836) programmati in spazi adatti come la Salle Saint-Jean dell'Hotel-de-Ville.

[41].   I dati che seguono sono attinti dal database (anni 1794-1814) elaborato dall'équipe del *Projet RPCF* (Répertoire des Programmes de Concert en France) sotto la direzione scientifica di Patrick Taïeb, Cécile Duflo e Étienne Jardin, di prossima pubblicazione online sul sito <https://dezede.org/>. Ringrazio sentitamente Étienne Jardin per avermene permesso la consultazione in anteprima.

opzionalmente, epilogo — sinfonico per lo più haydniano, seguito da avvicendamenti di pezzi solistici vocali e strumentali con o senza orchestra), si sottolinea come questi due siano stati tra gli ultimi dei Concerts de l'Académie de Musique tenutisi nel Pavillon d'Hanovre in rue Louis-Legrand, uno spazio che il recensore stesso dichiara ormai insufficiente a ospitare il cospicuo concorso di uditorio, con gli abbonati in crescita[42]. Di lì a poco (36ª *séance* del 20 novembre 1803) quei Concerts si sposteranno nella nuova Salle des redoutes in rue de Grenelle-St-Honoré, uno spazio assai più ampio, accogliente e capiente (1200 posti), insomma più squisitamente 'pubblico': ciò consiglierà però gli organizzatori ad annunciare una distinzione tra programmazione cameristica e sinfonico-solistica (vocale o strumentale), l'unica, quest'ultima, a trovare posto (forse anche per il maggior richiamo su un pubblico pagante potenzialmente più numeroso) nella nuova sede in occasione dei partecipati concerti della domenica pomeriggio, mentre studio ed esecuzione di musica da camera sarebbero stati indirizzati ad altro giorno e orario (non è chiaro se nello stesso luogo)[43]. È significativo come, da allora in avanti, le cronache (puntuali quelle della *Correspondance des amateurs musiciens*) perdano le tracce della *tranche* cameristica dell'iniziativa (nonostante essa, costituzionalmente, riunisse in ogni settore *professeurs de musique* e *amateurs*), mentre nei programmi domenicali i brani per piccolo organico non scompaiono del tutto, ma non comprendono più il trio a due violini e si volgono piuttosto al repertorio con pianoforte.

Quanto alla ricezione nella letteratura critica del tempo, i materiali ripubblicati e commentati da Unverricht (riguardanti recensioni editoriali uscite sulla *Allgemeine musikalische Zeitung* tra il 1811 e il 1816, e relativi a libri di *trios brillants* sempre per 2 violini e violoncello/basso) evidenziano l'assenza di sintonia — e la conseguente diffidenza, ora palese ora ironicamente malcelata — per una condotta così smaccatamente solistica e pertanto differente dalla tendenziale parità di ruolo sulla quale veniva lì misurato il grado di elaborazione artistica[44]. Di seguito, una scelta dai passi d'esordio di queste

---

[42]. *Correspondance des amateurs musiciens*, 29 ottobre 1803: «[…] Si le zèle des fondateurs de l'Académie se soutient, la salle ne suffira bientôt plus pour recevoir tous les amateurs qu'attire la séance du dimanche. Leur empressement à s'y rendre n'avait point encore été aussi marqué».

[43]. *AAA*, a. 12 (24 novembre 1803): «[…] On ne peut douter du succès que doivent obtenir les concerts donnés par cette réunion des professeurs de l'Opéra, de Feydeau, de l'Opéra-Buffa, du Concert Cléry, qui s'est formée rue Louis-Legrand, sous le titre d'Académie de musique. C'est satisfaire les amateurs que de leur apprendre qu'il y aura trois séances par semaine: elles auront lieu les mardis, samedis et dimanches. La première sera consacrée à l'étude des quatuors, *quintetti*, etc. que les amateurs, réunis aux professeurs, exécuteront. Cette séance aura lieu le soir, depuis six heures jusqu'à neuf. La seconde à une heure après midi, aura pour objet la répétition du concert qui doit avoir lieu le dimanche. La troisième à une heure précise, sera remplie par un concert formé par les artistes et amateurs réunis. Le prix de la souscription est de douze livres».

[44]. Unverricht, Hubert. *Op. cit.* (si veda nota 1), p. 237: «Das brillante Trio ist im deutschen Raum nur mit mehr oder weniger heimlichen oder offenen Ressentiments aufgenommen worden. Besprechungen

recensioni, che tuttavia non lesinano considerazioni benevole su altri aspetti delle composizioni:

• [sul Trio Op. 8 n. 2 di Gerke, presumibilmente August G., in *Allgemeine musikalische Zeitung*, XVIII (1816), col. 675] «Nicht eigentliches Trio, sondern Solo für die Violin mit Begleitung der beyden andern Instrumente. Ein lebendiger, kräftiger Geist spricht aus den beyden Allegrosätzen, un ein feiner Sinn aus dem Cantabile [...]. Auch der harmonische Antheil ist bedeutend und kunstgetmäss»;

• [sui tre Trii, Opp. 2, 4 e 9, di Polledro, in *Allgemeine musikalische Zeitung*, XIV (1812), coll. 368 e sgg.] «Die Trios des Hrn. Polledro [...] gehören, streng genommen, nicht in die Klasse der Trios, sondern sind mehr als Solos für die Violin mit zweystimmiger Begleitung zu betrachten. Als solche haben sie einen ausgezeichneten Werth [...]. Das erste [...] hat einen heitern Charakter, der sich durch die Einheit der Figuren, besonders im ersten Satze, sehr bestimmt ausspricht [...]»;

• [sui Trois Trios brillans Op. 13 di A. Bohrer, in *Allgemeine musikalische Zeitung*, XIII (1811), coll. 445 e sgg.] «Drey glänzende Trios! Es ist zwar nicht alles Gold, was glänzt: inzwischen braucht das auch nicht eben Gold zu seyn, was blos glänzen soll [...]»[45].

Tale sotterranea polemica contro il luccichio esteriore sembra distante, per ragioni soprattutto geo-culturali, dall'entusiasmo (10-15 anni prima) dell'adolescente Fétis all'ascolto dal vivo di un trio *brillant* suonato a Parigi dallo stesso Baillot: ma una valutazione sull'accoglienza critico-musicale delle successive stampe nel genere anche in ambiente parigino, progressivamente impregnato dalla diffusione — e modellizzazione — di musica da camera d'impianto più 'mitteleuropeo', dovrà essere condotta a partire dallo spoglio sistematico dei periodici del tempo.

L'esistenza e la pratica assidua di questa produzione non contraddicono tuttavia l'immagine del Baillot divulgatore del repertorio cameristico più classico[46], piuttosto la

---

in der Leipziger Allgemeinen musikalischen Zeitung betonen meist, daß es sich bei diesen virtuosen Stücken eigentlich um ein Trio handele und außerdem durch die einseitige Bevorzugung des Virtuos-Technischen nur äußerer Glanz den Kompositionen aufgelegt würde und der eigentliche Kunstwert fehle [...]». In coda alle recensioni di disistima, Unverricht colloca per contrasto una critica positiva (ancora dall'*Allgemeine musikalische Zeitung*, XXXI [1829], p. 283) di un *opus* proprio per due violini e basso (una delle ultime stampate, l'Op. 63 di Aloys Schmitt, c1826), ovvero l'organico predisposto alla formula *brillant*, lodante dei brani proprio la distanza dal protagonismo solistico relegante le altre parti ad accompagnamento («Es gehört nicht zu denen, wo es bloss darauf abgesehen ist, die erste Violine glänzen, und die übrigen Stimmen nur begleitend nebenher gehen zu lassen [...]»), di conseguenza l'equa distribuzione e la relazione 'dialogica' per il melos più rilevante, e l'appartenenza alla 'vera' categoria del trio d'archi («[...] die Melodieen sind für alle drey Instrumente wohl vertheilt und so in einander greifend, als es wünschenswerth ist, und wie es einem eigentlichen Trio zukommt»; *ibidem*, p. 241).

⁴⁵.   *Ibidem*, pp. 238-240.

⁴⁶.   Peraltro, ancor prima delle *Séances de quatuors et quintettes*, Baillot era stato coinvolto (forse insieme al violinista Grasset, al cantante Plantade e a un 'Frédéric', forse il cornista F. Duvernois o il polistrumentista F. Blasius) in una serie di concerti pubblici — da camera? — tra la fine del 1797 e l'aprile del 1798; delle

integrano e la precisano, allargandone l'azione anche al repertorio *brillant*, la cui distinta funzione di surrogato da camera del *grand-genre* del concerto vigeva non solo a Parigi, ma a livello internazionale. Si apre così una finestra di conoscenza su quanto i virtuosi-compositori del violino proponevano presumibilmente nei concerti privati o semi-pubblici per una cerchia ristretta di amici ed estimatori. Che siffatto 'solismo da camera' abbia eletto la formazione dei due violini e violoncello/basso quale sede — tra altre — privilegiata di apparizione, non sorprende: la discendenza da un genere quale la sonata a tre che, nella sua tarda esistenza trans-corelliana, era apparso spesso come una sonata a solo accompagnata — ma amplificata nella corposità delle parti di accompagnamento — ne ha senz'altro favorito la filiazione. Ne ha però anche decretato la sua scomparsa allorché quell'organico, ceduta definitivamente la funzione didattico-violinistica al duo e quella di accompagnamento alla *partition vivant* (definizione estrapolata proprio dall'*Art du violon* di Baillot)[47] incarnata dal pianoforte[48], si è trovato privo di finalità performative specifiche e tagliato fuori da un gusto musicale ormai polarizzato su generi definitivamente assestati tra modelli cameristici e sinfonico-concertistici.

Post scriptum. Chi scrive ha potuto prendere visione diretta del *Catalogue de mes œuvres de musique* autografo di Baillot, citato nella nota a) alla Tavola 2, solo dopo la consegna del presente articolo alla redazione del volume: la verifica dei dati lì presenti, e già utilizzati — attraverso la loro parziale apparizione in altri testi scientifici — in vari punti dell'articolo, ha permesso di apportare correzioni o integrazioni rilevanti (che qui riassumerò complessivamente) ad alcune risultanze altrimenti errate o lacunose. Va premesso che

---

traversie economiche, ma anche degli apprezzamenti ottenuti da questa iniziativa, il musicista racconta in lettere all'amico Montbeillard, del 21 novembre 1797, 13 gennaio 1798, 22 febbraio 1798 e 3 aprile 1798 (estratti riportati in François-Sappey, Brigitte. 'Pierre Marie François de Sales Baillot (1771-1842) par lui-même', *op. cit.* [si veda Tavola 2, nota a], p. 177). Su questo aspetto dell'attività (promozione ed interpretazione in serie di concerti più o meno regolari e più o meno pubblici, in Francia e all'estero), nonché su tutti gli altri legati alla figura di Baillot e toccati qui in precedenza (composizione di musica da camera e di concerti solistici, stesura di trattati violinistici, rapporti epistolari e musicali ecc.), si segnala il convegno *L'homme-violon. Pierre Baillot (1771-1842)*, organizzato dal Dipartimento di Musica della Bibliothèque national de France, l'Institut de recherche en musicologie (CNRS) e il Palazzetto Bru Zane, con la collaborazione del museo Denon, Parigi, 9-10 gennaio 2015, il cui svolgimento è previsto in data successiva alla chiusura del presente contributo, e che presenterà i primi risultati di nuove ricerche condotte sui fondi legati agli eredi Baillot e in parte già pubblicamente accessibili in forma digitalizzata.

[47]. Baillot, Pierre(-Marie-François de Sales). *L'Art du violon: nouvelle méthode*, Parigi, Au Dépôt central de la musique, [1835], p. 8 (nel manoscritto preparatorio dell'autore, conservato nel fondo Baillot e consultabile online [si veda nota 31] all'indirizzo <http://bruzanemediabase.com/Fonds-d-archives/Fonds-Baillot/Manuscrit-de-l-Art-du-violon-Pierre-Baillot-1-4/(offset)/28>, il passo testuale figura a p. 25).

[48]. L'introduzione del pianoforte nella serie delle *Séances* è dapprima (anni '20 dell'Ottocento) sporadica, poi — proprio nel decennio di pubblicazione di *L'Art du violon* — più assidua, in chiave sia cameristica sia propriamente solistica (eventualmente con orchestra), grazie alla costante partecipazione di Ferdinand Hiller. Nell'annata 1835, ad esempio, la prima metà dei 4 appuntamenti sarà espressamente votata al duo violino-pianoforte (*Séances de musique de piano et violon*), e nel 1836 le manifestazioni assumeranno la denominazione più generica di *Soirées* [o *Séance*] *de musique instrumentale*.

il *Catalogue* (sesto *cahier* del volume con segnatura già indicata) si presenta in realtà come un diario della composizione dei lavori dal 1798 al 1821 (una pagina per ogni anno), con il titolo/contenuto dell'opera al centro della pagina, più informazioni di luogo e data (spesso precisa fino al giorno esatto) di ultimazione della composizione nella colonna sinistra, e *Observations* — ovvero dati di eventuali edizioni a stampa — nella colonna destra. Rispetto alle date di composizione finora note, è stata corretta — già nella Tavola 2 — quella dei *Trois Trios* Op. 4 (Trio 1 inserito all'8 novembre 1802, Trio 2 al 5 gennaio 1803, Trio 3 al marzo 1803); solo due dei Trii poi pubblicati come Op. 39 sono inseriti nel *Catalogue*, prima dell'interruzione della sua redazione (verso la fine del 1821): il Trio 1 in Si♭ magg., ottobre 1818, e il Trio 2 in Fa min., 1 novembre 1821; ciò non esclude che anche il Trio 3 sia stato composto per la fine di quell'anno, ma rende improbabile una pubblicazione della raccolta entro quel termine. La consultazione diretta del *Catalogue* ha risolto anche l'individuazione dei temi di due *airs variés* non indicati nelle stampe né nella bibliografia secondaria: per l'Op. 5 n. 1, 'J'ai vu Lise hier au soir', una *ariette populaire* all'epoca assai diffusa, variata — tra gli altri — anche da Muzio Clementi nel secondo movimento della Sonata Op. 23 n. 3 in Mi♭ magg.; per l'Op. 33 (composta a Liegi, ma di cui è segnalata anche una versione *à 4 parties* realizzata a Belleville nel 1818), 'Tandis que tout sommeille', rinomata *serenade* da *L'Amant jaloux* di Grétry. Il *Catalogue* riporta infine due altri lavori per trio senza che siano presente i dati di edizione, e perciò si tratta presumibilmente dei due rimasti manoscritti (citati nella nota d'apertura al presente saggio): un *Morceau détaché, à 3. parties, en Si bémol* (aprile 1803), e un *Air de la Rosière* [vale a dire *La rosière de Salency*, di Grétry]: *Chantez, Dansez. Varié en Trio* (*mis à 4 parties en 1819 = avec un refrain et d'autres Variations*; 17 gennaio 1814); di essi, rimane tuttavia incognita la sopravvivenza e l'eventuale localizzazione.

LES CONCERTOS POUR VIOLON DE PIERRE RODE: UNE VIRTUOSITÉ INNOVANTE

Priscille Lachat-Sarrete
(PARIS)

> *Le talent de Rode était fait surtout de charme, de tendresse et de suavité [...]*
> *La franchise et la hardiesse des traits dont sont parsemées ses compositions*
> *nous font voir que le virtuose joignait à ces qualités la solidité du style,*
> *la fermeté d'archet, et une ardeur plein de noblesse*[1].

SURNOMMÉ LE 'CORRÈGE DU VIOLON', en honneur de son art voluptueux et suave, Pierre Rode fut l'un des plus talentueux violonistes français de la fin du XVIIIe et du début du XIXe siècle. Il était aussi compositeur. Certains de ses concertos étaient joués par Paganini[2]. Dans ses œuvres comme dans son jeu, il associait la tendresse et le lyrisme à une virtuosité qui époustoufla ses contemporains.

Né à Bordeaux en 1774, Rode eut comme premier professeur Fauvel. Ce dernier, conscient du talent remarquable de son élève, décida de l'emmener à Paris en 1787 (Rode est âgé de treize ans), où il est présenté à Giovanni Battista Viotti, qui était directeur du Théâtre de Monsieur (théâtre Feydeau). Il prit alors le garçon comme élève et le fit entendre au Concert spirituel. Rode y fit aussi la connaissance de deux autres jeunes violonistes talentueux de sa génération, Rodolphe Kreutzer[3] et Pierre Baillot[4]. Musicien militaire comme clarinettiste en 1793, il partit ensuite à Rouen, puis fit un long séjour en Espagne où il se lia d'amitié avec Boccherini. En 1800, il fut choisi comme violon solo de la musique du Premier consul (Napoléon). Il partit ensuite en Russie, où il fut nommé maître de Chapelle par le tsar Alexandre Ier. Rentrant en France en 1806, il ne connut qu'un succès d'estime; piqué au vif il préféra se produire à Paris uniquement dans des concerts

---

1. POUGIN, Arthur. *Notice sur Rode*, Paris, Pottier de Lalaine, 1874, p. 45.
2. CONESTABILE, Giancarlo. *Vita di Niccolò Paganini da Genova*, Perugia, Tip. V. Bartelli, 1851, in: HUET, Félix. *Étude sur les différentes écoles de violon depuis Corelli jusqu'à Baillot: précédée d'un examen sur l'art de jouer des instruments à archet au XVIIe siècle*, Châlons-sur-Marne, F. Thouille, 1880, p. 106.
3. Élève d'Anton Stamitz, Kreutzer fut professeur au Conservatoire de Paris depuis sa fondation en 1795 jusqu'en 1826. Il dirigea aussi à l'Opéra de Paris et en fut directeur.
4. Élève de Viotti, Baillot fut admis dès 1791 à l'orchestre du Théâtre de Monsieur (l'Opéra-Comique) et devint professeur au Conservatoire de Paris en 1795.

privés. Il séjourna à Berlin de 1814 à 1820, où il fut un proche de la famille Mendelssohn, puis retourna en France, où il s'éteindra en 1830, dans sa cinquante-septième année.

De cette brève biographie de Rode, quelques points méritent d'être développés. D'abord, on ne peut appréhender Rode sans insister sur le rôle joué par Viotti, son professeur. Ce dernier exerça une influence considérable non seulement sur son jeune élève Rode, mais sur toute cette génération de violonistes, avec notamment Kreutzer et Baillot. Viotti fut l'élève de Pugnani à Turin, lui-même élève de Tartini et de Somis de qui il reçut les traditions de Corelli. Virtuose très apprécié, voyageant dans toute l'Europe, il se produisit en 1782 au Concert spirituel à Paris où il vécut à partir de cette date. Il fut un moment au service de la reine Marie-Antoinette, puis s'exila à Londres lors de la Révolution française pour retourner dans la capitale française après 1818. A un siècle d'intervalle, Viotti joua pour le concerto pour violon un rôle similaire à celui que remplit pour l'opéra français un autre italien de naissance, Jean-Baptiste Lully[5]. Il transforma le genre en lui donnant des caractéristiques expressives nouvelles.

Puis, il convient d'évoquer l'école française de violon qui connut plusieurs époques fastes, marquées chacune par une certaine unité stylistique. Entre celle de Jean-Marie Leclair et de Gaviniès durant la première moitié du XVIIIe siècle et celle de Viotti, prolongée par Rode, Kreutzer et Baillot, il n'existe pas de filiation directe[6]. Les contemporains de Viotti furent impressionnés par la nouveauté de son jeu et de ses compositions; son premier concert parisien au Concert spirituel en 1782 marqua les esprits. Ainsi peut-on lire dans l'*Encyclopédie du dix-neuvième siècle* d'Ange de Saint-Priest: «C'est en mars 1782 qu'il débuta au concert spirituel par un concerto de sa composition, et justifia, surpassa même, dès cette première épreuve, ce que la renommée s'était plu à publier de son talent merveilleux [...]. Il devint le fondateur d'une école nouvelle, à qui l'école actuelle doit tout ce qu'elle a de réel et de durable»[7]. La Laurencie considère Viotti comme un «tournant dans l'histoire du violon»[8]. Entre ses œuvres et celles de Pugnani existe une différence telle que l'on change de paradigme. Gelrud[9] pense qu'il y a sans doute plus de dissemblances de jeu entre Viotti et son professeur Pugnani qu'entre Viotti et Menuhin, bien qu'un siècle les sépare. Portée par Viotti, Rode, Kreutzer et Baillot, l'école française de violon essaima, avec notamment

---

5. Lavignac, Albert – La Laurencie, Lionel de. *Encyclopédie de la musique et dictionnaire du Conservatoire*, Paris, Delagrave, 1931, p. 1524.

6. Pierre Gaviniès (1728-1800) resta proche de la génération précédente, publiant par exemple des sonates avec basse chiffrée selon la tradition baroque. Etant plus âgé, il n'enseigna que brièvement au Conservatoire de Paris aux côtés de Rode, Baillot et Kreutzer.

7. Saint-Priest, Ange de. *Encyclopédie du dix-neuvième siècle: répertoire universel des sciences, des lettres et des arts, avec la biographie de tous les hommes célèbres*, 27 vol., Paris, Au bureau de l'Encyclopédie, 1838-1853, vol. XXV, p. 355.

8. La Laurencie, Lionel de. *L'école française de violon de Lully à Viotti: études d'histoire et d'esthétique*, 3 vol., Paris, Delagrave, 1922-1924, vol. I, 'Avant-propos'.

9. «Unbridgeable gap»; Gelrud, Paul Geoffrey. *Foundations and Development of the Modern French Violin School*, M.A. Thesis, Ithaca (NY), Cornell University, 1940, p. 4.

Hubert Léonard et Joseph Lambert Massart à Paris, puis Charles-Auguste de Bériot et Henry Vieuxtemps à Bruxelles. La troisième génération est celle d'Eugène Ysaÿe. La tradition fut ensuite transmise à des violonistes de talent tels Arthur Grumiaux et Ginette Neveu.

Le premier genre dans lequel les compositeurs de l'école française de violon s'illustrèrent, furent des concertos pour leur propre instrument, qu'ils jouaient eux-mêmes. Viotti, Rode, Baillot et Kreutzer composèrent un total de soixante-dix concertos d'une remarquable homogénéité. Ils composèrent aussi de nombreux airs variés pour violon, seul Kreutzer composa près de quarante opéras, genre qu'il connaissait parce qu'il fut chef puis directeur de l'Opéra de Paris. Rode composa treize concertos pour violon, dont certains furent réimprimés sans interruption, et pour lesquels de grands violonistes, tel Wieniawski, composèrent des cadences.

Dans les concertos pour violon de Rode, la virtuosité est omniprésente. D'aucuns ont pu la trouver excessive[10]. Au-delà du goût des critiques ou des considérations patriotiques qui fondent en partie le jugement de Schering, il est indéniable que Rode imprima son style personnel aux traits de bravoure de ses concertos et que sa conception de la virtuosité eut une influence sur les générations suivantes de violonistes.

Une virtuosité omniprésente

Les passages virtuoses des mouvements extrêmes des concertos de Rode se distinguent nettement de ceux du mouvement lent central. Mais dans les trois mouvements, l'intérêt pour certaines sonorités est à l'origine d'une forme particulière de virtuosité.

Une virtuosité démonstrative dans les mouvements extrêmes

Les mouvements extrêmes des concertos ont une virtuosité similaire. Rode recherche la variété des coups d'archet. L'opposition entre le caractère souvent héroïque du premier mouvement et celui dansant du final est rehaussée par les différences de rythme. Le binaire domine les premiers mouvements et le ternaire s'impose souvent dans le final.

Les sections virtuoses des mouvements extrêmes sont nombreuses et irriguent l'ensemble de l'œuvre. La virtuosité y est exubérante, conçue pour impressionner. Elle se caractérise par les courbes mélodiques et les coups d'archets utilisés et s'appuie sur de longs passages de stabilité rythmique, souvent des doubles-croches ou plus rarement des triolets de croches ou de doubles-croches. Aucune monotonie n'est tolérée du fait de l'enchaînement constamment renouvelé de coups d'archets différents et d'articulations variées. Dans chaque passage virtuose, les formules évoluent au fur et à mesure; la même est parfois répétée deux fois au même degré, ou à un degré différent à l'occasion d'une marche d'harmonie, mais la caractéristique principale des passages des concertos de Rode,

---

[10]. SCHERING, Arnold. *Geschichte des Instrumentalkonzerts bis auf die Gegenwart*, Leipzig, Breitkopf & Härtel, 1905 (Kleine Handbücher der Musikgeschichte nach Gattungen), p. 171.

comme plus généralement de ceux de l'école française, est la modification progressive des formules, ce qui confère un dynamisme propre.

Dans le premier solo du 11ᵉ Concerto (Ex. 1), une section virtuose de dix-neuf mesures s'inscrit entièrement sur des doubles-croches. Il n'y a pas plus de deux mesures successives avec des articulations identiques, on trouve des liaisons par seize notes, puis par seize notes mais avec articulation par deux, des notes piquées avec accents sur la deuxième (passé à la postérité sous le nom de 'coup d'archet Viotti'), des liaisons par huit, par quatre, un accord de septième de dominante orné, mis en valeur par un trille sur chaque note réelle, une mesure de changement rythmique avec un motif en croche doublement pointée — triple-croche, des groupes de huit notes avec une piquée, deux liées, une piquée, quatre détachées, des groupes similaires avec ajout de trille, et enfin des liaisons longues dont certaines enjambant la barre de mesure. Dans ce passage, le rythme est stable, l'harmonie claire et les contours mélodiques simples — seules les mesures 89 et 90 s'appuient sur les notes principales du premier thème, les autres sont de nature harmonique avec gammes et arpèges. L'extrême variété du passage provient de l'articulation et des coups d'archet.

Ex. 1: Pierre Rode, Concerto Op. 23 n° 11 en Ré majeur, 1ᵉʳ mouvement, partie de violon solo, mes. 74-98.

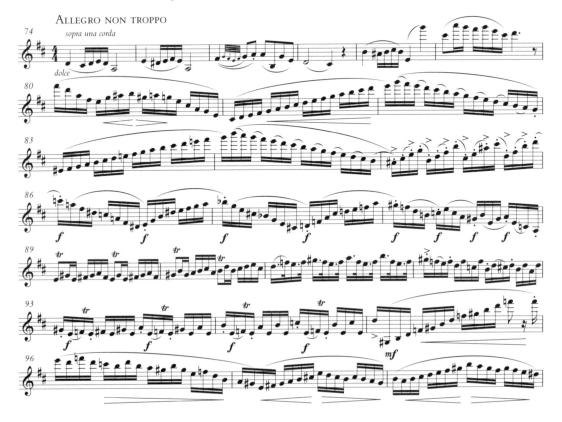

A l'intérieur d'un mouvement d'un concerto, chaque section virtuose a des contours mélodiques et des articulations similaires mais différents de ceux de la section précédente, afin de créer une impression d'unité tout en attisant la curiosité de l'auditeur. Dans ce même Concerto n° 11, la section virtuose suivante de vingt-quatre mesures s'appuie aussi sur un rythme de doubles-croches. Deux mesures utilisent des doubles-croches pointées — triples, mais soit les liaisons sont différentes de celles de la section précédente, soit des appogiatures sont ajoutées. On trouve des liaisons par deux entre 4e-1e et 2e-3e doubles-croches d'un groupe de quatre, deux temps avec des triolets de doubles-croches, du staccato, et mélodiquement des intervalles plus grands (Ex. 2).

Ex. 2: Pierre Rode, Concerto Op. 23 n° 11 en Ré majeur, 1er mouvement, partie de violon solo, mes. 144-168.

La virtuosité de Rode n'est pas recherche de vitesse. Les indications de tempo des premiers mouvements de ses concertos sont *Allegro moderato, Moderato, Maestoso, Allegro giusto, Allegro commodo, Allegro non troppo*. Dans les finals, on trouve parfois seulement le terme *Rondo*, ou des indications de tempo comme *Allegretto* et *Allegretto moderato*. Jamais le tempo demandé n'est *Allegro assai, Vivace* ou *Presto*. Les thèmes ne sont pas le lieu d'acrobaties virtuoses; on y rencontre peu de doubles-cordes et des notes souvent conjointes. Ils nécessitent un son plein et un vibrato intense. Le tempo modéré permet au son de s'épanouir, laisse le temps au soliste de produire des inflexions dans la mélodie et les formules virtuoses peuvent être énoncées très distinctement. Un tempo non exagérément rapide permet aussi de rendre lyriques et vibrants les passages de trait.

Une virtuosité d'ornementation dans les deuxièmes mouvements

Dans les mouvements lents, les passages virtuoses sont à rapprocher de la tradition non-écrite issue de la période baroque. La virtuosité est conçue comme une ornementation au service d'un thème chanté. C'est là que le brillant s'affirme. Contrairement aux mouvements extrêmes, il n'existe pas de sections virtuoses longues nettement séparées des parties thématiques. Par exemple dans l'*Andante* du Concerto n° 12 (Ex. 3), l'écriture est très clairement inspirée par la tradition d'ornementation baroque, avec des trilles, des gruppettos. Certaines terminaisons sont écrites, par exemple à la mesure 16, et de manière plus expansive aux mesures 19 ou 28. Le canevas du thème pourrait se résumer à des notes longues, mais elles sont reliées entre elles par des formules rapides, par exemple aux mesures 18 et 20. Cette écriture ornée présente des similitudes avec celle qu'un auditeur de Corelli a rapportée à propos de ses Sonates Op. 5, antérieures de plus d'un siècle. En effet, la première édition de Corelli (qu'il avait datée du 1er janvier 1700 pour annoncer une nouvelle écriture pour le siècle naissant) est épurée, ne comprenant que les notes thématiques, alors qu'une quatrième édition de 1715 retranscrit une version avec de nombreuses ornementations telles que le compositeur les aurait jouées lui-même[11]. L'observation de ce mouvement lent du concerto de Rode permet de se rendre compte que la tradition du XVIIIe siècle est encore bien vivante. On ne s'étonnera pas que dans son *Art du violon* publié en 1834, Baillot consacre encore de nombreuses pages à l'ornementation[12].

Egalement en lien avec la tradition baroque de l'improvisation, le compositeur note volontiers lui-même les cadences, souvent nommées 'point d'orgue'. Celles-ci peuvent se trouver dans tous les mouvements, mais elles sont surtout importantes dans le deuxième. Les grandes sections formelles de ces mouvements bi- ou tripartites sont séparées par de tels passages. La virtuosité permet d'en mettre en relief la structure. Par exemple dans l'*Adagio* du Concerto n° 12 se trouvent deux cadences, l'une sépare les deux sections (mesures 22 à 24 de l'Ex. 3), l'autre étant placée à la fin du mouvement.

---

[11]. Les deux versions peuvent être comparées dans l'édition CORELLI, Arcangelo. *Zwölf sonaten / Douze sonates / Twelve sonatas Op. 5*, Bernhard Paumgartner éd., Mainz, Schott, 1953.

[12]. Baillot propose d'orner des pièces de Corelli et donne aussi un exemple d'ornementation d'un mouvement lent d'un concerto de Viotti; BAILLOT, Pierre(-Marie-François de Sales). *L'Art du violon: nouvelle méthode*, Paris, Au Dépôt central de la musique, [1835], pp. 156-164. Des pages encore plus nombreuses sont consacrées aux points d'orgue et préludes (pp. 165-186).

Ex. 3: Pierre Rode, Concerto Op. 27 n° 12 en Mi majeur, 2ᵉ mouvement, partie de violon solo, mes. 9-29.

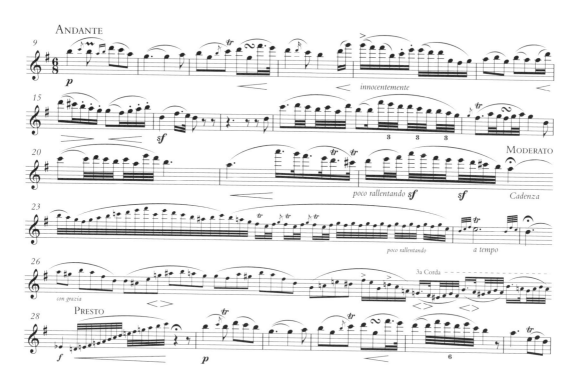

Une virtuosité au service de la recherche du timbre

Dans les concertos de Rode, beaucoup de thèmes portent des indications sur le choix de la corde sur laquelle il convient de les interpréter. Jouer tout un thème sur une seule corde exige une forme de virtuosité, car il ne s'agit pas du doigté le plus sûr ou le plus facile. Dans l'*Art du violon*, Baillot donne des indications précieuses sur les différences de jeu entre les plus grands violonistes français[13]. Il dit que Viotti démanchait peu, Kreutzer beaucoup ce qui convient aux thèmes hardis, et que Rode restait toujours sur la même corde. Le jeu de Rode permettait donc plus que celui de ses contemporains de créer une unité de timbre.

En effet, chaque corde a son timbre propre. Pour appuyer le lyrisme et varier les inflexions, les violonistes français de l'époque de Rode accordaient une importance toute particulière au nuancier de timbres que l'on peut obtenir sur chaque corde. Baillot y consacre un chapitre dans l'*Art du violon*, expliquant dans quel registre et sur quelle corde le son du violon peut imiter celui de la flûte, du cor, de la trompette, de l'harmonica ou de la harpe. La corde de *mi* qui produit un son argentin et clair convient particulièrement

---

13. *Ibidem*, pp. 149-150.

aux passages brillants et peut imiter la flûte, celle de *la* est plus douce et pénétrante et peut rappeler le hautbois ou la musette, celle de *ré* a un caractère noble et velouté. Enfin la corde de *sol* plaît surtout à Baillot par sa puissance car «elle favorise l'expression pour atteindre le sublime»[14] mais peut se prêter aussi aux imitations du cor ou de la trompette.

Un même thème est souvent donné successivement à des octaves différentes et pour que chaque occurrence ait son caractère propre, le compositeur demande à ce que chacune soit jouée sur une corde en particulier. Ceci oblige le violoniste à démancher souvent, mais permet de garder une unité de timbre pour chaque phrase. L'Ex. 4, extrait du 2e solo du premier mouvement du Concerto n° 8 illustre cette manière de composer. Le thème énoncé d'abord sur la corde de *mi* est ensuite transposé deux octaves plus grave et prolongé entièrement sur la corde de *sol*. Beethoven, sans doute sous l'influence des violonistes français qu'il admirait, a repris ce procédé dans le final de son Concerto pour violon Op. 77. Ce type d'indications de doigté, existant mais rare chez d'autres compositeurs, est courant aussi chez les compositeurs français des siècles suivants, fussent-ils ou non violonistes. Par exemple dans son quatuor à cordes, Ravel précise très fréquemment sur quelle corde doit être joué un passage déterminé. L'attention portée au timbre est une préoccupation récurrente chez les musiciens français que l'on trouve sous des formes différentes aussi bien chez Couperin que chez Debussy.

Si des effets d'imitation existaient déjà, par exemple dans la *Sonata Representativa* de Heinrich Ignaz Biber[15], et si le jeu sur une seule corde sera exploité très habilement par Paganini, par exemple dans ses *Variations sur le Moïse de Rossini*[16], l'utilisation qu'en fait Rode tient moins de la démonstration ou du coup d'éclat mais participe à la recherche d'une grande expressivité dans le respect du «bon goût».

Ex. 4: Pierre Rode, Concerto Op. 13 n° 8 en Mi mineur, 1er mouvement, partie de violon solo, mes. 68-81.

---

14. *Ibidem*, p. 142.

15. Heinrich Ignaz Biber (1644-1704). Dans sa *Sonata Representativa*, plusieurs animaux sont imités, par exemple le rossignol, la grenouille ou le chat.

16. Dans ces variations sur le thème 'Dal tuo stellato' de l'opéra *Mosè in Egitto* de Gioachino Rossini, le violoniste joue exclusivement sur la corde de sol et imite tour à tour d'autres instruments, la flûte, la clarinette, le violoncelle.

Une virtuosité expressive

Chez Rode comme chez les autres compositeurs de l'école française de violon de la fin du XVIIIᵉ et du début du XIXᵉ siècle, la virtuosité et l'énoncé des thèmes sont essentiellement le fait de la partie du soliste. L'école française est restée fidèle à la tradition baroque et à l'école italienne d'un soliste dominant l'ensemble. Cette conception de la musique dépasse le cadre du concerto, puisqu'elle se trouve aussi dans les quatuors concertants, dans lesquels le premier violon porte tout le chant avec le soutien harmonique des trois autres instruments. Le premier violon pouvait même jouer debout et les autres assis. Cette approche est radicalement différente de celle des quatuors de Haydn qui, au plus tard à partir de l'Op. 33, peuvent rappeler une aimable conversation[17], et dans lesquels chaque instrument peut endosser le rôle de meneur et où toutes les combinaisons instrumentales sont possibles.

La virtuosité déployée par Rode est d'importance non seulement parce qu'elle est impressionnante et omniprésente mais aussi parce qu'elle joue un rôle structurel dans les concertos.

L'orchestre au service de la virtuosité

Dans les concertos pour violon de Rode, la splendeur de l'orchestre se manifeste pleinement dans le premier tutti. De même que dans les concertos de son professeur Viotti, le premier tutti est généralement long et finement orchestré. Ce souvenir de Baillot d'une exécution d'un concerto de Viotti illustre l'importance et la beauté du premier tutti: «Le tutti du dix-huitième fut applaudi comme une des plus belles symphonies de Haydn»[18]. Tous les autres tuttis des trois mouvements de concerto sont très brefs. Dans le premier mouvement, l'orchestre y joue souvent le thème principal comme une ritournelle; dans le second, l'orchestre reprend son rôle d'annonce de l'entrée du soliste puisque le seul tutti, bref cette fois-ci, est au début avec huit ou douze mesures d'introduction; dans le troisième mouvement, le tutti joue souvent tout ou partie du thème de refrain du rondo, mais ses interventions sont toujours courtes. La différence entre la richesse et la longueur du premier tutti et la brièveté des suivants est frappante.

Pourquoi l'orchestre ne joue-t-il un rôle important que dans le premier tutti du premier mouvement? Celui-ci prend la forme d'une exposition orchestrale, comme dans

---

17. «Une femme d'esprit disait qu'en entendant les quatuors de Haydn, elle croyait assister à la conversation de quatre personnes aimables»; *Lettre italiennes sur Haydn* de Giuseppe Carpani, repris par Stendhal dans sa *Vie de Haydn*.

18. BAILLOT, Pierre(-Marie-François de Sales). *Notice sur J.-B. Viotti, né en 1755 à Fontaneto, en Piémont, mort à Londres, le 3 mars 1824*, Paris, Imprimerie de Hocquet, 1825, pp. 6-7.

tout concerto influencé par la forme sonate. Mais le choix de n'accorder à l'orchestre que le premier tutti correspond à une conception différente, héritée du théâtre classique. De même qu'un roi ne s'y présente que précédé de sa garde et entouré de sa cour, les deux premières scènes sont souvent consacrées à l'explication de la situation par des valets, soubrettes ou confidents, mais rarement par les personnages principaux. Dans son *Discours sur le poëme dramatique* de 1660, Corneille reprend en les développant les idées d'Aristote: «Il [le prologue] doit contenir les semences de tout ce qui doit arriver [...] Communément on y faisait l'ouverture du sujet, pour instruire les spectateurs de tout ce qui s'était passé avant le commencement de l'action qu'on allait représenter, et de tout ce qu'il fallait qu'il sût pour comprendre ce qu'il allait voir»[19]. La conception du concerto mise en œuvre par Rode et formalisée par Baillot semble parallèle à cette pratique théâtrale: «Dans le concerto: le Violon doit y développer toute sa puissance, né pour dominer, c'est ici qu'il règne en souverain et qu'il parle en maître [...] un orchestre nombreux obéit à sa voix et la symphonie qui lui sert de prélude, l'annonce avec noblesse»[20].

Le violon soliste domine l'orchestre. Il ne s'agit ni d'un rapport d'égalité, ni même de rivalité. Tant par la richesse de son introduction que par sa discrétion ultérieure, l'écriture orchestrale est entièrement dévolue à la mise en valeur du soliste. L'orchestre et le soliste ne dialoguent ni ne s'opposent. Après avoir annoncé par un tutti long et somptueux l'arrivée du violon qui dominera en maître, l'orchestre joue de brefs tuttis qui permettent de créer un contraste. Dans les solos, l'orchestre accompagne avec discrétion, sans porter le discours musical, ayant un rôle de soutien harmonique sans être chargé d'énoncer les éléments thématiques ou de s'opposer au soliste. Un extrait du premier mouvement du Concerto Op. 9 n° 7 (Ex. 5) illustre la place respective de l'orchestre et du soliste dans les solos. Après le premier tutti joué par tout l'orchestre et qui se termine par un grand unisson, le soliste est accompagné par un tapis de cordes très léger, fait de notes longues tenues et de battements lents legato, les vents n'intervenant jamais pendant tout le solo.

D'autres compositeurs avaient des conceptions très différentes du lien entre orchestre et soliste. Dans son *Versuch*, Heinrich Christoph Koch avait pris pour modèle les concertos de Mozart et décrit ainsi les rapports entre le soliste et l'orchestre:

> Il me semble que l'on doive juger le concerto d'un tout autre point de vue que celui du solo. L'expression des sentiments du soliste est un monologue au ton passionné, le soliste est replié sur lui-même, rien de l'extérieur ne peut avoir la moindre influence sur l'expression de ses sentiments. Si l'on observe un concerto bien pensé, dans lequel pendant le solo les parties accompagnantes ne sont pas seulement là pour combler un vide entre la partie supérieure et la basse, alors l'on trouve un dialogue passionné du soliste et de l'orchestre

---

19. Corneille, Pierre. 'Trois Discours sur le poëme dramatique', in: *Théâtre complet*, Pierre Lièvre, éd., 2 vol., Paris, Gallimard, 1950 (La Pléiade, 19), vol. 1, pp. 79-81.

20. Baillot, Pierre(-Marie-François de Sales). *L'Art du violon, op. cit.* (voir la note 12), p. 267.

Ex. 5: Pierre Rode, Concerto Op. 9 n° 7 en La mineur, 1ᵉʳ mouvement, mes. 42-61.

l'accompagnant; il lui expose ses sentiments, bientôt celui-ci lui adresse de courtes phrases d'approbation, bientôt il [l'orchestre] essaye dans l'allegro d'attiser encore ses sentiments; bref, je m'imagine le concerto comme quelque chose de semblable à la tragédie des anciens, où l'acteur n'exprimait pas ses sentiments à l'auditoire mais au chœur, et celui-ci était intimement lié à l'action et était en même temps habilité à prendre part à l'expression des sentiments. Ainsi l'auditeur, sans y perdre quelque chose, est seulement la troisième personne qui prend part à l'exposé passionné du soliste et de l'orchestre l'accompagnant[21].

[21]. «Mir scheint es überhaupt, als müsse man das Concert aus einem ganz anderen Gesichtspunkte beurteilen, als das Solo. Der Ausdruck der Empfindungen des Solospielers ist ein Monolog in leidenschaftlichen Tönen, der Solospieler ist dabey gleichsam in sich selbst gekehrt, nichts äußerliches hat den geringsten Einfluß auf den Ausdruck seiner Empfindungen. Betrachtet man aber ein gut gearbeitetes Concert, in dem während des Solo die begleitenden Stimmen nicht blos da sind, um dieses oder jenes, zwischen der Oberstimme und dem Basse fehlende Intervall der Accorde anzuschlagen, so findet man eine leidenschaftliche Unterhaltung des Concertspielers mit dem ihn begleitenden Orchester; diesem trägt er seine Empfindungen vor, dieses winkt ihm durch kurze eingestreute Sätze bald Beyfall zu, bald bejaht es gleichsam seinen Ausdruck; bald sucht es im Allegro seine erhabenen Empfindungen noch mehr anzufachen; kurz ich stelle mir unter dem Concerte etwas ähnliches mit der Tragödie der Alten vor, wo der Schauspieler seine Empfindungen nicht gegen das Parterre, sondern gegen den Chor äußerte, und dieser hingegen auf das genaueste mit in die

Ce *dialogue passionné*, échange complexe entre les différentes parties, correspond à une interaction riche, une écriture avec des parties instrumentales variées à l'orchestre. L'orchestre a de courtes interventions, soit en tutti, soit réservées à certains instruments qui répondent à un motif énoncé par le soliste. Fréquente dans les concertos de Mozart, ce type d'écriture est totalement absent dans l'école française de violon.

La virtuosité comme amplification

Les passages virtuoses ne peuvent se résumer à une démonstration d'agilité et de bon goût, ils occupent dans les concertos pour violon de Rode une place structurelle. Leur fonction est de prolonger les thèmes. Après chaque énoncé thématique, le soliste poursuit le discours musical par une séquence virtuose en perpétuelle évolution. Cette manière de développer est construite différemment dans les œuvres d'autres compositeurs de la même époque, en particulier de ceux de l'école viennoise.

Par exemple, dans son Concerto pour violon Op. 77 en Ré majeur, Beethoven insère aussi de nombreux passages virtuoses. Il était un admirateur des violonistes français, notamment de Kreutzer à qui il dédia sa neuvième Sonate pour violon et piano, et de Rode à qui il dédia la dixième. Son écriture violonistique dans le concerto était largement influencée par eux, ainsi qu'en témoigne la similitude des passages virtuoses[22]. La différence entre le concerto de Beethoven et ceux de Rode ne réside pas dans le choix des cellules virtuoses (par exemple figurations en arpèges, octaves ou tierces, rythme en doubles-croches ou en triolets en doubles-croches, coups d'archet alternant notes détachées ou liées, accentuées ou piquées) mais dans la manière de les utiliser. Pour chaque section virtuose, Beethoven n'utilise qu'une seule formule et construit un développement à partir des thèmes de son concerto en les morcelant, en modulant, en les ornant de formules virtuoses. Au contraire, Rode ne développe pas les thèmes mais les prolonge, les amplifie par des sections virtuoses aux formules extrêmement variées. Les passages virtuoses sont souvent non-thématiques, s'appuyant sur une succession d'accords sans lien avec les principaux thèmes du mouvement. Ce type d'écriture, avec une harmonie assez simple, est plus décoratif que dans l'école viennoise.

L'analyse actuelle tend à valoriser davantage le développement tel qu'il était pratiqué par l'école viennoise. Cette tendance peut s'expliquer par le fait qu'historiquement Mozart,

---

Handlung verflochten, und zugleich berechtigt war, an dem Ausdrucke der Empfindung Antheil zu haben. Alsdenn aber ist dem Zuhörer, jedoch ohne etwas dabey zu verlieren, erst die dritte Person, die an dem leidenschaftlichen Vortrage des Concertspielers an das ihn begleitende Orchester theilnehmen kann»; Koch, Heinrich Christoph. *Versuch einer Anleitung zur Composition*, 3 vol., Leipzig, Adam Friedrich Böhme, 1782-1793, vol. III, pp. 331-332.

[22]. Schwarz, Boris. 'Beethoven and the French School', in: *Musical Quarterly*, XLIV/4 (octobre 1958), pp. 431-447.

Haydn et Beethoven ont brillé plus que leurs contemporains qu'ils ont relégués à la seconde place. Mais la prépondérance de ces trois compositeurs ne justifie pas que leurs œuvres servent de canon formel exclusif et de jauge qualitative aux autres œuvres qui leur sont contemporaines. Certains auteurs ont montré les limites du modèle viennois pour l'analyse de genres variés allant de la pièce pour piano au quatuor à cordes[23]. Christian Speck en particulier montre que le caractère exemplaire du style des quatuors à cordes de Haydn et Mozart s'imposa progressivement comme canon formel[24]. Les concertos de l'époque viennoise peuvent servir de contre-corpus, comme outil de comparaison[25] mais leur analyse ne devrait pas induire des jugements de valeur négatifs sur les concertos de l'école française, et de Rode en particulier, du fait qu'ils correspondent à un autre idéal esthétique.

Sans doute s'agit-il là d'une caractéristique générale de l'esthétique de la musique française. Debussy affirmera: «On combine, on construit, on imagine des thèmes qui veulent exprimer des idées; on les développe, on les modifie à la rencontre d'autres thèmes qui représentent d'autres idées; on fait de la métaphysique, mais on ne fait pas de musique»[26], ou aussi «Je me persuade de plus en plus que la musique n'est pas par son essence une chose qui puisse se couler dans une forme rigoureuse et traditionnelle»[27].

Dans L'Art du violon, Baillot insiste sur ce que la tâche première de la musique est d'attirer l'auditeur dans un émerveillement au-delà du rationnel[28]. Cette approche peut expliquer que dans ses concertos Rode ait choisi d'assigner aux passages virtuoses la place qui aurait pu être dévolue au développement thématique. Les traits ne développent pas au sens viennois, ils amplifient les thèmes principaux, en prolongeant leur caractère et en l'intensifiant par une écriture toujours renouvelée.

---

[23]. Par exemple: FEND, Michael. 'The problem of the French Revolution in Music Historiography and History', in: *Musicology and Sister Disciplines. Past, Present, Future: Proceedings of the 16th International Congress of the International Musicological Society, London, 1997*, David Green, Ian Rumbold et Jonathan King éd., Oxford, Oxford University Press, 2000, pp. 239-250; GERHARD, Anselm. *London und der Klassizismus in der Musik: die Idee der «absoluten Musik» und Muzio Clementis Klavierwerk*, Stuttgart-Weimar, J. B. Metzter, 2002.

[24]. «Das konzertante Quartett wird durch den Quartettstil von Haydn und Mozart nicht sogleich verdrängt, sondern besteht zu Beginn des 19. Jahrhunderts auch dann weiter, als die Theorie bereits dem Wiener Klassischen Quartett den Rang des Mustergültigen zugesprochen hatte»; SPECK, Christian. 'Einige Bemerkungen an den Quartetten Op. 22 von Viotti', in: *Giovanni Battista Viotti: A Composer between the Two Revolutions*, Massimiliano Sala éd., Bologne, Ut Orpheus, 2006 (Ad Parnassum studies, 2), pp. 337-361: 359.

[25]. L'analyse, et *a fortiori* la réflexion sur un style, ne peut se pratiquer que par référence à un contre-corpus; LACHAT-SARRETE, Priscille. 'The Setting-Up and the Role of a Couple «Corpus/Counter-Corpus»: The Example of the Nineteenth-Century Student Concertos', in: *Musical Explorations*, XIII (2012), pp. 59-92.

[26]. DEBUSSY, Claude. 'La musique d'aujourd'hui et celle de demain', in: *Monsieur Croche et autres écrits*, édition complète de son œuvre critique avec une introduction et des notes par François Lesure, Paris, Gallimard, 1971, p. 281.

[27]. ID. *Lettres de Claude Debussy à son éditeur*, Paris, A. Durand et fils, 1927, p. 55, lettre de 1907.

[28]. SCHUENEMANN, Bruce R. *The French Violin School, Viotti, Rode, Kreutzer, Baillot and Their Contemporaries*, préface par William E. Studwell, bibliographie par María de Jesús Ayala-Schueneman, Kingsville (TX), The Lyre Orpheus Press, 2002, p. 10.

UNE VIRTUOSITÉ D'AVENIR

La virtuosité de Rode s'inscrit dans le cadre d'une technique de violon renouvelée par les musiciens de l'école française de violon; cette modernisation de la technique fut rendue possible par l'adoption du nouvel archet de Tourte. La technique de Rode, Kreutzer et Baillot essaima ensuite au travers de leur enseignement et de leurs compositions pour devenir le langage violonistique universel du violoniste moderne.

L'adoption de l'archet de Tourte

Au XVIIIᵉ siècle, les musiciens se servaient de plusieurs types d'archets selon l'œuvre qu'ils interprétaient, l'archet était plus court pour la musique dansante et plus long pour les sonates[29]. Considéré comme le Stradivarius de l'archet, François-Xavier Tourte (1747-1835) conçut un nouvel archet qui fut adopté par Viotti. Rode jouait ce même archet qui permettait une virtuosité d'archet nouvelle.

L'ancien ouvrier horloger François-Xavier Tourte était capable de travailler à la fois le bois et le métal, qu'il savait manier de par sa formation d'horloger, et non un seul de ces matériaux car il était établi «hors les murs» de Paris, dans un lieu où le régime corporatiste ne s'appliquait pas. Ses archets comportaient des pièces métalliques: il ajouta une plaque d'argent fixée par une goupille pour garnir le bouton, et une autre pour pincer les crins à la hausse[30]. Tourte fut l'initiateur d'une normalisation tacite[31] tant de la longueur de la baguette (environ 74-75 cm), de la longueur des crins (environ 65 cm) que de la largeur du ruban (11 mm). Alors que les archets plus anciens étaient fabriqués dans une grande variété de bois indigènes, ceux de Tourte, surtout s'il s'agissait d'instruments de haut de gamme, étaient taillés systématiquement dans du bois de Pernambouc importé du Brésil. L'usage de cet archet, normalisé dans ses dimensions et son bois, s'est généralisé en Europe dans les années 1830. Dans sa *Méthode pour le violon* de 1798, Michel Woldemar[32] présentait le 'modèle Tourte' comme celui joué par Viotti, puis en 1833, Louis Spohr en fait l'éloge dans sa *Violinschule*[33]. On assiste conjointement à une réduction du nombre de types d'archets, puisqu'auparavant chaque école avait le sien, et à une uniformisation de la tenue

---

[29]. Voir GEMINIANI, Francesco. *L'art de jouer du violon*, Paris, aux adresses ordinaires où se vend la musique, s.d., traduction augmentée de la version publiée à Londres en 1751.

[30]. Une autre pièce métallique, la plaque de coulisse garnissant la glissière sous la hausse qui coulisse sous la baguette d'archet, fut ajoutée par Nicolas Lupot.

[31]. BOYDEN, David D. 'The Violin Bow in the 18ᵗʰ Century', in: *Early Music*, VIII/2 (avril 1980), pp. 199-212: 199.

[32]. Michel Woldemar (1750-1815), violoniste français, auteur d'une *Grande méthode ou étude élémentaire pour le violon* en 1798, augmentée de quinze leçons faciles pour la 2ᵉ édition de 1800.

[33]. SPOHR, Louis. *Violinschule*, Hermann Schröder éd., Vienne, Haslinger, 1832.

de l'archet[34], à la hausse et non plus haut comme il était d'usage dans l'école italienne[35]. Des images d'époque de Geminiani, Corelli ou d'autres musiciens italiens montrent cette tenue, même les gravures de Paganini le présentent tenant l'archet très haut.

Ce nouvel archet, très équilibré, permet de maîtriser facilement un large spectre de coups d'archets, depuis les coups d'archets sautés tels le ricochet ou le sautillé jusqu'au jeu *cantabile*. Sans peine le violoniste peut obtenir une grande continuité dans le son; cet archet se prête particulièrement aux longs legatos qui s'accordent avec la sensibilité romantique naissante. Certains coups d'archet tels le martelé peuvent être exécutés tant au talon qu'à la pointe. La technique de violon présente dans les concertos de l'école française exige qu'ils soient joués avec ce nouvel archet. Les descriptions du début du XIXᵉ siècle sur le jeu de Viotti, Kreutzer, Rode et Baillot insistent sur la sonorité, l'élégance, la flamme; toutes ces caractéristiques ne sont pas liées à la technique de la main gauche mais à celle de l'archet. Le lyrisme et la virtuosité propres aux concertos de l'école française de violon sont donc intimement liés à l'utilisation de ce nouvel archet.

La postérité de la virtuosité de Rode

Les coups d'archets des traits virtuoses des concertos de Rode sont toujours très panachés, par opposition à la technique de la variation, où une seule formule est répétée, comme par exemple dans les airs variés. Chaque trait virtuose ne se définit pas par ses coups d'archets mais par le caractère qui doit y être exprimé. Dans son *Art du violon*, Baillot distingue les traits brillants, chantants, élégants, légers ou délicats. Des coups d'archets similaires peuvent servir pour des traits au caractère différent, celui-ci est donné par leur association à la courbe mélodique, à une nuance ou à des accents. Baillot demande à ce que l'on s'attache «à rendre le trait avec toutes ses intentions jusques dans les plus petits détails». L'agencement des coups d'archets variés «renferme un des principaux secrets du génie qui le distingue»[36].

En tant que professeur du Conservatoire de Paris, Rode transmit son mode de jeu mais aussi ses goûts esthétiques à ses élèves. Le plus célèbre d'entre eux est sans doute Joseph Böhm (1795-1876) lui-même professeur de Joseph Joachim (1831-1909)[37]. Rode enseigna bien moins longtemps au Conservatoire que Kreutzer ou Baillot, puisqu'il voyagea de nouveau à partir de 1805, mais sa volonté de transmettre son art ne fait pas doute; il aurait

---

[34]. GAUDFROY, Bernard. *Histoire de l'archet en France au dix-huitième siècle*, Paris, L'archet éditions, 2000 (L'Archet, 1), p. 25.

[35]. DELL'OLIO, Pepina. *Violin Bow Construction and Its Influence on Bowing Technique in the Eighteenth and Nineteenth Centuries*, D.M.A. Diss., Tallahassee, Florida State University, 2009 <http://etd.lib.fsu.edu/theses/available/etd-04202009-155942/unrestricted/Dell'OlioPTreatise.pdf> (29 janvier 2015).

[36]. BAILLOT, Pierre(-Marie-François de Sales). *L'Art du violon, op. cit.* (voir la note 12), p. 112.

[37]. Joseph Joachim fut l'ami et le dédicataire du concerto pour violon de Johannes Brahms, ainsi que de ceux d'Antonin Dvořák et Max Bruch et de la Fantaisie pour violon et orchestre de Robert Schumann.

voulu demander au Conservatoire cinq ou six élèves pour les former gratuitement, afin que l'école de Viotti soit propagée[38].

L'influence de Rode au travers d'ouvrages pédagogiques mérite d'être examinée de près. Il ne participa pas activement à la rédaction de la *Méthode du conservatoire*, par manque d'intérêt mais non par opposition à ce qu'elle contiendrait. Le comité du Conservatoire, soucieux d'obtenir une unité dans l'enseignement, arrêta dans une de ses séances que des ouvrages élémentaires seraient rédigés par les professeurs pour le solfège, le chant, l'harmonie et tous les instruments. Rode, Kreutzer et Baillot devaient travailler conjointement à cette méthode, mais Rode manqua d'entrain comme il l'explique à Baillot à la veille de son départ pour Saint-Pétersbourg en 1802:

> Je te jure qu'avec la meilleure volonté du monde, toutes les fois que j'ai voulu travailler à cet ouvrage, ces détails minutieux et ennuyeux m'en dégoûtaient aussitôt. […] Il est difficile à notre âge de s'occuper sérieusement d'une chose qui n'intéresse ni nos goûts ni notre talent. C'est quand on n'a plus la tête pleine de projets de toutes les couleurs qu'on renonce à soi pour s'occuper des autres, enfin quand on a rempli sa carrière qu'on peut se hasarder d'entreprendre une besogne comme celle-là. Aussi je t'assure que je suis encore à concevoir comment il t'est possible d'y mettre autant de suite. Quant à moi, je ne me sens ni assez de patience ni assez d'habitude d'un travail sérieux pour me charger désormais de pareille corvée. Mais si jamais le démon de faire une méthode me prend, ce ne sera que lorsque l'âge aura un peu calmé ma tête et que je pourrai me livrer tout entier à une occupation aussi importante et qui exige bien du dévouement[39].

Finalement, la *Méthode de violon* fut rédigée par Baillot et publiée chez Nadermann, conjointement avec Rode et Kreutzer, en 1802[40].

L'on joua «à la Rode», comme plus tard l'on jouera «à la Paganini»[41]. Il ne s'agit pas que d'une mode ou d'une célébrité passagère. Alors qu'il se rendait à Saint-Pétersbourg, Rode s'arrêta à Braunschweig et y donna un concert le 5 juillet 1802. Le jeune Louis

---

[38]. FAYOLLE, François. *Paganini et Bériot, ou Avis aux jeunes artistes qui se destinent à l'enseignement du violon*, Paris, Legouest, 1831, p. 40.

[39]. Voir MIGNOT, Jean. 'Pierre Rode, le violonniste virtuose de l'empereur', <http://www.napoleon.org/fr/salle_lecture/articles/files/@482171.asp>.

[40]. FÉTIS, François-Joseph. *Biographie universelle des musiciens et bibliographie générale de la musique, Supplément et complement*, 2 vol., Paris, Firmin-Didot, 1878-1880, vol. II, p. 20: «Rode, Kreutzer et Baillot se réunirent donc pour former une méthode de violon; mais si grand que fût le mérite des deux premiers, les études classiques de Baillot, ses habitudes de méditation et sa facilité à s'exprimer en termes élégans et précis, lui donnaient un avantage reconnu sur ses collaborateurs, pour la rédaction d'un tel ouvrage. D'un commun accord, il fut convenu que ce travail lui serait alors départi». La méthode fut retravaillée par Baillot qui publia *L'Art du violon* en 1835; cet ouvrage contient, outre des explications et recommandations techniques, des études et des conseils généraux pour les futurs artistes.

[41]. PINCHERLE, Marc. *Les violonistes compositeurs et virtuoses*, Paris, Laurens, 1922, p. 108.

Spohr qui connaissait et admirait déjà ses œuvres fut bouleversé par le jeu de Rode. Dans ses mémoires[42], il explique qu'il n'eut de cesse d'étudier les compositions de Rode afin de s'imprégner de son style. Il est intéressant qu'il ait choisi en priorité les concertos et non un autre genre, par exemple les airs variés qui n'ont pour certains rien à envier aux concertos en difficulté. La préférence de Spohr s'explique par le caractère exemplaire des concertos dont il estimait qu'ils contenaient la quintessence de l'art de leur auteur. Les compositions de Spohr portent aussi des traces de son admiration pour le violoniste français; ainsi par exemple les traits du Concerto n° 8 de Spohr ont des similarités frappantes avec ceux du Concerto n° 7 de Rode[43].

La diffusion de la technique et du mode de jeu de Rode doit aussi beaucoup à ses *24 Études ou caprices* qui sont d'excellents entraînements à ses concertos. En effet, l'accent est mis sur les traits, avec des études en rythme binaire qui permettent d'aborder plutôt l'exécution du premier mouvement, et d'autres en rythme ternaire qui préparent au troisième mouvement. On y trouve beaucoup de coups d'archet variés. Ces études sont aussi intéressantes car la virtuosité n'est jamais abstraite ou desséchée, chaque étude ayant un caractère particulier. La présence de nombreux mouvements lents introductifs qui facilitent l'apprentissage du jeu des passages chantées des mouvements rapides et du mouvement lent est également significative. Les études de Rode proposent une approche complète des difficultés rencontrées par le violoniste et ne s'arrêtent pas aux seules questions de célérité et de dextérité. Par exemple, pour appréhender le trait extrait du Concerto n° 11 présenté dans l'Ex. n° 1, l'on pourrait conseiller de travailler l'Études 3 (avec ses coups d'archet liés) et l'Étude 6 (pour l'enchaînement des gammes et des arpèges). La connaissance de l'ensemble des études de Rode constitue une excellente préparation pour jouer ses concertos, car tous les problèmes techniques spécifiques au compositeur y sont abordés.

Les études de Rode furent rééditées sans interruption jusqu'à aujourd'hui et furent adoptées, conjointement à celles de Kreutzer, non seulement en France[44] mais également

---

[42]. «Ich war schon eifrigst beflissen, sie [Rodes Spielweise] mir durch ein recht sorgfältiges Einüben der Rodeschen Kompositionen, die ich von ihm bei Hofe und in Privatgesellschaften gehört hatte, möglichst anzueignen»; Spohr, Louis. *Lebenserinnerungen*, Folker Göthel éd., 2 vol., Tutzing, Schneider, 1968, vol. 1, p. 66.

[43]. Brown, Clive. *Louis Spohr: eine kritische Biographie*, Berlin, Merseburger Verlag, 2009 (Edition Merseburger, 1555), pp. 68-69, version révisée par l'auteur de son propre ouvrage en anglais, *Louis Spohr: A Critical Biography*, Cambridge, Cambridge University Press, 1984.

[44]. Par exemple, Alexis Galpérine, professeur de violon au CNSMD de Paris et responsable de la formation des futurs professeurs, accorde aussi une place de choix aux études de Kreutzer et Rode, qu'il conseille de travailler intégralement, contrairement à celles de Gaviniès, Mazas ou Fiorillo, où un choix de quelques études suffit. Il conseille aussi de travailler des concertos de ces compositeurs. Galpérine, Alexis – Reverdito-Haas, Ana. *Un cursus de dix ans à la classe de violon*, Sampzon, Delatour, 2012.

par les écoles russe (Leopold Auer[45], Yuri Yankelevitch[46]) et américaine (Ivan Galamian[47]). D'autres violonistes proposèrent des exercices préparatoires à ces études[48], des méthodes de travail[49] ou des éditions commentées et annotées d'exercices et d'explications[50]. Les ouvrages pédagogiques de Rode et de Kreutzer constituent encore de nos jours des références reconnues et couramment utilisées. En quelque sorte, elles établissent la grammaire du violoniste. C'est pourquoi l'originalité des formules virtuoses de Rode, ainsi que celles de Kreutzer ou de Baillot, est de nos jours quelque peu émoussée. A l'époque d'une standardisation de la manière de jouer, d'une centralisation de l'enseignement, le style développé par ces violonistes s'impose indirectement comme norme de jeu.

L'école française de violon s'est si bien répandue qu'elle est devenue la norme pour les musiciens quelle que soit leur origine. En se propageant, l'apport des violonistes français s'est banalisé. De même, ils furent parmi les premiers à adopter l'archet de Tourte, et leur technique est parfaitement adaptée à ce nouvel archet. Devenu l'archet usuel, les musiciens ont adopté la technique la plus adaptée à cet archet. Comme Monsieur Jourdain faisait de la prose sans le savoir[51], tout violoniste suit la technique de l'école française de violon sans le savoir.

CONCLUSION

Apprécier à leur juste valeur les concertos de Rode suppose regarder de près les passages virtuoses. Ce sont eux qui portent sa signature la plus personnelle. Parmi les

---

[45]. AUER, Leopold. *Violin Playing as I Teach It*, (1921), New York, Dover, 1980 (Dover books on music, music history), p. 220. Les études de Kreutzer, Rode et Dont sont le répertoire pédagogique de base indispensable que tout élève doit maîtriser, maîtriser n'étant pas jouer tant bien que mal. Ensuite seulement l'étudiant pourra s'aventurer dans le grand répertoire.

[46]. BRUSSILOVSKI, Alexandre. *Yuri Yankelevitch et l'école russe du violon*, traduit du russe par Anna Kopylov, Fontenay-aux-Roses, Suoni e colori, 1999. Dans les exemples de programmes de travail (pp. 295-310), les études de Kreutzer et de Rode occupent une place importante. On y trouve aussi des concertos de l'école française, considérés comme préparatoires à ceux de Mendelssohn et Tchaikovsky, et même aux sonates de Brahms.

[47]. GALAMIAN, Ivan. *Enseignement et technique du violon*, avec une postface de Elisabeth A. H. Green, traduit de l'anglais par Gérard Mannoni, [Fondettes], Van de Velde, 1993 (Les maîtres de musique); édition originale ID. *Principles of Violin Playing and Teaching*, Londres, Faber & Faber, 1962.

[48]. DONT, Jacob. *24 Exercices pour le violon préparatoires aux études de R. Kreutzer et P. Rode*, Op. 37, (1852), Londres, Augener & Co., [c1900], pub. n° 7604.

[49]. MASSART, Joseph Lambert. *L'art de travailler les études de Kreutzer*, Paris, Leduc, 1893; Massart (1811-1892) avait pris des leçons particulières avec Kreutzer et fut professeur pendant quarante-sept ans au Conservatoire de Paris. Ses élèves les plus célèbres sont Fritz Kreisler, Eugène Ysaÿe, Henryk Wieniawski.

[50]. Léon Heymann, élève de Massart, édita les 12 caprices de Baillot avec de nombreux conseils de travail et commentaires chez Leduc en 1917.

[51]. Molière, *Le Bourgeois gentilhomme*, acte II scène 6 «Par ma foi! il y a plus de quarante ans que je dis de la prose sans que j'en susse rien, et je vous suis le plus obligé du monde de m'avoir appris cela».

violonistes de sa génération, son écriture contient moins de sauts brillants que celle de Kreutzer, mais est plus élégante, la plus raffinée. La richesse des coups d'archet et leur variété au sein d'un même passage sont des éléments novateurs par rapport à d'autres grands virtuoses du passé, tels Tartini ou Locatelli.

L'analyse formelle des concertos de Rode ne livre que peu d'indications. La construction du développement par un travail thématique ou contrapunctique n'est pas sa priorité; les traits virtuoses permettent le prolongement et l'amplification des passages lyriques. Pour être compris de l'intérieur, ces concertos nécessitent d'être joués, ou du moins déchiffrés. La variété et la richesse des coups d'archet peuvent se décrire mais leurs subtilités se ressentent encore davantage par le jeu.

Presqu'oubliées des salles de concert, les œuvres de Rode restent très présentes dans les salles de cours. Tant les *24 Études ou caprices* que ses concertos, en particulier les sixième, septième et neuvième, et les premiers solos des autres concertos, sont joués par les jeunes violonistes de toutes nationalités. Alors qu'il n'enseigna que pendant quelques années au Conservatoire, Rode exerça — et exerce encore dans une moindre mesure — une influence importante au travers de ses œuvres, influence discrète mais non moins réelle.

La virtuosité des concertos de l'école française de violon de la fin du XVIIIe et du début du XIXe siècle, et celle des concertos de Rode en particulier, s'est transmise par la diffusion de ses œuvres. Considérés surtout comme des compositions pédagogiques, leur appartenance au répertoire des violonistes reste invisible. Ils sont pourtant pour beaucoup de violonistes une sorte de langue maternelle dont ils se sont imprégnés. C'est toujours par référence à sa langue maternelle que l'on apprend d'autres langues. De même, c'est en s'appuyant sur les techniques violonistiques acquises, parmi lesquelles la virtuosité de Rode occupe une place de choix, qu'un violoniste appréhendera un langage propre à d'autres compositeurs.

Nicolò Paganini e la nuova semantica della passione[*]

Renato Ricco
(Salerno)

Igiudizi parziali o errati su Nicolò Paganini sono in larga parte dovuti a una costante, se non capziosa, attenzione a particolari fattori biografici letti sovente attraverso la lente deformante del basso aneddoto. A ciò si sono uniti un insufficiente o superficiale studio e contestualizzazione della sua produzione musicale collateralmente a un mancato esame delle fonti dirette, come ad esempio il *corpus* epistolare[1]. Il vero problema, quindi, non sono state tanto le inesattezze, sbavature, forzature o calunnie di cui il ritratto dell'autore dei *Capricci* è venuto caricandosi ancor prima della sua morte, quanto il fatale scivolamento di queste dall'ambito letterario e fantastico in cui hanno preso vita a quello propriamente storico-musicale[2].

Solo di recente è stato fatto un fondamentale passo in avanti, analizzando sotto molteplici aspetti la figura di Paganini da un punto di visto storico, sociologico e propriamente musicologico[3]. L'oggettivo valore artistico di Paganini emerge dal fatidico scarto tra la concreta realtà storica e la leggenda, in questo caso gravata di deteriori e falsi pregiudizi. La definitiva depurazione della figura paganiniana da incrostazioni di vario tipo (critico,

---

[*] Dedico questo lavoro a mio padre, primo e fondamentale artefice del mio amore per Nicolò Paganini.

[1] Solo recentemente è stato possibile avere a disposizione una prima *tranche* delle lettere di/a Paganini in un'edizione filologicamente corretta e attendibile: Paganini, Nicolò. *Epistolario: Volume I, 1810-1831*, a cura di Roberto Grisley, Milano, Skira, 2006 (L'arte armonica, serie III. Studi e testi, II/1).

[2] È il caso, ad esempio, di *Hoffmann et Paganini: conte fantastique* di Jules Janin, pubblicato sul *Journal des débats* del 17 marzo 1831, anno successivo alla prima esibizione parigina di Paganini: nelle intenzioni dell'autore, in questo racconto «Paganini incarna il musicista che Hoffmann avrebbe voluto divenire»: Rybicki, Marie-Hélène. 'Janin et Paganini', in: *Quaderni dell'Istituto di studi paganiniani*, n. 12 (2000), p. 41. Ma già lo stesso Julius Max Schottky, primo biografo di Paganini, parlando di questo in termini di «romanhafte Erscheinung» (*Paganini's Lebens und Treiben als Künstler und als Mensch*, Praga, J. G. Calve, 1830, p. 3), aveva stabilito una connessione tra il violinista genovese e il versatile artista tedesco. Un'analisi circostanziata dei vari articoli relativi ai concerti europei di Paganini si ritrova in Gooley, Dana. '«La Commedia del Violino»: Paganini's Comic Strains', in: *The Musical Quarterly*, LXXXVIII/3 (autunno 2005), pp. 370-427.

[3] Uno degli esempi più recenti di questa 'Paganini Renaissance' è il volume *Nicolò Paganini: Diabolus in musica*, a cura di Andrea Barizza e Fulvia Morabito, Turnhout, Brepols, 2010 (Studies on Italian music history, 5).

letterario, sociologico) viene inoltre a porsi quale operazione preliminare necessaria al fine di chiarire alcuni snodi focali della questione: il rapporto Paganini/romanticismo, con conseguente riflessione circa le origini del 'demonismo' che lo caratterizzò, e secondo quali parametri egli possa essere posto in relazione con la più importante tradizione violinistica coeva, quella francese, e in particolare con Pierre Baillot, suo più rappresentativo elemento.

I

In apertura, s'impone un'altra doverosa e più generale riflessione, valida in primo luogo per Paganini, ma anche per gli altri violinisti — e, a più largo raggio, strumentisti — virtuosi del XIX secolo[4]. Pur con la significativa eccezione di Liszt, il fine precipuo del virtuoso consisteva nell'impatto con cui egli si rivolgeva al pubblico, mirando a suscitare stupore, fanatico entusiasmo e immediata gradevolezza[5]. In virtù di ciò, risulterebbe improprio voler individuare complessi ragionamenti di carattere teorico o profonde innovazioni di natura formale in relazione a questo tipo di repertorio, ed esattamente in questo senso ha valore la parafrasi goethiana formulata da Charles Rosen[6]. Un corretto, obiettivo ed esaustivo inquadramento tanto della innovazione di Paganini quanto della portata del suo lascito non può quindi prescindere da una valutazione di questa produzione secondo i canoni del gusto coevo: «il contenuto di una musica che ha valore è dato non dalla storia empirica, ma dal significato che questa riveste per la coscienza e per l'inconscio dell'uomo»[7]. In altri termini, estrapolare Paganini dal suo *Zeitgeist*, identificato da Johann

---

[4]. Aldilà di una parziale e timida riscoperta moderna, drastica e senza possibilità d'appello è stata la condanna nei confronti dei violinisti virtuosi che s'inserirono nel solco paganiniano: «l'imitazione di modelli, la copia stilistica [...] venivano ritenute fino all'inizio del Settecento tanto legittime quanto indispensabili. Erano anzi segno della solidità dei fondamenti tecnici della musica e del devoto attaccamento alla tradizione piuttosto che indizio di un disonorevole difetto di idee proprie»; DAHLHAUS, Carl. *Analisi musicale e giudizio estetico*, edizione italiana a cura di Antonio Serravezza, traduzione italiana di Susanna Gozzi, Bologna, Il Mulino, 1987 (La nuova scienza. Serie di musica e spettacolo), p. 33. Necessario specificare, però, che queste osservazioni si riferiscono al XVIII secolo e proprio nel perpetrarsi di questi schemi, in seguito alle *tournées* paganiniane oltre i confini italiani (quindi a partire dal 1828), può ravvisarsi la ragione principale di scarsa incidenza e limitata importanza di questi virtuosi.

[5]. «[...] alla fama di Paganini in un certo senso corrisposero [...] i valori più legati alla cultura *Biedermeier*, perché la sua musica non era portatrice di tensioni e dialettiche complesse per il suo pubblico [...]: si poneva anzi come aproblematica trascinatrice per mondi sentimentali e meravigliosi, in fondo assai semplici e rassicuranti»; PAGANINI, Nicolò. *Epistolario* [...], *op. cit.* (si veda nota 1), p. 13.

[6]. Dopo aver citato l'assunto, tratto dai *Wilhelm Meisters Wanderjahre*, secondo cui «il reale è già teoria», e l'ammonimento «L'azzurro dei cieli ci svela la legge cromatica dell'ottica. Ma non guardate dietro i fenomeni, sono essi stessi la dottrina», Charles Rosen parafrasa «non guardate dietro le note, sono esse stesse la dottrina»; *Il pensiero della musica*, traduzione italiana di Anna Bassan Levi, Pietro Soresina e Angelo Zanardini, Milano, Garzanti, 1995 [Saggi blu], pp. 95-96.

[7]. DAHLHAUS, Carl. *Analisi musicale* [...], *op. cit.* (si veda nota 4), p. 22.

Gottfried Herder con opinioni, costumi e consuetudini dominanti di una determinata fase storica[8], sarebbe quindi un grave errore metodologico.

Il mito costruito sulla figura di Paganini ha determinato una serie di dannosi fraintendimenti, dovuti alla confusione tra le varie interpretazioni del mito stesso e i tentativi di indagine sulla sua origine, ritenuta quanto meno misteriosa quando non diabolica, unitamente alla sovrapposizione dei molteplici significati di cui si è caricata la leggenda paganiniana rispetto alla sua effettiva sostanza artistica e storico-musicale[9]. D'altronde, se è vero che «il mito non si definisce dall'oggetto del suo messaggio, ma dal modo in cui lo proferisce»[10], nel caso di Paganini possono allora spiegarsi i fraintendimenti e i difetti d'impostazione critica, data la portata rivoluzionaria del suo virtuosismo trascendentale, dell'impatto di questo non solo nell'universo musicale, bensì anche a livello sociale e di costume. In termini semiologici, si tratta allora in primo luogo di capire la natura dei rapporti vigenti tra i due sistemi (il linguaggio-oggetto e il metalinguaggio[11]) alla base dell'alone leggendario che avvolge Paganini, per poi analizzare lo svolgersi della parabola paganiniana alla luce dei tre concetti basilari che reggono la struttura barthesiana del mito: «il significante, il significato e il segno»[12]. Se con il primo elemento si potrebbe intendere lo stile paganiniano in senso lato (comprensivo di tutte le peculiarità tecnico-stilistiche del virtuosismo violinistico ottocentesco, con i relativi rapporti con le modalità compositive e i nuovi orizzonti timbrici), il secondo si potrebbe riferire al tipo di ideale estetico proprio di questo nuovo modo di 'sentire' il violino — senza dimenticare le relazioni con la tradizione precedente e il lascito per le generazioni successive. Infine, con il terzo, ci si potrebbe riferire ai principali tratti distintivi della scrittura paganiniana, cercando d'indagarne le effettive innovazioni[13].

---

[8]. *Cfr.* HERDER, Johann Gottfried von. *Briefe zu Beförderung der Humanität, Zweite Sammlung*, in: *Sämtliche Werke*, ristampa anastatica dell'edizione di Berlino 1877-1913, a cura di Bernhard Suphan, 33 voll., Hildesheim, Olms, 1967-1968, vol. XVII, p. 95.

[9]. Per tali problematiche, che affondano le radici nello studio strutturalista dell'istanza mitica, *cfr.* SEBAG, Lucien. *Mitologia e realtà sociale*, traduzione italiana di Maria Solimini, Bari, Dedalo Libri, 1979 (La scienza nuova, 67), p. 280. Riflessioni sulla nascita, lo sviluppo e la diffusione del mito paganiniano sono state compiute da TOSCANI, Claudio. 'Odore di zolfo: il diavolo e il solista', in: *Il diavolo all'opera: aspetti e rappresentazioni del diabolico nella musica e nella cultura del XIX secolo*, a cura di Marco Capra, Venezia-Parma, Marsilio-Casa della musica, 2008 (Musica in atto, 5), pp. 9-26.

[10]. BARTHES, Roland. *Miti d'oggi*, traduzione italiana di Lidia Lonzi, Torino, Einaudi, 1974 (Gli struzzi, 50), p. 191.

[11]. *Ibidem*, p. 197.

[12]. *Ibidem*, p. 196.

[13]. Sulla natura del mito paganiniano, recentemente Massimiliano Sala ha affrontato alcuni punti cruciali che permettono di inquadrare meglio la questione, apportando diversi e fecondi spunti di riflessione. Sala individua come tratto caratterizzante del fenomeno paganiniano l'essere parte di quello che si definisce oggi 'mito da pop starts': «Myths are expressions of the society from which they originate, since they articulate its values, fears and yearnings; principally, in the contemporary era heroes are by products of the cultural industry

Racconti di varia natura, di valore letterario alterno e raramente degno di nota, di prevalente taglio romanzesco, talvolta avallati dal diretto contributo degli stessi eredi di Paganini[14], hanno fatalmente sconfinato dal loro legittimo campo d'azione o dalla loro più appropriata area di pertinenza, sino a sostituire una serena e obiettiva lettura della vicenda biografica e artistica paganiniana.

Parlando di Paganini, si è registrata una costante insistenza sull'aspetto 'patologico' caratterizzante la sua natura artistica, in tutta la pregnanza letteraria e romantica dell'accezione, intendendo esattamente per 'patologia' una «esasperazione della sensibilità che porta ad una condizione di malattia fisica»[15], giocando quindi sullo slittamento semantico di questa parola e dando così vita a una infinita serie di interpretazioni distorte. Lo stato di salute di Paganini è stato costantemente precario per cause esclusivamente fisiologiche e naturali, cui si possono e devono fornire spiegazioni afferenti unicamente al campo medico. Ciò non toglie che lo stesso Paganini, ad esempio nella lettera del 15 gennaio 1832, abbia voluto alludere, con la frase «l'elettricismo che provo nel trattare la magica armonia mi nuoce orribilmente»[16], all'idea romantica di uno scotto che il 'genio' è costretto a pagare in termini di stress psicofisico. Se nel 1820 Leopardi annotava, attingendo dalla medesima sfera lessicale, «l'effetto naturale e generico della musica in noi non deriva dall'armonia ma dal suono, il quale ci elettrizza e scuote al primo tocco quando anche sia monotono [...]»[17], sensazioni simili susciterà, anni dopo, Henryk Wieniawski, stando alla testimonianza di Sam Franko:

---

and of the process of "democratization" of culture»; SALA, Massimiliano. 'Paganini and his Myth', in: *Henryk Wieniawski and the Bravura Tradition*, a cura di Maciej Jabłoński e Danuta Jasińska, Poznań, Henryk Wieniawski Musical Society, 2011 (Henryk Wieniawski, Complete works, B series), pp. 133-148: 142. A ciò connesso, Sala sostiene che «Paganini embodies the paradigm of the modern artist, inescapably bound to the masses: the same masses that he strove to mesmerize through his art»; *ibidem*, p. 143.

[14]. È il caso (solo per citarne alcuni) dei testi di Oreste Bruni, autore di *Niccolò Paganini celebre violinista genovese. Racconto storico* (Firenze, Galletti e Cocci, 1873), il cui sottotitolo specifica «racconto romanzato, sulle testimonianze del nipote Attila Paganini», e di Elise Polko *Niccolò Paganini* (traduzione italiana di Lodovico Ravasini, Milano, Treves, 1876), che è una biografia romanzata «pubblicata per cura di Achille Paganini e del Traduttore».

[15]. *Cfr.* FORNARO, Sotera. 'Introduzione', in: GOETHE, Johann Wolfgang von. *Achilleide*, Roma, Salerno editrice, 1998 (Omikron, 61), pp. 29-30.

[16]. *Cfr.* BERRI, Pietro – MOMPELLIO, Federico. 'Certamente di Paganini è il ritrovato concerto in 'mi' minore', in: *Genova*, LVI (1976), p. 27. Sintomatico che, più o meno negli stessi anni, anche Zelter usi, nelle sue conversazioni con Goethe, una metafora praticamente identica al termine usato da Paganini: «Using the modern metaphor of electricity (the players are "electrified"), Zelter invoked music's power to awaken the deep, seemingly nonrational aspects of human nature, a point decisively argued ten years earlier by Schopenauer [...]»; BOTSTEIN, Leon. 'The Patrons and Public of the Quartets: Music, Culture and Society in Beethoven's Vienna', in: *The Beethoven Quartet Companion*, a cura di Robert Winter e Robert Martin, Berkeley (CA), University of California Press, 1994, p. 80.

[17]. LEOPARDI, Giacomo. *Zibaldone di pensieri*, [155], 6 luglio 1820, edizione critica in CD-ROM a cura di Fiorenza Ceragioli e Monica Ballerini, Bologna, Zanichelli, 2009 (Dizionari in CD-ROM).

> I was electrified by Wieniawski's playing. I have never heard anyone play the violin as he did, either before or since. His wonderfully warm tone, rich in modulation, his glowing temperament, his perfect technique, his captivating élan — all threw me in a land of hypnotic trance[18].

L'alone di mistero che ammantava il magistero artistico di Paganini, già notato da Balzac, era d'altronde un dato riconosciuto già prima del 1840, come sembra testimoniare anche questa anonima fonte

> Afferma Schottky che Paganini possiede un segreto musicale ignoto a tutti Conservatorii, e per mezzo di cui basterebbero tre anni ad un allievo per conseguir tutta la immaginabile perfezione sul violino. Lo stesso Paganini affermò tal cosa, e disse che un solo, il maestro Gaetano Ciandelli di Napoli, conosceva quel suo segreto, cui egli lo comunicò, e che in tre giorni riuscì a suonare il violoncello assai meglio di quanto avesse ottenuto con lunghissimi studii[19].

Sull'aspetto più prettamente coreografico e teatrale Paganini avrebbe volutamente concentrato la sua attenzione, non lasciando nulla al caso: ad esempio, durante l'introduzione orchestrale de *Le Couvent du Mont Saint-Bernard*, per la cui esecuzione l'autore aveva esplicitamente richiesto delle quinte raffiguranti un paesaggio montano, il solista, non presente dall'inizio sulla scena, sarebbe infatti comparso in un secondo momento, eseguendo arpeggi e suoni richiamanti le campane del convento durante il suo ingresso[20]. La componente istrionica di Paganini costituisce un elemento tanto marcato da caratterizzarne le stesse modalità compositive diventando, non a caso, la cifra caratterizzante le critiche dei suoi concerti europei come emerge dalle righe della *Allgemeine musikalische Zeitung*:

> Dazu neigt sich, wie wir an allen scenischen Formen der italienischen Comödie, am Pantalon, Arlechino u.s.w., am Buffo caricato u.s.w. sehen, der italienische Nationalcharakter sehr zum Uebertreiben des Komischen, also zu dem, was wir im jetzigen Sprachgebrauche grotesk nennen[21].

Da ciò deriva il taglio particolarmente roboante di alcune recensioni, tendenti a descrivere un'atmosfera quasi innaturale cui Paganini, nella sua dimensione pubblica, viene solitamente associato:

---

[18]. FRANKO, Sam. *Chords and Discords: Memoirs and Musings of an American Musician*, New York, Viking Press, 1938, p. 46.

[19]. ANONIMO. *Iconografia musicale ovvero 24 ritratti e biografie di varj dei più celebrati maestri, professori e cantanti moderni*, Torino, Fratelli Reycend e Cª, 1838, pp. 26-27.

[20]. *Cfr.* SAUZAY, Eugène – FRANÇOIS-SAPPEY, Brigitte. 'La vie musicale a Paris a travers les Mémoires d'Eugène Sauzay (1809-1901)', in: *Revue de Musicologie*, LX/1-2 (1974), pp. 159-210: 194.

[21]. ANONIMO. 'Noch etwas über Paganini', in: *Allgemeine musikalische Zeitung*, VII (16 febbraio 1829), col. 109.

> Un immense cadre gothique est tombé des hautes frises autour de cet homme. J'ai vu le Christ, comme le peignent les artistes du Moyen-Age et à ses côtés les Saintes Femmes fondre en prières et en larmes [...]. Il souffrait visiblement, ses mouvements nerveux trahissaient son émotion[22].

Come già dimostrato da Arnold Niggli[23], le *tournées* di Paganini, così come degli altri virtuosi, avevano d'altronde un grande successo, anche perché intorno al concerto, da un punto di vista di *marketing*, era attiva una complessa macchina organizzativa, che sovente velava l'evento musicale di aloni misteriosi o aneddoti ricchi di eccentricità, riguardanti il virtuoso protagonista, da cui sarebbero poi scaturiti fenomeni di irrazionale e spasmodica esaltazione da parte del pubblico[24]. In realtà lo stacco tra dimensione pubblica e privata per Paganini si rivela particolarmente importante. Aldilà di alcuni atteggiamenti tacciabili di divismo, favoriti dall'indubbia consapevolezza della forza d'impatto sulle platee insita nella propria fisionomia, emerge dalle lettere un carattere profondamente ironico e interamente dedito all'amore per il proprio strumento[25], capace al contempo di riconoscere e apprezzare artisti a lui coevi, come ad esempio Berlioz, la cantante Angelica Catalani, il già citato violoncellista Gaetano Ciandelli, i violinisti Charles Philippe Lafont o Josef Slavík, oltre che i connazionali Giovanni Battista Polledro e Antonio Rolla, come anche di esprimere al contempo severi e obiettivi apprezzamenti su se stesso[26].

Riguardo poi l'insistenza delle voci circa l'avarizia[27], Paganini fu sempre molto attento all'amministrazione dei suoi capitali, dimostrandosi talvolta capace di grandi slanci di generosità, come attestato dalla donazione di ventimila franchi elargita il 16 dicembre 1838 a Berlioz, dopo l'insuccesso del *Benvenuto Cellini*. Lo stesso dicasi per il legame tra Paganini e Parma, testimoniato, oltre che dal fallito tentativo di riforma dell'orchestra ducale[28], anche

---

[22]. MIRAMON FITZ-JAMES, Bérenger de. *Paganini à Marseille: 1837-1839*, Marsiglia, à la Librairie Fuéri, 1941, p. 30.

[23]. *Cfr.* NIGGLI, Arnold. 'Nicolo Paganini', in: *Sammlung musikalischer Vorträge*, IV/44-45 (1882), p. 312.

[24]. *Cfr.* GOOLEY, Dana. *The Virtuoso Liszt*, Cambridge-New York, Cambridge University Press, 2004 (New perspectives in music history and criticism), pp. 201-262 (§ 'Anatomy of «Lisztomania»: The Berlin Episode).

[25]. «[...] testi vivi, immediati e spontanei, in cui il violinista non si trova quasi mai in condizione di dover operare un mascheramento delle proprie idee, anzi è spesso colloquiale e diretto»; GRISLEY, Roberto. 'Scrivere come parlare: la comunicazione epistolare di Paganini', in: *Paganini divo e comunicatore. Atti del convegno internazionale (Genova, 3-5 dicembre 2004)*, a cura di Maria Rosa Moretti, Anna Sorrento, Stefano Termanini ed Enrico Volpato, Genova, Serel International, 2007, p. 204.

[26]. *Cfr.* VÝBORNÝ, Zdenek. 'Paganini as Music Critic', in: *The Musical Quarterly*, XLVI/4 (ottobre 1960), pp. 468-481.

[27]. Accusa da cui non fu del resto immune neanche Gioachino Rossini, come dimostra l'episodio della donazione di soli due cavalli «da macello» fatta alle «legioni civiche» e ai «volontari dello stato pontificio» in partenza, nel 1848, per combattere gli austriaci; *cfr.* ZANOLINI, Antonio. *Biografia di Giochino Rossini*, Bologna, Zanichelli, 1875, p. 109.

[28]. *Cfr.* RICCO, Renato. 'Virtuosismo violinistico e direzione orchestrale: rapporti storici e scissione dei ruoli', in: *Orchestral Conducting in the Nineteenth Century*, a cura di Roberto Illiano e Michela Niccolai, Turnhout, Brepols, 2014 (Speculum musicae, 23), pp. 95-133.

dall'entusiasmo manifestato a favore del concerto del 5 novembre 1834 (poi posticipato di una settimana a causa di problemi di salute del violinista), il cui incasso di £ 3902 fu devoluto interamente in beneficenza a favore dei poveri della città[29]. Inoltre, circa l'arrivo a Londra, preceduto da una serie di maldicenze relative a una sua inguaribile esosità, Simon McVeigh ha finalmente inquadrato in maniera corretta e obiettiva la questione, spiegando come Paganini sia semplicemente stato un antesignano di un nuovo modo di condurre e gestire una *tournée* concertistica[30]. Da un punto di vista strettamente economico, Paganini fu, molto semplicemente, uno dei primi musicisti a organizzare le sue *tournées* secondo un'ottica di profitto economico[31]. Il suo contemporaneo Louis Spohr mostrò doti manageriali ben più spiccate, riuscendo a far coesistere le varie attività e i differenti incarichi di solista, direttore d'opera di corte (e di cori non professionistici), nonché organizzatore di concerti sinfonici[32]. Così Giuseppe Verdi che, in vista della prima rappresentazione napoletana della *Luisa Miller*, avendo saputo da Cammarano che la situazione del teatro San Carlo era tutt'altro che florida, si premunì chiedendo la garanzia dei 3000 ducati pattuiti, pena la rescissione del contratto[33].

---

[29]. Cfr. DALL'ACQUA, Marzio. 'Paganini e l'orchestra ducale', in: *Orchestre in Emilia-Romagna nell'Ottocento e Novecento*, a cura di Marcello Conati e Marcello Pavarani, Parma, Orchestra Sinfonica dell'Emilia Romagna Arturo Toscanini, 1982, pp. 147-148.

[30]. «Typically […] a performer would give as many concerts as the market could stand, taking care to move on before attendances declined. The appearance of Paganini in 1831 was not only the most sensational of these, but also the first organized in this manner: a long series of showpieces concerts at the end of the season, promoted not as benefit but as unashamed vehicles for solo display and adulation. […] Critics, carping as usual at the extortionate ticket-prices, calculated that Paganini would receive some £ 2000 per concert; but in the end the prices were reduced and receipts were apparently more of the order of £ 1000 per concert. Paganini followed his usual practice of giving as many concerts in a short time as the market would sustain (or slightly more) […]»; McVEIGH, Simon. 'The Musician as Concert-Promoter in London, 1780-1850', in: *Le concert et son public: mutations de la vie musicale en Europe de 1780 à 1914, France, Allemagne, Angleterre*, a cura di Hans Erich Bödeker, Patrice Veit e Michael Werner, Parigi, Éditions de la Maison des sciences de l'homme, 2002, p. 87. Proprio ad una ragione economica, in particolare ai prezzi dei biglietti troppo alti, Paul Metzner attribuisce la causa della freddezza con cui Paganini fu accolto a Praga; *Crescendo of the Virtuoso: Spectacle, Skill, and Self-Promotion in Paris during the Age of the Revolution*, Berkeley-Los Angeles, University of California Press, 1998 (Studies on the history of society and culture, 30), p. 127 .

[31]. «He [Paganini] attempted to give far more concerts than was the norm, often daily appearances in opera halls, locales holdings hundreds more people than the usual concert space»; WEBER, William. 'The Origins of the Concert Agent in the Social Structure of Concert Life', in: *Le concert et son public* […], *op. cit.* (si veda nota 30), p. 129. Molti cenni alle attenzioni di Paganini sull'aspetto economico delle proprie *tournées* sono contenuti in ID. 'From the Self-Managing Musician to the Independent Concert Agent', in: *The Musician as Entrepreneur, 1700-1914: Managers, Charlatans, and Idealists*, a cura di William Weber, Bloomington, Indiana University Press, 2004, pp. 105-129.

[32]. Cfr. SPOHR, Louis. *Louis Spohr's Selbstbiographie*, 2 voll., Kassel-Göttingen, Georg H. Wigand, 1860-1861, vol. I, p. 145.

[33]. Cfr. BUDDEN, Julian. *Le opere di Verdi*, 3 voll., Torino, EdT, 1985-1988, vol. I: *Da «Oberto» a «Rigoletto»*, p. 459.

Nella storia della ricezione paganiniana, infine, poca attenzione è stata sinora data a due voci, entrambe del XIX secolo, che gettarono su Paganini una diversa luce rispetto agli scritti fin qui riportati: lo scrittore Giuseppe Rovani e il violinista Carl Guhr. Il primo infatti scrive:

> Una cosa per ogni onest'uomo assai deplorabile si è la facilità con la quale i ribaldi accolgono ogni giorno le nuove più erronee, e spesse volte le imputazioni più scandalose, inventate dalla calunnia o dalla passione del sarcasmo. Paganini, già fatto segno, vivente, di rimproveri senza fondamento, d'ingiurie gratuite e persino d'accuse atroci, non fu risparmiato nemmeno dopo morte [...][34].

Il secondo, mettendo in chiaro di avere avuto la fortuna d'ascoltare Paganini in più occasioni, e pur ammettendo alla fine che talvolta, nelle esecuzioni paganiniane, il fine musicale poteva essere offuscato da intenti più scopertamente acrobatici, specifica che tutte le varie dicerie e pettegolezzi sprecati sul suo conto avevano in ultima analisi pochi fondamenti concreti[35]. In realtà, una cifra peculiare della natura paganiniana si potrebbe forse ravvisare proprio in questa contraddittorietà, questa sì tutta romantica: «spontaneity and reflection, exaltation and contemplation, a relish for the theatrical gestures and a retreat into the inner world»[36]. In ultima istanza, secondo questa impossibilità di coerente e logica *reductio ad unum*, Paganini viene a porsi quale insuperabile vetta della musica strumentale che però, nella sua più intima e ispirata natura cantabile, finisce per mostrare non pochi tratti d'analogia con il melodramma: «Paganini est Rossiniste»[37], paradigmatico modello di lirismo, che si coniuga e compendia nel primo esempio compiuto di teatralizzazione del virtuosismo.

II

Concetti come 'magnetismo' e 'demonismo' hanno provocato una catalogazione troppo frettolosa di Paganini come violinista *tout court* romantico, mentre in realtà i suoi rapporti con il romanticismo, innegabili per alcuni aspetti, non sono né scontati né diretti:

[34]. ROVANI, Giuseppe. 'Nicolò Paganini', in: ID. *Storia delle lettere e delle arti in Italia: giusta le reciproche loro rispondenze ordinata nelle vite e nei ritratti degli uomini illustri dal secolo XIII fino ai nostri giorni*, 4 voll., Milano, Francesco Sanvito, 1855-1858, vol. IV, p. 391.

[35]. GUHR, Carl. *Ueber Paganini's Kunst die Violine zu spielen: ein Anhang zu jeder bis jetzt erschienenen Violinschule nebst einer Abhandlung über das Flageoletspiel in einfachen und Doppeltönen*, Magonza, B. Schott's Söhnen, 1830, p. 3.

[36]. SUCHOWIEJKO, Renata. 'Virtuoso: an Incarnation of God or Evil? Some Thoughts about Violin Virtuosity in the 19th Century', in: *Instrumental Music and the Industrial Revolution*, a cura di Roberto Illiano e Luca Lévi Sala, Bologna, Ut Orpheus Edizioni, 2010 (Ad Parnassum studies, 5), p. 102.

[37]. IMBERT DE LAPHALÈQUE, George. *Notice sur le celèbre Nicolò Paganini*, Parigi, Guyot, 1830, p. 40.

proprio l'analisi della loro complessità può risultare utile per una più precisa collocazione di Paganini all'interno della temperie culturale dell'800. Se è innegabile che «[...] vitalità, ribellione al precetto, tendenza autobiografica, grande fervore, fantasia e sregolatezza»[38] possono essere tutte caratteristiche riscontrabili nella parabola del violinista, l'associazione del suo nome alla temperie romantica è sicuramente condizionata, più genericamente, da una semplificazione del mito dell'individualità di marca byroniana[39] e, con più specifico riferimento a Paganini, dalle *Florentinische Nächte* di Heine. Aldilà delle traversie che hanno costellato la sua vita, Paganini non rientra nel modello di artista disegnato da Liszt nella lettera del 7 aprile 1837 a George Sand:

> L'artiste vit solitaire. Si les événements le jettent au sein de la société, il crée à son âme, au milieu de ces bruits discordants, une solitude impénétrable dans laquelle nulle voix humaine a plus accès. La vanité, l'ambition, la jalousie, l'amour même, toutes les passions qui remuent les hommes restent au dehors du cercle magique qu'il a tracé autour de sa pensée. Là, retiré comme en un sanctuaire, il contemple et adore le type idéal que toute sa vie tendra à reproduire[40].

Conformemente a quanto delineato da Wackenroder e Hoffmann in letteratura, il pianista ungherese descrive infatti il musicista romantico come un *Sonderling*, un eccentrico, praticamente tagliato fuori dal consorzio civile e con questo non comunicante. Tracce di questo ineluttabile e doloroso isolamento — di cui un caso paradigmatico può vedersi nel testamento beethoveniano di Heiligenstadt, del 1802 — sono difficilmente verificabili, tanto per Paganini quanto per altri violinisti suoi contemporanei o successori. Se è mediante la musica che il Berglinger di Wackenroder riesce a far emergere la sua più pura *Innerlichkeit*, fuggendo dagli uomini verso i quali elabora una incomunicabilità sempre più paralizzante e angosciosa, al contrario Paganini e i virtuosi che si inseriscono nel suo solco, proprio mediante la loro arte, costituiscono a pieno titolo un fenomeno di comunicazione nella vita quotidiana, diventando anzi un fenomeno di costume e vantando, non di rado, molti contatti con le più alte e influenti sfere della società, e sovente con la massoneria[41]. In altri

---

[38]. Rietmann, Carlo Marcello. 'Paganini primo romantico', in: *Genova*, LVI (1976), p. 44.

[39]. «The Romantic virtuoso [...] stood for freedom, for Faustian man, for the individual in search of self-realisation-free, isolated, striving, desiring. Heroically overcoming his instrument, he was a powerful symbol of transcendence»; Samson, Jim. *Virtuosity and the Musical Work: The Transcendental Studies of Liszt*, Cambridge-New York, Cambridge University Press, 2003, pp. 75-76.

[40]. Liszt, Franz. 'Lettres d'un bachelier ès musique', in: *Gazette musicale de Paris*, IX (16 luglio 1837), pp. 309-310.

[41]. Giovanni Battista Viotti, nel suo periodo parigino, ebbe stretti legami con le logge più importanti (*cfr.* Dellaborra, Mariateresa. *Giovanni Battista Viotti*, Palermo, L'Epos, 2006 [L'amoroso canto, 4], pp. 24-28), mentre Rodolphe Kreutzer viene nominato espressamente nel *Discours sur l'histoire de la Loge 'Les Frères Unis Inséparables'* pronunciato dal 'fratello archivista' Octave Brimont (Parigi, F. L. Hugonis, 1875, p. 4). Il nome di Ole Bull ricorre nel registro dei visitatori delle Logge 'S. Cecilie' di New York e 'St. Andrew' del Massachusetts, mentre Henry Vieuxtemps viene citato in uno dei *Livres d'architecture* della Loggia di

termini, quella che Herbert Marcuse icasticamente identifica come la «scissione dolorosa che pone la natura e la vocazione dell'artista in contrasto col mondo circostante e che gli impedisce di trovare soddisfazione e compimento nelle sue forme di vita»[42] — anticipata in campo letterario dall'assunto leopardiano, secondo cui «eccellenza e infelicità straordinaria sono sostanzialmente una cosa stessa»[43] — non risulta essere una caratteristica saliente di Nicolò Paganini o degli altri violinisti virtuosi del XIX secolo. D'altronde né Paganini né altri violinisti virtuosi della sua epoca o di generazioni successive si sentirono investiti dal compito di rivelare «die geheimnisvolle, in Tönen ausgesprochene Sanskritta der Natur»[44], secondo l'affascinante espressione del Kreisler hoffmaniano, limitandosi piuttosto a sottolineare, molto più superficialmente, l'aspetto sentimentale e passionale su cui si basava la loro arte strumentale e compositiva. L'arte paganiniana non deve quindi implicare nessun'altra spiegazione che tracimi dalla sfera strettamente storica e musicale, e quando il musicista si trovò a vivere una condizione di isolamento fu solo per cause contingenti, e in questo senso dati paradigmatici sono tanto il fallimento della collaborazione con il violinista austriaco Joseph Panny[45] quanto la delusione ricevuta dalla parte solistica per viola dell'*Harold en Italie* di Berlioz.

In Paganini, come d'altronde in Rossini, non è quindi possibile trovare — e sarebbe anche fuori luogo cercarla — una riflessione estetica sull'arte musicale paragonabile, per profondità e innovazione, a quanto elaborato da Schumann o da Liszt. In questo senso, senza alcun intento denigratorio o riduttivo nei confronti dell'arte violinistica paganiniana, il solo ambito di pertinenza e d'indagine a questa relativo resta sempre quello direttamente collegato all'attività strumentale, senza che a questo siano connesse riflessioni teoriche o approfondimenti estetici di sorta[46]. In virtù di ciò, difficilmente si adatta alla

---

Bruxelles 'Les vrais amis de l'Union et du Progrès reunis' (*cfr.* il capitolo a Vieuxtemps dedicato in *Illustres et francs-maçons*, edito da Luc Nefontaine, Bruxelles, Labor, 2004 [La Noria]). Anche Charles-Auguste de Bériot, il cui nome è contrassegnato con «matricule 876» all'interno del *Livre d'or n. 2*, fece parte della Loggia bruxelliense degli 'Amis Philanthropes'. Questa cosa rappresenta peraltro una sensibile differenza tra Paganini e la stragrande maggioranza dei musicisti a lui coevi e successivi: nella lettera del 3 Maggio 1820, scritta a Germi da Napoli, egli manifesta infatti un atteggiamento estraneo, se non dichiaratamente ostile, verso questo tipo d'ambiente politico: «Qui certi così detti Carbonari li frustano non gentilmente sul ciuccio; ma a mio parere meritano il peggio»; PAGANINI, Nicolò. *Epistolario* […], *op. cit.* (si veda nota 1), p. 183.

[42]. *Cfr.* DI STEFANO, Giovanni. *La vita come musica, il mito romantico del musicista nella letteratura tedesca*, Venezia, Marsilio, 1991 (Saggi Marsilio. Musica critica), p. 64.

[43]. LEOPARDI, Giacomo. 'Dialogo della Natura e di un'Anima', in: *Operette morali*, introduzione di Antonio Prete, Milano, Feltrinelli, ²1981, p. 88.

[44]. HOFFMANN, Ernst Theodor Amadeus. 'Gedanken über den hohen Wert der Musik', in: *Sämtliche Werke*, 6 voll., a cura di Friedrich Schnapp, Monaco, Winkler Verlag, 1960, vol. I, p. 39.

[45]. I due violinisti scrissero insieme *La tempesta* M.S. 52, proposta senza successo prima a Vienna poi a Praga nel luglio e nel dicembre 1828.

[46]. Vladimir Jankélévitch, in *Liszt et la rhapsodie: essai sur la virtuosité* (Parigi, Plon, 1989 [De la musique au silence, 5]), chiarisce questo punto, spiegando come l'essenza stessa del virtuosismo sia da ravvisare nella

Weltanschauung di Paganini e, più in generale, di tutti i violinisti virtuosi che dopo di lui sono venuti, la comparazione schlegheliana secondo cui le modalità di proposizione, sviluppo e contrasto tematico in musica mostrerebbero molte affinità con l'enucleazione di un pensiero filosofico[47]. E se è innegabile che a Paganini manchi la caratura intellettuale per dirsi entusiasticamente immerso in una molteplicità di impegnative letture — come fa invece Liszt nella lettera a Pierre Wolff del 2 maggio 1832, citando la Bibbia, Platone, Locke, Byron, Hugo, Lamartine, e Chateaubriand[48] —, tuttavia la sua idea di violino e la produzione musicale a questa connessa vengono a costituire una premessa assoluta e ineliminabile all'interno del percorso evolutivo dell'arte lisztiana. Al contempo, Paganini si rivela tramite cruciale per il processo di trasferimento dell'istanza più poeticamente virtuosistica della letteratura — identificabile con Victor Hugo — al mondo della musica, con indubbio riferimento alle composizioni orchestrali di Berlioz. Questo procedimento, già evidenziato da Carl Dahlhaus[49], si poggia sulla nuova e rivoluzionaria idea che Paganini afferma e trasmette, quella di un virtuosismo che ormai è parte integrante del tessuto connettivo della composizione e non mero pretesto dimostrativo di funamboliche abilità strumentali, come nel caso di tanti epigoni paganiniani.

Oltre il riconoscimento della strabiliante tecnica, Paganini spalanca a Liszt nuovi e ignoti orizzonti timbrici e sonori, unendo a una bravura esecutiva inaudita, una pregnanza e una qualità di contenuti che gettano una luce diversa su quel funambolismo che «fin dall'infanzia lo aveva schiacciato come un peso e che ormai gli pareva assurto a tratto caratteristico della musica contemporanea»[50]. In maniera fondamentalmente involontaria e inconsapevole, il primo conduce il secondo al disvelamento di quella natura *trascendante* — magistero unico di conchiusa perfezione, e perciò capace di 'trascendere' i limiti dell'abilità digitale fine a se stessa, rivelando l'intima essenza del 'poetico' — che è un elemento focale nella concezione musicale lisztiana. Ma in Paganini tutto resta sempre circoscritto al solo mondo del violino, escludendo quelle connessioni spirituali e religiose presenti nell'orizzonte artistico lisztiano virtuoso della tastiera, e di

---

possibilità, potenzialmente illimitata, del creare (inteso come puro e semplice produrre musica) piuttosto che in un sostrato teorico o sapienziale a questo collegato.

[47]. «Muss die reine Instrumentalmusik sich nicht selbst einen Text erschaffen? Und wird das Thema in ihr nicht so entwickelt, bestätigt, variiert und kontrastiert wie der Gegenstand der Meditation in einer philosophischen Ideenreihe?»; SCHLEGEL, Friedrich von. *Athenäum Fragment, Nr. 444*, in: *Charakteristiken und Kritiken. 1. (1796-1801)*, a cura di Hans Eichner, Monaco-Zurigo, Schöningh-Thomas, 1967 (Kritische Friedrich Schlegel Ausgabe, II/1), p. 254.

[48]. *Cfr.* LISZT, Franz. *Letters of Franz Liszt*, raccolte ed edite da La Mara, traduzione inglese di Constance Bache, 2 voll., New York, Haskell House, 1968, vol. I: *From Paris to Rome: Years of Travel as Virtuoso*, pp. 8-9.

[49]. *Cfr.* DAHLHAUS, Carl. *La musica dell'Ottocento*, traduzione italiana di Laura Dallapiccola, Scandicci, La Nuova Italia, 1990 (Discanto/contrappunti, 28), p. 145.

[50]. DALMONTE, Rossana. *Franz Liszt: la vita, l'opera, i testi musicati*, Milano, Feltrinelli, 1983 (Biblioteca di musica), p. 28.

cui una perfetta esemplificazione letteraria è ravvisabile nel personaggio wackenroderiano di Joseph Berglinger. Innegabile quindi, benché estraneo alle intenzioni di Paganini, il suo contributo, seppur indiretto, all'elaborazione del concetto lisztiano di *Tondichtung*. Tuttavia, in inconsapevole ma significativa coincidenza cronologica con quanto realizzato da Wilhelm Heinrich Wackenroder in campo letterario e da Friedrich Schlegel e Novalis in sede estetica, in Paganini si mette in atto, per la prima volta in maniera significativa nel campo della musica strumentale, una dialettica contraddittoria tra due differenti istanze: forma ed espressione. Se Wackenroder, in particolare, e Paganini sembrano inoltre mettere in relazione la musica, in modo quasi esclusivo, con la sfera della sensibilità, a differenza di quanto di tragico accade al musicista immaginario Berglinger, in Paganini non si giunge all'esito estremo dell'annullamento del musicista — ultima ripercussione di un individualismo portato alle estreme conseguenze. Un implicito e importante *trait d'union* con Wackenroder, con l'amico Ludwig Tieck, e più che tutti con Ernst Theodor Amadeus Hoffmann, è infine possibile rintracciarlo nel parallelo tra le celebrazioni della musica strumentale che questi autori compiono nelle loro opere e quello che Paganini effettivamente rappresenta: la punta di diamante dello strumentismo solista. Benché vada evitato l'errore di stabilire facili o dirette connessioni tra due contesti affatto diversi e non direttamente comunicanti, come per quel che riguarda l'universo di Wackenroder «nell'operare del musicista cade ogni traccia di rispetto che la *Vernunft* poteva conservare per sé nel ripiegarsi su di sé»[51], il rifiuto paganiniano delle forme classiche trova una sua coerente ragion d'essere a vantaggio di una predilezione per la pratica improvvisativa[52], e proprio in questa accezione acquisterebbe valore la supposta osservazione di Giacomo Meyerbeer «Paganini inizia là dove finisce la nostra ragione»[53]: è d'altronde sintomatica l'osservazione di Berlioz, secondo cui Paganini «dédaignait les procédés connus, annonçait l'impossible et le réalisait»[54].

Alcune contingenze cronologiche vanno inoltre messe in luce. Nel 1809, abbandonando la corte di Lucca, Paganini dà vita *ipso facto* alla figura moderna del concertista, e nel 1810, anno della nascita di Fryderyk Chopin e Robert Schumann, egli inizia la sua carriera da solista, suonando in vari centri della Toscana e dell'Emilia Romagna: negli stessi anni

---

[51]. JESI, Furio. 'Romanticismo', in: *Dizionario critico della letteratura tedesca*, ripubblicato in appendice a ID. *Esoterismo e linguaggio mitologico: studi su Rainer Maria Rilke*, Macerata, Quodlibet, 2002 (Quaderni Quodlibet, 13), p. 223.

[52]. *Cfr.* BORER, Philippe. 'Paganini's Virtuosity and Improvisatory Style' e RICCO, Renato. 'Charles-Auguste de Bériot e l'improvvisazione virtuosistica per violino', in: *Beyond Notes: Improvisation in Western Music of the Eighteenth and Nineteenth Centuries*, a cura di Rudolf Rasch, Turnhout, Brepols, 2011 (Speculum musicae, 16), rispettivamente pp. 191-215 e 218-236.

[53]. Riportata in PASQUALI, Giulio. *L'imitazione di Paganini: memoria letta nella seduta pubblica del 31 marzo 1940*, Firenze, La Stamperia, 1941, p. 31 e in SCHWARZ, Boris. *Great Masters of the Violin: From Corelli and Vivaldi to Stern, Zukerman, and Perlman*, New York, Simon & Schuster, 1983, p. 175.

[54]. BERLIOZ, Hector. *Les Soirées de l'orchestre*, Parigi, Michel Lévy Frères, 1852, p. 212.

Hoffmann lavora alla recensione — pensata in origine per l'*Allgemeine musikalische Zeitung*, poi confluita nei *Phantasiestücke in Callots Manier* — della Quinta Sinfonia di Beethoven, in cui parla di quella «unendliche Sehnsucht»[55] affatto simile a quella capacità di commuovere, far vibrare le più intime fibre dell'anima e del sentimento, che costituisce la *condicio sine qua non* dell'arte paganiniana. Nel 1815, anno in cui Paganini presenta al pubblico della sua città natale il suo primo concerto in Mi minore, Hoffmann commenta positivamente un concerto eseguito da un organico misto di elementi dell'Orchestra reale e del Teatro nazionale, chiedendosi se proprio in questo non si possa ravvisare un cruciale segno dei tempi, indicativo di come la musica strumentale venga acquistando sempre maggiore audacia, finendo quasi per eliminare del tutto le catene che la vincolano alla parola[56].

La forza d'impatto del genio paganiniano è tale da sconvolgere canoni e prospettive date per certe: quantunque frutto di un'evoluzione coerente della tecnica strumentale, essa sembrerebbe collegarsi — anche in base alla sua matrice anti-accademica — a quanto già esemplificato, in ambito letterario settecentesco, dal gesuita Saverio Bettinelli:

> L'uomo di genio risentesi di se stesso, perché nasce con lui quell'ardore e quell'impazienza che il regge. A dispetto talor d'un maestro e d'una metodica disciplina se ne veggono sino ne' fanciulli le prime scosse, e una certa loro indocilità ne fa segno […][57].

Le riflessioni appena citate suonano particolarmente calzanti per inquadrare l'unicità di Paganini e la sua sostanziale indipendenza da ogni concetto di 'scuola' troppo strettamente inteso — fatti salvi tutti gli importanti legami di natura tecnica vigenti con Locatelli[58]. Nell'Ottocento, con il concetto di 'genio', che attirò l'attenzione anche di Mazzini e Foscolo, si vuole esprimere una personalità dalle straordinarie potenzialità che si erge — unico e solo — a inarrivabili altezze, esattamente come quello che si enuclea concettualmente in quanto scritto da Baillot, Rode e Kreutzer nella *Méthode de violon*[59]

---

[55]. «Si noti che la parola *Unendliche* (infinito), definita come l'"intenzione" (*Vorwurf*) della musica, che come tale si dischiude soprattutto nella musica strumentale, rinvia al saggio di Schiller *Über naive und sentimentalische Dichtung* […], nel quale essa è vista come il tratto caratteristico dell'*arte sentimentale* moderna di contro alla "perfezione del limite" (*Begrenzung*) propria dell'arte classica»; GUANTI, Giovanni. *Estetica musicale: la storia e le fonti*, Milano, La Nuova Italia, 1999 (Biblioteca di cultura. Storie di idee, 7), p. 285.

[56]. *Cfr.* HOFFMANN, Ernst Theodor Amadeus. 'Briefe über Tonkunst in Berlin: Erster Brief', in: *Allgemeine musikalische Zeitung*, XII (11 gennaio 1815), coll. 17-27.

[57]. BETTINELLI, Saverio. *Opere dell'abate Saverio Bettinelli*, 8 voll., Venezia, Zatta, 1780-1782, vol. II: *Dell'entusiasmo delle belle arti*, p. 147.

[58]. Sintomatica, a questo proposito, l'osservazione di François-Joseph-Marie Fayolle (*Paganini et Bériot: Avis aux jeunes artistes sur l'enseignement du violon*, Parigi, M. Legouest, 1831, p. 5): «Paganini n'a formé son talent prestigieux que sur les documents que les grands maîtres avaient rejetés de l'école du violon».

[59]. «Le génie, ce don du ciel que l'on reçoit en naissant, est toujours accompagné dans les arts d'une profonde sensibilité et d'une force de conception qui l'oblige à sortir du cercle ordinaire […] il imagine, il

e, non molti anni dopo, da Johann Nikolaus Forkel in relazione a Bach[60]. Questa idea trova una realizzazione compiuta sul piano pratico e artistico proprio in Paganini: «un des examples les plus frappants de la force presque surhumaine qui résulte de l'exaltation produite par le génie»[61].

IV

Berlioz racconta di come, subito dopo la fine del citato concerto parigino del 16 Dicembre 1838, Paganini, quasi completamente afono, pregasse il figlio Achille di riferire allo stremato direttore/autore francese la sua profonda ammirazione[62], mentre alla domanda di Julius Max Schottky circa quale particolare frase si potesse scegliere come esemplificativa del suo stile, Paganini avrebbe risposto: «Bisogna forte sentire per far sentire!»[63]. Proprio in questo assunto, che può esser considerato come il vero asse portante dell'estetica paganiniana, è possibile vedere una strettissima analogia, se non una vera e propria coincidenza, con il principio romantico secondo cui la musica si configura come un linguaggio dotato di assoluta autonomia, non riducibile o analizzabile razionalmente, quindi — forse anche in virtù di ciò — perfettamente funzionale alla più pura espressione del sentimento. Già Carl Philipp Emanuel Bach, nella prima parte del suo *Versuch*, aveva puntato l'attenzione precisamente sulla necessità, da parte del musicista, di sapere come trasfondere la medesima emozione e commozione provata nell'animo dell'ascoltatore. E se anche Carlo Gervasoni scrive

> Non è da porsi in dubbio che per commuover gli altri, è forza sentir se stesso vivamente commosso; e tutta l'arte onde ciò ottenere, consiste nel destare ed accendere nel proprio cuore quel fuoco che nel cuor degli altri portar si pretende [...][64]

è lo stesso Paganini a ribadire questo concetto-cardine, riferendosi esplicitamente a «cette faculté qui fait passer l'âme d'un exécutant au bout de ses doigts pour traduire en sons

---

crée, il fraye une route nouvelle, il recule les bornes de l'art, il donne l'élan à son siècle, et sert de modèle à la postérité»; BAILLOT, Pierre(-Marie-François de Sales) – RODE, Pierre – KREUTZER, Rodolphe. *Méthode de violon*, Parigi, Au Magasin de musique du Conservatoire, [1803], p. 2.

[60]. FORKEL, Johann Nikolaus. *Über Johann Sebastian Bachs Leben, Kunst und Kunstwerk. Für patriotische Verehrer echter musikalischer Kunst*, Lipsia, Peters, 1855, pp. 45-46.

[61]. IMBERT DE LAPHALÈQUE, George. *Op. cit.* (si veda nota 37), p. 53.

[62]. «Mon père m'ordonne de vous assurer, monsieur, que de sa vie il n'a éprouvé dans un concert une impression pareille; que votre musique l'a bouleversé et que s'il ne se retenait pas il se mettrait à vos genoux pour vous remercier [...]»; BERLIOZ, Hector. *Mémoires*, edizione presentata e annotata da Pierre Citron, Parigi, Flammarion, 2010 (Harmoniques: Série écrits de musiciens), p. 292.

[63]. SCHOTTKY, Julius Max. *Op. cit.* (si veda nota 2), p. 281.

[64]. GERVASONI, Carlo. *La scuola della musica*, Piacenza, Niccolò Orcesi, 1800, pp. 210-211.

les émotions»[65]. Ancora, se Hector Berlioz parla della musica come «art d'émovoir par les sons les êtres sensibles»[66], George Imbert de Laphalèque pone l'accento sull'inaudita capacità del genovese di avvicinarsi alla voce umana, mediante un canto commovente come nessun'altro mai udito sino a quel momento:

> […] jusqu'ici ce n'avait été qu'une indication isolée, qu'un accent transitoire; Paganini, avec des sons de cette nature, est parvenu à former des phrases entières de chant, dont l'effet, tant il est doux, pénétrant et pathétique, rappelle ces belles voix de femmes dans lesquelles on dit il y a des larmes[67].

Da un punto di vista tanto sociologico quanto storico-artistico, i virtuosi si pongono come gli antesignani della fatidica trasformazione del momento performativo in azione rituale e spiritualizzata in cui solista e ascoltatori si fondono in un unico nesso di soggettività. Per questa ragione il virtuosismo paganiniano acquista un valore che va ben oltre la mera abilità digitale, prefigurandosi invece quale mezzo privilegiato mediante cui una determinata competenza s'innalza a essenza stessa dell'auto-espressione. Non va d'altronde dimenticato che, per quel che concerne in particolare l'Italia, questa insistenza sull'istanza sentimentale sembra godere di una più vasta diffusione in ogni dominio dell'arte, come dimostrano vari esempi in campo letterario[68]. In virtù di ciò, fatta salva l'assoluta estraneità al contesto culturale in cui vengono concepiti, in Paganini è forse possibile scorgere la prima compiuta e reale incarnazione dei tre concetti basilari dell'estetica del romanticismo musicale tedesco, rappresentati dai termini *Empfindung*, *Gefühl* e *Ausdruck*. Il delicato equilibrio tra il fattore strettamente digitale e quello di natura più spirituale, inerente sia l'evoluzione della tecnica strumentale quanto il dischiudersi di nuovi orizzonti timbrici, costituisce il nucleo centrale dell'istanza rivoluzionaria paganiniana. Questo è infatti il lascito più artisticamente valido che dal maestro eredita Camillo Sivori, prima ancora dell'esorbitante bagaglio di funambolismi tecnici che quest'ultimo pur impiegherà, in modo sfrenato, in composizioni come *Fiori di Napoli* Op. 22, *Folies espagnoles* Op. 29, o in alcuni degli *Études – Caprices* Op. 25[69]. In pieno spirito schumanniano, un tratto autenticamente romantico di Paganini

---

[65]. Per la frase, contenuta nella lettera parigina a Douglas Loveday del 14 luglio 1838, *cfr.* Paganini, Nicolò. *Epistolario*, a cura di Edward Neill, Genova, La Comune, 1982, p. 306.

[66]. Berlioz, Hector. 'Deux aperçus', in: *Le correspondent* del 22 ottobre 1830, ora in Id. *Cauchemars et passions*, a cura di Gérard Condé, Parigi, J.-C. Lattés, 1981, p. 92 (Musique et musiciens).

[67]. Imbert de Laphalèque, George. *Op. cit.* (si veda nota 37), p. 17.

[68]. A questa è infatti connessa la fortuna in letteratura del romanzo, hegelianamente inteso quale unica epica borghese possibile, e come rimarcato anche da Silvio Pellico in una recensione di un romanzo inglese per *Il Conciliatore*: «non è meraviglia se le donne gustano sovra ogni altra la lettura de' romanzi, di quelli cioè dove la società è ritratta nel vero, e dove il cuore umano è analizzato con la più minuta esattezza»; *Il Conciliatore: foglio scientifico-letterario*, a cura di Vittore Branca, 3 voll., Firenze, Le Monnier, 1953, vol. II: *Anno II (gennaio-giugno 1819)*, p. 17.

[69]. *Cfr.* Ricco, Renato. 'L'eredità di Nicolò Paganini nelle musiche di Camillo Sivori e Antonio Rolla', in: *Nicolò Paganini: Diabolus in musica, op. cit.* (si veda nota 3), pp. 469-433. A differenza di Sivori, Franz

si può quindi identificare nell'inseparabile nesso vigente tra la sua persona e la sua arte, con la prima che si identifica e si fonde armonicamente nella seconda, senza una netta linea di demarcazione: questo aspetto è reso bene dal ritratto di Delacroix, in cui lo strumento del violino si pone come centro focale dell'opera, in quanto mezzo attraverso cui si attua l'osmosi tra sofferenza fisica e produzione di un fenomeno artistico. Per Paganini, lo strumento è infatti un organismo vivo e palpitante, capace anche di esser «scorrucciato» con il suo possessore, come dichiarato nella lettera a Germi del 23 Dicembre 1836[70], mentre due anni dopo, in occasione della seconda riparazione al Guarnieri, assistendo all'apertura della cassa da parte di Jean-Baptiste Vuillaume, Paganini avrebbe commentato: «fu come se uno scalpello penetrasse nella mia carne»[71]. A differenza di Schumann, però, la musica non viene investita — o a volte forse anche gravata — da Paganini di significati simbolici, che talvolta possono schiacciare l'obiettivo valore artistico della composizione musicale. Per contro, analogamente al Berglinger di Wackenroder, Paganini sembra, come dimostrato in alcuni passi di varie lettere, quasi annullare se stesso in nome di una totale devozione all'arte.

V

Al fine di capire le radici del 'demonismo' paganiniano sono necessarie indagini che riguardano tanto una determinata produzione letteraria quanto un particolare tipo di critica musicale. Per quanto riguarda il primo aspetto, vari esempi di connessione tra il virtuosismo violinistico e il sovrannaturale a questo sovente associato meritano d'essere messi in luce[72]. Uno dei primi casi è la figura di Franzesco, diabolico musicista di origini italiane, che nella novella epistolare di Friedrich Rochlitz, *Aus dem Leben eines Tonkünstlers: Fragment* (1802), presenta, non a caso, vaghe ma significative somiglianze con Paganini, come il viso emaciato e la chioma bruna e riccia. L'equivalenza violino = strumento del diavolo è palese anche nella novella hoffmanniana *Rat Krespel*, compresa nell'ampio progetto dei

---

Liszt, sulla scia di quanto metabolizzato dalla lezione paganiniana, riuscirà nell'ardua impresa di sviluppare, integrare ed inquadrare il virtuosismo in una più complessa problematica formale. Se è innegabile che Sivori può effettivamente configurarsi come allievo di Paganini, come anche altri violinisti italiani poterono giovarsi dei suoi consigli — su tutti Antonio Rolla, Nicola de Giovanni, Carlo Bignami, Onorio de Vito, Giuseppe Grasso D'Anna —, per indole e temperamento Paganini non sembrò avere particolarmente a cuore, a differenza di Alessandro Rolla, il concetto di 'scuola'.

    70. PAGANINI, Nicolò. *Epistolario, op. cit.* (si veda nota 65), p. 223.

    71. Per la frase, riferita dallo stesso Vuillaume a Louis Vidal, *cfr.* BORER, Philippe. 'Le corde di Paganini: some Reflections on Paganini's Strings', in: *Recupero e conservazione del violino Guarneri del Gesù (1743) detto «Cannone». Atti del Convegno Internazionale di Liuteria (Genova, Civica Biblioteca Berio, giovedì 14 ottobre 2004)*, a cura dell'Assessorato comunicazione e promozione della città, Genova, Assessorato comunicazione e promozione della città, 2006, p. 86.

    72. *Cfr.* SUCHOWIEJKO, Renata. *Op. cit.* (si veda nota 36), p. 103.

Serapionbrüder, cui l'autore lavora tra il 1819 e il 1821, quindi con Paganini attivo ancora su suolo esclusivamente italiano. In particolare, il 1820 è un anno fondamentale per la letteratura romantica europea, poiché vedono la luce *Melmoth the Wanderer* di Charles Robert Maturin[73], magistrale esempio inglese di romanzo *noir*, in cui «il tipo byronico finisce per confondersi col Mefistofele del grande tedesco»[74], e le *Méditations poétiques* di Alphonse de Lamartine, che si impongono per il trattamento sentimentale di temi intimi e religiosi: proprio nel 1820 — anno cruciale per il romanticismo musicale francese[75] — viene pubblicata, presso Ricordi, una delle opere più rappresentative di Paganini, i *24 Capricci* Op. 1. Da un punto di vista storico, inoltre, per i destini italiani questa annata rappresenta un passaggio importante, dal momento che nel 1819 viene chiuso dalla censura austriaca *Il Conciliatore*, nel luglio del 1820 si verificano i moti rivoluzionari di Napoli e Palermo, e nell'ottobre vengono arrestati Pellico e Maroncelli. Non è d'altronde secondario il fatto che Paganini sia stato il primo musicista a scegliere il rivoluzionario tema de *La Carmagnola* per farne oggetto di variazioni virtuose. Dopo l'arrivo dei federati marsigliesi in Liguria, nell'agosto del 1792, la popolazione locale fraternizzò con i francesi, innalzando l'Albero della Libertà in piazza Acquaverde — gesto di ripresa del *planter un mai* parigino — e ballandovi intorno. Ai fischi destinati alle danze d'estrazione aristocratica, come ad esempio la *Controdanza inglese*, in teatro il popolo chiedeva a gran voce la *contraddanza genovese*, cioè appunto *La Carmagnola*[76]. Queste constatazioni di carattere storico-letterario sono inoltre da connettersi con le coincidenze cronologiche che inseriscono Paganini all'interno del momento cruciale della stagione artistica ottocentesca, di svolta rispetto al secolo precedente. Paganini appone ai *Capricci* la dedica «Alli Artisti», mettendo in risalto la piena consapevolezza del suo ruolo di musicista e la novità dell'approccio[77]: questa particolare dedica assume valore sinesteticamente pregnante — come implicito riconoscimento di

---

[73]. «Paganini's concerts gave audiences the same kind of thrill they experienced from reading Gothic literature»; Kawabata, Maiko. 'Virtuosity, the Violin, the Devil…: What Really Made Paganini «Demonic»?', in: *Current Musicology*, n. 83 (primavera 2007), p. 98. Seguendo questa metodologia comparativa musica/letteratura, è utile notare come il 1794 veda sia la pubblicazione del primo concerto di Pierre Rode, in cui sono già presenti quasi tutti i tratti stilistici peculiari della nuova produzione brillante ottocentesca di marca viottiana, nella quale anche Paganini s'inserisce, sia — sempre per rimanere in contesto letterario anglosassone — la prima edizione de *The Mysteries of Udolpho* di Ann Radcliffe, archetipo del romanzo gotico.

[74]. Praz, Mario. *La carne, la morte e il diavolo nella letteratura romantica*, Firenze, Sansoni, 1966 (Biblioteca Sansoni, 14), p. 113.

[75]. *Cfr.* Reynaud, Cécile. 'Comment on devient romantique: Berlioz et la génération de 1820', in: *Paris 1820: l'affirmation de la génération romantique. Actes de la journée d'étude organisée par le Centre André Chastel le 24 mai 2004*, a cura di Sébastien Allard, Berna, Peter Lang, 2005, pp. 171-184.

[76]. *Cfr.* Neill, Edward. 'Paganini oltre il virtuosismo', in: *La Casana*, n. 4 (1978), pp. 8-9 e Id. 'Introduzione', in: Paganini, Nicolò. *Variazioni sulla Carmagnola: per violino e chitarra*, a cura di Salvatore Accardo, Genova, Istituto Studi Paganiniani, 1980, p. 3.

[77]. Benché l'interpretazione da parte di Israil Markovitch Yampolski dei *Capricci* come possibile manifesto della musica romantica sia indubbiamente forzata; *cfr.* Borer, Philippe. *The Twenty-four Caprices of*

autonomia e dignità artistica — se messa in relazione con l'*incipit* della *Préface des Orientales*, del 1829, in cui Hugo dichiara: «Le poëte est libre». Solo un anno prima Paganini iniziava la *tournée*, inaugurata col concerto viennese del 16 marzo, in cui si cristallizza la sua immagine 'demoniaca', sancita dall'appellativo di *Hexensohn* attribuitogli da Zelter, e sempre nel 1828 compare la prima traduzione, ad opera di Gérard de Nerval, del *Faust* goethiano, che già tanto impressionò il giovane Berlioz. In Paganini, o meglio nell'immagine che di lui viene quasi subito data, sembrano inoltre coesistere entrambe le sfaccettature derivanti dalla relazione con il demoniaco: sia quella più propriamente legata al terrore e al sentimento di paura sia quella — come dimostra numerosa iconografia fiorita con Paganini ancora vivo — più caricaturale e tendente al grottesco. Anche se non esclusivo appannaggio di Paganini[78], è comunque innegabile che egli sia il vero polo catalizzatore dell'idea luciferina del violino. Se la cifra dell'irrazionalità diventa distintiva dell'arte di Paganini in nome di una non spiegabile, strabiliante, abilità tecnica[79], il 'demonismo' paganiniano ha una precisa origine e spiegazione nelle parole di Johann Wolfgang von Goethe che, nella conversazione con Johann Peter Eckermann, spiega:

> Desgleichen [dämonisch] ist in der Musik im höchsten Grade, denn sie steht so hoch, dass kein Verstand ihr beikommen kann, und es geht von ihr eine Wirkung aus, die alles beherrscht und von der niemand imstande ist, sich Rechenschaft zu geben[80].

Poco prima lo stesso Goethe aveva specificato che «Bei Paganini zeigt es sich im hohe Grade»[81]. È opportuno porre nuovamente attenzione ad alcune contingenze cronologiche: la conversazione goethiana reca la data 2 marzo 1831, al contempo il biennio 1830-1831 risulta cruciale per il romanticismo, non solo musicale. Nel 1830, se in letteratura Hugo, nella prefazione a *Hernani*, individua le istanze liberali proprie del movimento, in musica Berlioz termina la *Symphonie fantastique*, mentre Schumann pubblica la sua Op. 1 e Mendelssohn il

---

Niccolò Paganini and Their Significance in the Romantic Era, Zurigo, Stiftung Zentralstelle der Studentenschaft der Universität Zürich, 1997, pp. 44-45.

[78]. Léon Escudier (*Littérature musicale: mes Souvenirs: les virtuoses*, Parigi, Dentu, 1868, p. 229) racconta ad esempio dello strumento di Henry Vieuxtemps che, causa una tempesta in mare, durante un viaggio transoceanico, fu ritenuto «le violon du diable», correndo perciò seri rischi d'esser gettato tra le onde.

[79]. Anche per questo, probabilmente, nei confronti di Paganini Goethe non dimostrò particolare apprezzamento: l'impossibilità di ascrivere una certa idea di musica come anche una determinata prassi esecutiva al regno della *Vernunft* non poteva che essere associata alla follia di cui non a caso paradigmatico esempio è il personaggio dell'arpista dei *Wanderjahre*, «risultato di un soggettivismo esasperato che si è posto fuori della sfera dei legami sociali e di un misticismo religioso che oscura il richiamo della ragione naturale»; DI STEFANO, Giovanni. *Op. cit.* (si veda nota 42), p. 67.

[80]. ECKERMANN, Johann Peter. *Gespräche mit Goethe in den letzen Jahren seines Lebens*, Monaco, Beck, ²1984, p. 407.

[81]. *Ibidem*, p. 405.

suo primo fascicolo di *Lieder ohne Worte*; dal canto suo, Paganini, già oggetto di monografie di vario tipo[82] e all'apice della sua parabola, presenta a Francoforte il suo Concerto per violino e orchestra n. 4 in Re minore. Il 21 novembre 1831, Giacomo Meyerbeer presenta a Parigi *Robert le diable*, il cui libretto di Scribe e Delavigne fornisce un intreccio romanzesco perfetto per le atmosfere macabre e fantastiche realizzate musicalmente dal compositore tedesco, ed elementi ugualmente demoniaci — in diretta discendenza dal *Don Giovanni* mozartiano — erano stati anche tratto saliente di *Zampa, ou la fiancée de marbre* di Louis-Joseph-Ferdinand Hérold, eseguito per la prima volta il 3 maggio con immediato successo. Proprio in questo contesto Paganini, esattamente una settimana dopo la data della conversazione goethiana, cioè il 9 marzo, esordisce all'*Académie Royale de Musique*, presente Franz Liszt[83]. All'aprile 1830, secondo la testimonianza di Eduard Genast[84], risale inoltre l'iniziale reazione negativa di Goethe all'ascolto dell'*Erlkönig* schubertiano, a causa dell'insistenza, da parte del musicista, sullo *Schauerlich*[85]; non è casuale che proprio questo *Lied* di Schubert sarà in seguito fatto oggetto di un arrangiamento, oltre che da parte di Liszt, anche da parte di Heinrich Wilhelm Ernst, forse unico autentico violinista erede del lascito paganiniano[86].

Per meglio comprendere la ricezione della figura di Paganini, e soprattutto la distorsione che questa subisce, è necessaria però anche un'altra riflessione. Durante la primavera del 1832, a Parigi, scoppia la grande epidemia di colera che, stando alle descrizioni heiniane[87], ha un influsso di straordinaria portata anche sulla letteratura, come dimostrano, ad esempio, i racconti di Edgar Allan Poe *King Pest* e *Mask of Red Death*. Nello stesso anno Eugène Delacroix dipinge il ritratto di Nicolò Paganini[88], la cui seconda *tournée*, da marzo a

---

[82].   Oltre i lavori citati di Guhr, Schottky e Imbert de Laphalèque, *cfr.* anche Harrys, George. *Paganini in seine Reisewagen und Zimmer, in seinen redseligen Stunden, in gesellschaftlichen Zirkeln und seinen Concerten*, Brunswick, F. Vieweg, 1830; Anders, Gottfried Engelbert. *Nicolò Paganini, sa vie, sa personne et quelques mots sur son secret*, Parigi, Delunay, 1831; Guibal du Rivage, Alexandre. *Réflexions d'un artiste sur le talent de Paganini*, Parigi, Dentu, 1831.

[83].   Della Seta pone l'attenzione dell'influsso paganiniano sul virtuosismo pianistico, dal momento che, stabilmente o di passaggio, nella capitale francese gravitavano, oltre a Liszt e Chopin, anche John Field, Frédéric Kalkbrenner, Johann Peter Pixis, Ignaz Moscheles, Ferdinand Hiller, Sigmond Thalberg, e Stephen Heller; Della Seta, Fabrizio. *Italia e Francia nell'Ottocento*, Torino, EdT, 1993 (Storia della musica, 9), p. 27.

[84].   *Cfr.* Genast, Eduard. *Aus dem Tagebuche eines alten Schauspielers*, 4 voll., Lipsia, Voigt & Günther, 1862-1866, vol. II, pp. 280-281.

[85].   *Cfr.* Byrne, Lorraine. 'Perceptions of Goethe and Schubert', in: *Music and Literature in German Romanticism*, a cura di Siobhán Donovan e Robin Elliott, Rochester (NY), Cadmen House, 2004, in particolare pp. 64-66.

[86].   *Cfr.* Rowe, Mark W. *Heinrich Wilhelm Ernst: Virtuoso Violinist*, Aldershot, Ashgate, 2008.

[87].   *Cfr.* Huet, Marie-Hélène. *The Culture of Disaster*, Chicago, Chicago University Press, 2012, pp. 72-75.

[88].   *Cfr.* Athanassoglou-Kallmyer, Nina. 'Blemished Physiologies: Delacroix, Paganini and the Colera Epidemic of 1832', in: *The Art Bulletin*, LXXXIV/4 (dicembre 2001), pp. 686-710.

giugno dello stesso anno, viene a capitare proprio nel momento cruciale dell'esplosione del fenomeno epidemico: il primo concerto di Paganini — in data 25 marzo — anticipa infatti solo di pochi giorni l'annuncio del primo morto a causa del colera. Se Parigi era la vera capitale della musica europea, particolarmente per gli strumentisti[89], l'arrivo di Paganini[90], sul cui conto, grazie principalmente a Jules Janin, aleggiavano menzogne di varia natura (la più diffusa era relativa a una permanenza in carcere, durante cui egli sarebbe entrato in contatto con il maligno), viene a cadere in un momento in cui l'immaginario collettivo era già scosso dal colera, anche alla luce delle conseguenze politiche, sociologiche e spirituali che il morbo comportò: il terrore del contagio che assale e mina le fondamenta della tranquillità della 'società civile'. I due fattori — colera e Paganini[91] — vengono subito accostati dalla stampa parigina, come dimostra ad esempio il *Journal des débats* del 23 aprile, in cui la descrizione fisiologica di Paganini sembra mettere in evidenza gli aspetti più inquietanti della sua figura:

> Paganini […] reparait dans ces jours de peste, cet homme noir. Ce sombre génie à la tête penchée, aux cheveux flottants, au corps brisé et qui plie sur la hanche droite; le voilà qui rejette en l'air son archet et son âme […] c'est certainement la plus bizarre et la plus sublime créature des temps modernes, — tout cela un jour de peste — un vendredi saint […][92].

Ancora, è utile riportare, per la particolare scelta dei vocaboli volutamente indirizzata a confondere il fenomeno infettivo con lo svolgersi delle varie stagioni concertistiche, quanto scritto nel terzo numero de *L'Artiste*, sempre del 1832; ovvi sono i ricorrenti riferimenti a Paganini:

---

[89]. «During the Age of the Revolution, Paris became the center of a cyclone of virtuosity, as increasing numbers of highly skilled performers arrived from around Europe and the rate of their exhibitions accelerated. Paris was at the same time the center of an anticyclone, as native or naturalized virtuosos flew out from there to tour Europe»; METZNER, Paul. *Op. cit.* (si veda nota 30), p. 2. A ciò si aggiunga che «la *democratizzazione* della musica e l'apertura dei teatri d'opera e delle sale da concerto al pubblico e al gusto di massa hanno accresciuto l'importanza del critico che, come Berlioz, poteva scrivere con intelligenza e raffinatezza e, soprattutto, con competenza»; RAYNOR, Henry. *Storia sociale della musica*, a cura di Ettore Napoli, traduzione italiana di Cristina Petri, Milano, Il Saggiatore, 1990 (La cultura), p. 445.

[90]. L'attesa per l'arrivo del virtuoso italiano, nella capitale francese, era spasmodica. Eccone una dimostrazione, a puro titolo d'esempio: «Voilà déjà plus d'un an qu'on nous annonce la venue de Paganini; il est vrai que ce merveilleux violiniste s'est mis en route pour notre capitale; les chevaux attelés à son char galopent tout aussi vite que ceux d'un courrier diplomatique, et pourtant Le bien aimé n'arrive pas! Disent les *dilettanti* désappointés […]»; *Journal des débats*, 9 febbraio 1830, p. 1.

[91]. «Paganini's "cadaverous" appearance was elsewhere interpreted as a symptom of cholera and the horrors and degenerative effects of cholera epidemic provided a metaphor for contemporary aesthetics»; KAWABATA, Maiko. 'Virtuosity, the Violin, the Devil […]', *op. cit.* (si veda nota 73), p. 89.

[92]. 'Les consolations', in: *Journal des débats*, 23 aprile 1832, p. 1.

> Cette année, le concert donne prodigieusement. Nous en sommes non pas accablés, mais infectés. C'est une rage, une épidémie [...]. Quoi qu'en soi le concert foisonne [...] sous toutes ses formes [...] instrumental, vocal [...] classique, romantique [...] soporifique [...] et quelquefois même cholérique [...] Paris est envahi par le concert et le cholera. Ce contraste du plaisir et de la mort est partout [...]. Les conversations, les journaux, les rues, les murs, tout est tapissé de musique et de peste. La mort a revêtu son grand uniforme moitié noir, moitié rose [...]. Au dehors, le rappel, le tocsin, la fusillade, les empoisonneurs, les cadavres violacés; au dedans les fêtes, l'archet de la folie [...][93].

Paganini, quindi, come «King Pest»[94]. Un'anticipazione di questo *trend* sembra aversi già nel 1831, con l'utilizzo, sempre a proposito di Paganini, del termine di «cadavérisation», presente nella *Notice physiologique sur Paganini* di Bennati[95]; ulteriore conferma di tutto questo si può scorgere inoltre anche in quanto riportato dallo scultore Pierre-Jean David d'Angers:

> Ricorderò a lungo l'espressione di Paganini nel giorno in cui gli vennero estratti dei denti [...] "Ho avuto qualche dente estratto, ma voglio tirarli via tutti". Egli disse queste parole con una di quelle espressioni terribili capaci di rendere il suo viso terribilmente selvaggio [...]. Dopodiché scoppiò in una prolungata risata, che non aveva nulla di umano, ma assomigliava piuttosto ad un rantolo di uno stomaco malato. Al contempo, del sangue scorreva agli angoli della sua bocca, il che gli conferiva un aspetto orrido[96].

Se la connessione violino/inferi non nasce *ex novo* con Paganini — basti pensare alla definizione di «arcidiavolo» che Arcangelo Corelli attribuì al violinista Nicolas Strunk per la sua 'diabolica' abilità nell'uso delle doppie corde[97] — è sicuramente l'autore de *Le Streghe* a porsi, anche in virtù della sua «fictionalized persona»[98], come l'incarnazione artisticamente

---

93. *L'Artiste: Journal de la littérature et des beaux arts*, I/3 (1832), p. 109.

94. Cfr. Athanassoglou-Kallmyer, Nina. *Op. cit.* (si veda nota 88), p. 699.

95. Bennati, Francesco. 'Notice physiologique sur le célèbre violoniste Niccolò Paganini', in: *Revue de Paris*, XXVI/17 (maggio 1831), pp. 52-60. Per un inquadramento della vicenda biografica e artistica di Paganini da una prospettiva di chiaramente medica cfr. O'Shea, John. *Musica e medicina. Profili medici di grandi compositori*, traduzione italiana di Marina Verna, Torino, EdT, 1991 (Biblioteca di cultura musicale. Improvvisi, 2), pp. 61-82.

96. La traduzione italiana è di Neill, Edward. *Nicolò Paganini il cavaliere filarmonico*, Genova, De Ferrari, 1990, pp. 346-347, mentre per la versione originale cfr. David d'Angers, Pierre-Jean. *Les carnets de David D'Angers*, 2 voll., Parigi, Plon, 1958, vol. I: *1828-1837*, p. 201.

97. Tempo, Claudio. 'Il virtuosismo e Paganini', in: *Incontri con la musica di Paganini. Atti del Seminario di studi a cura dell'Istituto di Studi Paganiniani (Genova, 5-6 Marzo 1982), in occasione del secondo centenario della nascita di Niccolò Paganini)*, Genova, Comune, 1984, p. 82 e Wilkins, Nigel Edward. *La musique du diable*, Sprimont, Mardaga, 1999 (Musique-musicologie), pp. 120-124.

98. Athanassoglou-Kallmyer, Nina. *Op. cit.* (si veda nota 88), p. 688.

più compiuta e attraente del virtuoso mefistofelico, ponendosi al contempo come estrema appendice di quel processo le cui basi sono rintracciabili nei procedimenti monodici del violinismo del '600 e '700[99]. È d'altronde innegabile che senza Paganini non sarebbe forse neanche del tutto spiegabile la fortuna che il soggetto faustiano, grazie all'opera di Gounod, ebbe presso i virtuosi[100]: il tema tratto dall'opera goethiana si prestava infatti a una perfetta e quasi teatrale resa strumentale, con la giustapposizione di una serie di episodi in cui il contrasto dei caratteri, che si svolge esclusivamente sul piano timbrico e sonoro, è legato alla messa in mostra di tutti gli artifici virtuosistici, come la danza di Mefistofele della *Fantasie brillante* Op. 20 di Wieniawski ben dimostra. Per la sua intrinseca volontà di oltrepassare i limiti umani, d'altronde, la figura di Faust ben si associa a quella del virtuoso, e in particolar modo a Paganini, che mira a trascendere, ampliandoli iperbolicamente, i limiti oggettivi dello strumento. Figura infernale, in virtù del patto con Mefistofele, Faust è però visto anche in un'accezione positiva quale nuovo Prometeo, «archetipo del genio incompreso, un portatore di luce ignorato dalla comunità chiusa nelle tenebre dei pregiudizi e dell'ipocrisia»[101]. Ponendosi come colui che affascina e disorienta mediante un'arte tanto prodigiosa da trovare nella collusione con il maligno l'unica possibile giustificazione, Paganini scardina completamente la precedente idea del violino, dischiudendo nuovi orizzonti tecnici e timbrici. Non a caso, connesso al tema faustiano, tra i fondanti l'intera cultura europea moderna, vi è anche quello della fascinazione, che comporta una nuova idea di corporeità inaugurata da Paganini e Liszt, veri creatori dell'immagine 'eroica' dello strumentista[102]. Se per quest'ultimo sono sufficienti le parole di Schumann, circa la necessità

[99]. *Cfr.* DAHLHAUS, Carl. *La musica dell'Ottocento, op. cit.* (si veda nota 49), p. 145. A tale proposito, Franco Piperno cita Marini e Monteverdi quali primi autori nelle cui musiche sia ravvisabile «una prima consapevole risposta alla questione più problematica posta da una musica strumentale intenzionata a sottrarsi al ruolo di surrogato o imitazione della vocalità per porsi in emulazione/competizione con essa»; PIPERNO, Franco. 'Modelli stilistici e strategie compositive della musica strumentale del Seicento', in: *Enciclopedia della musica*, diretta da Jean-Jacques Nattiez, con la collaborazione di Margaret Bent, Rossana Dalmonte e Mario Baroni, 5 voll., Torino, Einaudi, 2001-2004, vol. IV: *Storia della musica europea*, 2004, p. 433.

[100]. Mori, Sivori, Wieniawski, Vieuxtemps, Alard, Sarasate (in due differenti composizioni), Léonard, Dancla, Bezekirsky, Bertuzzi, Anzoletti: questo un elenco non completo di violinisti che composero virtuosistiche fantasie, o comunque utilizzarono temi, in relazione all'opera di Gounod. Una delle prime significative associazioni Paganini-Mefistofele pare sia da attribuirsi a Joseph d'Ortigue: «Oui, c'est bien lui, Méphistophélès, que j'ai vu et entendu jouer du violon, et plus d'un millier d'auditeurs l'ont entendu et vu comme moi»; D'ORTIGUE, Joseph-Louis (attribuito a). 'Paganini', in: *L'Avénir*, 12 marzo 1831, p. 1. Utile a tale proposito la tabella 'Paganini's "Demonic" Monikers' in KAWABATA, Maiko. 'Virtuosity, the Violin, the Devil [...]', *op. cit.* (si veda nota 73), p. 87.

[101]. MARCHAND, Guy. 'Il mito di Faust e la musica nel secolo XIX', in: *Enciclopedia della musica, op. cit.* (si veda nota 99), p. 1003.

[102]. *Cfr.* SACHS, Harvey. *Virtuoso: The Life and Art of Niccolò Paganini, Franz Liszt, Anton Rubinstein, Ignace Jan Paderewski, Fritz Kreisler, Pablo Casals, Wanda Landowska, Vladimir Horowitz, Glenn Gould*, New York, Thames & Hudson, 1982, p. 12; KAWABATA, Maiko. *Paganini: The 'Demonic' Virtuoso*, Woodbridge,

di vedere, oltre che di ascoltare, il pianista ungherese[103], su Paganini si sono sprecati ritratti e descrizioni volti a mettere in luce ogni tratto più bizzarro, sinistro, eccezionale, mirabile, inquietante relativo alla sua fisiognomica o alla sua corporeità. Ciò è assolutamente coerente con la capitale importanza assunta dal momento esecutivo, che acquista medesimo valore rispetto a quello compositivo, e proprio in quest'ottica, un ruolo di assoluta centralità riveste la pratica improvvisativa, di cui sia Paganini[104] che Liszt diedero magistrali esempi. In Paganini, quindi, per la prima volta, si realizza compiutamente un perfetto equilibrio tra i tre elementi della composizione, dell'esecuzione e dell'interpretazione, dove quest'ultima si configura quasi come prolungamento/completamento del suo atto creativo di composizione[105].

VI

Gli anni che vanno dalla pubblicazione dei *Capricci* alla prima *tournée* paganiniana fuori dall'Italia sono anche quelli del massimo fulgore, in terra francese, di Pierre Baillot, la cui formazione violinistica, a differenza di quella paganiniana, risulta essere saldamente basata sull'attento studio del repertorio del secolo precedente. Un'altra significativa differenza riguarda il lato caratteriale: al divismo di Paganini si contrappone infatti, a detta dei contemporanei, la natura timida e riservata di Baillot[106]. Convinto diffusore, al pari di Liszt, della musica di Beethoven, Baillot pubblicò la sua *Art du violon* nel 1831, contemporaneamente alla *Violischule* di Louis Spohr, nell'anno forse del picco massimo del genio paganiniano a conquista dell'Europa, con concerti in Germania, Francia, Inghilterra e Irlanda. Contrariamente alla tendenza improvvisativa e alla labilità del concetto di *Urtext* propria di Paganini, Pierre Baillot si propone invece come castigato e severo esecutore di autori classici e di vari periodi stilistici, in contrasto con altri virtuosi che si limitavano,

---

Boydell & Press, 2013, e RAYKOFF, Ivan. *Dreams of Love: Playing the Romantic Pianist*, Oxford, Oxford University Press, 2014, in particolare il decimo e conclusivo capitolo 'Virile Virtuosity', pp. 199-222.

[103]. *Cfr.* SCHUMANN, Robert. 'Franz Lißt', in: *Neue Zeitschrift für Musik*, XII/26 (27 marzo 1840), pp. 102-103. Le osservazioni schumanniane ricalcano quanto scritto da Hoffmann venticinque anni prima: «Ich sage mit Bedacht: sehen und hören. Die allgemeine Begierde, im Konzert nicht allein zu hören, sondern auch zu sehen, das Drängen nach Plätzen im Saal, wo dies möglich ist, entsteht gewiß nicht aus bloßer, müßiger Schaulust: man hört besser, wenn man sieht; die geheime Verwandtschaft von Licht und Ton offenbart sich deutlich; beides, Licht und Ton, gestaltet sich in individueller Form, und so wird der Solospieler, die Sängerin selbst die ertönende Melodie»; HOFFMANN, Ernst Theodor Amadeus. 'Briefe über Tonkunst in Berlin […]', *op. cit.* (si veda nota 56), col. 20.

[104]. *Cfr.* BORER, Philippe. 'Paganini's Virtuosity and Improvisatory Style', *op. cit.* (si veda nota 52), pp. 191-215 e ILLIANO, Roberto. 'Paganini. A Virtuoso Composer', in: *Henryk Wieniawski and the Bravura Tradition*, *op. cit.* (si veda nota 13), pp. 149-157.

[105]. *Cfr.* SUPIČIĆ, Ivo. *La musique expressive*, Parigi, Presses Universitaires de France, 1957 (Bibliothèque international de musicologie), p. 87.

[106]. *Cfr.* PROD'HOMME, Jacques-Gabriel. 'The Baron de Trémont. Souvenirs of Beethoven and Other Contemporaries', in: *The Musical Quarterly*, VI/3 (luglio 1920), pp. 373-374.

nelle pubbliche esecuzioni, alle loro opere[107]. Il francese, secondo i giudizi dell'epoca, è un artista di rango perché «dépouille son moi»[108], riuscendo a essere di volta in volta Haydn, Boccherini, Mozart e Beethoven: è il violinista stesso, d'altronde, a specificare che al fine di ottenere un'ottima interpretazione è necessario «tout traduire, tout animer, faire passer dans l'âme de l'auditeur le sentiment que le compositeur avait dans la sienne»[109]. Baillot, pur non condividendone sino in fondo alcune soluzioni stilistiche più audaci, nutre una sincera stima nei confronti di Paganini, come dimostra questo passaggio della lettera del 20 marzo 1831 indirizzata all'amico Montbeillard:

> Je vais ce soir au troisième concert de Paganini: c'est un talent admirable, vraiment prodigieux, un phénomène en musique, faisant des choses merveilleuses et les faisant avec une facilité et une perfection dont rien ne peut donner une juste idée. [...] N'attendez donc pas de moi une critique, je ne puis voir en ce moment que ses éminentes qualités, justesse à toute épreuve, aplomb que je ne puis comparer qu'a celui de Viotti, netteté et facilité inouïes, tout cela joint à beaucoup de chaleur, de sentiment et d'originalité: voilà Paganini[110].

Ancora più chiaro, del resto, quanto scritto nel trattato *L'art du violon*:

> Inscrire dans cet ouvrage le nom de Mr Paganini au moment où le succès qu'il vient d'obtenir à Paris justifient sa réputation est pour nous un devoir et un honneur indépendamment du plaisir que nous éprouvons à lui rendre justice[111].

La puntuale disamina, da parte di Baillot, dei vari problemi tecnici, l'approfondimento di quelli sino ad allora meno trattati, le minuziose osservazioni relative ai differenti colpi d'arco in relazione al tempo e al carattere del pezzo, vengono quindi a porsi, seppur con le dovute e indubbie distinzioni, come una ulteriore — e coeva di Paganini — evoluzione della maniera di percepire, vedere e vivere il violino, con tutte le ovvie conseguenze sul repertorio relativo. Paganini e Baillot sembrano inoltre essere accomunati, ognuno in linea con la propria natura artistica, da due fattori fondamentali. In primo luogo, la convinzione, chiaramente esplicitata dal francese[112], della centralità del momento esecutivo, vissuto ormai

---

107. *Cfr.* PORTA, Enzo. *Il violino nella storia: maestri, tecniche, scuole*, Torino, EdT, 2000 (I manuali EdT/SIdM), p. 252.

108. FAYOLLE, François-Joseph-Marie. *Op. cit.* (si veda nota 58), p. 41.

109. BAILLOT, Pierre(-Marie-François de Sales). *L'Art du violon: nouvelle méthode*, Parigi, Au Dépôt central de la musique, [1835], p. 266. Altrettanto importante, al fine di una distinzione tra i ruoli dell'esecutore e del compositore, è il seguente passaggio: «"l'exécutant" parvient à exprimer la pensée d'un autre à l'aide des signes qu'il convertit en idées, tandis que le "compositeur" réussit à peindre la sienne à l'aide des idées qu'il converti en signes»; *ibidem*, p. 261.

110. Citato in SAUZAY, Eugène – FRANÇOIS-SAPPEY, Brigitte. *Op. cit.* (si veda nota 20), p. 194.

111. BAILLOT, Pierre(-Marie-François de Sales). *Op. cit.* (si veda nota 109), p. 6.

112. «L'exécution est le premier moyen de création»; *ibidem*, p. 261.

come atto propriamente creativo. In secondo luogo, l'idea del 'sentimento' posta come insostituibile fondamento dell'arte musicale. Se Paganini sembra dare di ciò un'icastica definizione nella frase — già citata — dettata a Schottky e relativa all'importanza del 'sentire', Baillot definisce come fine ultimo della musica quello «d'émouvoir, de parler à l'âme en charmant l'oreille, de faire naître une image dans l'esprit, et plus souvent encore, un sentiment dans le cœur»[113]. D'altronde, sempre con un riferimento che dal mondo del violino si allarga alle altre arti, Henri Blanchard aveva scritto: «être maître de soi pour émouvoir, enchanter et dominer la foule; telle est enfin la mission du musicien, du peintre, de l'artiste supérieur en général»[114]. Lungo questa precisa direttiva estetica si pone Charles-Auguste de Bériot, che studia solo per pochi mesi con Baillot, metabolizzando al contempo la lezione tecnico-stilistica paganiniana, come testimoniano sia diverse sue composizioni solistiche sia l'assunto «la musique étant, avant tout, une langue de sentiment, sa mélodie renferme toujours en elle un sens poétique […]»[115]. L'idea della centralità del 'sentimento', concetto-cardine tanto per i musicisti francesi quanto per Paganini, già messa in rilievo evidenziata dal maestro di contrappunto di Baillot, Anton Reicha[116], trova una prima importante formulazione nell'opera di Charles Battreux, *Les beaux arts réduits à un même principe* dove, se l'attenzione viene posta sul «sujet», viene anche instaurato un paragone tra la musica e l'oratoria che, successivamente, verrà sviluppato sia da Baillot che da Bériot:

> Le caractère fondamental de l'expression est dans le sujet: c'est lui qui marque au style le degré d'élévation ou de simplicité, de douceur ou de force qui lui convient. […] le compositeur trouve dans l'unité même de son sujet, les moyens de le varier. Il fait paraître tout à tour, l'amour, la crainte, la tristesse, l'espérance. Il imite l'Orateur, qui emploie toutes les figure set les variations de son Art, sans changer le ton général de son style[117].

L'opera di Batteux è importante perché anticipa proprio quella che sarà la principale regola estetica e artistica dei violinisti del xix secolo, Paganini e Baillot in testa: l'equivalenza tra l'espressione musicale e la descrizione di affetti, i cui effetti migliori si registrano

---

[113]. *Ibidem*, p. 163. Baillot torna su questo punto-cardine dell'istanza sentimentale in vari punti del suo trattato (*cfr.* ad esempio p. 267: «Le violon […] parcourant l'espace, il va frapper l'oreille de l'auditeur le moins attentif et chercher au fond de son cœur la corde sensible qu'il fait vibrer»).

[114]. Bʟᴀɴᴄʜᴀʀᴅ, Henri. 'Le violonistes', in: *Revue et Gazette musicale de Paris*, n. 39 (25 settembre 1842), p. 390.

[115]. Bᴇ́ʀɪᴏᴛ, Charles-Auguste de. *Méthode de violon divisée en 3 parties, Op. 102*, Parigi, chez l'Auteur, 1857-1858, p. ii.

[116]. «La musique est par essence un art de sentiment. Les véritables idées musicales sont le produit de ce que nous sentons»; Rᴇɪᴄʜᴀ, Anton. *Vollständiges Lehrbuch der musikalischen Composition* […], 4 voll., Vienna, Diabelli & Co., [1832], vol. ɪᴠ, p. 1101.

[117]. Bᴀᴛᴛᴇᴜx, Charles. *Les beaux arts réduits à un même principe*, Parigi, Durand, 1746, p. 288.

nell'ambito del timbro e del 'colore'. Infatti, come la radicale innovazione apportata da Paganini è da riferirsi soprattutto ai nuovi orizzonti timbrici e sonori[118], più che al mero aspetto digitale, anche Baillot viene più volte lodato per il suo suono, che però brilla al meglio — a differenza di quanto avviene per il genovese — nel repertorio cameristico[119]. Anche in virtù di una più chiara, lunga e ponderata riflessione da parte di Baillot sul repertorio classico del proprio strumento, i due violinisti possono quindi essere inseriti nelle due differenti classi in cui erano inquadrati, a partire dagli inizi del secolo XIX, tutti gli esecutori: se in una questi vengono infatti giudicati come grandi interpreti dei capolavori musicali, nell'altra, sono invece visti come *circus performers* o *devil's servants*, oppure come ispirati incantatori capaci d'esprimere in modo magico e mitico le passioni dell'animo umano attraverso il linguaggio musicale trascendentale[120].

VII

La svolta lucchese acquista per Paganini valore paradigmatico: da questo momento l'artista, *faber fortunae suae*, tronca i vincoli con aristocrazia e protettori, per essere, anche in linea con il crescente individualismo che permea la cultura romantica, arbitro assoluto di se stesso. Tra l'interprete e questo nuovo pubblico il rapporto diventa particolarmente cogente[121]; in questa particolare relazione il virtuosismo assume, rispetto al passato, un significato affatto nuovo, anche alla luce delle mutate condizioni socio-economiche, con una nuova classe, la borghesia, sempre più influente (con i propri gusti e le proprie richieste anche nello specifico del campo musicale), un mercato in espansione, una maggiore

---

[118]. Proprio nell'ottica della sperimentazione timbrica e del contrasto di diversi 'caratteri' vanno inquadrate composizioni minori di Paganini, come ad esempio il *Duetto amoroso* per violino e chitarra M.S. 111, *cfr.* GOOLEY, Dana. '«La Commedia del Violino» […]', *op. cit.* (si veda nota 2), pp. 483-485.

[119]. Anche Charles Dancla, allievo del primo, si mostra poco convinto del senso stesso di un accostamento Baillot/Paganini, e annota a riguardo: «On ne pouvait du reste faire de comparaison entre ces deux grands artistes. Certes Paganini n'eût pas joué comme Baillot le sublime *quatuor en re mineur* de Mozart ou le *Septuor* de Beethoven, mais, par contre, Baillot aurait été peu à son aise dans l'exécution diabolique de la musique de Paganini. Non que Baillot manquât de mécanisme, mais son tempérament le portait à éviter ce qu'il appelait les grandes excentricités»; DANCLA, Charles. *Notes et Souvenirs*, Parigi, Delamotte, 1893, pp. 9-10.

[120]. *Cfr.* GOEHR, Lydia. *The Quest for Voice: On Music, Politics, and the Limits of Philosophy*, Oxford, Clarendon Press, 1998 (The Ernest Bloch lectures, 1997), p. 140.

[121]. Renata Suchowiejko (*Op. cit.* [si veda nota 36], p. 99) parla a questo proposito di «mutual bond, […] code of communication, especially striking at the beginning of the century». Enrico Fubini invece sostiene che «il musicista nella sua qualità di creatore può permettersi di rendere sempre più complessa e articolata internamente la struttura della sua opera ma a patto di renderla al tempo stesso rigida e inalterabile, creando così un conflitto latente con l'interprete. Ma la rigidità dell'opera musicale si riflette soprattutto nel suo svolgersi come un discorso serrato, come una creazione in cui le complesse tensioni e risoluzioni interne concorrono tutte a creare l'opera come un grande monumento»; FUBINI, Enrico. 'Implicazioni sociologiche nella creazione e fruizione della musica d'avanguardia', in: *International Review of the Aesthetics and Sociology of Music*, V/1 (giugno 1974), pp. 171-172.

circolazione di informazioni e un proliferare di case editrici. Ma Paganini — a differenza di Chopin e di Liszt — non seppe o non volle sfruttare questa novità: a una fortissima ritrosia nella diffusione della sua musica, di cui era estremamente geloso, s'aggiunsero i problemi di salute sempre più gravi che gli impedirono di portare a termine il progetto di pubblicazione di una cospicua parte delle proprie opere, come dimostrato dalla lettera che Paganini scrisse, in data 28 ottobre 1835, al periodico tedesco *Intelligenz-blatt*:

> Indigné par tant des ouvrages de musique que l'on publie avec mon nom, et qui ne sont que de plagiats malheureux, ou des faussetés, je déclare qu'qu'à l'exception de 1) 24 Capricci e Studi per il violino (op.1); 2) 12 Sonatine di violino e chitarra (op. 2 e 3); 3) 6 quartetti per violino, viola, violoncello e chitarra (op. 4 e 5) le tout par moi, cédé en propriété à l'Etablissement de Musique de Mr. Jean Ricordi à Milan (Italia) tous les ouvrages sont apocryphes, comme l'on reconnaîtra lorsque, ainsi que je me propose de publier entièrement ma musique.
> Signé Paganini[122]

Proprio in questo contesto — in cui si evince un sensibile abbassamento del livello degli ascoltatori, proporzionale a un allargamento del bacino d'utenza della musica strumentale — è significativo che Fétis, con specifico riferimento al capitolo *De l'exécution instrumentale*[123], porti proprio l'esempio di Paganini per illustrare i progressi della prassi esecutiva: è subentrata ormai la logica dell'agonismo, tipicamente borghese, implicante il gusto spettacolare della competizione in pubblico. Se il virtuosismo è infatti interpretabile come sfida con se stessi perennemente rinnovantesi, dal momento che «La difficulté vaincue est une beauté», secondo quanto osservato da Camille Saint-Saëns a proposito di Liszt[124], particolare significato assumono i certami musicali. Negli anni a cavallo tra XVIII e XIX secolo, appena dopo il ritorno da Vienna di Kreutzer e prima della partenza di Rode per la Russia, tra questi due artisti vi è uno spiccato, seppur sempre amichevole, spirito competitivo; significativo, a questo riguardo, il parere espresso da Baillot:

---

[122]. Paganini ribadisce tale concetto in un'altra lettera del 26 novembre dello stesso anno, indirizzata a un critico ferrarese di nome Zaffarini, che aveva lodato un concerto, evidentemente attribuito a Paganini in maniera erronea, eseguito da un certo «signor Bianchi»: «Io non ho il vantaggio di conoscere questo signore; io non ho fatto dono né a lui né ad altri di verun mio concerto, non potevo per altro impedire le rapsodie e di queste molte se ne contano, anzi si è spinta la cosa al segno di stampare pubblicazioni, come mia musica, delle cose accozzate, storpiate, mal conciate, soprani, chiari, tessiture non mie dacché non lascio come vedete di provarne dispiacere, anche per l'inganno che si commette a carico del pubblico»; *cfr.* Berri, Pietro. *Paganini, la vita e le opere*, a cura di Mario Monti, Milano, Bompiani, 1982, pp. 404-405.

[123]. *Cfr.* Fétis, François-Joseph. *La musique à la portée de tout le monde: exposé succinct de tout ce qui est nécessaire pour juger de cet art, et pour en parler sans l'avoir étudié*, Parigi, Alexandre Mesnier, 1830, pp. 276-277.

[124]. La frase, riferita da Théophile Gautier, è citata da Bloom, Peter. 'Virtuosités de Berlioz', in: *Romantisme*, n. 128 (2005), p. 83. Sulla stessa linea di pensiero lo stesso Fétis (*La musique à la portée de tout le monde* […], *op. cit.* [si veda nota 123], p. 276), che osserva a proposito dello stesso Paganini: «Une nouvelle ère a commencé pour le violon: c'est celle de la difficulté vaincue».

[…] l'art gagne toujours aux rivalités; la rivalité d'ailleurs, perdant ici tout ce qu'elle a d'hostile, agit en faveur de l'union, le combat tourne au profit de tous les combattants, le bonheur commun est la récompense du parti vainqueur, et l'art seul étend sa nomination, aspirant toujours à des nouveaux triomphes[125].

Giovanni Mane Giornovichi[126] e Viotti sono messi sovente a confronto, in termini di duello artistico, durante il periodo londinese del secondo: Paganini stesso si confronta alla Scala con Lafont, nel 1816, e a Piacenza con Karol Józef Lipiński, due anni dopo. Una testimonianza ottocentesca, di carattere aneddotico, racconta a tale riguardo:

Talora piacevasi il Paganini di mettere a posto un presuntuoso; e se questi fosse stato degli amici d'oltre Alpe, uno straniero burbanzoso, gongolava di poter rintuzzare quell'inessicabil vena di vanità e di superbie. Una sera un di costoro suonava a competenza con lui un difficil pezzo di Tedesco indiavolato. Lo eseguiva, non c'è che dire, con singolare maestria; ma, cessato il suono, guastò ogni pregio con la jattanza, dicendo all'Italiano: "Voilà comme on joue à Paris". Paganini zittì; ma venuta la sua volta nel sonare, strappò dal leggio la musica non ancora vista e ve la capovolse. Poi mise mano a suonare con quella guida tedesca a ritroso; e quei muti segni arrovesciati pigliavano dalla sua destra vita e forma sì pellegrine che il francese penò di molto a chiuder la chiostra dei denti. Quando lo scoppio degli applausi frenetici lasciò via alla voce, il Paganini sussurrava di rimbecco nell'orecchio del vantatore, queste parole: "Voilà comme on joue en Paradis", e non mentiva[127].

Solo per restare nell'ambito violinistico, l'esecuzione a Mosca nel 1872 di una composizione per due violini di Spohr, da parte di Joseph Joachim, accompagnato dal virtuoso cecoslovacco Ferdinand Laub, fu definita «a competition of two heroes»[128], mentre il rapporto tra Sivori e Bazzini, aldilà della reciproca gentilezza di facciata esibita nelle lettere, fu dominato da una costante rivalità, e questo dato acquista un'importanza ancora maggiore alla luce delle difficoltà che rendono il violino uno degli strumenti oggettivamente più complessi, per quel che concerne esecuzione ed espressività[129].

125. BAILLOT, Pierre(-Marie-François de Sales). *Op. cit.* (si veda nota 109), p. 10.

126. Arthur Pougin (*Viotti et l'école modern de violon*, Parigi, Schott, 1888, p. 18 n. 2), riporta il seguente episodio riguardante ancora Giornovichi e Le chevalier de Saint Georges: «Jarnowick avait souvent maille à partir avec le chevalier de Saint-Georges, aussi fameux comme violoniste que par son habilité à l'escrime, et il s'oublia un jour jusqu'à lui donner un soufflet; fort heureusement pour lui, Saint-Georges se contenta de dire: "J'aime trop son talent pour me battre avec lui". Mais plus tard, à Londres, comme il avait grossièrement insulté le fameux pianiste J. B. Cramer, celui-ci voulut le forcer à se battre; Jarnowick fut lâche, refusa absolument, et se vit obligé de quitter Londres».

127. *Cfr.* GARASSINI, Giuseppe. *Niccolò Paganini*, in: *Rivista universale*, n.s., II/7 (1868), pp. 87-88.

128. *Cfr.* in SCHWARZ, Boris. *Op. cit.* (si veda nota 53), p. 268.

129. «[…] tout le monde sait que le violon est, de tous les instruments, le plus difficile à apprendre»; HÉDOUIN, Pierre. *Mosaïque: peintres, musiciens, artistes dramatiques: à partir du XVe siècle jusqu'à nos jours*, Valenciennes, Heugel, 1856, p. 399.

VIII

Se è nella *Filosofia della musica* mazziniana che avviene una delle prime, significative, associazioni del nome di Rossini al movimento romantico[130], solo pochi anni prima Balzac aveva compiuto osservazioni analoghe proprio in relazione a Paganini:

> Le Napoléon du genre […]. Le secret de la création artistique, quel est-il? Quelle trajectoire artistique a pu suivre, par exemple, la force qui anime cet homme malingre? Et cette force, d'où lui vient-elle? Le miracle le plus extraordinaire qui me surprenne en ce moment, c'est celui que Paganini sait opérer. Ne croyez pas qu'il s'agisse de son archet, de son doigté, des sons fantastiques qu'il tire de son violon […]. Il y a sans doute quelque chose de mystérieux dans cet homme[131].

L'esecuzione, parte integrante dell'istanza paganiniana, si pone come euristica rivelazione secondo cui viene espresso un rapporto di potere e di dominio (solista/ *audience*) mediante l'evocazione di straordinarie emozioni e dando allo stesso tempo una realizzazione artisticamente compiuta e coerente delle aspettative proprie di un particolare tipo di pubblico. Libero da doveri nei confronti di nobili protettori, non più vincolato a un dover comporre a contratto, il musicista deve necessariamente concentrare le sue attenzioni sulle modalità di presentazione delle proprie musiche in pubblico, secondo variabili di situazioni e contesto: paradigmatica, in questo senso, la svolta lucchese del 1809.

---

[130]. «Rossini è un titano. Titano di potenza e di audacia. Rossini è il Napoleone d'un'epoca musicale. Rossini, a chi ben guarda, ha compíto nella musica ciò che il romanticismo ha compíto in letteratura. Ha sancito l'indipendenza musicale: negato il principio di autorità che i mille inetti a creare volevano imporre a chi crea, e dichiarata l'onnipotenza del genio»; MAZZINI, Giuseppe. *Filosofia della musica*, con note di lettura di Stefano Ragni, Pisa, Domus mazziniana, 1996 (Collana scientifica [Domus mazziniana, 23]), p. 22. Lo stesso Mazzini non fu per nulla tenero nei confronti dei virtuosi violinistici — Paganini e Sivori — suoi concittadini. Dopo la morte di Paganini, «Quando la sorella annunciò a Giuseppe (esule in Svizzera) che la città di Genova e il marchese De Nigro in particolare avrebbero offerto a Paganini un busto, il patriota rispose ferocemente: "[…] Certo l'Italia è la più grande fra tutte le nazioni, dacché Paganini suona bene il violino – stolidi, quelli che non si contentano di questo e cercano altro"»; *ibidem*, p. 60. Sivori, invece, non si fece mai coinvolgere nei concerti benefici organizzati da Mazzini a Londra per la scuola di Hatton Garden, quasi sicuramente per timore che una così netta presa di posizione politica avrebbe potuto pregiudicare la sua futura carriera musicale (*ibidem*).

[131]. Lettera del 18 marzo 1831, citato in BALZAC, Honoré de. *Œuvres complètes: édition nouvelle établie par la Société des études balzaciennes*, a cura di Jean Adhémar e Jacques Lethève, Parigi, Club de l'Honnête homme, 1956-1963, vol. XXII: *Les cents contes drolatiques: premier dixain, deuxième dixain, troisième dixain, fragments […]*, p. 490. Per l'importanza della figura di Napoleone quale simbolico riferimento in termini di eroismo romantico trasposto in musica *cfr.* GOOLEY, Dana. 'Warhorses: Liszt, Weber's *Konzertstück*, and the Cult of Napoléon', in: *19th-Century Music*, XXIV/1 (estate 2000), pp. 62-88 (poi ripubblicato come secondo capitolo in ID. *The Virtuoso Liszt, op. cit.* [si veda nota 24], pp. 78-116) e, con particolare riferimento all'ambito estetico-musicale tedesco, RUMPH, Stephen. *Beethoven after Napoleon: Political Romanticism in the Late Works*, Berkeley-Los Angeles, University of California Press, 2004 (California studies in 19th-century music, 14), pp. 11-33.

Questo radicale cambio di prospettiva implica che il testo di musica sia visto e concepito in funzione dell'esecuzione e non il contrario[132], e a tale riguardo è significativo quanto prescritto da Bériot:

> [...] lorsqu'un motif revient plusieurs fois dans le même *adagio*, on l'exposera d'abord dans toute sa simplicité pour en bien faire comprendre le dessin, on augmentera peu à peu les fioritures chaque fois que le même chant se reproduira[133].

Tanto Paganini quanto Rossini appaiono quindi fatalmente lontani e estranei all'idea, affermatasi per la prima volta nel saggio di Karl Philipp Moritz *Von der bildenden Nachahmung der Schönen* (1788)[134], secondo cui l'opera, per essere veramente tale da un punto di vista ontologico e artistico, debba configurarsi come *opus conclusum*. Su suolo germanico, dopo aver sostenuto che l'esecuzione consiste nella piena rappresentazione del carattere e dell'espressione della composizione, Johann Adam Peter Schultz spiega che sia a livello globale che in ogni singola parte devono essere resi suono, spirito, *Affekt* e chiaroscuro esattamente così come erano stati concepiti dall'autore in funzione di quella specifica composizione[135]. In Italia Galeazzi, similmente, sostiene la necessità d'intendere la musica «come se fosse parto di una stessa mente»[136], in riferimento alle idee del compositore e a quelle dell'esecutore. Questo concetto viene poi approfondito nella *Méthode des méthodes de piano* di Fétis, redatto con l'ausilio di Moscheles, e pubblicato proprio nell'anno della morte di Paganini (1840), in cui si spiega come, per l'esecutore, sia necessaria una riflessione sull'opera del compositore, affinché ne venga compenetrato lo spirito: verso di essa il musicista dovrà nutrire infatti il medesimo rispetto che egli pretende verso le proprie[137]. Sulla stessa linea e sempre nel medesimo anno, Richard Wagner, nell'articolo 'Du métier des virtuoses et de l'indépendence des musiciens', sostiene che il compito dell'interprete è quello di mirare a una perfetta penetrazione del pezzo in esecuzione, guardandosi bene dall'introdurre modifiche e variazioni scaturite dall'estro dello strumentista[138]. In campo

---

[132]. REYNAUD, Cécile. 'Présentation: Misère et accomplissement de l'art dans la virtuosité romantique', in: *Romantisme*, n. 128 (2005), p. 13.

[133]. BÉRIOT, Charles-Auguste de. *Op. cit.* (si veda la nota 115), p. 191.

[134]. *Cfr.* DAHLHAUS, Carl. *Estetica della musica*, Roma, Astrolabio, 2009 (Adagio), p. 25.

[135]. *Cfr.* 'Vortrag', in: SULZER, Johann Georg. *Allgemeine Theorie der Schönen Künste in einzeln, nach alphabetischer Ordnung der Kunstwörter auf einander folgenden, Artikeln abgehandelt*, 4 voll., Lipsia, Weidmannschen Buchhandlung, ²1792-1794, vol. IV, in particolare p. 706.

[136]. GALEAZZI, Francesco. *Elementi teorico-pratici di musica con un saggio sopra l'arte di suonare il violino: analizzata, ed a dimostrabili principi ridotta, opera utilissima a chiunque vuol applicare con profitto alla musica*, 2 voll., Roma, Stamperia Pilucchi Cracas, 1791-1796, vol. I, p. 230.

[137]. FÉTIS, François-Joseph. *Méthode des méthodes de piano*, Parigi, Schlesinger, 1840, p. 75.

[138]. WAGNER, Richard. 'Du métier des virtuoses et de l'indépendence des musiciens: Fantaisie esthétique d'un musicien', in: *Revue et Gazette musicale de Paris*, VII/58 (18 ottobre 1840), pp. 496-498.

violinistico, secondo questo spirito, Pierre Baillot e Léonard-Joseph Gaillard, elementi fondanti delle 'scuole' violinistiche rispettivamente francese e belga, appaiono nella duplice veste di virtuosi e raffinati musicisti da camera rispettosi del testo scritto, oltre che di insigni didatti. Allo stesso modo è possibile cogliere la novità, rispetto al solco paganiniano di provenienza, di Camillo Sivori, che si pone da un lato, proprio a partire dal 1840, come massimo interprete e diffusore della musica del suo maestro, gettando al contempo le basi per la sua attività quartettistica, in cui, negli anni a venire, riceverà significativi riconoscimenti — sarà infatti il protagonista della prima esecuzione londinese dei quartetti beethoveniani, e a lui Giuseppe Verdi si affiderà per la 'prima' del suo Quartetto per archi in Mi minore. Tanto Paganini quanto Baillot, d'altronde, convergono su consigli relativi a tali prassi improvvisative che, specie nei tempi lenti, continuavano ad abbondare: se infatti nella lettera dell'8 agosto 1828, il primo raccomanda a Gaetano Ciandelli di tenersi «curtino negli Adagj»[139], il secondo ammette che, dopo Haydn e Mozart, si è affermata la prassi di concedere «presque rien à l'arbitraire de l'exécutant»[140]. Tanto per Rossini quanto per Paganini, quindi, «il […] centro estetico non era l'opera ma l'esecutore o il cantante»[141], e una chiara dimostrazione di ciò è nell'evidente differenza che vi è tra la versione della *Sonata a preghiera*, sul tema 'Dal tuo stellato soglio' dal *Mosè* di Rossini, sulla corda di Sol[142] e quella, dello stesso brano, tramandata da François Habeneck[143]. Indipendentemente dal contesto specifico in cui nasce o per cui è concepita, la musica virtuosistica si inserisce quindi

---

[139]. *Cfr.* PAGANINI, Nicolò. *Epistolario* […], *op. cit.* (si veda nota 1), p. 406.

[140]. BAILLOT, Pierre(-Marie-François de Sales). *Op. cit.* (si veda nota 109), p. 157.

[141]. DAHLHAUS, Carl. *La musica dell'Ottocento, op. cit.* (si veda nota 49), p. 149.

[142]. Di cui comunque non si è possesso né delle parte del violino solista né della partitura autografa, e la cui prima edizione è quella postuma (1855), Hamburg, Schuberth & Co., con il titolo *Variations de bravure sur des Thèmes de Moïse de Rossini, sur la 4ᵐᵉ corde, cfr.* PREFUMO, Danilo. *Niccolò Paganini*, Palermo, L'Epos, 2006 (L'amoroso canto, 5), p. 231.

[143]. HABENECK, François. *Méthode théorique et pratique de violon*, Parigi, Canaux, [1842], pp. 171-175. Nonostante i propositi di fedeltà all'originale espressi in apertura («Nous donnons ici *sa prière de Moise* suivie d'un *Thême varié* qu'il exécutait entièrement sur la 4ᵉ corde», p. 171), dopo una *Introduction* e un *Récitativo* non presenti nella partitura paganiniana, il tema propriamente rossiniano, oggetto delle variazioni, è riportato da Habeneck in forma e tonalità differenti da quelle paganiniane. Se entrambi prevedono infatti l'innalzamento della quarta corda di una terza minore, mentre in Paganini si ha un *Adagio* (Do minore) in cui il tema rossiniano è esposto senza abbellimenti, in Habeneck questo viene presentato in un *Andante* (Re minore), in cui la linea melodica, ricca di fioriture, differisce sensibilmente dalla versione paganiniana. Ancora, nella seconda sezione della prima variazione riportata da Habeneck, si trovano diversi passaggi basati su un dialogo abbastanza serrato tra suoni armonici e suoni naturali che, pur essendo assolutamente coerente con lo stile di Paganini, non risulta tuttavia presente nella versione di quest'ultimo, che però contiene un altro tema (che compare come II variazione), tratto dall'opera *Castore e Polluce* di Georg Joseph Vogler, non citato da Habeneck. Stessa prassi per le generazioni successive di violinisti virtuosi: non è infatti un caso che Alberto Bachmann (*An Encyclopedia of the Violin*, New York, Da Capo Press, 1975, pp. 196 e 193), allievo di Jenő Hubay, riporti acriticamente le variazioni ritmiche operate da Eugène Ysaÿe nell'*incipit* dell'*Allegro giocoso, ma non troppo vivace* conclusivo del Concerto per violino e orchestra Op. 77 di Johannes Brahms e le variazioni ritmiche

a pieno titolo, e con una propria coerenza, riguardo al rapporto vigente tra strumentista e momento performativo, forte dei mutamenti in corso, nella linea di quella 'fluidità' che viene normalmente riconosciuta alla prassi esecutiva del XIX secolo[144].

La svolta lucchese del 1809 acquista particolare valore anche alla luce di un'altra importante contingenza cronologica: gli anni 1810-1813 sono quelli dei primi trionfi rossiniani (*La cambiale di matrimonio*, *L'inganno felice*, *La scala di seta*, *L'occasione fa il ladro*, *Il signor Bruschino*): proprio nei contrasti di 'carattere' che innervano la tessitura di queste farse è da vedersi un comune denominatore fondamentale con la nuova idea di allargamento della tessitura timbrica propria del violino. Questa è a sua volta da connettere a un altro fattore determinante, il legame con il mondo del ballo: se infatti un'analogia con la logica del contrasto di 'colore', tipica delle più significative composizioni paganiniane, può ravvisarsi nella differenza di ruoli affidati rispettivamente a *ballerini seri* e *ballerini grotteschi*, non è da sottovalutare che i programmi dei più importanti palcoscenici in cui Paganini si esibì erano sempre caratterizzati da una costante mescolanza di repertorio strumentale, arie o interi atti melodrammatici e musiche di balletto con eventuali coreografie. In questa ottica — con particolare attenzione alla vicenda amorosa dei protagonisti Roberto e Dorilla, in riferimento ad esempio al citato *Duetto amoroso* M.S. 111 — emerge tutta la pregnanza estetico-stilistica, aldilà del mero virtuosismo strumentale, di una composizione rappresentativa come *Le streghe* M.S. 19, la cui fonte, il «ballo allegorico in quattro atti» *Il noce di Benevento*, con musiche di Franz Xaver Süssmayr e coreografia di Salvatore Viganò, ebbe, in occasione della presentazione scaligera del 1813, recensioni estremamente simili a quelle ottenute dai concerti paganiniani[145]: è in questa istanza propria del 'grottesco' che gli articoli della *Allgemeine musikalische Zeitung* rinvengono la cifra — tutta italiana — caratterizzante l'arte paganiniana[146].

Se proprio attraverso la lente di lettura della «tragische Ironie»[147] di matrice hegeliana/schlegeliana, utilizzata da Ludwig Rellstab, l'approccio esecutivo paganiniano rivela tutta

---

e testuali licenziosamente eseguite da César Thomson in un segmento (bb. 134-135) del *Finale marziale (Andante – Allegro)* del Concerto per violino e orchestra Op. 31 n. 4 di Henry Vieuxtemps.

[144]. *Cfr.* SAMSON, Jim. *Op. cit.* (si veda nota 39), p. 26.

[145]. Si parlò infatti non a caso di «capolavoro di piacevole bizzarria» e «bisticcio di diaboliche e grottesche invenzioni»; *cfr.* ROSSI, Luigi. *Il ballo alla Scala: 1778-1970*, Milano, Edizioni della Scala, 1972, p. 52. Per le molteplici interconnessioni tra mondo dell'opera e del melodramma, doveroso il rinvio a HANSELL, Kathleen Kuzmick. 'Il ballo teatrale e l'opera italiana', in: *La spettacolarità*, a cura di Lorenzo Bianconi e Giorgio Pestelli, Torino, EdT, 1988 (Storia dell'opera italiana, II/5), pp. 175-306.

[146]. *Cfr.* 'Noch etwas über Paganini', *op. cit.* (si veda nota 21).

[147]. «Wenn eine neuere philosophische Schule als das höchste Prinzip der Poesie die tragische Ironie aufstellt, sich aber vergebens nach einem Repräsentanten dieses Prinzips umgesehen hat, so könnte man Paganini als einen solchen bezeichnen, der mit dem Höchsten, was er eben erschuf, nur zu scherzen scheint, indem er es selbst wieder zerstört, diese Zerstörung jedoch immer wieder zu einem neuen Kunstwerke zu gestalten weiss», citato in SCHOTTKY, Julius Max. *Op. cit.* (si veda nota 2), p. 172. In questa sede ci si limita a rinviare a BEHLER, Ernst. 'The Theory of Irony in German Romanticism', in: *Romantic Irony*, a cura

la sua portentosa innovazione — questa connessione del resto non è sfuggita allo stesso Schottky —, solo secondo questa specifica prospettiva analitica acquista valore l'eventuale accostamento di Paganini, «paradox as an 'un-Romantic Romantic'»[148], al romanticismo. In ultima istanza, posto che il dibattito romantico italiano era, negli anni della fase ascendente dell'astro paganiniano, quasi esclusivamente centrato su problematiche letterarie, o legate alla librettistica, ma certamente non includeva — a differenza di quanto avveniva contestualmente in Germania — speculazioni relative alla musica strumentale, è all'interno di un più ampio orizzonte estetico e culturale, secondo questa duplice ambivalenza estetica «dämonisch»/«himmlisch»[149], che può ravvisarsi il più fulgido valore del magistero paganiniano, oltre alle innovazioni più apertamente legate al funambolismo strumentale.

---

di Frederick Garber, Budapest, Akadémiai Kiadó, 1988 (A comparative history of literatures in European languages, 8), pp. 43-81.

[148]. Kawabata, Maiko. *Paganini: The 'Demonic' Virtuoso*, op. cit. (si veda nota 102), p. 9.

[149]. *Cfr.* Puppo, Mario. 'Divinità e demonismo della musica nella cultura romantica', in: *Nicolò Paganini e il suo tempo. Atti del convegno internazionale (Genova, 27-29 ottobre 1982)*, a cura di Raffaello Monterosso, Ufficio Stampa e Pubbliche Relazioni del Comune di Genova, 1984, pp. 79-99.

Interactive Strains of Virtuosity in the Violin Concertos of Louis Spohr:
Figuration, Lyricism, Motivic Development and the Expansion of Distant-Key Relations[1]

Rohan H. Stewart-MacDonald
(Stratford-upon-Avon, UK)

Spohr, Virtuosity and the Franco-Belgian Violin Tradition

Hartmut Becker's assertion that «Spohr has to be regarded as Paganini's antipode»[2] is justified in part. About Louis Spohr's pedagogical work, the *Violinschule*, biographer Clive Brown writes the following:

> The *Violinschule* covers every aspect of violin playing as Spohr practised it, from the most basic elements to the most advanced techniques [...]. [...] Spohr's rigid artistic creed excluded from the true canon of violin playing a

---

[1]. I am indebted to Majella Boland who provided a copy of the fourth chapter of her Ph.D. Dissertation: Boland, Majella. *The Reception and Analysis of John Field's Piano Concerti*, Ph.D. Diss., Dublin, University of College Dublin, 2013. Orchestral scores of Spohr's Violin Concertos are scarce. One significant source, containing Nos. 10 and 12, is the facsimile edition *Louis Spohr (1784-1859): Concertos*, edited by Clive Brown, New York, Garland, 1987 (Selected works of Louis Spohr, 7). Brown explains that none of Spohr's Violin Concertos were published in score during the composer's lifetime. The only ones to have appeared subsequently in this form are No. 7, No. 8 (in 1894) and WoO 12 (in 1955) (p. viii). Cambridge University Library contains several manuscript sources that include piano reductions alongside scores assembled from orchestral parts by Richard Pendlebury (1847-1902). Those consulted for the present study were: Spohr, Louis. *Neuvième Concerto pour le violon avec accompagnement d'orchestre*, Op. 55, 1 ms. score, 59 pp., MS.Add.9077(2); Id. *Violin Concerto No. 7 in E minor, Op. 38*, 1 ms. score, 92 pp., MS.Add.9075(2). The musical excerpts in this chapter are based, either on the orchestral scores included in the aforementioned sources or piano reductions. The following shorthand, derived from Hepokoski, James Arnold – Darcy, Warren. *Elements of Sonata Theory: Norms, Types, and Deformations in the Late Eighteenth-Century Sonata*, Oxford-New York, Oxford University Press, 2006, will be used to refer to specific components of the Concerto opening movement's structure: 'R1', *ritornello* 1; 'S1', first solo; 'R2', *ritornello* 2; 'S2', second solo; 'R3', *ritornello* 3; 'S3', solo 3.

[2]. Becker, Hartmut. Liner notes to *Louis Spohr: Violin Concertos*, Ulf Hoelscher (violin), Christian Fröhlich (conductor), Rundfunk-Sinfonieorchester Berlin, CPO 999 067-2; 145-2; 187-2; 196-2; 232-2; 403-2 (6 CDs), 1993-1999, p. 23.

number of techniques which were then gaining currency [...]. The techniques employed by Paganini and his imitators, which opened up a whole range of new possibilities for the instrument, were anathema to Spohr.

In fact, there was a strong element of ambivalence running through Spohr's attitude towards Paganinian virtuosity that Becker's statement does not encompass. Brown continues:

> After hearing [Paganini] play during a visit to Kassel in June 1830 Spohr had written: «In his compositions and performance there is a strange mixture of the highest genius, childishness and tastelessness, so that one feels alternately attracted and repelled»[3].

This same ambivalence — alongside great curiosity and some bewilderment — can be detected in Spohr's other accounts of his meetings with his illustrious Italian contemporary[4].

Paganini belonged to a Franco-Italian tradition of violin playing that had at its core the Italian Giovanni Battista Viotti (1755-1824) and the Frenchmen Pierre Rode (1774-1830) and Rodolphe Kreutzer (1766-1831)[5]. Spohr's strong connection to this tradition is unequivocal. He desired instruction from Viotti; Viotti was no longer teaching, so Spohr was instead taught by Franz Eck (1744-1804)[6]. Despite belonging to the Mannheim tradition, Eck had been influenced by the French school[7]. The playing and the compositions of Rode were strongly formative for Spohr[8]; Brown postulates a «strong debt» in the Violin Concerto No. 2 in D minor, Op. 2 (1804) to Rode's Concerto No. 7 in E minor,

---

3. BROWN, Clive. *Louis Spohr: A Critical Biography*, Cambridge-New York, Cambridge University Press, 1984, p. 212, quoting SPEYER, Edward. *Wilhelm Speyer der Liederkomponist, 1790-1878: sein Leben und Verkehr mit seinen Zeitgenossen dargestellt von seinem jüngsten Sohne*, Munich, Drei Masken Verlag, 1925.

4. See SPOHR, Louis. *The Musical Journeys of Louis Spohr, Being Extracts from Spohr's Diaries*, translated and edited by Henry Pleasants, Norman, University of Oklahoma Press, 1961, pp. 155-157 and 158-159. See also BROWN, Clive. *Louis Spohr: A Critical Biography*, op. cit. (see note 3), pp. 111-112.

5. Paganini is known to have performed Concertos by Viotti; and Massimiliano Sala notes that «Paganini's correspondence contains "frequent references" to the compositions of Viotti, Kreutzer, Rode and other earlier figures [...]». STEWART-MACDONALD, Rohan H. 'Approaches to the Orchestra in the Violin Concertos of Nicolò Paganini', in: *Ad Parnassum: A Journal of Eighteenth- and Nineteenth-Century Instrumental Music*, XI/21 (April 2013), pp. 57-119: 65, quoting SALA, Massimiliano. 'Paganini and his Myth', in: *Henryk Wieniawsky and the Bravura Tradition*, edited by Maciej Jabłoński and Danuta Jasińska, Poznań, Henrik Wieniawski Musical Society, 2011 (Henryk Wieniawski, Complete works, B series), pp. 133-148: 135. See also VÝBORNÝ, Zdenek. 'Paganini as Music Critic', in: *The Musical Quarterly*, XLVI/4 (October 1960), pp. 468-481.

6. BROWN, Clive. *Louis Spohr: A Critical Biography*, op. cit. (see note 3), p. 12.

7. *Louis Spohr (1784-1859): Concertos*, op. cit. (see note 1), p. viii.

8. Brown considers the influence of Rode on Spohr's chamber music and Concertos: see BROWN, Clive. *Louis Spohr: A Critical Biography*, op. cit. (see note 3), pp. 47, 51, 57, 78.

Op. 38 (published 1816)[9]. In fact, Franco-Italian elements can be traced in many of Spohr's Concertos. They are conspicuous in the regularly structured Rondo finales, whose refrains are laced with stereotypically French dotted rhythms[10]. Equally Franco-Italian are those opening movements that maintain clear structural demarcation and that alternate between expressive lyricism and figurative virtuosity: like Kreutzer, Rode, Viotti and also Paganini, Spohr seems to have endeavoured, in his opening movements, to attain an ideal balance between virtuoso figuration and expressive lyricism[11]. Like Paganini, Rode and Kreutzer, Spohr often evokes Italian opera in his Concertos. This is achieved most radically in No. 8 in A minor, Op. 47. Subtitled «In Form einer Gesangszene», this Concerto includes sections of recitative and arioso that Christopher Headington connects with Rossinian *cavatina-cabaletta* forms[12]. The first movement of the Concerto No. 12, Op. 79 ('Concertino No. 1') has a 'recitative' leading to an 'aria', much like the second movement of the Concerto No. 6, Op. 28, composed for Spohr's Italian tour of 1816-1817. Benjamin Swalin interprets Spohr's «sudden interchanges of major and minor tonalities» as evidence of a «new Romantic mode of expression»[13]; such interchanges also pervade the Concertos of Paganini where they continue much earlier, specifically Italian, traditions that some scholars have traced back to the Concertos of Antonio Vivaldi[14]. Spohr's intermixing of major and minor modes is epitomised by the *Siciliano* of the Concerto No. 3. The orchestral prelude begins in A minor, strongly emphasising the relative major. The solo eventually enters in the parallel major and sustains this key (with periodic minor-mode inflections) until the orchestra's next entry. The orchestra briefly restores the minor, again emphasising submediant and relative major, before coming to rest on the prolonged dominant that leads directly into the finale. The finale's tonic key

[9].   *Louis Spohr (1784-1859): Concertos, op. cit.* (see note 1), p. ix.

[10].   Benjamin Swalin detects the influence of Rode in the *Rondo alla polacca* of Spohr's First Concerto and in the *Rondo Allegretto* of the Fourth. SWALIN, Benjamin Franklin. *The Violin Concerto: A Study in German Romanticism*, New York, Da Capo Press, 1973 (Da Capo Press music reprint series), pp. 14-15.

[11].   I discuss structuring principles in Concertos by Kreutzer and Paganini in: STEWART-MACDONALD, Rohan H. 'Approaches to the Orchestra […]', *op. cit.* (see note 5), pp. 93-100. On French stylistic characteristics more generally in this period, see SCHWARZ, Boris. *French Instrumental Music between the Revolutions (1789-1830)*, New York, Da Capo Press, 1987.

[12].   HEADINGTON, Christopher. 'The Concerto after Beethoven: The Virtuoso Concerto', in: *A Companion to the Concerto*, edited by Robert Layton, London, Christopher Helm, 1988, p. 133.

[13].   SWALIN, Benjamin Franklin. *Op. cit.* (see note 10), p. 9.

[14].   On the origination of this phenomenon in Vivaldi, see TALBOT, Michael. 'Modal Shifts in the Sonatas of Domenico Scarlatti', in: *Chigiana*, XL/20 (1985), pp. 25-43, and BROVER-LUBOVSKY, Bella. «*Die Schwarze Gredel*», or the Parallel Minor Key in Vivaldi's Instrumental Music', in: *Vivaldi*, edited by Michael Talbot, Farnham, Ashgate, 2011 (Baroque composers), pp. 105-131. The first movement of Paganini's Concerto No. 5 is in A minor, but the parallel major intervenes periodically, during R1 and S1. Furthermore, the transposition, to the tonic major, of the material associated with the relative key in S3 almost causes the movement to end in A major — before an almost incongruously brief final orchestra coda restores the minor.

of C major is therefore approached via a Phrygian cadence — an archaism harking back to the Concertos of Vivaldi and Corelli.

Spohr's Concertos nonetheless exhibit strongly 'Germanic' motivic processing, reflecting the composer's early interaction with the string quartets of Haydn, Mozart and Beethoven and other Austro-German instrumental music[15] that, according to Brown, pre-dated his engagement with Franco-Italian violin repertory[16]. The often contrapuntal orientation of Spohr's Concerto textures could also be connected with his interest in seventeenth- and eighteenth-century sacred vocal music[17]. Motivic continuity, evident in certain of Spohr's opening movements, can work in conjunction with the systematic exploration of distant key relationships: in at least two examples a third- or even chromatically-related key centre appears as a series of periodic digressions, sometimes interlinked by recurrent modulatory processes, occasionally underpinned by motivic relationships. This device, with obvious parallels in the instrumental works of Haydn and Beethoven, can also be connected with Italian models: Luigi Cherubini has been regarded as «significant [...] for the development of Spohr's [chromatic] harmonic idiom»[18], and Viotti sometimes cultivated distant-key networks over the course of a multi-movement composition[19].

It is generally concurred that Spohr's Violin Concertos represent a complex amalgam of Italian, French and German elements. His undoubted effort, in the words of Swalin, «to make the Violin Concerto a substantial and superior composition, free from the artificial bravura practices of the time»[20] seems to have involved the importation of techniques cultivated by contemporary Austro-Germans in the full range of instrumental genres — and also by Spohr himself in his own chamber works. Brown identifies a

---

[15]. *Louis Spohr (1784-1859): Concertos, op. cit.* (see note 1), p. vii.

[16]. Brown, Clive. 'The Chamber Music of Spohr and Weber', in: *Nineteenth-Century Chamber Music*, edited by Stephen E. Hefling, New York-London, Schirmer-Prentice Hall International, 1998 (Studies in musical genres and repertories), pp. 140-169: 148.

[17]. Becker, Hartmut. *Op. cit.* (see note 2), p. 18. Contrapuntal textures are quite strongly exemplified by the first movement of the Concerto No. 5 in E-flat major. In R1, immediately after the opening statement involving a dotted motif, a quaver motif is introduced that is imitated between first violins and solo woodwinds. This texture also includes odd references to the initial, dotted motif (by the first clarinet, for instance). A similarly imitative orchestral texture appears at the very end of the movement, when there are even melodic interspersions by the first horn.

[18]. Brown, Clive. 'The Chamber Music of Spohr and Weber', *op. cit.* (see note 16), p. 148.

[19]. Both Concertos sustain networks of third-relations, placing both slow movements in E major, approached respectively from G major (Concerto No. 23) and C major (Concerto No. 27). E major is anticipated in both opening movements and recollected in the finales. Cfr. Stewart-MacDonald, Rohan H. 'Elements of «Through-Composition» in the Violin Concertos Nos. 23 and 27 by Giovanni Battista Viotti', in: *Ad Parnassum: A Journal of Eighteenth- and Nineteenth-Century Instrumental Music*, III/6 (October 2005), pp. 99-131.

[20]. Swalin, Benjamin Franklin. *Op. cit.* (see note 10), p. 8.

heightened preoccupation with motivic integration in the chamber compositions dating from Spohr's three years in Vienna, 1813-1816[21]. The first movement of the String Quintet in G major, Op. 33 No. 2 contains a figure that «appears in more than 150 of the first movement's 228 bars»; in the Nonet in F major for Winds and Strings, Op. 31 «the first four notes of the piece not only permeate the first movement […], but recur as well in the main theme, codetta and coda of the Adagio […], and are also jokingly alluded to in the second subject of the high-spirited finale […]»[22].

With their strategic blend of diverse stylistic elements Spohr's Concertos call for a multi-dimensional concept of virtuosity, encompassing more than simply solo pyrotechnics. Cliff Eisen traces the meanings of the word 'virtuoso' through several historical epochs[23]. A virtuoso was once «someone accomplished in [musical] art, whether theoretically, compositionally or practically»[24]; in the eighteenth century a virtuoso could be a «scientist-collector» of *objets d'art*[25]. Most significant is the criterion that emerged of the 'true' virtuoso being an upholder of tradition. The 'meretricious' purveyor of 'empty' or aesthetically (and ethically) dubious virtuosity was defined in contradistinction to the «'true' virtuoso […] the custodian of some greater good, a traditional value or even a traditional virtue […]»[26]: whereas Joseph Joachim was venerated for his blending of technical accomplishment with «artistic earnestness of purpose and truly Classical dignity of style», Paganini was «dismissed from the canon of 'true' virtuosos» because of his failure to «worship at the altar of the great»[27]. Spohr, whose veneration of Austro-German Classic models was underpinned by an unimpeachable playing technique, fortified by receptiveness to the best (or most 'desirable') of Franco-Italian influences, emerges as another candidate for categorisation as a 'true' virtuoso. His works, accordingly, embody the dimensions of 'figurative' virtuosity (associated, Michael Thomas Roeder observes, with «a very active left hand» rather than the «vigorous, convoluted bow movements» for which Paganini was infamous[28]), counterbalanced by quasi-operatic, expressive lyricism, periodically overlaid with motivic and harmonic manipulations — the latter qualifying as 'learned', explicitly 'intellectual', or 'compositional' virtuosity. The analysis

---

[21]. On Spohr's 'Viennese' spell, see BROWN, Clive. *Louis Spohr: A Critical Biography*, *op. cit.* (see note 3), Chapter V, pp. 75-109.

[22]. ID. 'The Chamber Music of Spohr and Weber', *op. cit.* (see note 16), p. 157.

[23]. EISEN, Cliff. 'The Rise (and Fall) of the Concerto Virtuoso', in: *The Cambridge Companion to the Concerto*, edited by Simon P. Keefe, Cambridge-New York, Cambridge University Press, 2005 (Cambridge companions to music), pp. 177-191.

[24]. *Ibidem*, p. 178.

[25]. *Ibidem*, p. 185.

[26]. *Ibidem*, p. 186.

[27]. *Ibidem*, p. 189.

[28]. ROEDER, Michael Thomas. *A History of the Concerto*, Portland (OR), Amadeus Press, 1994, p. 211.

of Spohr's Violin Concertos might involve tracing the interaction between these distinct but compatible modes of 'virtuosity'.

A multivalent concept of virtuosity (figurative, lyrical and 'learned') is implicit in many Concertos of the period, not just Spohr's. Scrutiny of a range of early nineteenth-century Violin Concertos reveals varied engagement with those virtuosic modes by all members of the Franco-Italian group, in a manner that resists schematic geographical distinction. The extent to which Franco-Italian composers remained indifferent to compositional techniques more readily associated with the Austro-German canon has been asserted too readily; even Paganini did not eschew the conceptually 'Germanic' realm of motivic processing and structural enterprise, particularly in the Concerto No. 1 in D/E-flat major, Op. 6[29]. Similarly, Spohr was not consistently preoccupied with 'learned' motivic elaboration and harmonic sophistication throughout his Concertos. Examples like the 'operatic' Concerto No. 8 are obvious exceptions, but in specific structural regions such as the second solo (S2) the approach often lies surprisingly close to Franco-Italian repertory; rigorous thematic manipulation is often absent, with a correspondingly greater prioritisation of the 'figurative' and 'lyrical' strains of virtuosity.

The ensuing section of this chapter explores a facet of Spohr's compositional style that is more familiar from his chamber music: linear motivic processes and the 'structural' expansion of distant-key relations, sometimes inter-movementally[30]. The following section, on Spohr's second solos, takes up an aspect of Concerto structure that is relatively neglected throughout the literature on both violin and piano repertory[31] (see TABLE 1).

[29]. *Cfr.* STEWART-MACDONALD, Rohan H. 'Motivic Processes, Dramatic Dialogue and Narrativity in Paganini's Violin Concerto No. 1 in E-flat Major, Op. 6', in: *Nicolò Paganini: Diabolus in Musica*, edited by Andrea Barizza and Fulvia Morabito, Turnhout, Brepols, 2010 (Studies on Italian music history, 5), pp. 141-166.

[30]. Specialised studies of Spohr's Violin Concertos are scarce. Most receive a brief commentary in BROWN, Clive. *Louis Spohr: A Critical Biography, op. cit.* (see note 3). Dissertations include: BERRETT, Joshua. *Characteristic Conventions of Style in Selected Instrumental Works of Louis Spohr*, Ph.D. Diss., Ann Arbor (MI), University of Michigan, 1974; SONNLEITNER, M. *Spohrs Violinkonzerte*, Ph.D. Diss., Graz, University of Graz, 1946; STURM, Jonathan A. *The Evolution of a Dramatic Compositional Style in the Violin Concertos of Louis Spohr*, D.M.A. Diss., Bloomington (IN), Indiana University, 1995.

[31]. In the third section of this chapter I build on two recent pieces of work: STEWART-MACDONALD, Rohan H. 'Approaches to the Orchestra [...]', *op. cit.* (see note 5), and ID. 'The Second Solo in the Opening Movements of Early-Romantic Parisian Piano Concertos: Frédéric Kalkbrenner (1785-1849) and His Contemporaries', in: *Piano Culture in 19th-Century Paris*, edited by Massimiliano Sala, Turnhout, Brepols, 2015 (Speculum musicae, 26), pp. 151-205.

TABLE 1
THE VIOLIN CONCERTOS OF LOUIS SPOHR*

CONCERTO	YEAR OF COMPOSITION	YEAR OF FIRST EDITION
Concerto in G major, WoO 9	1799	–
No. 1 in A major, Op. 1	1802	1803
Concerto in E minor, WoO 10	1803-1804	–
Concerto in A major, WoO 12	1804	1955
No. 2 in D minor, Op. 2	1804	1805
No. 4 in B minor, Op. 10	1805	1808
No. 3 in C major, Op. 7	1806	1806
No. 5 in E-flat major, Op. 17	1807	1810
No. 6 in G minor, Op. 28	1808-1809	1813
No. 10 in A major, Op. 62	1810	1824
No. 7 in E minor, Op. 38	1814	1816
No. 8 in A minor, Op. 47 («In Form einer Gesangszene»)	1816	1820
No. 9 in D minor, Op. 55	1820	1822
No. 11 in G major, Op. 70	1825	1827
No. 12 in A major, Op. 79 ('Concertino No. 1')	1828	1829
No. 13 in E major, Op. 92 ('Concertino No. 2')	1835	1837
No. 14 in A minor, Op. 110 (Concertino No. 3, «Sonst und Jetzt»)	1839	1840
No. 15 in E minor, Op. 128	1844	1846

*. Shading indicates Concertos excluded from this study, due to their employment of alternative formal schemes that omit conventional opening-movement second solos. The information is taken from GÖTHEL, Folker. *Thematisch-bibliographisches Verzeichnis der Werke von Louis Spohr*, Tutzing, Hans Schneider, 1981.

MOTIVIC CONTINUITY AND REMOTE-KEY DIGRESSIONS IN SPOHR'S VIOLIN CONCERTOS

In some Concerto movements Spohr maintains typically Franco-Italian structural demarcation, whereas in others he heightens the motivic continuity. In four cases he adds motivically generative slow introductions (see TABLE 2).

Table 2
Violin Concertos by Spohr beginning with Slow Introductions

Concerto	Introductory tempo marking	Notes
No. 3 in C major, Op. 7	*Adagio*	A 6-bar introduction to a full *ritornello* 1
No. 7 in E minor, Op. 38	*Allegro*	Despite the quick tempo designation, the minims predominating for the first 15 bars produce the effect of a slow introduction followed by a quicker main body to *ritornello* 1
No. 10 in A major, Op. 62	*Adagio*	The 27-bar slow introduction is followed by S1 ('*Allegro*')
No. 11 in G major, Op. 70	*Adagio*	A 22-bar slow introduction to a short introduction to S1 ('*Allegro vivace*')

In No. 11 the opening *Adagio* introduces two motifs; the second, dotted one resurfaces at the start of the *Allegro* of R1, and punctuates the orchestral parts during S1. The motif is especially prominent during the approach to the second theme, whose bass-line revives the *Adagio*'s initial minim motif. The Concerto No. 7 begins with a 15-bar, solemnly homophonic unit — marked *Allegro* but heard as a slow introduction because of its organ-like minim movement. Its principal motif reappears at the beginning of S1, in the orchestra. In bars 16-18 R1 also introduces a melodic gambit whose dotted motif dominates the transition to the relative major[32]. This motif is exchanged imitatively between solo and orchestra; from bar 108³ it is detached and reiterated by the woodwinds. S1 of No. 7 is therefore firmly attached to R1, but the links are forged by the orchestra rather than the solo violin. No. 2 differs, deriving S1's lyrical melody from the march-like opening of R1[33]. Motivic processing is highly conspicuous in the first movement of No. 5 in E-flat major. The quaver motif ('motif b'), introduced in R1 as a foil to the opening, dotted motif ('motif a')[34], is ubiquitous and often serves as the basis for imitation, either within the orchestra or between orchestra and solo. Closer scrutiny of R1 and S1 shows how motif b is used as a 'binding agent'. Reintroduced early in R1, motif b also 'introduces' the 'second' theme[35]. The solo first enters with motif b, and the figuration during the transition to the dominant is accompanied by the orchestra's truncated version

---

[32]. This is closely preceded, in bars 86-88, with a modified reference to the 'minim' motif, by both solo and orchestra.

[33]. Swalin, Benjamin Franklin. *Op. cit.* (see note 10).

[34]. See *supra*, footnote 17. A score of this Concerto was unavailable to me at the time of writing.

[35]. Motif b is also used in this 'introductory' manner at the start of S2, where it is shared between solo and orchestra.

of the motif. The solo statement of the dominant-key theme is preceded by another 'introductory' unit featuring motif b, the motif then being quoted by the woodwinds during the solo's reiteration of the second theme an octave lower.

Tonally, the first movement of No. 5 is less complicated than the Third Concerto, composed the previous year (see again TABLE 1). No. 3 sustains a network of distant-key digressions across its three movements. Bars 34-53 (R1) engage expansively and emphatically with the key of A-flat major, as if expanding the prominent upper chromatic neighbour to the *Adagio*'s final dominant — a conventional ramification of its minor mode: significantly, the digression in bars 34-52 grows out of a shift to the minor; and in bars 51-53 the same augmented sixth that preceded the introduction's final dominant restores the major. The next flatwards excursion involves a gradual recline into E-flat major in S2. A-flat major resurfaces in bars 226-236 (S3) as a modification of the original digression in R1. A-flat major reappears once again as the key of the Rondo's second couplet (bars 143ff) where it follows an unexpected turn to the parallel minor: this seems to affirm the origin of these A-flat digressions in the first movement's initial, 'rejected' minor mode. The second movement also contributes to the inter-movemental continuity, as a rare instance, in Spohr, of an 'open-ended' unit resolving directly into the finale[36]. The major-/minor-mode intermixing of the outer movements can be connected with the *Siciliano*'s tonal behaviour: its 'rightful' tonic, A major, predominates throughout the main body of its interior (dominated by the solo), whereas its orchestral outer parts engage with centres like C major and F major that belong to (and mediate with) the 'outside world' of movements I and III.

In the Third Concerto, then, rather than infusing the slow introduction with generative motifs, Spohr exploits it as the basis of subsequent harmonic excursions, so that E-flat and A-flat majors function like recurring 'motifs' in movements I and III, and II is implicated through its major-minor ambivalence, and its 'open-ended' construction. Motivic and harmonic techniques are combined in Nos. 10 and 15. The first movement of No. 10 has a much more protracted minor-mode slow introduction (shown below in Ex. 1c) whose relative major (C major) reappears as a digression within the subsequently 'sharper' world of the home key of A major. Bars 82-89 (S1) contains a digression *en route* to the dominant, whereby C major intervenes as the flattened submediant of V; S1's principal theme is quoted in this key (see Ex. 1a). C major later becomes a fully structural centre, as the principal key of S2 (see Ex. 1b). These two bouts of C major are connected by Spohr's derivation of the solo melody of bars 157-159 from the orchestra's semiquaver scalar descent in bar 82 (compare Exs. 1a and 1b).

---

[36]. Becker conjectures that this «may well have been a bow to Kreutzer, whose slow movements, in contrast to Spohr's adagios, exhibit an intermezzo character»; BECKER, Hartmut. Liner notes to *Louis Spohr: Violin Concertos 3, 6 & A major, op. cit.* (see note 1), CPO 999 145-2 (1993), p. 27.

Ex. 1a: Louis Spohr, Violin Concerto No. 10 in A major, Op. 62, first movement, bars 82–89.

Ex. 1b: Louis Spohr, Violin Concerto No. 10 in A Major, Op. 62, first movement, bars 155–164.

S1, R2 and S2 contain numerous motivic recollections of the introduction, via another dotted motif introduced in bars 5-7 and subsequently reiterated (see Ex. 1c). Bars 12-13 reappear transposed and repeated in bars 140-148, as part of R2's conduit to

Ex. 1c: Louis Spohr, Violin Concerto No. 10 in A major, Op. 62, first movement, bars 1-13.

S2[37] (see Exs. 1c [bars 12-13] and 1d [bars 140-148]). Bars 12-14 also provide the explicit point of reference for bars 182-187: their melodic outline can be traced in the orchestra's melodic initiations and the solo's responses (compare Exs. 1c and 1f). The orchestra reproduces the exact pitches at a faster speed; the solo embellishes the original version with semiquavers, but the original pitch-framework of A-flat–G–C–B is still clearly discernible. Spohr also generates structural continuity through a 'subdominant recapitulation' (not shown). In bars 196ff S2 comes to rest on a purportedly re-transitional dominant. The harmony then veers flatwards when, in bars 209ff, the opening of S1 is transposed to D major. The subdominant transposition continues through to bar 243 where the equivalent of the passage containing the original digression to C major is rewritten as a conduit to the tonic's restoration, whereupon the recapitulatory process regularizes.

---

[37]. Such explicit recollection of introductory contents also occurs in the first movement of the Octet in E major for Winds and Strings, Op. 32 (1814): «there are only 10 bars of development before the Adagio introduction returns notated in long note values in the Allegro tempo […]»; BROWN, Clive. 'The Chamber Music of Spohr and Weber', *op. cit.* (see note 16), p. 158. A similar process takes place in the first movement of the Symphony No. 3 in C minor, Op. 78 (1828) where a development section is substituted with a re-run of the *Andante grave* slow introduction, reconciled with the 6-8 *Allegro*; ID. *Louis Spohr: A Critical Biography, op. cit.* (see note 3), p. 195.

Ex. 1d: Louis Spohr, Violin Concerto No. 10 in A major, Op. 62, first movement, bars 140–150.

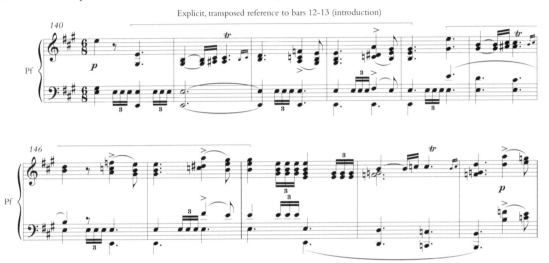

Ex. 1e: Louis Spohr, Violin Concerto No. 10 in A major, Op. 62, first movement, link from R2 to S2, original version.

Ex. 1f: Louis Spohr, Violin Concerto No. 10 in A major, Op. 62, first movement, bars 182-187.

Ex. 1g: Louis Spohr, Violin Concerto No. 10 in A major, Op. 62, first movement, opening of S1.

Ex. 1h: Louis Spohr, Violin Concerto No. 10 in A major, Op. 62, first movement, bars 188-195.

Spohr subjected the Concerto No. 10 to significant revision. The original version, composed in the Summer of 1810, originated in a *Konzertsatz* in F major, WoO 16 (1809). Although the Concerto remained unpublished until 1824, Spohr performed it regularly, referring to it as his «showpiece». In a letter to publisher Ambrosius Kühnel Spohr expresses his intention to simplify both solo and orchestral parts, and in his subsequent performances of the work, Spohr sometimes substituted the second movement with the one from No. 6. He eventually replaced the original slow movement with the *Adagio* he ultimately included in the Ninth Concerto (1820). When the A-major Concerto was published as Spohr's Tenth, it included an *Adagio* from his earlier, unpublished Concerto in A major, WoO 12, dating from 1804[38]. The principal revisions, then, concerned the slow movement, Brown describes the changes to the first movement as «largely superficial». There is one significant exception to this, however. In the revised version (shown in piano reduction in Ex. 1d) the passage towards the end of R2 just discussed, that quotes and transposes bars 12-13 from the slow introduction, is written in doubled note-values compared with its equivalent in the original version (shown in score in Ex. 1e)[39]. In the revised version, therefore, Spohr reinforces the

---

38. *Louis Spohr (1784-1859): Concertos, op. cit.* (see note 1), pp. ix-x, and Stewart-MacDonald, Rohan H. 'Approaches to the Orchestra [...]', *op. cit.* (see note 5), p. 87, n. 87.

39. Ex. 1e is based on the version included in Brown's facsimile edition: *Louis Spohr (1784-1859): Concertos, op. cit.* (see note 1), pp. 61-62.

connection between the *Adagio* introduction and the linking passage between R2 and S2 by restoring the *Adagio*'s approximate speed — implying a preoccupation with structural cogency as well as the 'simplification' mentioned above in the letter to Kühnel.

With its connecting passages between all three movements No. 15 in E minor recalls the 'through-composed' strategy of No. 8. It also evokes the consciously 'modern' experiments of contemporary pianists like Ignaz Moscheles (1794-1870), who in his later Concertos cultivated various forms of explicit inter-movemental continuity[40]. In the first movement of No. 15 Spohr builds on the motivic continuity of Nos. 7, 10 and 11 by dispensing with a substantial R1 and cultivating a closer, more 'dialogic' relationship between solo and orchestra, as if responding to Robert Schumann, who in his reviews of piano concertos advocated a more equal weighting of solo (piano) and orchestra to forestall 'excessive' solo domination[41]. Spohr's reconfiguration of the solo/orchestral relationship in No. 15 encompasses a more egalitarian sharing of thematic material that departs from his previous confinement to the orchestra of references to previously introduced motifs. In the first half of S1 Spohr conforms to his by-now familiar procedure of introducing a motif at the start of R1 (again, dotted) and making subsequent (orchestral) references to it during S1. From bar 22, however, the solo begins also to partake of the dotted motif; but the dialogue does not get into full swing until the onset of theme B (see Ex. 2): a buoyantly militaristic orchestral melody incorporating the opening's dotted motif, and introducing a triplet, is answered by a conciliatory legato violin phrase, in which the triplet is taken up and expressively reconfigured.

The opening movement of No. 15, radically, stations much of S2 in the chromatically related key of E-flat major. In fact, this key is encountered several times in the Concerto. Bars 83-95 introduce the initial digression to E flat as an expanded upper neighbour to V of the relative major (see DIAGRAM 1, stave 1). E-flat major is approached and departed via a diminished seventh that reappears in S2 (bar 135) as the pivot leading ultimately to the re-transitional dominant (see DIAGRAM 1, staves 2-3). Significantly, this same diminished seventh is the first harmony to be heard in bar 1 (see DIAGRAM 1, stave 1). It surfaces again in the passage connecting movements 1 and 2 where the move from E to A major is adorned with a series of chromatically ascending diminished sevenths (see bars 267-269 in DIAGRAM 1, staves 4-5). The chord makes a further appearance in the passage connecting the slow movement with the finale (see bars 37ff in DIAGRAM 1, stave 6). Here, it functions as a pivot, linking the C[7] (reached via a flatward cycle-of-fifths progression from A major, bars 34-36) with IV of A-flat major, prolonged in bars 39-42: Spohr reinstates the finale's E

[40]. Moscheles's Concerto No. 7 in C minor, Op. 93 (1835) has a second movement that alternates between slower and faster material, as if combining a slow movement and scherzo. The movement gradually prepares the theme of the finale, into which it runs directly. On Moscheles's 'progressive', later Concertos, see LINDEMAN, Stephan D. *Structural Novelty and Tradition in the Early Romantic Piano Concerto*, Stuyvesant (NY), Pendragon Press, 1999, pp. 249-250.

[41]. See MACDONALD, Claudia. *Robert Schumann and the Piano Concerto*, New York, Routledge, 2005.

Ex. 2: Louis Spohr, Violin Concerto No. 15 in E minor, Op. 128, first movement, bars 44-52.

major obliquely, through an enharmonic link between A flat and G sharp. The link is emphasised by the solo's insistent reiteration of A flat in bar 42, which is transmogrified into the prominent initial G sharp of the Rondo refrain (see again DIAGRAM 1, stave 7). This link synthesises the previous flatwards orientations: E-flat major serving as V of A-flat major, 'reconciled' with the tonic major. Alternatively, it can be seen as a 'learned' display of modulatory sophistication ('compositional virtuosity') that is redundant, structurally speaking: Spohr could have accomplished the link simply by moving down one notch in the cycle of fifths. Indeed, the transformation of the solo's A flat into G sharp recalls the famous enharmonic relationship in Beethoven's Piano Concerto No. 3 in C minor, Op. 37 (1800) where the *Largo*'s third scale-degree (G sharp) becomes the finale's submediant (A flat), projected as the second pitch of the Rondo's refrain (see Exs. 3a and 3b). Beethoven's Third Concerto contains other inter-movemental harmonic relationships. One is the slow movement's prolongation, at its centre, a third away from the *Largo*'s E major (not shown). More explicit is the finale's direct recollection of the *Largo*'s E major, reached through the A-flat/G-sharp pivot (see Ex. 3c). Spohr's finale is shot through with flatwards slips that connote the first movement's dissonant extremes — albeit often indirectly. Bars 62-64 and 80-86 move towards D major; C major appears in bars 108-111, as the flattened supertonic of V. The couplet in bars 164ff is set in A minor, and soon slips to B-flat major, as if paving the way for the brief, residual digression to E-flat major in bars 231-239 (see again DIAGRAM 1, staves 7-9).

Diagram 1: Spohr, Violin Concerto No. 15 in E minor, Op. 128, movements I–III: modulatory processes

There is no way of proving that Spohr had Beethoven's Third Piano Concerto specifically in mind when composing the Violin Concerto No. 15; but he may well have been instilling into his final solo Violin Concerto techniques purveyed by a wide range of sophisticated instrumental works of the 1790 onwards, featuring heightened chromaticism and the structural deployment of third- and chromatically-related centres, often inter-movementally. As Stephan D. Lindeman has comprehensively demonstrated, this type of 'compositional virtuosity' also became a hallmark of the virtuoso Piano Concerto. Nonetheless, a distinction is needed between the remote-key «dreamy, lyrical passages» Lindeman highlights in the Concertos of Dussek, Field and others that seem to be designed to «create an exclusive world for the soloist [...]»[42], and the conceptually more 'learned' equivalents in works like Spohr's Concertos Nos. 10 and 15.

42. LINDEMAN, Stephan D. *Structural Novelty and Tradition* [...], *op. cit.* (see note 40), p. 23. See also ID. 'An Insular World of Romantic Isolation: Harmonic Digressions in the Early Nineteenth-Century Piano Concerto', in: *Ad Parnassum: A Journal of Eighteenth- and Nineteenth-Century Instrumental Music*, IV/8 (October 2006), pp. 21-80.

Ex. 3a: Ludwig van Beethoven, Piano Concerto No. 3 in C minor, Op. 37, second movement, last 3 bars.

Ex. 3b: Ludwig van Beethoven, Piano Concerto No. 3 in C minor, Op. 37, third movement, bars 1-4.

Ex. 3c: Ludwig van Beethoven, Piano Concerto No. 3 in C minor, Op. 37, third movement, bars 258-265.

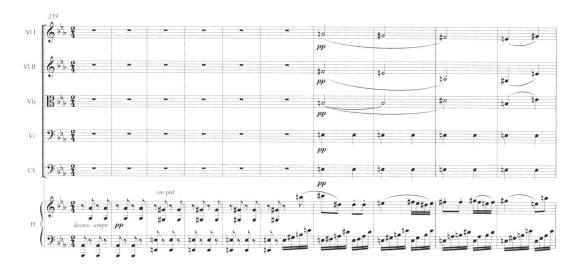

Spohr's Second Solos

The Concerto S2 is normally considered equivalent to a Sonata or symphonic development section. William Caplin laconically describes S2 as «a solo section functioning as a sonata development [...]»[43]. Writing specifically about the Violin Concerto, E. Chappell White asserts that «[t]he second solo section occupies the position and performs a parallel function to the development section [...]»[44]. Particularly in Violin Concertos, however, the quota of true developmental activity in S2s is often low: the S2 «almost never assumes a developmental character in the symphonic sense. Only rarely does the melodic material relate specifically to previous themes [...]»[45]. This is particularly true in Franco-Belgian Concertos[46]; nonetheless, Swalin cavils at Spohr for the «[l]ittle effort» he makes in S2 of the Concerto No. 1, «to manipulate and exploit thematic material». He identifies this as «a weakness that may be regarded as persistent and typical»[47]. The priorities of violin-Concerto S2s simply encompass more than motivic development; figurative virtuosity often takes centre stage, as does the lyrical expansion of themes that may be new, established, or if previously introduced, radically modified.

---

[43].   Caplin, William Earl. *Classical Form: A Theory of Formal Functions for the Instrumental Music of Haydn, Mozart, and Beethoven*, Oxford-New York, Oxford University Press, 1998, p. 243.

[44].   White, Edwin Chappell. *From Vivaldi to Viotti: A History of the Early Classical Violin Concerto*, Philadelphia, Gordon and Breach, 1992 (Musicology, 11), p. 76.

[45].   *Ibidem.*

[46].   Stewart-MacDonald, Rohan H. 'Approaches to the Orchestra [...]', *op. cit.* (see note 5), pp. 83-84.

[47].   Swalin, Benjamin Franklin. *Op. cit.* (see note 10), p. 11.

More often than in Franco-Italian Concertos, Spohr's S2s conform to a blueprint of two successive modules, of which the second is often (but not always) the longer. The first involves melodic statement, and often prolongs a single key centre; the second module connotes the Erwin Ratz/Caplin 'developmental core'[48] in its sequential patterning and periodic incorporation of developmental activity[49]. By conforming to this blueprint, Spohr's S2s lie closer than those of Paganini, Rode and Kreutzer to Piano Concertos and to contemporary theoretical descriptions of piano-Concerto S2s. Concerning the S2, Carl Czerny wrote:

> A new, extended, and elegantly embellished melody is generally the most suitable for the opening of this new Solo, to which succeed modulating brilliant passages, which may be accompanied by the orchestra *piano*, whilst it repeats and develops single ideas of the principal theme[50].

Also with Piano Concertos in mind, John Rink describes «a new solo theme, usually long-breathed and richly embellished; a virtuoso development of exposition analogous to the first and second *Spielepisoden*»[51]. Claudia Macdonald writes of «a closed, *espressivo* thematic statement usually in a remote key» which «is then always followed by passagework that modulates back home»[52]. Notable is Macdonald's identification of a «remote key» as a consistent trait of the virtuoso piano-Concerto S2: remote keys are also often found in Spohr's S2s, and again more frequently than in the works of Viotti, Paganini, Rode and Kreutzer (see TABLE 3).

---

48. CAPLIN, William Earl. *Op. cit.* (see note 43), p. 249. See also RATZ, Erwin. *Einführung in die musikalische Formenlehre. Über Formprinzipien in den Inventionen und Fugen J. S. Bachs und ihre Bedeutung für die Kompositionstechnik Beethovens*, Vienna, Universal Edition, ³1973.

49. The S2 of the Fifth Concerto almost departs from this by replacing a substantial sequential module with a rather concise modulation from C major, the principal key of S2, to the re-transitional dominant. The 'developmental' process (to be discussed below) is instead instilled into the initial, 'thematic' module.

50. CZERNY, Carl. *School of Practical Composition or Complete Treatise on the Composition of all Kinds of Music* […], translated into English by John Bishop, London, Robert Cocks, 1848, p. 159, quoted in BOLAND, Majella. *Op. cit.* (see note 1), p. 122.

51. RINK, John. *Chopin: The Piano Concertos*, Cambridge-New York, Cambridge University Press, 1997, (Cambridge music handbooks), p. 5, citing AMSTER, Isabella. *Das Virtuosenkonzert in der ersten Hälfte des 19. Jahrhunderts, ein Beitrag zur Geschichte des deutschen Klavierkonzertes*, Wolfenbüttel-Berlin, G. Kallmeyer, 1931. Quoted in BOLAND, Majella. *Op. cit.* (see note 1), p. 133.

52. MACDONALD, Claudia. *Op. cit.* (see note 41), p. 20, quoted in BOLAND, Majella. *Op. cit.* (see note 1), p. 137.

TABLE 3
HARMONIC POINTS OF FURTHEST REMOVE IN THE SECOND SOLOS
OF SPOHR'S VIOLIN CONCERTOS

CONCERTO	KEY CENTRE	RELATIONSHIP TO HOME KEY
No. 1 in A major, Op. 1	C major	Flattened mediant
No. 2 in D minor, Op. 2	B minor	Sharpened submediant
No. 3 in C major, Op. 7	E-flat major	Flattened mediant
No. 4 in B minor, Op. 10	B-flat major	Chromatic alteration of tonic
No. 5 in E-flat major, Op. 17		
No. 6 in G minor, Op. 28	E minor	Sharpened mediant
No. 7 in E minor, Op. 38	C major	Submediant
No. 9 in D minor, Op. 55	A-flat major; E major	Tritonal; supertonic with sharpened third
No. 10 in A major, Op. 62	C major	Flattened mediant
No. 11 in G major, Op. 70	F major	Flattened leading-note
No. 15 in E minor, Op. 128	E-flat major	Chromatic alteration of tonic

Both Czerny and more recently Rink ally *new* themes with the initial, 'thematic' module of the (piano-Concerto) S2. Like his Franco-Italian violinist-contemporaries, Spohr quite often introduces thematic material into this region that is either new or only freely associated with an earlier theme or themes. This is exemplified in the Concerto No. 3. The melody's predominating minims resemble the second theme of S2, but only casually. Similarly, the opening of the S2 of No. 4 has dotted rhythms that recall the B theme of R1; but a second version of the theme intervenes in S2 that seems less closely related to the S2 version, undermining any sensation of a chain of linear derivation between the three thematic statements. The initial module of No. 6's S2 contains freely virtuosic material, motivically unrelated to any previous theme. The melody that inhabits S2 of No. 15, perhaps because of the tonal distance (see *supra*, TABLE 3), is heard as a self-contained lyrical idyll resembling the 'nocturne' episodes that appear in the Concertos of pianists like John Field, Jan Ladislav Dussek and Schumann[53]. Spohr's melody makes no motivic reference to any previous theme; consequently, the taut motivic construction of S1 is juxtaposed with the rhapsodic expanse of S2. In the initial modules of his S2s Spohr is more inclined than his violinist contemporaries to resurrect earlier themes. This is seen in Nos. 2, 9, 10 and 11. In No. 2 the opening of R1 transposes the main theme

---

[53]. STEWART-MACDONALD, Rohan H. 'The Second Solo in the Opening Movements of Early-Romantic Parisian Piano Concertos […]', *op. cit.* (see note 31), pp. 167-176.

of R1 from G major to E minor. More subtly, in No. 9, Spohr begins S2 with a direct transposition of the opening of S1 (to the tritonally-distant key of A-flat major), expanding the dotted motif of bar 3 of R1 (see Exs. 4a, 4b and 4c). This is followed, in bars 162⁴-168, by an explicit reference to a motif originating from bars 104⁴-106 (the secondary-key region of S1, not shown)[54].

Ex. 4a: Louis Spohr, Violin Concerto No. 9 in D minor, Op. 55, first movement, bars 1-4.

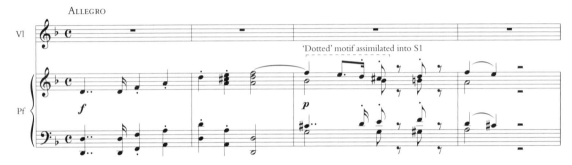

Ex. 4b: Louis Spohr, Violin Concerto No. 9 in D minor, Op. 55, first movement, bars 57-60.

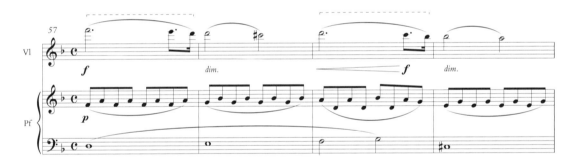

Ex. 4c: Louis Spohr, Violin Concerto No. 9 in D minor, Op. 55, first movement, bars 155-158.

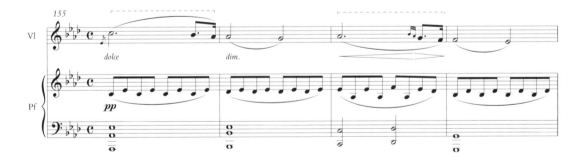

---

54. Swalin identifies the initial presentation as «the second theme»; SWALIN, Benjamin Franklin. *Op. cit.* (see note 10), p. 23.

In other cases previous and new material is presented in succession. In No. 1 the (rather prolix) initial module of S2 begins with a new theme; but the sudden intervention by C major halfway through directly recalls R1's opening theme. Both Swalin and Brown interpret the melody that opens No. 7's S2 as new[55], but it is actually a direct derivative of the opening of R1 (see Exs. 5a and 5b).

Ex. 5a: Louis Spohr, Violin Concerto No. 7 in E minor, Op. 38, first movement, bars 1-4.

Ex. 5b: Louis Spohr, Violin Concerto No. 7 in E minor, Op. 38, first movement, bars 192-195.

The references to this minim-theme are, however, interspersed with unrelated material that perhaps masks the connection. As shown above, No. 10's S2 begins with a melody subtly derived from an orchestral interspersion during the transition to V (see *supra* Exs. 1a and 1b); but thereafter the melody diverges from previous thematic events.

The expressive disposition of the initial modules of Spohr's S2s is highly variable. In Nos. 10, 14 and to some extent No. 3, the point of reference seems to have been the operatic aria — encoded not only in the solo's melodic style, but also in the orchestral accompaniment, whose reiterated bass-notes and ostinato-like string figuration strongly resembles what is so often found in Italian operatic arias of the time (see *supra*, Ex. 1b); and Italian aria accompaniments were often imitated by composers of Violin Concertos, both Italian and French[56].

---

55. *Ibidem*, p. 18; Brown, Clive. *Louis Spohr: A Critical Biography*, *op. cit.* (see note 3), p. 100.

56. I have explored this in Stewart-MacDonald, Rohan H. 'Approaches to the Orchestra […]', *op. cit.* (see note 5), pp. 100-109.

The 'thematic' module of Spohr's S2s is followed by a 'sequential' compatriot whose twin priorities are virtuoso elaboration ('figurative virtuosity') and motivic reference, occasionally extending to thematic development. In Spohr, thematic references are usually confined to the orchestra, underpinning, but not encroaching upon, the solo figuration. Typical is No. 3, where the solo's triplets overlay orchestral references to the 'dotted' motif from the slow introduction. In No. 9 the cellos home in on the opening motif of R1 (and R2), extracting from it a two-crotchet-minim motif that proceeds beneath the solo's semiquavers. In No. 7 the orchestra alights on the second thematic element of R1. The sensation, here, is of a more genuinely 'learned', 'developmental' texture, because of the imitation in the orchestral parts, and also the orchestration: the motif is exchanged between different instrumental sections (including solo woodwinds). The same process of quasi-imitative motivic exchange[57] between different orchestral parts occurs in No. 11. The sequential modules of Nos. 2 and 4 are unusual — for Spohr — in eschewing thematic references altogether. Once the initial module of No. 2 has relinquished the opening theme it dissolves into solo semiquavers underlain with a lightly-scored, thematically non-referential accompaniment. The solo part of No. 4's sequential module, although melodic to some degree, has no thematic reference-point in R1, S1 or R2.

Examples of the paradigmatic, 'Mozartian' developmental dialogue involving quasi-contrapuntal, motivic exchanges between solo and orchestra are rare in the Concertos of Spohr, just as they are in those of his Franco-Italian contemporaries and forebears. In the sequential module of No. 1 there is some sharing of a variant of the R1 theme between solo and orchestra; but after only 8 bars the solo turns to triplet figuration and drops the theme. In bars 179ff of No. 6 a sequential dialogue between solo and orchestral woodwinds emerges that appears to be 'developmental' in character: but the 'subject' of the dialogue, a triplet figure in thirds, has no clear precedent in the movement and therefore lacks 'thematic' status[58]. No. 10 has one of the few sequential modules that processes an established theme. As already noted, bars 182-187 distribute the melodic line of bars 12-13 between woodwinds and solo in 'dialogic' fashion (see *supra*, Exs. 1c and 1f). Once the sequential module is under way (bars 188ff) the woodwinds reiterate an excerpt from the main theme of S1 (see *supra*, Exs. 1g and 1h)[59]. The solo line appears to have thematically neutral figuration[60]; but the arpeggio descent in each alternate bar (bars 188; 190; 192; 194) refers in retrograde to the initial 3 pitches of the S1 motif. This is not, of course, a *dialogue* and the connection just proposed between the violin's figuration and the theme could be dismissed as abstruse; but it does typify Spohr's especially perspicacious pursuit,

---

[57]. The dotted motif is introduced in the *Adagio* introduction and assimilated into the main theme of the *Allegro* component of R1.

[58]. STEWART-MACDONALD, Rohan H. 'Approaches to the Orchestra [...]', *op. cit.* (see note 5), p. 87.

[59]. I am elaborating on some observations on this passage I made in *ibidem*, p. 87 and pp. 91-93.

[60]. As I interpreted in *ibidem*, p. 87.

in this movement, of subtle motivic connections. A more genuinely dialogic texture had been cultivated in the S2 of the slightly earlier Fifth Concerto, but in the 'thematic' module rather than the (truncated) sequential unit. The S2's principal key of C major is reached, and then the orchestra revives the main motif of the dominant-key theme; the solo responds by quoting motif b, and a solo/orchestra dialogue ensues, albeit briefly, before mobilising a sequential approach to the re-transitional dominant.

Genuinely developmental, dialogic textures thus remain a rarity in Spohr's S2s — perhaps surprisingly, given his evident predilection for 'Germanic' compositional techniques. One of his most sustained dialogic textures occurs, not in a first-movement S2, but in an intriguing, lengthy episode interpolating the *minore* couplet and ensuing refrain of the finale of No. 1 (see Ex. 6).

Ex. 6: Louis Spohr, Violin Concerto No. 1 in A major, Op. 1, third movement, bars 129-136.

The episode traverses a wide harmonic expanse: the first module begins in F major, the second in E flat, the third in D flat; the tonic is then reinstated enharmonically. The whole episode lasts for some 61 bars. Although one of the most flamboyantly 'learned' passages in Spohr's Violin Concertos, its thematic 'subject' — a rather extroverted arpeggio figure with off-beat accents — is newly (and rather unexpectedly) introduced in bar 129.

Those sequential modules by Spohr (and others) in which the solo maintains figuration whilst the orchestra cites motifs belonging to principal themes raise questions concerning the intended focus of the listener's attention: is the perceived foreground dominated by the solo figuration, by the orchestra's motivic references, or by both in equal measure? Expressed differently, which virtuoso strain is seen to predominate, the violin's 'figurative' virtuosity or the more conceptually 'learned' contributions of the ensemble? The experience is ultimately determined by the mode of listening adopted: prioritisation of the linear, structural dimension (arising, perhaps, from more detailed, prior knowledge of the work, or an 'analytical' mentality) would create a sensation of the soloist accompanying the melody-bearing orchestral sections or solos; a mode of listening foregrounding soloistic display would perceive a feat of 'figurative' virtuosity with the orchestra in the background, the motivic references, perhaps, remaining unrecognised. In such contexts the interaction between the strains of virtuosity is affected by variables beyond what is encoded in the written score.

CONCLUSION

The motivic and harmonic processes traced in section 2 of this chapter may well stand as evidence of Spohr's close study and emulation of those chamber works and Concertos that lay at the epicentre of the Austro-German, 'Classical' tradition, that were accruing canonicity during the first half of the nineteenth century. This is likely to have been motivated at least in part by Spohr's ambivalence about Franco-Italian instrumental virtuosity. The above discussion confirms, however, that Spohr by no means eschewed Franco-Italian approaches. Operatic models always lie in close proximity; and in his second solos Spohr adopts an approach that stands midway between the Franco-Italian (relative) indifference towards motivic processing and the greater rigour of the Mozartian piano-Concerto tradition. All parts of the discussion point to the question of whether and to what degree the Mozartian model of the piano-Concerto first movement serves (or served) as a criterion for composers of Violin Concertos. Recent scholars have critiqued the uncritical application of 'Mozartian' approaches and models to the totality of early-Romantic pianists, including those who, like Field and Dussek, were geographically and culturally removed from its influences[61]. Majella Boland succinctly observes:

> [T]he possibility that all piano concerti from this period are [...] deformations in comparison with the Mozartian model, and the extent to which the works of a single composer can dominate a genre, is suspicious. Even if one believes that Mozart's concerti are in many ways superior, it is important to note that they are merely representative of a particular thread within the genre's development[62].

---

[61]. See BOLAND, Majella. *Op. cit.* (see note 1), Chapter IV, pp. 108-144, and, for instance, HORTON, Julian. 'John Field and the Alternative History of Concerto First-Movement Form', in: *Music & Letters*, XCII/1 (February 2011), pp. 43-83.

[62]. BOLAND, Majella. *Op. cit.* (see note 1), p. 144.

Although figures like Paganini, Viotti, Rode and Kreutzer operated at an even greater distance from the Mozartian orbit, and were in any case contributing to a genre of Violin Concertos that had its own distinct and longer-established traditions, the lacuna of theoretical models devised specifically for the Violin Concerto exposes these works to applications of 'Mozartian' criteria, however covert; and any such application is disenfranchising when it leads to criticism of the alleged lack of structural/motivic cogency in the structuring of individual movements or, with regard to second solos, complaints about lacking 'thematic development' of the prescribed, 'dialogic' kind.

Mozartian criteria might, of course, have been consciously invited by a figure like Spohr. Nonetheless, close examination of his Violin Concertos discloses markedly fluctuating priorities. Some, like No. 8, face the world of Italian opera head on, and Nos. 2 and 4 embrace Franco-Italian structural clarity whilst prioritising the 'figurative' and 'lyrical' virtuoso strains; Nos. 3, 7, 10 and 11 (3 and 10 especially) do certainly pursue 'Germanic' linear processes, as if keeping the string quartets of Haydn and Beethoven within sight. No. 15 achieves an intriguing synthesis that tempers the structural radicalism of No. 8 whilst pursuing certain of the processes explored in Nos. 3, 7, 10 and 11 to enterprising extremes. Importantly, Spohr's Concertos chart no smooth 'evolution' towards ever-increasing cogency and rigorously 'linear' syntactical continuity; and the second solos disclose several viable approaches including — or excluding, as the case most often is — 'motivic development'. In his manipulation of the changing faces of virtuosity, 'learned', figurative and lyrical, Spohr simultaneously embraces and critiques both Franco-Italian and Germanic streams of influence, in much the same way that he was fascinated, perplexed and repelled by the playing, compositions and demeanour of the mercurial Italian violinist he met for the first time in Venice on 20 October 1816.

L'OPERA VIOLINISTICA DEL VIRTUOSO BELGA
ALEXANDRE-JOSEPH ARTÔT
E IL CASO DELLE *VARIATIONS CONCERTANTES*, OP. 17[*]

Fabrizio Ammetto – Alejandra Béjar Bartolo
(GUANAJUATO, MX)

NEI MODERNI DIZIONARI ENCICLOPEDICI musicali il nome di Alexandre-Joseph Artôt compare quasi di sfuggita. Poche righe gli vengono dedicate in *The New Grove Dictionary of Music and Musicians* del 2001[1] — che ricicla integralmente, con pochissime aggiunte, il contenuto della stessa voce dell'edizione del 1980[2] —, mentre nel volume del 1985 del *Dizionario Enciclopedico Universale della Musica e dei Musicisti* alle scarse notizie biografiche sull'autore fa seguito un'incompleta e imprecisa lista delle sue composizioni[3]. L'unico contributo bibliografico di un certo rilievo — seppur di trent'anni fa — è un saggio (pure piuttosto inaccessibile) di José Quitin, intitolato 'Un grand violoniste belge injustement oublié: Alexandre-Joseph Artôt', apparso nel *Bulletin de la société liégeoise de musicologie*[4]. L'interesse di quell'articolo risiede nel fatto che l'autore riporta varie citazioni tratte soprattutto dalla *Gazette musicale de Paris* relative ai programmi musicali eseguiti da Artôt e ai commenti successivi alle sue *performances*. Per contro, il saggio non si sofferma particolarmente sugli aspetti analitici delle composizioni di questo violinista.

---

[*]. Il presente articolo rielabora e amplia la relazione 'L'opera violinistica del virtuoso belga Alexandre-Joseph Artôt' presentata al Convegno internazionale *The 'Franco-Belgian Violin School' from G. B. Viotti to E. Ysaÿe*, La Spezia, Centro di Arte Moderna e Contemporanea, 9-11 luglio 2012.

[1]. CHITTY, Alexis – PARIKIAN, Manoug. 'Artôt, Alexandre [Montagney, Joseph]', in: *The New Grove Dictionary of Music and Musicians, Second edition*, a cura di Stanley Sadie, 29 voll., Londra, Macmillan, 2001, vol. II, pp. 92-93.

[2]. ID. – ID. 'Artôt, Alexandre [Montagney, Joseph]', in: *The New Grove Dictionary of Music and Musicians*, a cura di Stanley Sadie, 20 voll., Londra, Macmillan, 1980, vol. I, p. 645.

[3]. 'Artôt, Alexandre-Joseph', in: *Dizionario Enciclopedico Universale della Musica e dei Musicisti*, diretto da Alberto Basso, 13 voll., Torino, UTET, 1983-1990, *Le Biografie*, vol. I, p. 153.

[4]. QUITIN, José. 'Un grand violoniste belge injustement oublié: Alexandre-Joseph Artôt', in: *Bulletin de la société liégeoise de musicologie*, n. 44 (1984), pp. 1-21.

Ma chi era questo Artôt, oggi sconosciuto virtuoso della tradizione violinistica franco-belga, ma alla sua epoca stimato strumentista e compositore, per il quale nel 1839 Hector Berlioz scrisse l'elegante romanza per violino e orchestra *Rêverie et caprice*, Op. 8 (H 88)?

Nato a Bruxelles il 25 gennaio 1815, Alexandre-Joseph Artôt apparteneva a una famiglia di musicisti d'origine francese trapiantata a Bruxelles all'inizio del 1800. Alexandre-Joseph iniziò giovanissimo gli studi del violino con il padre Maurice Montagney, detto Artôt, che oltre a essere primo corno nel teatro della città era anche un buon chitarrista, violinista e cantante. Sempre a Bruxelles Alexandre-Joseph Artôt fu istruito anche da Joseph-François Snel, un violinista di talento. Nonostante una frattura a un braccio occorsa quando aveva sei anni, i progressi del giovane Artôt furono talmente rapidi che all'età di sette anni eseguì in pubblico un concerto di Viotti e l'anno seguente fu accompagnato dal padre al Conservatorio di Parigi, dove studiò con Rodolphe e (successivamente) con Auguste Kreutzer. Appena tredicenne Artôt vinse il Primo Premio di violino dell'École Royale davanti ad altri diciassette concorrenti, risultando il più giovane. Da quel momento in avanti la sua carriera fu tutta un crescendo di successi fino alla morte prematura, avvenuta nei pressi di Parigi il 20 luglio 1845, quando aveva appena trent'anni.

I successi internazionali della carriera artistica di Artôt, sia come violinista sia come compositore, sono puntualmente registrati nella *Gazette musicale de Paris*: in particolare, le annate che vanno dal 1839 al 1845 ci forniscono molte informazioni in merito alle sue applauditissime tournée in Belgio, Olanda, Francia, Italia, Austria, Germania, Inghilterra, Spagna, Russia, Stati Uniti, Cuba e Messico.

In questo articolo si farà un po' d'ordine tra le composizioni di Artôt, presentando per la prima volta una lista e (ove possibile) una sommaria descrizione di esse. Conformemente al gusto dominante negli anni Trenta e Quaranta dell'Ottocento, i generi praticati da Artôt furono essenzialmente quelli del tema con variazioni, della fantasia su arie d'opera, del rondò, della serenata e della romanza. Accanto a queste pagine — tutte per violino con accompagnamento d'orchestra (o di pianoforte) — figura anche un concerto per violino e, soltanto secondo il *New Grove* del 2001, alcuni quartetti per archi e un quintetto con pianoforte manoscritti (sebbene di queste composizioni cameristiche non venga fornita la relativa localizzazione). La produzione di Artôt — che si concentra in un periodo piuttosto ristretto, compreso tra l'inizio degli anni Trenta e il 1845 — fu pubblicata dall'editore Schott (salvo un'unica eccezione): i numeri d'*opus* registrati dall'editore non sempre coincidono con la sequenza cronologica delle prime esecuzioni in concerto realizzate dallo stesso Artôt.

Le Opp. 1 e 2 sono *Airs variés* per violino e orchestra/pianoforte, rispettivamente in Re maggiore e in Mi maggiore. Il frontespizio dell'edizione a stampa della prima composizione recita:

> Premier | AIR VARIÉ | Pour le Violon | avec Accompagnement |
> d'Orchestre ou de Piano | dédié à M.ʳ Emerigon, | Officier de l'Ordre Royal
> de la Légion d'Honneur, | President du Tribunal Civil de Bordeaux. | PAR |
> J. ARTOT. | N.º 6521. | MAYENCE, | ANVERS ET BRUXELLES | chez
> les fils de B. SCHOTT | Dépôt général de notre fonds de Musique: à Leipzig
> chez G.ᵐᵉ Haertel. à Vienne chez H. F. Müller. | Paris, chez J. Meissonnier.

Il frontespizio dell'edizione a stampa della seconda *Air varié* riporta:

> Deuxième | AIR VARIÉ | Pour le Violon | avec Accomp.ᵗ d'Orchestre |
> ou de Piano | Dédié à Sa Majesté | LÉOPOLD I.ᴱᴿ | Roi des Belges | PAR | J.
> ARTOT. | N.º 6522. | MAYENCE, | ANVERS ET BRUXELLES | chez les
> fils de B. SCHOTT | Dépôt général de notre fonds de Musique: à Leipzig chez
> G.ᵐᵉ Haertel. à Vienne chez H. F. Müller. | Paris, chez J. Meissonnier.

I numeri d'*opus* non compaiono nelle pubblicazioni ottocentesche di Schott, ma si ricavano dalla lista delle composizioni di Artôt contenuta nell'edizione della sua Op. 4[5]. I numeri di catalogo (6521 e 6522) suggeriscono la pubblicazione quasi contemporanea di queste prime due opere: per il fatto che l'Op. 2 venne dedicata a Leopoldo I, re del Belgio, che salì al trono il 26 giugno 1831, si può considerare questa data come *terminus ante quem*. Le Opp. 1 2 condividono la medesima struttura formale: introduzione, tema con sei variazioni e finale. Nell'Op. 1 Artôt richiede la scordatura della quarta corda del violino, che deve essere innalzata di un tono (*la₂*).

Del contenuto dell'Op. 3 non è stato possibile rintracciare informazioni, mentre l'Op. 4 — la *Fantaisie brillante «Souvenirs de Bellini»*, in Re minore-maggiore, per violino e orchestra/pianoforte — dev'essere stata una delle composizioni favorite dal pubblico dell'epoca, a giudicare sia dal numero di esecuzioni menzionate nella citata *Gazette musicale de Paris*[6] sia dalle differenti versioni manoscritte (con accompagnamento d'orchestra, di pianoforte o d'archi) oggi conservate in alcune biblioteche italiane[7] e tedesche[8]. Il frontespizio dell'edizione a stampa dell'Op. 4 recita:

> SOUVENIRS DE BELLINI | *Fantaisie Brillante* | *Pour Violon avec*
> *accompagnement d'Orchestre ou de Piano* | par | J. ARTOT. | Op: 4. | 6170.

---

5. Il frontespizio della parte del pianoforte contiene una lista (incompleta) delle composizioni pubblicate di Artôt («J. ARTOT | Compositions pour Violon | avec Accomp: de Piano.») corrispondenti alle Opp. 1, 2, 4-8, 11, 13-20, oltre alla *Romance de Lucrèce Borgia* senza numero d'*opus*.

6. Nelle annate 1839-1840.

7. In I-BREd, senza segnatura [RISM 650006445], con accompagnamento orchestrale: flauto, oboe (o clarinetto in Do?), 2 corni in Re e archi (violini I, violini II, viole e bassi). In I-Vlevi, CF.C.87 [RISM: 850011346], con accompagnamento pianistico.

8. In D-MT, Mus. ms. 440 [RISM 454001461], con accompagnamento d'archi (violini I, violini II, viole, violoncelli e bassi). In D-NBss, Mus. ms. 357 [RISM 455010476], con accompagnamento pianistico.

Proprieté des Editeurs. | SCHOTT & C.° | LONDON | 157 & 159 Regent Street. | SCHOTT FRÈRES | BRUXELLES | Montagne de la Cour. | B. SCHOTT'S SOHNE | MAYENCE | Weihegarten 5. | Le droit d'exécution publique est réservé. | Printed in Germany.

La struttura dell'Op. 4 prevede un'introduzione, un tema con tre variazioni e finale. Un'esecuzione (la prima?) dell'Op. 4 avvenne l'11 aprile 1839 all'Opéra-Comique di Parigi e fu annunciata nella *Gazette musicale de Paris* il 7 aprile di quell'anno[9].

L'Op. 5 di Artôt è un altro omaggio al repertorio operistico italiano, stavolta donizettiano: si tratta della *Fantaisie sur le scène des tombeaux de «Lucie de Lamermoor»*, in Mi minore, per violino e orchestra/pianoforte. Il frontespizio dell'edizione a stampa riporta:

[…] à son Excellence | Le Duc de San Lorenzo | SCÈNE DES TOMBEAUX | DE | Lucie de Lamermoor | Fantaisie | pour le VIOLON avec Acc.ᵗ | d'Orchestre ou de Piano | PAR | J. ARTOT | Op. 5. | N.° 6461. | MAYENCE CHEZ LES FILS DE B. SCHOTT. | Bruxelles chez Schott frères: Londres chez Schott & C.ⁱᵉ

La composizione di questa fantasia è senz'altro successiva al 6 agosto 1839, data della prima rappresentazione a Parigi (nel Théâtre de la Renaissance) della versione francese dell'opera di Donizetti. Un'interpretazione di Artôt della sua Op. 5 è attestata il 18 marzo 1840, stessa data in cui l'autore presentò per la prima volta al pubblico parigino anche la sua Op. 6, «Le Rêve» (*Scène*), in Sol maggiore, per violino e pianoforte[10]:

LE | RÊVE. | SCÈNE | POUR | Violon | avec Accompag.ᵗ de Piano, | dédiée à son ami F. Ledoux, de Varsovie, | PAR | J. ARTOT | Op. 6. | N.° 6323. Proprieté des Editeurs. – Enregistré aux Archives de l'Union. | MAYENCE, | ANVERS ET BRUXELLES | chez les fils de B. SCHOTT | Dépôt général de notre fonds de Musique: à Leipzig chez G.ᵐᵉ Haertel. à Vienne chez H. F. Müller. | Paris, chez J. Meissonnier.

Anche l'Op. 7 è una composizione che prevede soltanto l'accompagnamento del pianoforte: si tratta di uno *Scherzo*, in Si minore, del quale si conosce almeno un'interpretazione dell'autore offerta al pubblico di Parigi il 27 aprile 1841. Questo il titolo dell'edizione a stampa:

---

9. «[…] Le onze de ce mois MM. Doëhler et Artôt, ces artistes si jeunes et déjà célèbres, donneront un concert à l'Opéra-Comique, dont voici le programme: […] 5° *Souvenir de Bellini*, caprice et andante pour violon, composés et exécutés par M. Artôt; […] 10° Grandes variations pour violon, sur un air russe, composées et exécutées par M. Artôt […]».

10. «[…] Le concert de M. Artôt aura lieu mercredi 18 mars, chez MM. Pleyel et Cⁱᵉ, 20, rue Rochechouart. Voici le programme: […] *Le Rêve*, scène de violon, exécutée pour la première fois par M. Artôt. […] Fantaisie pour violon, sur la dernière scène de la *Lucie*, exécutée par M. Artôt […]»; *Gazette musicale de Paris* del 15 marzo 1840.

SCHERZO | POUR | VIOLON | avec Accomp.ᵗ de Piano, | dédié |
à Monsieur le V.ᵗᵉ de Latour Dupin | PAR | J. ARTOT. | Op. 7. | PARIS,
chez J. MEISSONNIER, Editeur, Rue Dauphine, N.° 22. | Mayence et
Anvers chez Schott | J. M. 1259.

Un altro dei cavalli di battaglia di Artôt fu la sua *Fantaisie brillante «Hommage à Rubini»*,
in Re maggiore, Op. 8, per violino e pianoforte/orchestra, la cui prima esecuzione assoluta
venne recensita assai positivamente dalla *Gazette musicale de Paris* del 31 gennaio del 1841:

> […] M. Artôt, notre brillant, impressionnable et impressionnant violoniste, a
> exécuté, pour la première fois, un morceau de concert intitulé: *Hommage à
> Rubini*. Son introduction en *si* mineur est un large et beau dialogue entre le
> violon et l'orchestre, dans lequel intervient surtout la flûte par des rentrées
> ravissantes d'effet. Dans ce morceau comme dans la grande *Fantaisie* qu'il e dite
> ensuite, ce violoniste distingué a constamment été noble, chanteur expressif,
> profond, dramatique; et ces deux morceaux finissent par des octaves en double
> corde qui donnent une puissance extraordinaire au violon, qui dans les mains de
> M. Artôt, mérite plus que jamais le titre de roi des instruments[11].

La dedica nel titolo di questa fantasia fa riferimento a Giovanni Battista Rubini (1794-
1854), il leggendario tenore italiano dell'opera lirica di primo Ottocento. Il frontespizio
dell'edizione a stampa recita:

> Hommage | à | RUBINI. | FANTAISIE | brillante | Pour le
> VIOLON | avec Acc.ᵗ | de Piano, | PAR | J. ARTOT. | Op. 8. | N.° 6324. |
> Proprieté des Editeurs. - Enregistré aux Archives de l'Union. | MAYENCE, |
> ANVERS ET BRUXELLES | chez les fils de B. SCHOTT | Dépôt général
> de notre fonds de Musique: à Leipzig chez G.ᵐᵉ Haertel. à Vienne chez H. F.
> Müller. | Paris, chez J. Meissonnier.

Una versione manoscritta con accompagnamento d'orchestra di questa Fantasia è
conservata a Metten[12], in Germania.

Delle Opp. 9 e 10 di Artôt si ignora, al momento, il contenuto. L'Op. 11 è la *Grande
fantaisie sur l'Hymne national russe*[13], in Sol maggiore, per violino e orchestra/pianoforte.
Nonostante nell'edizione Schott appaia tale numero d'*opus*, questa maestosa composizione
era già stata eseguita in pubblico nel citato concerto parigino dell'11 aprile 1839[14]. Il
frontespizio dell'edizione a stampa riporta:

---

[11]. *Gazette musicale de Paris* del 31 gennaio 1841, p. 70.

[12]. In D-MT, Mus. ms. 439 [RISM 454001460]. L'orchestrazione prevede: 2 flauti, 2 oboi, 2 clarinetti,
2 fagotti, 2 corni, 2 trombe, 2 tromboni, timpani e archi (violini I, violini II, viole, violoncelli e bassi).

[13]. 'Bože, Carja chrani!' ('Dio, proteggi lo Zar!') è stato l'ultimo inno nazionale dell'Impero russo:
venne scelto a seguito di un concorso di composizione tenutosi nel 1833 e rimase l'inno ufficiale dell'Impero
fino alla Rivoluzione russa del 1917.

[14]. Si veda nota 9.

Grande | FANTAISIE | sur l'Hymne National Russe | POUR |
Violon | dédiée | à S.A.R. et I. Le Grand Duc héréditaire de Russie, | PAR |
J. ARTOT | A. J. | Œuv: 11. | Paris, au BUREAU CENTRAL de Musique
29, Place de la Bourse. | Mayence fils B. Schott. Milan, Luca | B. C. 671.

La seguente opera di Artôt è frutto di una collaborazione compositiva col
pianista tedesco Frédéric Kalkbrenner (1785-1849): si tratta del *Duo brillant sur le ballet
de «Giselle»*[15], in La maggiore, per violino e pianoforte. La composizione è menzionata,
tra le novità editoriali, nella *Gazette musicale de Paris* del 17 ottobre 1841. Nell'edizione
Schott questa composizione è segnalata come Op. 154 di Kalkbrenner — responsabile
dell'accompagnamento pianistico — e come Op. 12 di Artôt, a cui si deve la parte
violinistica:

DUO | brillant | POUR | Piano et Violon | sur le Ballet
de | GISELLE | d'Ad: Adam, | PAR Frédéric Kalkbrenner Op: 154. | et
J. ARTOT. | Op: 12. | N:° 6586. | Proprieté des Editeurs. - Enregistré aux
Archives de l'Union. | MAYENCE, | ANVERS ET BRUXELLES | chez les
fils de B. SCHOTT | Dépôt général de notre fonds de Musique: à Leipzig chez
G.^me Haertel. à Vienne chez H. F. Müller. | Paris, chez J. Meissonnier.

L'Op. 13 di Artôt, la *Fantaisie sur la «Norma» de Bellini*, in Mi minore-maggiore, per
violino e orchestra/pianoforte[16], è un ulteriore omaggio all'operista catanese. Il frontespizio
dell'edizione a stampa recita:

Fantaisie | POUR | VIOLON | avec Acc.^t d'Orchestre ou de Piano |
Sur la NORMA de Bellini. | dédiée | à sa Majesté | l'Impératrice de Russie |
PAR | J. ARTOT. | Op: 13. | N:° 6700. | Proprieté des Editeurs. Enregistré
aux Archives de l'Union. | MAYENCE | ANVERS ET BRUXELLES | chez
les fils de B. SCHOTT. | Dépôt général de notre fonds de Musique: à Leipzig
chez G.^me Haertel. à Vienne chez H. F. Müller. | Paris, chez J. Meissonnier.

Di questa composizione esistono anche due esemplari manoscritti in Germania[17] e
in Italia[18], nella versione con accompagnamento pianistico. La prima esecuzione assoluta
della *Fantaisie* Op. 13 («un caprice pour le violon sur *Norma*, composé par M. Artôt dit par
l'auteur pour la première fois») fu splendidamente recensita nella *Gazette musicale de Paris*
del 19 aprile 1840.

---

[15]. *Giselle*, balletto in due atti con musica di Adolphe Charles Adam (1803-1856), venne rappresentato
per la prima volta a Parigi nella Académie royale de musique (oggi Opéra de Paris) il 28 giugno 1841.

[16]. Nella lista delle composizioni di Artôt contenuta nell'edizione della sua Op. 4 non viene menzionata
la versione per orchestra.

[17]. In D-OLl, Cim I 456, 38 [RISM 451504485].

[18]. In I-Vlevi, CF.C.88 [RISM 850011347].

L'Op. 14 è una *Sérénade*, in La maggiore, per violino e pianoforte, dedicata alla celebre cantante Laure Cinti-Damoreau (1801-1863), della quale Artôt fu fedele partner artistico negli ultimi anni della sua intensa carriera concertistica. Questa serenata è segnalata, tra le novità editoriali, nella *Gazette musicale de Paris* del 27 ottobre 1844. Il frontespizio dell'edizione a stampa riporta:

> SÉRÉNADE | pour le | VIOLON | avec accompagnement de Piano | dédiée | à Madame | Cinti Damoreau | PAR | J. ARTÔT. | Op. 14 | N.° 7975. | Proprieté des Editeurs Enregistré aux Archives de l'Union. | MAYENCE | ANVERS ET BRUXELLES | chez les fils de B. SCHOTT. | Paris, au Bureau Central de Musique. | Milan, chez Ricordi. | Dépôt général de notre fonds de Musique: à Leipzig chez C. F. Leede à Vienne chez H. F. Müller

L'Op. 15 è un *Rondo*, in La minore-maggiore, per violino e pianoforte (di datazione incerta). Il frontespizio dell'edizione a stampa menziona:

> RONDO | POUR | Violon, | avec accompag.ᵗ de PIANO | dédié | à son ami Stunz Maitre de Chapelle à la Cour de Bavière | PAR | J. ARTOT | Op: 15. | N:° 8041. | Proprieté des Editeurs Enregistré aux Archives de l'Union. | MAYENCE | ANVERS ET BRUXELLES | chez les fils de B. SCHOTT. | Paris, au Bureau Central de Musique. | Milan, chez Lucca. | Dépôt général de notre fonds de Musique: à Leipzig chez C. F. Leede à Vienne chez H. F. Müller

La successiva pubblicazione di Artôt è la *Grande fantaisie de concert*, in Re maggiore, per violino e orchestra/pianoforte:

> GRANDE | Fantaisie de Concert, | POUR | VIOLON | avec | Accomp.ᵗ d'Orchestre, ou Piano | DÉDIÉE À | M.ʳ le Comte Eugène de Cessole. | PAR | J. ARTOT | Op: 18. | A Villèe. | Paris, au BUREAU CENTRAL de Musique, Place de la Bourse, N.° 29. | Mayence fils B. Schott. Milan, Lucca | B. C. 675.

Sebbene nell'edizione Schott appaia il numero d'opera 18, questo è senz'altro un errore: infatti, nella lista delle composizioni di Artôt contenuta nell'edizione dell'Op. 4 questa *Grande fantaisie de concert* è registrata come Op. 16. Nella *Gazette musicale de Paris* del 23 aprile 1843 si annuncia il programma del Concerto del 2 maggio, che include tra le composizioni di Artôt, l'esecuzione di una «Fantaisie de concert sur un théme original»: forse potrebbe essere proprio questa Fantasia Op. 16?

L'Op. 17 di Artôt è una composizione assai singolare. Si tratta di una serie di *Variations concertantes*, in Mi bemolle maggiore, per canto, violino e pianoforte, su un'aria di Antonio Pacini (1778-1866)[19]:

---

19. Musicista napoletano trasferitosi a Parigi nel 1804.

> Variations | Concertantes | POUR | CHANT ET VIOLON | Avec
> Accomp.ᵗ de Piano | Sur une Romance | de Paccini | Composées pour | M.ᵐᵉ
> Cinti-Damoreau | PAR | J. ARTOT | Op. 17. | N:° 8076. | Proprieté des
> Editeurs Enregistré aux Archives de l'Union. | MAYENCE | ANVERS ET
> BRUXELLES | chez les fils de B. SCHOTT. | Paris, au Bureau Central de
> Musique. | Milan, chez F. Lucca. | Dépôt général de notre fonds de Musique:
> à Leipzig chez C. F. Leede à Vienne chez H. F. Müller

In questa composizione le quattro corde del violino devono essere accordate tutte mezzo tono sopra: $la\flat_2$-$mi\flat_3$-$si\flat_3$-fa_4. Le *Variations concertantes* Op. 17 vennero presentate a Parigi il 2 maggio 1843, nell'interpretazione dell'autore e della dedicataria, il soprano francese Laure Cinti-Damoreau.

Nella stessa data venne eseguito anche il Concerto per violino in La minore, Op. 18[20]. Questa composizione — che Artôt dedicò al violinista e compositore francese François-Antoine Habeneck (1781-1849) — risale tuttavia ad almeno un paio d'anni prima, quando venne presentata (probabilmente per la prima volta) a Monaco di Baviera il 6 ottobre 1841[21]. Il Concerto è articolato in tre movimenti (*Allegro, Larghetto, Allegro*): la fine del movimento iniziale si innesta direttamente nel tempo lento (secondo una struttura adottata anche da Mendelssohn nel suo celebre Concerto per violino in Mi minore, Op. 64). Il Concerto Op. 18 di Artôt fu co-pubblicato dagli editori Lucca di Milano, Ducci di Firenze e L'Euterpe Ticinese di Chiasso (quest'ultima stamperia aveva iniziato la propria attività intorno al 1833):

> CONCERTO | POUR | VIOLON | avec accompag.ᵗ de Grand
> Orchestre ou Piano | DÉDIÉ À | M. HABENECK | Professeur au
> Conservatoire Royal de Musique etc. | PAR | J. ARTÔT | Op. 18 | N.°
> 5166 | Prop. des Editeurs | Milan chez F. Lucca vis à vis le Grand Théâtre |
> Florence chez les Fréres Ducci Chiasso l'Euterpe Ticinese

L'orchestrazione prevede 2 flauti, 2 oboi, 2 clarinetti in La, 2 fagotti, 4 corni, 2 trombe, 3 tromboni, timpani, triangolo, grancassa e archi (violini I, violini II, viole, violoncelli e bassi). Dello stesso concerto esiste, inoltre, una versione manoscritta con accompagnamento pianistico conservata nella piccola città tedesca di Harburg (Schwaben)[22].

L'Op. 19 di Artôt è la *Grande fantaisie sur des motifs de «Robert le diable»*[23], in Mi minore-maggiore, per violino e orchestra/pianoforte[24]. La *Gazette musicale de Paris* registra

---

[20]. Nella lista delle composizioni di Artôt contenuta nell'edizione della sua Op. 4 questo Concerto è indicato come «Premier Concerto», ma non risulta che Artôt abbia composto altri lavori di questo tipo.

[21]. L'esecuzione è registrata nella *Gazette musicale de Paris* del 14 novembre 1841.

[22]. In D-HR, III 4 1/2 2 | 0 1108 [RISM 450023690].

[23]. La prima rappresentazione di *Robert le diable* di Giacomo Meyerbeer avvenne all'Opéra de Paris il 21 novembre 1831.

[24]. Nella lista delle composizioni di Artôt contenuta nell'edizione della sua Op. 4 non viene menzionata la versione per orchestra.

un'esecuzione dell'autore di questa *Fantaisie* il 27 aprile 1841. Anche in questo caso il numero d'*opus* dell'editore Schott non segue la cronologia delle composizioni di Artôt. Il frontespizio dell'edizione a stampa recita:

GRANDE | FANTAISIE | sur des motifs de | ROBERT LE DIABLE | POUR | VIOLON | avec accompagnement de Grand Orchestre ou Piano | DÉDIÉE À S. M. | l'Impereur de toutes les Russies | PAR | J. ARTÔT | Op. 19 | N.° 8127 | Proprieté des Editeurs. Enregistré aux Archives de l'Union. | MAYENCE | ANVERS ET BRUXELLES | chez les fils de B. SCHOTT. | Paris, au Bureau Central de Musique. | Milan, chez F. Lucca. | Dépôt général de notre fonds de Musique: à Leipzig chez C. F. Leede à Vienne chez H. F. Müller

Infine, con il numero d'Op. 20, Schott pubblica la *Romance de Field*, in Si bemolle maggiore, per violino e pianoforte: si tratta della trascrizione di un Notturno del compositore e pianista irlandese John Field (1782-1837). Il frontespizio dell'edizione a stampa registra:

Romance | DE | FIELD | Transcrite pour le Violon avec accompagnement | de | PIANO | PAR | J. ARTOT | Op: 20. | N.° 8043 | Proprieté des Editeurs Enregistré aux Archives de l'Union | MAYENCE | ANVERS ET BRUXELLES | chez les fils de B. SCHOTT. | Paris, au Bureau Central de Musique. | Milan, chez Lucca. | Dépôt général de notre fonds de Musique: à Leipzig chez C. F. Leede à Vienne chez H. F. Müller

A questa lista di composizioni di Artôt si devono aggiungere, inoltre, poche altre pagine pubblicate senza un numero d'opera, o trasmesse in versioni manoscritte:

1. la trascrizione per violino e pianoforte di una *Romance dans «Lucrèce Borgia» de Donizetti*, in Do maggiore:

à son ami Alp. Paranque. | ROMANCE | chantée par Mario[25] | DANS | LUCRÈCE BORGIA | de Donizetti. | transcrite pour VIOLON avec accomp.ᵗ | DE PIANO | PAR | J. ARTOT | N.° 6462 | MAYENCE, | ANVERS ET BRUXELLES | chez les fils de B. SCHOTT | Dépôt général de notre fonds de Musique: à Leipzig chez G.ᵐᵉ Haertel. à Vienne chez H. F. Müller.

2. Un *Tema con variazioni brillanti (sulla «Figlia del Reggimento»)*[26] *per violino con accompagnamento di violino 2.do, viola, cello e baßo v. J. Artot. u. a.* [?], in La maggiore, il cui manoscritto è conservato a Bressanone[27].

---

[25]. «Mario» è il tenore italiano Giovanni Matteo de Candia, detto 'Mario' (1810-1883), interprete — nel ruolo di Gennaro — nella rappresentazione parigina della *Lucrezia Borgia*, il 31 ottobre 1840, nel Théâtre des Italiens.

[26]. *La Fille du régiment* di Donizetti fu rappresentata per la prima volta all'Opéra-Comique di Parigi l'11 febbraio 1840.

[27]. In I-BREd, senza segnatura [RISM 650005770].

3. Un *Duo sur l'«Elissire d'Amore»*, per violino e pianoforte, scritto in collaborazione col pianista irlandese George Alexander Osborne (1806-1893). Un'esecuzione di questa composizione venne annunciata nella *Gazette musicale de Paris* del 25 aprile 1841. Il 5 settembre 1841 lo stesso periodico segnala questo *Duo* tra le novità editoriali.

4. Una *«Sérénade» de Rossini*, per violino e violoncello, composta in collaborazione col violoncellista olandese Alexandre Batta (1816-1902). Un'esecuzione di questa *Sérénade* venne annunciata nella *Gazette musicale de Paris* sempre del 25 aprile 1841.

In generale, la scrittura violinistica di Artôt alterna un accentuato virtuosismo strumentale a un'estrema cantabilità, grazie alla quale il virtuoso belga fu sempre lodato dalla critica dell'epoca, che lo paragonò spesso alle migliori voci dei cantanti a lui contemporanei. Già a partire dalla prima pubblicazione a stampa si incontrano numerosi ingredienti del suo violinismo sfavillante, tanto per la mano sinistra come per l'arco: doppie corde e accordi, posizioni acute, armonici, ampio uso della quarta corda o di lunghi passaggi su una sola corda, picchettati, *ricochet*, ecc.

Vale la pena — in questa sede — soffermarsi sulle *Variations concertantes*, Op. 17 per canto (soprano)[28], violino e pianoforte, una composizione di Artôt non propriamente rappresentativa della sua tecnica violinistica, ma senz'altro assai singolare. Come è stato segnalato anteriormente, questo brano fu scritto, dedicato ed eseguito assieme a Laure Cinti-Damoreau, celebre interprete rossiniana. Nelle *tournées* dell'epoca la combinazione cantante-violinista era piuttosto frequente: celebri, per esempio, quelle tra Maria Malibran (1808-1836) e Charles-Auguste de Bériot (1802-1870), o di Antonia Sitches de Mendi (1827-1914) con Hubert Léonard (1819-1890). Nel caso del duo Cinti-Damoreau - Artôt, la *Gazette musicale de Paris* registra una collaborazione costante a partire dal 1842: questo fatto potrebbe giustificare la necessità del violinista belga di dotarsi di un 'pezzo forte' a duo per le esibizioni concertistiche col celebre soprano.

Nell'Op. 17 Artôt utilizza il testo 'Sommo Ciel, che un padre amato', tratto da un'aria (bipartita) in Mi maggiore, per soprano con violino obbligato, di Antonio Pacini[29], articolata in una sestina di ottonari e quattro quartine di senari (cabaletta):

> Sommo Ciel‹o›, che un padre amato
> dar ti piacque a questo core,
> un amante sventurato
> salvo rendi e guidi a me.
> Abbia fine il mio dolore,
> sommo Ciel‹o›, confido in te!

---

[28]. Con estensione si_2-si_4.

[29]. Il cui manoscritto è conservato in F-Pn, Département de la musique, D 18028.

L'eccesso di gioia
che l'alma m'inonda
ti parli, risponda,
o padre per me.

Al petto io stringo
lo sposo diletto,
spiegare l'affetto
possibil non è!

Felice respiro
nel seno d'amore
contento maggiore
bramare non so.

Cessati gli affanni,
svanite le pene,
fra dolci catene
spirar[e] potrò.

Da un punto di vista musicale, la struttura formale delle *Variations concertantes*, Op. 17 è quella maggiormente adottata da Artôt nelle sue fantasie violinistiche: introduzione, tema con tre variazioni e coda.

Seguendo la bipartizione testuale dell'aria di Pacini, Artôt utilizza la sestina di ottonari per il *Grave* introduttivo e le seguenti quartine di senari per il resto della composizione: le prime due quartine per il Tema, la terza quartina ('Felice respiro') per la I variazione, una rielaborazione testuale delle prime due quartine per la II variazione, e l'ultima quartina ('Cessati gli affanni') per la III variazione. Infine, per la Coda, Artôt riutilizza porzioni testuali della prima e dell'ultima quartina di senari.

Dopo una breve introduzione pianistica dal carattere marziale, la prima parte del *Grave* è affidata al violino, che sfoggia una melodia riccamente fiorita (batt. 3-17), mentre nella seconda parte si aggiunge il canto (batt. 17-36), prima accompagnato sia dal pianoforte sia dal violino, poi in stretto dialogo concertante con quest'ultimo (Es. 1).

Il tema (*Andante con moto*, Es. 2) è strutturato in forma bipartita (16+16 battute) ed è concluso da una breve coda (di 4 battute) affidata al pianoforte solo. Nella prima variazione (Es. 3) il violino *tacet* (e il canto omette la ripetizione della prima parte). Nella seconda variazione (*Un poco più stretto*, Es. 4) il violino accompagna la melodia del canto con un *ricochet* alternato ad altri agili colpi d'arco in staccato e in picchettato. Nella terza variazione (*Tempo I*, Es. 5) voce e strumento ad arco alternano scale parallele (diatoniche e cromatiche) in trentaduesimi ad altre rapide figurazioni virtuosistiche, sfociando infine in una cadenza 'a due'.

Es. 1: Alexandre-Joseph Artôt, *Variations concertantes*, Op. 17, Introduzione.

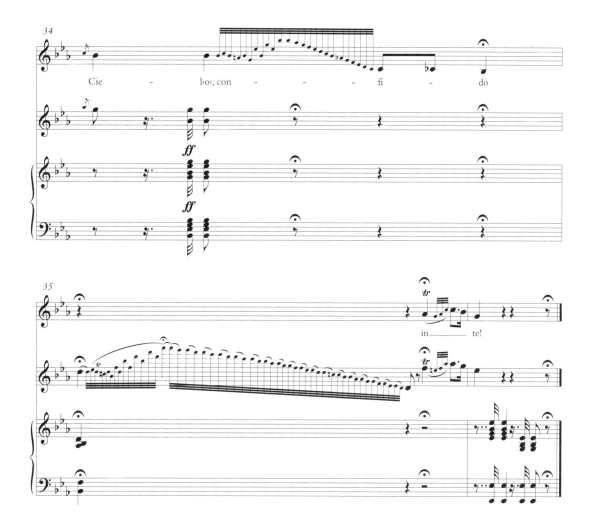

Le *Variations concertantes*, Op. 17 costituiscono una delle rare composizioni per canto e violino scritte nella prima metà dell'Ottocento, epoca in cui non esisteva ancora l'abitudine al concerto esclusivamente strumentale.

Queste variazioni vennero ampiamente apprezzate anche dal pubblico del continente nord-americano quando, tra l'autunno del 1843 e la primavera dell'anno seguente, Artôt e Cinti-Damoreau realizzarono una fortunatissima tournée negli Stati Uniti (New York, New Orleans, etc.), a Cuba (L'Avana)[30] e in Messico (Città del Messico): in quest'ultimo paese l'arrivo di Artôt precedette quello del conterraneo Henry Vieuxtemps (1820-1881)[31].

---

[30]. La tournée americana venne annunciata nella *Gazette musicale de Paris* del 30 luglio 1843: «NOUVELLES. [...] Mme Damoreau et M. Artôt doivent être à Liverpool au mois de septembre, et s'y embarquer pour New-York, d'où ils comptent aussi se rendre dans le courant de l'hiver à la nouvelle-Orléans et à la Havane».

[31]. E anche quello del violinista norvegese Ole Bull (1810-1880).

Es. 2: Alexandre-Joseph Artôt, *Variations concertantes*, Op. 17, Tema (batt. 1-16).

Es. 3: Alexandre-Joseph Artôt, *Variations concertantes*, Op. 17, Variazione 1 (batt. 1-16).

Es. 4: Alexandre-Joseph Artôt, *Variations concertantes*, Op. 17, Variazione II (batt. 1-8).

Es. 5: Alexandre-Joseph Artôt, *Variations concertantes*, Op. 17, Variazione III (batt. 1-8).

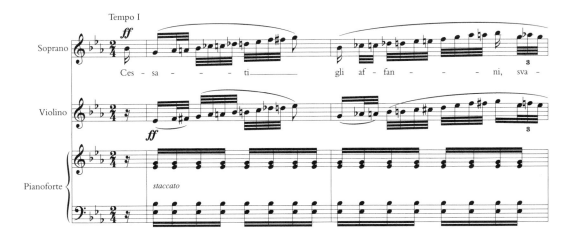

Infatti, come registra la *Gazette musicale de Paris* del 31 marzo 1844, «[…] Vieuxtemps et sa sœur se sont embarqués le 1ᵉʳ de février à la Nouvelle-Orléans pour le Mexique, où M. Artôt et Mᵐᵉ Damoreau les ont précédés […]».

Il quotidiano messicano dell'epoca *El siglo diez y nueve* dedicò per tre giorni consecutivi — dal 7 al 9 febbraio 1844 — varie colonne alla descrizione delle qualità artistiche di Artôt e di Cinti-Damoreau, esaltando il carattere straordinario delle loro *performances*. Il giorno del loro ultimo concerto nella capitale messicana (7 febbraio 1844) il periodico annunciò entusiasticamente:

> […] ¡No lo olviden, pues, los artistas! Nueva-York aprecia más lo de Londres que lo de París, y no hay para ella más celebridades que las que son recomendadas en los periódicos ingleses. Mlle. Damoreau, a quien se ha llamado *Cerito*, y Artot a quien se ha llamado *Artol* durante ocho días en la prensa de Nueva-York, son dos ejemplos graciosos y divertidos que confirman nuestro aserto. Estos dos

grandes artistas dan esta tarde su última representación en el teatro de Park. El programa está lleno de atractivos, y los aficionados a la verdadera música, vocal e instrumental, no dejarán de aprovechar, como esperamos, esta última ocasión que se les ofrece de ver y oír, por última vez, lo que no volverán a ver ni a oír en mucho tiempo[32].

Speriamo che la musica di Alexandre-Joseph Artôt possa uscire presto dall'oblio in cui è caduta al giorno d'oggi: come esortava il quotidiano *El siglo diez y nueve*, non dimentichiamola.

---

[32]. *El siglo diez y nueve*, 7 febbraio 1844, p. 3.

Between Continuity and Change: Eugène Ysaÿe's Six Sonatas, Op. 27, for Solo Violin

Jessika Rittstieg
(Milton Keynes, UK)

Introduction

THE DISTINGUISHED BELGIAN violinist Eugène Ysaÿe (1858-1931) is mainly remembered today for his role in the development of modern violin playing. He was particularly important to the increased use of highly nuanced *vibrato*[1] and admired for synthesising «technical perfection and the greatest intensity of expression»[2]. At the same time, «Eugène Ysaÿe is often spoken of as the last representative of the romantic trend in violin playing, a trend initiated by Paganini, whose exponents — in a greater or lesser degree — were Josef Slavík, Henryk Wieniawski, Henry Vieuxtemps, Pablo de Sarasate and some other virtuosi of the past century»[3]. Similarly, Joseph Szigeti states that Ysaÿe «was perhaps the last representative of the truly grand manner of violin-playing, the living link with Vieuxtemps, the dedicatee of the César Franck Sonata and of Chausson's *Poème*, and the first interpreter of the Debussy Quartet […]»[4].

But Ysaÿe's importance to music history extends beyond his impact on violin playing. Through his close ties with a number of contemporary mainly French and Belgian composers, he shaped their music, for instance, through his encouragement of and practical advice on compositions for violin and his subsequent tireless promotion of them. Ernest Chausson's *Poème* Op. 25 for violin and orchestra (1896) is known to have particularly

---

[1]. See, for example, STOCKHEM, Michel. *Eugène Ysaÿe et la musique de chambre*, Liège, Pierre Mardaga, 1990 (Musique musicologie), p. 236.

[2]. See FLESCH, Carl. *The Memoirs of Carl Flesch*, edited by Hans Keller and Carl Flesch, English translation by Hans Keller, Harlow, Bois de Boulogne, ²1973, p. 79.

[3]. GINSBURG, Lev. *Prof. Lev Ginsburg's Ysaÿe*, edited by Herbert R. Axelrod, English translation by X. M. Danko, Neptune City (NJ), Paganiniana, 1980, p. 260.

[4]. SZIGETI, Joseph. *With Strings Attached: reminiscences and reflections*, New York, Alfred A. Knopf, ²1967, p. 117.

benefitted from Ysaÿe's input[5]. The violinist's importance to Debussy is indicated in the latter's letters. For instance, following the 1894 all-Debussy concert at *La Libre Esthétique* he writes to Chausson: «Ysaÿe a joué comme un ange! et le quatuor a donné une émotion qu'il n'avait pas eue à Paris [...]»[6]. Debussy's letter of 22 September 1894 to Ysaÿe also testifies that Ysaÿe inspired him: «Mon cher grand ami, [...] Je travaille à trois nocturnes, pour violon principal et orchestre [...] J'espère que cela t'intéressera et le plaisir que tu pourras en avoir est la chose qui m'intéresse la plus»[7].

Ysaÿe also composed. Although his works, in themselves, have not had a great historical impact, they are of considerable interest, for example, when studying his artistic identity. However, this area of research has, so far, been somewhat neglected despite its relevance to a greater insight into both Ysaÿe as an artist and his impact on musical development.

The Sonatas Op. 27 (1923/1924) are especially valuable in this regard because they convey, more or less consciously, important aspects of his aesthetic disposition. The work «constitute[s]» as his son puts it, «the best of a vibrant, artistic personality [... and] contain[s] as much science as art»[8]. Stylistically multifaceted, Ysaÿe's intensive engagement with different aspects of musical tradition is particularly striking.

His commitment to the violin *virtuoso* tradition is reflected in a number of ways. For instance, he dedicates each Sonata to a different violinist friend of the younger generation.

SONATA	DEDICATEE
No. 1	Joseph Szigeti (1892-1973)
No. 2	Jacques Thibaud (1880-1953)
No. 3	Georges Enescu (1881-1955)
No. 4	Fritz Kreisler (1875-1962)
No. 5	Mathieu Crickboom (1871-1947)
No. 6	Manuel Quiroga (1892-1961)

In addition, Ysaÿe very much draws on J. S. Bach and the Baroque, late-nineteenth-century music and thought and more contemporary, mainly Debussyian, trends. Embedded in an imaginative and improvisatory musical fabric, the different aspects of musical tradition interact and are expanded. This seems to reflect a particular focus in Ysaÿe's aesthetics: the conviction that the musical past, present and future are part of a constantly evolving process to which the musician, guided by their individual musical heritage, contributes.

---

[5]. Also Chausson's *Concert in D* for piano, violin and string quartet (1889-1891).

[6]. DEBUSSY, Claude. *Claude Debussy: Lettres 1884-1918*, edited by François Lesure, Paris, Hermann, 1980, p. 64 (also in STOCKHEM, Michel. *Op. cit.* [see note 1], p. 116).

[7]. DEBUSSY, Claude. *Op. cit.* (see note 6), p. 69.

[8]. YSAŸE, Antoine. *Historique des Six sonates pour violon seul Op. 27 d'Eugène Ysaÿe et résumé chronologique des événements importants de la vie et de la carrière du maître suivi du catalogue de ses œuvres et d'un essai discographique*, Bruxelles, Les Editions Ysaÿe, 1967, p. 13.

This chapter will begin with a biographical contextualisation of Ysaÿe's aesthetics, and then explore compositional strategies in the Sonatas through which Ysaÿe seeks to incorporate and build on the musical past and present within the context of his individual musical heritage. It is hoped that this will help to strengthen the overall understanding of Ysaÿe's artistic identity as well as his impact on music history.

Background

Throughout his life Ysaÿe identified himself as a «Romantic»[9] and maintained deep roots in the nineteenth century. His artistic identity was fundamentally shaped by both his violinistic vocation and his lifelong commitment to the modern French and Belgian music of his youth, above all that of Franck and his circle.

The Violin Tradition

Ysaÿe's artistic outlook and musical goals were particularly shaped by his violin teacher Henry Vieuxtemps, with whom, he felt, a violin tradition going back, via Viotti, to Corelli had culminated[10]. This affinity was probably increased by their shared Belgian (Walloon) origin[11]. Ysaÿe judged Vieuxtemps to have possessed exceptional artistic integrity and the 'double genie' of the nineteenth-century composer-performer tradition[12]. He particularly admired Vieuxtemps's ability to fuse complementary stylistic aspects. His teacher, he felt, had achieved a unique and highly personal fusion of past and present as well as greatly contributed to the development of musical expressiveness and *virtuosity*.

> L'art d'Henri Vieuxtemps est fait d'une forme large; de traits nouveaux; de détails et de dessins dont la variété et la richesse étaient avant lui inconnues. Si Corelli, Viotti, de Bériot furent ses maîtres; s'ils lui ouvert la voie, il y a marché sans guide — d'un pas assuré et confiant. La plus grande partie de ce que l'art post-paganinien crée d'intéressant est due à Vieuxtemps. Son œuvre résume tous les efforts de ses devanciers. Elle forme un cycle accompli. Grace a ses forces créatrices, qui n'ont d'autres sources qu'elles-mêmes, Vieuxtemps achève le monument érigé par les anciens; il en affermit les bases et le rend impérissable. [...]
>
> Il ne faut être surpris que le romantique, tel que je fus et tel que je reste, soit attiré par ses penchants naturels vers l'art des Corelli, Geminiani (un des plus beaux poètes du violon), Nardini, Viotti, de Bériot, Léonard, Vieuxtemps — qui, tous, furent essentiellement des 'expressifs'.

---

[9]. See YSAŸE, Eugène. *Henri Vieuxtemps mon maître*, edited by Paul André, Bruxelles, Editions Ysaÿe, 1968 (Les Cahiers Ysaÿe, 1), p. 8.

[10]. *Ibidem*, pp. 7, 9.

[11]. *Ibidem*, p. 10.

[12]. *Ibidem*, p. 7.

> Chez notre grand homme, au demeurant, la conception diffère de celle de
> Tartini, Locatelli, Paganini. Il écrira comme eux des traits, des passages difficiles,
> des combinaisons sonores de tous genres. Mais il y ajoutera des sentiments, des
> couleurs; il en fera des tableaux évoquant des joies et des douleurs. Il y aura là
> le langage de la vie. Bref, toute une poétique. Ainsi, Vieuxtemps s'intégrera
> aux expressifs précités. Les tendances littéraires et poétiques du moment l'y
> aideront pour leur part. Tout en gardant, extérieurement, les grandes lignes du
> classicisme, il opérera l'évolution qu'il a rêvée. Il l'opérera par les magistrales
> trouvailles de sa science et par les géniales inspirations de son cœur. Telle est son
> œuvre. Elle est réformatrice et progressiste[13].

Ysaÿe felt these values had become neglected, even disdained, and needed to be revived[14].

Franck and His Circle

During his two stays in Paris (1876-1879 and 1883-1886) Ysaÿe formed artistic bonds that would prove decisive for the rest of his life[15]. He grew particularly attached to the composers around César Franck, though he also highly valued others, such as Camille Saint-Saëns, Gabriel Fauré and Claude Debussy.

> Les œuvres que j'ai eu le bonheur de révéler ont constitué pour moi
> la nourriture esthétique et spirituelle sans laquelle je serais resté exclusivement
> dans ma carcasse de virtuose violoniste, et que je ne renie pas.
> Franck, Saint-Saëns, Fauré, Debussy, d'Indy, Chausson, Duparc,
> Bordes, Magnard, Lekeu, Ropartz, Dalcroze et bien d'autres ont été pour moi
> des guides et des éducateurs […][16].

And: «Je me tiens à Franck, surtout»[17].

Anne-Marie Mathy characterises Franck's aesthetics as of «[…] l'éloquence à la fois vigoureuse, méditative, sentimentale et austère […]»[18], «[…]constamment renouvelé dans sa polymorphie fondée sur les principes unitaires d'un souple classicisme […]»[19]. Stylistic hallmarks of the works of Franck and his followers include very rich chromaticism, modal

---

[13]. *Ibidem*, pp. 7-8.

[14]. See Christen, Ernest. *Ysaÿe*, Geneva, Labor et Fides, ²1947, p. 195 and Ysaÿe, Eugène. *Op. cit.* (see note 9), p. 16.

[15]. See Stockhem, Michel. *Op. cit.* (see note 1), p. 16.

[16]. In Christen, Ernest. *Op. cit.* (see note 14), p. 179.

[17]. *Ibidem*, p. 63.

[18]. Mathy, Anne-Marie. 'Introduction', in: *César Franck et son temps. Actes du colloque de l'Université de Liège (novembre 1990)*, edited by Philippe Vendrix, Bruxelles, Société belge de musicologie, 1991 (Revue belge de Musicologie, 45), p. 9.

[19]. *Ibidem*, p. 10.

inflections, a flexible syntax, intense expressiveness and cyclic construction (the return of thematic material in one or more movements). The music also tends to have a strong historical perspective and the use of counterpoint and Classical genres, such as the sonata and the string quartet, are characteristic. Though increasingly considered reactionary in the new century, the composers around Franck originally constituted the musical *avant-garde*[20]. This was partly due to their intent, fuelled by the, to the French, humiliating defeat in the Franco-Prussian war in 1871, to create specifically French instrumental music in a climate that valued above all operatic music, especially *grand opéra*. Other factors, such as a somewhat Wagnerian use of chromatic harmony, further distinguish their works from most other contemporary French music.

Thus, like Vieuxtemps, the aesthetics of these composers comprise two complementary sides: a commitment to both tradition and to progress. It may be that a certain aesthetic affinity between Vieuxtemps and Franck is partly explicable by a link with Antonín Reicha (1770-1836). Resident in Paris, he was most influential as a composition teacher and theorist and his treatises were widely used for training purposes. As boys, both Vieuxtemps and Franck briefly studied with Reicha[21].

Past and Future

Like many of his contemporaries, including Debussy and Franck's circle, Ysaÿe was very interested in music from the eighteenth century and before. He greatly admired Bach and often performed his music, especially the Chaconne BWV 1004 and the Adagio and Fuga BWV 1001 from the Sonatas and Partitas for solo violin[22]. The violinist acknowledges that «[l]e génie de Bach effraie celui qui voudrait suivre la voie de ses sonates et partitas. Il y a là un sommet et il ne sera jamais question de le dépasser»[23].

As noted, Ysaÿe attached great importance to fostering musical progress. He felt that, as a violin *virtuoso*, it was his responsibility to contribute through the development of new violin technique. Technical innovation was, in his opinion, prompted by the need to render new harmonic processes and effects on the instrument. However, the ultimate purpose of technical progress was to achieve greater musical expressiveness[24]. Thus, ideally

---

[20]. For an excellent discussion of the development of modern French music see Duchesneau, Michel. *L'avant-garde musicale et ses sociétés à Paris de 1871 à 1939*, Sprimont, Mardaga, 1997 (Musique musicologie).

[21]. See Schwarz, Boris – Hibberd, Sarah. 'Vieuxtemps', and Trevitt, John – Fauquet, Joël-Marie. 'Franck, César', both articles in: *Grove Music Online*, <http://www.oxfordmusiconline.com> (accessed 6 December 2014).

[22]. The Bach performances in chamber music settings are charted by Stockhem, Michel. *Op. cit.* (see note 1).

[23]. In Ysaÿe, Eugène. *Op. cit.* (see note 9), p. 4.

[24]. See Martens, Frederick Herman. *Violin Mastery: Talks with Master Violinists and Teachers, Comprising Interviews with Ysaye, Kreisler, Elman, Auer, Thibaud, Heifetz, Hartmann, Maud Powell and Others*, New York, Frederick A. Stokes, 1919, pp. 9-10.

instrumental technique and musical content would work together and grow out of each other. He called this composition «pour et par le violon»[25]. In particular, the violinist hoped to draw on a Debussyian harmony to extend the technical possibilities of the violin. He explains that «[w]e have the scale of Debussy and his successors to draw upon, their new chords and successions of fourths and fifths — for new technical formulas are always evolved out of and follow after new harmonic discoveries […]»[26].

However, he felt alienated from the modern music of the early twentieth century, experiencing it as chaotic, technically incompetent (particularly in violin technique) as well as lacking beauty and grandeur. Remaining devoted to the aesthetic values of his youth and seeing music as «un monument unique et perpétuellement inachevé, auquel chaque génération, chaque école viennent apporter leur pierre […]»[27], he sought to develop, for instance, innovative timbres and fingerings, that would renew and extend this tradition from within. Therefore, although estranged from much contemporary musical development, he had found a way to participate in shaping the musical future without breaking with the past.

The dedication of each Sonata to violinists younger than himself is significant too. Inspired by a concert he attended in about 1923 in which Joseph Szigeti performed Bach's G minor Sonata BWV 1001, Ysaÿe set out to write his own Sonatas[28]. He envisioned the Sonatas to be «une expérience "pour et par le violon", en tentant de suivre parfois le jeu spécifique de tel ou tel grand violoniste actuel»[29]. Perhaps it matters less if such references are audible. More importantly, even if private, they offer Ysaÿe a further way to establish «le point de contact nécessaire entre le passé et le présent»[30] for which he was longing. Moreover, through these dedications Ysaÿe may be symbolically passing on the violin tradition he so treasured to the next generation.

ANALYSIS

When listening to the Sonatas their multifaceted and seemingly improvisatory idiom stands out in particular. Stylistic fluidity is, to a greater or lesser degree, present not only within each Sonata but also between Sonatas. For instance, whereas the First Sonata, despite its internal stylistic fluidity, very much draws on Bach and the Baroque, the Fifth is

---

[25]. See YSAŸE, Eugène. *Op. cit.* (see note 9), p. 15 and QUITIN, José. *Eugène Ysaÿe: étude biographique et critique*, Bruxelles-New York, Bosworth, 1938, p. 35.

[26]. MARTENS, Frederick Herman. *Op. cit.* (see note 24), p. 10.

[27]. In CHRISTEN, Ernest. *Op. cit.* (see note 14), p. 180.

[28]. YSAŸE, Eugène. *Op. cit.* (see note 9), p. 4.

[29]. *Ibidem*, p. 4.

[30]. In CHRISTEN, Ernest. *Op. cit.* (see note 14), p. 181.

overwhelmingly Debussyian in character and the flamboyant Sixth most openly draws on the nineteenth-century violin *virtuoso* tradition of Ysaÿe's youth.

Fantasia Tradition

The very improvisatory and multifaceted nature of the Sonatas suggests a possible link to the fantasia tradition, and this is supported by Ysaÿe's own statements, such as,

> [...] j'ai laissé voguer une libre improvisation. Chaque sonate [in Op. 27] constitue une sorte de petit poème où je laisse le violon à sa fantaisie. J'ai voulu associer l'intérêt musical à celui de la grande, de la vraie virtuosité, trop négligée depuis que les instrumentistes n'osent plus écrire et abandonnent ce soin a ceux qui ignorent les ressources, les secrets du métier. J'aurais pu appeler ces sonates, Caprices; mais on y aurait vu une analogie avec Locatelli et Paganini[31].

Jean-Pierre Bartoli and Jeanne Roudet trace the development of this tradition in some detail[32] although mainly with regard to the free (that is, not based on pre-existing popular melodies) fantasia for keyboard other than organ[33]. Suffice it to say here, as an introduction to the following discussion, that the fantasy tradition, which, in its different manifestations was already in existence in the sixteenth century, plays a vital role in J. S. Bach's oeuvre for solo violin, too.

Bartoli and Roudet explain that around the turn of the nineteenth century an aesthetic of the individual and subjective developed and became the basis of Romanticism. At its core lay values, such as the idealisation of genius, free inspiration, sensitivity, sentiment, expressiveness, the sublime and transcendence of physical reality. They observe that the ideal of the Romantic artist was to 'poeticise' (to instil a poetic feeling rather than to put into verse) the arts and literature. Because instrumental music is not limited by words in its expressiveness, it became considered the highest of the Romantic arts. «Mais dans cet art supérieur, c'est avant tout le genre de la fantaisie — en tant que réalisation objective de la spontanéité et accès naturel à l'absolu au-delà du rationnel — qui devient l'archétype de la création»[34]. And:

> [P]ar sa vertu abstraite, en tant que musique instrumentale, et par-
> dessus tout autre genre, la fantaisie et ce que nous avons désigné par l'*écriture*

---

[31]. *Ibidem*, pp. 195-196.

[32]. Bartoli and Roudet note that in the French sphere of influence the term 'fantasy' as used in the Germanic tradition was often substituted by 'caprice'; see Bartoli, Jean-Pierre – Roudet, Jeanne. *L'Essor du Romantisme: la fantaisie pour clavier de Carl Philipp Emanuel Bach à Franz Liszt*, Paris, Vrin, 2013 (Musicologie), p. 11.

[33]. *Ibidem*.

[34]. *Ibidem*, pp. 23-40 and 344-346.

> *improvisatrice* dans leur capacité à être pure présence de l'esprit créateur, ne représentent pas les sentiments ni les secrets du monde, même les plus indicibles d'entre eux: ils en sont la directe *incarnation*. Rejetant la 'signification restreinte' de l'allégorie au profit de 'l'interprétation infinie et inépuisable' du symbole comme immanence de l'absolu, l'esthétique romantique trouve son idéal dans la musique et tout particulièrement dans la fantaisie instrumentale. [...] Lorsque l'esprit de fantaisie se dilue dans les autres genres, c'est aussi le romantisme qui arrive à son zénith[35].

In fact, some writers, such as A. B. Marx, consider it, in its most masterful realisation, as the most evolved and perfect musical genre, transcending the sonata[36]. It is, therefore, not surprising that Ysaÿe, who very much identified with Romanticism and greatly admired Bach's Solo Violin Sonatas, would have been drawn to this tradition.

It is difficult to define the fantasia genre compositionally because of the great variety of forms the individual works take. Yet, certain traits appear to be characteristic. These include an often sectional construction with a strong element of variation technique and one or more recurring themes. Rondo, ternary or variation form are common. Frequently aspects of sonata form are also incorporated and the mixing of genres is widespread. Interruptive musical processes, such as thematic discontinuities and juxtaposition of materials, are important to the fantasia though linking these coherently is no less important[37].

The primary points of reference in Op. 27 with regard to style have been identified as Bach and the Baroque, the nineteenth century and a Debussyian idiom. Ysaÿe alludes to the individual styles by means of a variety of musical parameters, such as melody and harmony. For instance, the Baroque might partly be evoked through compositional techniques, such as thoroughbass, and genres associated with the period, such as the *sonata da chiesa*. The violin tradition, too, is consistently a key concern. On the whole, the bond that is strongest in both areas is that to the nineteenth century. As a result, especially in terms of musical style, elements of the Baroque and Debussyian idioms appear to be used in relation to those of the nineteenth century; they are merged or contrasted with it. Throughout the Sonatas, allusions to the different styles interact within the music's improvisatory fabric and the exploration of violinistic possibilities equally develops within this context.

The Sonatas' pronounced improvisatory quality and their association with the fantasia tradition rests on inner-musical processes, such as widespread harmonic and

---

[35]. *Ibidem*, p. 347 (internal quotation marks added by Bartoli and Roudet with reference to Le Blanc, Margantin and Schefer).

[36]. See COPPOLA, Catherine. 'The Elusive Fantasy: Genre, Form and Program in Tchaikovsky's «Francesca da Rimini»', in: *19th-Century Music*, XXII/2 (Autumn 1998), pp. 169-189: 177-178.

[37]. *Ibidem*, pp. 171, 177.

metric ambiguity and frequently deflected melodic-thematic processes. Stylistic fluctuations within and between the Sonatas also contribute. Nevertheless, each work maintains a substantial degree of coherence. For example, large-scale harmonic schemes tend to be simple and some motivic-thematic material recurs. Moreover, the music's firm footing in the nineteenth century is a unifying factor, particularly through the extensive chromatic and modally inflected tonal harmony.

First Sonata (Grave)

The First Sonata, too, is closely linked to the nineteenth century, especially through its chromatic harmony, but also includes distinctly Debussyian traits. In addition, references to Bach's G minor Sonata BWV 1001 stand out. In fact, the entire cycle refers to Bach's solo Sonatas. Not only does it consist of six sonatas, the keys of the outer sonatas (G minor and E major respectively) correspond to those of Bach's outer Sonatas. Specific parallels between Ysaÿe's and Bach's First Sonatas include, in addition to the overall key, a third movement in the relative major and a *sonata da chiesa* design in four movements with a fugue-like second movement. Ysaÿe's extensive use of counterpoint in a work for unaccompanied violin also recalls Bach's Sonatas.

The musical discussion will focus on the first movement of the First Sonata, the *Grave*, because, perhaps partly related to its position as the opening movement of the entire sonata cycle, it seems to reflect Ysaÿe's aesthetic concerns and compositional strategies especially vividly. Stylistically, the *Grave*, too, is firmly rooted in a late-nineteenth-century aesthetic. Characteristics associated with the Baroque and a Debussyian idiom are woven into the musical fabric and appear, at times, with great clarity. Moreover, throughout the piece Ysaÿe explores and seeks to extend the technical possibilities of his instrument.

Baroque and the Nineteenth Century

The beginning of Ysaÿe's *Grave* is especially reminiscent of its counterpart, Bach's *Adagio*. This reminiscence largely stems from the contrapuntal texture and the shape of the melodic line, though the serious *Affekt* and the quasi-improvisatory musical fabric also contribute. The counterpoint in the *Grave*, as in the *Adagio*, is grounded in tonal harmony in which chords, like pillars, buttress the melodic line. The latter is woven into the chordal structure and, moving through the different voices, gives a somewhat sinuous impression. Moreover, the melodic line in the *Grave*, though less continuous and florid as well as rhythmically less even than in the *Adagio*, tends to also emphasise stepwise movement.

Ex. 1.1: Eugène Ysaÿe, *Grave*, Op. 27/1, bb. 1-4.

Ex. 1.2: Johann Sebastian Bach, *Adagio*, BWV 1001, bb. 1-2.

The harmony, as in much music of the late nineteenth century, is markedly chromatic and also modally inflected. Chromatic and extended chords are widespread and often used relatively autonomously, as elaborations of simpler chords. Like the modal inflections which Ysaÿe employs, such as the Lydian fourth (the melodic *g*♯ in b. 1 [3]), their function is colouristic. Such concern with timbre is characteristic of the period's music, especially within in the French sphere of influence[38]. The second bar will serve to illustrate Ysaÿe's kaleidoscopic use of harmonic colour (see Ex. 1.1). The bar consists of a gradually transforming and stabilising G major harmony[39]. As the sonority unfolds, the harmony slowly resolves from within and the colour progressively shifts. Only after the pure fifth *g-d* is distilled does the music move on to a C minor chord (b. 3 [1]).

Harmony, rhythm and meter work together to create the improvisatory quality of the music and its association with the fantasia tradition. The chromaticism is an important

---

[38]. See MORGAN, Robert P. *Twentieth-Century Music: A History of Musical Style in Modern Europe and America*, New York-London, Norton & Company, 1991 (The Norton introduction to music history), pp. 3-5; and BARTOLI, Jean-Pierre. *L'harmonie classique et romantique (1750-1900): éléments et évolution*, Clamecy, Minerve, 2001 (Musique ouverte), pp. 179-203.

[39]. The initial b♭o/7 is interpreted as a G7/9 without root.

factor because it tends to obscure basic underlying harmonic progressions. For instance, the simple cadential nature of the initial phrase (bb. 1-5 [2]) is significantly blurred through chromatic alterations and added notes in chords and melody. Rhythmic and metric ambiguities intensify this effect. The melodic line is almost immediately syncopated and meter and phrasing do not entirely coincide either. The phrase is four and a half bars long and overlaps with the next, producing a three-quaver elision in b. 5 (b. 5 itself contains four crotchets rather than the three of the surrounding measures). In addition, the climax of the phrase falls on a metrically weak beat (b. 2 [2]). As a result, from the very beginning of the *Grave*, Ysaÿe creates a constant musical flux. Wagner's statement that the secret of musical form is to be the «Kunst des feinsten allmählichen Überganges»[40] (referring to the *Tristan* Act II love-duet) neatly encapsulates an important aspect of Ysaÿe's compositional approach. Compositional processes, such as these, are typical for the entire sonata cycle and emphasise its link to both the nineteenth century and the fantasia tradition. They also suggest a significant association between the two for Ysaÿe.

Although in the discussion of the initial bars of the *Grave* only references to the Baroque, specifically to Bach, and the nineteenth century have been considered, it illustrates important ways in which Ysaÿe tends to draw on and merge the two throughout the Sonatas. Associations with the Baroque often stem from the use of extensive counterpoint as well as from the integration of musical genres typical of the Baroque. Allusions to individual pieces from the period also occur. The bond with the nineteenth century, on the other hand, tends to be strongest in the harmony and in the substantial ambiguities present often from the very beginning. Consequently, both styles become integral to the musical structure. In fact, as in the majority of music contemporary to Ysaÿe, allusions to the Baroque generally do not occur on their own but merge with more recent styles. Ysaÿe integrates Baroque references most often and most clearly into a nineteenth-century context but they also arise in a Debussyian context. On the other hand, both a nineteenth-century and a Debussyian style often occur on their own (though, because of a certain amount of stylistic overlap the two cannot always be clearly delineated)[41]. The fluctuating allusions constitute a further way in which Ysaÿe creates ambiguity. These ideas are being further explored in the doctoral thesis on which the author is currently working.

Debussy

Nonetheless, at times a Debussyian idiom is clearly foregrounded in the *Grave*. Perhaps the two most striking occurrences are in bb. 15-17 and in bb. 42 to the end.

---

40. Quoted in ABBATE, Carolyn. 'Wagner, «On Modulation», and Tristan', in: *Cambridge Opera Journal*, I/I (March 1989), p. 43.

41. Two important sources of this overlap include the impact especially Wagner's work had on Debussy and his, albeit ambivalent, relationship with the Franckists.

Despite a smooth transition from and to surrounding material, both passages are stylistically very distinct. They abandon the strong emphasis on a late-nineteenth-century aesthetic as well as the reminiscences of Bach and the Baroque.

Ex. 2: Eugène Ysaÿe, *Grave*, Op. 27/1, bb. 15-17.

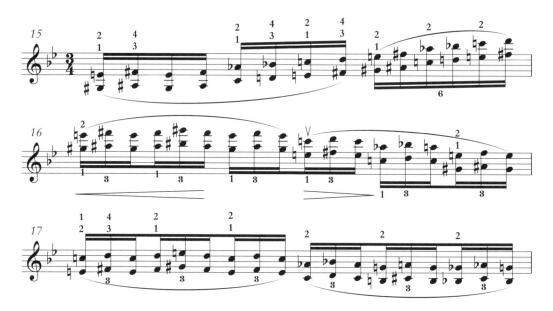

Ex. 3: Eugène Ysaÿe, *Grave*, Op. 27/1, bb. 42-end.

At the end of the *Grave*, the music's Debussyian quality stems largely from the use of timbre. The timbre itself, created by combining very soft *ponticello tremolo* with left-hand *pizzicato*, is novel. The dynamics are very soft and the music gradually fades out. However, though typical in Debussy, the use of distinctive timbres had become increasingly important during the nineteenth century, especially in France since Berlioz[42]. The stylistic proximity to Debussy stems notably from the importance Ysaÿe confers on tone-colour in these bars. As often in Debussy's music (much more so than in that of his predecessors), timbre becomes a structural element to which melodic-rhythmic-harmonic considerations are subordinated[43]. In the final bars of the *Grave* Ysaÿe similarly prioritises colour. Harmonic activity ceases and, remaining on G, a pedal (*g* or *g-d*) is introduced. Harmonic changes are limited to the surface and have an exclusively coloristic function. As frequently in Debussy, the musical fabric itself comprises distinctive layers. The two layers at the end of the *Grave* differ greatly, for example, in timbre, texture and rhythm, though each layer is homogenous within itself. Moreover, the construction of these bars might be described as somewhat 'additive' in that an initial four-note unit is gradually transformed through subtly changing repetitions[44]. This, again, is characteristic of a Debussyian idiom. The additive construction causes the emphasis to be placed on the present moment and the musical surface, that is, away from deeper harmonic-thematic processes.

In bb. 15-17 it is especially the evenly undulating whole-tone scale in parallel sixths that creates a stylistic link to Debussy. Here, too, attention shifts from harmonic-thematic processes to the musical moment. Harmonic direction is suspended through the relatively sustained use of the whole-tone scale. In the absence of leading tones melodic direction is also reduced, which the undulations with their parallel motion and even rhythm further decrease. This creates a soft musical outline and a floating feeling so that the musical moment becomes the main focus. These examples indicate that Ysaÿe's Debussyian allusions are differentiated in a number of ways, such as through harmonic organisation, phrase structure, rhythmic organisation and absence of counterpoint. Also, on both occasions, there is no stylistic fusion.

At the same time, the allusions to the different styles all share the improvisatory and explorative character, linking them to the fantasia tradition. A vital unifying force in the *Grave*, this bond is emphasised through the inner-musical processes with their recurrent

---

[42]. An insightful contemporary account is: MacLean, Charles. 'On Some Causes of the Changes of Tone Colour Proceeding in the Most Modern Orchestra', in: *Proceedings of the Musical Association*, XXI Sess. (1894-1895), pp. 77-102.

[43]. For a discussion of Debussy's innovative use of colour see, for example, Wenk, Arthur B. *Claude Debussy and Twentieth-Century Music*, Boston (MA), Twayne, 1983 (Twayne's music series), pp. 122-126.

[44]. The term 'additive' has been adopted here following Morgan who uses it to describe similar techniques in Debussy (see Morgan, Robert P. *Op. cit.* [see note 38], p. 48).

and substantial though never abrupt shifts in rhythm, harmony and melodic material. In turn, the waxing and waning of stylistic references contributes to the fluidity of the musical structure. Thus, references and inner-musical processes interact and reinforce each other; they become inseparable.

Violin Tradition

So far, the role of the violin tradition in the *Grave* has only been touched on. Here too, Ysaÿe is deeply rooted in the nineteenth century but includes allusions to different periods in history. He creates a confluence of traditions by employing technical means that have strong traditional associations, such as fingering and bowing techniques that accommodate the use of a counterpoint reminiscent of Bach, as well as technical innovations that, for instance, allow the creation of novel timbres.

The innovations are perhaps most perceptible in the more contemporary, Debussyian passages discussed earlier (that is, the whole-tone passage (bb. 15-17 [see Ex. 2]) and the *ponticello tremolo* with left-hand *pizzicato* (bb. 42 to the end [see Ex. 3]). In the first case, it is the fingering for the undulating whole-tone sixths that is novel. It enables the clean playing of such passages, sidestepping undesired bowing noises from avoidable string changes and audible shifting. The innovative aspect of the ending, on the other hand, lies in the special sound quality created by the combination of *sul ponticello tremolo* with left-hand *pizzicato*. Both times, Ysaÿe enables the creation of effects on a single violin which were previously impossible. Particularly in light of the increasing importance of both non-diatonic scales and sonority in music, this contributes two valuable assets to help future composers to realise their musical intentions.

Violinistic exploration and development, however, is not limited to a contemporary context as here, too, traditional and innovative aspects tend to merge. For instance, Ysaÿe develops fingerings and bowings to extend the contrapuntal possibilities of the violin in harmony and voicing (see Ex. 1.1). Unusual intervals and progressions, such as the move through the double-diminished F-sharp minor chord in b. 3 (3) need to be negotiated. Creative bowing solutions are, for example, required for both chords in b. 2. For the first chord the difficulty consists in giving prominence to the melodic line, which is placed in the lowest voice. This might suggest the breaking of the chord from the top down. The second chord, on the other hand, contains five notes and the melodic line lies in the second voice. The difficulty here is to convincingly convey a chord as a vertical entity that has more notes than the violin has strings, that is, cannot even be attempted to be played simultaneously. At the same time, the melodic line has to receive due attention. Thus, tradition and innovation constantly interact on a technical level as much as they do on a stylistic level. The *Grave*, of course, reflects the uniqueness of Ysaÿe's violinistic style in many other ways too, such as in the careful fingering, bowing and *agogic* markings that concern matters of style and expressiveness much more than innovation.

As suggested above, the dedication of the Sonatas to the younger dedicatees constitutes a link with the future in itself. Interestingly, although the immediate inspiration for the Sonatas stems from Szigeti's Bach playing, Ysaÿe also very much appreciated a rare ability he perceived in Szigeti to «assouplir son talent aussi bien aux voix âpretés modernes»[45], and, thus, to convincingly perform the music of very different periods. By dedicating the initial Sonata to Szigeti and modelling it on the Bach Sonata he had heard Szigeti perform, Ysaÿe acknowledges the immediate inspiration he received from Szigeti's Bach performance. Moreover, Szigeti's stylistic versatility may have encouraged Ysaÿe to explore the interaction of different traditions in the sonata cycle. The dedication, therefore, also becomes a way in which Ysaÿe is able to bring different parts of history together.

Again, the fantasia with its inherent freedom is well suited to Ysaÿe's objective to experiment with and explore the incorporation of a range of previous and current violinistic achievements as well as innovations of his own[46]. In turn, the explorative nature of the technique strengthens the music's improvisatory feeling and, hence, its association with the fantasia tradition. Thus, style, technique and structure are intimately linked. Given that Ysaÿe considered violin technique and musical content to be inseparable and interdependent, the fantasia tradition inevitably accommodates violinistic issues as much as the musical content.

Finally, living on the cusp of sound recording, Ysaÿe only made a few recordings of very limited scope and quality. The Sonatas with their detailed notation, on the other hand, provide him with an effective vehicle to communicate his aesthetic and violinistic concerns and to transmit his exploration of a multiplicity of musical and technical issues to future generations of musicians. Therefore, the composition of the Sonatas in itself becomes a means to bridge the divide that separates himself from future generations of musicians; to link different historical periods.

Conclusion

The foregoing discussion has identified a number of characteristics to be central to Ysaÿe's *Grave*. The piece is very much a work for violin in which Ysaÿe explores and

45. In Ysaÿe, Antoine. *Op. cit.* (see note 8), pp. 3-4.

46. For a more in-depth discussion of Ysaÿe's violin technique and technical contributions see Hoatson, Karen D. *Culmination of the Belgian Violin Tradition: The Innovative Style of Eugène Ysaÿe*, D.M.A. Diss., Los Angeles (CA), University of California, 1999.

develops a wide range of violin techniques, from counterpoint to innovative colouristic effects. While the compositional idiom is deeply rooted in the nineteenth century, he also clearly draws on earlier and later music, in particular on Bach and the Baroque and on a Debussyian idiom. Even references to the Sonata's dedicatee may be detected. The manner in which the music proceeds is imaginative and explorative. The different musical styles and traditions wax and wane within an improvisatory musical fabric. They often merge and are elaborated. The *Grave*'s stylistic fluidity, multifaceted and often innovative nature mirrors Ysaÿe's belief in the continuity of history, the value and inseparability of past, present and future. They testify to his commitment to balancing the continuation of musical tradition with making a unique and personal contribution to its development.

Musical expressiveness was fundamental to Ysaÿe's aesthetics. His search for it is especially palpable in his resourceful and innovative use of violin technique, the intensely chromatic and modally inflected harmony and the music's improvisatory nature. The different ambiguities and divergences from convention intensify the sense of freedom and spontaneity. Again, exploration is a primary issue. In his verbal discourse Ysaÿe had identified the development of expressiveness without neglect of the various aspects of musical tradition as the true purpose of musical progress, and this objective he pursued continuously throughout the *Grave*. Thus, a comparison between his verbal discourse about his musical identity and aesthetic aspirations, and the compositional idiom of the *Grave* reveals great consistency between the two.

Ultimately, Ysaÿe's identity is perhaps best described as multifaceted. He was both proudly traditional, yet always sought to explore and innovate; he openly emulated music from a variety of periods and traditions, yet was very personal in his choices on whom to draw and how to do so. He constantly sought for ways to increase musical expressiveness and beauty, yet was very focused on the technical possibilities of his instrument. His music is carefully planned and constructed, yet gives an improvisatory impression. On first sight this may appear somewhat contradictory. For Ysaÿe, however, these aspects were complementary and formed his artistic personality and identity.

Moreover, the Sonatas reflect his passion to communicate and transmit his aesthetic convictions — which he considered immutable throughout history — in a world he feared had abandoned them in favour of chaos and ugliness[47]. He intended Op. 27 to offer new violinistic resources and to illustrate ways in which to respect and creatively follow traditional aesthetic values in the early twentieth century, while always remaining committed to musical progress. This suggests that, to Ysaÿe, his identity as a 'Romantic' included an openness to and inclusiveness of compositional approaches from

---

[47]. See CHRISTEN, Ernest. *Op. cit.* (see note 14), pp. 179-181.

different periods and traditions, both past and present, while maintaining a strong vision of musical progress. Although deeply rooted in the past, he was profoundly concerned with the future and focused perhaps as much on this as he did on the past.

Therefore, when evaluating Ysaÿe's identity and music, it may be advisable to leave aside labels, such as Romantic, modern, reactionary or progressive, and to follow his advice: «Ne jugez pas un artiste […] d'après ce que vous voulez qu'il soit, mais d'après ce qu'il vous donne»[48]. This offers an excellent way to consider Ysaÿe in his individuality and multifaceted nature, with as few preconceptions as possible of what he should or should not have been.

---

[48]. In *ibidem*, p. 151.

Contributor Biographies

A Doctor of Music candidate in Early Music Performance at McGill University, Sallynee Amawat's performance research is focused on violin repertoire from France in the early-to-mid eighteenth-century. As a player of both baroque- and modern-era violin repertoire she has performed extensively with ensembles throughout Canada, the United States, and Asia. Her chamber ensemble, *Infusion Baroque*, was awarded Grand Prize and Audience Prize at the Early Music America Baroque Performance Competition in 2014, and is preparing for a tour of the United States and CD release in 2016. She also holds a Master's Degree in Violin Performance from the Hartt School (Connecticut, USA) and a Master's of Music from McGill University (Canada) in baroque violin performance.

Performer and musicologist, Fabrizio Ammetto is professor of violin, chamber music, baroque music, musical analysis, and musical philology at the Music Department of the University of Guanajuato, Gto., México. He is also a member of the 'Academia Mexicana de Ciencias' (AMC) and 'Sistema Nacional de Investigadores' (SNI) of México. He holds degrees in violin, viola and electronic music, and received his Ph.D. in musicology from the University of Bologna. As violinist, violist and conductor he has given over 700 concerts in Europe and America, and has produced numerous critical editions and recordings of eighteenth- and nineteenth-century instrumental music. He has published articles in *Ad Parnassum*, *ArteConCiencia*, *Esercizi*, *Musica e spettacolo*, *Hortus Musicus*, *Per Archi*, *Studi vivaldiani*, and *The Consort*. He is the founder and director of *L'Orfeo Ensemble* of Spoleto and the *Baroque Ensemble* of the University of Guanajuato. He is a member of the international Editorial Committee of the Istituto Italiano Antonio Vivaldi (Fondazione Giorgio Cini), Venice.

Alejandra Béjar Bartolo is professor at the Music Department of the University of Guanajuato, Gto., México. After obtaining a degree in piano performance she studied musicology at the Universidad Autónoma de Madrid, and received her Ph.D. in Arts from the University of Guanajuato. As pianist and harpsichordist (with the *Baroque Ensemble* of the University of Guanajuato) she has given over 200 concerts in México and Italy. Her book *Scherzi musicali, [Op. II] e Duetti e terzetti, Op. III* by Francesco Antonio Pistocchi, a critical edition with Italian text, is forthcoming (Libreria Musicale Italiana).

Paola Besutti is Associate Professor at the University of Teramo (Faculty of Sciences of Communication); she is also member of the Ph.D. Program on *Musica e spettacolo* of the University of Rome 'La Sapienza'. From 2003 to 2010 she was director of *Rivista Italiana di Musicologia*. She is full member of the Accademia Nazionale Virgiliana di Scienze Lettere ed Arti (Mantova) and artistic director of "I concerti dell'Accademia" (from 2006). Her publications as author and editor include *inter alia*: *Claudio Monteverdi. Studi e prospettive* (Olschki 1998), 'The "Sala degli Specchi" Uncovered: Monteverdi, the Gonzagas and the Palazzo Ducale, Mantua' (*Early Music* 1999), *L'oratorio musicale italiano e i suoi contesti (secc. XVII e XVIII)* (Olschki 2002), 'Spaces for Music in Renaissance Mantua' (CUP 2007), *Carlo Tessarini da Rimini. Violinista, compositore, editore nell'Europa del Settecento* (LIM 2012).

Gregorio Carraro is a musicologist and performer (recorder, traversa, oboe, harpsichord). His Ph.D. (University of Padua) focuses on the eighteenth-century violin, particularly the sonatas of Giuseppe

Tartini (Autograph I-Pca 1888-1). He is currently preparing a critical edition of these sonatas, as well as an Italian translation of Paul Brainard's dissertation *Die Violine Sonate Giuseppe Tartinis* (Göttingen, 1959). Carraro has also written about Tartini's ornamentation and musical theories, focusing in particular on the connections between violin playing, the human voice and nature. He has edited the *Six Sinfonias* for Solo Violin by Angelo Berardi (Bologna, 1670) for Ut Orpheus Edizioni, Bologna.

CANDIDA FELICI obtained diplomas in piano and harpsichord, a degree in musicology at Rome University, a Ph.D. at Fribourg University (2003) and a post-doctoral scholarship at Bologna University (2005-2007). From 2006 she has been teaching music history in various Italian Conservatories of Music. Her research focuses on Baroque music (early Baroque keyboard repertoire, performance practice, eighteenth-century violin music, gender studies) and on contemporary music (Luciano Berio, Franco Donatoni, Jonathan Harvey). She has published two books, two critical editions and several essays. She regularly performs contemporary music with the *Dynamis Ensemble*.

ÉTIENNE JARDIN obtained a Ph.D. in history from the École des Hautes Études en Sciences Sociales (Paris). His reserch concerns musical life in France during the nineteenth century: concerts, music schools and lyric theatres. Co-founder and director of publication for the eletronic journal *Transposition. Musique et sciences sociales* (2010), he is now in charge of publications and conferences for the Palazzetto Bru Zane – Centre de musique romantique française (Venice).

A graduate of the University of Windsor, Western University, and Yale University (M.Phil. and Ph.D. in Musicology), WALTER KURT KREYSZIG is professor of musicology at the University of Saskatchewan and a member of the Center for Canadian Studies at the University of Vienna. He has published on eighteenth- and nineteenth-century music in *Ad Parnassum*, *Boccherini Studies*, *Jahrbuch für Internationale Germanistik*, *Mozart-Jahrbuch*, *Musicologica Austriaca*, *Musikgeschichte als Verstehensgeschichte*, *Revista de Musicología*, *RILM Perspectives*, *Schriften des Händel-Hauses*, *Studien zur Musikwissenschaft*, *Speculum musicae*, *Studien zur Musik*, *Studies in Music from the University of Western Ontario*, *Wiener Veröffentlichungen zur Theorie und Interpretation der Musik*, *Wissenschaft und Kunst*, and in *The Cambridge Handel Encyclopedia*.

PRISCILLE LACHAT-SARRETE is a violinist, presently working as a professor at the Conservatoire (CRD) of Chartres. She is also a researcher affiliated to the IreMus of the CNRS/Paris-Sorbonne University/BNF Library. She studied at the Paris Conservatoire (CNSM) and the Paris-Sorbonne University where she was granted a doctorate with honors in 2010, with the dissertation *L'entrée du soliste dans les concertos de 1750 à 1810, à travers les œuvres de Johann Christian Bach, Haydn, Mozart, Viotti et Beethoven*. She has published articles on eighteenth and nineteenth-century music, in particular on violin concertos and nineteenth-century student concertos. Performing on both Baroque and modern violins she appears in duos and chamber ensembles in Paris and its surrounding region.

SIMONE LAGHI is a violin and viola player. He studied early music at the Conservatorium Van Amsterdam. Particularly interested in Italian string quartet music from the Classical period, he has published and recorded works by Pietro Nardini, Ferdinando Bertoni, Bartolomeo Campagnoli and others. In 2012 he founded the *Ensemble Symposium* with the aim of promoting research and the historical performance practice of unpublished repertoire. In 2013 he joined Cardiff University to work on a Ph.D. in performance related to the string quartets of Venanzio Rauzzini (1746-1810) and, more broadly, to Italian composers working in the United Kingdom at the end of the eighteenth century. He has performed and recorded with renowned ensembles such as *Europa Galante*, *Arte dell'Arco*, *Accademia degli Astrusi*, *Collegium Pro Musica*, and others.

ALESSANDRO MASTROPIETRO graduated in composition, electronic music and orchestral conducting from L'Aquila Conservatory, and in musicology from the University of Rome 'La Sapienza' with a dissertation on Luigi Nono. He is now Professor in Musicology and History of Music at the University of Catania. His scholarship deals mostly with the music of the last 60 years, in particular with composers of the avant-garde who were active in Rome and whose theatrical works he has investigated in his Ph.D. Dissertation (*Nuovo teatro musicale tra Roma e Palermo, 1961-1973*). His research also encompasses instrumental music from the second half of the eighteenth century, above all on the music of Boccherini. He has participated in numerous international conferences, as well as publishing essays in various books and journals. He has produced a critical edition of the writings of D. Guaccero in *Le Sfere* series and has edited, for the publishing house LIM, monographs on P. Renosto (2013) and F. Pennisi (2014).

Musicologist, archivist and, until December 2013, librarian at the Public Library and Historical Archives 'Angelo Mai' in Bergamo, PAOLA PALERMO is currently Head of the Archives of the City of Bergamo. She has produced numerous publications and participates in conferences and round-table discussions on composers including Locatelli, Leoncavallo, Donizetti and Mayr. She has worked for many years on the reconstruction of the musical Chapel of the Basilica of Santa Maria Maggiore in Bergamo, devoting particular attention to the seventeenth and eighteenth centuries. Together with Giulia Pecis Cavagna she has published the volume *La cappella musicale di Santa Maria Maggiore a Bergamo dal 1657 al 1810* (Brepols, 2011). She also contributed the entries 'Francesco Ballarotti' and 'Giovanni Battista Quaglia' for *The New Grove Dictionary of Music and Musicians* (2001) and 'Carlo Antonio Marino' for the *Biographical Dictionary of Italians* (2008).

RUDOLF RASCH studied musicology in Amsterdam with Karel Philippus, Bernet Kempers and Joseph Smits van Waesberghe. He wrote a dissertation on seventeenth-century polyphonic carols in the Spanish Netherlands (Utrecht, 1985) and from 1977 was affiliated to the Institute of Musicology of Utrecht University. His main research interests are the musical history of the Netherlands, tuning and temperament, and the works of composers such as Corelli, Vivaldi, Geminiani and Boccherini. He has published articles, books and editions in these fields, including contributions to *Music Publishing in Europe 1600-1900* (a collection of essays published in 2005), *Driehonderd brieven over muziek* (letters on music passing from and to Constantijn Huygens, 2007), *Understanding Boccherini's Manuscripts* (a collection of essays, published 2014), and several volumes of the Italian National Edition of the complete works of Luigi Boccherini (since 2007). In 2014 he was appointed General Editor of the *Opera Omnia* of Francesco Geminiani.

After obtaining a first-class diploma in violin, RENATO RICCO graduated from the University of Naples 'Federico II' with a dissertation on the evolution of the violin concerto in the years 1900-1940. In 2012 he received his Ph.D. at the Faculty of Letters and Philosophy at University of Salerno; his monograph *Sulle tracce di Didone fra Età Classica e Rinascimento, l'evoluzione letteraria di un mito*, is to be published by Guida (Naples). In addition to his research on Italian literature (leading to publications on Giraldi Cinzio, Metastasio, Mazzini, Foscolo, Verga, d'Annunzio, Moravia and Sanguineti), his musicological interests are centered chiefly on the instrumental music of the nineteenth century, in particular Italian and French violin music. He's actually Research Fellow at the University of Salerno.

JESSIKA RITTSTIEG is a musicologist and violinist. Educated in Germany, the USA and England, she is currently studying for a Ph.D. at the Open University, Milton Keynes (UK) and has given papers at conferences in the UK and abroad. The title of her thesis is *The Compositional Style of Eugène Ysaÿe: The Six Sonatas, Op. 27, for Solo Violin*. Her papers include 'Towards an Elucidation of Eugène Ysaÿe's Aesthetic Persona' (La Spezia, 2012) and 'Eugène Ysaÿe and the Legacy of Debussy: Ysaÿe's Sonata, Op. 27/5, for Solo Violin' (Liverpool Hope 2013). Jessika's research focuses particularly on Eugène Ysaÿe, and she is also interested in French and Belgian music of the late nineteenth and early twentieth centuries, as well as issues of violin performance.

Honorary member of the Centro Studi Opera Omnia Luigi Boccherini, Rohan H. Stewart-MacDonald studied at St Catharine's College, Cambridge between 1993 and 2001 and worked as Director of Studies in Music and Director of Music at Murray Edwards College, Cambridge, from 2004 until 2009. Since completing the Ph.D. he has specialized in British music of the eighteenth and nineteenth centuries, publishing *New Perspectives on the Keyboard Sonatas of Muzio Clementi* in 2006 (Quaderni clementiani, 2). In 2012, with Roberto Illiano, he co-edited and contributed to *Jan Ladislav Dussek: A Bohemian Composer «en voyage» through Europe* (Quaderni clementiani, 4). His research interests have broadened to encompass eighteenth-century Italian symphonism; nineteenth-century British symphonism and early nineteenth-century British concert life and the early-Romantic virtuoso (both piano and violin). Stewart-MacDonald has returned to performing as a solo pianist, with programmes that include his own arrangements of American popular music from the middle decades of the twentieth century.

Michael Talbot is Emeritus Professor of Music at the University of Liverpool and a Fellow of the British Academy. He is best known for his studies and editions of Italian late Baroque music, especially those concerning Albinoni, Vivaldi and other Venetian composers. His most recent book is *The Vivaldi Compendium* (The Boydell Press, 2011). Particular interests, reflected in the present essay, are the connections of Italian musicians with their colleagues in the rest of Europe during the eighteenth century and the reception of Italian music there during the same period.

Canadian violinist Guillaume Tardif (DMA, Eastman) is Associate Professor of Violin, String Coordinator, and Interim Chair at the Department of Music, University of Alberta. He performs internationally as a soloist and chamber musician, produces concert series and recordings, arranges and composes music, and develops scholarly projects, mostly on topics relating to string literature and string pedagogy. He has been a guest professor at various universities in Europe, Asia, and in North and South America, and his research has been supported by various agencies, including the Alberta Foundation for the Arts and the Social Sciences and Humanities Research Council (Canada).

Neal Zaslaw is the author of numerous books and articles on European music of the seventeenth and eighteenth centuries. His new edition of Ludwig Köchel's *Verzeichnis der Werke von W. A. Mozart* is in production. Currently his research concerns opera and its precursors in Italy in the late sixteenth and early seventeenth centuries. He is the Herbert Gussman Professor of Music at Cornell University, where he has taught since 1970.

Index of Names

TAPPERT, Wilhelm 124

TARADE, Théodore-Jean 111

TARDIF, Guillaume 95

TARTINI, Giuseppe x-xii, 33, 40, 47-50, 53, 73, 96, 99, 107, 109-110, 112-113, 123, 125, 127-130, 144-146, 165-185, 191-193, 200-201, 203-207, 220, 226, 231, 252, 258, 276, 368

TASKIN, Pascal Joseph II 45

TAYLOR, Jane 123

TCHAIKOVSKY, Pyotr Il'yich 104

TELEMANN, Georg Philipp 63, 68, 77, 92, 98, 106, 145, 235

TEMPO, Claudio 297

TERBY, François 176

TERBY, Joseph Jr 176

TERBY, Joseph Sr 176

TERMANINI, Stefano 282

TESSARINI, Carlo 12, 107, 110, 131-152, 209-212

TESSARINI, Caterina 134

TESSARINI, Elisabetta 134

TESSARINI, Francesca 134

TESSARINI, Giovanni Francesco 135, 138, 143

TESSARINI, Pasqua 134

THALBERG, Sigmond 295

THIBAUD, Jacques 366

THIEME, Ulrich 64

THOM, Eitelfriedrich 67-68

THOMAS, Downing A. 200

THOMSON, César 308

TIBY, J.-F. 117

TIECK, Ludwig 288

TISHKOFF, Doris P. 67

TODD, R. Larry 87

TORELLI, Giuseppe x, xii, 12, 106

TOSCANI, Claudio 279

TOUCHEMOULIN, Joseph 175, 200

TOURTE, François-Xavier xi, 271, 275

TRAPPES-LOMAX, Richard 173

TRAUB, Andreas 76

TRAVASSOS, Elizabeth 97

TREMAIS, de 110, 145, 200

TREVITT, John 369

TRONCHET, Jeanne, *dite* 'de Mainville' 168, 173

TROTTO, Buono 19, 23

TROTTO, Lucia *see* CROCCHI, Lucia

TROTTO, Margherita 19

TÜBEL [LEBUTINI], Christian Gottlieb 14

TUMARKIN, Anna 68

TUNLEY, David 70

TWITTENHOFF, Wilhelm 60

U

UCCELLINI, Marco x

UNVERRICHT, Hubert 231-232, 253-254

V

VACHON [VASSON, WASCHON], Pierre 108, 186

VALENTINE, Robert 102, 107

VALENTINI, Giuseppe 144-145

VANÇON, Jean-Claire 43, 58

VAN DEN BREMT, Frans 110

VAN HEYGHEN, Peter 91

VAN REIJEN, Paul Wilhelm 126-127

VEINUS, Abraham xiii

VEIT, Patrice 283

VENDÔME, Marie-Charlotte 140

VENDRIX, Philippe 368

VERACINI, Antonio 213

VERACINI, Francesco Maria x, xii, 12, 107, 109, 127, 144-145, 213-214, 226

VERDI, Giuseppe 283, 307

VERNA, Marina 297

VETTER, Walther 77

VIAL, Stephanie D. 63, 106

VIBERT, Nicolas 103, 106

VIDAL, Jean 45

VIDAL, Louis 292

VIERHAUS, Rudolf 59

VIEUXTEMPS, Henry xi, 96, 117-118, 259, 285, 294, 298, 308, 357, 365, 367-369

VIGANÒ, Salvatore 308

VIOTTI, Giovanni Battista xi-xii, 45, 47-48, 108-109, 111, 113, 115-117, 201, 220, 232-233, 235, 242-243, 245-246, 248-252, 257-260, 262-263, 265, 271-273, 285, 304, 312-313, 332, 339, 342, 367

VITALI, Danilo 73

VITALI, Veronica 24

VIVALDI, Antonio ix-x, xii, 33, 79-80, 96, 99, 107, 144-145, 149, 165-167, 171, 179-181, 183-185, 187-190, 192, 202, 209-212, 215-220, 226, 313-314

VOGLER, Georg Joseph, Abbé 12, 126, 307

VOLPATO, Enrico 282

VUILLAUME, Jean-Baptiste 292

VÝBORNÝ, Zdenek 282, 312

W

WACHER, Pierre Jean 236
WACKENRODER, Wilhelm Heinrich 285, 288, 292
WADE, Rachel W. 67
WAELTNER, Ernst Ludwig 75
WAGNER, Günther 60, 67
WAGNER, Richard 56, 306, 375
WAITE, William R. 75
WALDEN, Valerie 116
WALDURA, Markus 63-65, 68, 78
WALKER, Paul 77
WALLACE, Barbara K. 65
WALLON, Simon 124-125
WALLS, Peter 80, 85, 105, 214
WALSH, John xii, 4, 141, 211-212, 215
WALTHER, Johann Gottfried 14, 79
WASSENAER, Unico Wilhelm van, Count 11
WATELET, Claude-Henri 142-143
WEBER, Petra 67
WEBER, William 43, 283
WEBSTER, James 87
WECKERLIN, Jean-Baptiste 124
WEGMANN, Nikolaus 66
WEINMANN, Alexander 115
WEISS, Zoe 42
WEN, Eric xiii
WENK, Arthur B. 377
WERKMEISTER, Andreas 61
WERNER, Michael 283
WESSELY, Othmar 115
WHITE, Edwin Chappell 109-110, 112-113, 232, 331
WHITMORE, Philip 180, 193
WIENIAWSKI, Henryk 104, 118, 259, 275, 280-281, 298, 365
WIENS, Victor D. 72
WIER, Albert E. 105, 118
WILCOX, Beverly 167-168, 171, 173, 200, 206
WILHELMJ, August xii
WILKINS, Nigel Edward 297
WILLEM I, King of the Netherlands 117
WILLEM IV, Prince of Orange-Nassau 5
WILLEM V, Prince of Orange-Nassau 11
WINKLER, Gerhard J. 87
WINTER, Robert 280
WIRSTA, Aristide 200
WITTING, Carl 90

WITVOGEL, Gerhard Fredrik 13, 133, 141, 174
WOLDEMAR, Michel 89, 271
WOLF, Eugene K. 114
WOLF, Jean K. 114
WOLFF, Christoph 63, 77, 113
WOLFF, Pierre 287
WOLLHEIM, Heinrich 70
WOLLNY, Peter 61
WOOD, Anthony 38
WOODCOCK, Robert 216
WOODFIELD, Ian 225
WORNELL ENGELS, Marjorie 86
WRANITZKY, Antonin 115
WRANITZKY, Paul 115
WUIDAR, Laurence 76
WYZEWA [WYŻEWSKI], Théodore de [Teodor] 126

Y

YAMPOLSKI, Israil Markovitch 293
YANKELEVITCH, Yuri 275
YEARSLEY, David Gaynor 71
YSAŸE, Antoine 118, 366, 379
YSAŸE, Eugène xi, 96, 104, 118, 259, 275, 307, 365-381

Z

ZAMINER, Frieder 75
ZANARDINI, Angelo 278
ZANI, Andrea 145
ZANOLINI, Antonio 282
ZAPPALÀ, Pietro 113
ZAPPULLA, Robert 86
ZASLAW, Neal xiv, 4-5, 7, 29, 36, 59, 70, 73, 80, 88, 92, 95, 97, 99, 101, 105, 107, 111, 154-156, 196, 199
ZELTER, Carl Friedrich 280, 294
ZIINO, Agostino 72
ZINGERLE, Hans 61
ZINGONI, Giovanni Battista 12
ZOFIA, Lissa 72
ZOHN, Steven 66
ZONCA, Andrea 24
ZUCCARI, Carlo 166